MAGILL'S
LITERARY ANNUAL

1984

MAGILL'S LITERARY ANNUAL

1984

*Essay-Reviews of 200 Outstanding Books
Published in the United States during 1983*

With an Annotated Categories Index

Volume One

A-Lo

Edited by
FRANK N. MAGILL

SALEM PRESS
Englewood Cliffs

LIBRARY OF CONGRESS CATALOG CARD NO. 77-99209
ISBN 0-89356-284-X

FIRST PRINTING

PRINTED IN THE UNITED STATES OF AMERICA

PUBLISHER'S NOTE

Magill's Literary Annual, 1984, is the twenty-ninth publication in a series that began in 1954. The philosophy behind the annual has been to evaluate critically each year a given number of major examples of serious literature published during the previous year. Our continuous effort is to provide coverage for works that are likely to be of more than passing general interest and that will stand up to the test of time. Individual critical articles for the first twenty-two years were collected and published in *Survey of Contemporary Literature*, in 1977.

For the reader new to the Magill reference format, the following brief explanation should serve to facilitate the research process. The two hundred works represented in this year's annual are drawn from the following categories: fiction; poetry; literary criticism and literary history; essays; literary biography, autobiography, memoirs, diaries, and letters; and miscellaneous. The articles are arranged alphabetically by book title in the two-volume set; a complete list of the titles included can be found at the beginning of volume 1. Following a list of titles, the user will find the titles arranged by category, in an annotated listing. This list provides the reader with the title, author, page number, and a brief one-sentence description of the particular work. All contributing reviewers for the literary annual are listed alphabetically in the front matter as well as at the end of their review. At the end of volume 2, there is a Cumulative Author Index from 1977 to 1984. Beneath each author's name are the titles of any of his or her work reviewed in the Magill annuals since 1977. Next to each title, in parentheses, is the year of the annual in which the review appeared, followed by the page number.

Each individual article begins with a block of standard top matter that indicates the title, author, publisher, and price of the work. When possible, the year of the author's birth is also provided. The top matter also includes the number of pages of the book, the type of work, and, when appropriate, the time period and locale represented in the text. Next, there is the same capsulized description of the work that appears in the annotated list of titles. When pertinent, a list of principal characters or of personages will introduce the review.

The articles themselves are approximately two thousand words in length. They are original essay-reviews that analyze and present the focus, intent, and relative success of the author, as well as the makeup and point-of-view of the work under discussion. To further assist the reader, the articles are supplemented by a list of sources for further study in a bibliographic format.

Until 1983, history-oriented books were included in *Magill's Literary Annual*. Readers who are interested in history, biography, and current affairs are invited to consult *Magill's History Annual*, 1984, a companion to *Magill's Literary Annual* and the twelve-volume *Great Events from History*.

LIST OF TITLES

TITLES BY CATEGORY

ANNOTATED

FICTION

xix

xxv

LITERARY CRITICISM
LITERARY HISTORY

ESSAYS

page

AUTOBIOGRAPHIES
MEMOIRS
DIARIES
LETTERS

CONTRIBUTING REVIEWERS FOR 1984 ANNUAL

Michael Adams

Andrew J. Angyal

Stanley Archer

Edwin T. Arnold

Jean W. Ashton

Dean Baldwin

Paul A. Bateman

Carolyn Wilkerson Bell

Gordon N. Bergquist

Gerhard Brand

Peter A. Brier

Jeanie R. Brink

Karen Carmean

John J. Conlon

Julian W. Connolly

Mark Conroy

Susan M. D'Antuono

J. Madison Davis

R. H. W. Dillard

Alice Drum

Gweneth A. Dunleavy

Sandra Dutton

Bruce L. Edwards, Jr.

Robert P. Ellis

John P. Ferré

Daniel Mark Fogel

Margot K. Frank

Eberhard Frey

Faith Gabelnick

Kristine Ottesen Garrigan

Georg Gaston

Leslie E. Gerber

Scott Giantvalley

Clareece Godt

Sidney Gottlieb

Peter W. Graham

William E. Grant

Angela Hague

Cathryn Hankla

Terry Heller

Greg E. Henderson

John T. Hiers

Janet H. Hobbs

Theodore C. Humphrey

Roseline Intrater

Philip K. Jason

Ronald L. Johnson

Carola M. Kaplan

Joanne G. Kashdan

Steven G. Kellman

Henderson Kincheloe

Jeanne Larsen

Leon Lewis

Elizabeth Johnston Lipscomb

Mark McCloskey

Margaret McFadden

Ric S. Machuga

Charles E. May

Laurence W. Mazzeno

Walter E. Meyers

Jim W. Miller

Sally H. Mitchell

Leslie B. Mittleman

Robert A. Morace

Katharine M. Morsberger

Robert E. Morsberger

Carole Moses

Stella Nesanovich

Olga S. Opfell

David B. Parsell

L. W. Payne

Edward L. Queen II

Thomas Rankin

James R. Reece

Bruce D. Reeves

Ann E. Reynolds

Michael S. Reynolds

J. Thomas Rimer

Mary Rohrberger

Carl E. Rollyson, Jr.

Stephanie Sandler

Roberta Sharp

T. A. Shippey

Thomas J. Sienkewicz

Gilbert Smith

Michael Sprinker

Rae H. Stoll

Gerald H. Strauss

Mary J. Sturm

Charles Johnson Taggart

Daniel Taylor

Henry Taylor

John G. Tomlinson, Jr.

William B. Toole III

Janet Tucker

Ronald G. Walker

John N. Wall, Jr.

Norbert Weinberg

Craig Werner

Mary C. Williams

John Wilson

James A. Winders

MAGILL'S
LITERARY ANNUAL

1984

ABOUT MY TABLE

Author: Nicholas Delbanco (1942-   )
Publisher: William Morrow and Company (New York). 203 pp. $11.95
Type of work: Short stories
Time: The 1970's and 1980's
Locale: The Northeast United States

Nine stories about nine men in a particularly traumatic time of their lives—when the approaching age of forty can be personally terrifying but where the trivial events of life go on in more or less expected ways.

About My Table is Nicholas Delbanco's first volume of short stories, though he is the author of ten novels and a biographical study of writers in community, *Group Portrait: Conrad, Crane, Ford, James, and Wells* (1982). Reviewers of Delbanco's novels have placed him squarely in the modernist tradition, commenting on his emphasis on fictional techniques, poetic style, verbal agility, and sometimes structural discontinuity.

Delbanco's short stories, too, are thoroughly modernist in character, the surfaces rendered with care, the characters revealed through ironic juxtapositions, the situations ordinary but where ordinariness takes on symbolic dimension by virtue of its commonality. In fact, when read in sequence, the stories take on a dreary repetitiousness. There is a sameness not only about the characters and the point of view but also in the very structure, the skeleton of the pieces. One is struck by the fact that the first five stories are all exactly twenty pages long; the remaining four stories do not stray far from this model, numbering twenty-four, thirty, twenty-four, and sixteen pages respectively. The fifth story, "Ostinato," is the only one where point of view shifts from third-person limited to the male protagonist to third-person omniscient. The climax of each story occurs within one to two pages to the end, and each story is divided into sections with such regularity as to suggest a wearisome and soporific monotony. Nevertheless, this may be the point of it all—an indirect revelation of a burdensome past forever giving way to an expected future ending in nothingness.

The title piece, "About My Table," is the concluding story in the volume. It begins:

Death visited him daily. He did what he could to deny it but could not avert his eyes. Headlines blazoned and newscasters announced it: bombs and strangulations and cancer were the news. Arson increased. The alarm in his smoke detectors at home whistled at him shrilly for no apparent reason in the night.

It ends:

He set himself to comfort her. Death visited him nightly. It comes when it will come. It

could be a furnace malfunction, allergic reaction, rabid bat, oncoming drunk in a van in
his lane, suicide, undiagnosed leukemia, handgun in a shopping mall, pilot error, stroke,
the purposive assault of some unrecognized opponent, earth, air, water, flame.

In between the first and last paragraphs are references to war, to slaughter,
to torture, to revolution, to frigid weather with frost six feet deep, to the
corpses of rats in basements, to three deaths, each one touching the protagonist, Daniel, more deeply. Along with the "male" world of "consequential"
events foremost in Daniel's consciousness, however, is a "female world imaged
in the birthday party prepared by Daniel's wife, Ann, for their four-year-old
daughter, Adriana. There are sixteen women and nine little girls. The women
cause Daniel to feel out of place. The little girls play "pass the apple" and
"musical chairs" but cannot quite manage the latter. They display little competitive sense, and Daniel and Ann make them all winners. The cake is in
the shape of a Tootsie Roll two feet long. One of Adriana's candles, the fifth
one, is a trick candle and will not blow out. "It's for good luck," Daniel tells
his daughter, but to his wife he says: "These beautiful, clean children . . . I
wish that this could last." It will, his wife tells him, "in memories," "in
photographs."

Daniel is a free-lance journalist, but he takes no comfort in the memories
he will leave behind. He recalls his wedding day and the detour he and his
wife took before going to the reception, but though this moment with his
wife has remained vivid to him in every detail, he has never again been able
to find the place on the road where they turned off on that magical detour.

The story ends on Friday the thirteenth. Adriana is watching the Cookie
Monster on television. War is all around just outside the television set; Daniel
and Ann have a glass of wine together and look at the photographs of the
birthday party. Ann, thinking of their dead dog and the war and a photograph
of her daughter whose mouth is so stuffed with cake that it "looked like she'd
swallowed the tootsie roll whole," begins to cry. Daniel tries to comfort her.
"Not everything," he says, "is awful."

The protagonists of the nine stories in this collection are all men in their
late thirties, all successful in their chosen occupations, all from the same
region of the country; most are comfortably married and have one or two
children. They are the generation of the 1960's marked by their time but now
comfortably in the mainstream—writers or architects or art dealers or musicians or lawyers or professors, all playing the roles expected of them. They
love their wives and children, but, as the years pass, they experience a growing
sense of discontinuity and despair, brought to climax by the approach of their
fortieth year. Mortality is upon them, but, despite it, they need to go on. All
manage to survive the turning point, step back on the treadmill, whatever
the delays and accidents and misunderstandings and frustrations, and thwarted
desires, and deaths.

"What You Carry," the first story in the collection, announces major themes that will continue throughout the volume. The protagonist, Kenneth Perrera, is a doctor whose Jewish parents fled from Hitler's Germany to London, where they arrived in the middle of the Blitz. When Hitler turned on Russia, Kenneth's mother turned to her husband and asked to be made pregnant. In 1952, the Perreras sailed to the United States. Kenneth is an only child. Not at all religious, Kenneth marries Susan, a lapsed Catholic, who is as photogenic as Kenneth's mother, on whom he lavished both love and respect. Six months after his marriage, his mother has a massive heart attack, and he and Susan fly to her bedside. Kenneth's mother asks for a grandchild, seeking life in a period of impending death, as she had earlier sought pregnancy in wartime. Kenneth obeys. That night, he makes such urgent love to his wife that he worries that his father down the hall will hear her cries.

Kenneth's mother dies during Susan's pregnancy, and Kenneth is comforted by the fact that what is carried in the head cannot be destroyed. Members of his mother's family had survived Dachau by reciting *Faust* when no books had been available. The grandson his mother had hoped for is a girl named Elizabeth, after his mother.

Elizabeth is a precocious child, but from the beginning she is somehow different from what Kenneth and Susan expected—a difference reflected in their calling her first Liz, then Lizzie, then Elizabeth. She is self-contained, introspective, controlled, "tight." Susan says: "One button out of place and she wants to start all over."

The crisis comes when Kenneth learns that Elizabeth has formed a picture of God in the image of a statue of Henry of Portugal, stern-visaged and Christian. Kenneth is alarmed. He wants his daughter to know of her heritage, which he himself has neglected. For him, his mother was his past and his future, his attachment to a heritage, but she is gone, and the next generation is cut off from her memory. Kenneth identifies the important point in the last sentence of the story: "I'm sorry. I so much wanted you to meet." The sentence, addressed to his daughter, is as much about his mother as it is about himself.

The placement of the story "Ostinato" in the center of the collection is a signal that the thematic motifs introduced in the first stories will continue to the volume's end, but it is a signal, also, that the author is aware of the role he has assigned to the women in his stories. In "Ostinato," for the first and last time, Delbanco enters the mind of a woman character. In most of these stories, women play the role of the protagonist's helpmate, his understanding wife, and the mother of his children. Only here does Delbanco reveal directly that women may not be entirely happy in this role.

Though Delbanco's male characters in *About My Table* view themselves as hosts, providers, owners, and overall benefactors of wife and children, they never seem to realize that maintaining this role is a terrible burden and a primary reason for their despair. Thus, each of the protagonists makes his way through a crisis, but nothing is ever resolved because the characters never really understand their problems. This lack of understanding contributes further to the feeling of despair, so that—in and between the stories—form and content merge.

Delbanco's skill as a craftsman is obvious, but he contributes nothing unique to the form of the short story or to the dominant thematic content of the twentieth century. The young people of the 1960's grow up, too, to take their places as a group alongside all the other groups making up lost generations, and Delbanco falls in place, following the leaders, in the tradition of such early masters as James Joyce, Ernest Hemingway and William Faulkner.

Mary Rohrberger

Sources for Further Study

Boston Review. VIII, October, 1983, p. 36.
Hudson Review. XXXVI, Winter, 1983, p. 751.
Library Journal. CVIII, September 1, 1983, p. 1720.
Los Angeles Times Book Review. August 7, 1983, p. 2.
The New York Times Book Review. LXXXVIII, September 18, 1983, p. 14.
Publishers Weekly. CCXXIV, July 15, 1983, p. 40.
Times Literary Supplement. October 22, 1982, p. 1148.

AIMÉ CÉSAIRE
The Collected Poetry

Author: Aimé Césaire (1913-
Translated from the French, with an introduction and notes, by Clayton Eshleman
   and Annette Smith
Publisher: University of California Press (Berkeley). 408 pp. $25.00
Type of work: Poetry

*A bilingual edition which offers the first translation into English of the collected poetry
of Aimé Césaire*

Nearly three-quarters of a century after Ezra Pound argued that translation was a valid means of expression for the most serious and inventive of poets, contemporary American writers have finally begun to apply the full power of their imagination to the finest poetry of other cultures and continents. Richard Howard's rendering of Charles Baudelaire typifies this kind of commitment, following the lead of Robert Fitzgerald, whose 1961 translation of the *Odyssey* (c. 800 B.C.) is an exemplum of how a classic might be translated into contemporary English, but few poets of the absolute first rank have attempted a full-scale translation of a major contemporary poet. This very ambitious edition features a poet with a unique and powerful voice, whose translators are faithful to all of his skills and concerns.

Césaire is known in this country as a man of diverse, even exotic accomplishments, including the writing of poetry; he is best known as the cocreator (with Léopold Senghor of Senegal) of the concept of *négritude*, as a maverick member of the Communist Party, and as an active supporter of a progressive, Socialist movement in his native Martinique, which he has represented in the French Chamber of Deputies for many years. As a Communist comfortable neither with Party doctrine nor professional anti-Communists, an eloquent advocate of black culture and black studies, and an intellectual with a command of European history and literature, Césaire has been pigeonholed under the heading exotic; the singularity of his life has obscured, for the most part, his continuing production as a poet and diverted attention from the fact that the prime strength of his poetry is the integration of many diverse interests into a distinct, powerful poetic voice. To use Charles Olson's phrase, it is the "complex of occasions" in Césaire's work which makes it so fascinating and unusual.

Césaire was born in Martinique in 1913; his father was a tax collector, his mother a dressmaker. Césaire's grandmother taught him to read French by the age of four, and his parents, despite their simple circumstances, maintained high intellectual standards. Césaire's father refused to settle for the Creole folk culture that captured most of the population of the island, encouraging his six children to read the world-famous French prose classics and reciting

Victor Hugo's poetry at home. The family moved to Fort-de-France, the nation's capital, so that Césaire might attend the only secondary school in that region of the French colonial empire. Césaire continued his education in France, where he became part of a community of black students from the colonies who attended the École Normale Supérieure in Paris. There, he studied traditional European history and literature as well as literary modernism and also became familiar with the Harlem Renaissance and black American literature; his thesis for the Diplôme d'Études Supérieures was on the image of the South in black American writing. In 1937, Césaire met and married Suzanne Roussy and founded with her the magazine *Tropiques*, which included studies of African archetypes among various literary and cultural topics.

Césaire traveled in Europe during his student years in France but returned to Martinique just before the outbreak of World War II. The island was under the control of the Vichy regime until 1943, and the racism of the thousands of French sailors garrisoned there (and contained by the United States Navy) may have politicized his thinking in certain specific ways. Although apparently apolitical to this point in his life, he agreed to the request of some friends to run for the municipal council on the Communist ticket. The party had never received more than a few hundred votes before the war, but the general dislocation of the war led to what was described as a "shocking upset," and the Césaire group won a majority in the parliament. He was elected mayor of Fort-de-France and was thus appointed a member of the French Première Assemblée Nationale Constitutante to participate in the formation of a new constitution of the Fourth Republic. In 1957, in response to the Russian invasion of Hungary in the fall of 1956, he broke with the Communist Party and became a leading member of the independent Socialist Martinique Progressive Party in 1958.

Césaire's experiences have all been gathered into his poetry, and the mixture is a challenge for most readers, even those familiar with the separate aspects of the style and attitude that he has organized into his poetic voice. The problems that the translator must face are no less daunting, but Clayton Eshleman and Annette Smith are superb guides to Césaire's work. Eshleman is the editor of *Sulfur*, a poetry journal that reflects his place in the center of the Ezra Pound-Charles Olson-William Carlos Williams line of poetic expression. His translation (with José Rubia Barcia) *César Vallejo: The Complete Posthumous Poetry* (1978) won a National Book Award, and his own poems have earned for him a position of some stature in the chaotic and competitive arena of contemporary American poetry. Smith is French but was born and reared in Algeria amid the struggle for independence. Eshleman and Smith are thus very well prepared for the task of translating Césaire and have put an enormous amount of energy into their work. Nevertheless, while their work is excellent in many aspects and indispensable for the reader with no knowledge of French, one simply cannot claim, as the publisher's blurb does, that their translation "will remain the definitive Césaire in English." This is not to demean their achievement, but to recollect, as Walter Benjamin argues persuasively in "The Task of the Translator," that "a translation comes later than the original, and since the important works of world literature never find their chosen translators at the time of their origin, their translation marks their stage of continued life." Eshleman and Smith give Césaire "life" in English and have responded brilliantly to Benjamin's insistence that translation be criticism, telling readers something about the original.

When one considers, even briefly, the method of Césaire's modes of creation, the great effort that went into the translation becomes clear. Benjamin also demands that the translator "liberate the language imprisoned in a work in his re-creation of that work," and while Eshleman and Smith have produced a strong foundation for knowing Césaire, they have not produced the definitive—which is to say, *final*—version in English of Césaire's work. It is difficult, Benjamin observes, to "release in one's own language, that pure language which is under the spell of another." It is particularly difficult when one considers the components of Césaire's "spell."

Césaire's university education centered on French literature—in the classic French style—and it covered to some degree writers of other nationalities. There are echoes of the English Romantics, particularly William Blake and Percy Bysshe Shelley in the strophe from his *Notebook of a Return to the Native Land* (1947) that begins

> I would rediscover the secret of great communications and great combustions. I would say storm. I would say river. I would say tornado.

The tone of measured grandeur which Césaire develops is designed to convey something of Blake's vision of the cosmos, something of Shelley's prophetic politics, and it complements the central influence on Césaire's style: the work of the French *Symboliste* poets and their confreres, the Surrealists, especially Comte de Lautréamont, Stéphane Mallarmé, and André Breton (an acquaintance in Paris). For Césaire, Surrealism offered more than a mode of expression, with its emphasis on bizarre juxtapositions of metaphor and object and its use of rhythm as chant to induce ecstatic states of consciousness. Surrealism was also more than a source of black humor, with its manipulation of words into neologisms and multilevel megapuns. In addition to these primarily linguistic devices, Surrealism provided a stance for opposition to the dominant white culture which suppressed and degraded black cultural forces, particularly of African origin—sources which Césaire had discovered and which he regarded as a vital, untapped reservoir of energy. In a continuing clash with white, Western materialistic values, Césaire regarded Surrealism as a "beneficial madness" that could reach a powerful, overlooked aspect of black culture—a close kinship to the primitive earth. He also regarded Surrealism as an instrument, in Robert Duncan's words, "to break into the forbidden."

Césaire believes that poetry can restore a clarity of vision to both black and white society, and that his role as a politician is to work toward the gradual improvement of social conditions. His concept is that poetry can sustain "the wounded self" in its struggles, whereas a violent revolution would merely exchange oppressors. This gradualist, practical approach is typical of Césaire's historical perspective and truly civilized temperament, thus permitting the subtle mixture of styles and subjects that make his work unique.

Within the Surrealist mode, Césaire has emphasized certain subjects of particular personal importance. From his university days, Césaire's continuing fascination with African studies (especially the work of Leo Frobenius) led to an examination of African fauna that produced a matrix of vegetal images. He ties personal growth, for example, to the growth of a tree, using its thrust toward the sky, its continual regeneration and its roots in the earth to suggest a figure for black people to follow. Similarly, his use of pre-Christian myth culminates in his metaphorical consideration of cannibalism as a symbol for devouring experience, for devouring a colonial administration, for developing a special awareness of the spiritual need for nourishment, and for the idea of an imaginative absorption of experience. The Surrealist approach works perfectly here to transform the literal into the transcendent.

Césaire's voice is a product of all of these factors as well as other less prominent but important features such as his interest in black musical forms and his employment of "chains" of images which ignite one another in accordance with Olson's idea (from the seminal essay "Projective Verse") that one perception should lead directly and immediately to another. The "spell" that Césaire's voice casts is composed of his political principles: a larger version of a life beyond politics; a commitment to poetic inspiration as a source of personal growth; a love of learning for its own sake; a belief in the revitalization of old myths to form the foundations of new ones; and a profound love of language. It is a voice that is often almost oratorical, a voice that does not flinch from rhetorical devices but reinvigorates them with a stunning subjectivity. It is a voice that can blend ferocity and tenderness, European culture and African primitivism in a unique synthesis.

Eshleman and Smith have obviously immersed themselves in every aspect of Césaire's life and work and have also brought their own gifts of language, imagination, judgment, and contemplation to the task of re-creating Césaire's voice in English. Their success is indisputable, yet theirs is not the only way to approach Césaire in English. Although the magnitude of Césaire's work precludes the possibility of a sustained examination of large segments of the translation, a brief consideration of a few lines will demonstrate both the success of the Eshleman-Smith version and the potential of other approaches to rendering Césaire in English.

In their translation of *Notebook of a Return to the Native Land*, Eshleman and Smith begin the section of the poem subheaded "ENOUGH OF THIS OUTRAGE!" with

> So here is the great challenge and the satanic
> compulsion and the insolent
> nostalgic drift . . .

from Césaire's

> Alors voilà le grand défi et l'impulsion
> sataniques et l'insolente
> dérive nostalgique . . .

There is an appropriate distancing in the initial exclamation, but it lacks the arresting power of the French. One might begin

> So then, see the great challenge, the satanic
> compulsion, the insolent nostalgia . . .

This alternative is both more direct and more forceful. The repetitious word "et" becomes the cumbersome, redundant "and" in English and can be eliminated. In the next stanza, Eshleman and Smith render "la même pauvre/ consolation" as "the same indigent/ solace," where the word "meager" (for "pauvre") would be more precise and less self-conscious. In the next stanza, Eshleman and Smith translate "des continents en délire" as "delirious continents"; here, it would be preferable to foresake literal correctness for an extension to "continents in delirium," which comes closer to getting the personal note for which Césaire is reaching: a suggestion of land mass as living entity.

Further along in the same text, there is an extremely interesting stanza in which Césaire writes:

> Et à moi mes danses
> mes danses de mauvais nègre
> à moi mes danses
> la danse brise-carcan
> la danse saute-prison
> la danse il-est-beau-et-bon-et-légitime-d'être-nègre
> A moi mes danses et saute le soleil sur la raquette
>   de mes mains

Here is the Eshleman/Smith version:

> Rally to my side my dances
> you bad nigger dances

    the carcan-cracker dance
    the prison-break dance
    the it-is-beautiful-good-and-legitimate-to-be-a-
        nigger dance
    Rally to my side my dances and let the sun bounce
        on the racket of my hands

An alternative version might read:

    Come to me
    my bad nigger dances
    come to me
    the dance of the collar-cracker
    the dance of the prison-breaker
    the dance of the beautiful-legitimate-good nigger
    Come to me my dances and let the sun explode off
        the battering ram of my hands

To tighten and intensify the rhythm, and thus capture fully the seductive tone of Césaire's beckoning song, this second version omits clearly superfluous words (Pound's old principle of *condensare*). Perhaps more significant is the change from "carcan" to "collar," which is what the word means in Old French. This makes the change in the last line from "racket" to "battering ram" consistent because the Old French for "raquette" is "battledore"— which, in this stanza, works very well as "battering ram" even when the seemingly obvious cognate is lost. "Saute" can certainly be translated as "explode," which is actually a more conventional use of the word than "bounce."

The point in suggesting these alternatives is not to find fault with Eshleman and Smith or to start an endless debate on each line's merits à la Edmund Wilson. Eshleman and Smith have done an excellent job with a vast and challenging mass of material, but, as Benjamin insists, "translation marks the stage of continued life." This book is a testament to the continuing life of Aimé Césaire's work, a true version of his poetry, and a convincing basis for the judgment and pleasure of the reader. It gives English-language readers access to a poet whose elements are never employed formulaically yet are alive in the dynamic flux of an active energy field. Indeed, this book is a persuasive justification for any award that Césaire's poetry might yet receive, even an award from the Nobel selection committee—a fitting tribute to the collected poetry of one of the premier poets of the twentieth century in any language.

Leon Lewis

Sources for Further Study

Los Angeles Times Book Review. December 4, 1983, p. 1.
The New York Times Book Review. LXXXIX, February 19, 1984, p. 14.
Virginia Quarterly Review. LX, Spring, 1984, p. 62.

ALICE IN BED

Author: Cathleen Schine (1953-   )
Publisher: Alfred A. Knopf (New York). 228 pp. $12.95
Type of work: Novel
Time: One year in the mid-1970's
Locale: New York and suburban Connecticut

Wry yet unembittered humor distinguishes the heroine of this sparkling first novel about a young woman immobilized by an undiagnosed disease

>   *Principal characters:*
>   ALICE BRODY, a nineteen-year-old Sarah Lawrence College student
>   BRENDA BRODY, her mother, who is being divorced
>   WILLIE BRODY, Alice's seventeen-year-old brother
>   STEPHANIE CARTER, an understanding nurse
>   DR. DAVIS, an eye surgeon who loves helplessness
>   SIMCHAS FRESSER, a hypnotist and expert on pain
>   CHRISTOPHER, a beautiful (if brainless) surfer

Cathleen Schine, whose writing has appeared in *The New Yorker* and the *Village Voice*, makes her debut as a novelist with a very readable book that dances past the quagmires lurking in her subject and sails lightly over the usual tones and topics of first novels. Indeed, in defining Schine's achievement, it is easier to talk about what *Alice in Bed* is not than what it is. It is not grim and depressing, nor is it brave and inspirational. It has little suspense in the ordinary sense of the word, no moments of significant crisis and climax, no startling incidents pulled out of the novelist's bag of tricks. There is hardly any action—after all, the central character is immobile in bed for most of the novel. There are no extended flashbacks or highly significant dreams that reveal the development of her character or clarify the meaning of her life. Schine has not written a novel with a message, though one might (at the cost of misrepresenting the book's spirit) write about her skill in making readers aware of topics that could be rendered in jargon, such as the sexuality of the disabled, medical incompetence, and the dehumanization of patients in the service of advanced technology.

Furthermore, although the central character is a woman of nineteen, the novel is not about typical adolescent angst or coming of age. It does not yield any deep meanings or metaphors for contemporary life. Despite its abundant wit and sometimes surreal exaggeration, the book is not pure comedy either. Finally, although the appeal of the novel derives from its protagonist, the story does not offer a development of character in the conventional sense— there is no crucial change in the central character's voice or personality or understanding. What *Alice in Bed* does offer is the thoroughly old-fashioned pleasure of reading a book about someone who is very likable. Schine's conceptualization and her narrative control in the novel have produced a wholly engaging central character.

Alice Brody, a nineteen-year-old girl from a suburban Connecticut family, is a sophomore at Sarah Lawrence College when, while babysitting one night, she is suddenly struck down by weakness, fever, and pain in her legs. After four weeks in bed at home (hooked up to a traction device which, she says, looks like one of the slicing-dicing-mashing-whipping machines on late-night television commercials), she is moved to a fashionable New York hospital. Her parents are in the process of a divorce, and her father takes off for Vancouver (from whence he eventually reappears with a new young wife); her mother, Brenda, a resolute optimist who lives in a state of continual distraction, is apparently studying for her doctoral orals in psychology and determinedly seeing the best in an unappealing hustler named Louis Scifo.

Schine deliberately limits her characters to the aspect they show to Alice at her bedside. Visitors are afraid of her illness; other patients are as self-involved as she is. The doctors are arrogant and insecure; they avoid telling Alice anything meaningful, change treatments without explanation, conceal their inability to diagnose her illness by ordering ever more radical tests. Nurses follow orders so they will not have to think or feel, even when the orders are doing obvious damage to the patient.

Alice uses humor as a defense—as a means of preserving some sense of control over her situation. The humor gains depth because, beneath it, the reader is aware of Alice's physical pain and the terrifying helplessness that grows from loss of control of one's body and one's fate. It is humiliating to be ill and weak. Furthermore, it violates one's unexamined assumptions concerning the order of things: Alice's illness has no explanation, no relationship to cause and consequence or to justice.

To cope with this frightening uncertainty, Alice regards her experiences with a studied detachment:

> She pulled the large red plastic mirror out of the drawer next to her bed. Her complexion was grayish, pale, and circles as dark as caves surrounded her eyes. She let her lids droop and tried to look vampy. Her lips looked a little blue, but at least they weren't chapped. There were hollows beneath her cheekbones, which she rather liked, and a small spray of pimples across her forehead. She watched two tears swell over her eyelids to slide dramatically down her pallid cheeks. Pain pounded through her body. I know I don't deserve this, she thought.
>
> She put her watch on. She put her watch on every day. Remnants of her old routine clung to her new life. Others had dropped away. She had stopped brushing her teeth, but still used deodorant.

This passage illustrates Schine's control of narrative tone throughout the novel. Although Alice's story is told in the third person, the narrative frequently employs the language which Alice herself would use to relate her experiences ("tried to look vampy," for example)—a device increasingly common in contemporary fiction.

The book's title carries deliberate double meaning. After her fever subsides, Alice begins to grow more aware of the people who surround her. She is a bedridden adolescent woman, paying a great deal of attention to her own body. Her hips and thighs are fixed in one position. Inevitably, sex occupies a great deal of her attention. Two doctors present themselves as lovers. In each of the book's sexual passages, Alice reveals her basic good humor and recovering self-possession. Dr. Davis, the family eye surgeon, visits her bedside and desires her, but as she recovers, she realizes that his sexual attraction stems from a yearning pity that makes him treat her like an infant. More promising (and entertaining) is Simchas Fresser, a hypnotist and expert on pain. ("How to inflict it?" she asks when she first hears him described—and events prove that she may well have been right.) He is a splendidly realized comic character, a psychologist who overflows with life and yet needs his patients' gratitude and admiration (as well as their fees) much more than they need his help. The prospect of going to bed with Simchas Fresser gives Alice a goal for getting on her feet. The happy event, however, does not take place. In his own apartment Fresser is not the man he was in the hospital. He has lost his power, Alice realizes, because she is getting better. Finally, in the rehabilitation hospital, among the sweaty male bodies in physical therapy, Alice experiences a full-blown adolescent passion for a beautiful man and realizes what she has missed in her cool, intellectual rejection of athletes and crushes. She even distracts herself momentarily with romantic fantasies before admitting to herself that she and Christopher have nothing in common except the rehabilitation institute.

The novel's other developing thread is Alice's attitude toward her parents. In childhood, she idolized her father, and despite her wry and realistic acceptance of the divorce ("They've been fighting for ten years, so what's the big deal?"), both Alice and her brother feel deeply angry and betrayed. Alice writes, but does not send, a bitterly sarcastic answer to a letter from her father. Toward her mother, Alice feels a baffled mixture of warmth, condescension, and empathy. Mrs. Brody's relentless suppression of all unpleasantness is laughable—but it may also be, in part, the source of Alice's sound good nature. Through the process of her recovery, a more womanly friendship with her mother grows, without Alice losing her unsentimental awareness of Mrs. Brody's failings.

Most of the book's characters are, as Alice would say, terminally isolated. Her letters to a college friend who is in a mental hospital show that Alice has as little comprehension of mental illness as her own hospital visitors do of physical illness. Alice feeds on the human interchange with her private-duty nurse Stephanie Carter and is surprised to discover, late in the book, how little she has understood of Stephanie's own problems and traumas. Schine, however, is not necessarily criticizing human failures of communication. The characters in this book who most desperately need other people are, at least as Alice observes them, the most ridiculous.

It is inevitable that Alice herself should be self-centered. Her world has diminished to her self and her own body in her bed. She sees other people and events only as they refer to her. Like adolescents in general, she is preoccupied with sex, unable to control the events in her life, struggling with ambivalent feelings toward her parents. To an extent, she becomes identified with her illness. She is deeply depressed when she begins to recover—struggling toward health had given her an objective in life as well as a lot of concentrated attention from other people. The book does not move to any conclusive achieving of adulthood—the final passage indicates that she may, for the moment, have taken her identity from her experience as a patient— but genuine good nature goes deep in Alice. It is not simply superficial good spirits nor her wryly comic perspective that makes Alice so appealing; her irony is refreshingly free of cynicism. Thus, one resists making the obvious comparison between *Alice in Bed* and *The Catcher in the Rye* (1951). Holden Caulfield disintegrates, but Alice Brody uses her intelligence and humor as glue to keep herself together.

Sally H. Mitchell

Sources for Further Study

Antioch Review. XLI, Fall, 1983, p. 509.
Library Journal. CVIII, May 1, 1983, p. 921.
Los Angeles Times Book Review. June 1, 1983, p. 8.
Ms. XII, July, 1983, p. 22.
The New Yorker. LIX, August 1, 1983, p. 87.
Newsweek. CI, June 13, 1983, p. 74.
Publishers Weekly. CCXXIII, March 18, 1983, p. 53.

AN AMATEUR'S GUIDE TO THE NIGHT

Author: Mary Robison (1949-   )
Publisher: Alfred A. Knopf (New York). 129 pp. $11.95
Type of work: Short stories
Time: The mid-1970's to the early 1980's
Locale: The United States

Thirteen stories of contemporary life in the United States

During the past few years, Mary Robison has won increasing recognition as one of the finest of a new generation of American writers. *An Amateur's Guide to the Night* is her second collection of short stories. In addition to her first collection, *Days* (1979), she has published a novel, *Oh!* (1981). Six of the thirteen stories in *An Amateur's Guide to the Night* originally appeared in *The New Yorker*. It is not surprising that such a high percentage of Robison's stories should appear in one of America's most prestigious markets for short fiction, for Robison's fiction is at once accessible and highly distinctive. With her precise control of language and her rigorous selection of detail and event, she places the reader in the center of her characters' emotional lives. Robison found her unique voice at a relatively young age, and in this second collection of stories, that voice continues to develop. She has the ability to write such completely rendered stories—within the confines of her narrative approach—that the widespread assumption about necessary apprenticeship years does not seem applicable to her. Raymond Carver has noted that Robison is one of a handful of contemporary short-story writers who are capable of rendering the world according to their own vision. That vision is tempered by a sense of humor, and although some critics have complained about the bleakness in many of her characters' lives, almost all have responded to her humor and touches of irony. Among the stories in *An Amateur's Guide to the Night* that first appeared in *The New Yorker*, "Coach" was selected for *Best American Short Stories 1982*, while "You Know Charles" (previously "Happy Boy, Allen"), first published in *The Mississippi Review*, was included in *The Push-cart Prize, VII*. Of the five previously unpublished stories in the collection, two—"An Amateur's Guide to the Night" and "Look at Me Go"—are among Robison's best.

Robison generally eschews authorial comment, so that motivation of characters and meaning of event must be deduced largely from what the characters say or from their actions. The advantage of such an approach, and one achievement of the stories, is that her characters and their environments become vividly real for the reader. Robison does not indulge in fantasy or in the morbid and sensational, nor are her stories highly plotted with sharply defined climaxes and epiphanies. Rather, Robison presents a "slice of life"—as in certain stories by Anton Chekhov or Ernest Hemingway—but in a manner that suggests the great complexities of the human world. This approach is very much in the tradition of the American short story, from Hemingway's "Hills Like White Elephants" and much of John O'Hara to stories by such contemporaries as Richard Yates and Andre Dubus. The achievement of Robison's best stories is to make the commonplace significant, to suggest the tensions that lie beneath the surface of everyday life.

In many of Robison's stories, a character's natural impulse toward compassion and a sense of meaning is limited or thwarted by his circumstances. Robison's characters are ordinary people—usually good, decent people, although such a classification would not occur to most of them—who are often confused by the shifting values of contemporary life. They are football coaches, optometrists, high school art teachers, housewives, laborers, college and high school students; they are not intellectuals, and they rarely reflect on the fragmented nature of society. Many critics have found in Robison's work a sense of disengagement, an anomie that characterizes many contemporary short-story writers—Carver, Yates, William Kittredge, and Ann Beattie to name only a few. Many of Robison's stories, however, deal with family relationships, and her characters are often compassionate and committed to one another. For the most part, they are not alienated in traditional existential terms but are simply people living common lives in everyday American society.

Robison's narrative method is to present her stories through several small dramatic sections—often only a page or two, at times less—which suggest the central importance of individual moments in the lives of her characters. In the best stories in this collection—"An Amateur's Guide to the Night," "The Dictionary in the Laundry Chute," "Coach," "Smart"—these individual moments add up to a revealing portrait of modern society, in which the past and the future are often disjointed from the present. Indeed, Robison suggests that people achieve a sense of meaning in their lives primarily through such individual moments; there is little sense of the past working through her characters and little promise of a future in which those characters will achieve a larger significance in their lives.

The danger of Robison's method is apparent in such stories as "Nothing's It," "Falling Away," and "You Know Charles," where her slice-of-life portraits are cut too thin. On the surface, these less successful stories exhibit the deft use of language, the tight structure, and the economical use of detail characteristic of her best work, but at their center, the characters are too fragmented; they do not generate that vital sense of life which is necessary for a Robison story to work. Other writers—Donald Barthelme, for example, or Robert Coover—with different approaches can create successful fictions without that vital sense of character, but Robison's fiction becomes flat and uninteresting without it.

Because Robison does not directly explore the psychological motivations of her characters, dialogue and action become the focus of narrative attention.

A feel for spoken language is one of Robison's greatest strengths as a writer. Critics agree on the precision of her rendering of speech; the poet and critic Katha Pollitt has said that Robison has the ear of a playwright, and repeatedly in these stories, a telling line of dialogue illuminates the inner world of a character. Many of Robison's most successful stories are first-person narratives in which the speaker's voice is unmistakably authentic.

The title story, "An Amateur's Guide to the Night," is narrated by Lindy, a seventeen-year-old senior in high school. The story moves forward with incidents presented in a brisk, straightforward, and very readable sequence, as is typical of Robison, and yet the narrative voice is distinctive: Every incident is filtered through Lindy's consciousness. Her world is limited by her relationship with her thirty-five-year-old divorced mother, Harriet. Lindy and her mother double-date, and on such occasions, Lindy, who is an "old seventeen," and her mother, who is five feet tall and who "looks young for her age," pass as sisters. In Lindy's perception, this situation is not bizarre; she is a levelheaded, vital young woman who is maturing into adulthood without the cynicism typical of many adolescents in contemporary fiction. Hers is a life filled with healthful curiosity—her hobby, astronomy, suggests a larger world of beauty and possibility—and despite the behavior of her mother, who requires periodic hospitalization for an emotional problem, Lindy's outlook is essentially positive. The "night" in the title connotes the unknown forces that Lindy must eventually confront, chief of which is her mother's condition, but for the moment, Lindy simply cares for her mother, "mothering" her in a reversal of the normal mother-daughter relationship.

"The Dictionary in the Laundry Chute" explores the parent-child bond from another angle. Margaret Anne, the twenty-two-year-old daughter of Ed and Angela, requires psychiatric attention. As she has done in other stories, Robison here treats in an unsensational manner a character suffering from emotional disturbance. Margaret Anne refuses to eat, and her parents' lives revolve around their attempts to bring her out of her depression. Ed and Angela care, they care deeply, but they are so limited in their own lives that they are ineffective in attempting to deal with their daughter's problems. A psychiatrist, Dr. Sid Grosh, visits the home to treat Margaret Anne, and his treatment begins to bring her back into the realm of normal life; she begins to eat. Dr. Grosh has assumed the authority that the father, in his pain and confusion, cannot. As the story draws to a close in the middle of the night, with the mother crying in fear and pain over the condition of her daughter, the father wonders aloud: "I don't see why we aren't happier and why we can't *all* get a little sleep around here." His plea is indicative of these characters' lack of control of their lives. That this malaise is expressed in dialogue is typical of Robison's narrative approach.

In contrast to the ineffectual father in "The Dictionary in the Laundry Chute," Harry Noonan, the title figure in the story "Coach," exerts considerable control over his family and over his situation in life. Coach Noonan has recently moved to a college town in Pennsylvania with his wife and fifteen-year-old daughter to become the freshman football coach, a move up after years of high school coaching. Noonan's attitudes regarding sexual roles are limited: When his daughter Daphne dates a student reporter from the college newspaper, Noonan disapproves because the student does not display the macho characteristics which the coach values—the student is too mature, too comfortable in his own identity for that. Coach makes his disapproval known to Daphne when he tells her that she is wasting her time: "You'd be trying to start a fire with a wet match," he says. The undertone of sexuality is not lost on Daphne, and she replies, "That's sick!" Such an exchange is indicative of Robison's ear for colloquial speech.

Although Robison satirizes Coach's stereotypical attitude toward male and female roles, she makes his character far more complicated than that of the typical butt of satire. When his wife, Sherry, explains that she feels confined by her role as mother and wife—she wants to rent a studio away from home to paint, to attempt to assume some kind of identity outside the family— Coach agrees to her request and supports her in her efforts. Although he occasionally resents his wife's ambitions, he keeps his resentment to himself, explaining to his daughter, who fears that her parents are headed for a divorce, that his wife genuinely needs a life of her own.

A number of the stories in *An Amateur's Guide to the Night* are quite short, ranging from one to two thousand words. Several of these fail, largely because in them Robison presents characters who call for further development. The tantalizing story "In Jewel," for example, narrated by a high school art teacher in a small mining town, leaves the reader yearning for a fuller treatment of character and situation; the same might be said of "I Am Twenty-one" and "The Nature of Almost Everything." All of these stories lack the sense of fulfillment—that "silence [of the] imagination," in Truman Capote's words— that one should feel upon completing an outstanding short story. In contrast to these stories, "Yours," which is only about one thousand words long— three pages—illustrates what can be accomplished in such a demanding form. Here, Robison maintains a distance from the characters, allowing for the kind of objectivity that such a length seems to require. Clark, a retired seventy-eight-year-old doctor, has remarried. His relatives write to tell him that he is being "cruelly deceived." They assume that Allison, his thirty-eight-year-old new wife, has married for her own gain. Ironically, however, it is Allison, not Clark, who is dying from cancer. At Allison's death, in a moving moment of pathos, Clark realizes what she has meant to him. It is in such stories that Robison displays her ability to make the limitations of the short-story form work for her, so that the form exhausts the content, and there is nothing left to be said. In such cases, the complexities of the deceptively simple action reverberate in the reader's mind long after the story has been put aside.

This suggestive power is evident in "Look at Me Go," a story not quite fifteen hundred words long. The story is divided into two sections: In the first section, the narrator sets the scene. She has come to the beach (the setting is the New England coast) with her fourteen-year-old son, Paul. The narrator recalls an argument which she has had earlier that morning with her husband, a furniture salesman. The husband believes that Paul is a "fraud." The mother knows that their son is immature for his age, but in her love for him, she is content simply to allow him to be what he is. Paul, who has a "girlish giggle" and who is not muscular, is their only child. Although the husband declares his love for Paul, he is greatly dissatisfied with his son. In the second section of the story, the narrator becomes engaged in conversation with a Russian immigrant who has brought his own son to the beach. The Russian, who has the "big girth and rolling muscles of a laborer," watches his son and Paul playing, and he comments to the mother that "some kids get big real fast" while "some other kids get to be kids a long time. I think they're more lucky." (The phrase "more lucky," instead of the more idiomatic "luckier," again demonstrates Robison's exact ear for speech.) The Russian does not wish Paul to be something other than what he is—he does not view the boy with the aspirations and demands typical of many middle-class parents. In the closing sentences of the story, Robison achieves a kind of lyricism which makes plain language beautiful: The Russian "smiled as though he loved all boys and took pride in them—even mine. He smiled as though he loved *me*. I let it come, so much love so easy." This love is not sexual love; it is the love of one human being for another—just for being human. Thus, Robison suggests the compassion that is possible between strangers, the harmony of the world as it sometimes can be.

Many critics have described Mary Robison's work as "promising," but in such stories as "An Amateur's Guide to the Night," "Coach," and "Look at Me Go," she already has attained considerable achievement. On reading such stories, one has that "absolute and final" feeling to which, in Truman Capote's formulation, the short story aspires.

Ronald L. Johnson

Sources for Further Study

Christian Science Monitor. January 11, 1984, p. 19.
Los Angeles Times Book Review. December 9, 1983, p. 38.
The New York Times Book Review. LXXXVIII, November 27, 1983, p. 13.
Publishers Weekly. CCXXIV, September 30, 1983, p. 106.

AMERICAN FICTIONS, 1940-1980
A Comprehensive History and Critical Evaluation

Author: Frederick R. Karl (1927-   )
Publisher: Harper & Row, Publishers (New York). 637 pp. $32.50
Type of work: Literary criticism

A reader's guide to the contemporary American novel in which fiction is examined in its cultural context

Structuralism, semiotics, and deconstruction have no place in *American Fictions, 1940-1980*, for Frederick R. Karl believes it is the Americanness of American literature that is most important—a position that is sure to appeal to those who have grown weary in recent years seeing distinctive national literatures turned into grist for the various mills of European formalist theories. Karl is not, however, an isolationist critic; in fact, he argues that the strength of recent American fiction derives from the American writer's willingness and ability to adapt American materials to the ideas and techniques of European modernism, which had surprisingly little influence on American novelists (except for William Faulkner and John Dos Passos) prior to World War II. Karl deliberately labels the innovative fiction of the postwar years "American modernism," avoiding the more common term, "postmodernism," in order to stress (as that high modernist T. S. Eliot would have said) the continuing presence of the past in contemporary American literature, which involves not a renunciation of the modernist legacy but instead a dialectic of old and new, European and American, tradition and the individual talent. In Karl's view, the basic test of the American modernist writer is whether he can make his language accommodate his subject matter. Those who continue to employ traditional narrative techniques, and as a result improve their chance of winning popular approval, fail to measure up to Karl's standard. The writers who pass are those who have demonstrated the ability to move beyond the naturalistic style of their early work—Norman Mailer in *Why Are We in Vietnam?* (1967), for example, or Joyce Carol Oates in *Bellefleur* (1980)—and more especially the formally innovative writers—Walter Abish, John Barth, Donald Barthelme, William Burroughs, William Gaddis, John Hawkes, Joseph McElroy, and Thomas Pynchon. However inaccessible, even unreadable their experimental fictions may be to the general reader (with whom Karl has very little patience or sympathy), they represent the writer's provisional triumph over his voracious, media-driven American audience and the best reflection of the paradoxes inherent in American life.

What Karl promises in this ambitious survey is a threefold project: a cultural as well as aesthetic interpretation of contemporary American fiction that will demonstrate the superiority of nontraditional fiction over traditional; a "comprehensive history" that—unlike the *Harvard Guide to Contemporary Ameri-*

can Writing (1979), for example—will be broad, deep, and coherent; and an analysis that will improve on such well-known critical assessments as Tony Tanner's *City of Words* (1971), Raymond Olderman's *Beyond the Waste Land* (1972), Alfred Kazin's *Bright Book of Life* (1973), and Jerome Klinkowitz's *Literary Disruptions* (1975). What Karl actually delivers, however, is considerably less, despite his extensive reading and the more than six hundred double-column pages of this book. The problem (as Karl is so fond of saying) begins with the title. Karl's subject is not American fictions but American novels; the period under study is not 1940 to 1980 but the postwar era, including a number of novels published after 1980 and, oddly, earlier works such as Henry Roth's *Call It Sleep* (1934) and Dos Passos' *U.S.A.* trilogy (1930-1936). The "comprehensive history" is little more than a confusingly organized survey, heavy on plot and platitude, and the "critical evaluation" is tacked on, rather than integral.

The chief way in which Karl attempts to prove the continuity of the postwar novel with the rest of American literature is by identifying the major themes and motifs that run throughout both: the pastoral impulse, "the regaining of paradise by means of spatial movement," the individual self versus the Procrustean system, resurrection-regeneration, imaginative alternative realities, dissipation of talent (no second acts, as F. Scott Fitzgerald pointed out). The noting of such continuity is commendable; the author's presentation of these themes as his own discoveries is not. His failure to credit Leo Marx's *The Machine in the Garden* (1964), Richard Poirier's *A World Elsewhere* (1966), Leslie Fiedler's "No! in Thunder" and his *Love and Death in the American Novel* (1960), R. W. B. Lewis' *The American Adam* (1955), Gerald Graff's *Literature Against Itself* (1979), and a number of other influential works would have been understandable had Karl written his book as a general survey for students on the order of Malcolm Bradbury's *The Modern American Novel* (1983), and had he not created the illusion of scholarly documentation in his twenty pages—forty columns—of notes (mainly identifying quotations taken from various novels). Given this failure or, more charitably, omission, it is ironic that Karl should fault George Steiner for his "derivative and stereotypical" views or William Styron for being unaware that the material he used in one of his novels "had been exhausted well before he got to it."

Despite its great length, *American Fictions, 1940-1980* is a rather thin book in terms of its argument. Derivative as many of its cultural ideas may be, they are nevertheless correct, and Karl might have spent his and the reader's time demonstrating their presence in the postwar American novel. Instead, the cultural commentary is kept distinct from the usually rather general discussions of the novels, which as a result appear to be little more than summaries spiced now and then with a few lines of hit-and-run "critical evaluation." (A noteworthy exception is all but the last few pages of chapter 10, "The Female Experience"; tightly focused and truly evaluative, it is significant both for Karl's discussion of the spatial metaphor in women's literature and for his remarks on the rather conservative narrative approach of many women writers.) What is wanted here is less summary, more demonstration, not of points that have already been amply proven, such as the pastoral idea in American literature, but of the many significant issues Karl raises in passing—the problem, for example, of American comedy—which, in taking the side of the individual rather than the community, runs counter to the cultural impulse that gives rise to the comic mode in other societies.

The raising of such points—and there are many of them—is one of the virtues of this exasperating work. Another is the author's willingness to praise new and unusual talents—Joseph McElroy, for one—without feeling compelled to praise all innovative writers indiscriminately. Much of what is heralded as unique is not, as Karl notes, very good or even very new—the apocalyptic postmodernist tag notwithstanding. He understands that the fictions of Abish, Barthelme, Ronald Sukenick, and Raymond Federman rest on a common aesthetic foundation, but Karl also understands—as many of these writers' advocates seem not to—that the quality of Abish's and Barthelme's fiction is far superior to that of their fellow experimentalists. Karl, to his credit, is not content to take either all of the new fiction or none of it. Robert Scholes showed the same courage in his *Fabulation and Metafiction* (1979) and was promptly condemned as a traitor to the innovative fiction movement that he had helped make respectable with the publication of *The Fabulators* in 1967. Karl's own conservative approach to literary criticism, with its stress on character, structure, and cultural content, undermines, at least in part, his commitment to and understanding of many of the innovative works he discusses. Conversely, although Karl argues convincingly that Hawkes's *The Cannibal* (1949) is superior to Mailer's *The Naked and the Dead* (1948) on the basis of narrative technique—the one innovative and modernist, the other conservative and naturalistic—he proves rather dogmatic when it comes to appreciating or even recognizing the narrative experiments of less overtly innovative writers, such as "pastoralists" John Cheever and John Gardner or "didactics" Saul Bellow and Walker Percy (whom Karl confuses with the first-person narrator of Percy's fourth novel, *Lancelot*, 1977). Similarly, for all of his stress on "paradox" in American literature, Karl provides rather literal-minded readings of a number of works—Bernard Malamud's *The Tenants* (1971), for example, or "The Magic Barrel"—that simply defy such closed, determinate interpretations. On the other hand, his penchant for paradox leads him on more than one occasion beyond criticism to something a little closer to bathos, as in this comment on Peter S. Beagle's *The Last Unicorn* (1968): "The last unicorn cannot mate, since no mate exists, and yet she is immortal—here is the paradox of an American fate."

American Fictions, 1940-1980 demands to be read as a unified work of literary criticism rather than as a work merely to be consulted (this despite its already having been shelved in the reference section of several university libraries). Not only does it not repay the reader's commitment to it; every chapter raises serious questions about its author's method and critical sensibility. It becomes increasingly difficult to trust a critic who detects in McCarthyism "a profound [but unexplained] radicalism," or who dismisses the effect of the stock market crash of 1929 on all but the five percent of the population who owned one-third of the nation's property and wealth, or who claims that Franz Kafka "had no doubts" about the beyond; a critic who believes, again without bothering to explain himself, that Pynchon's achievement is "hobbled" by his inability to write about love, that the title *Naked Lunch* "has a traditional ring to it," that Robert Coover's *The Universal Baseball Association, Inc. J. Henry Waugh, Prop. (1968)* is a pastoral novel, that William Gass's *Willie Masters' Lonesome Wife* (1971) is about the female experience, that Joan Didion's fiction is marred by her self-pity, that Maria Wyeth's is the only voice in Didion's 1970 novel *Play It As It Lays* (what about the "Helene" and "Carter" sections and the third-person narrator?), and that Didion's characters are too well heeled to be existential. How—or why—is the reader to accept Karl's judgment that John Barth's "summa theologica," *Giles Goat-Boy* (1966)—"an immense, self-indulgent, overbearing novel"—fails as art, whereas Barth's *Letters* (1979)—"immense, overdrawn, indulgent"—is "a landmark fiction"? More important, what is one to make of a critic who establishes major cultural themes and then uses them as weapons to bludgeon the very authors who fictionalize those themes in their novels? If Saul Bellow fears allowing the self too much space or fails to resolve the tension between the individual character and his world or does not provide the reader with characters who mature during the course of a novel, is Bellow somehow remiss (as Karl claims) or is he perhaps to be applauded (as Burroughs and Pynchon are) as a "quintessentially American author"?

Such are some of the fruits of reading *American Fictions, 1940-1980* in its overdrawn entirety; there are others. One of the most annoying is Karl's habit of finding fault with nearly every novel he discusses: because it is too ambitious or too ideological or not ideological enough or not sufficiently modernist or imperfectly executed—usually because of the author's failure to maintain his distance, the modernist stick which Karl uses to beat offenders and non-offenders alike. More objectionable are Karl's suggestions for ways offending writers could or *should* have improved their novels. What makes these suggested revisions so nettlesome is the overwhelming evidence that Karl revised his own work little if at all. Not only is the book poorly organized, but it is also wordy, at times factually incorrect, and incredibly repetitive, partly the result of the haphazard organization and partly because of the kind of carelessness so glaringly obvious on pages 211 and 212, where Burroughs' description of his "nova technique" is quoted twice. Other kinds of repetition are only slightly less annoying; the favorite words (dialectic, paradox, hover, hobble, dilemma, problem, seam, seamless, palimpsest), and the frequent, usually unilluminating, and often gratuitous comparisons of recent American novels to Kafka's writings, Ivan Goncharov's *Oblomov* (1958), Friedrich Nietzsche's "last man," Albert Camus' *L'Étranger* (1942; *The Stranger*, 1942) and *La Chute* (1956; *The Fall*, 1956), Delmore Schwartz's "In Dreams Begin Responsibilities," and the novels of Joseph Conrad, whose influence Karl, Conrad's biographer, finds nearly everywhere.

Had Professor Karl looked over his manuscript more thoughtfully, he undoubtedly would not have found Barthelme's Snow White an "avatar" of Ernest Hemingway's Lady Ashley; nor would he have had Sylvia Plath's Esther Greenwood attempt suicide in the breezeway of her mother's basement. He might also have trimmed his manuscript and organized it more logically and consistently. Once the focus had been made clear—the Americanness of the postwar American novel—he might even have considered the significant consequences of an innovative fiction entirely free of the limitations of the general reading audience. This point, which Karl sidesteps entirely, lies at the heart of all postmodernist art and literature, as Christopher Butler demonstrated so brilliantly in his *After the Wake* (1980). What Karl might have written, then, is the book *American Fictions, 1940-1980* promised to be. In its published form, it constitutes what Karl would call an ambitious failure. As a guide to the contemporary American novel, it does not replace such standard reference works as the volumes in the *Dictionary of Literary Biography* devoted to the postwar American novel. As a work of criticism, it certainly does not supplant Tony Tanner's *City of Words*.

Robert A. Morace

Sources for Further Study

Christian Science Monitor. April 6, 1984, p. 24.
Los Angeles Times Book Review. January 15, 1984, p. 4
The New York Times Book Review. LXXXVIII, January 8, 1984, p. 11.
Saturday Review. X, February, 1984, p. 54.

THE ANATOMY LESSON

Author: Philip Roth (1933-   )
Publisher: Farrar, Straus and Giroux (New York). 291 pp. $13.95
Type of work: Novel
Time: 1973
Locale: New York City and Chicago

The further misadventures of the novelist Nathan Zuckerman, who, at the age of forty and stricken with pain from a mysterious orthopedic ailment, feels that he has lost his subject and thus contemplates becoming a medical doctor

> Principal characters:
> NATHAN ZUCKERMAN, an afflicted novelist
> DIANA, JENNY, GLORIA, JAGA, his secretary-confidante-cook-housekeeper-companion harem
> MILTON APPEL, Zuckerman's nemesis, a critic
> BOBBY FREYTAG, Zuckerman's old friend, now a doctor
> MR. FREYTAG, Bobby's father
> RICKY, a female limousine chauffeur

Since *The Anatomy Lesson* is Philip Roth's third novel in which Nathan Zuckerman is the central character, a few words of background may be helpful to place Zuckerman's current fictional dilemma in perspective. Zuckerman was first introduced in *My Life as a Man* (1974) as the fictional creation of Roth's fictional creation, Peter Tarnopol, in two stories by Tarnopol entitled "Salad Days" and "Courting Disaster." In 1979, Zuckerman emerged as the central figure in his own right of Roth's short novel *The Ghost Writer* (1979). In that first-person narrative, Zuckerman recounts his visit as a promising young writer of twenty-three to the country home of E. I. Lonoff, an older writer whom he greatly admires. Witness to Lonoff's Jamesian disengagement for the sake of his art, Zuckerman ends the novel fairly clear about the kind of books he wants to write but less clear about the kind of life he wants to lead.

Roth's 1981 novel *Zuckerman Unbound* picks up its title character at the age of thirty-six, following the publication of Zuckerman's best-selling novel, *Carnovsky* (clearly the equivalent of *Portnoy's Complaint*—which, like the fictitious *Carnovsky*, was published in 1969). Here, Zuckerman must cope with fame and fortune and ponder his brother's accusation that he caused the death of his father with his autobiographical and anti-Jewish novel. At the end of *Zuckerman Unbound*, Nathan is left feeling that he has lost his father, his wife, his brother, and his heritage. One would think that with all of these ghosts exorcised, Nathan would finally be free—or at least that Roth would be free of Zuckerman. As this new Roth novel makes clear, however, such is emphatically not the case.

What began in *My Life as a Man* as an interesting experiment with the problematical relationship between fiction and reality becomes in *The Anatomy Lesson* forced and tedious. The basic trope that Roth uses to unify this new Zuckerman misadventure is a mysterious and undiagnosable back ailment which renders Zuckerman immobile, reduced to lying on his back on a child's play mat—an ailment that, although Zuckerman denies it, seems clearly a psychosomatic illness brought on by the guilt he feels for *Carnovsky*. The further and most obvious irony is that the ailment represents the generalized Jewish guilt which Zuckerman both writes about and denies in his infamous novel itself; as Roth says of his persona, "He hadn't spent 20 years writing about irrational guilt to wind up irrationally guilty." The key to the central trope of physical pain is given in a prefatory quotation from a textbook of orthopedic medicine: "The chief obstacle to correct diagnosis in painful conditions is the fact that the symptom is often felt at a distance from its source."

Much of the first chapter of the book presents extensive excruciating detail about the pain itself, for if the novelist cannot analyze the cause of the pain (which, after all, is the job for the critic), he can at least graphically describe its symptoms. Lying on his play mat, unable to move his neck and looking at the world around him through grotesque prism glasses, Nathan welcomes both the companionship and the sexual favors of the four women who visit him and play the roles of lost mother and lost wives. Although Nathan denies the diagnosis a psychoanalyst offers him—that he is "the ineradicable infant, the atoning penitent, the guilty pariah"—it seems clear that the book depends on the reader's perceiving Nathan in just this way. To interpret his pain in any other way is to see it as the unmotivated and thematically uninteresting cause of his loss of his subject, to see it as a mere contingency of fate that makes him unable, either physically or morally, to find a posture for his writing. On the other hand, however, to see the pain as the objectification of Nathan's guilt is likewise to see it as the thematically motivated creation of Roth and thus to see it as stereotypical and banal.

Although the previous Zuckerman novels deprive Nathan of his father, his brother, and his birthplace, *The Anatomy Lesson* must take away still more and thus begins with the loss of his mother, his health, his hair, and—most important, according to the fictitious critic Milton Appel—his talent. It is indeed this final father figure (at least the reader can hope that Appel is the final one) who must be dealt with before Nathan can finally be free to live his life and Roth can be free to write of something else besides his own ghosts. Appel, who in 1959 had called Zuckerman a "wunderkind" for his early stories (an appellation lavished on Roth himself after the publication of *Goodbye, Columbus* in 1959), reconsiders "The Case of Nathan Zuckerman" in a harsh criticism of what he calls Zuckerman's anti-Jewishness after the publication of *Carnovsky*. Appel charges that Zuckerman feels as Carnovsky does—that the "Jews can stick their historical suffering up their ass." It is a criticism that rankles Zuckerman to the point of obsession.

When Diana, one of Zuckerman's female confidantes, tells him, "You cannot make yourself a life of misery out of a book that just happened to have been a roaring success," the reader begins to wonder if Roth is determined to persist in using Zuckerman as expiation for the roaring success of *Portnoy's Complaint.* Throughout *Zuckerman Unbound* and *The Anatomy Lesson*, Nathan insists on the separation between reality and fiction, personal life and created life, and he even attacks Appel in a virulent telephone call for confusing the two, yet it seems clear that the interest of the Zuckerman novels resides in the parallels that compel one to read the trilogy as a commentary on Roth's career.

Whether Roth in fact feels guilty for betraying both his immediate family and his larger cultural family in *Portnoy's Complaint* is not the point; he certainly has attempted in his last three novels to encourage the reader to believe that he has. Thus, Roth covertly refers to one of his best-known early short stories when Zuckerman mocks Appel as a self-styled "Defender of the Faith." It is a cute little in-joke but perhaps, like much of *The Anatomy Lesson*, a bit too cute. Such self-referential devices allow Roth to justify his previous work while at the same time seeming to accept his responsibility for it. After three volumes of this, the reader begins to feel that Zuckerman indeed protests too much.

At any rate, in *The Anatomy Lesson*, one finds Zuckerman finally insisting that he wants a second life; that he is tired of being chained to self-consciousness, introspection, and his own "dwarf drama" until he dies; that he wants to hear stories not his own, stories from patients with a clear and practical purpose: "Cure me." *The Anatomy Lesson* itself may be understood as a means by which Roth/Zuckerman attempts to cure himself, for it is an intellectual analysis of his own novelist's nature in terms of physical pain, just as Robert Burton's *Anatomy of Melancholy* (1621) is an intellectual analysis of society in terms of the central conception of the humors. The "lesson" Zuckerman both teaches and learns here relates not to his physical body but to the body of his work.

The second half of the book narrates Nathan's return to Chicago, where he had earlier begun his intellectual life in an attempt to enter medical school. Doped up on Percodan, marijuana, and vodka, Zuckerman takes his self-indulgent and self-satisfied revenge on Milton Appel by pretending to be a professional pornographer of that name, publisher of a sleazy magazine named *Lickety Split.* Indeed, a great deal of the last half of the novel offers Nathan-as-pornographer-Appel justifying his life and his work, first to a fellow airplane passenger and then to Ricky, the female limousine chauffeur he has hired. In long monologues, Zuckerman justifies the essential fantasy nature of pornography and in so doing presents himself-as-Appel as the most unregenerate and notorious pornographer in the United States. Such a role-playing projection allows Zuckerman to create an image he feels has been imposed upon him and give it back in spades to the one who he feels has imposed it on him in the first place. It also allows him to play the role of Carnovsky as the reader might imagine him, yet the only justification for such an interpretation—Zuckerman's novel existing only as a title—is the reader's prior knowledge of *Portnoy's Complaint*: Zuckerman's apologia for a hedonistic search for sexual pleasure sounds very much like the justification of Alexander Portnoy. The rambling monologues constitute the release of a long pent-up need for self-expression—made possible, ironically, by Zuckerman's role-playing reversal of his enemy.

In the final chapter, entitled "The Corpus"—a not-too-subtle pun suggesting both the physical body and the body of a writer's work—the dope, the vodka, and the Percodan, not to mention the obsessive nature of the role he has been playing, finally prove too much for Zuckerman. In a cemetery scene, he attacks his friend Bobby's elderly father for talking about the "sacred genes" of the Jews, then falls and lacerates his face on the tombstone of the old man's brother. Ricky, the strong and independent female chauffeur (very much like the powerful female Jewish freedom fighter at the end of *Portnoy's Complaint*), plays both forbidding and succoring mother to Zuckerman at the moment of his collapse.

Still, Roth is not finished with Zuckerman. In the last pages of the book, with his mouth clamped shut, silenced at last, Zuckerman allows his tongue to explore the "Heart of Darkness" of his mouth, as he ponders in another much-too-cute allusion: "I am the Marlow of my mouth." During his recuperation, he considers his experience and the clever jokes that fate plays but thinks to himself, "Just don't make me write about it after." Realizing that not everything has to be a book, he further knows that "everything *can* be a book. And doesn't count as life until it is." He goes the rounds with the doctors, introduced as "Dr. Zuckerman . . . resident humanist," confronting reality at last, as he believes: "*This is life. With real teeth in it.*" Roth leaves Zuckerman making his rounds, however, with a final ironic observation that he acts as if he "still believed that he could unchain himself from a future as a man apart and escape the corpus that was his."

One fears that such an ending is no ending at all and that Zuckerman at forty still has yet to become Roth at fifty in his next book. Roth has said that what readers often take as "veiled autobiography" is only a "useful fiction," a kind of "idealized architect's drawing for what one may have constructed—or is yet to construct—out of the materials actuality makes available." *The Anatomy Lesson* suggests that the previously "useful fiction" of Nathan Zuckerman has perhaps outlived its usefulness. Nathan may not be able to escape his body, but surely Roth has now fully exorcised his own demons and can now at least escape the cannibalizing of the body of his own work. Although in *Reading Myself and Others* (1975), Roth said he was involved in the writer's "seemingly interminable task of self-justification"—a job that he felt may not be within his power or his best interest ever to complete—one can hope that, in his next, inevitable novel, he will find a less obvious and less tediously self-indulgent means to pursue this interminable task.

Charles E. May

Sources for Further Study

America. CL, March 10, 1984, p. 179.
Commentary. LXXVII, January, 1984, p. 63.
Hudson Review. XXVII, Spring, 1984, p. 152.
Los Angeles Times Book Review. November 13, 1983, p. 1.
The New York Times Book Review. LXXXVIII, October 30, 1983, p. 1.
Publishers Weekly. CCXXIV, October 7, 1983, p. 89.
Saturday Review. IX, December, 1983, p. 57.

ANCIENT EVENINGS

Author: Norman Mailer (1923-   )
Publisher: Little, Brown and Company (Boston). 709 pp. $19.95
Type of work: Novel
Time: 1290-1100 B.C.
Locale: Egypt

This profoundly imaginative but belabored novel is a culmination of the author's principal themes and a daring synthesis of his previous experiments in fiction and nonfiction

> *Principal characters:*
> MENENHETET I, the protagonist and narrator
> MENENHETET II, his great-grandson
> HATHFERTITI, the daughter of Menenhetet I
> NEF-KHEP-AUKHEM, her husband and the father of Menenhetet II
> PTAH-NEM-HOTEP (RAMSES IX), the Pharaoh who, on the "Night of the Pig," requests that Menenhetet I tell the story of his four lives
> USERMARE (RAMSES II), the great Pharaoh whom Menenhetet I first served and whom Ptah-nem-hotep venerates
> NEFERTIRI, Usermare's queen
> RAMA-NEFRU, a Hittite queen favored by Usermare
> HONEY-BALL, one of Usermare's queens, a lover of Menenhetet I

On the first page of *Advertisements for Myself* (1959), Norman Mailer announces that he has been "imprisoned with a perception which will settle for nothing less than making a revolution in the consciousness of our time." In all of his subsequent work, he has put himself forward as a great novelist in the making, and many critics have regarded him as America's most prominent contemporary literary voice. Even in a seemingly self-effacing book such as *The Executioner's Song* (1979), one is reminded of Mailer's huge ambition. At the same time, however, each new book has been offered as a provisional product of the author's evolving existential vision and not as a definitive utterance. Thus, Mailer has been opportunistic and eclectic, taking what comes to hand—no matter whether it is Marilyn Monroe or a moon shot—and turning it toward his sensibility. Not until *Ancient Evenings*, written with much deliberation during a period of approximately ten years (1972-1982), has he dared to call one of his works his magnum opus.

Ancient Evenings is a summing-up and a testament wherein Mailer appears to have concentrated his whole will on expressing in their entirety the themes implicit in his career. *Ancient Evenings* is also a cosmological treatise in which the author of *An American Dream* (1965) and *Why Are We in Vietnam?* (1967) wants nothing less than to discover the sources of his imaginative power by returning to the origins of modern consciousness. If modern man could experience the very birth of consciousness, then perhaps his awareness of all things, or of how human consciousness participates in all things, would mitigate the overpowering sense of alienation that pervades twentieth century literature. This is the revolutionary premise of Mailer's long Egyptian novel.

Reviewers have been quick to grasp *Ancient Evenings* as the embodiment of Mailer's metaphysics and poetics. Throughout his career, Mailer has argued the interdependence of fact and fiction, of observation and imagination, and *Ancient Evenings* constitutes his supreme demonstration of that interdependence, first explicitly enunciated in *Advertisements for Myself*: "There is finally no way one can try to apprehend complex reality without a 'fiction.'"

The time and place of Mailer's novel are historical: Egypt in the nineteenth and twentieth dynasties (1290-1100 B.C.). Many of the characters and the events are also historical and based upon his extensive reading of the literature on ancient Egypt. The frequent evocations of the country's geography and topography, of its architecture and climate, and of its varied sights and smells, reflect the author's effort to encompass the whole of a civilization. Beginning with the first sentence—"Crude thoughts and fierce forces are my state"— the reader is immersed in a style that confounds expectations—above all, the expectation of Mailer's active authorial voice transforming everything it articulates, even when that voice hides behind the conceit of having been "imprisoned with a perception." In *Ancient Evenings*, the imprisonment is palpable, for "my state" is governed by "crude thoughts and fierce forces." Something very strange is happening to the passive voice of the novel's first narrator-protagonist. This is, Mailer would have the reader believe, Egyptian consciousness, premodern; the "I" is not even yet born. The narrator-protagonist quite literally does not know who he is and therefore does not have the faintest idea of who he has been or who he might become. As the reader eventually figures out, Menenhetet II is undergoing the painful process of rebirth, a rebirth that is portrayed, however, not as merely the development of a personal identity but as a phenomenon of nature, a geological upheaval: "Mountains writhe. I see waves of flame. Washes, flashes, waves of flame."

This first book of the novel is awesome and quite wonderful in its depiction of a consciousness trying to differentiate itself from all that surrounds it. It is tempting to see here an allegory of the artist's search for a personal voice and vision that is also analogous to each sentient person's wish to know himself and his world. In his other writings, Mailer has approached much more tentatively and speculatively the idea of humanity's karmic roots. He posits a common consciousness and a kind of *spiritus mundi* out of which human beings originate and to which, in some sense, they return. In *Marilyn* (1973), for example, he imagines the actress' death scene as possibly also a rebirth: " . . . out there somewhere in the attractions of that eternity she has heard singing in her ears from childhood, she takes the leap to leave the pain of one deadened soul for the hope of life in another. . . . " In *Ancient Evenings*, the reader senses just such a transformation, so that Menenhetet II has not one life but as many as he is able to enter, for human minds are porous and are simultaneously both male and female, young and old. Some readers will no doubt be disgusted by Mailer's frequent use of sexual and scatological language, but it is his contention that human beings are entering one another, seeking power over one another, through every conceivable orifice, all of the time, and he is determined to explore every route, physical and metaphorical, to human identity—as he makes clear in his *People* magazine interview: "In Egypt, given the Nile flooding its banks and turning villages into islands in the river, with detritus everywhere, animals living in the houses, everyone huddled together, one knows that it was an incredibly fecal place. . . . It's no secret that Freud gave us a firm set of connections between anality and power . . . and what I learned about Egypt seemed a kind of confirmation."

After the first book, much of the novel is narrated by Menenhetet I, the great-grandfather of Menenhetet II. Menenhetet I has learned the secret of rebirth, and from the perspective of his fourth life he reflects upon his three former selves for the benefit of his Pharaoh, Ptah-nem-hotep (Ramses IX), who, in turn, is obsessed with his predecessor, the great Usermare (Ramses II), whom Menenhetet I has served and fought alongside in the historic battle of Kadesh. The parallels between the two Menenhetets and the two Ramses reflect the concern with doubling and with a divided world that has informed much of Mailer's work. Because Egypt itself is split between upper and lower parts, it is called the land of the two houses, and the Pharaoh is called "Divine Two-House." Similarly, there are "two houses of the mind" which must be reconciled, just as one life can only be understood in terms of another, one emotion in the context of its opposite: "I do not believe we can ever know a great emotion until the noblest and commonest impulses in ourself are present at once," says Menenhetet I in recalling the profound mixture of love and hate he held for Usermare. He has only come to know himself through his many lives as charioteer, general, harem master, high priest, and grave robber.

Menenhetet I's long narrative covers not only his several lives but also the ages of a civilization and of his listeners. His daughter Hathfertiti; his great-grandson, Menenhetet II; and his Pharaoh, Ptah-nem-hotep—all of whom, at various stages of his narrative, are able to take on his thoughts and to participate in his involvement with all levels of society and periods of history. Their participation in Menenhetet I's memories is a way of reclaiming the past, of understanding an Egypt that has forgotten the primal sources of its power: "Of course," Menenhetet I remarks, "in these years, we are not close to the Gods." Of "The Book of the Gods," which follows Menenhetet II's rebirth, the reviewer in *The New Republic* observes: "Mailer's gods are metaphors for the permanent energies of the human psyche and for the character types these energies produce." Egypt, under Ptah-nem-hotep, seems roughly parallel to the America of Mailer's other work, the America that lacks but yearns for an occult connection with the mysteries of existence. Finally, in this fiction, Mailer is free from the constraints of books such as *An American Dream*, where such an intermingling of characters, ages, and worlds beyond the present one could only be essayed, not accomplished. At the end of that earlier novel, Stephen Rojack puts in a phone call to his dead lover, Cherie, and ". . . a voice came back, a lovely voice, and said, 'Why, hello, hon, I thought you'd never call. It's kind of cool right now, and the girls are swell. Marilyn says to say hello.' "

It is a curious circumstance that what Mailer could not do for America— penetrate to its very core—he tries to do for ancient Egypt. Apparently, at the inception of his novel, he believed that his very distance from that land and that time would enable him to release a certain inventiveness lacking in his previous fiction, which was set in a country that he knew too well—a country that provided him with plots ready-made. Conceptually, then, *Ancient Evenings* towers over his past achievements; heretofore, Mailer has had to explain his epistemology on the run, so to speak, while delving into his characters' minds.

In *Ancient Evenings*, the prose is driven by what Menenhetet II calls "the long slow current of my great-grandfather's mind," and that mind is the receptacle for "what any of us might wish to put within it." Coming to *Ancient Evenings* from Mailer's previous work, one has to learn to read him anew, and not all readers have been willing to grant him the luxury of this latest style. On the one hand, it embeds the reader in the lush details of ancient Egypt, in the rhythms of an alien time that eventually become strangely familiar. On the other hand, even the most sympathetic readers have noted a numbing sameness in the prose, a univocal quality which suggests that the author has striven too hard for unity, for the merging of the opposites that create so much exciting tension in *The Naked and the Dead* (1948), *The Armies of the Night: History as a Novel, the Novel as History* (1968), and *The Executioner's Song*. *Ancient Evenings* is Norman Mailer at his neatest; the loose ends of his philosophy and his prose are tied together rather impressively, but the novel seems static, a little too thoroughly thought-out. Absent from it is the rough-edged stimulation of a writer on the make, a writer who is at his best when he is suggestive rather than explicit, when he is promising to complete the circle and join its halves without ever quite doing so.

Carl E. Rollyson, Jr.

Sources for Further Study

Christian Science Monitor. July 6, 1983, p. 9.
Esquire. C, July, 1983, p. 116.

Hudson Review. XXXVI, Autumn, 1983, p. 560.
Library Journal. CVIII, April 1, 1983, p. 759.
Los Angeles Times Book Review. April 24, 1983, p. 1.
Ms. XII, August, 1983, p. 33.
The New York Times Book Review. LXXXVIII, April 10, 1983, p. 1.
Psychology Today. XVII, June, 1983, p. 16.
Saturday Review. IX, June, 1983, p. 53.
Time. CXXI, April 18, 1983, p. 85.

ARARAT

Author: D. M. Thomas (1935-   )
Publisher: The Viking Press (New York). 191 pp. $13.50
Type of work: Novel
Time: 1981, 1837, and 1825
Locale: Gorky, Moscow, Petersburg; shipboard in the Atlantic; New York; and
  Yerevan, Soviet Armenia

A narrative puzzle of embedded and interlocking stories about improvisation and its relationship to cruelty and sex

> *Principal characters:*
> SERGEI ROZANOV, a fifty-year-old Russian poet
> OLGA, a blind doctoral student writing a thesis in Gorky on Rozanov
> VICTOR SURKOV, a fifty-year-old Russian poet, biographer, and
>   novelist
> MARIAN FAIRFAX, an Armenian-American writer of romantic fiction
> ARAM KHANDJIAN, an Armenian storyteller who teaches at Yer-
>   evan University
> ANNA POLANSKI, a Polish gymnast traveling to the United States
> FINN, an elderly Scandinavian ship passenger, a participant in
>   numerous atrocities
> NAYIRIE, a Turkish athlete whom Surkov marries aboard ship to
>   enable her to enter the United States
> DONNA ZARIFIAN, an Armenian-American sculptor at whose
>   Brooklyn apartment Surkov stays
> C. P. CHARSKY, an aristocratic young Petersburg poet in Alexander
>   Pushkin's "Egyptian Nights"
> KATERINA ORLOV, a consumptive Moscow woman courted by
>   Charsky
> NEAPOLITAN *IMPROVISATORE*, a performer

D. M. Thomas' third novel *The White Hotel* (1981), which brings Freudian fantasy to the theme of Nazi extermination of the Jews, became a publishing legend. When first released in the author's native Great Britain, the novel did not receive much more notice than that which had been accorded Thomas' two previous novels, *Birthstone* (1980) and *The Flute-Player* (1982). The American edition, however, was soon enormously successful, outselling everything, including novels that were far more accessible and conventional. Thomas, an obscure Cornish don better known in literary circles for his poetry and his translations of Russian verse than for his fiction, was transformed into a celebrity, the object of lavish attention, both positive and negative—several critics noted that long passages in *The White Hotel* and other works by Thomas were appropriated from the writings of others.

Ararat, Thomas' latest novel, has been reviewed widely and prominently in both the United States and the United Kingdom. Although it has not been the best-seller that *The White Hotel* was, *Ararat* likewise has provoked strong and disparate reactions. Some have praised its spare construction and narrative inventiveness, while others have denounced it as a self-indulgent and gratuitously unpleasant game. In *Ararat*, Thomas once again makes use of other authors' texts, most notably of Alexander Pushkin's poetry-prose fragment "Egyptian Nights," which Thomas translates and completes. *Ararat* marshals Thomas' talents as Slavicist, translator, poet, and novelist and recapitulates his preoccupations with genocide, sexuality, and the nature of creativity. An improvisation on the theme of improvisation, it is in part a rejoinder to those critics who have stigmatized Thomas' work as derivative and contrived.

The intricate plot of *Ararat* resembles a Russian *matrushka*, a set of dolls within dolls within dolls, except that it is impossible to determine with absolute certainty which of the book's several story lines frame which others. The novel begins with a visit by Sergei Rozanov, a Russian poet of Armenian descent, to the city of Gorky in order to meet and bed a blind admirer, a doctoral student named Olga. Rozanov is soon disappointed with her, and, unable to sleep, he agrees to while away the rest of the night in the hotel room by improvising a story for her. He begins by recounting the tale of three authors—a Russian poet, an Armenian-American writer of romances, and an Armenian storyteller—who, thrown together at a congress, agree to improvise on a common theme.

The next section of *Ararat* recounts a ship voyage to the United States by Victor Surkov, who may or may not be the Russian poet who is vying with the Armenian-American and the Armenian in the improvisational competition that is the premise of Rozanov's frame tale. Surkov does, in any case, have much in common with Rozanov, including a considerable reputation and an ambivalent relationship with the authorities. Like Pushkin and Boris Pasternak, whom Surkov imagines himself to be, both Rozanov and Surkov are torn between a wife and a mistress. Extratextual speculation suggests that Surkov also derives some characteristics from the contemporary Russian poet Yevgeny Yevtushenko. During the journey, Surkov seduces Anna Polanski, a Polish gymnast preparing for the Los Angeles Olympics. He soon grows bored with her but finds that while in a drunken stupor, he offered to marry her. He extricates himself from this predicament through the ostensibly magnanimous gesture of marrying Nayirie, a Turkish athlete who learns that she would be unable otherwise to enter the United States.

Suffering from insomnia, Surkov imagines himself to be Pushkin writing "Egyptian Nights." In that work, left unfinished at the time of Pushkin's death in a duel, C. P. Charsky, an aristocratic young Petersburg poetaster, is asked by a Neapolitan *improvisatore*, who never reveals his name, to help him find employment. Charsky arranges for the *improvisatore* to perform at the salon of a Petersburg princess. In response to suggestions from his audience, the *improvisatore* recites a variation on the theme of Cleopatra and her lovers. In his version, which he improvises in Italian, the beautiful queen offers to spend a night with each of three men, provided they be willing to relinquish their lives in the morning. Surkov completes Pushkin's unfinished text by writing of how the *improvisatore* is challenged to a duel by a gentleman who believes his mother has been slandered in this portrait of Cleopatra. The *improvisatore* flees ignominiously, but Charsky, as his double, is obligated to go through with the duel, averted at the last moment only by the scandal of Pushkin's death. As sovereign creator, Surkov decides he does not like this ending and proceeds to move his story back twelve years, where he is now able to have the *improvisatore* beheaded during the Decembrist revolt.

The next section of *Ararat* has Surkov arriving by plane (suggesting that he—or one of the other improvisers—might have imagined the sea voyage) in New York. After a comical press conference with American reporters, Surkov stays at the Brooklyn apartment of Donna Zarifian, an Armenian-American sculptor. Disappointed with the possibilities of a sexual encounter with her, Surkov goes off (or imagines going or is imagined going off) to Mexico with a beautiful young American admirer.

In the penultimate chapter of the novel, Marian Fairfax, an Armenian-American writer; Aram Khandjian, an Armenian storyteller; and an unnamed Russian (probably the trio of Rozanov's frame tale, unless he is a creation of theirs) find themselves in a hotel in Yerevan, the capital of Soviet Armenia. By the time Marian and Aram have concluded an unsatisfying attempt at lovemaking, the Russian, referred to now as *"improvisatore"* (as if it is his version of the theme that one has been reading) has disappeared. Rozanov reappears at the very end of the book, finishing his night of improvisations in the hotel room with Olga and thinking about a long poem that he intends to write concerning the murdered Russian director, Vsevolod Meyerhold.

Thomas' involuted novel defies plot summary. Its labyrinthine metafictional design resembles an M. C. Escher visual puzzle in its refusal to provide a comfortable vantage point for ascertaining what is central and what is peripheral. To read *Ararat* is to proceed through a series of variations on a few basic themes. Almost all the characters are writers, and almost all of them are disagreeable. The men are abusive toward women, and sex is invariably cruel.

Ararat, the sacred Armenian mountain where Noah's Ark is supposed to have found its final resting place after the Flood, provides Thomas with a title and a pervasive image. A rallying point for Armenian identity and majestically visible from Yerevan, Ararat remains just across the border from contemporary Armenia, and hence inaccessible. As his flight rushes toward Kennedy Airport, Surkov speculates that the universe itself is a vast work of improvisation: In such a universe, Ararat is the stable vantage point just beyond man's reach. Ubiquitous, despite and through its absence from *Ararat*, Ararat is this deconstructed novel's impossible center.

Ararat is further appropriate as a memorial to the victims of one of the twentieth century's several attempts at genocide. During his sea voyage, Surkov encounters an elderly Scandinavian named Finn who insists on recounting his numerous experiences as a soldier. In a dispassionate style disturbingly at odds with the horrors he recounts, Finn tells of his active participation in some of civilization's most heinous atrocities, including the Turkish massacre of the Armenians, the Nazi extermination of Jews and Gypsies, and the Stalinist liquidation of kulaks, Jews, and dissidents. If history is indeed a series of improvisations by an unsavory author or authors, it has been on an appalling theme. Mount Ararat remains outside all of that, as a distant, haunting dream and an angle of repose. Speaking of improvisations, Rozanov says to Olga: "It's just a game, like doing crosswords." Thomas' detractors describe his books as derivative and cerebral toys. *Ararat* suggests that originality is a convention and spontaneity a contrivance, that there is nothing beyond the brutal sports of history but the legendary Ararat.

Steven G. Kellman

Sources for Further Study

Antioch Review. XLI, Fall, 1983, p. 510.
Boston Review. VIII, October, 1983, p. 36.
Hudson Review. XXXVI, Autumn, 1983, p. 556.
Library Journal. CVIII, March 1, 1983, p. 518.
Los Angeles Times Book Review. April 3, 1983, p. 1.
The New York Review of Books. XXX, June 16, 1983, p. 34.
The New York Times Book Review. LXXXVIII, March 27, 1983, p. 7.
Newsweek. CI, April 4, 1983, p. 75.
Time. CXXI, April 25, 1983, p. 114.
Virginia Quarterly Review. LIX, Summer, 1983, p. 91.

ARCHES & LIGHT
The Fiction of John Gardner

Author: David Cowart (1947-   )
Publisher: Southern Illinois University Press (Carbondale). 228 pp. $19.95
Type of work: Literary criticism

A critical study of the ways in which John Gardner fashioned novels and stories that not only acknowledged the fact of man's existential situation but also provided alternatives to Existentialist despair

For a writer who, since the publication of *On Moral Fiction* in 1978, has been under almost continual attack and whose literary reputation reached its lowest point in the time between the appearance of his ninth novel, *Mickelsson's Ghosts*, in June, 1982, and his death three months later, John Gardner has received a surprising amount of attention from academic critics, who have made him the subject of no fewer than seven books in the past four years: *John Gardner: A Bibliographical Profile* (1980), by John Howell; *Moral Fiction: An Anthology* (1980), edited by Joe David Bellamy; *John Gardner: Critical Perspectives* (1982), edited by Robert A. Morace and Kathryn VanSpanckeren; *John Gardner: True Art, Moral Art* (1983), edited by Beatrice Mendez-Egle; *A World of Order and Light: The Fiction of John Gardner* (1984), by Gregory Morris; *John Gardner: An Annotated Secondary Bibliography* (1984), by Robert A. Morace; and the book under review here, *Arches & Light: The Fiction of John Gardner* (1983), by David Cowart.

On the strength of his earlier critical study, *Thomas Pynchon: The Art of Allusion* (1980), Cowart's view of Gardner demands the serious attention of anyone interested in Gardner and his work. Briefly stated, that view is as follows. Gardner believed that

> the artist must, in his work, make the world over from scratch. This creation is by no means irresponsible or escapist, because the world becomes what art says it is. To put it another way, the artist must shoulder responsibility for what he creates at first hand—his art—and for what he creates at second hand—the world shaped by that art. Gardner thus modifies the traditional dictum that art uncovers changeless, preexistent truths; he makes of the proposition "life imitates art" something more than a parlor witticism.

As an artist, Gardner acknowledged the horror of the world but refused to succumb to despair. Against the darkness of the abyss, Gardner posited what he called the "arches and light" of aesthetic creation, in particular the effect of such art on the reader for whom it would act as "an antidote to despair." Gardner's characters, many of them artists or surrogate artists, face the same choice; they must choose between negation and affirmation, between the acceptance of a "narrowly defined existential truth" and "some finer, more complex, less accessible truth that is no less real for being created, at least in part, by the artist in the process of uncovering it."

No one familiar with Gardner's work will find Cowart's position especially startling or even new, for it derives in large measure from *On Moral Fiction*. At his best, however, Cowart does add significantly to the reader's understanding of and appreciation for Gardner's artistry. In writing his three "early pastoral novels," *The Resurrection* (1966), *The Wreckage of Agathon* (1970), and *Nickel Mountain* (1973), Cowart explains, Gardner "sets himself the task of making positive stories out of the grimmest possible material," realizing "that his creed as a novelist—affirmation—was nugatory unless it could be practiced in the face of the ugliest truths about the human condition." By manipulating narrative points of view and combining the conventions of distinct literary forms, the novel and the pastoral, Gardner was able to transform morbid subjects, such as the death of *The Resurrection*'s protagonist, James Chandler, into affirmations of certain basic human values such as responsibility and community. Cowart's chapter on Gardner's most frequently discussed work, *Grendel* (1971), is nearly as good. Cowart's lucid treatment makes clear exactly how much previous commentators have missed, even in the by now overworked relationship between the novel and the Anglo-Saxon epic from which it derives. *Beowulf* (c. 1000), Cowart points out,

> at once endorses and questions the values of the society it describes; it glorifies the ancient, heroic ideals espoused by the pagan ancestors of its Christian audience at the same time that it reveals how little those ideals mean without the rationale provided by Christian faith. With *Grendel* the situation is exactly reversed. Where the earlier audience could look back on the pagan past and congratulate itself on its spiritual enlightenment, the modern audience looks back on a Christian past and laments its disillusionment. The desperate spiritual situation of the Scyldings mirrors our own.

Cowart's success in these chapters, and in his Jungian analysis of *The Sunlight Dialogues* (1972), in which Taggert Hodge is discussed as the trickster figure who becomes Fred Clumly's shadow and eventually his savior, derives from his critical method. A reviewer once complained that Gardner's mind was too well stocked with literary matter, matter which the professor-as-novelist turned into grist for the mill of academic fiction. Cowart's mind appears to be just as well furnished. Works by William Blake, Richard Wagner, Sir Philip Sidney, André Gide, Sir Thomas Malory, Dante, Geoffrey Chaucer, Henry James, William Butler Yeats, John Gay, Sir James Frazer, Carl Jung, and filmmakers Jean Cocteau, Akira Kurosawa, and Michael Cimino are among the many sources of and analogues to Gardner's fiction identified by Cowart. Many of these deserve and require fuller treatment than Cowart provides, but all of them shed new light on Gardner's accessible yet highly allusive and richly textured novels and stories. Had Cowart concentrated on these matters, as he did in his Pynchon study, *Arches & Light* would have been a far better book than it is. As it stands, however, *Arches & Light* (like Morris' more recent *A World of Order and Light*) functions chiefly as a general introduction. Cowart may be interested in illuminating Gardner's allusive style, but he is apparently intent on explaining the fiction for an interested but largely uninformed audience of undergraduates who, for example, might still not know that Gardner modeled the dragon in *Grendel* on the philosopher Jean-Paul Sartre. What is needed here is not a mere restatement of this obvious connection but an examination of the precise nature of Gardner's self-confessed love-hate relationship with Sartre (and with Existentialism as well).

Because this is essentially an introductory study, Cowart discusses the fiction comprehensively, novel by novel, story by story, down to the very least of the tales written for children. (Unwisely, Cowart does not include the epic poem *Jason and Medeia*, 1973, among Gardner's fictions despite the author's fondness for Chaucerian "genre-jumping" and the general breakdown of literary categories which characterizes literary postmodernism, with which Gardner had another of his love-hate relationships.) Because he is an astute critic, Cowart does raise significant points, but because he has committed himself to slogging his way through all the fiction, he often fails to pursue these points (often presenting them as if they are self-evident facts) or to treat them consistently. Does Gardner's "willingness to raise the question of whether the phenomenal world is fundamentally orderly or chaotic" really evidence his "integrity," as Cowart claims? Should the critic simply agree with Gardner's belief that the test of art is the effect it has on its audience? Did Gardner maintain throughout his career (or only during his "new fiction" phase) that "the proper task of the artist . . . is at once to create illusion and to penetrate it"? Can the artist be said to create *ex nihilo* the truths he affirms in his work *and* to uncover them as if they were preexistent eternal verities? Cowart makes both claims but makes no effort to resolve the inconsistency (his as well as Gardner's); in fact, he seems to be unaware that the inconsistency even exists and is certainly unconcerned about what it implies about Gardner's art, as distinct from his well-intentioned posturings in *On Moral Fiction*. A deconstructionist would have made too much of the discrepancy; Cowart makes too little.

The most serious limitation of *Arches & Light* derives from Cowart's unwillingness to consider the issue of Gardner's aesthetic development. That Gardner's general subjects, major themes, character types, and dramatic conflicts have remained constant throughout his career is an established fact and as such hardly requires or deserves the lengthy and generally predictable attention Cowart gives it. Serious questions have been raised, however, concerning the appropriateness of "moral fiction" in the postmodern age of uncertainty; some critics have suggested that Gardner's fiction written after *On Moral Fiction* suffers from the author's commitment to his literary theory. Committed to proving that Gardner's fiction forms a seamless whole, Cowart can only offer generalizations concerning the progress of the author's literary career. Cowart writes that Gardner involved himself in "a career-long quest for fictive strategies to gainsay this horror," but he fails to situate this "quest" in the larger literary context of innovative versus traditional fiction, of the novel as play versus Gardner's odd claim that the novel has its own "built-in metaphysic" (*The Art of Fiction*, 1984). Further, Cowart contends that those writers and critics who have dismissed Gardner as being "ridiculously quixotic" will "in time" come to realize that he was "more admirable than absurd," but surely the time to convert these skeptics and infidels who have worshiped at the altar of immoral fiction is the now of *Arches & Light*, not some happy future of literary faith, hope, charity, and built-in metaphysics.

Unfortunately, Cowart does not make a convincing case for either the cultural importance or the literary merit of Gardner's fiction. Instead of assessing the fiction with some degree of critical detachment, Cowart praises every scrap of it indiscriminately. *The King's Indian* (1974), for example, cannot in good conscience be favorably compared with James Joyce's *Dubliners* (1914); nor is the title story of the collection *Grendel*'s equal in wit and invention; nor is *In the Suicide Mountains* (1977) "a perfect hybrid" of adult and children's fiction; nor do Gardner's four books for young readers prove that children's literature can be "major" (presumably on a par with Fyodor Dostoevski's *Crime and Punishment*, 1866, and Gustave Flaubert's *Madame Bovary*, 1857); nor, finally, do works such as "Gudgekin the Thistle Girl" evidence "the awesome power of art to deliver us from dragons, from darkness, from despair itself." Even Gardner's most sympathetic readers will find this kind of praise overblown and unconvincing. Instead of establishing and clarifying Gardner's place in contemporary American literature, *Arches & Light* only makes clear that these tasks remain to be done.

Robert A. Morace

Source for Further Study

Los Angeles Times Book Review. February 12, 1984, p. 4.

ART & ARDOR

Author: Cynthia Ozick (1928-   )
Publisher: Alfred A. Knopf (New York). 305 pp. $16.95
Type of work: Essays

A collection of essays, reviews, and occasional pieces by a contemporary novelist and short-story writer, centering on the conflict between artistic creation and religious belief

In this brilliant collection of essays, Cynthia Ozick, primarily a fiction writer, reveals her central concerns as a moral critic, her responses to contemporary politics and social developments, and her conflicts as a Jew in diaspora who chooses art as her home. The collection is aptly titled. Art and ardor, artistic creation and religious belief: These are the polarities of Ozick's dialectic, the nice alliteration of the title revealing the ever so slight tipping of the scales in favor of art. What emerges from this dialectic is not so much a series of distinct pieces, despite the fact that they were commissioned by a variety of journals and interest groups over the course of fifteen years, as variations on a theme. This theme is the conflict between religious commitment and artistic creation, more particularly the conflict between the primary, central, and historical covenant of Judaism and the siren song of art in contemporary America, a Gentile culture which encourages assimilation, rewards trendiness, and dismisses history as bunk.

The greatest attraction of these essays is their passionate intensity, their moral urgency, and their belief in the power of ideas. Ozick's mind is hard and brilliant, her judgment often severe and occasionally unjust. With a sense of urgency, she examines the claims of modern culture, adjusting her glasses to look ever more penetratingly, more honestly, more critically at current writers, such as Truman Capote and John Updike, and at current trends, such as the recent tide of black anti-Semitism in America. Fearlessly, she examines ideas and assumptions in the harshest light and exposes the flaws in some of the most fondly held contemporary beliefs, such as in the existence of a separate female consciousness, psychology, and art. At best, her high seriousness, stern morality, and unswerving commitment argue tellingly for the importance and meaningfulness of art in the modern world. She persuasively maintains, "Fiction will not be interesting or lasting unless it is again conceived in the art of the didactic. (Emphasis, however, on *art*.)" At other times, however, she sounds severe and unjust, her assertions those of a Jewish fundamentalist who fails to understand other minority groups because she fails to sympathize.

Ozick's major preoccupation as an essayist is one of her major preoccupations as a novelist and short-story writer. Her primary concern is with the risk and temptation of idolatry. This theme runs throughout her work:

in *The Pagan Rabbi and Other Stories* (1971), *Bloodshed and Three Novellas* (1976), *Levitation: Five Fictions* (1982), and *The Cannibal Galaxy* (1983). As Ozick notes, idolatry is the substitution for the creator of any other good, whether nature, art, literature, or philosophy. For the novelist, whose delight is in the sensuous world, the risk of nature worship is very great. Indeed, the line is fine between praising God's creation and worshiping it. Thus, the practice of any art is a risk because the artist, like the pagan rabbi, who falls in love with a dryad, may so exult in the beauty of the world as to forget the source of this beauty. Not surprisingly, then, some of Ozick's short stories are explicitly directed against storytelling. Many of her essays, as well, criticize idolatry and idolmakers, no matter how brilliant. Indeed, the more brilliant, the more seductive. For this reason, in "Literature as Idol: Harold Bloom," she condemns the critical system that would make literature an object of worship, while appreciating the brilliance and sensitivity of the critic who devised it.

Clearly, then, Ozick's concern is to preserve her identity as a Jew first, as a writer, second. Viewing the modern world from an absolute religious outlook, judging its actions in the light of an unvarying standard, she speaks with tough-mindedness and backbone against trendiness and solipsism. Repeatedly, she speaks for the highest standards in literature, because she sees literature as redemptive. In "Innovation and Redemption: What Literature Means," she speaks against the narcissism in art which she maintains is now in fashion. She insists, rather, "What literature means is meaning" and "literature is for the sake of humanity." Her literary sympathies being largely nineteenth century, she renews the Arnoldian dialogue between Hebraism and Hellenism with a new urgency in the wake of the Holocaust, the single historic event that demonstrated for all time the inadequacy of a purely aesthetic response to life. Above all, she is a polemicist, like all the cultural models she admires, among them the biblical Moses and the twentieth century historians Gershom Scholem and Maurice Samuel. A polemicist is one who argues most profoundly for a certain position because he feels most keenly the lure of the opposite side. Just as Moses became most effectively a Hebrew champion because he knew at firsthand the lure of Egyptian power and indolence, Ozick is most insistently the exponent of a Jewish, sacral view of human life because she so intimately feels the lure of an art that is secular and self-contained, the art of Henry James, E. M. Forster, and Virginia Woolf, whom she considers appreciatively in essays throughout the book.

Underlining the force of Ozick's logic is her astonishing precision of language. She uses words with surgical accuracy. She delights in definition, building her austere edifice on a bedrock of axioms: "Culture is the continuity of human aspiration." Her style is tight, lucid, aphoristic: "There is no predicament that cures itself so swiftly as that of belonging to 'the young.'" Often, however, her relentlessly precise language ignores ambiguity; in general, she is not comfortable with muddle. (Perhaps this discomfort explains her ambivalent fascination with E. M. Forster: His is the murky terrain which she chooses not to explore.)

Some of her finest essays are missiles of provocative dissent. The most controversial of these are her denunciations of the self-segregation of the women's movement in the United States. In "The Hole/Birth Catalogue" and "Justice to Feminism," two of her most playful and wicked pieces, she decries the idea of anatomy as destiny and the assertion that the minds of men and women are fundamentally different, pointing out that in accepting these notions, women are willingly imposing on themselves the most constraining of earlier male stereotypes.

Not only is she arguing against the self-isolation of the women's movement in the United States, but also she is arguing for a return to what she sees as the much larger claims of classical feminism. As she views it, classical feminism, which originally gained women the vote and which later demanded equal pay for equal labor, broadened the concept of mankind to humankind and offered women equal access to the delights and burdens of the world. Such freedom of access to experience, Ozick argues, is essential for the imaginative writer, who must never operate under the self-limiting assumption that there is a separate and particular female nature and therefore a separate and distinct subject matter about which she must write. Ozick's argument concerning women writers is part of her larger argument against narcissistic literature in general. "Self-discovery," she maintains, "is only partial discovery. Each human being is a particle of a generation, a mote among the revealing permutations of Society."

Whereas Ozick's denunciation of the idea of the "woman writer" seems to be in the interest of greater liberation for writers, her dogmatic assurance makes her oddly blind and obtuse at times. One of these instances is her peremptory dismissal of E. M. Forster's *Maurice* in "Morgan and Maurice: A Fairy Tale." It is not that Ozick is inaccurate in citing the flaws in Forster's *Maurice*—indeed, even the staunchest admirers of Forster's writing would have to acknowledge them—but that she is intemperate and one-sided in her reading of the novel. As she points out, the central character is unconvincing because he is too much a mix of Forster and Fantasy Lover; the book is too timid rather than too bold in championing a permanent homosexual union across class lines. The novel's premise calls for explicit sexual passages; instead, as in fairy tales, episodes of libidinous satisfaction are assumed rather than depicted. In fact, the title of her essay is a cheap shot, despite Ozick's disclaimer, and is reinforced by the malice of some of her remarks: "Forster, prodding the cosmos to do its job of showing us how puny we are, is left holding his little stick." Ozick refuses to acknowledge the force of *Maurice* as a fairy tale because she does not recognize the indeterminate nature of fairy tales. No matter that the hero is divided between gratification and conscience, or between what Forster secretly considers his higher and lower natures. Fairy tales, like dreams, allow the hero and the audience to have it both ways, to be both the kind sister and the cruel one, to have one's folly met by both the devouring wolf and the rescuing woodcutter. Fairy tales and dreams do not resolve the conflict between wish and misgiving: They create a world that simultaneously gratifies desire and placates conscience. Such is the world of Forster's *Maurice*—a world in which, as Forster would have it, two men "fall in love and remain in it for the ever and ever that fiction [read: fairy tale] allows."

Ozick is not at her best when she cavils and excludes; she is at her best as a celebrant. In some of her finest critical essays, she rediscovers either an overlooked work or an underappreciated writer. Among these essays are "The Fourth Sparrow: The Magisterial Reach of Gershom Scholem," her affectionate tribute to the heir of an assimilated German Jewish family who transformed himself into a leading chronicler of Jewish history. Ozick esteems Scholem as one who refused to turn out as predicted, who repudiated the estrangement from Jewish history that was to be his fate, and who chose instead to create himself by fashioning the contents of his own mind. Another such essay is "Out of the Flames: The Recovery of Gertrud Kolmar," an elegy for a gifted German Jewish poet who perished at Auschwitz, but whose newly discovered body of mature poetry is a lasting memorial.

Ozick celebrates with equal originality the achievements of the already famous; her critical essays are distinguished by a trait that she applauds in a former student: "the askew glance of the really inquisitive." In "Mrs. Virginia Woolf: A Madwoman and Her Nurse," Ozick asks the question that most admirers of Virginia and Leonard Woolf would like to have answered but avoid asking: Why did Leonard Woolf marry Virginia Stephen? Why did a talented, even brilliant young man, attractive to women, choose to marry a fragile, self-absorbed young woman whose lesbian tendencies and episodes of madness were known to him before the marriage? Ozick's answer, if conjectural, is fascinating: Leonard Woolf, the provisionally accepted grandson of Jewish shopkeepers, could not resist the opportunity to gain the social eminence enjoyed by the Stephen family. For this position, he was willing to spend a lifetime as a nurse. Ozick's point is not to reproach Leonard Woolf for social climbing but to point out how precarious is the position of even a very talented and advantaged Jew in England, where, under a veneer of social acceptance, there remains a thick layer of anti-Semitism. Equally intriguing is Ozick's essay "I. B. Singer's Book of Creation," in which she applauds the Nobel Prize-winning author, not as a fabulist but as a moralist, not for his imagination and invention but for his celebration of ordinary people and daily life.

As Cynthia Ozick points out in the foreword to this collection of essays, the essay is a lesser form than fiction because it generally summarizes rather than invents. She acknowledges, however, that occasionally, even in an essay, all is not foreknown: "even an essay can invent, burn, guess, try out, dig up, hurtle forward, succumb to that flood of sign and nuance that adds up to intuition, disclosure, discovery." In all of her essays, Ozick shows herself to be a preeminent discoverer of the extraordinary in the ordinary. For this reason, many of these essays burn with the urgency of new knowledge, of understanding achieved not beforehand but at last. For this reason, they are what Ozick hoped they would be: "as much scouted and discovered as stories themselves."

Carola M. Kaplan

Sources for Further Study

Georgia Review. XXXVII, Fall, 1983, p. 676.
Library Journal. CVIII, May 1, 1983, p. 907.
Los Angeles Times Book Review. May 29, 1983, p. 2.
Ms. XI, June, 1983, p. 38.
Nation. CCXXXVII, July 23, 1983, p. 87.
The New York Times Book Review. LXXXVIII, May 22, 1983, p. 7.
Newsweek. CI, May 30, 1983, p. 91.
Publishers Weekly. CCXXIII, March 18, 1983, p. 59.
Saturday Review. IX, July, 1983, p. 54.
Virginia Quarterly Review. LIX, Autumn, 1983, p. 115.

THE ART OF TELLING
Essays on Fiction

Author: Frank Kermode (1919-   )
Publisher: Harvard University Press (Cambridge, Massachusetts). 229 pp. $15.00
Type of work: Essays and literary criticism

Drawing upon a richly diverse body of postwar literary criticism, the author demonstrates, through analysis of modern and classic texts, the usefulness of new theories in the analysis of the novel and makes a case for pluralistic interpretation

Frank Kermode writes with an awareness that the New Criticism that dominated literary analysis in academic circles from the 1930's through the 1950's has experienced an eclipse. Indeed, he studiously avoids the commonplace expressions of the New Criticism—ambiguity, point of view, tone, irony—preferring a new and more arcane set of analytical terms. Even at the height of its influence, the school initiated by Cleanth Brooks, Robert Penn Warren, William Empson, and I. A. Richards, among others, revealed limitations. It treated literary texts as artifacts, isolated from the periods and cultures that produced them, and it advocated intensive analysis. As a result, the novel suffered critical neglect, because it is too unwieldy and amorphous to lend itself readily to close analysis. Kermode's chief interest lies with the novel, and so it is natural that he should turn to newer theories.

No clearly dominant school, however, has emerged to replace the New Critics. Instead, there developed in the 1960's a reexamination of the use of theories and methods from other fields—anthropology, linguistics, psychology (Freudian), political science (largely Marxist), folklore and myth—to illuminate literary texts. Ways of interpreting reality that theorists devised for these fields shaped the theory of criticism in the direction of new movements, notably the Structuralist and Deconstructionist movements that originated in France. At the same time, a few critics—the best known in this country being Stanley Fish and Louise Rosenblatt—turned from the text (or poem) to the reader (or audience) to examine in thorough detail the experience of reading. Others, such as Northrop Frye, intensified their exploration of texts from the perspective of myth.

Kermode's measure of independence from new theoretical currents is secured by three factors prominent in the book: his stated awareness that he is seeking a neutral ground amid the battles being waged by advocates of various schools; his continuing interest in literary history, including the history of genres, interpretation, and reading; and an inclination, long conspicuous in his work, to analyze beginnings of lengthy texts. The book makes an extended plea for careful, yet pluralistic, readings of novels, first by tracing changes in the genre and then by exploring the varied responses of readers and critics. Throughout his work, Kermode incorporates memorable aphorisms or sentences on the nature and purpose of literary criticism—criticism being to him an ethical act that has illumination as its main function. He is inclined to accept a range of modes as contributing to this end, though he has serious reservations—both theoretical and pedagogical—about Deconstructionism. He is fond of quoting important expressions of critics and gauging the extent to which they are true or useful.

The title of Kermode's book, it might be observed, does not suffice. It is more clearly about the art of reading or the art of critical interpretation than the art of narrative, though it does in fact include important ideas on the subject. The subtitle, *Essays on Fiction*, indicates more accurately the nature of the book's contents, which derive from lectures and papers written over a period of a dozen years or more. All of the material, except for a lengthy prologue, has been previously published, though Kermode has made revisions for the present volume. The book has two major thrusts: the theoretical influence and the formal (or institutional) influence on interpretation. The second concerns university faculties and their influence over canon (texts that are selected for analysis) and hermeneutics (critical methods and approaches).

To clarify a few of the theoretical problems involved in interpreting the novel, Kermode selects data for an examination of the genre. In his first chapter, "The English Novel, *Circa* 1907," he turns to once popular but now forgotten works. Kermode's analysis reveals that novelists of that period were seeking to incorporate contemporary themes of importance to society—sex, the class struggle, imperialism—into their works instead of relying upon history and romance, a thematic development which Kermode names "the condition of England." The more significant novelists of the period, however, were those concerned with innovation not in theme but in technique, in the craft of fiction. Here, the names are neither obscure nor forgotten—Henry James, Joseph Conrad, Ford Madox Ford—novelists who blazed a trail leading away from more traditional men of letters such as John Galsworthy, Arnold Bennett, H. G. Wells, and G. K. Chesterton. The innovators made special demands upon their readers by withdrawing or withholding authorial guidance, by making their narratives indirect and complex, and by relying upon symbols and subtle patterns of repetition and allusion.

The nature of complex narrative is further clarified in the second chapter, which focuses on E. C. Bentley's classic detective novel, *Trent's Last Case* (1912). This work raises the problem of how authors involve the reader by presenting the same event from different and conflicting accounts, from clues, from the introduction of "irrelevant" and sometimes misleading material. In addition to the traditional puzzle at the heart of the whodunit, Bentley incorporates cultural and symbolic meanings and themes that invite pluralistic interpretation. The detective novel thus represents a departure from the traditional narrative, in which the author sequentially develops recognizable themes. Later novelists, largely in France, began to consider the detective story with its indirect narrative, its clues, its lack of emphasis upon character, a narrative model more useful than the mainstream novel. The advent of a complex narrative art prompted Roland Barthes to distinguish between *lisible* (readable) texts, which refer to a closed system of reality, and *scriptible* ("writable") texts, which lack closure or well-defined limits and thus require the reader to become involved in discovery of possible meanings.

The codes that Barthes developed for narrative analysis in *S/Z* (1970; English translation, 1974), his book-length study of a Balzac novella, exert a strong influence on Kermode's subsequent chapters. According to Barthes, in analyzing a text a reader examines five aspects: the proairetic, concerned with the sequence of events; the hermeneutic, concerned with solving enigmas of the plot caused by delay, deception, concealment; the semic or semantic, concerned with character; the cultural, concerned with the world-view represented by the text; and the symbolic, concerned with underlying meanings, particularly mythical. Kermode will not go so far as to say with Barthes, "dans le texte, seul parle le lecteur" ("in the text, the reader alone speaks"), but in analyzing narratives he relies heavily on Barthes's second and fifth codes, and he finds Barthes's distinction between *lisible* and *scriptible* texts useful enough to point out that a reader who comes to terms with *scriptible* texts will begin to see *scriptible* dimensions of classic (*lisible*) texts. Indeed, "for Barthes, the only hope for *lisible* texts is that they allow themselves, in limited ways, to be treated as modern," though Kermode rejects this attitude as too extreme.

In chapter three, "The Use of the Codes," Kermode applies Barthes's approach to Anthony Burgess' *MF* (1971), Thomas Pynchon's *The Crying of Lot 49* (1966), and Henry Green's *Loving* (1945), stressing the hermeneutic and symbolic (mythic) codes. This method does not permit one to arrive at a single, final meaning; indeed, Kermode holds that the business of the modern critic is "to read in order to maximize plurality, not in order to understand secrets."

To illuminate the challenge posed by modern texts and their narrative techniques, Kermode turns to the opening of Ford Madox Ford's *The Good Soldier* (1915). The point of view is that of a character who, it turns out, deceives the reader through his innocence and naïveté. Having turned his narrative over to a character, the author thus deceives the reader, who must read on to other points of view before discovering his error. The opening passage of the novel also introduces symbolic references whose meanings elude the character but later become significant to the reader, who is forced to read recursively.

Even a work such as George Eliot's *Adam Bede* (1859) reveals more complexity than what Kermode calls a normal reader would perceive. Kermode analyzes two passages in detail, applying approaches that Barthes would have included in his semic and cultural codes. Joseph Conrad's *Under Western Eyes*

(1910) reveals that when one encounters difficulties, or turbulence, in the straightforward narrative (proairetic), there are likely to be fruitful results when one applies the hermeneutic code. In the Conrad novel, one finds a series of patterns echoing black and white, somewhat reminiscent of the image patterns in *Heart of Darkness* (1902).

Given Kermode's insistence upon plurality of reading, his view that a single correct reading can never be achieved, his demonstration, beyond reasonable doubt, that readers respond quite differently and that the same person will never reread a complex work the same way, one may ask whether Kermode leads readers into a kind of antinomianism, where all readings have equal value, where none can be considered more perceptive—or, to use Kermode's term, illuminating. If the reader creates the text (*scriptible*), is alone with the text, then what can fend off chaos and confusion? Encouraging overreading, as Kermode (citing Freud) does, invites the reader to ignore any limits and boundaries. Kermode turns to this problem in the seventh chapter, "Can We Say Absolutely Anything We Like?" A commonsense answer is yes, of course, but the question also implies, "will what we say be taken seriously?" Kermode has no difficulty demonstrating that some interpretations must be dismissed. A reading that is lexically naïve, or blatantly ahistorical, or dependent upon an analogy that sheds no light on the subject will be discounted. For example, the critic who interprets William Shakespeare's Caliban as an effort to create the missing link between man and ape must be dismissed as too ahistorical. Further, a critic's tone may at times be so shrill as to indicate a paucity of clear analysis and thus may undermine the writer's position.

In the final analysis, Kermode points out, institutions such as the church and the university control interpretation by approving the canon of works and by approving hermeneutics (or modes of interpretation). The canon of literature is more loosely formulated and more subject to alteration than that of Scripture, yet university faculties undeniably exert control over the process. Whether this control results in progress and enlightenment, as Kermode seems to think, or a somewhat arbitrary series of judgments by a hieratic caste, the reader must decide, but Kermode's knowledge of the history of interpretation makes the case for progress seem plausible. He demonstrates through the use of New Testament passages how over a long span of time both hermeneutics and man's understanding of texts alter.

Kermode shows that he is steeped in all of the newer currents of criticism, though he does not profess adherence to any one. In particular, he has clearly been influenced by the work of Roland Barthes and by the hermeneutic criticism of Hans-Georg Gadamer, though he maintains a critical distance from both. Throughout these essays, Kermode's analysis is timely and perceptive, yet it is somewhat arcane and perhaps too tentative to be highly influential or appealing to a large audience outside the circle of literary specialists.

Like the innovative novelists whose strategies he admires, Kermode himself makes demands upon the reader by shifting points of view or by shifting abruptly from reader to text to author, yet apparent contradictions are only apparent. With his terminology, however, the problems are potentially more serious. It is unclear whether one gains anything when, instead of labeling a passage as *ironic*, one describes it as *deceptive*. Further, the word *hermeneutic* is used with two separate meanings in the text, one to indicate any method of interpretation, another in the limited application indicated by Barthes. As for the codes suggested by Barthes, they do not appear to be defined narrowly enough for a critic to apply them consistently and to avoid overlapping. For the reader who confronts *The Art of Telling* armed with patience and determination, the main rewards are likely to be Kermode's perceptive interpretation of passages from novels, his account of the development of the novel as a narrative genre, and his subtle analysis of the critical theories that inform his own interpretations.

Stanley Archer

Sources for Further Study

Christian Science Monitor. January 17, 1984, p. 20.
Los Angeles Times Book Review. December 8, 1983, p. 46.

THE ASSASSINATION OF JESSE JAMES
BY THE COWARD ROBERT FORD

Author: Ron Hansen (1947-   )
Publisher: Alfred A. Knopf (New York). 304 pp. $14.95
Type of work: Novel
Time: 1865-1892
Locale: Primarily the midwestern United States

An account of the exploits of the notorious James Gang, the slaying of Jesse James by Robert Ford, and the subsequent triumphs and trials of Robert Ford

> *Principal characters:*
> JESSE JAMES, a robber, killer, and folk hero
> ROBERT FORD, the killer of Jesse James
> FRANK JAMES, a robber, killer, Jesse's brother
> ZEE JAMES, Jesse's wife
> THE JAMES GANG, an assortment of characters who rode with the Jameses
> THE LAW ENFORCEMENT OFFICERS, pursuers of the James Gang

The way in which Americans choose their heroes and create their myths is a curious process which seems to draw more or less equally from the dark side and the bright side of the human spirit. A case in point is Jesse James, a vicious robber and killer who was widely admired by his contemporaries as a sort of Robin Hood figure and who was immortalized after his death in songs, tales, books, and films. The well-known folk song expresses the prevailing attitude quite correctly and quite tersely: "But that dirty little coward that shot Mister Howard, he laid poor Jesse in his grave." Mister Howard was an alias which was often used by Jesse James, and "that dirty little coward" was, of course, Robert Ford. The story contained in the song is the skeleton of this excellent novel. It is a story that has often been told; the quality of the novel lies in Ron Hansen's fleshing out of the familiar tale.

Hansen's Jesse James is a complex, contradictory, enigmatic figure. Early in the novel, the reader is told that Jesse

> practiced out-of-the-body travel, precognition, sorcery . . . sucked raw egg yolks out of their shells and ate grass when sick, like a dog . . . was a faulty judge of character, a prevaricator, a child at heart . . . was persistently vexed by insomnia and therefore experimented with a vast number of soporifics . . . could intimidate like King Henry the Eighth . . . could be reckless or serene, rational or lunatic, from one minute to the next . . . regretted neither his robberies nor the seventeen murders that he laid claim to, but he would brood about his slanders and slights, his callow need for attention, his overweening vaingloriousness, and he was excessively genteel and polite in order to disguise what he thought was vulgar, primitive and depraved in his origins.

Furthermore, Jesse is depicted as faithful to his rather mousy wife, Zee, and as a rather fastidious person in sexual matters. Before their marriage, he asks Zee if he can be "liberal" with her, and upon being refused he becomes embarrassed and does not persist. Years later, when Robert Ford passes on to Jesse a story suggesting that Jesse would take advantage of female robbery victims, he is offended.

Despite the intriguing catalog of Jesse's characteristics, traits, quirks, and eccentricities with which the reader is provided, two facets of Jesse James are not so clearly spelled out: his reasons for pursuing a life of thievery and murder, and the strange, hypnotic effect which he seemed to have on his followers and on the public who followed his exploits from a distance. The narrator asserts that "rooms seemed hotter when [Jesse] was in them, rains fell straighter, clocks slowed, sounds were amplified." Although Hansen sketches in the background of bitterness and violence from the Civil War that preceded Jesse's life of crime, the reader is largely left to puzzle out for himself the James enigma. This is an intelligent decision by Hansen. A glib psychological explanation of Jesse's motives would trivialize the character. Furthermore, too much explanation of his effect on others would constitute mythmaking, something Hansen mostly avoids. Show, do not tell, states the old narrative rule, and Hansen wisely obeys.

What of the antagonist, Robert Ford, "the dirty little coward"? In this book, Ford is, in fact, treated rather nicely. The reader first meets him in an encounter with Frank James while the James Gang is busy preparing for a train robbery. Frank is unimpressed: "He looked to Frank like a simp and a snickerer, the sort to tantalize leashed dogs." Despite Frank's misgivings, Ford manages to ingratiate himself with Jesse, with Ford serving as court jester and sycophant, listening avidly to Jesse's stories, laughing at Jesse's jokes, and telling stories himself about the deeds of the gang. This, however, is not all there is to Robert Ford: "I'm afraid of being forgotten. . . . I'm afraid I'll end up living a life like everyone else's and me being Bob Ford won't matter one way or the other," he tells Jesse shortly before the assassination. Still more revealing is Ford's comment to a law officer when he decides to betray Jesse for reward money:

> I've been a nobody all my life. I was the baby; I was the one people picked on, the one they made promises to that they never kept. And ever since I can recall it, Jesse James has been big as a tree. I'm prepared for this, Jim. And I'm going to accomplish it. I know I won't get but this one opportunity and you can bet your life I'm not going to spoil it.

Thus, Ford moves from wimp to Judas to assassin, and still later one step further, to celebrity.

Hansen's manipulation of narrative chronology is deft yet unobtrusive. He begins in September of 1881, only a few months before the assassination, showing the gang at work on a train robbery. Here he introduces Jesse and

Ford as well as most of the other important characters in the book. Hansen then backs up some fifteen years to Jesse's younger days, telling of Jesse's lengthy romance with Zee and describing many of the crimes committed by the gang. Hansen then slows the pace and takes the reader almost week by week through the final months before the assassination. Remarkably, given the reader's knowledge of the outcome, Hansen manages to build suspense and tension until the moment when Jesse, standing on a chair and tending to a picture, is gunned down. "Gunpowder and gun noise filled the room and Jesse groaned as a man does in his sleep and then sagged from his knees and tilted over and smacked the floor like a great animal, shaking the house with his fall."

After the killing, Ford sends telegrams to the governor and others with the simple declaration, "I have killed Jesse James. Bob Ford." Thus Hansen shifts the focus to Ford, tracing his life through the next ten years, culminating in his own death by shooting. This final section of the novel, entitled "Americana," seems to be Hansen's ironic way of suggesting that publicity seeking, celebrity status, and the merchandising of personalities are not concepts newly arrived on the American scene. If there had been late-night television in 1882, Hansen seems to suggest, Robert Ford would have been invited. There was, of course, no television, but there were interviewers and carnival goers anxious to see a reenactment of the killing by one of the principals. At last, Robert Ford told himself, his name would be known—respect and fame and, yes, even heroism would be his—but it was not to be. Jesse remained the hero, and Ford remained the Judas. "Do you know what I expected? Applause. I thought Jesse James was a Satan and a tyrant who was causing all this misery, and that I'd be the greatest man in America if I shot him. I thought they would congratulate me and I'd get my name in books. I was only twenty years old then. I couldn't see how it would look to people. I've been surprised by what's happened."

A nice contrast between Jesse and Ford that is subtly drawn by Hansen is in the manner of their deaths—or, more precisely, in their spiritual readiness for death. In both cases, Hansen gives a vivid description of the violence of death by gunshot. When Jesse is killed, the reader is told that "Ford's .44 ignited and a red stamp seemed to paste against the outlaw's chestnut brown hair one inch to the rear of his right ear, and his left eyebrow socked into the glass watercolor. . . ." The description of Ford's death is even more graphic: ". . . the shotgun ignited once and again from five feet away, clumped sprays of shrapnel ripping into the man's neck and jawbone, ripping through his carotid artery and jugular vein, stripping skin away. . . ." Outwardly then, both men died sudden, violent, bloody deaths, but in Hansen's account there is a marked difference in the way in which they meet death. Hansen's Jesse meets death with awareness, peace, readiness. Asked by Ford if he feels anything for his victims, Jesse says, "I've been forgiven for all that. . . . I've already been forgiven." A couple of days before his death, Jesse gives Robert Ford a gift, a pearl-handled .44 caliber Smith and Wesson revolver, the soon-to-be instrumentality of Jesse's death. When the day of death arrives, Jesse seems to know it and plays his role accordingly, unbuckling his holster and standing up on a chair as if offering himself to the executioner. Robert Ford, on the other hand, has seen his dream of fame and respect elude him and has only just remarked to a companion, "My luck isn't very good as it is," when he walks out onto the street, is blasted by a shotgun, and dies with "the light going out of his eyes before he could say the right words."

While Jesse and Ford are the dominant characters in the book, it should be noted that Hansen does a fine job of presenting lesser characters with depth and individuality: Jesse's brother Frank, a moody, reserved man frequently not on speaking terms with Jesse; Zee, the woman who nursed Jesse back to health from pneumonia and a chest wound, was engaged to him for nine years, and married him and bore his children, a rather drab woman who becomes increasingly resigned to her husband's livelihood, in the process losing her vitality; the members of the gang, particularly the Younger brothers; and the various politicians and law enforcement officials who sought to destroy Jesse James and his gang.

This is a book which is filled with factual material—dates, particular incidents, specific individuals—and Hansen acknowledges several sources upon which he relied. Throughout the narrative, the reader is compelled to ask the question: What is actual fact, and what is the creation of Ron Hansen? With the exception of several very inventive and very literary passages, this book could almost pass as a biography. This is not to suggest that Hansen's achievement should be diminished. His was the organizing mind that selected the material and the narrative voice that succeeds in retelling oft-told material in a fresh and compelling manner. While a purist might, perhaps, argue that fiction should be entirely the product of the writer's imagination, there are several examples in recent fiction of an author relying on factual material. William Kennedy's *Legs* (1976) comes to mind, as does E. L. Doctorow's *Ragtime* (1975), in which actual characters flit in and out of the story among the fictional creations of the author. Quibbles aside, this is a novel which contains the elements that are common to most good fiction—well-drawn characters and a strong narrative drive. *The Assassination of Jesse James by the Coward Robert Ford*, nominated for the 1984 P.E.N./Faulkner Award for Fiction, is only the second novel by Ron Hansen, but it is a work that displays considerable talent and maturity. The past few years have seen the arrival on the literary scene of a number of impressively skilled young writers. The name of Ron Hansen should be added to the list.

L. W. Payne

Sources for Further Study

Christian Science Monitor. December 28, 1983, p. 18.
Hudson Review. XXXVII, Spring, 1984, p. 160.
Los Angeles Times Book Review. November 20, 1983, p. 8.
Newsweek. CII, November 14, 1983, p. 112.
Publishers Weekly. CCXXIV, September 9, 1983, p. 49.

AT THE BOTTOM OF THE RIVER

Author: Jamaica Kincaid (1949-   )
Publisher: Farrar, Straus & Giroux (New York). 82 pp. $9.95
Type of work: Short stories
Time: Unspecified
Locale: The West Indies

A collection of ten brief sketches recounting memories of the author's childhood in the Caribbean

> *Principal character:*
> A YOUNG GIRL, the first-person narrator

Occasionally a new literary voice emerges that is so distinctive, so original, that critics and readers have difficulty in knowing exactly how to respond to the work. Such is the case with Jamaica Kincaid, a young Caribbean writer whose first collection of short stories, *At the Bottom of the River*, has recently appeared. Kincaid, who was born on the island of St. John, Antigua, in the West Indies, is now a staff writer for *The New Yorker*. Her stories have been published in *The New Yorker, Rolling Stone*, and *Paris Review*. This first collection of her short fiction is a slim volume of pieces reprinted from these magazines, where they originally appeared. Several critics, including Susan Sontag and Derek Walcott, have praised Kincaid's work, while others, such as *The New York Times* book reviewer Edith Milton, have expressed reservations about her lack of clear characterization and plot and the resulting obscurity of some of her sketches.

Part of the difficulty in responding to Kincaid's work is the lack of any of the conventional elements of fiction. One might almost say that her work is "deconstructed" to the point of presenting a pure, unstructured narrative of her major character's memories, impressions, and recollections of her Caribbean childhood. Time, place, and point of view are scrambled in a collage of physical sensations, dreams, and disembodied voices. Her style, so intensely lyric, so rhythmic and evocative, approaches that of the prose poem. She presents a world of fresh, urgent, unmediated childhood impressions, some pleasant and comforting, others threatening and disturbing, a compilation of raw and undigested experiences of her family, village life, and the lush physical environment of the Caribbean islands. Her stark and vivid impressions of her world leap from the pages like disturbing dreams, graphic and unforgettable but puzzling and indecipherable. Often, more than one character is present in a sketch, and Kincaid leaps from consciousness to consciousness with few narrative hints as to who is speaking or thinking. The result is an almost surrealistic sensation of a frightening and disturbing world about to overwhelm the small, vulnerable, childish consciousness of the narrator.

The reader may infer a few clues about the continuity and meaning of these ten sketches from the dominant, first-person point of view of the narrator, a young Caribbean girl, at times a small child, in other sketches an adolescent or a young woman. The jacket illustration, the painting *Green Summer* (1868) by Edward Burne-Jones, sets the tone for the collection in its depiction of a group of wistful, Pre-Raphaelite maidens sitting in a lush green meadow listening to one of the young women reading from a book. The dominant feminine perspective of Kincaid's sketches ranges from the matter-of-fact, domestic quality of the first story, "Girl," to the darkly Freudian, dreamlike mood of the title piece, "At the Bottom of the River," which appears last.

Many of Kincaid's pieces are very short; such is the case with the opening selection, "Girl," a set of household and domestic instructions narrated in a singsong, staccato manner which suggests English spoken with a Caribbean accent. Here, a mother seems to be lecturing her young daughter about the household skills she needs to learn in order to become a woman in her culture. The mother's advice is frank, practical, and colloquial, as she instructs her daughter when to wash which clothes and where; how to dry and iron them; how to prepare and cook fish, pumpkin fritters, and pepper pot; how to walk and behave like a lady "and not like the slut you are so bent on becoming"; how to clean and sweep the house; whom to speak with at church and Sunday school; how to set the table; how to shop for fresh bread and produce; how to garden and fish; and how to treat men in all of their moods. This three-page "story" consists of a single continuous sentence, a Joycean sentence flavored with Kincaid's distinctive blend of shrewdness, common sense, folklore, and superstition.

The second selection, "In the Night," shifts from the daytime world of domestic chores to the nocturnal world of mysterious sounds and impressions. Here, the author does a marvelous job of evoking the hot, lazy night rhythms of Caribbean life, as recorded in the child's consciousness. "What is the Night?" this sketch seems to ask, in all of its dark, mysterious, palpable immediacy. A jumble of commonplace sounds—the chirp of a cricket, the house creaking, a distant radio playing, a restless sleeper, a domestic argument, the rain falling on a tin roof—is mixed in the child's consciousness with the sounds of ghosts, vampires, a jablesse (a female vampire). As the child sinks into sleep, sounds from the outside world are mingled with dreams in a Blakean account of babies turning into lambs and eating green grass, interrupted when her mother awakens her—she has wet the bed. Impressions of her father follow—random associations, disjointed memories of his job as a night soil man, his favorite clothes, birthday celebrations, the time he went to the hospital, his favorite songs and interests. The child's dream then shifts to flowers and to a confused sense of adulthood; she imagines marrying an older, "red-skin woman" who will take care of her.

In the next piece, "At Last," the dream sequence seems to shift to adulthood in a confusing dialogue between the narrator and an unidentified voice, the two perhaps being mother and daughter. The impressions here are of house and yard, representing the protective world of the home as mediated by dreams. Perhaps this is the fearful child's sense of adulthood, womanhood, motherhood, with its threats of death, decay, and loss, or perhaps it is the mother's brooding regret for the loss of her daughter, now grown to be a young woman and gone from home. The mother's memories of her life with her daughter come rushing back in a torrent of powerful recollections as she sits musing about the past. Past and present are telescoped in the mind's attempt to hold onto threads of memory as the narrator's life unravels before her.

The following sketch, "Wingless," projects the child's wistful and girlish sense of her own innocence, fear, and vulnerability. The sketch opens with a group of small children reading a passage from the Victorian children's story *The Water Babies* (1907) by Charles Kingsley and quickly moves to a bewildering set of impressions of childhood games, songs, fears, anxieties, and questions. The narrator sees herself as "a defenseless and pitiful child," quick to tears and sorrow, a "primitive and wingless" creature, now frail and vulnerable but hoping someday to "grow up to be a tall, graceful, and altogether beautiful woman" capable of imposing her will "on large numbers of people." For now, though, she must endure the small hurts and disappointments of childhood. The schoolroom, especially, is a place of great risks and dangers, where one must learn to please the teacher and to choose one's friends carefully. Kincaid's sketch suggests how difficult it sometimes is for the child to guard against all the imagined threats and dangers of the outside world and how the smallest disappointment can bring tears to the eyes of a sensitive child. Even the world of nature seems by turns fascinating and terrifying in its various moods. Above all, the child in this sketch seeks reassurance from her mother as she reaches out and explores the world outside her home.

"Holidays" records a variety of the child's physical sensations and moods associated with the lazy, idle hours of holiday time. It is a time for the child to luxuriate in doing nothing: to sit on a wicker couch and look out the window at a "field of day lilies"; to wander about the house and glance idly at books lying on the table; to take a barefoot walk down the road to the village store to buy peaches; to daydream on the porch; or to make up songs and rhymes. She lives in the "eternal now," and this sketch captures the luxurious ease of those timeless moments of indolence. It is a composite sketch of typical kinds of pleasant, summertime experiences that everyone remembers from childhood.

"The Letter from Home" returns to the theme of the palpable sense of mystery that haunts ordinary moments of domestic life in Kincaid's sketches. It answers that most mundane of questions, "What did you do today?" as the mother recounts a typical day's chores in a singsong style of short, declarative phrases that trip after one another in one long paragraph composed of a continuous sentence. So much is packed into this involved narrative of continuous action that one begins to suspect that it is an account not of a single day but of a lifetime. This sketch contains some particularly lovely cadences of almost biblical simplicity; here, time blends into eternity as artlessly as in an Emily Dickinson poem.

"What I Have Been Doing Lately" also evokes the mysterious qualities of ordinary life, but this sketch is narrated from the child's point of view. Kincaid's style here is one of almost pure free association, as the child's attention leaps from sensation to sensation. The author also makes effective use of a litanylike refrain as the child repeats key phrases; the entire sketch circles on itself and ends by repeating the opening phrases. Images float before the reader and change with bewildering rapidity, often with no external frame of reference. The child steps out from her house to encounter a series of bizarre, "Alice in Wonderland" adventures, during which she meets, coming down the road, a strange woman to whom she repeats her account of her adventures. The tale is whimsical and fanciful but difficult to follow, because the dream sequence seems so private and cryptic.

"Blackness" reintroduces the mood of "In the Night," except that the focus seems to be on the mother's identity rather than on nocturnal sounds and impressions for their own sake. The sketch addresses the child's bemused question, "Who am I?" The surrealistic set of impressions that Kincaid presents may be externalizations of the mother's feelings about herself and her child. The mother falls asleep at her table and dreams of an army that comes marching through her house, weakening its foundations and destroying her flowers. Then she looks up lovingly to watch her child admire herself in the mirror. Her daughter's kindness and cruelty are perplexing, as she first teases and then cares for a hunchback boy. One lovely passage in particular describes the anguish of all parents in watching anxiously over the small lives they have brought into existence: "Though I have summoned her into fleeting existence, one that is perilous and subject to the violence of chance, she embraces time as it passes in numbing sameness, bearing in its wake a multitude of great sadnesses." The great love she bears toward her child allows the mother to shrug off her "mantle of despair" and "move ever toward that silent voice," which enfolds her, so that "even in memory the blackness is erased." This is beautiful and evocative writing, almost elegiac in its haunting and plaintive qualities. It expresses the hopes and fears and longings of all parents for their children, their progeny, their answer to the "silent voice" of personal oblivion.

"My Mother" expresses the child's deep and impetuous love for her mother, an affection capable of sudden, irrational bursts of anger and tenderness. The child rashly wishes her mother dead, then immediately regrets her terrible wish with bitter tears and lamentation. She craves tenderness and intimacy, yearning to be enveloped in her mother's arms and protected from the world. Her mother's moods can be terrible and mysterious, so that she looms large and reptilian in the child's frightened imagination, but most of the time her mother is soothing and gentle. There is a graceful description in this sketch of mother and daughter undressing by candlelight, as the flickering shadows of the candle make the mother loom larger than life against the dark shadows in the background of the room. Then mother and daughter seem to launch out in a dreamlike adventure, almost an allegory of the daughter's transition from girlhood to adolescence to womanhood. They experience several metamorphoses, as the daughter first turns into a lamb and then becomes an earth-burrowing creature. Images of the moon, caves, ponds, and sea voyages preside over these feminine mysteries. The sketch shifts abruptly to a dreamlike allegory of life, with the daughter bidding farewell to her mother before she departs on a sea voyage that will take her to another island similar to the one she left; there a woman exactly like herself awaits to greet her and the two gradually merge into one person. Signs of fertility abound in their house as the mother dresses her daughter with flower petals and a hummingbird nests on her stomach. Fishermen pull in nets of fish from the sea and lambs bound in the pasture. Mother and daughter inhabit a "bower of bliss."

The last piece in the collection, "At the Bottom of the River," is both the longest and perhaps the most difficult to explicate because of its bewildering variety of mythical episodes and images. The sketch seems to present a version of the creation story, an account of Adam and Eve without the Fall, with the narrator blessing the variety and abundance of the natural world. The sketch opens with a tropical, mountainous landscape inhabited by a single man. This world, though beautiful, is "bereft of its very nature" because it is untouched by human hands. This paradise knows nothing of human joys and sorrows until, in a sudden transition, the man wakes from his dream into his ordinary domestic life of breakfast and greetings from his wife and daughter. The man, apparently a carpenter, then departs for his day's work, contemplating his projects. The mystery of the ordinary is compounded as the narrator asks, "And who is this man, really?" The rest of the first part of the sketch seems to be a hymn of praise for the beauty and variety of the natural world, as the man contemplates with satisfaction the house he has built with his own hands, the food and shelter he has provided for his wife and daughter, and the "tenderness and love and faith" they have shared. He seems to take great pleasure in "the beauty of the common thing" and the tranquility of the scene.

The mood of the sketch shifts abruptly to images of death and decay as the narrator contemplates how vainly the man has struggled against the threat of death. All that he has done seems to vanish in the darkness and into oblivion. The remainder of the sketch is an extended meditation on death. The narrator mocks the notion that "Death is natural" and argues that people must hold on to what they have. "Is life, then, a violent burst of light, like flint struck sharply in the dark?" the narrator wonders. Maternal love reaches out across the darkness and the years as the narrator recalls the deep love and affection that her mother had lavished upon her.

The meaning of the story's title becomes evident in the final section, which opens like an apocalyptic vision, with the narrator viewing her house at the bottom of the river, as if from the other side of life, as all of the flowers, grass, birds, and creatures that represented the beauty of life flow past her. Then she seems to become transfigured and the heavens revolve about her as she "stood above the land and sea and looked back up at myself as I stood on the bank of the mouth of the river." Liberated from her physical body, she reunites with the elements in the freedom of her new existence.

A collection as rich and varied as Jamaica Kincaid's *At the Bottom of the River* does not exhaust its possibilities after a first or even a second reading. The sketches included here leave the reader marveling at the richness and dexterity of her language yet puzzled over their meaning, if indeed they are intended to convey any meaning in the conventional sense of the word. Kincaid reveals a genuine poetic talent in these sketches, yet part of her problem is that she is basically a poet rather than a storyteller, neglecting the storyteller's art of engaging the reader through the conventions of plot and character. Here, character emerges primarily through narrative tones of voice, and one is left with a sense of Kincaid's persistent elusiveness. The strength of these stories is in their rich, evocative lyricism; they are small gems of poetry masquerading as prose.

Andrew J. Angyal

Sources for Further Study

Los Angeles Times Book Review. December 15, 1983, p. 46.
Ms. XII, January, 1984, p. 15.
The New Republic. CLXXXIX, December 31, 1983, p. 32.
The New York Times Book Review. LXXXVIII, January 15, 1984, p. 22.
Publishers Weekly. CCXXIV, October 14, 1983, p. 45.

AXE HANDLES

Author: Gary Snyder (1930-   )
Publisher: North Point Press (San Francisco). 114 pp. $12.50; paperback $7.50
Type of work: Poetry

The first new collection in a decade by the Pulitzer Prize-winning poet

Gary Snyder's new volume of poems, *Axe Handles*, is the first he has published since *Turtle Island*, which was awarded the Pulitzer Prize in 1974. This beautifully crafted book of seventy-one poems includes brief, haiku-like lyrics; riddles; and free-verse narratives. Snyder's publisher, North Point Press, has quickly acquired a reputation as one of the finest small presses in the country, and their craftsmanship is evident throughout this book, from the cover design to the handsome layout and the poet's careful arrangement of his material. The dust jacket features an exquisite illustration of Gaia, the Earth Goddess, depicted as a goddess of snow by artist Mayumi Oda. Taken from the artist's collection, *Goddesses*, the jacket illustration is entitled "Treasure Ship, Goddess of Snow." The delicate Oriental quality of the cover design complements the series of haiku poems in the second part of the collection, "Little Songs for Gaia."

West Coast poet Snyder has been associated with the Beat movement—notably with his longtime friend Allen Ginsberg—and the San Francisco poet Kenneth Rexroth, who encouraged the young Snyder in his study of Oriental languages and culture. Snyder has always been distinguished from the Beats, however, by his disciplined imagination, tempered by his long study of Buddhism in Japan, where he lived for some years. In his early poems of the 1950's, he anticipated many of the concerns of the counterculture, blending Eastern thought with environmentalism, and he has not swerved from those commitments. In his poetry, Snyder has tried to articulate this sensibility, one based on a rejection of technology and affluence, a harmony with nature, and a Buddhist inner discipline and tranquility. Snyder's mastery of his form is evident in the firm, clean lines of verse, reminiscent of Ezra Pound's *Rock-Drill* cantos (1955). Pound's ideogramic technique stands behind Snyder's work, though Snyder's extensive familiarity with Oriental languages and thought has permitted him to surpass Pound in his fidelity to the values that inform his Japanese and Chinese models. The poems in *Axe Handles* are marked by simplicity and understatement, sharpness of image and syntactical spareness, discipline and restraint.

The collection is unified by Snyder's awareness of the resources of language as a tool for shaping and crafting his verse, a theme suggested by the epigraph, a fifth century B.C. Chinese folk song about shaping axe handles from the pattern of an already existing handle. As he implies in his title poem, "Axe Handles," poetry is language used as a tool to make other tools. Like the axe handle, poetry is both a tool and a model for shaping other tools. Snyder borrows his metaphor from Lu Ji's *Wên Fu*, a fourth century A.D. "Essay on Literature," which begins, "In making the handle/ Of an axe/ By cutting wood with an axe/ The model is indeed near at hand." The theme of cultural continuity, present in many of the poems in this collection, appears in the title poem as a wonderful parable of the transmission of culture implicit in the poet's simple act of showing his son Kai how to shape a new hatchet handle from a broken-off axe handle. Teaching and learning, from master to pupil, father to son, is like shaping a new handle to the form of the old handle in one's hand. The pleasure Snyder takes in his work reminds him of a phrase first learned from Ezra Pound, who in turn borrowed it from its Chinese original. Thus, in the cycle of renewal, "Pound was an axe,/ Chen was an axe, I am an axe/ And my son a handle, soon/ To be shaping again, model/ And tool, craft of culture,/ How we go on."

Many of the poems describe the daily life of Snyder and his family at their homestead in the foothills of the California Sierra Nevadas, where he lives with his Japanese wife, Masa, and their two sons, Kai and Gen. The deep and abiding pleasure he finds in the details of ordinary life are registered in these poems, which together evoke a sense of a healthy, harmonious, and productive life-style in which rearing children and bringing the soil back into production through composting and recycling are part of the same caring, nurturing concern.

The poems in *Axe Handles* are divided into three sections: "Loops," "Little Songs for Gaia," and "Nets." They range outward from family, to community, to national government, to a global environmental concern of the kind that Snyder first articulated in *Turtle Island*. Judging from the subject matter of many of his poems, Snyder likes tools and uses them well. He values honest labor and the things of the earth as self-disciplines that provide serenity and repose.

These poems record a wonderfully vivid and exact sense of a man's life rich in ordinary moments—gardening, cutting firewood, painting a school-house, repairing an old Willys pickup truck, putting in fenceposts, enjoying time spent with his two sons, and noticing what is in bloom as the seasons progress. These experiences are the Tao, or "given" of life. Although a deep imprint of Eastern sensibility is evident in Snyder's work, he is no recluse, as the poems describing his work with the California Arts Council and his conversations with then Governor Jerry Brown testify. Rather, Snyder represents a unique blend of American environmentalism and love of the wilderness with an Oriental serenity, self-discipline, and restraint. This melding of East and West is what accounts for the distinctiveness of his poetic voice, though Snyder resists thinking in these dualistic cultural terms. "Better," he has said, quoting a Zen saying, "the perfect easy discipline of the swallow's dip and swoop, 'without east or west.'"

The poems in part 1, "Loops," emphasize the natural cycles and continuity of family, community, and land. In an obliquely personal poem, "For/From Lew," a dead friend advises the poet to "teach children about the cycles./ The life cycles. All the other cycles./ That's what it's all about, and it's all forgot." This respect for the balance of nature is evident throughout this section, as Snyder celebrates natural events such as the nesting of swallows and the flow of rivers. "Where do rivers start?" his son asks in the poem, "Rivers in the Valley," and the answer comes in the form of a verse meditation on the cycles of water. Another poem, "Among," describes West Coast forest succession, as the tiny Douglas firs, the climax tree, reseed themselves among a stand of ponderosa pine. What rescues these poems from banality is the remarkable discipline and control that Snyder exercises over his material. The craft of writing good free verse is as demanding as writing traditional verse, and Snyder makes effective use of variable line and stress and elliptical syntax. "On Top," a poem about composting, uses the metaphor of building soil to suggest how the poet works over his materials for creative inspiration.

Many of Snyder's poems are meditations inspired by the physical work of homesteading. Throughout this collection, he emphasizes the dignity and value of manual work as a means of getting back in touch with oneself. "Bows to Drouth," for instance, was inspired by a summer drought in 1974 that kept the poet busy pumping water to his apple trees. Throughout these poems, Snyder's outdoor work helps him to keep in touch with the physical world around him—the land, weather, seasons, moods of nature. As a young man, Snyder worked summers with the Forestry Service, and he retains his love of the high country of the Sierras and Sawtooth Ranges. Many of his poems were inspired by camping trips and his time spent outdoors. He feels little but contempt for the great urban sprawl of coastal California, preferring the small communities and relative isolation of the foothills.

Like the California poet Robinson Jeffers before him, Snyder perceives the reckless transiency of white American settlement in contrast to the permanence of the land itself. His poems yearn for the serenity and order of a Native American or Oriental outlook in place of the waste and heedlessness of modern American life. There is, however, little of Jeffers' stark "inhumanism" in Snyder's outlook. Instead, his work celebrates a mellowed and matured counterculture, still critical of prevailing American values but offering its own alternative set of values in communal cooperation, conservation, and a nonexploitative way of life that shows respect for the land. The military serves as a particular object for Snyder's scorn, whether it be the futile display of American and Soviet jet maneuvers and aerial confrontations that waste millions of gallons of kerosene or the satellites and jet vapor trails seen at night during a Sierra camping trip. The vanity and futility of these cultural gestures contrast sharply with the serenity and repose of the natural world.

Perhaps the best poem in part 1 is "Working on the '58 Willys Pickup," a free-verse manifesto of Snyder's hard-won values and wisdom. This personal narrative, occasioned by the poet's need to rebuild an old pickup truck that he hopes to use to haul rotten sawdust for his garden, encompasses both the poet's personal development and a cultural confrontation between East and West. As he repairs the truck's brakes, Snyder recalls that he was studying Chinese and Japanese the year this truck was built, but in his education he learned nothing of practical matters such as truck repair. Now, some twenty years later, the cycles of his life have brought him back to a California homestead where he works to restore the abandoned truck. As he works, he admires its compact utility, thinking that ". . . a truck like this/ would please Chairman Mao." Now Snyder and his other formerly academic friends attempt to recycle what their culture has discarded so wastefully. Snyder puts the truck back into use. Thus in his labor, theoretical and practical knowledge are united, and the pleasure of working with his hands and doing something useful complements his academic background. East meets West in the practical agrarian utility of the poet and his associates, who use what their culture has discarded in order to bring the land back into fruitful production. Other poems such as "Getting in the Wood" also celebrate the satisfactions of hard work done cooperatively among good friends as a means of building community and living the values in which they believe.

The second part, "Little Songs for Gaia," is a set of twenty-one exquisite haiku-like lyrics that record glimpses of the natural world in a manner as elegant and stylized as an Oriental landscape painting. Snyder uses words as gracefully as brush strokes to evoke, in an act of poetic meditation, strong, clear images of the natural world. These sharp pieces remind the reader of Ezra Pound and William Carlos Williams at their best and demonstrate how thoroughly Snyder has assimilated the techniques of Oriental poetry and made them part of his own voice and style. Lyric grace and movement abound in these glimpses of hawks circling over marshes, the ouzel diving in a stream, the call of the red-shafted flicker, the rattle of buck antlers, or the dream of Corn Maidens dancing. All of these visions are part of the seamless web of the ever-changing natural cycles of nature. These brief verse meditations bespeak a mind trained to look beyond the temporary, transient world of man to the permanence of the natural world.

Part of the discipline of Zen is knowing the proper place and use of things, so that they serve people instead of dominate them. That discipline is sometimes depicted in the metaphor of the archer and the bow, in the effortless fusion of arrow and flight. Snyder demonstrates such discipline and detachment in part 3, "Nets," a more eclectic selection of verse about the human and natural worlds. Divided into four sections, "Nets" opens with several poems based on Snyder's numerous camping trips into Yellowstone National Park and Montana, which offer vivid glimpses of the pristine wilderness. "Geese Gone Beyond" describes an experience of spotting a flock of Canada geese while the poet and his companion are canoeing on a mountain lake. Their experience of kneeling and watching from the canoe is likened to a Japanese tea ceremony or watching a Nō play, as the poet and his friend stop to gaze in rapt admiration as the geese take off and fly honking overhead. In another short piece with a title longer than the text, a sudden Nevada snow-storm inspires the poet to bow to Mother Gaia (the Earth Goddess) in the roadside gravel. Snyder's act of veneration serves as the perfect tribute to the austere beauty of the Western American landscape.

The second part of "Nets" shifts to the Western American cultural landscape with a varied series of poems, one describing the commercial vulgarity of a Nevada county fair rodeo contrasting with several more dignified pieces ded-icated to then California Governor Jerry Brown. The concluding poem, "What I Have Learned," is the strongest in the section, an ode to the discipline of the proper use of hand tools.

The third part of "Nets" opens with an occasional poem, "A Maul for Bill and Cindy's Wedding," which offers the wish that the newlyweds may never be divided as easily as the poet's maul splits his rounds of oak. Following are two Alaska poems about the desecration of the natural environment by the crude-oil pipelines and the stampede for development, as Snyder depicts redneck construction workers brawling in bars when they are not out wrecking the natural world. These Alaskan scenes of environmental vandalism remind the poet of a Native American legend of a greedy one who failed to "master his Ally correctly" when he was young but instead became greedy and imitated the white man's ways, so that he became a threat to his tribe and his people. Such behavior was "crazy" from the Indians' perspective and the renegade among them should have been killed, but instead he lived and prospered at the expense of others. That Zen of the proper mastery of things is best illustrated by a short lyric about the hydraulic system of a backhoe, in which the poet takes delight in machinery that is designed well and works well to serve its function.

Finally, in the fourth part of "Nets," the poet turns to themes of illusion and aging. The illusory lure of money and power is treated metaphorically in "Breasts," the organs of nourishment which concentrate the environmental toxins (the metaphorical equivalent of cultural illusions) that the mother takes in with her own food. The work of life is to "burn the poison away" to reveal the gaiety of parents in old age. In the memorable poem "Old Rotting Tree Trunk Down," human aging is contrasted with other cycles of death and decay in the natural world. The poem traces the process of decay and disintegration of a massive tree trunk, which serves as a host to fungi, beetles, and larvae, and as a food source for woodpeckers, as life passes to death and then to myriad other forms of life as the natural cycles perpetuate themselves. There follow in this last section a poetic tribute to a mummified Bäckaskog woman in a Stockholm museum, who is likened to "Old Woman Nature"; and "The

Canyon Wren," a moving tribute to the soon-to-be dammed Stanislaus River, on which Snyder rafted with several friends in April of 1981, shortly before the river was scheduled to be impounded by the New Mellones Dam. The song of the Canyon Wren stayed with them during the entire voyage. The collection concludes with "For All," a facetious ecological parody of the Pledge of Allegiance, in the form of an ecological pledge to all forms of life in the ecosystem of "Turtle Island," the Native American mythological concept of the world.

The careful selection and arrangement of the poems collected in *Axe Handles* demonstrates Gary Snyder's steady development and maturity as one of America's foremost contemporary poets. This fine new collection shows that there has been no decline in Snyder's art since the publication of *Turtle Island*; rather, the poet has used the intervening years to strengthen and deepen his poetic vision. *Axe Handles* offers a sensible and coherent vision of a poet engaged not with the cultivation of a private personal vision but with the hard and earnest business of crafting a life and community for himself, his family, and friends. Snyder's poetry offers a healthy antidote to the stultified irrelevance of most contemporary American poetry. The poems in *Axe Handles* demonstrate Snyder's ability to whet and hone the tools of language to shape and craft his poems with fine precision. He is a poet well worth reading.

Andrew J. Angyal

Sources for Further Study

Booklist. LXXX, October 15, 1983, p. 324.
Nation. CCXXXVII, November 19, 1983, pp. 501.
Publishers Weekly. CCXXIV, September 16, 1983, p. 123.

THE BACK ROOM

Author: Carmen Martín Gaite (1925-   )
Translated from the Spanish by Helen R. Lane
Publisher: Columbia University Press (New York). 210 pp. $17.95
Type of work: Novel
Time: The 1970's
Locale: Spain

The narrative of a conversation between a novelist and her mysterious visitor, whose critical probing of her literary work prompts her to recall intimate memories of her past

> *Principal characters:*
> CARMEN, the novelist
> ALEJANDRO, the visitor in the black hat
> CAROLA, a woman who telephones the novelist during her interview with the visitor
> RAFAEL, a man who interrupts Carola during her telephone conversation with the novelist

Carmen Martín Gaite is one of a group of Spanish women novelists who began writing in the period about ten or fifteen years after 1939, the year that marked the end of the Spanish Civil War and the triumph of Francisco Franco's Fascist government. Of this group, which includes Carmen Laforet, Dolores Medio, and Ana María Matute, Martín Gaite was perhaps the most immediately successful. In 1954, her first novel, *El balneario* won the prestigious fiction prize awarded by the Café Gijón, the traditional gathering place of Madrid's artistic intelligentsia. Three years later, *Entre visillos* received the Premio Nadal, and in 1962, her novel *Ritmo lento* was the runner-up for the coveted Premio Biblioteca Breve. During that period of prolific writing, she published in 1960 a collection of short stories, *Las ataduras* (attachments), which bears the same title as the popular novel published years later by the American writer Judith Rossner. It is a curious coincidence, for the fiction of Martín Gaite is dominated by the same feminist concerns that characterize Rossner's work.

In the male-dominated Spanish society of the 1950's and 1960's, Martín Gaite's success was aided to some extent by the fact that she was married to Rafael Sánchez Ferlosio, himself a noted novelist and winner of the Premio Nadal. After the publication of *Ritmo lento*, Martín Gaite abandoned fiction and turned to scholarly research and writing. She published first a history of an eighteenth century literary inquisition and then her doctoral dissertation in Romance philology at the University of Madrid on the courtship habits of eighteenth century Spaniards. During the 1960's, she also published articles in the most prestigious literary and cultural journals of Spain, articles which were later collected in *La búsqueda de interlocutor y otras búsquedas*.

In 1974, Martín Gaite returned to her exploration in fiction of the significance of being a woman in Spain: *Retahílas* is the story of a young girl's attempts to escape the web of submission that binds Spanish women. In 1978, Martín Gaite published *El cuarto de atrás* (*The Back Room*), for which she received the important Premio Nacional de Literatura. The translation, done by Helen R. Lane with the polish and elegance that she has bestowed on the works of other contemporary Spanish novelists, is the first of Martín Gaite's works to appear in English and is part of a series initiated in 1983 by Columbia University Press to publish translations of contemporary Continental fiction.

One of the most significant facts about Martín Gaite's novel is that it is her first work of fiction after the death of Franco, her first novel in the post-censorship era. *The Back Room* is a synthesis of evocations of memories of the narrator's life and of the narrator's earlier fictional works. Because the remembered episodes correspond so closely to the details of Martín Gaite's life—indeed, Martín Gaite and the narrator share the same first name, Carmen—and because the fictional works attributed to the narrator bear the titles of Martín Gaite's own novels, *The Back Room* is dominated by an autobiographical tone. The back room of the title is a metaphor for her place of retreat and escape, and this fictional narrator-novelist takes refuge in that haven from the world to explore the significance of the episodes of her past, a significance that until this period of free expression could not be addressed.

This new freedom embraces not only liberation from the strictures of the Franco era, but also freedom from the tyranny of social norms, and particularly from the sex-role stereotyping that characterized the society in which Martín Gaite was trained and educated. The enormous changes that took place in Spain and throughout the Western world during the period of Martín Gaite's retreat from fictional writing are reflected here in *The Back Room*, in the form of revaluations not only of her autobiographical narrator's historical life, but also of her fictional inventions.

The stimulus for the narrator's introspection is a visit from a mysterious man in a black hat. The man knows her literary work by heart and possesses an extraordinary ability to criticize her fiction and elicit from her the most intimate details of her life. Early in the interview, he identifies the essential fact of her literary activity—that it is a refuge, a sort of "back room" of her existence. Through the emphasis that Martín Gaite gives to the unconscious motivation of her narrator's literary work, she creates an interesting parallel between this fiction—the novel *The Back Room* as a Martín Gaite novel—and the novels of Carmen, the protagonist-narrator. In each case—the fictional and the historical—the novelist becomes aware of the evasion of reality disguised as a creative impulse. This moment, however—the moment of the fictional narrator's introspection and the moment of the historical Martín Gaite's creation of *The Back Room*—is a time of confronting the truth of existence and reworking the literary expressions of the past.

As Martín Gaite creates the novel, the hidden truth emerges. As the narrator creates her introspective narrative, her truth emerges, not only in her spoken words but also in the stack of typed pages that mysteriously grows and grows on the table beside the strange interlocutor in black. When the narrator begins to read those pages the next morning, wondering what became of the man in black, the text corresponds exactly to the text of Martín Gaite's novel *The Back Room*.

Here, the novelist makes use of a narrative trick that has become rather common in twentieth century Hispanic fiction. One of the assumptions of fictional narrative has always been that the narrator does not *write*, but *tells* a story. The written text exists only because that is the convenient way—or perhaps the only way—to relay to the audience the oral narrative that is the story. In certain types of fiction, however, such as the epistolary novel, the text represents a written text in the fictional world. In fiction such as *The Back Room*, the text seems to be a report of an oral narrative up to a certain point—in this case, to the very end of the book. When Carmen reads the typewritten manuscript and realizes that her experience has somehow been transformed into written text, the reader realizes that the novel *is* the manuscript that Carmen is reading. The implication, then, is that the narrator's experience related in the novel has been in fact one and the same with her experience of writing the manuscript.

If this is true, it is certainly a mysterious, fantastic process. The novel becomes a personal memoir typical of autobiographical fiction within the framework of an episode typical of the fantastic novel. For obvious reasons, *The Back Room* is dedicated to Lewis Carroll, "who still consoles us for being so sensible and welcomes us into his world turned topsy-turvy." It also contains a number of references to Tzvetan Todorov's work in the genre of fantastic fiction. The narrator is reminded several times during her strange experience with the man in the black hat of Todorov's observation that "the time and space of supernatural life are not the time and space of daily life." Alice is able to experience the topsy-turvy world of Wonderland precisely because she allows it to happen, and Martín Gaite's narrator pursues her interview with the mysterious visitor with an openness that surprises and pleases her. As she does, the meaning of her past experience and fictional expressions of experience begin to make sense to her.

Todorov, in *Introduction à la littérature fantastique* (1970; *The Fantastic: A Structural Approach to a Literary Genre*, 1973), identifies three essential elements in successful fantastic fiction. The reader must consider the world portrayed in the fiction to be real; the reader and the narrator are not certain whether what they perceive derives from commonly held perceptions of reality; and there is no attempt in the fiction to explain the unexplainable through an allegorical interpretation. Only if these elements persist can the necessary balance of total faith and total incredulity be maintained. Carmen the narrator has read Todorov and has promised herself that she will write a fantastic novel. In fact, she is struggling with the first few pages when she receives the call from the mysterious man in the black hat. The episode that follows, constituting the novel, is perfect Todorovian fantastic fiction. The perfect interlocutor appears in the middle of the night, keeping a date that the narrator never made. A woman calls, claiming to have read the letters that the narrator wrote to the man in the black hat, letters that Carmen did not write but wishes that she had.

The theme of the writing of fiction as a means of evading reality and retreating into solitude is constant throughout this novel. The writing of the fantastic novel, paradoxically, is the moment of confronting reality, although it seems that this kind of writing would represent the greatest escape. The encounter with the mysterious man, whose presence cannot be explained rationally, evokes painful memories. Most of those memories reveal the pattern of escape that has characterized the existence of the narrator—refuge in the back room of her childhood home, flights into the unreality of children's fantasies, complete immersion in her work. This confrontation with a supernatural event, however, liberates her from her own evasions, in much the same way that the death of Franco liberated her from the old patterns of antifeminist social norms and state-imposed censorship.

Throughout this novel, the narrator is aware that even though her experience has been conditioned by those societal forces, she has reinforced them by her acquiescence to the kind of world in which she has lived. The strange events that occur toward the end of the novel—the telephone call from the woman who claims to have read the letters and the interruption by a man identified only as Rafael—disrupt to some extent the flow of *The Back Room*. Suddenly, the tone of the narrative changes, and the novel seems less effective than it did before. This disruption, however, is important to the significance of this fantastic, autobiographical memoir. The text does not offer any interpretation of these events, as Todorov suggests that it should not. The woman on the telephone encourages the narrator to reject the man in the black hat, and Rafael berates the woman for her relationship with the interlocutor. In the irrational experience of this narrative—the experience that in retrospect seems to be the actual writing of the fantastic novel—the woman on the telephone represents the socially restricted personality of the narrator, and Rafael the oppressive masculine influence that she has allowed to determine much of her past experience. The man in the black hat, with his attitude of probing and analyzing, offers the possibility—threatening as it may be—of liberation from an existence the boundaries of which have always been determined by others.

Of the many memories evoked by the interlocutor, the most significant is the image of Carmencita Franco, in mourning, attending the funeral of her father. Surely, only the Spanish can fully understand the meaning of that ceremony; the funeral marked the end of a block of frozen time, a self-contained era that spanned most of the life of Martín Gaite and the women of her generation. Ironically, Carmen the narrator watches the ceremony on television, the vehicle of modern mass culture. Spain and the narrator, on the threshold of the contemporary culture, confront reality with all avenues of escape suddenly closed.

In *The Back Room*, Martín Gaite has created a profound statement of feminist liberation in a form quite different from that of much of the literature of that contemporary movement. This is a narrative of a woman whose self-discovery comes through the process of rigorous introspection that constitutes her fictional, fantastic text. Thus, Martín Gaite has created a remarkable work of fiction that is a composite of intimate experience and artistic creativity.

Gilbert Smith

Sources for Further Study

Kirkus Reviews. LI, October 1, 1983, p. 1063.
Los Angeles Times Book Review. December 26, 1983, p. 38.
The New York Times Book Review. LXXXVIII, December 11, 1983, p. 11.
Publishers Weekly. CCXXIV, October 14, 1983, p. 44.

BANKER

Author: Dick Francis (1920-   )
Publisher: G. P. Putnam's Sons (New York). 306 pp. $14.95
Type of work: Novel
Time: The 1980's
Locale: England

After novice investment banker Tim Ekaterin loans a stud-farm owner money to purchase a stallion, disaster threatens banking firm and breeder because foals are born deformed

> *Principal characters:*
> TIM EKATERIN, an investment banker
> JUDITH MICHAELS, the wife of Tim's boss
> DISSDALE SMITH, a racing enthusiast
> OLIVER KNOWLES, a stud-farm owner
> GINNIE KNOWLES, his daughter
> CALDER JACKSON, a veterinarian
> PENELOPE WARREN, a pharmacist

In twenty-two mystery novels since he made his debut in 1962 with *Dead Cert*, Dick Francis has informed whodunit buffs about the intricacies, lore, and seamy underside of horse racing; as a former steeplechase jockey in England, he knows whereof he writes. Despite the predictability of his settings, Francis avoids sameness from one book to the next; he almost always has a different hero-detective (only Sid Halley has appeared in more than one book: *Odds Against*, 1965; and *Whip Hand*, 1979), an uncharacteristic practice for mystery writers. Further, the equestrian erudition is organically part of the plots, so the reader inevitably becomes involved in the world of jockeys, trainers, gamblers, and stud fees. To those who are indifferent to the turf world, John Leonard (in *The New York Times* review of Francis' *Reflex*, 1981) has said: "Not to read Dick Francis because you don't like horses is like not reading Dostoyevsky because you don't like God."

The practice of developing a whodunit around specialized subject matter—from gemology to philately—goes back to Arthur Conan Doyle and S. S. Van Dine, and as a boy Francis read Edgar Wallace's detective fiction, which features racing. In recent novels, Francis has joined other well-researched subjects to his usual backdrop, such as photography in *Reflex* and aeronautics in *Flying Finish* (1966). In *Banker*, there is a multiple backdrop, not merely a double one: racing, pharmacology, and investment banking. The book represents an advance for its author in another respect as well, for in it he travels the same route that Ross Macdonald and P. D. James, among others, have taken before him, transcending the limitations of the whodunit genre more fully than in any of his previous works. Indeed, not until past its midpoint does the novel become a full-scale mystery, and all of the preceding matter is not merely preamble for the subsequent detection; it has a life of its own.

Early in the novel, Francis begins to develop his two nonmystery plots, which are linked by the presence of his protagonist, investment banker Tim Ekaterin. In 1983, Francis said: "My heroes . . . are the sort of chaps I'd like to meet. . . . I do like to write about good types." Ekaterin is such a man, an unheroic type who copes with the unsought and unwanted challenges—emotional, physical, and professional—that he confronts, yet he retains his old-fashioned morality clear to the last page of the novel, which spans three years.

In the first year, Tim moves through his apprenticeship at Paul Ekaterin Ltd., an investment banking firm founded by his great-grandfather. Due to the temporary disability of Gordon Michaels, his boss, Tim becomes responsible for deciding whether to grant loans to such people as a cartoonist who wants to establish a film-editing studio and the owner of a stud farm who wants to purchase a thoroughbred for five million pounds. He decides that the firm will invest both in the cartoonist's talent (which turns out to be a profitable move) and the racehorse's fertility (which nearly ruins Ekaterin's budding banking career). Most of this first third of the book deals with the internal operations of the firm and tensions among its personnel, the latter initiated by a bimonthly gossip sheet, *What's Going On Where It Shouldn't*, which alleges a variety of questionable practices in London's banking firms. Tim helps Paul Ekaterin Ltd. deal with the innuendoes and develops procedures to forestall future difficulties; he also is instrumental in exposing an in-house contributor to the scandal sheet. The new job thus provides Tim with executive experience and, unexpectedly, an apprenticeship in detection. It is the means, too, by which he comes to know Sandcastle, the five-million-pound thoroughbred, and his milieu. Recovered from his illness, Gordon Michaels invites Tim to the Royal Ascot, where he meets Dissdale Smith and Calder Jackson, the former a heavy bettor, the latter an unconventional veterinarian who cures horses with odd medications and a mystical laying on of hands. As the party leaves the track, having profited from Sandcastle's success, Tim saves Jackson from a knife-wielding teenager who then flees into the crowd, an act that reveals Tim's instinctive (even foolhardy) fearlessness when confronted with danger. Francis also introduces a third major motif of the novel in this first part: the developing relationship between Tim and Judith Michaels, Gordon's young wife.

Although one realizes upon reflection that most of the first part of *Banker* provides expository background and foreshadows events to come, there is no clear indication of what form the crime and detection will take. With all the attention that Francis pays to Paul Ekaterin Ltd., the firm could prove to be a likely venue, and there are at least two potential suspects; the incipient affair between Judith and Tim also seems likely to have future ramifications insofar as the whodunit is concerned. Knowledgeable readers of Dick Francis, however, will confidently zero in upon Oliver Knowles's stud farm, his expensive purchase of Sandcastle, and the details of broodmares, stallion fees, the estrus, and breeding sheds. Are the banking scenes "perfunctory" and is the love interest "expendable," as *Newsweek*'s reviewer believes? Not at all; for while they may not bear directly upon the mystery, they are the means by which Tim becomes a credible character, a cut above the traditional two-dimensional series detective and a moral force working against the immorality pervading the different social strata through which he moves.

The section of *Banker* devoted to the second year of the three covered by the novel opens with news of the murder of Ian Pargetter, a veterinarian from whom Calder Jackson had received most of his referrals, but most of the opening chapter of this part is devoted to Tim's visit to Knowles's place, where he learns about breeding practices and becomes acquainted with Knowles's teenage daughter Ginnie, to whom he immediately is attracted. The idyllic link with Ginnie (which comes to a tragic end before it advances very far) is Francis' means of giving additional depth to Tim's character, demonstrating his sensitivity and highlighting his capacity for selfless love.

Another determinedly idyllic interlude in the second section is an Easter Monday trip on which Tim hosts the Michaels and Penelope Warren, a pharmacist friend of theirs. They first go to Jackson's place, where they view his patients in their paddocks, and then tour his laboratory; their next stop is Knowles's farm, where more details of the breeding process are explored. This sequence also further develops Tim's feelings for the maturing Ginnie and the married Judith. Penelope, neither teenager nor married woman, at first seems to have been introduced as an appropriate alternative for Tim, but Francis focuses upon her pharmaceutical knowledge, not her romantic availability, and Tim soon realizes the usefulness of that professional expertise. When he does, the plot of *Banker* moves forward. This practice of advancing his primary plot almost imperceptibly is common in Francis' novels; he introduces elements incidentally, then reintroduces them with elaboration much later. For example, just past the midpoint of the book, Tim is at a racetrack and by chance runs into the boy who had attacked Jackson a year earlier. He learns about the youngster's grievance against Jackson, details of which add to the pattern of questions developing in Tim's mind. In the same way, the brief mention of Ian Pargetter's murder early in the second section is recalled much later in the novel when that crime becomes a centerpiece in the emerging scheme, just as Penelope's specialized knowledge proves to be vital to the solution. More than simply the commonplace planting of fake and real clues, this is skillfully orchestrated plot development.

The seemingly casual and dilatory pace of the novel is necessary to Francis' design, for enough time must elapse so that the mares which Sandcastle has serviced can foal. In the third section, set two years after the opening scenes of the novel, the stallion's first progeny are born. The birth of these deformed foals—followed in rapid succession by an assault on Ginnie, the inexplicable discovery of a plastic bottle of shampoo, and an offer from Dissdale Smith to purchase the stallion—quickens the pace of the action, and *Banker* finally becomes an honest-to-goodness mystery. There is a difference, however. Whereas in traditional whodunits, the detective is a man or woman of keen insight whose perception outpaces his or her accumulation of facts and proof, *Banker's* Tim Ekaterin is a novice whose progress toward the resolution is even more tentative than the reader's. Some may see as a flaw the difficulty Tim has in putting together the pieces of the puzzle—he is an amateur detective who makes the reader look good—but his lack of superlative insight à la Sherlock Holmes or Hercule Poirot is the way it should be, for from the very start of the book he is confronted with challenges that require him to scale new heights or in some way test him. That he succeeds is as much a surprise to himself as to the reader, because he is as self-effacing a character as any who has served as a whodunit protagonist. For most of the novel, in fact, Tim is a learner—learning about investment banking, chemical compounding, and thoroughbred breeding. He is involved in much more than the standard pursuit of clues and facts that engages most whodunit detectives, amateurs or professionals; Tim is a young man in search of himself and his place in the world, and in this way he is not unlike Ross Macdonald's Lew Archer, albeit younger and not at all world-weary. Given Tim's personality and his inexperience, it would have been uncharacteristic for him to have acted more confidently and purposefully as a detective.

The ultimate test that Tim must pass is a physical one, and it is this test and its aftermath that link *Banker* (and each of Francis' other mysteries) to the hard-boiled tradition of Raymond Chandler and Dashiell Hammett. After being knocked unconscious, Tim comes to in a horse box at a stable. The person who carried him there makes a necessary final appearance and then leaves Tim to contemplate both his enlightenment and likely fate in the company of a horse who goes berserk: " . . . he whirled and kicked and hurled his bulk against the walls, and I, still attempting to jump through the tempest into the manger, was finally knocked over by one of his flailing feet." The "rearing, bucking, kicking, rocketing nightmare" breaks one of Tim's arms, crunches an ankle, gives him "a swiping punch in the chest," and lands a "crushing thud" on a shoulder. Tim concludes: "This is death . . . dreadful, pulverizing extinction." Unprepared though he is for "the onslaught of so much pain all at once, and also not quite sure how to deal with it," Tim manages to endure and at the same time belatedly reach some firm conclusions about the case. Since he is *Banker's* narrator (all of Francis' books are written in the first person, with the protagonist as narrator), readers know all that Tim knows, and many are likely to have pieced together the puzzle long before Tim has completed it. Though a primary aim of traditional whodunits is to keep readers guessing and lead them astray until the last possible moment, in *Banker*, Tim's personality is as important as his sleuthing skills and the Tim-Judith story line as important as the mystery.

This romantic relationship brings Tim to the brink of adultery, but he does not betray Gordon's friendship and trust. Near the end of the novel, Penelope advises him to let Judith go, to "Take out some other girl." She tells Tim that he is "a child of the light" and says, "You always take the sunshine with you . . . everything brightens when . . . you walk in." Finally, she tells him: " . . . carry the sunlight to a new young girl who isn't married to Gordon and doesn't break your heart." He does not take this "good pharmacological advice," and on a Christmas Eve Judith calls from India (where she and Gordon have gone on a post-retirement holiday): "Gordon's ill and I'm alone and I don't know, I don't know . . . I'm so afraid . . . I do so love him. . . . It's so much to ask . . . but I need . . . help." He goes to her, and the novel ends with Tim reporting: "Gordon died before I reached her, on the day after Christmas, like her mother." In Dick Francis' old-fashioned morality story, virtue prevails and presumably is to be rewarded. The message may be dated, but the story line has a more significant weakness, for Judith is no more than a two-dimensional character who pales beside Tim and lacks credibility; she is little more than a stereotype. So, too, are the other important females, Ginnie and Penelope, as well as such minor figures as Ursula Young and Bettina Dissdale. Francis admitted in 1983: "I can't really place myself in a woman's mind." Though G. P. Putnam's Sons, his publisher since 1980, has been promoting him as a best-selling novelist rather than as a mere mystery writer (a gap he began trying to bridge years earlier), the inadequate depictions of women delay the definitive breakthrough.

This weakness in characterization notwithstanding, *Banker* succeeds. It is an imaginatively crafted portrait of social climbers corrupted by their ambition and of a virtuous protagonist whose insistent pursuit of truth and justice is analogous to a ritual purgation, enabling him to overcome the stigma of profligate parents and to assert his own identity. Though Ross Macdonald already has worked this territory, Dick Francis brings to it his singular perspective.

Gerald H. Strauss

Sources for Further Study

The Atlantic. CCLI, May, 1983, p. 105.
Christian Science Monitor. April 20, 1983, p. 9.
Library Journal. CVIII, February 1, 1983, p. 223.
The New York Times Book Review. LXXXVIII, March 27, 1983, p. 15.
The New Yorker. LIX, April 11, 1983, p. 138.

Newsweek. CII, July 11, 1983, p. 70.
Publishers Weekly. XXXIII, January 28, 1983, p. 74.
The Times Literary Supplement. December 10, 1982, p. 1378.
West Coast Review of Books. IX, May, 1983, p. 34.

BARTLEBY IN MANHATTAN

Author: Elizabeth Hardwick (1916-   )
Publisher: Random House (New York). 292 pp. $15.95
Type of work: Essays

A wide-ranging collection of essays by a noted contemporary writer

One of the founding editors of *The New York Review of Books*, Elizabeth Hardwick has a formidable and well-deserved literary reputation. She is the editor of a selection of William James's letters and an eighteen-volume collection of fiction by American women. She is also the author of three novels and numerous articles and reviews. As a critic and essayist, Hardwick excels at elegantly written explorations of literary and cultural subjects. Writing in what Richard Locke has called an "anti-academic" style, Hardwick is a personal essayist whose wide reading, varied interests, and witty style elicit comparisons with the nonfiction of Virginia Woolf, Susan Sontag, and William Gass. Her subjects are cultural and social movements, historical and literary personalities, language and place, as well as drama and literature. Her probing studies are sometimes occasioned by a theatrical performance or the publication of a book, but her essays typically range far wider and deeper than most drama and literary reviews. Intelligent, thorough analyses, they have the excitement and learning of lively scholarship. Both keen moral and psychological insight and a vibrant, poetic prose style characterize Hardwick's writing.

Bartleby in Manhattan, Hardwick's third collection of essays, consists of twenty-four articles arranged in five parts. Nearly all originally appeared in *The New York Review of Books*. Selections date from as early as 1962 and as late as 1983; because there is no introduction to the book nor any precise dates accompanying the essays, it is unclear if the five-part arrangement is chronological. Subject dates several pieces and provides unity within two sections. "Out in the Country," the first division, contains essays of social criticism clearly dating from the 1960's. These include articles on the Selma, Alabama, civil rights marches; on Lee Harvey Oswald, the assassin of President John Kennedy; on the aftermath of the 1968 slaying of civil rights leader Martin Luther King, Jr.; and on evangelist Billy Graham. Other divisions include one of theater criticism and three combining social, cultural, and literary discussions. There are analytical essays on the lives of literary figures, such as Ring Lardner and Robert Frost, and on the novels of Thomas Mann, Thomas Hardy's *Jude the Obscure* (1895), and the university lectures of Vladimir Nabokov. Simone Weil, Svetlana Stalin, Lady Byron, and the Countess Tolstoy come under Hardwick's probing gaze, as do journalists John Reed and Louise Bryant and the landscape and history of Brazil. The title essay, "Bartleby in Manhattan," typifies Hardwick's eclecticism and broad interests.

Occasioned by "some lectures on the subject of New York City . . . the present landscape," the essay combines occasional social commentary with an astute and original analysis of Herman Melville's story "Bartleby the Scrivener" (first published in *The Apple-Tree Table and Other Sketches*, 1922). Though the essay's title suggests a discussion of setting, Hardwick's focus is in fact Bartleby's language, his cryptic and strangely empowering "I would prefer not to."

Because *Bartleby in Manhattan* covers such a variety of subjects and ranges over more than twenty years, it lacks the thematic unity and cohesiveness of Hardwick's two earlier books of nonfiction, *A View of My Own: Essays on Literature and Society* (1962) and *Seduction and Betrayal: Women and Literature* (1974). Nevertheless, *Bartleby in Manhattan* is coherent and consistent. In all of the essays, Hardwick exhibits a characteristic passion for understanding her subjects, a thorough and inviting probing of the concrete and abstract qualities of the experiences she describes, juxtaposing detail and philosophical inquiry in an attempt to understand the basis of the works and characters she analyzes.

This method is perhaps best illustrated in Hardwick's theater and film reviews, though it is evident throughout *Bartleby in Manhattan*. In an essay on Jerzy Grotowski's Polish Laboratory Theater, Hardwick focuses on the underlying abstract qualities of the productions, their haunting lyricism and liturgical character, their sense of "transcendent pity and terror." In succeeding passages, her vivid and thorough descriptions of staging, costuming, acting, and audience reaction permit the reader to envision the live performance. Hardwick's essay, however, is much more than an unusually evocative drama review. It also discusses the history of the Polish theater and Slavic drama. A similar analytic method informs Hardwick's essay on Warren Beatty's *Reds* (1981). Discontent with the film's portraits of John Reed and Louise Bryant and its insistent homage to "American radicalism," Hardwick draws on biographies and the works of Reed and Bryant in order to grasp fully their lives and personalities, the milieu in which they worked, and their accomplishments.

Delving beneath the surface of events and personalities, Hardwick explores incongruities of character while providing strong moral assessment. The hardness and cruelty of Ring Lardner's stories she finds inexplicable in the light of his background and apparent virtues: his "charming, talented family," his perseverance at work, his kindness and reserve. "Why he drank," Hardwick writes, "why his views were so bitter are a mystery." In discussing Robert Frost, Hardwick finds irony in the contrast between his "acute" public consciousness and the poetry that "grew out" of his "isolation." His lack of generosity and sense of "rivalry" with his contemporaries were evidence of "vanity . . . not simplicity of mind." Svetlana Stalin, Stalin's daughter, Hardwick describes as "a worthy and attractive person," but one who does not say what "she really feels. She doesn't love her father and she doesn't love Russia and she took her ultimate revenge on them by escaping to the enemy."

Hardwick's judgment of her subjects is not always so harsh. In "Wives and Mistresses," for example, she focuses on the reputations of those who enter "history" through association with "celebrated artists" and political figures. Among those whose lives have somehow become "footnotes" to biographies of the great are Lady Byron and the Countess Tolstoy. Hardwick characterizes the former as deceitful and morally culpable for her brief marriage and "the lifetime of poisonous preoccupation" that followed it. The Countess Tolstoy, however, demands vindication. Though her neurasthenia caused her "intolerable frenzies of distress" and led her husband to "murderous rages against carnal passion and marriage," the Countess' forty-eight years of marriage, her "thirteen confinements," and "seven copyings of *War and Peace*" cry "to Heaven" for justice.

To this insight into the characters of her subjects, Hardwick brings a poet's sense of language: vivid, precise, sometimes jarring imagery reflective of the intelligence and vision of the writer. Analyzing the Warren Commission Report on Lee Harvey Oswald, Hardwick finds a text that reads "as if it were the last chorus of a tragedy by Euripides." Oswald himself is "a ghostly anachronism in a cast of characters" that includes "seers who foretell the future and interpret the past: the social workers and psychiatrists" consulted by the Warren Commission. In "The Charms of Goodness," Hardwick captures the confrontation between civil rights demonstrators and angry white townspeople in dramatic, filmlike sequences aided by images from the Southern landscape and William Faulkner's novels. "The voteless blacks, waiting tentatively on the courthouse steps," face "the angry jowls of the racists." "The enduring Negroes, the police, the same old sheriff" act out roles seemingly created for television. In "Sad Brazil," one of the finest pieces in *Bartleby in Manhattan*, Hardwick vivifies her own sharp perceptions of the Brazilian landscape with the observations of anthropologist Claude Lévi-Strauss and South American writer Euclides Da Cunha. The result is a highly original study of Brazilian politics, literature, and history. Here as elsewhere, Hardwick's eye for the incongruous and her sharpened moral sense lend richness to the style. Brazil, personified as a giant, rises from "a thicket of sleep and the jungle of apathy." A fallen Eden, it is a place of "mysterious, ineffable plentitude," of "endless, blue shore lines," and buildings of "steel and concrete, a transfiguration of metals." Amid the activity of urban life, a "bereft, scabby" beggar sits against an old wall, "an eruption of the sores of underdevelopment." Near him, "an explosion of automobiles and their infinite signification" whiz past.

Such an eye for visual contrasts lends depth and insight to all of the essays in *Bartleby in Manhattan*. The collection is an important addition to Elizabeth Hardwick's oeuvre and a testament to her well-deserved reputation.

Stella Nesanovich

Sources for Further Study

Book Week. XIII, May 29, 1983, p. 7.
Hudson Review. XXXVI, Winter, 1983, p. 737.
Library Journal. CVIII, May 1, 1983, p. 907.
Los Angeles Times Book Review. May 29, 1983, p. 1.
The New Republic. CLXXXVIII, June 20, 1983, p. 32.
New Statesman. CVI, October 28, 1983, p. 28.
The New York Times Book Review. LXXXVIII, June 12, 1983, p. 7.
Newsweek. CI, May 30, 1983, p. 91.
Publishers Weekly. CCXXIII, March 18, 1983, p. 59.
Saturday Review. IX, July, 1983, p. 54.

BERTOLT BRECHT SHORT STORIES
1921-1946

Author: Bertolt Brecht (1898-1956)
Translated from the German by Yvonne Kapp, Hugh Rorrison, and Anthony Tatlow
Edited, with an introduction, by John Willett and Ralph Manheim
Publisher: Methuen (New York). 242 pp. $19.95
Type of work: Short stories

Thirty-seven stories and one biographical fragment, most of them with a message to ponder, ranging from parable and fairy tale to novella and detective story

Bertolt Brecht is generally recognized as one of the most revolutionary and influential dramatists in this century; the theory and practice of his non-Aristotelian Epic Theater has sparked controversy and emulation worldwide. Epic Theater is supposed to stimulate one's thinking through a "narrative" style of presentation, by telling a story calmly in a sequence of episodes, rather than by involving the audience emotionally in a dramatic plot. Stories, therefore, form the basis of much of Brecht's work, even his poetry, and they are often derived from folktales, ballads, newspaper reports, and other popular sources.

Nevertheless, Brecht's actual narrative works, his novels, short stories and anecdotes, are still not widely known, except for the occasional inclusion of one of his conveniently concise *Tales from the Calendar* in an anthology or language textbook. Brecht's fiction appears less revolutionary in style and content than his dramatic work, and Brecht himself seems to have given his stories low priority: Only one collection of stories, *Kalendergeschichten* (*Tales from the Calendar*), appeared during his lifetime, and even there the stories are interspersed with poems and anecdotes. It was not until 1965 that a relatively complete German edition of Brecht's short stories appeared in the context of his collected prose works. Since then, this small but fascinating segment of Brecht's creative output has attracted increasing attention.

The present volume, at last, contains all the major short stories of Brecht in highly competent English translations. It is based on volume 11 of Bertolt Brecht's *Gesammelte Werke in 20 Bänden* (1967), which is entirely devoted to the short stories but not a complete translation of that volume. As the title indicates, the selection is limited to stories written from 1921 to 1946. This seems to be a wise choice. In the German volume, which has the stories in approximate chronological order, the only works after 1946 are a few anecdotes about Eulenspiegel, the clever fool. Like the anecdotes about a certain Mr. Keuner, an unorthodox thinker, which are eliminated from both volumes, they are bits of worldly-wise Bert Brecht philosophy rather than genuine stories. For similar reasons, the editors of the English translation left out all other anecdotes, very short stories, any play summaries and film scenarios detectable as such, and also all fragments except for the unfinished "Life Story of the Boxer Samson-Körner," which appears as an appendix to the collection. The elimination of the stories before 1921 was obviously more a value judgment than a matter of genre; most of these early stories are somewhat sophomoric exercises that were first published in Brecht's school magazine and in local newspapers. In fact, they seem to embody the very vices and illusions Brecht attacked in his later writings.

The "hard core of genuine short stories" resulting from this process of elimination has been arranged chronologically and grouped into three creative periods coinciding with major waystations in Brecht's life: The Bavarian Stories (1920-1924), The Berlin Stories (1924-1933), and Stories Written in Exile (1934-1948). They were written predominantly in the early years of each period, while the rest of each period was almost completely devoted to poetry, drama, and theater production. Brecht's stories in this volume display a special and powerful talent: concise, concentrated, no-nonsense narration. This talent is visible in a variety of narrative modes and styles, from the factual report to the lyric setting of an atmosphere, from fairytale simplicity to the complexity of Lucretian hexameters or of a cleverly spun detective story. Brecht's stories have a variety of unforgettable characters, a clear message, and wit, irony, and punch.

Thus, it should come as no surprise that Brecht achieved his first literary success with a short story rather than a play. The story in question is the first in this collection and is entitled "Bargan Gives Up." Bargan, the brilliant and ruthless leader of a marauding band of buccaneers, becomes hopelessly addicted to a fat, clubfooted fellow "who had lain on the road like an unwanted dog till Bargan drew him to his bosom." Eventually, Bargan abandons ship, crew, and everything merely for the sake of this repulsive and devious creature. The wild buccaneer's unseemly fate is presented as a parable of the uncertainties of "life on this planet." This captivating pirate story already contains many characteristic elements of Brecht's fiction: evil but fascinating villain-heroes, stark macho and antimacho actions, the exotic atmosphere of faraway places and unusual social settings, the conscious attempt to convey a message or a moral (be it ever so unconventional), and a restrained, strangely rough-hewn language, equally distant from colloquial speech as it is from poetic diction, yet deriving its effects from both. More specifically, the story belongs to Brecht's early period of youthfully poetic nihilism best known from his plays *Baal* (1922; *Baal*, 1970) and *Trommeln in der Nacht* (1922; *Drums in the Night*, 1966). In these early works, Brecht's language is rich in earthy colloquialisms and poetic imagery. The buccaneers, invading a town, tread "carefully as if on eggs," whistle "like mad" for help, afraid of getting caught in "a damn rat-trap," and start "satisfying the women," whose "screaming filled the air like an icy mist." In this fashion, the fictitious pirate-narrator vacillates between colloquial speech, sober description, and expressive simile. Now and then, there is a sudden poetic moment, as when the buccaneers commemorate, with a few good gulps of brandy, the "dear corpses" of their fellow pirates "which now, as one of us put it rather nicely, were swimming up from the depths under the mild light of the stars, face upwards, towards some goal or other which had been forgotten and like someone who has no home and is homesick none the less." The image of the corpse drifting under a big sky and the motif of homesickness without a home are central to an underlying feeling of *Weltschmerz* in Brecht's early works, a feeling carefully checked by occasional irony (as in the aside in the quote above) and by long stretches of matter-of-fact narration, and dialectically balanced by lusty action and sly folk wisdom. Homesickness without a definite object is, in fact, the main topic of "Story on a Ship," which breathes the same drunken-sailor atmosphere and the important insight in "The Revelation" is that nobody cares whether you live or die, so why should *you* care? Nihilism, or at least a fundamental scepticism about the meaning of this world and the goodness of its people, are at the base of most of Brecht's stories, but there is a gradual shift from an attitude of "Live it up or give it up" to one of "Look out for yourself, and for your neighbor, if you can." On the whole, there are many more stories with a positive message than with a negative one, and, in later stages, as Brecht comes to embrace Communist doctrines, the positive stories become predominant.

One approach to such didactic stories is the parable or fairy tale, in which the author uses the simple, direct language of the Bible, the Brothers Grimm, or popular almanacs. The early stories "The Foolish Wife," "The Blind Man," "A Helping Hand," and "The Answer" all start with similar phrases, such as "A man had a wife who was . . ." or "In a harsh land there once lived an evil man . . ."; "The Good Lord's Package" starts with the cozy narrator saying "Draw your chairs up to the fire. . . ." "The Foolish Wife" and its complementary piece "The Answer" are virtually the only stories in the collection that approach the genre of the love story, a very rare species in Brecht's entire oeuvre; even these two stories are more concerned with marital loyalty, steadfastness, and mutual generosity than with romantic, emotional love.

The most memorable of Brecht's fictional characters, however, are not loving but mean and evil. They may well teach us what life and people can be like and help us to be wary of danger and exploitation but they are also extremely fascinating as evil individuals. The title "A Mean Bastard," for example, leaves no doubt about its main character—or does it? He unabashedly exploits a young widow sexually and financially, as he did others before her. They "need" him, and he uses them, at least until he becomes bored. The widow struggles valiantly to maintain her dignity but breaks down completely when she finds him in her own bed with her own maid. In "Bad Water," a husband murders his wife and her lover in bed, not out of jealousy, but because she has failed to do her housekeeping chores. Mean characters outdo one another in "The Death of Cesare Malatesta," when a ruthless ruler is slowly, sadistically destroyed by an even crueler enemy. Such are the faces of evil.

Nevertheless, the most evil persons are often the least obviously evil in appearance. "The Monster" is a Russian governor who has conducted horrible pogroms, but his face and manners are considered too bland when he later, anonymously, tries to play his own role in a motion picture. (The story could be seen as a perfect denunciation of ruthless Nazi leaders with petit-bourgeois faces, had it not been written years before they came to power.) In "Letter About a Mastiff," the fine instincts of a dog are required to sense the evil in the protagonist; ironically, the more the man tries to please and appease the dog, the more he discloses his evil potential. This eerie and compulsive confrontation with a terrified—and terrifying—animal appears to be symbolic of a person's confrontation with his conscience or his own true self—a disturbing experience reminiscent of stories by Edgar Allan Poe and Franz Kafka. In fact, Kafka was one of the very few contemporary writers whom Brecht respected and admired, and another story, "Gaumer and Irk," almost reads like a special tribute to Kafka's nightmarish parables. Gaumer has killed Irk and tries to get rid of the body, no easy task to begin with, when he suddenly realizes that the body is growing bigger, slowly but steadily. The author's cool, detailed description of Gaumer's increasingly desperate attempts to move the corpse highlights the grotesque, dreamlike, symbolic quality of the action.

The *Tales from the Calendar*, which are incorporated individually in the present volume, stand out by having the most positive, likable heroes and heroines. These tales all come from the last of Brecht's three creative periods and were selected for publication by Brecht himself, so one can assume that they represent most closely his later creative intentions. Major characters include one philosopher, two soldiers, three scientists, and five strong women. One of the soldiers is "The Soldier of La Ciotat." He is, in fact, the living statue of a soldier at a sideshow, who has acquired his uncanny ability to remain motionless for any desired length of time as a result of being buried alive at Verdun. Brecht sees him as a symbol of the indestructible soldier through the Millennia, "afflicted by the hideous leprosy of patience, sapped by the incurable disease of imperviousness." This strong antiwar stance pervades all of the stories dealing with war, where the only heroism is knowing how to survive, as does Anna in the "The Augsburg Chalk Circle" (a forerunner of *Der Kaukasische Kreidekreis*, 1949, 1956; *The Caucasian Chalk-Circle*, performed 1948, revised version published 1960); true courage is the ability to admit one's fear, which the philosopher-turned-soldier finally does in "Socrates Wounded." Hope for the future comes from the scientists, not because of expected technological advances (although Brecht obviously admires fast cars and airplanes), but because of science's eager pursuit of the truth, as exemplified in the young apprentice of "The Experiment." Most admirable, however, are the women in these stories—independent, hard-working, no-nonsense women with a sense of reality: Socrates' wife Xantippe, the tailor's wife in "The Heretic's Coat," and "The Unseemly Old Lady," who decides to live her last years exactly as she pleases. Such women represent the permanence of life against all odds and the hope that reason will prevail over evil and insanity.

The final publication of all of Brecht's major short stories in English is a noteworthy event. This collection will greatly help to round out the picture of Brecht as a writer and as a person and will provide some surprising new insights concerning his literary development. The volume is handsomely produced and carefully edited with an extensive introduction, an index of the German titles, and ample annotations helpful to the scholar as well as the casual reader. The translations have been done with stylistic sensitivity, accuracy, and attention to detail (except for some minor factual errors and omissions in "Life Story of the Boxer Samson-Körner"). It is impossible to render all the interesting peculiarities and stylistic allusions of Brecht's language into English, but enough has survived the translation to make for a rich and exciting reading experience.

Eberhard Frey

Sources for Further Study

Choice. XXI, October, 1983, p. 285.
New Statesman. CVI, July 15, 1983, p. 27.
The New Yorker. LIX, August 29, 1983, p. 92.
Observer. September 18, 1983, p. 31.
Publishers Weekly. CCXXIII, April 22, 1983, p. 85.

THE BIRTH OF THE PEOPLE'S REPUBLIC OF ANTARCTICA

Author: John Calvin Batchelor (1948-   )
Publisher: The Dial Press (New York). Maps. 401 pp. $16.95
Type of work: Novel
Time: 1973-2037
Locale: Sweden, the Atlantic Ocean, several South Atlantic islands, and Antarctica

A novel based on Scandinavian sagas, telling of the degeneration of modern civilization from the viewpoint of exiles unusually vulnerable to misfortune

> *Principal characters:*
> GRIM FIDDLE, the narrator, an illegitimately born Swedish exile who becomes King of Antarctica and is deposed
> LAMBA FIDDLE, the mother of Grim Fiddle, seen by her son as a sibyl and as an albatross
> MORD FIDDLE, Lamba Fiddle's father, a Swedish clergyman who becomes a political leader, then is exiled
> PEREGRINE IDE, Grim Fiddle's father, an American draft evader, and the ex-husband of Charity Bentham
> CHARITY BENTHAM, an American philosopher who shares exile with Peregrine Ide and the Fiddles
> CESARE FURORE, Charity Bentham's second husband who is murdered by Peregrine Ide
> CLEOPATRA FURORE, the daughter of Charity Bentham and Cesare Furore, also an exile
> LAZARUS FURORE, a political philosopher who is the adopted son of Charity Bentham and Cesare Furore
> GERMANICUS FRAZER, a military leader in South Georgia
> LEARNED SHARON LANGFAEROE, a clergyman in South Georgia
> ABIGAIL LANGFAEROE FRAZER, the widowed daughter of Learned Langfaeroe and mother of Grim Fiddle's son, Sam
> SAM, Grim Fiddle and Abigail Frazer's son, to whom Grim dedicates his autobiography

On the copyright page of *The Birth of the People's Republic of Antarctica*, John Calvin Batchelor acknowledges his debt to various editions of several Scandinavian sagas; in particular, there are parallels between the novel's protagonist, Grim Fiddle, and a certain saga hero, Skallagrim Strider. Batchelor's novel, however, is more than a retelling of the saga of Skallagrim Strider: It deals with questions which the authors of sagas did not ask, such as the origin of myth, the usefulness of ideas, and the causes of alienation. Batchelor also explores the meaning of guilt, a rare theme in sagas or in heroic literature, generally. Finally, despite its title, Batchelor's novel is more about degeneration than about origins.

Characters in *The Birth of the People's Republic of Antarctica* think and act in ways not strange to twentieth century readers, but their adventures are similar to those of heroes in Scandinavian sagas. Batchelor's exiles turn deprivation into opportunity, becoming leaders or rulers of lands in which they arrive by chance. Principalities rise and fall, largely because of the qualities of individuals, but no shift to an earlier—and more heroic—age is necessary. The action takes place in the immediate future—a modern adventure story made more exciting by implications involving entire countries.

To make plausible this kind of adventure story in the immediate future, Batchelor posits a decline of twentieth century institutions and a climatic catastrophe affecting a large part of the earth. Moreover, the novel's protagonist, for a peculiarly twentieth century reason, has an education similar to that of Skallagrim Strider and occasionally retreats into a way of thinking in which certain kinds of magic are possible.

In Batchelor's novel, the decline of twentieth century pluralistic states and other institutions creates a class of seaborne exiles. These exiles have adventures similar to those in Scandinavian sagas. The novel includes a detailed account of the replacement of Sweden's tolerant social democracy by a nationalistic, ostensibly Christian, authoritarian regime that consumes its own leaders. In flimsy boats named *Angel of Death* and *Black Crane*, Grim and others of foreign or suspect origin flee from Sweden in 1995. Denied landing rights by many countries, the exiles finish their journey in the desolate South Atlantic. Events outside Sweden are not discussed in detail, but it is obvious that nationalistic fervor is increasing in most countries and that land grabs are becoming commonplace.

Separated from the rest of his group, Grim briefly participates in international war—an unsuccessful defense of British rule in the Falkland Islands. He then settles in neighboring South Georgia, which is officially British but has effectively become autonomous. In six years, Grim rises from shepherd to president of the Assembly, then he is exiled again. Later, he establishes his own kingdom centered on another South Atlantic island, Anvers Island. Anvers and nearby islands, once sparsely inhabited, become refuges for persons deported during wars and disturbances, and Grim's monarchy fills a need for some kind of authority.

Eventually, Grim is overthrown and replaced by a self-proclaimed people's republic that subjects him to solitary confinement for more than twenty years. When he is finally released, he is exiled again—with at least the hope of more adventure.

Although the novel is rife with references to Scandinavian myths, the reader is not asked to believe that the gods of those myths exist objectively. A sudden change in the climate of Antarctica and the South Atlantic offers excitement similar to that offered by the anger of the gods in the sagas. Volcanic eruptions on South Atlantic islands lead to an extension of ice caps and the creation of an area of solid black ice. There is much suffering among South Atlantic refugees, but the black ice becomes a kind of territory for Grim's kingdom based on Anvers Island. Unpredictable and ateleological, the volcanic and climatic phenomena leading to the creation of black ice are, in a way, more frightening than the actions of angry gods.

Just as these natural phenomena provide a modern equivalent to the gods of yore, so Grim is the ironic modern counterpart of the saga hero. Born out of wedlock, he has no birth certificate and is denied formal schooling. An informal education—consisting largely of Scandinavian folklore—is substituted.

Grim does not objectively believe in the myths on which he is reared, but he does believe, at least on one level of consciousness, that his mother is a kind of Scandinavian sibyl. Grim acknowledges inventing a story of how his mother, Lamba Fiddle, planned to conceive and give birth to him after seeing a vision of him in a mirror—a method of foretelling which occurs in Scandinavian mythology—yet he almost believes his own story. His unusual education prepares him for his vision of Lamba Time-Thief (whom he later identifies with Lamba Fiddle)—a vision in which he learns that his life is to be similar to that of Skallagrim Strider. Later, Grim becomes convinced—or nearly so—that his mother has taken the form of an albatross and has talked to him.

In addition to such parallels, *The Birth of the People's Republic of Antarctica* contains two structural elements found in the saga: the recitation of a dying man and a funeral song for him after his death. Grim, after being exiled from South Georgia, meets his grandfather Mord Fiddle, the dying father of Lamba. A fanatical minister, Mord led the movement that destroyed Sweden's tolerant social democracy. Soon, however, the revolution he led turned against him, and he was forced to flee. The narrative of his death is followed by a long funeral song (albeit in prose).

Unlike its Scandinavian models, however, Batchelor's novel is narrated entirely in the first person. Even Mord's narrative is recounted from Grim's viewpoint; Grim paraphrases it instead of quoting it. Indeed, the novel purports to be Grim's autobiography; in the narrative, Grim refers to his solitary confinement and worries that his jailers may deny him writing materials. The autobiography is dedicated to Sam, the son of Grim and of Abigail Langfaeroe Frazer. Sam is born on South Georgia, and Grim's exile from that island denies him knowledge of his son's fate.

Guilt is not a common theme in the saga genre; the prevailing assumption is that heroism is admirable and makes all things right. Autobiographies, by contrast, frequently deal with guilt; it is no accident that the seminal autobiographies of Saint Augustine and Jean-Jacques Rousseau are both entitled *Confessions*. Thus, Batchelor plays the introspective moral intensity of the autobiography against the unreflective ethos of the saga. When Grim declares that his reign as king on Anvers Island was one of misrule and wanton plunder, he confesses to much that would have been considered heroic in the saga.

Batchelor also designs his allegory as a critique of rationalism, represented in the novel by the American philosopher Charity Bentham (whose name mocks the presumption of the utilitarian philosopher Jeremy Bentham and his rationalistic fellow spirits). Charity herself comes to see the hubris in all master plans to regulate human affairs. Like Grim, she learns that there is no real solution to alienation and misery.

The Birth of the People's Republic of Antarctica is an adventure story, exciting and suspenseful, but it leads to bleak conclusions. Grim Fiddle can turn exile into opportunity, but he cannot solve the real problems of his time.

Charles Johnson Taggart

Sources for Further Study

Choice. XXI, October, 1983, p. 272.
Christian Science Monitor. September 14, 1983, p. 11.
Commonweal. CX, May 20, 1983, p. 307.
Library Journal. CVIII, June 1, 1983, p. 1154.
Los Angeles Times Book Review. August 14, 1983, p. 8.
The New York Times Book Review. LXXXVIII, May 29, 1983, p. 1.
Newsweek. CI, May 9, 1983, p. 80.
Publishers Weekly. CCXXIII, March 11, 1983, p. 79.

BLUE HIGHWAYS
A Journey into America

Author: William Least Heat-Moon (William Trogdon, 1939-   )
Publisher: Little, Brown and Company (Boston). Illustrated with photographs by
  William Least Heat-Moon. 421 pp. $17.50
Type of work: Travel account
Time: March to June, 1978
Locale: The backroads of America, encircling the continental United States

A journey through obscure, fascinating corners of the United States

As it was for Herman Melville's Ishmael (*Moby Dick*, 1851), "it is a damp,
drizzly November in [his] soul" when William Least Heat-Moon embarks on
a journey of escape and exploration, a journey that in the tradition of other
great American travelers, is also a voyage of self-discovery. Separated from
his wife and laid off from teaching English at a Missouri college suffering
from declining enrollment, the author begins a trip around the country in
order to delve into the meaning of his life.

This is no solipsistic submersion into self, however, for Heat-Moon pene-
trates the surface of life in these United States to find the incredible diversity
that persists throughout the land. As he moves from state to state, following
a roughly circular pattern that takes him first to the Atlantic, then to the Gulf
of Mexico, the Pacific, back to the Atlantic, and finally home to Missouri, he
finds, behind the billboard veneer of modern mainstream America, people
and places as strange to a contemporary urbanite as any that Ulysses and
Gulliver encountered on their fantastic voyages.

How did Heat-Moon find them? Not by joining most American travelers
along the multilane interstates, where one can travel secure in the thought
that a McDonald's or a Howard Johnson's is never far away, where one can
leave home without abandoning its familiar comforts, though also without
experiencing a real sense of adventure. For some travelers, it is the destination
that gives the journey a purpose; for Heat-Moon, what matters is the journey
itself, an endless immersion in discovery.

So that he can avoid "the oranging of America," as Max Apple has whim-
sically but aptly termed Howard Johnson's expropriation of the country's
landscape, Heat-Moon steers clear of the interstates and takes his Ford van
Ghost Dancing (as he has named it) down the backroads of the United States.
These are the routes old highway maps traced in blue, in contrast to the red
of the main routes—hence the book's title.

Down these roads, Heat-Moon finds wonders that a generation raised on
Big Macs and television would never dream of. His journey becomes one
through time as well as space, as he peels away the billboards to discover not
only the land behind but also the fascinating stories of each region's past—

the derivations of town names like Dime Box, Texas; and Nameless, Tennessee; the waves of settlers and immigrants; distinctive customs that have survived the homogenization enforced by network television. Moving across the country, he comes into contact with living annals of American history as well as scenes of memorable moments of the past: Martin Luther King's Selma marches; the mining boom in the West; the opening of the Northwest, courtesy of Lewis and Clark and Sacajawea; battles of the Revolutionary War; the earliest English settlement in America, on Roanoke Island.

Beyond these stands the perseverance of the continent's earlier inhabitants, whose imprint remains not only on the map in the names of rivers, towns, and states but also in the memories of the current inhabitants. These more recent arrivals often, with admiration, acknowledge to Heat-Moon (whom they do not recognize as part Sioux) the skill and respect of the various Indian tribes in their use of the land—abilities that modern America has generally lost. ("Indian," not "Native American," is the author's preferred term.) Few pages go by without a reference to the tribal peoples and their place in the history of a particular region. In fact, any reader interested in the United States will be grateful for Heat-Moon's close attention to the history of the various scenes visited.

There are more things on this American earth, then, than are dreamed of in many contemporary philosophies. *Blue Highways* demands concentration, as Heat-Moon describes unfamiliar scenes with occasionally arcane vocabulary—chukars, drumlin, pocosins, tupelo, bugeye, skipjack—which will send the typical urban reader to the dictionary.

The land itself offers many surprises, asserting the tenacity of deserts and swamps, mountains and waterways that modern, technological man has not yet brought under his control, and vast stretches of territory still undeveloped. In North Dakota, Heat-Moon quotes Gertrude Stein: "In the United States there is more space where nobody is than where anybody is." So he comes to realize, at times to his own dismay, having voluntarily renounced the interstates with their assurances of food, gas, and lodging.

To his chagrin—but ultimately appreciative respect—the land sometimes even fights back, as if to say, "No man can win me so easily yet!" A late April snowstorm traps him overnight on a mountain road after he has ignored the warning: "ROAD MAY BE IMPASSIBLE DURING WINTER MONTHS." Heat-Moon learns it's springtime in the Rockies much later than anywhere else. He also discovers that even though man may install dams along the mighty Columbia, the Mississippi reserves its power to change course: "One day rain gonna start and keep on like it do sometimes. When the rainin' stop, the Missippi [sic] gonna be ninety miles west of N'Orleans and St. Martinville gonna be a seaport. And it won't be the firstest time the river go runnin' from Lady N'Orleans."

The Louisianian voicing this opinion is only one of many amazing characters whom Heat-Moon encounters on his odyssey. A Margaret Mead of his own homeland, Heat-Moon records speech and customs as alien to many Americans as those of Mead's Samoans. He includes his own photographs of many of these people, but even more striking is his ability to capture individual Americans' splendidly distinctive talk. In this, *Blue Highways* proves as gripping and as sharply observed as Studs Terkel's transcriptions of everyday speech in *Working* (1975) and many other books. With equal fidelity, Heat-Moon renders Southern volubility and Midwestern taciturnity, Western tall tales and Yankee understatement. Says a Maine fisherman when the author joins him on his daily ocean expedition, "In fifteen minutes, we'll find out if this pond's got any damn fish in it." The book is filled with the humor of the people, sounding much more natural than the standard snappy Hollywood or Manhattan one-liner.

A Texan tells about his uncle keeping sugar ants and feeding them molasses: "When they fattened up, he put them on a butter sandwich. Butter kept them from runnin' off the bread. . . . Claimed molasses gave them ants real flavor."

A North Carolinian complains about the tastelessness of contemporary cigarettes: " . . . maybe the popalation [sic] got scared by them mouse spearmints wheres they give a mouse a needle-shot of a substance ever day until he dies a cancer."

A Cajun waitress in Louisiana asks about Heat-Moon's crawfish order: "Did they eat lovely like mortal sin? . . . You know, the Cajun, he sometime call them 'mudbugs.' But I never tell a customer that until he all full inside."

In the tiny burg of Nameless, Tennessee, Mrs. Thurmond Watts boasts that "we had a doctor on the ridge in them days." One day, Mrs. Watts relates, she "took to vomitin'" from some bad ham and was "hangin' on the drop edge of yonder. I said to Thurmond, 'Thurmond, unless you want shut of me, call the doctor.'"

Many of the towns that Heat-Moon visits did have "a doctor on the ridge" in the old days. Towns are not founded merely to become ghost towns. The shifting winds of "progress," however, change the routes of the trade, the seats of industry, the demand for a region's goods, and the town fades to a few dilapidated buildings, a few old-timers hanging on, content to let the modern world pass them by.

Among the young people whom the author encounters on his travels, most leave him more depressed than hopeful. A student at Mississippi College in Clinton, Mississippi, plans "to use the computer to enrich spiritual life" by running prayers through twice a day for a week. A ten-year-old marvels at the author's van, not for the adventures it represents but for its surprisingly good gas mileage. In fact, many of the most vital people in the book are old—people such as Porfirio Sanchez, a sixty-seven-year-old part-Apache Mexican-American hitchhiker, and Alice Venable Middleton, an octogenarian schoolteacher on Smith Island, Maryland, eighteen years retired, who taught ecology long before it was fashionable. A notable exception to the dreariness of the young people whom Heat-Moon meets is Kendrick Fritz, a Hopi medical student who plans to return to his people's land and community (he refuses to call it the reservation) and meet their health needs while pre-serving the Hopi culture.

In rejecting neither the present nor the past, this Hopi student becomes an embodiment of the book's theme, while harborside Newport, Rhode Island, serves as a cautionary example: Newport tore down its atmospheric water-front—grubby but historic—to erect a shopping area for the affluent.

Heat-Moon's journey shows him how change can coexist with respect for tradition—a principle exemplified by a New Hampshire family that has been tapping the same maple trees for syrup for generations. Some changes are purely destructive, as when a powerful corporation seeks to buy up a small, centuries-old New Jersey town for industrial exploitation, against which the town's citizens struggle for the sake of their heritage. With books such as this one providing admonition—and ammunition—Americans may be moved to defend all the more vigorously the splendor in diversity that distinguishes their nation. The widespread popularity of *Blue Highways*—a surprise best-seller—suggests that Heat-Moon has spoken for many Americans who hope that regional traits will continue to flourish and that the far corners of the land will not succumb to franchised hamburgers and homogenized speech.

Scott Giantvalley

Sources for Further Study

America. CXLVIII, April 9, 1983, p. 284.
Christian Century. C, June 8, 1983, p. 590.
Christian Science Monitor. February 11, 1983, p. B1.
Library Journal. CVII, November 1, 1982, p. 2097.
Los Angeles Times Book Review. January 30, 1983, p. 3.
National Review. XXXV, May 13, 1983, p. 580.
The New York Times Book Review. LXXXVIII, February 6, 1983, p. 1.
Newsweek. CI, February 7, 1983, p. 63.
Publishers Weekly. CCXXII, November 5, 1982, p. 64.
Time. CXXI, June 24, 1983. p. 88.

BLUE PASTORAL

Author: Gilbert Sorrentino (1929-   )
Publisher: North Point Press (San Francisco). 315 pp. $18.00
Type of work: Novel
Time: The allegorical present
Locale: The United States

A brilliant comic commentary on American pastoral mythology, this novel challenges the aesthetic and political premises of modernist literature and consolidates its author's prominent position in a developing populist avant-garde

> *Principal characters:*
> SERGE "BLUE" GAVOTTE, a frustrated pianist and picaro
> HELENE, his wife
> ZIMMERMAN, his son
> DOCTOR VINCE DUBUQUE, a narrator
> DOCTOR CICCARELLI, a protean academic and another narrator
> BERNI M'INTOSH, a ghostly presence

More than sixty years have passed since T. S. Eliot accorded James Joyce's use of myth in *Ulysses* (1922) the "importance of a scientific discovery." Few would argue the point, although Joyce's employment of what Eliot called a "continuous parallel between contemporaneity and antiquity" had been anticipated both within and outside the Euro-American cultural continuum. In commenting on the significance of Joyce's discovery, Eliot issued a pronouncement that in some ways proved to be as influential as the "discovery" itself. Eliot described Joyce's use of myth as "simply a way of controlling, of ordering, of giving a shape and significance to the immense panorama of futility and anarchy which is contemporary history." Reading *Ulysses* as a fictional analogue to *The Waste Land* (1922), Eliot effectively claimed what he called the "mythical method" for the branch of modernism that, viewing the contemporary world and especially popular movements with disdain, treated literature as the province of a cultured elite (often located in academic institutions) capable of recognizing the superiority of antiquity. Although Joyce may not have shared Eliot's perspective, there is no doubt that Eliot's position, especially as developed, propagated, and frequently distorted by the New Criticism, largely determined the significance of the mythical method for Anglo-American modernism.

One by-product of Eliot's influence, which contributed to the identification of novelists such as John Barth as major contemporary figures, has been the absence of a populist avant-garde as a major force in American literary culture. Writers sharing Eliot's contempt for contemporary experience frequently employed the mythical method in part because it had become the *lingua franca* of academic discourse. Partly as a response to what they saw as the reactionary politics of Eliot's followers, writers with strong populist commitments (at least those not interested in arguing their case on academic premises) frequently avoided the mythical method for two basic reasons. First, many saw the myths of antiquity as hierarchical and antidemocratic in origin and implication. Second, they feared alienating themselves entirely from the nonacademic audience, which had come to see modern literature as inaccessible and irrelevant. The assumption of an underlying split between aesthetic sophistication and populist commitment became a central fact of American literary culture. Despite its origins in popular experience, myth came to be associated with the symbol-hunting academic elite.

This fabricated dichotomy between the popular and the mythical consciousness, however, has come under increasing scrutiny as contemporary writers, among them Gilbert Sorrentino, have turned away from Eliot's interpretation of the mythical method. Frequently, and Sorrentino's *Blue Pastoral* provides an excellent illustration of the movement, the repudiation of Eliot brings these writers closer to the view of the mythical method, and of avant-garde techniques generally, advanced by Bertolt Brecht, who viewed myth as a *part* of the perceptual system within contemporaneity. Sorrentino is not the first American writer to explore the Brechtian position. Prior to the 1960's, William Carlos Williams, Melvin B. Tolson, and the early Adrienne Rich intimated the possibility of reconceiving the mythical method by pointing out the Euro- and phallo-centrism of the ostensibly universal myths invoked, more by Eliot's followers than by Eliot himself, to validate their philosophical and aesthetic positions. Although populist in implication, these early arguments took place almost entirely within the confines of modernist discourse. Only in the early 1960's did serious attempts to liberate myth from the universality of the university begin to succeed. Gary Snyder, Amiri Baraka, and the later Rich simply (and complexly) refused to engage in battle on Eliot's premises; rather, they excavated and endorsed alternative mythical systems, which they believed to be of much greater relevance to the nonacademic communities that embraced their work than Sir James George Frazer's *The Golden Bough* (1922).

Brecht would accept this attack on cultural hegemony, could he be resurrected to pass judgment on it, but he would ultimately extend the attack in radical directions. Responding to the aesthetic conservatism of leftist political critic Georg Lukacs (which curiously parallels the split between aesthetics and politics in Anglo-American modernism), Brecht insisted on an aesthetic that would both express the full complexity of consciousness and make an active contribution to progressive politics. Carefully avoiding any temptation to pander to the conservative tendencies of his audience, Brecht emphasized *alienation* as an aesthetic and political strategy. Drawing on the full range of cultural expression, popular and elite, Brecht challenged his audiences to understand the ways they interpreted contemporaneity. For Brecht, the perception and interpretation of myth *within* a cultural context holds far greater significance than the attempt, which in any case he sees as futile, to see myth as a realm separate from that context. The view of antiquity as a repository of mythical order and contemporaneity as futile and anarchic is, from the Brechtian perspective, symptomatic of a profound cultural delusion.

Sorrentino is America's Brecht—or, perhaps more precisely, America's Brechtian Joyce. The Joycean aspect of Sorrentino's work takes on special significance in that it challenges Eliot's view of Joyce from a variety of angles.

Blue Pastoral, like Sorrentino's most recent novels *Mulligan Stew* (1979), *Aberration of Starlight* (1980), and *Crystal Vision* (1981), contains a multitude of complex allusions to Joyce. In *Blue Pastoral*, for example, Henry Flower and Martha Clifford continue the correspondence they began in *Ulysses*. Not content with simple allusion, which nevertheless emphasizes the overly serious nature of Eliot's Joyce, Sorrentino plays elaborate games with the fact that neither Flower (a Bloom pseudonym) nor Clifford (whose existence is a subject of some debate among Joyce critics) really exists in *Ulysses* to be alluded to. More important than such specifics, however, are Sorrentino's adaptations of the mythical dimension of the Joycean sensibility to the American context, adaptations that finally alienate the audience in classic Brechtian fashion. Emphasizing the American tendency to seek escape from contemporaneity, Sorrentino parodies the pastoral myth as it exists in classical literature, rock and roll, Jesuit lectures on sex, black nationalist rhetoric, Saint Patrick's Day oratory, academic discourse, "French letters," Southern Agrarianism, Renaissance poetry, pornography, bluegrass music: Sorrentino's love of Joycean catalogs would enable the unrestrained critic to extend the list almost indefinitely.

The underlying "plot" of *Blue Pastoral* is relatively simple. Frustrated pianist Serge "Blue" Gavotte, whose talents seem alternately nonexistent and Cagean, sometimes both, sets off from New York City in search of the "Perfect Musical Phrase." Accompanied by his wife, Helene, and son, Zimmerman (contemporary troubadour Bob Dylan was born Robert Zimmerman), and traveling in a pushcart covered with the mystic regalia of a frank vendor, Blue sets off on a picaresque quest. En route to a comic denouement in California, the archetypal emblem of America's pastoral impulse, the trio traverses the East, Midwest, South, and Southwest, encountering new variations of the pastoral myth in every region. While Blue seeks knowledge of the perfect musical phrase from academics, rednecks, and jazz musicians, Helene engages in a variety of sexual adventures. In the grand tradition of pastoral shepherds, Zimmerman does little or nothing. Between adventures, Blue reads a semipornographic play (apparently a literal English translation of a French original) titled "La Musique et les mauvaises herbes." Zimmerman, who has become an inconvenience to his parents, is misplaced in a cave. His magical reappearance suggests a multitude of mythical and literary analogues.

To concentrate on plot or character in a Sorrentino novel, however, is to miss the point entirely. The first two chapters of *Blue Pastoral*, narrated by Dr. Vince Dubuque of the "University" and Dr. Ciccarelli of Italy, draw attention in hilarious fashion to the insubstantiality of the fictional characters' experience. Just two of the novel's many parodic versions of Dr. Sorrentino (who teaches at Stanford), Doc Dubuque and Dr. Chick shift voices, slip in and out of ridiculous accents, and exhibit an extreme consciousness of their nonexistent "selves." Throughout the opening chapters, as in the rest of the novel, which shifts from prose to poetry to drama, Sorrentino emphasizes the irreconcilable demands that his narrative (and perhaps all narratives) make on reader psychology. Somehow, "we" can complain about "Doctor Ciccarelli's" inconsistent "voice" shortly before "you" are asked—ostensibly "orally"—to "turn the page." Sorrentino places the final phrase in quotation marks to emphasize the anomaly of the conventions that demand readers react to the text simultaneously as physical artifact and personal voice. The pursuit of this kind of aesthetic paradox is a major concern of the post-Eliot New Critics. By first establishing and then violating implied rules in nearly every chapter, Sorrentino both seduces the reader into participating in the academic game and withholds satisfying aesthetic coherence. Ultimately, however, to seek a Jamesian (or even a Joycean) consistency in *Blue Pastoral* is not only futile; it misses the point as completely as the naïve "realistic" analysis of plot and character. Conventions, as Sorrentino demonstrated in *Mulligan Stew*, are just that: conventions, ways of mediating between an author (who can be reflected in but never subsumed by the text) and an audience (which can be invited into but never included within the text).

Ultimately, *Blue Pastoral* implies that *all* mediations of experience, including those described by Eliot in his discussion of the mythical method, are simply conventions. Individuals create myths to help them order their experience. Ordering myths originating in Edmund Spenser and in Bob Dylan, in Hesiod, and in baseball deserve equally serious attention. Reveling in the Joycean juxtaposition of disparate types of pastoral mythology, Sorrentino effectively challenges the implied hierarchy of Eliot's mythical method. If contemporary reality presents nothing but futility, Eliot contributes to and participates in that futility. Eliot's attempt to withdraw to a separate mythic realm identified with antiquity is itself simply another version of the pervasive American pastoral impulse.

Sorrentino's satires of the glorious University and the somewhat less glorious Annex College, both characterized by self-deconstructing lectures and complicated sexual intrigues, emphasize that academics have no special relationship to contemporaneity. Nor do populist romantics. Shortly after parodying the Southern Idyll of Eliot's Agrarian heirs (who were instrumental in establishing the elitist perspective on myth in part to justify their social position in a segregated South), Sorrentino reveals the analogous delusion of "Big Black," who in the course of a militant harangue concerning "the Theft of

Black Flowers" provides a summary judgment of Andrew Marvell's poetry. This Brechtian passage critiques both the intellectual failure of emotional populism and the economic exploitation supporting the Euro-American pastoral tradition. Sorrentino subjects academic elitists and populist romantics to similar critiques in numerous passages, refusing to accept any version of the pastoral myth, contemporary or antique, as an objective or correct way of ordering experience.

The implications of this stance are complex. It would be possible to see *Blue Pastoral* as a repudiation of contemporaneity even more extreme than Eliot's, a repudiation that treats order as nothing more than the illusion of a particularly self-satisfied and deluded class. Although an abstract description of the novel might give credibility to this interpretation, an actual reading creates a radically different feeling. Where Eliot saw futility and tragic disharmony, Sorrentino sees futility tempered by comic connection. The excesses of academics and black militants, of narrators and characters, emphasize not the impossibility of order but the potential for perceiving an order based on shared experience—in this case, the desire for pastoral escape. By treating a wide variety of pastoral myths without establishing hierarchical relationships, Sorrentino invites his readers to recognize their excesses and absurdities as well as the nature of the cultural context shaping their desires. By implication, Sorrentino invites readers to extend their sympathy and empathy to fellow sufferers, however alien their form of expression. Nowhere is this invitation clearer than in the marvelously comic section in which Sorrentino constructs, deconstructs, and reconstructs a genealogy of "Nawlins" jazz bands manned by literary figures and their creations, among them the Beckettian "Murph Watt and the Mugs from Malone" and "Rambo Charlie and the Hell Raisers," no doubt known for their evil ways and flowery riffs.

A profoundly pluralistic sensibility shapes this passage, as it does *Blue Pastoral* as a whole. The synthesis of Euro-American avant-garde literature and Afro-American popular music intimates the potential for a populist avant-garde working in a language common to academics and nonacademics. Such a language can develop, however, only following the repudiation of the belief that contemporaneity is somehow distinct from and inferior to antiquity, that myths exist independent of context, and that some myths are better than others. Sorrentino ultimately resembles no writer, more than the Brecht of *Der gute Mensch von Sezuan* (1943; *The Good Woman of Setzuan*, 1961), which closes with the comic departure of the gods and the insistence that humanity bear full responsibility for its condition. Assuming his place in the tradition of comic iconoclasts, Sorrentino indicates that liberating the contemporary consciousness from the false dichotomy of Eliot's mythical method is necessary if humanity is to accept this responsibility with joy rather than despair.

Craig Werner

Sources for Further Study

The Atlantic. CCLI, June, 1983, p. 105.
Library Journal. CVIII, April 1, 1983, p. 760.
Los Angeles Times Book Review. August 7, 1983, p. 12.
Newsweek. CII, July 4, 1983, p. 73.
Publishers Weekly. CCXXIII, April 1, 1983, p. 51.

BLUEBEARD

Author: Max Frisch (1911-   )
Translated from the German by Geoffrey Skelton
Publisher: Harcourt Brace Jovanovich (San Diego, California). 134 pp. $10.95
Type of work: Novel
Time: The early 1980's
Locale: Zurich and Ratzwil, Switzerland

*The continuing self-interrogation of a physician who has been acquitted of murdering
his sixth wife but who is still tormented by the crime*

> Principal characters:
> FELIX THEODOR SCHAAD, a Zurich internist married seven times,
> tried for the murder of his sixth wife
> ROSALINDE ZOGG, Schaad's sixth wife, found in her apartment
> naked and strangled to death
> THE PUBLIC PROSECUTOR, the man who conducts the murder trial
> of Schaad in Zurich
> MAJOR ZOGG, the victim's father and a witness in the trial
> JUTTA SCHAAD, Felix's current, seventh, wife, a film editor
> HELENE MATHILDE JETZER,
> LILIAN HABERSACK SCHAAD,
> GISELA STAMM SCHAAD,
> CORINNE VOGEL SCHAAD, and
> ANDREA PADRUTT SCHAAD, former wives of Felix and witnesses
> at his trial
> HERMANN SCHAAD, Felix's dead father, a teacher

The agony of self-discovery has been a theme throughout the career of
Max Frisch, the most internationally celebrated of contemporary Swiss novelists. Frisch was an architect before he turned to writing, but his most recent
books have been appropriate to the deconstructionist *Zeitgeist.* Shunning the
amplitude of his earliest fictions, his recent works—including *Montauk: Eine
Erzählung* (1975; *Montauk,* 1976), *Der Mensch ersheint im Holozän* (1979;
The Man in the Holocene, 1980), and *Triptychon* (1978; *Triptych,* 1981)—
have been increasingly austere and lacerating probes into the deceptions that
constitute an individual identity. The austerity and reductiveness of these
works have provoked comparisons to Samuel Beckett.

Frisch has continued to practice this spare style in *Bluebeard* (published in
the Federal Republic of Germany in 1982 as *Blaubart*), which is cast entirely
in dialogue form, that of a personal inquisition. After the strangulation of
Rosalinde Zogg, his sixth wife, whom he had divorced, Felix Schaad is arrested
and tried for the brutal murder. He spends a total of 291 days in detention
before the verdict is rendered: acquittal because of "insufficient evidence"—
a phrase that echoes in Schaad's troubled brain. The novel begins some
months after the fifty-four-year-old doctor's release, but he is condemned to

replay the trial in his mind, this time augmented by harsher interrogation and by the testimony of his dead parents and of the victim herself. Herr Doktor Felix Theodor Schaad is a specialist in internal medicine, but he is unable to cure his own personal torments.

Bluebeard, then, is no ordinary whodunit. Despite the judicial finding of not guilty, much circumstantial evidence implicates Schaad in the crime. He had been obsessed with the sexual fidelity of Rosalinde, who after the divorce became a prostitute. He did visit her apartment on Saturday, February 8, the day of the homicide, and it is possible that the murder weapon was his own necktie. Schaad, who has been diagnosed as an alcoholic with paranoid tendencies, tries to allay his anxieties through travel and through such banalities as billiards and counting panels in the ceiling, but all to no avail; the culmination of the spiritual audit that constitutes this novel is Schaad's frantic drive from Zurich to Ratzwil, the town where he was born. There, he turns himself in to the police as the murderer of Rosalinde Zogg. The police, however, knowing that Schaad has already been acquitted and that someone else—a Greek student named Nikos Grammaticos—has been charged with the crime, refuse to accept Schaad's confession. Whether Schaad did or did not kill Rosalinde Zogg remains a mystery, but a rather trivial one compared to the more fundamental question of whether he *could* have killed her. Who is this perfectly miserable Felix Schaad, this masochist whose name seems such an apt oxymoron? All that the reader knows for certain is what a voice tells Schaad in the concluding words of the novel, as he lies hospitalized after attempting suicide by driving into a tree: "You are in pain."

Sixty-one people testified in Schaad's murder trial, and many of these voices, as well as those of others, continue to haunt him. His six surviving wives, Rosalinde's father, a waitress, a garage owner, a cleaning woman, a caretaker at the cemetery where he spends the night, a stranger whom he saves from suicide, his dead parents, and Rosalinde herself—each provides a distinct perspective on the accused. These diverse accounts are not strictly contradictory, but neither do they establish a coherent identity for their subject. The reality of Felix Schaad eludes adjudication. Even the swans he likes to feed at a Zurich lake no longer recognize him.

Jutta Schaad, a thirty-six-year-old film editor who is Felix's seventh wife, affectionately calls him "Chevalier Bluebeard," though she is convinced he is quite unlike the Charles Perrault knight "who killed his seven wives and concealed their corpses in the cellar." Theirs is a rather unconventional marriage, as she refuses to live with him; her work takes her out of the country much of the time, and she is in Kenya, making an ethnographic film, when Felix is released from jail. When she returns to Zurich, she announces that she has taken up with another man.

In *Bluebeard*, love is as fragile and unfathomable as it is compulsive. Schaad never understands any of the women who have assumed the burden of his name any more than any of them can give definitive testimony about him. His sixteen-year-old son—by second wife Lilian Habersack Schaad, a nursery-school teacher—sums up his father as "egocentric," and that is probably as reliable a description as is possible in Frisch's atomistic universe.

A collage, like *Tagebuch 1966-1971* (1972; *Sketchbook 1966-1971*, 1974), of memories, dreams, and meditations, *Bluebeard* asks its reader to assume the role of missing narrator, to undertake the impossible task of finding a figure in the carpet of Schaad's life when he is standing on a bare hardwood floor. Perhaps the systematic guilt from which Schaad suffers is less a matter of uxoricide or of cutting up a rabbit with a razor when he was seven than of his fundamental failure at the Socratic project of self-knowledge, or genuine knowledge of anyone. A baffling assemblage of fragments, *Bluebeard* succeeds admirably in communicating that guilt. It is an additional, concentrated demonstration of literary mastery by an author whose major accomplishments remain *Stiller* (1954; *I'm Not Stiller*, 1958) and *Homo Faber* (1957; English translation, 1959).

Steven G. Kellman

Sources for Further Study

Library Journal. CVIII, June 1, 1983, p. 1156.
The New Republic. CLXXXIX, July 11, 1983, p. 32.
The New York Review of Books. XXX, September 29, 1983, p. 14.
The New York Times Book Review. LXXXVIII, July 10, 1983, p. 9.
Newsweek. CII, July 18, 1983, p. 69.
Publishers Weekly. CCXXIII, June 10, 1983, p. 55.

THE BOOK OF QUESTIONS
Yaël, Elya, Aely

Author: Edmond Jabès (1912-   )
Translated from the French by Rosemarie Waldrop
Publisher: Wesleyan University Press (Middletown, Connecticut). 337 pp. $25.95
Type of work: Pensées

The fourth, fifth, and sixth volumes of Jabès' seven-volume work entitled The Book of Questions, *an aphoristic, deliberately fragmentary exploration of the nature of writing and the predicament of the Jew*

Edmond Jabès, born in 1912 in Cairo and now a citizen of France, is a writer known for bringing into his unusual books his own contradictory sense of identity as a Jew and as émigré writer within the twentieth century French literary tradition. Like the French Symbolists and their literary offspring, much of his concern as a writer is to make the very mysteries of writing his subject or his central problematic focus. Coupled with this sensibility is his keen awareness of the exiled condition of Jews, a people who, in their exile, are destined to be "people of the book." As a Jew, Jabès is condemned to dwell "within the book," but as the literary heir to Stéphane Mallarmé, he cannot regard even the book as home. The homeless condition of the poet is similar to the homeless condition of the Jew, or as Jacques Derrida has written in an influential essay on Jabès, "the Poet and the Jew are not born *here* but *elsewhere*." The writer cannot ever be found in his book. This is the central contradiction and dilemma behind the urgent tone of Jabès' own writing.

There is little in the foregoing account to suggest that Jabès would be of interest to anyone outside France except those with an interest in international Judaica. With the appearance in translation of Derrida's *L'Écriture et la différence* (1967; *Writing and Difference*, 1978), however, containing the essay "Edmond Jabès, and the Question of the Book," English-speaking readers began to be familiar with the name of Edmond Jabès as one whose texts served to raise questions similar or complementary to those introduced by Derrida. These include, most notably, explorations of the difference between writing and voice, the critical opposition with which Derrida is preoccupied. Derrida, who has been one of Jabès' foremost champions in France, insists on the prior status of writing; in thus consciously flaunting the historical priority of speech, Derrida challenges the claims on behalf of *voice* or *presence* (the presence of God in the book of nature, the voice or controlling presence of an author in his text) which he sees as central to the metaphysical tradition of Western man.

Jabès tends in his later texts to regard written language as a "silent scream," which is also the scream of the Jew, "the scream of the book before the book."

This might tempt one to say that *The Book of Questions: Yaël, Elya, Aely* (published in France in 1967, 1969, and 1972 as *Le Livre des questions: Yaël, Elya, Aely*) is about the Holocaust, especially because one gathers that these characters (Yaël, and her stillborn child Elya) are somehow related to earlier names in *The Book of Questions* such as Sarah and Yukel. In *The Book of Yukel* (volume 2) and *The Return to the Book* (volume 3), it becomes apparent that these figures have perished in the Holocaust. In such self-deconstructing texts as these of Jabès, however, the very "aboutness" of literature is called into question. The world outside the text is canceled out, and writing creates its own universe in which the marks on the page are silent screams rather than means of communication about the pain beyond or prior to the text. Questions about the book thus become inquiries into the nature of this uncertain universe, for which the writer himself is still only an imperfect cartographer.

This approach leads to attempts to theorize and problemize the realm of writing, or of *écriture* in the theory of Derrida or Roland Barthes. Here one is working in a recognizable French tradition of critical inquiry, whose antecedents include Gustave Flaubert and Marcel Proust. What is writing? According to what rules does it operate? What is the relationship between the author and the text? Such theorizing concerning the possibilities and modes of existence of texts have also, however, been central projects for the Gnostic and Cabalistic traditions of the Jews, as explained at length in recent writings of Harold Bloom. Here one confronts another source informing the texts of Jabès, who brings the power of these mystical approaches to the written word into the well-known modern French world of textual interpretation, exemplified by Derridean deconstruction and by Barthes's eroticizing of the text as a source of pleasure for the reader, but taking as its point of departure the celebrated observation by Mallarmé that, whatever world may be said to exist outside texts, *Tout, au monde, existe pour aboutir à un livre.* (Everything in the world exists in order to end up in a book.) Compare Derrida's gloss on the Mallarméan pronouncement: "Life negates itself in literature only so that it may survive better. So that it may *be* better."

Nevertheless, Jabès' consciousness, as he contemplates the book he cannot enter, is an unhappy one. At the very beginning of the first volume of *The Book of Questions*, Jabès' imaginary interlocutor inquires, "Are you in the book?" To which he must reply that he is only at the "threshold" of the book. In so doing, Jabès signals at the outset of his series of books of questions one of his central themes: the mysterious relationship between the author and the book, since Proust's *Contre Sainte-Beuve* (1954; *By Way of Sainte-Beuve*, 1958)—at least—the polemical focus of modern French letters. The relationship of the author to what he has written is not quite paternal, although Western culture has encouraged such a notion. It is not that the book is something brought into existence solely through the author's activity. It is true that the author is in a position to contemplate the book at close range, as a world to which he is somewhat more accustomed than his readers, but this world, for him, is still filled with mystery.

Perhaps the image that best captures Jabès' sense of the relationship between writer and text is that of the seasoned angler who, although he may know the stream well and may have acquired all sorts of tricks for making his catch, still cannot control the scene in its entirety. "A man at his desk," writes Jabès, "is in the position of an angler by the river. One looks for hours at an untouched sheet, the other at the water with a brighter circle on the surface, around the bait, the center of attraction. One spies on words, the other on fish." Or, even more strikingly: "Writing a book means joining your voice with the virtual voice of the margins. It means listening to the letters swimming in the ink like twenty-six blind fish before they are born for our eyes, that is to say, before they die fixed in their last cry of love." Perhaps Jabès as easily could have said that the writer listens to the letters buzzing like flies; writing is then the act of swatting the flies one by one. In either case, the writer is engaged in the murder of language or in an attempted murder in order to fix the meanings once and for all. The writer, however, is an imperfect assassin, for written language, phoenixlike, continually revives itself. The writer cannot leave his fishing bank or boat in order to live with the fish. In the latter of the two passages quoted above, the concern with the "virtual voice" of the margins recalls Derrida's concern with margins, while Jabès' wonderment over the contradictions and complications of the act of literary creation places his work within one of the major currents of modern French literature, from Mallarmé to, in their very different ways, such latter-day figures as Samuel Beckett and Philippe Sollers. For Beckett ("I can't go on. I'll go on.") the writer writes anyway, despite the futility of the act, while for Sollers, the act of writing always includes the experiencing of limits.

Limits, in the case of Jabès, include also the limits of the space of the book, across whose threshold the writer himself cannot pass. Like Vergil taking leave of Dante before the *Paradiso*, the writer cannot accompany the reader through the labyrinth of the text, but the advantage accorded the reader in this scheme of things must be weighed against the difficulty of locating the book within the book. Just as Derrida points to the mistaken nature of traditional notions of the book's closure, Jabès will caution against the assumption that the boundaries of the book are always determined by the physical dimensions of it between covers. In the dialogue of *Yaël*, one reads: "Where is the book found? In the book." Years earlier, Jabès had written, "Where is the way? The way is always to be found. A white sheet of paper is full of ways. . . ." The process of discovery begins within the pages of the book one reads. It is not a matter of planting one's flag and laying immediate claim to the book, having gained entry. In their differing ways, such twentieth century critics as Gaston Bachelard, Maurice Blanchot, and Georges Poulet all have drawn attention to literary space, and to the space of reading itself, as in

Poulet's sense of a phenomenological field within which reader and author confront each other. Jabès, too, forces the reader to consider the space of the book within which he must make his way. It is a space, like Albert Einstein's fourth-dimensional space-time, with physical laws and limitations all of its own. Allowing for this analogy from advanced physics, one could say that the space of the book leads into intense gravitational fields in which the material forces of the marks of writing are unleashed.

If likened to a more familiar local environment, the book is a setting in which profound silence is only occasionally punctuated by the "sounds" of written language. Or, as Jabès writes, "the book is the place where a writer offers his voice up to silence." The peculiar sense of space conveyed by a single page is vital for Jabès' project, and the appearance of the pages of *The Book of Questions* deserves comment. A typical page is mostly white space, marked here and there by the traces of Jabès' blind fish. In some ways, the silences are more eloquent than anything else in this text, and the whiteness of space in which words are relatively modest intrusions produces a feeling of peace and tranquillity in the reader. The white expanse of the page can also be a corporeal whiteness. Rather than the ether surrounding the words themselves, the page is often likened more to flesh itself, flesh bearing the wounds of inscription. In the first volume of *The Book of Questions*, Jabès wrote, *"Mark the first page of a book with a red ribbon, for the wound is inscribed at its beginning."* Like Yaël's imaginary lover, the writer wounds the object of his love, the blank page upon which his gaze is longingly fixed.

The book is then the place of contradiction, like the country of the exile. The book is the place where "writing means absence, and the empty page, presence." This paradox is compounded by the writer being Jewish, which means "exiling yourself in the word and, at the same time, weeping for your exile." He also writes, "Every letter . . . is the skeleton of a Jew." In the first volume of *The Book of Questions*, the imaginary Reb Lema said, *"To every question, the Jew answers with a question,"* but this is simply how books answer other books. If questions about acts of writing, reading, and interpretation have led only to still more questions, then perhaps the title of Jabès' limit-testing project can serve to designate all texts of criticism and theory. Is not every book a "book of questions"?

James A. Winders

Sources for Further Study

Library Journal. CVIII, June 1, 1983, p. 1157.
The New York Times Book Review. LXXXVIII, August 21, 1983, p. 13.

THE BREAKS

Author: Richard Price (1949-   )
Publisher: Simon and Schuster (New York). 446 pp. $15.95
Type of work: Novel
Time: June, 1971-November, 1972
Locale: Yonkers, the Bronx, Manhattan, and Buchanon (Ithaca), New York

A comic novel about the difficulty—or perhaps impossibility—of growing up in the United States where the national dream collides with the national reality

Principal characters:
  PETER KELLER, the narrator and protagonist
  MR. KELLER, Peter's ineffectual father
  JACK PETTY, professor of English and one of Peter's many surrogate fathers
  TONY FONSECA, a failed writer-in-residence and another of Peter's surrogate fathers
  KIM FONSECA, Tony's wife with whom Peter falls in love

It was inevitable, given the rough language and the graphic depiction of sex and violence, as well as the focus on the brutalizing effect of the urban environment (the Bronx) on young protagonists, that critics would place Richard Price's first two novels, *The Wanderers* (1974) and *Bloodbrothers* (1976) in the tradition of literary Naturalism and their author in the company of James T. Farrell, with a dash of William Burroughs, John Rechy, and Hubert Selby. Although accurate to a degree, the Naturalist tag fails to account for the comic grotesquerie that makes up a substantial part of Price's exploration of loneliness and failure in American life, particularly in the first-person works *Ladies' Man* (1978) and *The Breaks*. Both suggest a certain indebtedness to Nathanael West and, more important, Stanley Elkin. One finds in *The Breaks* many of the same qualities that have made Elkin one of the best— and the funniest—contemporary American writers: the pyrotechnic verbal display (less flamboyant and more accessible in Price's case), the understated theme-and-variation structure (often dismissed by plot-minded critics as digressive or episodic), and the recycling of the dreck of the popular culture in a way which is at once satirical and compassionate. Price's fiction may be as weighted with specific detail as Theodore Dreiser's, but the effect is different, emphasizing the incongruities and absurdities of modern life rather than its grim determinism. There are television shows (from "Joe Franklin" and "Topper" to "Mod Squad"), films, rock songs, cartoon strips, advertising slogans, name-brand cleansers (Bab-O, Comet), Flagg Brothers shoes, polyurethaned college diplomas, twenty-five-dollar gift certificates to E. J. Korvette's discount department store, The Official U. S. Navy Rock and Roll Recruiting Band, singles bars where patrons cha-cha to James Brown, a Greek luncheonette named Two Guys from Corfu, a supper-club menu written "in bar mitzvah French . . . Roast beef *au jus avec* French Fries," and shopping malls in which the air is alive with the sound of Muzak and the stores have been renamed Sheds, Attics, Corners, and the like. It is in such a world that Price's characters yearn for satisfaction and fulfillment and, quite understandably, fail to find them.

The odyssey of unfulfilled longing in *The Breaks* begins on a June graduation day in 1971 at Simon Straight College, "the Harvard of upstate New York" (or, more factually, Cornell University, from which Price was graduated the same year). Peter Keller is the pride of his family and the hope of their future, their first college graduate, "the happy ending to our private little American Everyman play." For Peter, however, American reality and American dream are incompatible. Unlike his well-connected college friends who have gotten "the breaks," Peter only makes the waiting list at Columbia University's law school. Prepared to move ahead in the world, he finds himself on hold or, worse, thrust back in time. Returning to Yonkers to live with his father and stepmother, Peter feels like a sixteen-year-old trapped in a slapstick Oedipal crisis—a crisis that teeters on the edge of something more significant both for Peter and for the reader, who understands that Peter's situation is cultural as well as individual.

Although Peter suffers from "the Gregor Samsas," his nemesis is quite unlike Franz Kafka's stern parent. The father with whom Peter struggles— or shadowboxes—is a silent, unambitious drone who has spent the last twenty years selling stamps at the city post office. The son realizes "how nothing" the father is, yet it is precisely this nothingness that hangs around his neck, more a millstone than an albatross. He responds to his parent ambivalently, alternating love and loathing, uncertain whether his father deserves to be kicked or cared for. Peter wants his freedom and manhood, but he also wants his father's recognition and love.

More troubling than who Peter's father is, is what his father represents: the (lower) middle-class dream of upward mobility and the good life on the one hand and the failure of that dream on the other. (When father and son move from the Hispanicized Bronx to what the father calls the country, Yonkers, they take up residence in a housing project originally intended for the well-to-do, but out of necessity, rented to refugees from the boroughs: failures entombed alive in another failure.) Peter responds to the American dream as ambivalently as he responds to his father, believing it one moment, despising it the next. Longing to be one of the famous (and feeling guilty because he is not), he pores over copies of *People* magazine, but in his real (not fantasy) life, he seems to court failure. The first time he takes the law boards, for example, he is hung over; the next time he scores a phenomenal 748 but perversely does not bother to reapply anywhere. Instead, he accepts a number of dead-end jobs. At American Communicators, a telephone sales operation, Peter meets a homosexual actor named James Madison and a too-large would-be dancer, Randye, the first of several surrogates for Peter's 250-pound mother, eleven years dead. Immediately, he mythologizes them, as well as all of the other workers hidden away in their phone cubicles, into a select group of theatrical people on the road to fame and wealth: aspiring, talented, determined. Believing his own mythology, Peter decides to forget law school and to follow James and Randye. "As a kid, my class-clown nickname had been Speedo. I wanted to be called Speedo again. Like all the dancers, the ventriloquists, the actors, I wanted to bask in my own brand of ace-hood." What he fails to understand is that for all of their acting lessons and dance practices, James, Randye, and the others are only a step above the losers to whom Peter tries to sell Power Plower exercise equipment over the phone. At the post office, where his father manages to summon enough energy to help secure a job for his son, Peter discovers "the flip side" of American Communicators, the "nickel and dime" dream of refrigerator repairman school, of becoming a policeman, and so forth. Something of a psychological chameleon, Peter naturally adapts to his new environment; no longer the aspiring ace comedian, he returns to his colorless dream of life as a lawyer with a house in the suburbs.

Peter's dream of future greatness as a comedian derives from his mother, who played the histrionic fool in order to mask her feelings of loneliness and vulnerability. Peter plays the same role for a similar reason. By improvising biographies for himself, he avoids having to put forth his real self, the nothing he (like his father) is. What distinguishes father from son in this regard is Peter's awareness of just how nothing they both are. Like T. S. Eliot's Prufrock, Peter is painfully self-conscious. He knows that his act does not equal a real life, but neither is it merely a comic entertainment. As he candidly admits, he would like to stand on a stage and chant (like Saul Bellow's Henderson the Rain King) "I want, I want, I want" until the audience applauds. What he wants is approval, especially from the nuclear audience of family and friends. The risk here is that all of Peter's relationships will be reduced to the level of performer and audience, but for the Peter who, in one of his most honest as well as theatrical moments, claims to be "drowning," the risk may be necessary.

Peter resembles J. Alfred Prufrock in yet another way, in his inability, or unwillingness, to act decisively. Although living with his father and stepmother only serves to erode further his already weak will and meager sense of self-identity, as he himself understands, he cannot bring himself to take the first step toward psychological maturity, "breaking" with his family. Instead he makes three phony bomb threats, hoping to be caught—hoping, that is, that his father will make the decisive act of forcing Peter out of the house. Like so many of Peter's plans, this one backfires. Fear, not anger, is what Mr. Keeler feels; sensing this fear, Peter makes his quiet exit, his "crisis" still unresolved.

What ought to constitute a step forward proves to be further evidence of Peter's regressive personality, his Gatsby-like refusal "to accept the ongoing-ness of things." Instead of moving ahead, Peter again moves back to another of his paradises lost, the upstate town of Buchanon (Ithaca) and the womb of his alma mater, Simon Straight. Neither wholly man nor wholly child, Peter resumes his old life in something of a postnatal daze, making a disconcerting pilgrimage back to his fraternity house, where he confronts the ghost of his undergraduate self in the person of Mark Schiff, loner and class clown. Not surprisingly, Peter does not like what he sees and rebuffs Schiff in his efforts to become close to his older "brother." Peter makes a similarly unsuccessful effort to befriend members of the college's English faculty, his former teachers now suddenly, if only nominally, his colleagues, when he is hired to teach a section of freshman composition to students only five years his junior. Peter's motivation here is more complex than it may at first appear. He wants to be treated as an equal, thus proving that his initiation into the adult world is complete, but he also wants to find for himself a suitable father-figure among the ranks of his former mentors.

The father-figures to whom he turns are drawn in half-realistic, half-cartoonish strokes. Bill Crown is the failed actor-turned-drama teacher whose greatest theatrical triumph occurs before an audience of his students when he climaxes his autobiographical confession by taking off his toupee and throwing it down with a flourish on the bar. Tony Fonseca, a failed writer-in-residence and closet Sephardic Jew, plays the part of charismatic extrovert to attract students but then uses his immense physical strength to keep them at a distance. The most effective of these surrogate fathers is the 366-pound Jack Petty, who hires Peter to teach composition partly because he likes his former student and partly because he wants to unload his freshman section on someone else. Though kind and protective toward others, Petty is himself suicidal; a paternalistic teacher and department chairman, he is nevertheless a failure as both a husband and a father. As he explains to Peter, he has left his wife and children because "I was scared to death of no more curves in the road." He is afraid, that is, of becoming like Peter's father—not satisfied exactly, but resigned, passive. The same fear haunts many of Price's characters because, Price seems to suggest, American life breeds not only dreams but also dissatisfaction. Walt Whitman's open road has transmogrified into the yo-yoing of Thomas Pynchon's Benny Profane (*V.*, 1963) and the frantic cross-country travels of Jack Kerouac's Neal Cassady (*On the Road*, 1957) and more especially Stanley Elkin's Ben Flesh (*The Franchiser*, 1976). In the land of Muzak, Bab-O, and James Bond movies, dreams of greatness are not elusive but illusive, even ridiculous. Desperate for any kind of greatness, including great size, Peter begins to lift weights and, dutiful son that he is, to emulate the larger and more experienced lifters, going so far as to buy the little blue gym bag "that made them [appear] larger than life and cartoon-hero powerful. It added perspective." If greatness is relative, however, then so too is failure. While Crown, Fonseca, and Peter strive after their various fames, they neglect the one thing they can do well: teach. Like Petty, they find it necessary to "shake things up."

Peter's uncertainty concerning who he is and what he wants intensifies when he meets Kim Fonseca, not realizing that she is Tony's wife. For Peter, she is lover, mother, sex object, audience, rival, and mirror image of his own loneliness, insecurity, and inability to resolve the contradictions that, in a sense, define him. He loves Kim (both as woman and as mother) but fears Fonseca (as her husband and as his father). Peter wants to be Kim's lover in Buchanon, but he also wants to be his father's boy in Yonkers. Although clearly trapped in—or between—various roles, Peter is paradoxically in motion throughout the entire course of his relationship with Kim. Geographically, he travels back and forth between Buchanon and New York City; psychologically, he vacillates between yearning, for Kim and for a vaguely defined "something *special*," on the one hand, and the discontent and loathing that seem inevitably to follow in the wake of his yearning, on the other.

That Price does not attempt to resolve this tension, or ambivalence, is one of the many strengths of *The Breaks*, for to have imposed any clear-cut solution, either optimistic or pessimistic, on his anti-*Bildüngsroman* would have falsified the experience Peter shares with those archetypal Americans Rip Van Winkle, Huck Finn, and especially Major Molineux's kinsman, Robin. Peter's Oedipal confrontation with Fonseca cannot serve to resolve his dilemma because their *High Noon* showdown is slapstick rather than mythic: The son, defending himself with a pair of pliers (he has deliberately avoided the phallic knife), breaks the father's collarbone with a bottle of cranapple juice. Although Peter is now willing to finish the semester at Simon Straight—Petty has reminded him of his responsibility to the college—and to live with Kim—"I'll meet you home," he tells her on the last page—the reader senses something other than resolution here. Petty's sense of responsibility must be weighed against his attachment not to wife and children but to his means of escape from them, his boat and motorcycle. Similarly, Peter's commitment to Kim must be weighed against his choosing to walk the three miles to her apartment in order to "keep in shape," ready to move on, to shake things up. *The Breaks*, like Richard Price's three earlier novels, comments ironically on the American dreams of home and freedom, stasis and motion—on the Ben-Linda antithesis dramatized in Arthur Miller's *Death of a Salesman* (1949). Price's riff-and-realism style does more than delight the reader; it illuminates the half-sad, half-silly uncertainties, the Prufrockian "do-I-dares" that lie at the heart of the American experience.

Robert A. Morace

Sources for Further Study

Antioch Review. XLI, Spring, 1983, p. 249.

Library Journal. CVIII, January 15, 1983, p. 146.

Los Angeles Times Book Review. April 17, 1983, p. 12.

The New York Review of Books. XXX, March 31, 1983, p. 28.

The New York Times Book Review. LXXXVIII, February 13, 1983, p. 14.

The New Yorker. LVIII, February 14, 1983, p. 114.

Publishers Weekly. CCXXII, November 19, 1982, p. 64.

Saturday Review. IX, March, 1983, p. 63.

BRECHT

Author: Ronald Hayman (1932-   )
Publisher: Oxford University Press (New York). 423 pp. $24.95
Type of work: Literary biography
Time: 1898-1956
Locale: Germany, Austria, Switzerland, Denmark, Finland, Sweden, Russia, and the United States

A comprehensive biography of Germany's leading twentieth century dramatist and poet

> *Principal personages:*
> EUGEN BERTHOLD BRECHT, a German poet and playwright
> HELENE WEIGEL, a Vienna-born actress who became Brecht's second wife and career partner
> MARIANNE ZOFF, an opera singer who was Brecht's first wife and bore him a daughter
> ELISABETH HAUPTMANN,
> RUTH BERLAU, and
> MARGARETE STEFFIN, Brecht's mistresses and collaborators
> STEFAN BRECHT, the son of Bertolt Brecht and Helene Weigel
> KURT WEILL, a brilliant composer who sometimes collaborated with Brecht
> ERWIN PISCATOR, a distinguished stage director who sometimes collaborated with Brecht
> OSCAR HOMOLKA, a distinguished actor who appeared in numerous Brecht plays
> CHARLES LAUGHTON, a film and stage actor with whom Brecht collaborated on revisions of his *Galileo*
> CASPAR NEHER, Brecht's lifelong friend who designed the sets for many of his plays

Bertolt Brecht's status as Germany's greatest twentieth century dramatist is by now securely established. Many critics also regard him as his country's leading modern poet, with an astonishingly wide lyric range spanning folk ballads, Rimbaudesque prose poems, political epistles, and luminously concrete sonnets. On a personal level, he struck many who encountered him as sly, cunning, guileful, opportunistic, and perfectly prepared to play devious, treacherous games with love, friendship, and ideological evil for the sake of some selfish advantage.

To do justice to such an ambiguous titan is an enormous task, at which no German, British, or American writer has yet succeeded. Among the many who have tried to take Brecht's measure, the most ambitious has been Klaus Volker, who compiled a faithful daily chronicle of Brecht's life and work (1971), then wrote a full-scale biography (1976) that makes him out to be a tame, comfortable bourgeois, with no awareness on Volker's part of the extraordinary complexity of his subject. Max Spalter, in *Brecht's Tradition*

(1967), traced his dramaturgy back to Georg Büchner, Friedrich Hebbel, and Frank Wedekind. Eric Bentley, who befriended Brecht in Santa Monica during World War II, translated most of Brecht's plays and many of his poems into sometimes brilliant but often unfaithful English and wrote a number of incisive introductions to their Grove Press editions. The most scholarly English edition of Brecht's plays is the British-American enterprise of Ralph Manheim and John Willett, published by Methuen in England and Random House in the United States. It has variant texts and scholarly notes for each play—a daunting achievement when one considers that Brecht loved nothing better than to revise continuously each of his texts, up to and often beyond their premieres.

The latest adventurer into the jungle of Brechtiana is Ronald Hayman, a Cambridge-educated man-about-the-British-theater who worked as an actor and director before turning critic and biographer. His two dozen books include short monographs on John Osborne, Tom Stoppard, Arnold Wesker, Harold Pinter, and Samuel Beckett, and biographies of the Marquis de Sade, Friedrich Nietzsche, and Franz Kafka. Hayman's biography of Brecht is obviously a painstaking, comprehensively researched text: He worked on it, off and on, for many years, consulted the authorized archive in East Berlin, and interviewed dozens of Brecht's relatives, friends, and foes. Like Volker's biography, his exceeds four hundred pages; also like Volker's, alas, his blurs the profile of Brecht's stormy personality and is generally unable to illuminate the masterpieces Brecht contributed to the canon of Western drama: *Die heilige Johanna der Schlachthöfe* (1931; *Saint Joan of the Stockyards*, 1956), *Der gute Mensch von Sezuan* (1943; *The Good Woman of Setzuan*, 1961), *Herr Puntila und sein Kneckt Matti* (1948; *Mr. Puntila and His Hired Man Matti*, 1954), *Der Kaukasische Kreide Kreis* (1949, 1956; *The Caucasian Chalk-Circle*, performed 1948, revised version published 1960), and what may be two of the contemporary theater's three greatest plays: *Mutter Courage und ihre Kinder* (1941; *Mother Courage and her Children*, 1948) and *Leben des Galilei* (1943; *Galileo*, 1947). The third is, of course, Beckett's *En attendant Godot* (1952; *Waiting for Godot*, 1954).

In an early ballad, Brecht told of having been descended from shrewd, hardheaded peasants, carried "from the black forests. . . into the towns" while in his mother's womb. Actually, Hayman notes, Brecht's genealogy was solidly middle-class and could be traced back to the sixteenth century. His father was managing director of a paper mill in Augsburg, forty miles northwest of Munich; he was Catholic, his wife Protestant, and both Brecht and his younger brother, Walter, were reared in their mother's faith and primarily by her—the father was a workaholic. Brecht's boyhood and adolescence were marked by self-confidence, quick-mindedness, and vitality—all characteristics that stood him in good stead throughout his life. His skill in manipulating people and his ruthlessness in pursuing his goals were also evident even in his youth.

During World War I, Brecht took up medical studies at the University of Munich to delay an early conscription call-up, but the only medical lectures he attended dealt with venereal diseases. Instead, he studied theater history with a Professor Artur Kutscher, the friend and biographer of Frank Wedekind, who became Brecht's idol. Wedekind not only wrote avant-garde Expressionistic plays advocating sexual liberation but also composed and sang ballads with enormously aggressive bravado. Wrote Brecht,

> Never has a singer made me feel so excited, so shaken. It was the enormous vitality of this man, his energy, that gave him his personal magic and enabled him, while showered with ridicule and scorn, to perform his brash hymn to humanity.

Like Wedekind, Brecht discovered that, given audacity, aplomb, and a guitar, one did not need a trained voice or handsome looks to excite and manipulate an audience. Not only did he compose and bawl out his own ballads, but also he wrote his first play, *Baal*, about an amoral, vagabond bard-balladeer who follows his instincts cruelly, exploiting and then discarding friends and lovers of both sexes. His only love is for the natural world, which he celebrates eloquently in lyrics of raw Expressionism.

Perhaps the best—and surely the most enigmatic—of Brecht's early works was *Im Dickicht der Städte* (1923; *In the Jungle of Cities*, 1961), in which two men, Shlink and Garga, engage in a relentless but seemingly motiveless duel of wills. Shlink, a Malaysian lumber dealer, seeks to buy Garga's soul but is himself shown to be a victim—one whose skin has been so toughened by life that he can no longer feel. He stages his battle with Garga to penetrate his own shell of indifference, crying out, "If you cram a ship full to bursting with human bodies, they'll all freeze with loneliness."

In the 1920's, Brecht became a celebrated personality in the urban jungle of postwar Berlin: sexually perverse, intellectually brilliant, brutally predatory toward women, affecting a part-bohemian, part-proletarian persona. His trademarks were a seminarian's tonsorial haircut, steel-rimmed spectacles, two days' growth of beard, a leather jacket and a trucker's cap, a cheap but large cigar, and chronic rudeness. People found him either charismatic or disgusting as he played ringmaster in Berlin's grotesque circus of artistic innovation and political savagery. Many women found him irresistible.

Hayman's biography is deficient in bringing to life the special texture of Berlin's atmosphere in the 1920's, but it does illuminate Brecht's voracious sexual appeal to a phalanx of gifted and harrowed women. There was the rich and darkly beautiful singer-actress Marianne Zoff, whom he charmed with his "grating metallic voice" and lack of inhibitions. They married in November, 1922, and she bore him a daughter, Hanne, the following March; they separated before the end of 1923 and divorced in 1927. In 1924, he met the blond, chubby-cheeked Elisabeth Hauptmann, who became a lifelong, on-and-off mistress and assistant. Hauptmann spent the exile years during World War II in Manhattan, where Brecht would occasionally visit her when working on a New York stage production; they collaborated most successfully in organizing adaptations for the Berliner Ensemble in the 1950's. His most turbulent relationship was with the alcoholic, manic-depressive photographer-actress Ruth Berlau: They met in Danish exile in 1934 and managed to form part of an erotic trio, quartet, or even quintet until his death. In 1944 in Los Angeles, she bore him a son who lived but a few days. Probably Brecht's most tender romance was with the tubercular, sacrificial Margarete Steffin, whom he loved from 1932 until her death in Moscow in 1941.

Withal, the most important woman in Brecht's life was the Viennese actress Helene Weigel, Jewish, Communist, and staunchly feminist, whom he met in 1923, married in 1929, and with whom he had a son, Stefan, in 1924, and a daughter, Barbara, in 1930. His decision to marry Weigel shocked his sexual commune—Elisabeth Hauptmann even attempted suicide—but it was eminently practical: Weigel was stable, strong, and protective; her devotion to his talent and person caused her to give up her stage career willingly for fifteen years during their wanderings through Europe and stay in the United States. On the deficit side, she was too masculine to fascinate him physically, and her party-line Marxism prevented him from examining Soviet policies with a sufficiently open mind. Weigel's greatest stage successes were as the protagonist of Brecht's *Die Mutter* (1932), his openly Communist play, and *Mother Courage and Her Children*, his most successful work. Her marvelously expressive face and superbly disciplined acting skills caused many theater critics to consider her the finest actress of her time on the German-speaking stage.

Even Weigel's patient, motherly tolerance of Brecht's libidinous gluttony had its limits: In Finnish exile, she refused Ruth Berlau entry into their home; the imperturbable Berlau thereupon pitched a tent in the garden. During the last weeks of his life, Brecht, troubled by cardiac seizures, made a will in which he left the proceeds of *Die Dreigroschen-oper* (1928; *The Threepenny Opera*, 1955) to Hauptmann; of *The Caucasian Chalk-Circle* to Berlau; of *Die Mutter* to Käthe Rülicke, his assistant for the past year; and of his most popular poems to Isot Kilian, a young actress who was his latest—and last—love. Kilian, however, neglected to have the will properly witnessed by a notary. Weigel consequently became Brecht's sole inheritor and paid comparatively scant sums to his other women.

A central problem for Brecht's biographers and critics is his adherence to Communism and its effect on his work. It is clear that from youth on he was in revolt against a middle class that led Germany to a wasteful war, bitter defeat, and extreme social disorder in the 1920's. Andreas Kragler, however, the protagonist of his second play, *Trommeln in der Nacht* (1922; *Drums in the Night*, 1966), while disillusioned with profiteering postwar capitalism, in the end decides not to join the Communist-led Spartakus uprising. He prefers a comfortable life with his shopworn, disloyal bride to strident heroism as a revolutionist: "I am a swine and the swine goes home." As so often with the enigmatic Brecht, one cannot be certain whether he shares his antihero's conclusion.

What *is* certain is that Brecht read a considerable amount of Karl Marx from 1926 to 1929 and was influenced by the Marxist sociologist Fritz Sternberg, to whom he gave a copy of an early play with the inscription, "To my first real teacher." When, however, a Communist demonstration was bloodily suppressed by the Berlin police on May Day, 1929, Brecht observed the event from a characteristically safe window. What attracted him to Marxism was largely its hostility to the crass and smug selfishness of Germany's business and military circles. The antibourgeois and anarchic individualist in him delighted in its savage opposition to the moral and economic failures of the ruling classes, and though his very membership in the Party remains disputed—did he join it in 1930? later? never?—one cannot doubt that Brecht was a Marxist from the late 1920's until his death. His adherence to Communism, however, remained consistently idiosyncratic, equally indigestible to the official Soviet cultural apparatus, to the great Hungarian Communist critic Georg Lukács, to the House Un-American Activities Committee (before which he made what would become a celebrated appearance on October 30, 1947), and to the mummified party-liners who ran East Germany after World War II.

What seems fundamental to Brecht's vision and his work is his derisive, misanthropic view of human nature. He had a fascinated obsession with human cruelty, deterioration, bestiality, grotesquerie. In common with such pre-Marxist playwrights as Ben Jonson and Molière, such satirists as Jonathan Swift and Voltaire, Brecht depicts man as a predatory animal motivated largely by his economic needs—"What keeps a man alive? He feeds off others" (*The Threepenny Opera*). Should a character speak of love, loyalty, friendship, honor, progress, religion—the chances are that he is merely masking a corrupt and greedy deal. His Joan of Arc (in *Saint Joan of the Stockyards*) is an evangelical Salvation Army lassie who tries to soften the heart of a Chicago meat magnate (well-named Pierpont Mauler) toward the plight of exploited stockyard workers; he tries to convince her of their alleged wickedness. In the end, starved and dying, sold out by her organization, hypocritically canonized by brutal capitalism, she converts to the class struggle:

. . .those who are below are kept below so that those above may stay above and the vileness of those above is measureless. . . . Only force helps where force rules, and only men help where men are.

Brecht wrote *Saint Joan of the Stockyards* during a phase in his life—the late 1920's and early 1930's—when Communism's dogmatic austerity and

monastic discipline mesmerized him as a counterforce to the amorphous nihilism and corrosive cynicism that pervaded his earlier years and plays. The
other masterpiece from this period is *Die Massnahme* (1930; *The Measures
Taken*, 1959), a harshly Stalinist and severely didactic dramatic cantata performed by four soloists who represent party agitators reenacting a mission in
China, as well as a Control Chorus representing the collective conscience of
the Communist Party. The agitators demonstrate to the chorus the necessity
of having killed an individualistic young comrade who preferred compassionate but impetuous idealism to planned, party-line orthodoxy. The chorus
acquits the agitators of any guilt—as does the young comrade, who consents
to be shot—as does the author. Hayman points out that the play's "liturgically
balanced phrases point to an affinity with T. S. Eliot, while the acquiescence
to martyrdom parallels that of Becket in *Murder in the Cathedral*. Brecht has
swung—both in form and in attitude—to the opposite extreme from *Baal*."
What Hayman does not point out is that *The Measures Taken* is one of two
great dramatizations, along with Arthur Koestler's *Darkness at Noon* (1941),
of the means-versus-ends moral dilemma engendered by Soviet totalitarianism.

What complicates Brecht's career are his constant self-contradictions. To
be sure, he committed himself to Communism like a submissive monk, trying
to lose himself in a secular faith that would satisfy both his desire to revolt
against established society and his desire to discipline his terrifyingly aggressive impulses. A hysteria of violence hovers constantly at the margins of his
dramas and poems, an awareness that the human will is weak and malleable,
that man's nature is savage, brutal, and uncontrolled, and that romantic
individualism is a luxury which man cannot usually afford—hence the mag-
netic appeal of systematic Marxism as a source for man's original sinfulness.

Brecht's personality and works also have a raffishly humane aspect that
charms and beguiles many readers and spectators. Many of his characters
may be sharklike in preying upon one another in monstrous fashion, yet in
his best plays Brecht often rises above his singular mixture of cynicism-
*cum*Communism. In *The Good Woman of Setzuan*, the heroine, Shen Te, is
naturally loving, kindly, selfless, motherly; she fulfills herself by giving, thrives
on sharing her feelings and goods. Alas for her, the world repays her virtues
with greed, betrayal, envy, spite, and ruthless exploitation. Hence she needs
to call, with increasing frequency, on the services of her calculating male
"cousin," Shui Ta, who meets the world on its own level of meanness and
deception. Shui Ta turns out to be Shen Te masked, the other half she needs
to protect her interests yet also the other self that denies Shen Te her essential
identity.

Beyond a brief reference to "the ambiguity of moral identity," Hayman
shows little interest in Brecht's dramatization of the dualism in human nature,
either as a parable of the permanent frustrations in store for man's quixotic
goodness or as an unconscious autobiography of Brecht's self-struggle with

conflicting drives. In a play he wrote in Finnish exile in 1940 to 1941, *Mr. Puntila and His Hired Man Matti*, Brecht invented one of his finest characters in the rich landowner, Puntila. When he is sober, Puntila personifies the harshest aspects of capitalism, treating his servants, particularly his intelligent chauffeur, Matti, with snarling arrogance and malevolence. Puntila drunk, however, is a benign, democratic rogue who wants Matti to marry his daughter and manages to get himself engaged to four girls in one evening. In the concluding scene, Matti decides to leave such unsettling employment: "It's time your hired hands showed you their rears. They'll quickly find good masters when the masters are the working men."

Brecht's persistent return to characters of goodness, compassion, and hence moving vulnerability is perhaps best illustrated in another parable play, *The Caucasian Chalk-Circle*. Its coprotagonists are Grusha, a kitchen maid in the mansion of a rich governor in Russian Georgia, and Azdak, an alcoholic village scribe. Both perform impulsive deeds of kindness: Grusha adopts the abandoned son of the governor's wife when she flees during an uprising; Azdak shelters a Grand Duke who has become an abject refugee in the same revolution. The scampish Azdak is rewarded with a judgeship which enables him to render verdicts combining the biting wit of Groucho Marx with the proletarian bias of Karl Marx. In the concluding courtroom scene, he awards Grusha permanent custody of the boy, then flees the powerful vengeance of the boy's genetic mother. His brief days of judgeship are celebrated in a closing ballad as a "Golden Age when there was almost justice"—as happy a period, Brecht indicates, as man can realistically achieve in a society plagued by the defeat of decency.

In *Mother Courage and Her Children*, his most famous work, Brecht seeks to present a relentlessly Marxist indictment of the economic causes of war. In his production notes, he states that the play is designed to demonstrate that "war, which is a continuation of business by other means, makes the human virtues fatal even to their possessors." In the drama's atmosphere of rape, pillage, and meaningless murder, where Protestants and Catholics slaughter each other in the Thirty Years' War, all human ideals degenerate into hypocritical cant, while heroism shatters into splinters of cruelty, madness, greed, or absurdity. The protagonist, owner of a canteen wagon who follows the seemingly endless war, is a shameless profiteer who cashes in on the troops' needs for alcohol and clothes; another character calls her "a hyena of the battlefield." Brecht clearly meant to draw her as a largely evil woman who haggled elsewhere while all three of her children lost their lives. She is another of his split characters who transcends her creator's original intent. Salty, shrewd, sardonic, skeptical, she is a full-blooded personification of the antiheroic view of life: Greed and motherly love stage a continuous contest in her heart. To Brecht's disgust, audiences would invariably weep at the play's end as Courage, a pathetic victim of the wrong dream, having sacrificed all of her human children to war's ravages, tied herself to her inhuman fourth child—her wagon—to trudge after the soldiers. She had become an indomitable symbol of man's capacity to suffer greatly and endure. Her world had moved from Falstaff's to Lear's.

Galileo is in some respects a companion piece to *Mother Courage and Her Children*. Both works are located in the seventeenth century. Both have protagonists who are egotistic opportunists, canny, shrewd, and resourceful— like their author—and both protagonists are self-divided. For Brecht's Galileo is not only a self-indulgent sensualist who loves to gorge himself with food and wine but also a masterly researcher and teacher, an intellectual locksmith picking at rusty incrustations of Ptolemaic tradition as he elucidates his proof that the Earth revolves around the sun. Surely influenced by his collaboration and friendship with Charles Laughton during his Southern California exile, Brecht has a cardinal describe Galileo as someone who "gets pleasure out of more things than any man I ever met. Even his thinking is sensual. He can never say no to an old wine or a new idea."

When Galilco rccants his revolutionary theories of cosmology before the Inquisition's threat of torture, it is not he but his disciples who are disillusioned. Says Galileo drily: "Unhappy the land that needs a hero." Such a view echoes Brecht's deep-lying sentiments. After all, he survived fifteen years of migration, poverty, tremendous personal traumas, grubby internecine rivalries, the whole bitter pathos of Adolf Hitler's demonic enmity to culture and Joseph Stalin's betrayal of left-wing idealism. Wherever Brecht was, and however sour his circumstances, he managed to pour out an impressive volume of distinguished plays and poems at full pressure. Like Galileo, he employed all of his sly tenacity to persist in his work.

Astonishingly, after the nuclear explosions over Hiroshima and Nagasaki, Brecht revised Galileo's last long speech to have him condemn himself for his recantation. "I have betrayed my calling," he tells his disciple. "A man who does what I have done cannot be tolerated in the ranks of science." Brecht clearly sought to shift the balance of the play so as to revile Galileo— that is, physics—for having failed to fulfill his (its) duty to society. Hayman states persuasively that "Blaming Galileo for Hiroshima was a naive mistake which Marx would never have made, believing as he did . . . that individual virtues and vices never determine the course of history."

A more autobiographical interpretation of the altered ending is possible: In changing his view of Galileo's conduct, Brecht may well have been changing his views of his own. The Galileo who lashes himself for his cowardice and lack of integrity may represent the author's own evaluation and condemnation of himself. For one brief stage in his foxy life, Brecht may have been seized by the seductive notion of absolutely intransigent morality. If so, however, the spell soon vanished: Brecht spent his last years living affluently in East Berlin, presented by the Communist regime with his own theatrical company, the Berliner Ensemble, and with virtually unlimited time and means to stage his own plays. He was shrewd enough to place the copyright of his works with a West German publisher, to give himself ample Western currency, and to obtain Austrian citizenship, to enable him to travel freely. Like Galileo, Brecht had checked his impulse toward forthright heroism by considerations of his comfort and safety. Like Galileo, Brecht insists on defying easy categories of understanding.

Gerhard Brand

Sources for Further Study

Library Journal. CVIII, October 1, 1983, p. 1871.
New Leader. LXI, December 12, 1983, p. 6.
New Statesman. CVI, September 30, 1983, p. 27.
The New York Review of Books. XXXI, March 15, 1984, p. 25.
The New York Times Book Review. LXXXVIII, November 27, 1983, p. 14.
Publishers Weekly. CCXXIV, September 9, 1983, p. 55.

THE BROTHERS SINGER

Author: Clive Sinclair (1948-   )
Publisher: Allison & Busby (New York). 176 pp. $14.95
Type of work: Literary criticism and biography

A study of selected works by Israel Joshua Singer in an effort to appreciate his achievement and measure his impact on his celebrated younger brother, the Nobel Prize-winning Isaac Bashevis Singer

Literary editor of the *Jewish Chronicle*, Clive Sinclair is also a young British writer of fiction and criticism. Besides shorter journalistic pieces on Isaac Bashevis Singer, he has published an interesting introduction to a recent translation of *Deborah* (first published in Yiddish as *Der Szejdym Tanc*, 1936), an autobiographical novel written by Esther Singer Kreitman, the Singer brothers' sister. Sinclair is particularly fascinated by the literary impact of Hasidism, and in his work on the Singer brothers this preoccupation is clearly evident.

The Brothers Singer, stresses Sinclair, "is a book about literary relationships." The work is thus not a careful investigation of the intertwined biographies of Isaac Bashevis Singer and his elder brother, Israel Joshua. To obtain clear familial chronologies, key facts about the two men's lives in Poland and the United States, a sense of their circles of friends and relations—one must search elsewhere. Sinclair's first chapter, "Fathers and Sons," does provide useful background material, but even here his determination to maintain a literary focus is evident. The Singer family's odyssey from the 1890's through the 1930's is viewed through the lens of the various autobiographical works later produced by Esther, Joshua, and Bashevis. In many cases, these works are infused with a fictive literary intentionality that makes them difficult sources. Sinclair copes with this problem mainly by attending to the inner dramas of the family's life; the year-by-year sequence of outer events is rendered impressionistically, if at all.

One can, however, piece together the general picture: a Hasidic rabbi father, impractical and creative; a strong, skeptical, fretful mother; before World War I, life lived in Russian-governed Polish villages; in the interwar period, Warsaw, literary careers, the coming of Fascism, emigration to the United States. Joshua was born in 1893, Bashevis in 1904. Besides Esther, the eldest, there was also young Moshe, who starved to death during World War II. (While Sinclair has much to say about Esther, he devotes exactly two sentences to Moshe.) Conscripted into the Russian army, Joshua eventually deserted, hid out in Warsaw, and then, in order to see the Revolution at close proximity, lived for a time in Kiev. By the mid-1920's, he was a rising literary figure in Warsaw. As coeditor of a journal, he supplied the young Bashevis with a proofreading job, "thereby rescuing him from the 'half-bog, half-village' in Galicia" where their father was rabbi. On the strength of a volume of short stories, Joshua became the Polish correspondent of *Der Forverts*, (*Jewish Daily Forward*), the largest Yiddish newspaper in the United States. Sent on assignment to the Soviet Union in 1926, Joshua developed a distinct hostility to the Soviet experiment. His subsequent series of political novels were searching criticisms of various movements of political salvation by a skeptical, self-consciously Jewish leftist intellectual. Joshua's death in 1944, after five major novels, ended prematurely a career which had inspired and then nourished that of the brilliant younger brother.

Sinclair's foremost concern in *The Brothers Singer* is to detail the divergent responses of the two brothers to the problem of the Enlightenment. Basically, this was a complex structure of ideas and attitudes: the scientific method, rational skepticism, the progressive nature of historical development, evolution through natural selection, materialistic modes of explanation, Deism, political Liberalism, and natural rights. Nevertheless, for Central European Jews, the Enlightenment always meant something more than mere ideas. Embodied as Napoleon's armies, the Enlightenment led to the razing of ghetto walls, the possibility of citizenship and assimilation, the reign of toleration, the promise of wealth. As such, it was Janus-faced. Rationalism threatened the revealed authority of the Pentateuch and the Talmud. Evolutionism undermined the presiding immanence of a sovereign God. Assimilation and citizenship attacked the organic unity of the chosen people. Skepticism played havoc with pious worship.

In the Singer household, the conflict between Enlightenment and tradition was embodied with an astonishing purity in the relationship of Bathsheba and her Hasidic husband, Pinchas Mendel—she, the unlettered rational pragmatist; he, the perfervid celebrator of an omnipresent God. In the Hasidic culture of the Pole, dybbuks, demonic possession, shamanistic healing, numerology, messianic expectation, sympathetic magic, and the transmigration of souls dominated ordinary consciousness. While Bathsheba moved warily, Pinchas embraced the totality of this "medieval" culture. For his part, Joshua forsook rabbinical studies, cultivated the cosmopolitan life-style, and sought in political struggle a more just, less superstitious world. Bashevis, as is well-known, has dwelt ambiguously and richly in the tension between skepticism and mysticism, resolving it (only when absolutely necessary) in favor of the mystical and the godly.

Sinclair ponders the brothers' common encounter with the antinomy of rationalism and pietism by comparing Joshua's major novels with key works from Bashevis' enormous canon. Thus, in chapter 2, "Reputations," Sinclair studies Joshua's *Sztol un Ajzn* (1927; *Steel and Iron*, 1969) and *Yoshe Kalb* (1933; originally published as *The Sinner*) in relation to Bashevis' *Shoten an Goray* (1935; *Satan in Goray*, 1955). The first of these was a considerable failure. Partially autobiographical, *Steel and Iron* traced the process of political disillusionment of one Benjamin Lerner, a Jewish deserter from the Czarist army who experiences a Warsaw brutally dominated by German occupation forces. The work is political in that it focuses on Lerner's attempts to rally working-class Jews to revolt against their condition. In the process, he must come to terms with his own essential misanthropy and classism. At the same time, he learns to distrust those with grandiose schemes of social salvation, especially the Bolsheviks. Sinclair agrees with the early critics of the book: "It failed in the mismatch between its episodic structure and epic traditions." More fundamentally, argues Sinclair, the novel's failure resulted from the nature of its protagonist: Lerner is a skeptic, and Joshua was to learn from Bashevis that the skeptic furnishes poor material for the fictionalist.

Joshua's second novel, *Yoshe Kalb*, enjoyed a completely different reception. In writing it, Joshua drew upon one of his father's favorite tales—thereby tacitly acknowledging the power of the Hasidic folk tradition which he pretended to despise. The protagonist, himself a rabbi's son, is seduced away from his bride by the libidinous fourth wife of Rabbi Melech. Though he occupies high office and is held to be a zaddik, or charismatic rabbi, Melech is crude and corrupt. The novel's events work toward his exposure and ruin. The victim of the seduction, Melech's own son-in-law, Nahum, exiles himself to a distant village where he constructs a new identity as the fool, Yoshe Kalb. Eventually he runs afoul of another group of superstitious rabbis, is forced into another arranged marriage, and flees to his former residence. There, Yoshe Kalb's foolishness is interpreted as saintliness. When he is finally accused of maintaining a double identity, a trail ensues which results in the downfall of Rabbi Melech's empire.

Its examination of female sexual passion, its attack on custom (especially that of arranged marriages), and its anti-Hasidic stance made *Yoshe Kalb* a popular and controversial work. The Yiddish Art Theatre of New York performed a dramatic version of the novel in 1932, and Joshua's career was rejuvenated. Bashevis was delighted with his brother's success, though the younger Singer's first novel, *Satan in Goray*, revealed a wholly different approach to the same folkloric materials. With themes of demonic possession, messianic expectation, sectarian bickering, asceticism, and sexual license, Bashevis implicitly sets the mystic, imaginatively expansive world of the shtetl against that of reductionist industrial modernity. The younger brother thus becomes a romantic champion of the Hasidic way; at the same time, he appreciates the traditional rationalism of the *misnagid* strain of Jewish sensibility. As Sinclair notes, the novel resonates with "the conflict between the Talmud, which teaches by reason and example, and the Cabala, which seeks knowledge through intuition and poetic imagery." Bashevis has said that had his brother lived longer, he might have come to see better the values of both sides of this conflict.

In succeeding chapters, Sinclair studies the divergent literary responses of the brothers to these tensions. Joshua's *The Brothers Ashkenazi* (1936) is paired with Bashevis' *The Manor* (1967; serialized in Yiddish in 1953-1955). The final chapter, "Politics," links Bashevis' *Di Familie Mushkat* (published in the United States as *The Family Moskat*, 1950) with the elder's *Khaver Nakham* (1938; *East of Eden*, 1939) and *Di Mishpokhe Karnovsky* (1943; *The Family Carnovsky*, 1943). Sinclair hazards no final conclusion about this fruitful literary relationship, though he clearly regards Bashevis as the more gifted writer. The Nobel Prize-winner has said, "Certainly, if my brother would have lived another twenty or thirty years, which he should have, he would have developed more and more, and he would have published stunning books— I'm absolutely convinced of that." Adds Sinclair, "It was left to Bashevis himself to fulfill this prophecy."

Of Sinclair's achievement in *The Brothers Singer*, one must judge it to be modest. The work suffers from a series of uncertainties and imprecisions. Sinclair did not decide on what sort of audience he wished to address. He most certainly is not addressing literary scholars, for there are impermissible instances of carelessness and omission. His bibliography does not include vital publication information about the Yiddish versions of the Singers' works. Sinclair alludes to Joshua's early collection of short stories but neither treats it in the text nor mentions it in the bibliography. More significantly, he neglects major works by Bashevis that bear the striking impact of Joshua's life and works—for example, the novel *Shosha* (1978), whose protagonist seems closely modeled on the elder brother.

Sinclair's book is equally ill-suited, however, to the needs of a wider, more popular audience. His failure to work in key biographical details about the two writers robs the book of tension and excitement. One learns almost nothing substantial about Joshua's American years—about his wife, his children, his friends, his premature death. Further, Sinclair has a perverse addiction to digression and drift. No clear theses overarch the chapters; no headings relieve and clarify the flow of text. The book's introduction provides only the barest clue as to the plan and strategy of the effort. Singer fans will probably lay the book quickly aside.

Finally, *The Brothers Singer* seems to proceed from the sexist assumption that only the male members of the family are worth concentrated attention. Sinclair makes much of his discovery of Esther Singer's literary vocation, yet he uses her only for the light she sheds on the brothers' artistic careers. His bibliography lists three novels by Esther, but only *Deborah* receives careful treatment. Why should not his "discovery" be trumpeted? Why should a chapter entitled "Fathers and Sons" contain mostly material from the daughter? It seems all too obvious that Sinclair needed to write *The Brothers Singer* in order to do justice to what was, in fact, a triangular literary relationship.

Leslie E. Gerber

Sources for Further Study

Choice. XXI, December, 1983, p. 581.
Commentary. LXXVII, February, 1984, p. 75.
Contemporary Review. CCXLIII, July, 1983, p. 52.
Esquire. CI, February, 1984, p. 96.
Los Angeles Times Book Review. September 11, 1983, p. 4.
New Statesman. CV, May 13, 1983, p. 28.
Time. CXXI, October 17, 1983, p. 95.

CAL

Author: Bernard MacLaverty (1942-   )
Publisher: George Braziller (New York). 170 pp. $12.95
Type of work: Novel
Time: The 1980's
Locale: A suburb of Belfast, Northern Ireland

A novel about the tragic guilt a nineteen-year-old Irish Catholic youth experiences after he helps to kill a reserve loyalist police officer

> *Principal characters:*
> CAL MCCRYSTAL, a nineteen-year-old Irish Catholic
> SHAMIE, his father
> CRILLY, a youthful, criminal IRA supporter
> SKEFFINGTON, Crilly's and Cal's friend
> MARCELLA, the woman with whom Cal falls in love

Obsession and guilt are the two forces that clash head-on in Bernard MacLaverty's second novel, *Cal*. His characters, many of whom have been stripped of their humanity, exemplify the human tragedy of Ireland's violent history. In *Cal*, MacLaverty continues to explore the subjects of loneliness, sin, freedom, and responsibility that preoccupied him in his critically acclaimed first novel, *Lamb* (1980) and his short-story collections *Secrets and Other Stories* (1977) and *A Time to Dance and Other Stories* (1982). Conflicts between sin and forgiveness, loyalty and betrayal, crime and punishment, violence and justice, maturity and responsibility permeate his works. In *Cal*, MacLaverty takes a particular family, and through them depicts the real victims of Ireland's struggle.

Cal, nineteen years old and unemployed, lives at home with his father; they are the only Catholics in a Protestant neighborhood. As the novel begins, Cal is besieged by guilt for helping in a murder and obsessed with desire for the woman he helped to make a widow. Guilt and desire combine to make Cal a psychological cripple. As his character unfolds in flashbacks, it is clear that he is a passive, sensitive youth, easily intimidated and manipulated by others. Although he is railroaded into rallying behind the Irish Republican Army (IRA), he cannot understand the hatred between Irish Catholics and Protestants. "It was the idea of people whose faces he did not know hating him that made his skin crawl," the omniscient narrator observes. "To be hated not for yourself but for what you were": this Cal cannot comprehend. Because he is easily manipulated, Cal is vulnerable to the likes of Crilly and Skeffington, two IRA supporters who enlist his aid. The consequences of his passive behavior are enormous and tragic. Overwhelmed by Skeffington's cold, cruel reasoning and intimidated by Crilly, a street thug, Cal agrees to assist in armed robberies to gain money for the IRA. Initially wavering, Cal finally succumbs to Skeffington's logic: "think of the issues, not the people." To Skeffington, who believes that sacrifices must be made for the movement, death and human suffering mean nothing. "The problem with this kind of thing," he lectures Cal, "is that people get hurt. But compared with conventional war the numbers are small." Initially, Cal's capitulation requires him only to drive the getaway car for several burglaries, but ultimately it means driving the getaway car for a murder. In one terrible moment of weakness, Cal sacrifices a human life for the sake of the issues.

The novel begins a year after the murder, with Cal trying to fill his empty days by strumming his guitar, going to the library, cooking for his working father, Shamie, fearing the Irish Protestant threats, and attempting to rid himself of guilt. Conflicts converge on him from all sides. His environment, an all-Protestant suburb of Belfast where hatred and violence are a way of life, poses daily threats. Both his friends and enemies intimidate him. Skeffington and Crilly threaten reprisal if he fails to assist in IRA-backed crimes, while Protestant youths threaten to firebomb his home. Finally, his psychological torment over killing reserve police officer Robert Morton gradually destroys his mental stability. To make matters worse, Cal is unemployed, providing more time for guilt to fester. Even his unemployment is a consequence of his guilt. He has quit his job at the abattoir where his father works because he does not have a "strong enough stomach." In short, he cannot stand the sight of blood pouring from the slaughtered beasts. This repulsion emerges as the first hint of guilt that continues to plague him throughout the novel. The blood as well as the "tumble of purple and green and grey steaming innards" falling to the ground "from the raised carcase" makes Cal sick. In contrast, Crilly, the thug who meticulously planned and executed the murder, has no trouble working at the abattoir and thus takes Cal's job.

Cal's guilt keeps him mentally imprisoned even though he is physically free. Images and dreams haunt him—above all the image of Robert Morton "genuflecting" as he called out to his wife, Marcella, after the first of three bullets tore through his skull at point-blank range.

Cal, whose name has obvious Catholic connotations, continues to attend Mass but not confession; "the thing he had done was now a background to his life, permanently there, like the hiss that echoed from the event which began the Universe." During one particular Mass, a priest's sermon suggests to Cal that he must experience pain to achieve forgiveness. The priest tells the story of Matt Talbot, a drunken derelict for ten years, who sought atonement for his decade of debauchery by wearing a chain around his waist so tight that it grew into his flesh. The sermon, like the recurring image of Robert Morton "genuflecting" as he falls from Crilly's bullets, haunts Cal. Physical pain Cal has not yet experienced; psychological pain is his constant companion.

On one of Cal's frequent trips to the library to borrow musical tapes, he sees a new librarian to whom he becomes attached before he learns her name: Marcella Morton. Although he realizes that she is the wife of the man he helped to murder, he becomes obsessed with her; he "couldn't get close enough to her." Constantly he feels the "enormous pull of her," but he knows that "because of what he had done, they would never come together."

In time, Cal discovers ways to do small favors for Marcella. He wants to get closer to her even though his guilt-ridden conscience tells him to stay away. This split is clearly imaged in a scene in which Cal is splitting wood for the Mortons. He says, as Marcella watches him, "Give me a big enough wedge and I'll split the world." His world, unfortunately, is split. He loves Marcella, "the one woman in the world who was forbidden him," but he hates what he has done to her and knows that "by his action he had outlawed himself from her. She was an unattainable idea because he had helped kill her husband." Just as Ireland is split between the Protestants and Catholics in a seemingly never-ending tragic struggle, so Cal is split, and his split widens after he is hired on at the Morton farm.

When the Protestant youths who have threatened to set his house ablaze make good their threat, Cal moves into a dilapidated farmhouse with no running water and no plumbing. This move provides an escape from the clutches of Crilly and Skeffington and the violence of Ulster; Cal is sure that the two IRA supporters will "never guess where he is." The move also brings him closer to Marcella; he becomes increasingly obsessed with his effort to "right the wrong he has done her." Starved for human affection and companionship, alienated from people, Marcella begins to reciprocate Cal's interest, and when her in-laws leave for a week, she and Cal become lovers. As their love develops, however, Cal's guilt intensifies.

Although Cal believes that he is safe from Crilly and Skeffington when he is on the farm, he fears encountering them while visiting his father. He knows that his disappearance and refusal to help them in the movement will be interpreted as betrayal, and betrayal in their minds demands reprisal. Finally, on a trip to the library, the inevitable happens. Cal meets Crilly, who is setting a bomb in one of the books, and Crilly insists that Cal come with him to talk with Skeffington. Although Cal initially refuses, Crilly's domineering attitude wears him down. He goes with Crilly to meet Skeffington, and the three of them are talking about loyalty and betrayal when the police knock on the door. Cal escapes, while Crilly and Skeffington are apprehended. Fleeing the area, Cal fulfills Skeffington's prophecy, anonymously notifying the police of the bomb in the library and thus becoming an informer.

After his traitorous phone call, Cal walks back to the farmhouse and Marcella. He realizes as they make love that only if he confesses can their relationship develop, but he cannot bring himself to confess, and so they never "truly come together." The next morning, Christmas Eve, Cal awaits arrest; in fact, he welcomes it. He is grateful "that at last someone was going to beat him within an inch of his life," for he believes, as Matt Talbot did, that he must pay for his sins with suffering.

Cal develops from a static character who capitulates to the pressure of his Catholic friends to a dynamic character who suffers for the murder in which he has allowed himself to become involved. His escape from the violence of Ulster and from Crilly and Skeffington does not reduce his guilt. Seemingly safe in the Morton tenant house, Cal is still haunted. As MacLaverty's omniscient narrator reveals: "Now that he felt safe from the world outside he was being attacked from within his own head." In confronting guilt, Cal ultimately recognizes that he must accept the consequences of his actions: He must lose his freedom to truly gain it. Cal's tragedy, like that of many Irish Catholic and Protestant youths, is that in his innocence he is easily persuaded to support and assist the IRA, just as the Protestant youths who beat him have been convinced to support their cause. Like others before him, Cal succumbs to peer pressure and forfeits his humanity. By capitulating, he takes a life and ruins his own. The destruction of his life is symbolic of the destruction of so many Irish Catholic and Protestant lives. Like all who support a cause through violence, Cal must suffer the consequences of his action, and those consequences are costly and tragic. The dream of driving a car that he cannot control, one dream among the many that plague him, is symbolic of his uncontrolled world, of the uncontrolled world which Ireland has become.

Crilly represents the violent members of society who serve misguided leaders. Skeffington uses him only when crime serves his purposes. A bully during his school years, Crilly remains a bully as an adult. In his mind, murder is acceptable "to win the war," to justify the Irish Catholic cause. He and Cal represent two opposing Catholic forces in Ireland: one seeking resolution of national and religious conflicts via peaceful means and the other via violence. Even Skeffington recognizes Crilly's vengeful character, but he sees Crilly as a "useful man" who you send for "if you have a war on your hands."

Skeffington, Crilly's sidekick, is the cold, calculating rationalist who intellectualizes the issues, the causes, and the movement, winning over others with his logic. Oppressed people, according to Skeffington's philosophy, have a "right to insurrectional violence. . . . There are no rules just eventual winners."

In contrast to Crilly and Skeffington is Shamie, Cal's widowed father, who lives in a world of illusions created from an overdose of Western movies. He begins to believe in the romanticized ideal depicted in those movies, where right always wins, where justice is always served. When Shamie and Cal receive a bomb threat from Protestants, Shamie accepts a gun from Crilly under the misguided belief that, like the cowboys, "he had right on his side and it was the baddies who would die." Unfortunately, the Irish struggle is not that simplistic. When Shamie's and Cal's home is firebombed, no one is apprehended, and Shamie's vision of right conquering wrong is shattered. He cannot cope with the loss of his illusions, and he suffers severe depression that soon becomes physically debilitating as well, resulting in his hospitalization.

Ireland's struggle victimizes Marcella, too. Like Cal, she is alienated from family and friends; they both seek the warmth of human affection which they have been denied. Cal's mother, whose name still brings "a lump to his throat," died when he was eight. Deprived of motherly love after her death, Cal "gave himself love-bites, sucking until he tasted the coppery blood coming through his skin." Marcella, who is from Portstewart and is of Italian descent, lost her husband to Ireland's violence, but long before his death, she lost her love and respect for him. As she tells Cal, "He was one of those people whose company you love for an hour or so, but you're glad you're not married to them." She is the object of Cal's desire but a thorn in his conscience; her warmth and innocence intensify his psychological turmoil.

In this, MacLaverty's second novel, his characters represent the middle-class working people of Ireland, the true victims of Ireland's violence. Cal symbolizes the psychological devastation of his people: He can only gain freedom by losing it; he can only atone for sin through suffering. MacLaverty's vision is clearly nonpartisan. He depicts the hopelessness of the Irish struggle in sharp and tragic detail.

Janet H. Hobbs

Sources for Further Study

Contemporary Review. CCXLII, April, 1983, p. 213.
Hudson Review. XXXVI, Winter, 1983, p. 750.
Library Journal. CVIII, June 15, 1983, p. 1275.
Los Angeles Times Book Review. August 21, 1983, p. 1.
The New Republic. CLXXXIX, September 19, 1983, p. 30.
New Statesman. CV, January 14, 1983, p. 26.
The New York Times Book Review. LXXXVIII, August 21, 1983, p. 1.
The New Yorker. LIX, October 24, 1983, p. 162.
Newsweek. CII, September 5, 1983, p. 68.
Publishers Weekly. CCXXIII, June 17, 1983, p. 62.

THE CANNIBAL GALAXY

Author: Cynthia Ozick (1928-   )
Publisher: Alfred A. Knopf (New York). 162 pp. $11.95
Type of work: Novel
Time: The early twentieth century to the 1980's
Locale: France, principally Paris, and the United States

A dense, allusive, stylistically complex allegory of modern Jewish history

> *Principal characters:*
> JOSEPH BRILL, a French Jew who survives the Holocaust and who,
> as the principal of a private school, brings a fusion of Jewish and
> European culture to the United States
> HESTER LILT, a scholar of modest accomplishment whose indepen-
> dence and abilities Brill recognizes as a reflection of himself as
> he might have been and might yet be
> BEULAH LILT, Hester's daughter, who absorbs nothing from Brill's
> educational system but blossoms into an accomplished, original,
> and world-famous artist
> IRIS GARSON, the school secretary, and wife of Joseph Brill
> NAPHTALI, the son of Joseph Brill, in whom Brill places high hopes

This latest achievement by Cynthia Ozick is another spellbinding, virtuoso performance, confirming her reputation as one of America's most brilliant writers. Ozick's craft is a national treasure. Her themes are of the highest importance. Her audience, however, will no doubt remain limited for a number of reasons. She is a fine literary writer in a culture in which higher literacy is quickly vanishing, the enjoyment of Ozick's work—its intricacy, its polish, its inherited and transformed traditions—is available to fewer and fewer readers. Perhaps more important, her settings, characters, and situations embrace a restricted milieu. Readers needing obvious mirrors of themselves or conventional escape worlds will struggle with Ozick's rarefied intellects, sophisticated immigrants, and devotees or transmitters of a Judaica nourished in ghettos. The clash of the Old World and the New in *The Cannibal Galaxy* is powerfully and wisely told, but its terms are very special; some of them already need footnotes.

Joseph Brill, the central character in this novel, is defined as a man caught, or stuck, in the middle. A man in middle age risen to middle heights of success (far less than could have been imagined for him), he is the architect and chief proponent of an eccentric educational curriculum that attempts to blend the two old worlds of his experience: Orthodox Jewish learning and tradition on the one hand, the noble achievements of European civilization on the other. That is, he would stabilize for the youth of the New World that volatile mixture whose explosion in the Holocaust Brill barely escaped. As the principal of a private primary school located right in the middle of the United States, he oversees the workings of his ideal compromise without ever seeing it as the paradox that it really is. His curriculum defines another kind of middle—a norm—but Brill himself sees it as something very special, something transcendent. It is his hope for a personal contribution of the highest order. How did Joseph Brill come to his sense of a special destiny?

Extended flashbacks begin to answer that question. Reared in the Jewish quarter of Paris, a prodigy in his Jewish learning under the revered Rabbi Pult, the young Brill slowly falls under the influence of the expressive non-Jewish culture that surrounds his tradition-bound, closed world. A maverick, he lingers at the monuments and museums of Paris, risking a contamination that could affect his Judaic studies. Particularly fascinating to him is the Musée Carnavalet, which contains the apartment of the legendary Madame de Sévigné, the molder of French literature whose "unreasonable passion for her undistinguished daughter had turned the mother's prose into high culture and historic treasure." Brill is awed by the richness of this culture, so different from his explorations into Torah and Talmud.

Brill pursues studies in literature and history at the Sorbonne, finding himself increasingly at home outside the Jewish community. His new friend, Claude, is his guide to Gentile culture, especially the latest fashions in European art and society. Brill trims his Jewish accent only to be wounded by the discovery of his friend's homosexuality. Avoiding Claude, Brill finds himself labeled "Dreyfus"; he begins to mistrust the enlightened Europe shaped by great men who, like Voltaire, were anti-Semites. Ozick writes: "He was sick of human adventure. He had felt an unknowable warmth and feared it. It had betrayed him and named him Dreyfus." Brill changes his course of study to astronomy, turning his attention from the deeds and expression of men to the passionless stars.

Suddenly, the Nazis are overrunning Paris. Brill, in attempting to find his old mentor, Rabbi Pult, finds instead a broken door, packed suitcases, and a pile of burned books. He grabs a briefcase containing Rabbi Pult's Venetian *Ta'anit* and, reeling with fear, tries to save himself. Although he loses his parents and five of his siblings in the Nazi death camps, his three older sisters manage to survive. Brill himself is taken in by nuns, who hide him in the cellar of a convent school. Here, he undergoes a kind of rebirth, emerging with a clear sense of mission. During this period of confinement, he finds a shadowy double, a figure from the past who helps him to articulate who he is and what he must do.

The nuns who shelter Brill have been charged with sorting out the library of an eccentric priest, and Brill volunteers to help. Among the volumes, he discovers a strange book by one Edmond Fleg entitled *Jésus, raconté par le Juif Errant*. "And who was Edmond Fleg?" Brill wonders. Fascinated, he searches for more books by this mysterious figure, finding volumes of plays, a cycle in verse, a long essay on Palestine, a metaphysical autobiography—

heavily annotated by the priest. From the idiosyncratic works of Fleg (né Flegenheimer), Brill takes a vision of a grand synthesis of Christian and Jewish traditions. Indeed, the priest's marginal notes in the various volumes point to a similar understanding of Fleg's work: "The Israelitish divinely unifying impulse and the Israelitish ethical inspiration are the foundations of our French genius. Edmond Fleg brings together all of his visions and sacrifices none. He harmonizes the rosette of the Légion d'Honneur in his lapel with the frontlets of the Covenant on his brow." Thus, in the wildest of ironic situations, Brill, tutored by the strange tastes and jottings of a dead priest and the harmonizing efforts of a Jewish Parisian playwright, emerges from the convent cellar with an ideal curriculum blooming in his mind. Ozick leaves nothing to mere logic but constantly invents portents for Brill and the reader. Here, the operative one is the virtually exact resemblance between the dark-green, leather binding of the old priest's volume of Pierre Corneille and that of Rabbi Pult's *Ta'anit*—the two cultures strangely twinned.

Discovered by one of the convent schoolgirls, Brill is relocated to a farm outside of Paris, where he spends the remainder of the war, sleeping in a hayloft and doing menial chores around the barn. Here, he is treated less kindly, and his human difference from the lower orders of creation is reduced even further than it was in the convent cellar. Brill's trials prepare him to emerge as some sort of hero, but the terms of his heroism are ambiguous.

Ozick has her hero discovered by a "rich benefactress" (that is what Ozick calls her, with depersonalizing irony, again and again) while he is working as a Hebrew teacher in a poor Milwaukee synagogue. Somehow, this nouveau riche Russian immigrant has heard of Brill's ideas. She is incapable of grasping them, but what matters to her is the cachet of European culture, and she underwrites a school based on Brill's curriculum: "Chumash, Gemara, Social Studies, French: the waters of Shiloh springing from the head of Western Civilization!" The Edmond Fleg Primary School is a success; that is, there are always enough students. Through years of warfare with parents and occasional skirmishes with teachers, Brill maintains his authority—and his curriculum. During her lifetime, his benefactress is loyal to Brill. The only problem is that, year after year, the school produces another crop of mediocre students. Worshiping this idol of his own making, Brill fights despair, but he is beginning to lose the fight.

Then, magically, Hester Lilt enters Brill's life. Hester, an abstruse philosopher with a formidable academic reputation and a mysterious European background, reawakens Brill's longings for a life of exceptional purpose and accomplishment. In part, this is the result of his desire to impress her; he thinks he has found a kindred soul—another exiled intellectual. Even more exciting, however, is Hester's desire to enroll her daughter, Beulah, in the Edmond Fleg School. Brill is convinced that the child of such a mother, nourished by the dual curriculum, will redeem his system and his life. When

Beulah fails the standard entrance tests, Brill admits her anyway. After all, the tests have only dealt with common clay in the past.

Brill tries to develop a relationship with Hester, but his progress is slow and faltering. He notices that she does not exhibit typical maternal mannerisms. He is perplexed by this, but all the ways in which Hester Lilt is different add to the mystery that attracts him. As the years go by, Beulah remains retiring and apparently slow, an abject follower. Brill tries many strategies to awaken her dormant genius, but nothing works. Frustrated by a dashed last hope, he imagines that Hester is either blind to Beulah's shortcomings or undergoing tremendous suffering because of them. When he discovers that Hester is in fact a loving mother, he imagines her another Madame de Sévigné, pouring her heart into her work. After Beulah graduates (the school runs up to the eighth grade), the Lilts move back to Europe.

When it becomes clear that the great opportunity for his system has been missed, Brill makes a reluctant peace with normality. To the surprise of many, he takes as the wife of his advancing years Iris Garson, the school secretary, an attractive younger woman with a son by a previous marriage. Brill gives his stepson special opportunities for enrichment, but the young man, like Beulah, disappoints him. His last hope is his own son by Iris, Naphtali, who like his father begins as a prodigy but seems destined to leave that early promise unfulfilled.

With a grim and grinning irony, Ozick gives her fable its final twist: Beulah Lilt develops into an original artist of world renown. None of her talents had been detected or fed by Brill's system. She had genius after all, but of her own kind. To face this truth is one of the final punishments for Brill's idolatry and pride.

It is not Ozick's plot, however, that gives her novel its appeal. In fact, the plot may be one of the novel's weaknesses; many of Ozick's decisions about how to balance summary with detailed narration seem questionable. The balance that is struck does not allow the world she is creating to maintain its credibility. Too often, these decisions are so obviously made for deepening thematic implications that the fun of getting lost in the novelist's imaginings of place, character, and event is lessened. The novel spans most of its protagonist's long life; the reader comes away with the feeling that there is enough Joseph Brill to make a rich short story but not enough to fill a novel.

The Cannibal Galaxy lives in its style. Ozick's genius for metaphorical invention and for linguistic virtuosity that stays, usually, on the right side of tact, gives her work its special power. This is a magnificent achievement, but one that will appeal to an elite readership whose reading pleasure can rest on appreciation of stylistic command. This command includes not only dazzling figures of speech but also every subtlety of diction, syntax, rhythm, and rhetoric. Again, it is difficult to devise a novel-length fiction so dependent on these interests. The excellence that Ozick has achieved in shorter forms escapes her here; her distinctive strengths as a writer handicap her chances for ultimate success in the novel form.

This is not to say that *The Cannibal Galaxy* is to be valued lightly. A writer with Ozick's vision, dedication to craft, and mastery of her subject is always worth attention. This novel is a very good one, and it is only by the standard of the author's achievement in the short story that it seems lacking. It is a novel with missing dimensions, or a fable gone on too long and stretched too thin.

After all, it is a fable. Brill's idolatry and his pride are made real, understandable, almost inevitable—and then, through a series of exposures, Brill and the reader are made to face humiliation. This is a version of the Pygmalion myth with Brill creating a system in his own image, a dual curriculum from his divided self. His dedication to the system is a form of self-love gone beyond healthy bounds, and his hopes for Beulah Lilt are vain in every sense of the word. Brill's vision, like everyone's, has been rooted in his experience. When, in retirement, he receives word that the school's name and character are being changed, that the old curriculum is no longer relevant, the question arises if it ever was. Certainly Beulah never needed it; it made no impression on her, yet she was the genius whom Brill yearned for to validate his life.

As a fabulist, Ozick is at pains to develop parallels within the story that underscore her meanings. Thus, Brill's exile in the hayloft is followed by a career in which his principal's quarters are in a converted hayloft. The fact of his isolation, whether in a state of helplessness or power, is thus reinforced. Ozick develops parallels to strands of myth outside of her story as well. In Joseph Brill's name and actions, there are allusions to Joseph of the Old Testament—a man of vision who escapes from bondage and rises to influence in a strange land. There are some hints, too, that Joseph of the New Testament is on Ozick's mind. In Hester Lilt's name, there may be echoes of the biblical Esther as well as of Lilith, an ungovernable, demonic female force. Hester is also a pariah, and thus reminiscent of Hester Prynne in Nathaniel Hawthorne's *The Scarlet Letter* (1850). The sounds of "Brill" and "Lilt" provocatively link and separate the characters so named, while "Beulah" suggests the promised land.

Beyond these rich trappings lies the possibility that Ozick's narrative is an allegory of modern Jewish history, a history understood as part of a cyclical pattern. In the novel, Brill's school is presented as a unique and isolated institution, an experiment in the middle of nowhere, but the dual curriculum is only a somewhat rarefied version of a familiar type of establishment—the Jewish day school—that has flourished in America since World War II. In part, the proliferation of such schools at the expense of synagogue-connected institutions has been a reaction to the Holocaust experience; in part, it has been a consequence of demographic changes in the Jewish population. In such schools, as in Brill's school, religious faith and fervor are rare; Judaism is a cultural heritage, a body of learning, an enormous conduct book.

The novel's metaphorical title—a cannibal galaxy devours smaller galaxies, as Gentile culture threatens to devour Judaism—suggests that Ozick must be aware of these parallels, and that her ultimate subject is assimilation. She may be defining the Judaism of survivors such as Brill as a godless Judaism, a shriveled, petty, rationalized thing; and she may be questioning the authority of this remnant to establish the terms of Judaism's survival. Ozick has full sympathy for what her character has suffered, full awareness of the colossal tragedy that Nazism was allowed to perpetrate—but still there is this daring, searing question: If the survivor's God is dead, how can his vision be whole?

Philip K. Jason

Sources for Further Study

Christian Science Monitor. November 4, 1983, p. B4.
Library Journal. CVIII, August, 1983, p. 1504.
Los Angeles Times Book Review. September 18, 1983, p. 1.
Ms. XII, December, 1983, p. 38.
The New York Review of Books. XXX, November 10, 1983, p. 27.
The New York Times Book Review. LXXXVIII, September 11, 1983, p. 3.
Newsweek. CII, September 12, 1983, p. 76.
Publishers Weekly. CCXXIV, July 8, 1983, p. 58.
Time. CXXII, September 5, 1983, p. 64.

CATHEDRAL

Author: Raymond Carver (1938-   )
Publisher: Alfred A. Knopf (New York). 228 pp. $13.95
Type of work: Short stories
Time: The 1970's and early 1980's
Locale: Various, usually unidentified locations around the United States

In these twelve disquieting stories, the characters struggle with the pain they feel over the intensely personal losses they have suffered, at times transcending their pain and bewilderment in a Chekhov-like moment of understanding

Raymond Carver's decision to dedicate *Cathedral* to the memory of John Gardner, from whom Carver took a writing course in the fall of 1958, may seem rather odd to many readers. Gardner's expansive stories and novels sprawl across page after page as the author seeks to affirm the eternal verities of moral fiction. Carver's fiction is written in an entirely different mode: concise, elliptical, and tightly controlled, suggestive rather than (as with Gardner) exhaustive. This style, which several reviewers have inaccurately termed minimalist, is as clipped as Ernest Hemingway's and as incisive and emotionally detached as Joan Didion's. Nevertheless, Carver and Gardner do resemble each other in one most important way: their shared commitment to "values and craft," as Carver phrases it in his foreword to Gardner's *On Becoming a Novelist* (1982).

Since the publication of his first collection of stories in 1977, *Will You Please Be Quiet, Please?*, Carver's distinctive prose style and commitment to the craft of fiction have provoked widely divergent critical judgments. Although his work has been richly and deservedly praised—his first collection was nominated for a National Book Award, while his second, *What We Talk About When We Talk About Love* (1981), helped Carver win the prestigious Mildred and Harold Straus Living Award—the two books (comprising thirty-nine at times *very* short stories) have led a few reviewers to question whether Carver's style and "terrifying vision of ordinary human life in our country" (as Leonard Michaels once described it) has hardened into fashionable despair and mere literary affectation. The criticism is understandable but by no means merited, especially now that *Cathedral* has appeared, a work which, even as it recalls the earlier stories, marks a distinct advance in both the author's vision and his narrative aesthetic.

Before discussing this advance, it is necessary to establish the chief object of Carver's concern, the lives of his characters. These characters are not, as one reviewer has complained, "morbid caricatures"; rather, they are only as monotonous and monochromatic as the featureless, middle-class or lower-middle-class America in which they live—a world, incidentally, that Carver has progressively stripped of particular geographical details in order to focus better and more intensively on the internal lives of his characters. Carver does for his segment of the contemporary American population what Didion has done for her more affluent characters; he has portrayed a world in which the individual has been stripped of all the usual forms of support—family, religion, politics, economic security, shared culture, and so forth. Radically cut off from what once served to preserve and sustain human life, his characters necessarily fall back on themselves and their own meager resources. One dreams of living "in an old house surrounded by a wall"; another believes that she and her husband will thrive within the self-contained world of their marriage, but then the husband-narrator unintentionally makes clear how impoverished their lives actually are: "Some nights we went to a movie. Other nights we just stayed in and watched TV. Sometimes Fran baked things for me and we'd eat whatever it was all in a sitting." Here is a quiet desperation such as Henry David Thoreau never could have imagined. For these people, transcendence seems less a problem than an impossibility. The simple, seemingly trivial ways in which their uncertainty manifests itself—what, for example, to bring one's nominal friends when invited to dinner at their house— suggests a deeper dis-ease. They begin to discover the drab truth of certain clichés—time is what passes you by, dreams "are what you wake up from." What they wake to is a dim perception of the fragility of their lives and of bad situations getting slowly but inexorably worse.

They do not concern themselves with the problems of radioactive waste, the greenhouse effect, or nuclear war; their disasters are not environmental or international but intensely personal. "Without looking, the birthday boy stepped off the curb at an intersection and was immediately knocked down by a car." In another story, J. P. gets everything he wants: marriage, good job, children, house. Then, slowly and inexplicably, he begins drinking, and his life falls apart. These characters come to realize that their seemingly safe domestic lives have transmogrified into minor, even commonplace tragedies in which, as helpless victims, they can at best hope to endure rather than, as William Faulkner had it, prevail. As Carver explained in an interview, "They'd like to set things right, but they can't" and so are left just trying to "do the best they can." Often, the best is not much. In the aptly titled story "Preservation," husband and wife spend a night discussing what he can do now that he has lost his job as a roofer, "but they couldn't think of anything," and so the husband spends the next three months lying on the living-room sofa. The narrator of "Where I'm Calling From" (the "where" refers to a rehabilitation house for alcoholics) adopts a similarly fatalistic view. "I've been here once before. What's to say? I'm back. . . . Part of me wanted help. But there was another part." In turning to alcohol, he is turning away from the pain of a failed marriage and eventually from all potentially painful human relationships. As he says in explaining why he will not call his girlfriend, also an alcoholic, who has recently learned she has vaginal cancer: "I hope she's okay. But if she has something wrong with her, I don't want to know about it." Given such an attitude, the reader usually finds it easier to understand and sympathize with Carver's *isolatos* than to like them.

In rehabilitation houses, furnished rooms, and rented apartments, loneliness stalks these characters, often driving them to acts that only further separate them from others. Wes, for example (in "Chef's House"), rents a house from his friend Chef and, like Carver, makes an apparently successful recovery from alcoholism. In Wes's mind, however, the recovery is mysteriously linked to the rented house, a home of sorts, and when Chef says he needs the house for his daughter, the recovery abruptly ends, leaving Wes and his wife (who left her lover for Wes's sake) homeless and alone. The story's closing lines effectively summarize just how transient their lives are and how precarious is their hold on everyday existence: "Wes got up and pulled the drapes and the ocean was gone just like that. I went in to start supper. We still had some fish in the icebox. There wasn't much else. We'll clean it up tonight, I thought, and that will be the end of it." As the narrator of "The Bridle" says about four different yet similar characters, "These people look whipped." In Carver's fiction, they often do.

The vision is bleak but convincing, the author relentless in his depiction of the darker side of ordinary American life yet compassionate as well, detached but never condescending. Something of a Samuel Beckett of the blue-collar classes, Carver has not until recently mixed his compassion for his characters with an equal measure of hope. It is precisely here that *Cathedral* represents a distinct advance over the previous works, a movement toward what Carver has called a more "generous" fiction that is particularly evident in the collection's two finest pieces, "A Small, Good Thing" and "Cathedral." A much shorter and much less "generous" version of "A Small, Good Thing" appeared under the title "The Bath" in Carver's second collection. In that earlier version, a mother orders a birthday cake for her son, Scotty, who, on the morning of his birthday, is struck by a car and falls into a coma. While in the hospital, the baker (without identifying himself and apparently without any knowledge of the accident) calls the house several times, asking the parents (whichever one happens to be home at the time) if they have forgotten Scotty—meaning the cake, though they immediately—and guiltily—think of their son. Reading the story is a painful experience, especially for the reader who also may be a parent. The longer version, of which "The Bath," slightly but significantly revised, forms the first half, is even more emotionally trying. In the second half of "A Small, Good Thing," Scotty dies, and his stunned parents return home to face both the loss of their only child and the sudden emptiness of their own lives as well. The wife says, "He's gone and now we'll have to get used to that." Before they can even begin to adjust, the phone rings; the wife realizes the caller's identity and demands that her husband drive her to the bakery. The confrontation very nearly turns violent, but then a transformation occurs; the anger turns into grief, the grief into a special kind of understanding. Realizing what he has done, the baker asks for forgiveness and explains that while he is not evil, as the woman has claimed, neither is he entirely human. Lonely and childless, he has somehow lost his humanity, and it is the sense of loss that binds these three people together. "You have to eat and keep going," the baker tells the grieving parents, offering them the rolls and bread he has made. "Eating is a small, good thing in a time like this." In this moment of communion (no other word will do to describe it), the baker regains what he has lost—as do the parents—becoming at once father and son to the childless couple, who, as the story ends, continue to sit at his table and "did not think of leaving."

"Cathedral"—the first to have been written of the twelve stories in the collection—is arguably the best, a tour de force in which Carver seems determined to prove to himself as well as to the reader that in the contemporary wasteland, redemption is still possible, as it clearly was not in most of the author's earlier fictions. As with all of his stories, the plot of "Cathedral" is simple and straightforward. A blind man named Robert visits the narrator and his wife, who worked for Robert some ten years before. The real story occurs not in the events of Robert's visit but in the narrator's changing attitude toward his unwanted guest. The blind man's presence makes the narrator feel self-conscious (as if he, not Robert, were the stranger), even jealous and resentful. Robert, he thinks, may actually know more about his wife than he does. (The wife and the blind man have exchanged tape-recorded "letters" throughout the ten years.) At first, the narrator mentally derides Robert as "spiffy" and "creepy," but gradually he begins to observe the blind man more closely. His scrutiny leads first to understanding and then, as in "A Small, Good Thing," to his sympathetic identification with his guest. Whereas earlier he found Robert's presence "disconcerting," now the narrator is glad to have his company and concerned that Robert may not be able to visualize a cathedral from his description of it on the television screen. The problem stems less from Robert's physiological blindness than from the narrator's spiritual blindness—his self-centeredness and lack of faith in anything or anyone, including himself. He cannot describe a cathedral adequately, even to himself, because cathedrals do not really mean anything to him; nothing does. In the story's remarkable conclusion, Robert asks the narrator to draw a cathedral while the blind man holds his hand. The narrator begins with a simple box that reminds him of his own house and then adds a roof, spires, arches, windows, flying buttresses: "I couldn't stop." Closing his eyes, he continues to draw, and as he draws he loses all of the anxiety, selfishness, and feeling of confinement that characterized him earlier. For the first time, he is free to understand, as the blind man has apparently understood all of his life despite the loss of his sight and of his wife, that "It's really something"—the mystical "it" being purposely left undefined.

   The blind man teaches the sighted narrator to see their shared world and to desire to live in it. The *seeing* in "Cathedral" corresponds to Carver's purpose in *writing* these stories. His characters have an urgent need to explain themselves, their lives, and more especially their failures, but, like the woman in "A Small, Good Thing" who "didn't know how to begin" or the man in "Careful" who "didn't know where to start," they are unable to articulate the point of their stories—the point, really, of their lives. Carver's purpose, however, is not to explain; it is, more humbly, to "allow certain areas of life to be understood a little better than they were before." These "certain areas" are only superficially socioeconomic in nature; as the resemblance between his fictions and those of Beckett, Didion, Renata Adler, John Cheever, and Walker Percy suggests, Carver's concern is not with the problems of any one class but rather with the universal condition of psychological and spiritual exhaustion that afflicts contemporary man.

   In his three collections, Carver has illuminated the darkened lives of his defeated and bewildered characters; only in *Cathedral*, however, has he begun to affirm, as John Gardner would have said, the emotional values that enable them to go on in the face of what appear to be overwhelming odds and certain defeat. His is a stoic vision, one that is tempered, however, by the possibility—no longer so terrifyingly remote—of understanding and perhaps even love.

Robert A. Morace

Sources for Further Study

Christian Science Monitor. November 4, 1983, p. B4.
Library Journal. CVIII, September 1, 1983, p. 1719.
Los Angeles Times Book Review. October 2, 1983, p. 3.
The New Republic. CLXXXIX, November 14, 1983, p. 38.
The New York Review of Books. XXX, November 24, 1983, p. 40.
The New York Times Book Review. LXXXVIII, September 11, 1983, p. 1.
Newsweek. CII, September 5, 1983, p. 66.
Publishers Weekly. CCXXIV, July 8, 1983, p. 58.
Saturday Review. IX, September, 1983, p. 61.
Time. CXXII, September 19, 1983, p. 95.

THE CHANGING LIGHT AT SANDOVER

Author: James Merrill (1926-   )
Publisher: Atheneum Publishers (New York). Illustrated. 560 pp. $25.00;
    paperback $12.95
Type of work: Poetry
Time: 1955-1978
Locale: Primarily Stonington, Connecticut, and Athens, Greece

A sacred epic for a postreligious age, revealing the dangers confronting the human race in a masterly work combining absorbing narrative, intense drama, lively humor, and impressive lyricism

> *Principal characters:*
> JAMES MERRILL, poet
> DAVID JACKSON, his lover
> WYSTAN H. AUDEN, the posthumous voice of the Anglo-American
>   poet
> MARIA MITSOTÁKI, the posthumous voice of a close Greek friend
>   of James and David
> EPHRAIM, the spirit of a Greek slave
> MIRABELL (741), the spirit of a batlike creature

It all started back in the summer of 1955.

Poet James Merrill (whose only significant publication to date had been *First Poems* in 1951) and his lover David Jackson gathered at a ouija board and began consulting the spirit world. David (called here DJ) served as "Hand," his fingers operating the willowware cup that under the guidance of the spirits pointed to the symbols on the board, while James (called JM) served as scribe, taking down these letters and numbers and eventually transforming them into poetry to fill the bulk of more than five hundred pages.

What is spelled out on the board is essentially a new metaphysics, including the past, present, and future of a world now confronted by overpopulation, pollution, and nuclear threats. Through communication with the spirits— from mortals now dead (both friends and the famous) through nonhuman beings who flourished on Earth before Homo sapiens through God's angels to God Himself (here aptly dubbed God B for Biology, suggesting the teeming life that is the greatest distinction of Earth)—JM and DJ learn about the transference of souls, the failures of God B's past experiments, and the danger to the souls of mankind through nuclear power and radiation.

The product of these communications—which transpire over nearly a quarter of a century, chiefly in JM and DJ's house in Stonington, Connecticut, and in a house outside Athens called Sandover—is a vast epic poem, originally published separately as "The Book of Ephraim" in *Divine Comedies* (1976), *Mirabell: Books of Number* (1978), and *Scripts for the Pageant* (1980). Now gathered under one cover, the trilogy is unchanged from the original publications except for the addition of a coda, "The Higher Keys," which unfortunately represents a severe comedown after the superb climactic action that closes *Scripts for the Pageant*.

Very much in the tradition of Dante (frequently alluded to here) and John Milton, Merrill's epic seeks to justify (or at least explain) the ways of God to men. Unlike those immortal forebears, however, Merrill lacks an audience that shares a single religious worldview. Indeed, as one of their major spirit-world contacts, Mirabell, notes about the spirits' increasingly unheard message: "MAN IS AMOK & CHAOS SLIPS IN (UPON/ COLLAPSE, IN INTELLIGENT MEN, OF RELIGIOUS BELIEF)." (Merrill consistently uses uppercase letters to indicate communications transmitted through the capital letters of the ouija board.) In the lack of such a prevailing faith, Merrill through this poem must create one, or at least record it as received from the spirits, for unlike Milton, Merrill needs to invite no "Heavenly Muse" to "sing"; rather, supernatural forces seek *him* out and invoke *his* aid in conveying their "message of survival."

Why? Because he and DJ are deemed worthy through their love, as well as by Merrill's talent, even though so recently launched upon the world— Merrill still in his twenties, Jackson a bit older, when they begin these communications. Some years later, in fact, there is a delightful moment for JM when Mirabell's choice of words and images indicates that he has read *First Poems*.

Eventually Merrill and Jackson discover that they have been chosen over a heterosexual couple because "SO CALLD NORMAL LOVERS" must reproduce, while "MIND IN ITS PURE FORM IS A NONSEXUAL PASSION/ OR A UNISEXUAL ONE PRODUCING ONLY LIGHT." To be sure, their relationship is not all "pure mind," for they enjoy some bawdy interplay with two other homosexual poets, W.H. Auden and Chester Kallman, who had also been lovers, and their twenty-fifth year together is initiated by an exquisite ceremony of the spirit world, accompanied by the music of Richard Strauss as James and David kiss.

The poem traces their relationship, through separations and reunions, through difficulties with aging and dying parents, and through their own aging processes. As they learn about themselves and grow emotionally, they also proceed into knowledge of the nonhuman world, for the movement of the poem is ever deeper, into longer books, into the further past, and into ever more profound revelations about humankind, the world, and God, and particularly their mission: JM's duty to write the poem disseminating these revelations. As a poet, Merrill has a further responsibility, especially to his audience: to create, from the letters that the cup on the board has pointed to, a work of art.

This Merrill has done with consummate grace and power, with a poet's catalog of exquisitely handled meters, a virtual rhyming dictionary of sound patterns, and a virtuoso ensemble of voices, all of which taken together may outdo anything this profound and versatile versifier has produced heretofore, if that is possible for such a master of metrical and metaphorical manipulation and aural originality and variety. The voices—from the campy gay innuendo of Auden, Kallman, and their first contact, Ephraim, to the measured warmth of God B's twin, Mother Nature; from the wry humor of their Greek friend Maria to the touching ingratiation of Unice, a unicorn from a race that preceded mankind; from the stately Latinate profundities of Archangel Michael, Lord of Light, to the remote uneasiness of God B Himself—may come from the other world, but the poem itself reveals, in "conversations" between JM and the spirit of Auden, that it was Merrill who selected the appropriate meters for his various spirit-world voices. He even admits to tinkering with an eight-line stanza voiced by the spirit of no less than W. B. Yeats, who himself sought spiritual contacts through the automatic writing of his wife, Georgie.

Occasionally Merrill emerges clearly from the medium's mode to indulge in some lyric flights wholly and undeniably his own, with the resounding cadences that characterized his work as early as "The Black Swan" of 1946. See especially "Samos," which opens the middle section of *Scripts for the Pageant*, a gorgeously manipulated yet utterly simple sestinalike lyric of five twelve-line stanzas, whose iambic pentameter lines bear no rhyme other than repetition of five key words: "sense," "light," "land," "fire," and "water." These are major controlling motifs of the poem, representing the four elements (and the angels who embody them in this poem) along with the human quality that creates perception of those elements. These words, however, are given multiple meanings in this poem—the same sound may be presented in "fire," "magnifier," and "sapphire," in "sense" and "scents." Such transformation of one sound into different words and senses reflects the book's pervasive theme of reincarnation—the transference of souls, the recurring presence of the same spirit within different existences—while the persistent repetition of the basic words suggests eternal recurrence.

Reincarnation, in a Buddhist-like progression toward emergence from the perpetual cycle of birth, death, and rebirth, becomes not only the truth through which JM and DJ enter more deeply into the world of the spirits but also becomes part of their most significant revelation. First, they learn of the Five: exalted spirits who have inhabited the bodies of some of the race's greatest geniuses, from Akhnaton and Nefertiti, through Plato and Homer, to Wolfgang Amadeus Mozart, Albert Einstein, and Mahatma Gandhi. These five, in their various avatars, lead the race to new heights.

Something, however, is threatening the human race: radiation from nuclear power, which was responsible for disasters on Earth even before the bombing of Hiroshima and Nagasaki in 1945. Merrill presents analogies of the atom to the apple in Eden, its splitting causing great harm to the human race.

Atomic explosions, it seems, kill not only bodies but souls as well, and one of the major spirit communicants, JM and DJ's friend Maria, proves to have a soul killed by the radiation of her chemotherapy treatments.

Here, unfortunately, the metaphysics gets rather murky. If Maria's soul is dead, how is she still able to communicate with the living? She proceeds to become a plant, appropriate for someone who loved gardening so dearly; this seems to be a permanent transformation. If the goal, however, of the spirits in their progressive lives is a state beyond human incarnation, what can be tragic about this new transformation? Further, if it is not tragic but rather glorious—as it seems to be in the closing sections of the book, when both Maria and Auden, who is associated with earth and is becoming stone (recall his great poem "In Praise of Limestone"), enter their vegetable and mineral forms in something approaching the exultation of Isolde's Liebestod or Daphne's transformation into a tree in Strauss's opera—what happens to the warning against radiation?

Actually, the warning against abusing the power of the atom remains strong, for the poem predicts destruction of the race as now known before the new race takes its place. This is the most political poem Merrill has ever written. After all, he wrote in "The Broken Home," "I rarely buy a newspaper, or vote," but in *The Changing Light at Sandover*, that earlier poem's dichotomy of "Father Time and Mother Earth" is much more elaborated, and Merrill becomes more comfortable with both. He learns that, despite threats to his future, Homo sapiens may stay on Earth a while yet, enjoying the richness of its beauties, advancing the knowledge and nobility of the race. Such too is the hope of God B Himself.

Usually heard only through the voices of His angels, on a few occasions God B's words appear unmediated upon the board, always with a keen sense of drama, whether anticipated or awaited with awe. They resound most chillingly in the intercepted fragment of endlessly repeated and rearranged phrases:

ALONE IN MY NIGHT BROTHERS DO YOU WELL
I AND MINE HOLD IT BACK BROTHERS I AND
MINE SURVIVE BROTHERS HEAR ME SIGNAL ME

It is these words that close the third book of Merrill's trilogy, after DJ and JM have broken the mirror through which the spirits and these two mortals communicated. How thrilling they are after the fears that DJ and JM have learned, experienced, and expressed—for themselves, their loved ones, and the human race. They experience then the true meaning of the title of this section of *Scripts for the Pageant*. The sections of each part of the trilogy follow the order of one part of the ouija board—the alphabet, the numbers from 0 to 9, and "Yes & No"—each section beginning with the appropriate letter, number (often in languages other than English), or word. Moving into the section "No," the reader joins Merrill and Jackson in fearing the worst for humankind, prepared for by the spirits' dark hints and repeated warnings. At the end, however, it appears that it is all humankind who will say the "No"—No to abuse of the atom, to the devastation of radiation, and to the threat of nuclear war. "I AND MINE SURVIVE," says God B. May we all join Him in "holding it back" and hope that indeed we do.

Scott Giantvalley

Sources for Further Study

Commonweal. CX, November 4, 1983, p. 585.
Harper's. CCLXVII, September, 1983, p. 69.
Hudson Review. XXXVI, Winter, 1983, p. 724.
Los Angeles Times Book Review. October 30, 1983, p. 12.
The New York Review of Books. XXX, June 16, 1983, p. 41.
The New York Times Book Review. LXXXVIII, March 13, 1983, p. 6.
Newsweek. CI, February 28, 1983, p. 70.
Yale Review. LXXIII, Autumn, 1983, p. R9.

CHARLES WILLIAMS
An Exploration of His Life and Work

Author: Alice Mary Hadfield (1908-   )
Publisher: Oxford University Press (New York). 268 pp. $24.95
Type of work: Literary biography
Time: 1886-1945
Locale: London and Oxford

One of the first biographers of Charles Williams, a personal acquaintance, revises and extends her earlier memoir, producing the most complete biography available of this remarkable writer

> *Principal personages:*
> CHARLES WILLIAMS, an English novelist and poet
> MARY AND WALTER WILLIAMS, his parents
> FLORENCE CONWAY (MICHAL), his wife
> SIR HUMPHREY MILFORD,
> PHYLLIS JONES, and
> GERARD HOPKINS, employees of Oxford University Press
> C. S. LEWIS and
> J. R. R. TOLKIEN, the other "Inklings"

In his fine collective biography of C. S. Lewis, J. R. R. Tolkien, and Charles Williams, *The Inklings* (1979), Humphrey Carpenter states that by 1927, Williams, then forty and married for ten years, had fallen in love with Phyllis Jones, the librarian at Oxford University Press, and that unknown to their coworkers, she returned his love. A footnote on the page catches the eye: "Nor was it known to Alice Mary Hadfield, Williams' friend and biographer, when she wrote *An Introduction to Charles Williams* (1959)."

Much new material has become available on Williams since Hadfield wrote in 1959, and this wealth of information fills the pages of *Charles Williams: An Exploration of His Life and Work*. Hadfield notes in her preface that since her first work she has had access to two thousand letters by Williams, including several hundred to Phyllis Jones, and to much of his unpublished work. In addition—and perhaps most important—Hadfield is now twenty years further away from her subject, able to test her evaluation of the man through two decades of consideration.

Hadfield's present work illustrates, among other things, the traps of writing biography, as one anecdote will show. One wonders how many university teachers have told their students that Williams wrote his novels to pay his son's tuition. Alice Mary Hadfield was herself the source of the story, relaying it in good faith in her *Introduction to Charles Williams*; as she now notes, though, the story cannot be true, because his son was only three when Williams began writing, and both Williams and his wife were then employed. Their financial position was reasonably secure, as Mrs. Williams indignantly pointed out in a letter responding to Hadfield's earlier work.

Here is the biographer's dilemma: The best biography can offer only fragments of its subject's personality, and a fragmentary picture may be worse than none at all. Williams is an especially dangerous subject when not presented completely, because some episodes from his life—taken out of context—paint a bizarre picture, one radically different from the testimony of those who knew the whole man. For example, as a young man Williams joined A. E. Waite's Order of Golden Dawn (of which William Butler Yeats was also a member), an offspring of Rosicrucianism, whose members sought mystical—even magical—knowledge. Although Williams outgrew the order and its rituals, Hadfield admits that "there was something of the Manichaean in him, but to torment, not to rule him."

The Manichaean surfaces, as Hadfield notes, in the question of Williams' "capacity for cruelty." Williams commanded a strong attraction for women and seemed to be constantly attended by disciples. One such was a young woman, a student in an evening lecture course he gave. Because she worked nearby the Press, he asked her to come to his office after work, and they would go to the lecture together. As Hadfield relates, Williams instructed the young woman to bend over

and in silence he took [a ceremonial sword] and made smooth strokes with it over her buttocks. He did not hit, nor touch with his hand. She was fully clothed. All was in silence. Afterwards, she said she did not like it. He replied, "This is necessary for the poem," and refused to allow the episode to be mentioned.

Such events lend themselves to facile and probably faulty psychoanalysis, but ultimately only Williams could have explained what these rituals meant to him, and perhaps not even he.

Williams did know that "our bodies go wrong; they torment us with diseases and irritate us with desires." As a practicing Anglican, he believed that one was obliged to check unlawful desire, as by all accounts he did. Hadfield reports the testimony of Phyllis Jones that their love was not accompanied by sexual intimacies: For Williams, romantic love provided a way to spiritual development.

The record of his progress in that development will change the minds of those who are used to thinking of Williams as a shadowy figure on the fringe of the Lewis-Tolkien group. At the outbreak of World War II, Oxford University Press moved its editorial offices from London to Oxford. Williams, then fifty-three years old, had published six novels, seven biographies, seven verse plays, three works of literary criticism, two of theology, and seven books of poetry in addition to those he edited. He was already a figure of reputation in London literary circles. Williams' theology is the thread that connects all of these works; in fact, except for his poetry, his earliest writing was "Outlines of Romantic Theology," a work never published but one whose ideas he developed all during his life.

Williams took his lead from Dante Alighieri's use of Beatrice as a guide to the way to Paradise: Rather than the ascetic practice of denial, Williams sought to develop a theology based on an affirmation of romantic love in marriage. Insisting on the Church's acceptance of the holiness of the body, Williams found the principle of Romantic Theology in "any two lovers who knew that their love was Christ, and that their marriage was His life." Each event of the marriage could be linked to some event of the divine life, whether success or failure, temptation, even death and resurrection to a new life. Hadfield words Williams' thoughts concerning the sexual consummation beginning the marriage in this way: "At our Bethlehem our bodies are the shepherds, our highest imagination the Magi, both finding the birth of love." He saw a likeness between the body of Christ and the bodies of true lovers and viewed sexual love as a kind of Communion.

Romantic Love was only a means, not an end for Williams. He regarded the assumption that it is sufficient as one of the three attacks that "Hell has made . . . on the Way of Romantic Love." Being *in* love must progress to *being* love. That is to say, Williams expected love to change the lover, who should reject the old self on the old way and become first the old self on the new way and ultimately the new self on the new way. Love shows its genuineness, one might say, in action.

This was the Williams whose ideas T. S. Eliot enjoyed and approved, and to whose influence W. H. Auden attributed his conversion to Christianity: ". . . for the first time in my life [I] felt myself in the presence of personal sanctity" (cited in Glen Cavaliero's *Charles Williams: Poet of Theology*, 1983, reviewed elsewhere in this volume). This Williams opened a new chapter in the life of as keen a mind as C. S. Lewis.

When Williams came to Oxford, he was already acquainted with Lewis. In 1939, by happy accident, each had admired one of the other's works, Lewis the novel *The Place of the Lion* (1951) and Williams *The Allegory of Love* (1936). They had discussed their works, yet the two were at heart creatures of vastly different worlds: For Williams, the city of London was a microcosm of existence, while the University was Lewis' center of reference. One intuits that these two could have been brought into close proximity only by changes as great as those of the war. Hadfield, however, believes that the move to Oxford for the first time put Williams in touch with people who were his intellectual equal.

The stay at Oxford reveals (perhaps "confirmed" is a better word) another of Williams' talents—that of an educator. Williams had for years taught in municipally sponsored evening courses for working people in London; yet, as one might expect, Oxford either did not know of or was unimpressed by those efforts. Nevertheless, people of discernment had discovered the electric effect of Williams' teaching. E. Martin Browne was a mature man and head of the Religious Drama Society when he first heard Williams lecture. Williams spoke on the poet John Milton, and, according to Browne, "set the room aflame. I have never met any human being in whom the divisions between body and spirit, natural and supernatural, temporal and eternal were so non-existent."

Lewis knew of Williams' thoughts on Milton—perhaps had even heard him speak—and arranged for Williams, though he lacked an academic degree, to give a series of lectures on Milton at Oxford's Divinity School. After the second of these, Lewis noted, "I have at last, if only for once, seen a university doing what it was founded to do: teaching wisdom." The Milton lectures generated invitations for others: on William Wordsworth, on William Shakespeare, on Dante. To qualify Williams for an official faculty position when he was scheduled to retire from the Press in 1951, the University awarded him (in 1943) an honorary degree of Master of Arts.

Ironically, the seclusion of Oxford made Williams much more of a public figure than London ever had. He met Dorothy Sayers, for example, and in an unofficial capacity, helped her with her study of Dante. (In acknowledgment, Sayers dedicated her translation of the *Divine Comedy* to Williams.) In the midst of this hectic activity (all in addition to his regular work at the Press), he contemplated retirement to the Oxford faculty. He wrote to his wife—who had remained in London—about the idea, characteristically adding that the retirement was subject to her approval, that they would not live anywhere that she did not wish. He continued to write more plays, another novel, and more poetry on the Arthurian cycle, which had occupied his attention through his adult life. Finally, he continued to attend to the spiritual supervision of the order that he had inspired: the Companions of the Co-inherence.

In 1939, his friends had persuaded Williams to let them found a lay organization based on his theological ideas and stressing the New Testament precept to bear one another's burdens. (Hadfield's book explains well both the order and Williams' notions of co-inherence, substitution, and exchange.) All through the war and its attendant duties (including, for example, standing fire-watch in buildings at night), Williams continued to guide the members of the growing society through his letters and his personal conversation. Still, in the midst of all of this activity, Hadfield and other friends noted a withdrawing and a tiring in him. A few days after the end of World War II, he was dead.

Charles Williams' work has not yet been fully appreciated, especially his drama, which audiences of all kinds warmly received, yet which is hardly known in the United States. He was a complex figure, one of great talent and depth, and Alice Mary Hadfield's biography will help immeasurably to present the whole man to a generation grown up since his death. At the last, perhaps the best test of Williams' influence is the vividness of his memory to his friends, to which Hadfield's book is a moving witness.

Walter E. Meyers

Sources for Further Study

Christian Science Monitor. April 23, 1984, p. 18.
Library Journal. CVIII, October 1, 1983, p. 1878.
Publishers Weekly. CCXXIV, September 23, 1983, p. 66.

CHARLES WILLIAMS
Poet of Theology

Author: Glen Cavaliero (1927-   )
Publisher: William B. Eerdmans (Grand Rapids, Michigan). 199 pp. $8.95
Type of work: Literary criticism

An eminent critic of Charles Williams provides a detailed study of the writing of the English novelist and poet

The year 1983 was a fortunate one for those studying the writings of Charles Williams. In addition to Glen Cavaliero's *Charles Williams: Poet of Theology*, the year saw the publication of Alice Mary Hadfield's impressive biography, *Charles Williams: An Exploration of His Life and Work* (reviewed elsewhere in this volume), and Thomas Howard's *The Novels of Charles Williams*. In particular, Cavaliero's and Hadfield's studies complement each other well. Hadfield has some things to say about Williams' writing, but her work is strongest as a biography and personal memoir, drawing as it does on a large number of Williams' letters. On the other hand, Cavaliero uses only a few pages to sketch the writer's life; most of his book details Williams' thought and themes.

Cavaliero does not approach Williams' works in strict chronological order. He begins with chapters on "The Early Poetry" and "Criticism, Biographies and Plays"; follows with "The Novels" and "The Arthurian Poems" (on which Williams worked throughout most of his life); and ends with "Theology" and a conclusion. The work also contains a very brief appendix concerning affinities in the symbolism of Williams, the poet William Blake, and the nineteenth century fantasist and religious writer, George Macdonald. Finally, there is a bibliography which includes a selection of critical and biographical sources as well as a list of Williams' principal works.

In Cavaliero's opinion, Williams' early poetry (which, to be sure, is not much read) follows in theology the late Victorian tradition of religious writers such as Coventry, Patmore, and especially Francis Thompson. Unfortunately, Williams did not bring the rhythmic freedom of Patmore or Thompson to his early work; rather, Cavaliero finds Williams hampered by "the jogging measures of a hundred hymn writers." He sees Williams in *Poems of Conformity* (1917) and *Divorce* (1920) attempting something like Blake's *Songs of Innocence* (1789) and *Songs of Experience* (1794); Williams contrasts earthly marriage, symbolizing the union of the human and the divine, with divorce, symbolizing separation on both levels. *Windows of Night* (1924) reveals Williams' increasing spiritual disquiet. Less traditional in form than its predecessors, the volume suggests an uneasy awareness of the claims of modernity. "In all this early work," Cavaliero concludes, "the artist is subordinate to the theologian."

As a critic, Williams was "personal, expository and receptive" in a manner now too easily dismissed as "superficial and belletrist." Cavaliero contrasts Williams' manner of reading with the professional criticism exemplified by F. R. Leavis, whose work grew out of the context of university teaching. The first people to encounter Williams' criticism were the students who, generally after a full day's work, attended the evening courses he taught for the Municipality of London. These courses offered neither degree nor diploma, nothing but knowledge itself. Cavaliero believes this early training to have been important in the development of Williams' thinking, particularly the idea that poets teach and that the best criticism of poetry is poetry itself. In fact, in his first work of criticism, *Poetry at Present* (1930), Williams appended short verses to each essay. Cavaliero suggests that in this early criticism may be found the attitudes and convictions that informed Williams' own writing, and indeed, his view of life.

Cavaliero pays particular attention to what he calls "the divided consciousness" in Williams' writing: the state that occurs in one who encounters a situation wholly contradictory to one's understanding of the world. An example that Williams provides in *The English Poetic Mind* (1932) is William Shakespeare's Troilus, who, in finding Cressida to have been untrue, experiences an undeniable reality that shows him "the union of incompatible experiences of one woman in her inseparate personality." The situation suggests to Williams the union of two natures in one person, leading to a discussion (not in theological terms but in poetic) of the nature of Christ. Through much of Williams' adult life, he referred to the union of opposites that is characteristic of human experience as "the Impossibility."

It was also in the early 1930's that Williams began to write biography—not from a spontaneous desire to discuss the lives of King James I or Queen Elizabeth I, but because his work at Oxford University Press often presented him with commissions for such projects. Cavaliero distinguishes Williams' biographies from the many popularizations then in vogue, observing that they tell as much about Williams as about their ostensible subjects. In the biographies, Williams used his notion of "the Impossibility" as an organizing principle, finding in a figure such as Francis Bacon or the poet John Wilmot, Earl of Rochester, a single animating conflict or contradiction. Although these commissioned works were necessarily ephemeral, Cavaliero's final assessment of the biographies is positive: He judges them sometimes mannered, but he finds much to praise in them in the honing of Williams' style, showed to better advantage when Williams wrote on subjects of his own choosing.

The plays are another story entirely: The annual Canterbury Festival provided an important stage for the presentation of verse plays with religious themes. One needs to be reminded of what Cavaliero notes—that the play in the festival of 1935 was T. S. Eliot's *Murder in the Cathedral* (1935), a hard act to follow. Thus, Williams' *Thomas Cranmer of Canterbury*, the play for

1936, brought his work before an important audience and likewise brought Williams to public attention. It was to be pleasant attention: Cavaliero describes Williams' dramas as "unconventional and daring"; they are also devout and powerful. There is an interesting detail in this section. When Williams wrote his *Judgment at Chelmsford* (1939), he used the pseudonym "Peter Stanhope," the name of a character (also a dramatist) who appears in his novel *Descent into Hell* (1937). In some ways, that character describes Williams' aims as a dramatist, and the comparison between author and character is fascinating. Had his personal history evolved differently, Williams might have been one of the century's outstanding dramatists (working actors testify—as do audiences—that his plays are "good theater"), and the reconstruction of Charles Williams' reputation as a dramatist may be one of the chief effects of the resurgence of interest in him as a writer.

Indeed, it is ironic that Williams is almost exclusively remembered as a novelist. Cavaliero argues that he was not primarily such, and that his works stand outside the English novelistic tradition—a tradition that Cavaliero describes as "naturalistic, faithful to observed reality and imagined within the confines of tangible experience." One might note in passing that Williams simply may be in a different tradition, the one that includes Mary Shelley, George Macdonald, H. G. Wells, James Joyce, and many others, yet Cavaliero surely is correct in making the division along different lines: Williams stood outside literary fashion, not in rejecting naturalism but in rejecting materialism. Coming to maturity in an era in which writers as diverse as Algernon Blackwood and Henry James were exploring themes of the supernatural, Williams the novelist was significantly influenced, Cavaliero suggests, by the "diverse but broadly Christian novels of Arthur Machen, Evelyn Underhill, and G. K. Chesterton."

Cavaliero's chapter on Williams' novels devotes a section to each in turn: to *Shadows of Ecstasy* (written in the 1920's but not published until 1933), *War in Heaven* (1930), *Many Dimensions* (1931), *The Place of the Lion* (1931), *The Greater Trumps* (1932), *Descent into Hell* (written in 1933, published in 1937), and *All Hallows' Eve* (1945). One does not, however, find ordinary literary criticism in these discussions; in keeping with the subtitle of his book, "Poet of Theology," Cavaliero is more intent on discussing how Williams' religious thought found expression in the novels than in dissecting his style or searching for sources. There are comments, often insightful, on style or sources, but the focus is on the maturing (and a very consistent maturing) of Williams as a combination of theologian and poet. From that point of view, a character such as Peter Stanhope mentioned above is interesting chiefly in that he provides a fictional example illustrating Williams' literal acceptance of the New Testament precept to bear one another's burdens. The Companions of Co-Inherence, a group which Williams later agreed to found, put heavy emphasis on this precept. Whatever his oddities or temptations, Williams did not proclaim one thing artistically and live another.

Williams' Arthurian poems are discussed in a chapter of their own, in keeping with the importance with which Williams himself must have regarded them; he returned to them repeatedly throughout his life. At one point in his career as an editor, Williams worked on the poems of Gerard Manley Hopkins (whose nephew, Gerard Hopkins, was one of Williams' coworkers at Oxford University Press), and Cavaliero finds Hopkins' beneficial influence in Williams' later Arthurian poems. In theme, Cavaliero shows that the idea of the Grail was central to Williams' conception of the Arthurian myth and argues that Williams' handling of it is not so much incomplete as unfinished. Cavaliero judges the two collections, *Taliessin Through Logres* (1938) and *The Region of the Summer Stars* (1944), as finished in themselves but adds that Williams planned to add a third collection. Because they fall outside the present academic canon of twentieth century verse, Williams' Arthurian poems are not well-known, and Cavaliero's close examination of them in a long chapter is most welcome.

In a chapter devoted to Williams' theology, Cavaliero argues that such idiosyncratic works as *He Came Down from Heaven* (1938) and *The Descent of the Dove* (1939) constitute Williams' most remarkable achievement, creating a genre for themselves, not polemical or apologetic or devotional or intellectual but rather visionary theology combined with "personal application." Cavaliero describes Williams' method as a commentary on the history of the Church, but drawing from that history (as a poet would) symbols through which one may interpret life.

Cavaliero calls *The Descent of the Dove* Williams' masterpiece. Here, Cavaliero finds the first detailed examination of Williams' notion of an approach to God not through the "Way of Rejection"—an ascetic turning from the world—but through the "Way of Affirmation." This is again a long chapter, studying Williams' theology with a thoroughness which it has not received before.

Many works of literary biography and criticism show a blindness to the faults of their subjects. Cavaliero's study is not one of these; his conclusion is, if anything, subdued. He gives praise where he feels it is due, observing that nature and grace were joined in Williams' life and work, and is candid about what he believes to be the limitations of the writer's work: "Williams reveals little interest in his contemporaries, and all his concerns are turned inward to his self-propagating personal myth." This judgment is a little harsh in a book that demonstrates Williams' real virtues as convincingly as does Cavaliero's. Williams' concern did not find a congenial outlet in political organizations but in social and religious ones. Future ages may find human goals and problems more meaningfully addressed by Charles Williams than by any of his contemporaries.

Walter E. Meyers

Sources for Further Study

Choice. XX, June, 1983, p. 1452.
Christian Century. C, August 3, 1983, p. 722.
Library Journal. CVIII, April 15, 1983, p. 824.

CHRONICLE OF A DEATH FORETOLD

Author: Gabriel García Márquez (1928-   )
Translated from the Spanish by Gregory Rabassa
Publisher: Alfred A. Knopf (New York). 120 pp. $10.95
Type of work: Novel
Time: 1950-1981
Locale: The Caribbean coast of Colombia

In this chronicle of a death widely foretold, García Márquez recounts the murder of a man believed to have been the lover of another man's new bride, the events leading up to it, its impact upon the town, and its long-term effects on those who must go on living

> *Principal characters:*
> GABRIEL GARCÍA MÁRQUEZ, a journalist, novelist, and chronicler of his own past
> SANTIAGO NASAR, the murder victim who died without understanding his death
> ANGELA VICARIO, the returned bride who names Nasar as her "perpetrator" and lives out her abandonment finally understanding her own life
> BAYARDO SAN ROMÁN, the groom who returns his dishonored bride and becomes, for the majority of people, the one victim of the tragedy

One of the foremost writers of *El Boom Latinoamericano* of the 1960's, Gabriel García Márquez has steadily produced a series of works that have won for him both popular international acclaim and the official recognition that attaches to the Nobel Prize for Literature (1982). While his reputation rests securely upon such epic works as *Cien años de soledad* (1967; *One Hundred Years of Solitude*, 1970), and *El otoño del patriarca* (1975; *The Autumn of the Patriarch*, 1976), and such short fiction as *Lo hojarasca* (1955; *Leaf Storm and Other Stories*, 1972) and *El coronel no tiene quien la escriba* (1962; *No One Writes to the Colonel and Other Stories*, 1968); his *Chronicle of a Death Foretold* (published in Colombia in 1981 as *Crónica de una muerte anunciada*) clearly contributed to his official recognition as a master storyteller and continues to bring him popular acclaim despite its mixed critical reception. Measured against his longer and more ambitious works, García Márquez's latest novel falls short of the virtuosity of *One Hundred Years of Solitude* and *The Autumn of the Patriarch*, but it is nevertheless a richly complex work, a monument to García Márquez's artistry.

A virtually undisguised García Márquez shuttles back and forth between August, 1950, and his present moment of writing to narrate a series of events based on historical fact, his own research into the facts of the case and their fictionalized outcome, and his quest that leads him, at various historical points, to return to his "forgotten village, trying to put the broken mirror of memory back together from so many scattered shards." One must approach these authorial and narrational shuttlings warily, particularly in those instances in which fact and fiction intersect: The narrator remains a fictional character of limited perspective and at times appears to be the victim of some authorial irony. One must also tread warily in the footsteps of the narrator, who leads the reader, familiarly and openly, to a place abutting that celebrated region of a mind's geography García Márquez calls the Macondo, the Caribbean coastal area of northern Colombia that has its North American counterpart in the famous Yoknapatawpha county of his avowed master, William Faulkner. The mind's geography also intersects that of cartographers: The unnamed village may not be unlike the author's native Aracataca; both Riohacha, where the Vicario brothers serve out their brief sentence, and Manaure, where the rest of the Vicarios live after Santiago Nasar's death, are surely on the map. These places also belong to a magical region filled with the incongruities, oddities, small insanities, and omnipresent hostilities that characterize its genuinely human, sometimes warm, and truly unforgettable populace. So, too, the facts upon which García Márquez weaves his fiction are verifiable: In 1951, two brothers murdered a man in Sucre, Colombia, for being the supposed lover of their sister, another man's bride. García Márquez, then a journalist, was acquainted with the victim. The fictional treatment of these bare facts is pure García Márquez and partakes of what has been termed his "magical realism,"6 a technique that superadds fantasy to the shards of history in surprising ways.

The chronicle García Márquez presents is a tale of slaughter that affects the village's entire population. Twin brothers, Pablo and Pedro Vicario, avenge the honor of their sister, Angela, a bride of five hours, returned home by her groom, Bayardo San Román, upon his discovery that she was not a virgin. Santiago Nasar, the man whom Angela names when asked who deflowered her, is an unlikely suspect; indeed, no one really believes that he is responsible. It is Nasar's death that is foretold in the novel's first sentence, variously heralded before the fact, and explicated, discussed, and rationalized once it has occurred. The chronicle is itself, however, incomplete, despite the fact that García Márquez has said it was thirty years in the making: The one shard of memory not found and replaced is the secret Angela Vicario never reveals— the name of her actual lover.

As author and narrator, García Márquez uses the improbabilities of life and the techniques of fiction to comment upon the nature of reality in a work that treats life in the spirit of art and art in the spirit of life. Early in the chronicle, the narrator refers to the door before which Nasar was murdered as having been "cited several times with a dime-novel title: 'The Fatal Door.'" Later, twenty-three years after the tragedy, the narrator, unlike his creator, finds himself in an uncertain period of his life selling encyclopedias and medical books in the towns of Guajira. There, he glimpses Angela Vicario, a figure with steel-rimmed glasses and yellowish gray hair, seated at her embroidery machine. "I refused to believe," he writes, "that the woman there was who I thought it was, because I couldn't bring myself to admit that life might end up resembling bad literature so much." The same motif appears in García Márquez's account of the investigating magistrate who visits the village twelve days after the crime: "he never thought it legitimate that life should make use of so many coincidences forbidden literature, so that there should be the untrammeled fulfillment of a death so clearly foretold." Here, fiction-as-fact is commenting on fiction-as-fiction in a multi-mirrored regression. The preoccupation with literature and its relation to life—and the creation of the chronicle is one example of such a preoccupation—extends to a preoccupation with the act of writing, ordering the perception and memory of experience and reordering experience itself.

Most of what the narrator learns comes from direct observation and conversation, but significant portions of knowledge come from written sources. He first learns of Bayardo San Román's entry to the village from his mother's letters to him, and his reconstruction of the judicial inquiry into Nasar's death is drawn from his five-year effort at rummaging around the sometimes flooded record offices of the Palace of Justice at Riohacha, where he secured only 322 pages of a much longer brief. The reordering of experience, the chronicling of a death foretold, represents a significant, long-term effort on the narrator's part, an effort that spans three decades and is, finally, an effort directed at fixing in words, at writing, the history of a calamity that befell Santiago Nasar, Angela Vicario, Bayardo San Román and, indeed, the whole town. This act of writing, arguably the unifying theme of the work, is mirrored and surpassed by the prodigious writing of Angela Vicario herself, writing that is entirely obsessive and that chronicles her own existence over approximately twenty-seven years. Angela, seized by the memory of San Román, who "had been in her life forever from the moment he'd brought her back home," writes him long letters with no future, letters he never answers until finally a fat, bespectacled and balding Bayardo San Román pays his visit and returns to her the nearly two thousand letters she has written him. A quintessential García Márquez touch closes the chapter: The two thousand letters are arranged chronologically in bundles tied with colored ribbons, "and they were all unopened."

At the heart of the novel is the double standard of sexual morality and, with it, the strange, dark power of sex and sexuality that pervades the culture García Márquez depicts. This double standard in its Latin-American form is part of a larger cultural phenomenon embraced by the term *machismo*, a phenomenon noted in many sociological and psychological works and summarized pithily in Manuel de Jesus Guerrero's *El machismo Latinoamericano* (1977). There is, for example, no thought that Angela Vicario could come legitimately to the marriage bed having had another lover, just as there is no thought that the amorous exploits of Santiago Nasar with Maria Alejandrina Cervantes and the girls of her bordello should interfere with his right to marry—and expect virginity from—his fiancée, Flora Miguel.

The lot of women, in fact, receives considerable attention in the novel. In Hispanic cultures, boys are brought up to be men while girls are "reared to get married." The Vicario girls, for example, are exemplary in their devotion to the cult of death and should make any man happy "because they've been raised to suffer." When Angela hints obliquely that, despite the fact that her parents arranged that she marry Bayardo San Román and obliged her to do so, she had an inconvenient lack of love for him, the matter is settled by her mother's phrase, "Love can be learned too." The one voice that undercuts the stereotypical view of Hispanic women is that of the narrator's mother, a voice that is not without humor. That Angela dons the wedding veil and orange blossoms is, after her return, interpreted as a profanation of the symbols of purity. Recognizing the courage it took for Angela to do so, she comments, "In those days God understood such things."

In a work that deals with the more somber elements of existence, with frustration, betrayal, and the imposition of a one-sided code of conduct, there are also many wryly humorous passages. One, for example, seems to parody Gustave Flaubert's famous operating-room scenes: The grisly, botched autopsy on Nasar leads to the conclusion that, based upon the weight of the encephalic mass, he had not only a superior intelligence but also a brilliant future. So outrageous is the autopsy and so poorly is it executed that Colonel Aponte, the mayor, whose personal logic is elsewhere presented for the illogic it is and whose responsibility for numerous massacres is clearly established, becomes a vegetarian as well as a spiritualist. Another instance illustrates both García Márquez's mastery of form and his pervasive sense of the incongruities of which humor is born. One of the dozens of minor characters who weave through the novel, Magdalena Oliver, is present on the boat when San Román arrives at the village and also witnesses his inglorious departure. On both occasions, she draws an incorrect conclusion based on his appearance, first thinking him a homosexual and then, as he leaves, concluding that he is dead and making a remark about waste which Gregory Rabassa wisely leaves untranslated. Magdalena thus frames San Román's entry and exit with complete understanding.

Elsewhere García Márquez has said that the historical personage he most detests is Cristóbal Colón (Christopher Columbus). It is not without significance that Bayardo San Román first meets his future bride "on the national holiday in October." This holiday, celebrated throughout the Americas as Columbus Day, is also known in Colombia as *Fiesta de la Raza*, a nomenclature devised early in this century to downplay the commemoration of colonialism and its oppressive legacy. October, one recalls from García Márquez's story "No One Writes to the Colonel," is an unpropitious time in general; in

Chronicle of a Death Foretold, October 12 is doubly unpropitious: It is the day when Bayardo (whose name is too close to the word *boyardo*, which Rabassa translates as "seigneur," to ignore) buys up all the raffle tickets from, and presents the prize (a music box) to, his intended conquest, Angela Vicario; it is also the unfortunate Angela's birthday.

These small touches, matter-of-factly stated, and scores of other similarly deft strokes combine to form a highly wrought vision of a tragic event. It is a deliberately fragmented vision, one more tentative addition to the one book of solitude that García Márquez claims, in *El olor de la Guayaba* (1982; *The Smell of Guava*, 1984), to be his life's work.

John J. Conlon

Sources for Further Study

Antioch Review. XLI, Summer, 1983, p. 380.
The Atlantic. CCLI, May, 1983, p. 103.
Christian Science Monitor. July 6, 1983, p. 9.
Hudson Review. XXXVI, Autumn, 1983, p. 552.
Library Journal. CVIII, April 1, 1983, p. 758.
Los Angeles Times Book Review. April 10, 1983, p. 1.
The New York Review of Books. XXX, April 14, 1983, p. 3.
The New York Times Book Review. LXXXVIII, March 27, 1983, p. 1.
Newsweek. C, November 1, 1982, p. 82.
West Coast Review of Books. IX, May, 1983, p. 40.

THE COFFIN TREE

Author: Wendy Law-Yone (1947-   )
Publisher: Alfred A. Knopf (New York). 195 pp. $12.95
Type of work: Novel
Time: 1963-1975
Locale: Burma and the United States

A Burmese refugee experiences confusion, breakdown, and ultimately recovery after affirming her own independence in the United States

> *Principal characters:*
> THE NARRATOR, a young Burmese woman
> SHAN, her half brother, ten years older
> FATHER, a general at the head of a rebel army in North Burma

In a striking and accomplished first novel, Wendy Law-Yone presents vivid pictures of Burma (where she lived until she was twenty), looks with wry irony at contemporary American customs and artifacts and creates a compelling central character whose experience transcends cultural barriers. The novel is permeated by death, ghosts, and the heavy burdens of the narrator's personal and cultural heritage, yet it finally affirms life. The unfamiliar background is only one of the interesting ingredients. Law-Yone's broader subjects are attachment and loss, the complex interweaving of isolation, individuality, and self-dependence, the continuity of personality, and the mature comprehension of the past that must occur if the central character—and the twentieth century urban human—is to adapt and survive.

The novel's opening plunges at once and without explanation into the center of a complex family situation in Burma. The unnamed narrator, a girl of fourteen, does not supply the exposition that would make everything clear to Western readers but does give such a compelling view of her immediate situation that one automatically accepts her values and behavior. She lives with two elderly aunts, an uncle who stays with them to avoid responsibility for his own wife and children, a grandmother (who dies in the book's opening passage), and a half brother, Shan, who is ten years her senior but seems—in his easy tears and casual irresponsibility—closer to childhood than does the narrator. Her own mother, who died at her birth, was a convert to Catholicism; the narrator attends a convent school run by Irish nuns. Her family is well-off if not wealthy; they live in a spacious compound inherited from a grandfather who was economic adviser to the last king before the Burmese monarchy was ousted. Her father became a revolutionary while at the university and commands a People's Army that has temporarily seized power. Another coup sends him fleeing back to the hills. When the narrator is twenty, she and Shan are bundled onto a plane and sent to the United States.

Baffled by New York and too inhibited to take the help some Americans would be willing to give, the narrator nevertheless contrives ways to eat, learns to type, preserves her identity, and eventually secures an adequate clerical job. While she feels that she is mastering her new life, Shan is rootless and disoriented. Lacking the dreams and the social support Burma had supplied, he withdraws increasingly into fantasies and paranoia. The narrator, trapped by her sense of responsibility for her brother, endures two years of drudgery, anxiety, isolation, and repressed resentment while she tries to take care of him. By the time Shan dies, his psychic illness has infected his sister. Burdened by guilt and lack of purpose, cut off from Burma by her father's death, she is committed to a mental hospital after a suicide attempt. The treatment she receives there may or may not do her any good, but the core of strength at the center of her personality allows her to reassert her independence and discover a way to meet life on her own terms.

The Coffin Tree, however, is not nearly so grim as the foregoing summary might suggest. The immediate pleasures of its tone grow from Law-Yone's sharp eye for incongruous detail and from the narrator's engaging personality. Even when she is a Burmese child conversing with her grandmother's ghost, she is accessible. Her emotionally deprived childhood and her sudden flashes of boldness (despite the extreme timidity fostered by her cultural tradition) may remind the reader of the protagonist of Charlotte Brontë's *Jane Eyre*, 1847—and some readers may see their own experiences reflected in those of the narrator. Even people not suddenly faced by the differences between Mandalay and New York can hang up a telephone a dozen times rather than commit a message to an answering machine or can be too shy to question their hosts. Like Jane Eyre, also, the narrator can be desperately and refreshingly frank, as when she gets a job by telling the bemused interviewer, in answer to his stock question about her strongest and weakest points, that she dislikes work because she is lazy, forgetful, and was never trained for any kind of job but that, on the other hand, she is in terrible need, which might make her willing to learn.

With a combination of acceptance and wry detachment, the narrator sees both Burma and the United States with extraordinary clarity, and sometimes from slightly odd angles. Aunt Lily and Aunt Rosie, in Burma, remain girlish despite their white hair and missing teeth; there is "enough left, all in all, to flirt with the male masseur who came twice a week, and after he left to discuss celibacy as though the alternative were still an issue." The signs in the mental hospital seem suspicious: "'BATH,' 'OFFICE,' 'SUPPLIES.' . . . It was the quotation marks on the signs that alarmed me. I took those marks to signify euphemisms. Surely some barbaric form of hydropathy went on behind the room marked 'BATH'. . . ." Law-Yone has a wonderfully sharp ear, always just short of satire, for the languages of such people as personnel managers, therapists, and social workers.

Aside from the narrator, the only character realized in depth is Shan.

Clearly, it is not America alone that drives him mad; for both Shan and the narrator, cultural shock simply emphasizes basic elements of personality that were partly masked by Burmese traditions. Even at twenty-four, he was more childish and less responsible than his fourteen-year-old sister. His society allowed men to be indolent and self-indulgent. He was involved with a gang of disreputable friends, telling stories, pursuing a dream, inspired by the tales of a Chinatown opium addict. Shan also bears the heritage of a more primitive layer of life in Asia. His mother was a woman from one of the hill tribes, and he was reared until the age of fourteen in a village near the opium fields that sheltered the People's Army. His retreat from reality and his need to construct a vindictive world to account for his own lack of success had seeds in his early falsehoods (encouraged by his aunts as mere entertaining play), fantasies about the sunken treasures he would find and the evil street gangs he and his friends had fought.

The bond between the narrator and her brother is exceptionally strong. For a girl circumscribed by Asian society and a convent school, he is the source of freedom and energy. He teaches her to swim and climb trees—forbidden skills—and takes her on excursions to the Thieves' Market. "Without him," she writes, "the world might have remained only as large as the compound in which I lived: a house bordered by hedges clipped in the shape of regimental birds just high enough to conceal the concertina coils of barbed wire." She has, however, the depth and strength that he lacks; when they begin to learn typing, for example, he memorizes the keyboard and then gets bored and goes to bed, while she practices late every night. He draws on her strength until she is drained nearly dry. He represents the weak dependence that must be purged from her life, yet he also embodies the anger and freedom of expression that she cannot show without threatening her self-esteem.

Shan, in other words, often seems to be the other half of the narrator's self, though their culture redistributes elements which the Western reader might otherwise be tempted to call "masculine" and "feminine." It is no wonder that she slips into a living death when he dies. There are echoes of Emily Brontë's *Wuthering Heights* (1847) here, as there are in other aspects of style and theme: the contrast between the casual sex and raw brutality of the mountain village and the artificial, pretense-ridden, virginal ease of the urban compound; the influence of past on present; the sometimes-puzzling ruptures of narrative sequence; and the permeable boundary between living and dead. Although the cumulative effect is unlike that of *Wuthering Heights*, the book does, like Emily Brontë's work, encourage readers to look beyond the narrative line for thematic meanings and allegorical interpretations.

In particular, *The Coffin Tree* suggests a resemblance between the all-powerful father of childhood memory and the Christian God Whom the narrator comes to know as a Catholic in a Buddhist society: "a God with many masquerades, disguised now as dove, now as mistreated man, now as king; a God that spoke in riddles to be accepted, not solved; a God that dreamed us up, let us loose, sat back to watch our mistakes, then held them against us, knowing all the while that we never stood a chance." The narrator's father, like the Christian God, keeps secrets and exercises absolute power over those around him, must be approached submissively, and can be irrationally cruel, but he also provides glimpses of a wider life and the materials for learning. He seems emotionally indifferent to his children, yet when he deserts them for the last time he sends them to safety in another country. These specifics drawn from Burmese life and individual history can be seen as metaphors for key facets of twentieth century urban society. In the asylum scenes, the Freudian father-God looms over everyone, regardless of cultural backgrounds or literal experience. All of the patients—and, one suspects, the therapists as well—are a "community of wronged children" haunted by the ghosts of their fathers.

The novel is also enriched by its ambivalence about emotion, repression, and the conventions of Western psychological theory. Both cultural and personal history make the narrator discipline her feelings almost out of existence. Thus, she avoids the pain of guilt and self-loathing—and she controls the adults who cannot provoke her to anger and tears. She also denies her womanhood; at fourteen, she is probably anorexic; at eighteen, she binds her breasts and even shrinks in height. On the other hand, this self-dependence—this unwillingness to draw on others for help or emotional support or even human interchange—makes her self-sufficient enough to survive the cultural shocks of America. In the psychiatric hospital, she is constantly urged to express her thoughts and explore her feelings. The hospital's intense human interaction and constant scrutiny of motives and sentiments, however, seem to parody the ideals of pop psychology. Because their feelings are freed from the real world's disciplines, the patients become, indeed, children—they are dependent on their fathers and unable to get along without supervision. The narrator does not begin to recover and heal until she independently takes charge of her own therapy.

Images of death pervade the book. It opens with the grandmother's dying and the taunts of the grandmother's ghost, who calls the narrator a killer because her mother had died in childbirth. It turns on Shan's belief in the legend of the coffin tree, whose discovery will make him rich because its wood has the rare power to keep souls safe in their passage through death to rebirth. The narrator feels enormous guilt when Shan dies, but in the depression that follows, her plans for suicide make her realize, ironically, that she is not powerless and enable her, day by day, to stave off the moment of her ending. When she slashes her arm, she knows it is the pain of living that she wants to kill, not life itself. The aphorism "Living things prefer to go on living" opens and closes the book. At the beginning, it is only a piece of traditional wisdom but by the end, it has come to define the narrator: a living thing, in contrast to those who did not prefer life. She has become her own coffin tree, making a safe passage to rebirth.

Sally H. Mitchell

Sources for Further Study

America. CXLIX, August 27, 1983, p. 96.
The Atlantic. CCLI, June, 1983, p. 105.
Library Journal. CVIII, May 1, 1983, p. 920.
Los Angeles Times Book Review. April 13, 1983, p. 12.
Nation. CCXXXVI, April 30, 1983, p. 551.
The New York Times Book Review. LXXXVIII, May 15, 1983, p. 12.
Publishers Weekly. CCXXIII, March 4, 1983, p. 86.

A COLDER EYE
The Modern Irish Writers

Author: Hugh Kenner (1923-   )
Publisher: Alfred A. Knopf (New York). 301 pp. $16.45
Type of work: Literary history and criticism
Time: The twentieth century
Locale: Ireland

An investigation of some of the principal figures of modern Irish literature and the historical context in which they worked

> *Principal personages:*
> WILLIAM BUTLER YEATS, a major Irish poet of the twentieth century
> JAMES JOYCE, an Irish writer who has produced some of modern literature's masterworks
> JOHN MILLINGTON SYNGE, an Irish dramatist
> SAMUEL BECKETT, an Irish poet, critic, and playwright
> PATRICK KAVANAGH, a leading poet of the Irish Literary Revival
> AUSTIN CLARKE, an Irish poet
> SEAN O'CASEY, an Irish dramatist
> GEORGE RUSSELL, an Irish poet better known as Æ

In *A Colder Eye: The Modern Irish Writers*, Hugh Kenner adds yet another to his impressive list of books on modern literature. Having previously published important studies of, among others, Ezra Pound (two), Wyndham Lewis, James Joyce (three), Samuel Beckett (three), and the American modernists, Kenner is one of the kings of twentieth century literary criticism. In *A Colder Eye*, he turns his attention to Ireland, re-creating in his own idiosyncratic way the milieu out of which came so much that is central to modern literature.

It is common in modern literature and art for technique or style to attract more attention than content in the traditional sense. In *A Colder Eye*, Kenner contributes to a similar trend of recent years in the formerly staid world of literary criticism. From his opening dedication of the book to the memory of a fictional character, Leopold Bloom, to his arch one- and two-word descriptions of each person listed in the index (Pablo Picasso: "modish painter"; Beckett: "immobilist"), Kenner gives a study in the manipulation of tone, juxtaposition, and anecdote to create an extended effect rather than a logical argument.

The "colder eye" of Kenner's title is not only that of William Butler Yeats's horseman in his poem "Under Ben Bulben"; it is Kenner's, too, as he surveys modern Irish culture. Although at times affectionate, Kenner's tone is essentially condescending. Many writers and critics, following John Millington Synge and Yeats, have seen Ireland as primarily tragic; others, following Joyce, as largely comic. Kenner follows the later tradition, but without the sympathetic identification that keeps the comic spirit from turning to detached cynicism. Of the 1916 Easter Uprising he says, "If you can suppress thought of the pain, the bloodshed, all the spilt idealism, much of what's left is Keystone comedy." It is clear here and throughout that Kenner has little difficulty suppressing such thoughts; he follows this observation with an anecdote about a carload of inept rebels driving off the end of a pier and drowning themselves. That this central event in Irish history has frequently been mythologized beyond recognition is a point often made and well-taken; that it should be depicted as merely the bumblings of fools seems less advisable.

Kenner's puckish air extends to the writers he treats individually, none more so than Yeats. Kenner, refreshingly at times, will have none of the heavy seriousness with which other critics have treated every aspect of Yeats's passion for the occult, for private symbolic systems, ancient towers, and the like. Instead, Kenner presents to the reader a thoroughly materialistic Yeats striding self-importantly up and down the aisles of the Abbey Theatre assessing the nightly take, a coddled Yeats playing the sensitive poet summer after summer at Coole Park. Which aspects of a writer's character one heightens for what effect is a critic's choice, made for distinct purposes. Interestingly, in his masterpiece *The Pound Era* (1971), Kenner chose to treat with tragic high seriousness two men, Pound and Wyndham Lewis, whose lives and personalities offer at least as much potential for caricature and deflation as those of Yeats and his countrymen.

Kenner prepares the groundwork for his deflationary treatment of twentieth century Irish culture in his opening chapter, entitled "Warning," with a discussion of what he calls "Irish Fact." Bluntly put, Kenner says that the Irish are liars, though for charming reasons. There is a preference in Ireland for the rhetorically satisfying over the merely true, and Heaven help the wandering critic who believes everything he is told by priests, peasants, pub keepers, or even fellow critics. Kenner adduces various entertaining "Irish Facts," but does not address one's suspicion that there is nothing uniquely Irish about misinformation, tall tales, leg-pulling, apocryphal stories, and the like. By so beginning his book, however, Kenner offers a clear "reader beware" for what follows, thereby both protecting himself from certain kinds of criticism and aligning himself with a typically modernist view of truth, memory, and the past.

The part of the past with which *A Colder Eye* is primarily concerned is that modern movement in Irish culture often called the Irish Revival. Again, Kenner finds mostly buffoonery and benightedness; his novelist's gift for setting a scene is particularly evident in his evocation of the 1907 Abbey Theatre outbursts over Synge's *The Playboy of the Western World* (1907). Kenner portrays the revival as doomed, in a sense, by inherent tensions within Ireland itself. The revivalists, led by the likes of Yeats and Lady Gregory, tended to be Protestant, Anglo-Irish, and aristocratic in a time when any of these were cause for suspicion. Conflicts with single-minded nationalists were inevitable and debilitating. Nothing, including pure acts of the imagination, could escape politicization. It was enough to make one want to wash one's hands of the whole mess, and Joyce, for one, did exactly that.

An early and central concern in the revival was the collection of Irish folklore and the preservation of the Irish language. Kenner finds fertile ground for mockery in the doings of these passionate amateurs whose missionary zeal and inevitable blunders make them easy targets. Kenner, who long ago abandoned dull scholarly prose in his books, entertains the reader by slipping into his own version of pseudoIrish to parody the ignorant popularization in Irish journalism of folk speech:

> The trick is to drop in many a *'tis* and *wisha* and *imbeersa*, and always spell "yellow" *yella*, faith an' begorra, and though you've no ear at all for the tune of a sentence 'tis *Ireland's Own* and *Our Boys* will have ye into print so fast they'll not even read proof, awonomsa, and . . . make believe yer the voice of the oul' sod itself, mossa, the same that is watered wi' th' blood o' saints, begannies, and it rich too with the spuds, the Lord save us all.

Kenner has a fondness in all of his books for the unnoted connection in temporally contiguous events, and such juxtapositions are frequently startling in their suggestiveness. In *A Colder Eye*, however, they often seem strained (the supposedly metaphysical language of Synge's *The Playboy of the Western World* comes "only six years before Grierson's edition of Donne") or even farfetched (Kenner sees a hitherto undiscovered "conjunction of timing" in Synge's death, Yeats's sister having a vision of a ship on the same night, and the laying down, a week later, of the keel of the *Titanic*). As with much contemporary criticism, one admires the ingenuity without being certain what one has learned.

The same can be said for the considerable space that Kenner devotes to prosody. His careful attention to the intricacies of the poetic and dramatic line yields enough light from time to time to give one faith that something worthwhile is also being said when one no longer quite follows the argument. The confident identification of specific sources for particular poems and forms, however, tests that faith, sometimes to the breaking point.

If there is a thesis to the book, it has to do with language. Kenner sees the Irish co-option of the conqueror's tongue as one of the central developments (and ironies) of modernism. Joyce's *Ulysses* (1922), Kenner suggests, was a more effective act of rebellion than the Easter Uprising in that it simultaneously completed and destroyed the 150-year tradition of the English picaresque novel. The assumption that the Irish use the English language in the same manner as the English themselves masks a subversive intent—the secret revenge of the protean, oral Irish language.

Kenner is at his best in exploring the qualities of Irish and Irish English and their implications for modernist literature. The primary illustration is Joyce, and the ultimate exhibit his *Finnegans Wake* (1939), a book the language of which "is like Irish in its capacity for assimilating anything at all, likewise for being open to infinite misinterpretation." Kenner cites a study of Celtic languages to support his contention that meaning in Irish words and syntax (not to mention pronunciation) is unusually fluid and contextual, congruent with the modernist sensibility that finds its beginning and fulfillment in Joyce.

It is worth noting that the strongest parts of *A Colder Eye* deal with Joyce and Beckett, on both of whom Kenner has written extensively; significantly, neither was a part of the Irish revival, which Kenner is simply unable to take seriously. Joyce avoided its energy-draining entanglements and soon left Ireland, while Beckett matured after it was spent and also left for good measure. Kenner treats each with more respect than those who dirtied themselves in the Irish mud.

Kenner's characteristic love of the unusual angle enjoys mixed success in *A Colder Eye*. An attempt to link Joyce's *Dubliners* (1914) with the Gospels is uninspired, and critical acrobatics with the significance of the number eleven in *Ulysses* are merely tedious, but these are compensated for by an intriguing connection between Joyce's work as a Berlitz language teacher and the structure of *Ulysses*. The Berlitz method forbade the teacher to speak anything other than the tongue to be learned, the initial total ignorance of the learner notwithstanding. It was learning by immersion, each lesson making the next slightly more comprehensible. Likewise, *Ulysses*, Kenner points out, is a new kind of text which provides only gradually within itself the skills necessary to understand even the first page. Hence, the familiar observation that *Ulysses* cannot be read but only re-read.

A Colder Eye offers brief treatments of other Irish writers: Sean O'Casey, George William Russell (Æ), Patrick Kavanagh, and Austin Clarke among others. They serve more as tools for Kenner's debunking than as subjects deemed worthy of study for their own efforts. O'Casey, for example, serves well to show the fate of those who challenged the heroic version of Irish history—in this case, of the Easter Uprising. The reception in 1926 of Sean O'Casey's *The Plough and the Stars* at the Abbey proved that the Irish had changed little since the time of Synge's troubles. Kavanagh helps Kenner skewer the mythic version of the wonderful Irish peasantry so central to nationalist propaganda.

A Colder Eye is not easily evaluated. When one removes all of that which is doubtful, strained, or simply sarcastic, what is left? Kenner's search for a biographical origin for the mythical Stephen Daedalus in Joyce's *A Portrait of the Artist as a Young Man* (1916) perhaps offers a clue. A certain physics professor, Kenner relates, tried to fly with mechanical wings in the park behind Dublin's Trinity College: ". . . if (as seems probable when you think how word of queer sights gets round Dublin) one of the faces one day at the College Park railings was that of thirteen-year-old Jim Joyce, then. . . ." It is not necessary to finish the sentence. A great improbability magically "seems probable," and the Irish character is invoked to harden the evidence. More than anything else in *A Colder Eye*, the reader is in the presence of a critic playing Irish storyteller. Warning readers from the beginning to beware of the "Irish Fact," Kenner has adopted a strongly oral and highly entertaining style, lapsing at times into the vernacular himself; as he has done in the past with books on Pound and T. S. Eliot, he has adopted the style of his subject. Those who object to the stereotype of the Irish as essentially comical, incompetent, born to futility, but lovable, especially when drunk, are not likely to be pleased by Kenner's book. The rest may be satisfied that they have heard a good story, even if not the truth.

Daniel Taylor

Sources for Further Study

Antioch Review. XLI, Fall, 1983, p. 507.
Choice. XXI, October, 1983, p. 278.
Christian Science Monitor. October 18, 1983, p. 25.
Library Journal. CVIII, April 15, 1983, p. 825.
National Review. XXXV, April 15, 1983, p. 444.
New Statesman. CVI, August 5, 1983, p. 26.
The New York Review of Books. XXX, May 12, 1983, p. 40.
Publishers Weekly. CCXXIII, March 11, 1983, p. 74.
Saturday Review. IX, July, 1983, p. 48.

THE COLLECTED LETTERS OF JOSEPH CONRAD
Volume I: 1861-1897

Author: Joseph Conrad (1857-1924)
Edited, with introductions by, Frederick R. Karl and Laurence Davies
Publisher: Cambridge University Press (Cambridge, England). Illustrated. 446 pp.
$39.50
Type of work: Letters

The first volume of the collected and newly edited letters of Joseph Conrad, covering the period from his childhood to the publication of The Nigger of the "Narcissus"

When complete, the Cambridge edition of Joseph Conrad's letters will mark the first time that all available letters from Joseph Conrad have been collected into one edition: 3,500 pieces of Conrad's correspondence, including telegrams, postcards, and brief notes, some fifteen hundred of which have never appeared before, will have been collected into eight volumes.

The only other attempt at a comprehensive edition of Conrad's letter was G. Jean-Aubry's *Joseph Conrad: Life and Letters* (1927). As Frederick R. Karl points out in his general editor's introduction to the Cambridge edition, however, Jean-Aubry's edition contains silent deletions of the text of letters, sometimes for reasons of delicacy, sometimes for no apparent reason. Nevertheless, even for the Cambridge edition, the editors have had to rely often on Jean-Aubry's printed text for letters now lost. Other editions of Conrad's letters have focused on particular correspondents but have generally complemented the earlier work of Jean-Aubry: Edward Garnett's *Letters from Joseph Conrad, 1895-1924* (1928); John A. Gee and Paul J. Sturm's *Letters of Joseph Conrad to Marguerite Poradowska, 1890-1920* (1940); William Blackburn's *Joseph Conrad: Letters to William Blackwood and David S. Meldrum* (1958); Zdzisław Najder's *Conrad's Polish Background: Letters to and from Polish Friends* (1964); and C. T. Watt's *Joseph Conrad's Letters to R. B. Cunninghame Graham* (1969).

Karl's general editor's introduction describes some of the difficulties remaining even to the editor of a modern novelist's letters. Many important letters are lost, notably many Polish originals destroyed in Warsaw in 1944. In these cases, the editors have had to rely on already published texts, with little to guide their editorial decisions except Jean-Aubry's unreliable English-printed text and his manuscript which he translated into French from the Polish. Nevertheless, the editors have vigilantly tried to avoid repeating the editorial errors of the past. Whenever possible—and this was done with the majority of the letters—the originals have been transcribed and, in the case of French or Polish letters, newly translated. For example, volume 1 contains many letters in French to Marguerite Poradowska, whom Conrad referred to as "Aunt" (they were distantly related). All of the original texts of their letters were available at Yale University, allowing for fresh translations of the text rather than relying on previously published English translations.

The general editor's aim "has been to furnish texts and notes useful to the scholar which, at the same time, do not discourage the general reader." For the scholar, this edition will be indispensable; the appeal of the letters to the general reader may not be so evident. However, for the scholar and indeed for any general reader interested in letters of this kind, Karl and Davies have provided a layout that is both pleasing in its clarity and complete in its annotations. The layout for each letter welcomes rather than thwarts the reader. Each letter's correspondent is indicated clearly in bold type, and below the correspondent's name is the source of the text. From this brief but important annotation, the scholar recognizes at a glance whether the text is from a manuscript at Yale, for example, or is a text based on a collation of Jean-Aubry's published English text of a letter with a French translation of the original. Similarly, notes concerning the dating of a letter are indicated clearly as footnotes, with the evidence for assigning a date to an undated or unclearly dated letter given.

Finally, the text itself reflects Conrad's hand, complete with capitalized "You" and "Vous." Occasional lapses of penmanship are corrected by means of square brackets in the text of the letter, as are obviously missing words and the occasional slip of the pen. Any Conradian spellings are left as they appear with an unobtrusive asterisk to note the spelling as such. For the scholar, the text as Conrad wrote it is easily appreciated; for the general reader, the text is clear, offering uninterrupted reading.

With an edition of this kind, one expects copious annotations. The editors have keenly kept both scholarly and general readers in mind by supplying appropriate footnotes to various points in the text, even to the extent of repeating a similar note in a later letter. Although this results in some duplication, it answers the needs of the general reader who may not read the letters in order. For the scholar, the repeated notes clarify vague points. The only shortcoming to the editors' style in this regard is that notes to those letters in French appear only below the French text, not below the English translation as well, so that readers unfamiliar with French may have some small trouble assigning a footnote to a place in the translated text. In all, though, the layout of the letters is exemplary.

It is, of course, the text of the letters themselves that should receive the most attention. Volume 1 comprises letters from the first forty years of Conrad's life—the beginning of his sea career, his four months in the Congo, his retirement from the sea, the publication of his first novel, *Almayer's Folly* (1895), his marriage to Jessie George in 1896, and the publication of his critically successful, *The Nigger of the "Narcissus"* in 1897.

This first volume, however, does have some remarkable biographical gaps that the scholar may expect but which the general reader will be disappointed to find. For example, there are no letters from Conrad as an adolescent and only a few letters detailing his early sea career. Therefore, the general reader will find biographies of Conrad far more helpful than the first volume of letters. Once Conrad left the sea, his circle of correspondents expanded to include not only relatives and family friends but also publishers and literary figures such as Stephen Crane, H. G. Wells, and Henry James. This period of Conrad's life as a novelist is already well documented, and the general reader may be disappointed here, too, for the letters do not reveal anything startlingly new. The scholar may expect less in this regard and will probably be delighted at the previously unpublished letters found in this volume.

The bulk of the letters in this volume are to Marguerite Poradowska, a distant aunt and possibly a romantic attachment for Conrad, and to Edward Garnett (the husband of Constance Garnett, the great translator of Russian literature), then a reader for the publisher T. Fisher Unwin, with whom Conrad shared his doubts about himself as a writer, and from whom Conrad sought business advice about contract terms with Unwin as well as about the placing of his fiction.

The letters to Marguerite Poradowska show Conrad as an admirer of a distant relative who has published—as well as the admirer of a beautiful woman. There has been much speculation about their relationship and its eventual cooling. The early letters to her indicate a dutiful, familial status, with Conrad often signing himself her "affectionate nephew," while a later letter in 1891 salutes her with "I admire you and love you more and more. I kiss your hands" (July 8, 1891). With Poradowska, he despairs at the mistake he had made in wanting the Congo assignment and refers to one of her letters "as a ray of sunshine piercing through the grey clouds of a dreary, winter day, for my days here are dreary" (September 26, 1890). The same letter describes his experiences while he waits for a new boat to command:

> Everything here is repellent to me. Men and things, but men above all. And I am repellent to them, also. . . . The new boat will not be completed until June of next year, perhaps. Meanwhile, my position here is unclear and I am troubled by that. . . . I suffered an attack of dysentery lasting five days. I feel somewhat weak physically and not a little demoralized.

This was the experience that provided the background for *Heart of Darkness* (1902).

By September, 1892, on returning to London after one of several passages as first mate aboard the *Torrens*, Conrad finds it "impossible . . . to break this solitude" of working onboard to see Poradowska and signs the letter "Your very devoted/ J. Conrad" (September 4, 1892), an obvious contrast to the warmth of a year or two before. The letters stop abruptly in June, 1895, not to appear again until April, 1900 (volume 1 extends only to 1897). It is not known whether there were any other letters, although, as the editors' note to a June, 1895, letter indicates, Conrad does mention "news" from his "Aunt Margot" in December, 1897, suggesting that their correspondence continued but was destroyed, suppressed, or lost. The latter seems unlikely, because so many of the Poradowska letters are extant.

It was with Poradowksa that Conrad showed his excitement at having the manuscript of *Almayer's Folly* accepted by the publisher T. Fisher Unwin. In the same letter, however, with a novel accepted and work on "The Two Vagabonds" in progress, Conrad's thoughts were still directed to finding work as a seaman: "Now, I need only a ship in order to be almost happy" (October 4, 1894). In fact, he was not to return to the sea except for occasional recreational outings and voyages as a passenger.

Laurence Davies notes the variety of audiences the letters address and the range of personalities Conrad offered his correspondents. One reading only those letters to a publisher, for example, might declare Conrad to be, as Davies puts it, "fussily professional," but it is the virtue of a collected edition to show readers all sides of the writer's personality. In his letters to family members, Conrad strikes an almost breathtakingly correct, yet warm and concerned tone, never forgetting to request embraces for the children (whom he could not have seen in years) and always offering kind remembrances to the older members of the family. Similarly, in matters of business with T. Fisher Unwin, whom he derides in his letters to Edward Garnett, he is professionally correct. This manner, Davies suggests, "is the expression both of a Polish gentlemen's loyalty to the code of his ancestors and of a ship's officer's conviction that everything must be done in the proper way."

With Garnett, Conrad was open and friendly, often relying on him for advice about his business dealings with his publisher. As the letters to him demonstrate, Garnett—later to become a celebrated editor—was more than simply a publisher's reader to Conrad; Conrad shares with him the joys of publication and the lows of facing blank sheets of paper each day. Clearly they were close, and on occasion, it would be Conrad consoling Garnett whose own work was sometimes rejected for publication. It was to Edward Garnett that Conrad first sent his famous preface to *The Nigger of the "Narcissus"* in August, 1897; Garnett suggested certain revisions to which Conrad in the main agreed.

The letters to Henry James and H. G. Wells—two letters each in this volume—are tentative. In 1896, Conrad wrote to the anonymous reviewer of *An Outcast of the Islands* in the *Saturday Review*. The reviewer was H. G. Wells. Conrad's happy surprise (he had been reading Wells's short stories) is evident in a second letter a week after the first but gives no indication that Wells would become one of Conrad's circle of friends. The letters to James, one in French, are formal letters of praise to explain Conrad's sending him copies of *An Outcast of the Islands* and later *The Nigger of the "Narcissus."*

The letters to Crane are less formal—they met in October, 1897—and Conrad is comfortable asking Crane his opinion of the ending of *The Nigger of the "Narcissus."* This letter is free of formality and full of a sincere affection, like that found in letters to Conrad's relatives.

The letters to his other correspondents of this period—the young seaman turned writer Edward Noble, Cunninghame Graham, the Briquel family, the Sandersons, and others—merely confirm what is already known about Conrad. Nevertheless, the first volume does provide a fine mix of the everyday and the aesthetic, with a glimpse into the ending of a career at sea and the beginnings of a great novelist.

Paul A. Bateman

Sources for Further Study

The Economist. CCXC, October 22, 1983, p. 99.
Harper's. CCLXVII, November 1983, p. 60.
Library Journal. CVIII, August, 1983, p. 1483.
Los Angeles Times Book Review. November 25, 1983, p. 40.
The New Yorker. LIX, January 9, 1984, p. 106.
Publishers Weekly. CCXXIV, August 26, 1983, p. 379.

COLLECTED POEMS, 1970-1983

Author: Donald Davie (1922-   )
Publisher: University of Notre Dame Press (Notre Dame, Indiana). 172 pp. $14.95
Type of work: Poetry

In these intellectually lively poems, the self is subordinated to the issue, the observation, the business of living in a complex world in which civilization's networks are always informing one's experience while simultaneously undergoing change

Donald Davie is one of those increasingly rare individuals who is a significant force both as a creative writer and as a critic. The shape of his career harkens back to the long line of English masters of letters that includes John Dryden, Samuel Johnson, Matthew Arnold, and—in the twentieth century—such American figures as T. S. Eliot and Allen Tate. Equally at home with the creative or critical act, knowledgeable about the literary and social issues in both Great Britain and the United States, Davie is a fine exemplar of a vanishing breed. As a critic and editor, he has grappled with such topics as diction and syntax in English poetry, the languages of science and literature, the literature of English dissent, Augustan poetry, William Wordsworth, Thomas Hardy, and Ezra Pound; he has translated poems by Boris Pasternak, among others. Davie's own poems have filled many volumes, beginning with *Brides of Reason* in 1955. His first twenty years of poetic activity were gathered in *Collected Poems: 1950-1970* (1972). The present volume is a retrospective of what he has accomplished since then.

Collected Poems, 1970-1983 brings together three full-length collections, a cluster of three long poems, an appendix of two previously uncollected poems, and an introductory piece, "Pilate," labeled "A Poem of the 1960s," that explores the psychology of the keeper of standards. In "Pilate," Davie makes an oblique assessment of his own role as a critic whose severity has been criticized in turn. The poem questions the motives and ultimate value of the keeper of standards in a political and moral context, but the literary context is easily imagined. One cannot be sure whether Davie wants mercy or justice for the poems that follow. Most readers will incline toward leniency.

In *The Shires* (1974), Davie presents an alphabet of England's political geography, beginning with Bedfordshire and ending with his native Yorkshire. Each poem is named, simply, for the shire it describes, though description is both more and less than what Davie attempts. *The Shires*, which can be thought of as one long poem, risks tedium and sameness while it gains a natural unity. To solve the problem of encyclopedic dullness, Davie has pushed for the greatest formal, stylistic, and tonal variety from segment to segment while maintaining throughout a recognizable, consistent voice. This tour de force is successful. Hints of landscape, historical significances, native sons, and literary anecdote are effectively mixed with the poet's subjective reactions to each place. Each poem takes a different shape, as if Davie sought to provide not only the appropriate images and language but also a formal objective correlative for his own inner sense of each locale.

Most of these poems are short sketches; as such, they illustrate Davie's ability to be brief without being superficial. His well-honed vocabulary allows economy through precision, as in the following lines on Robert Walpole from "Norfolk": "Walpole: heaven-high smell of/ Whitewash on tainted beef,/ Piquant in learning's nostril." While Davie's work maintains a clear literal level, each word is suggestively ripe, and word combinations reveal shadings that entertain and enrich.

Davie is called, and has called himself, a traditionalist. This label, however, is not warranted by slavish employment of traditional devices or models. Davie refashions what he inherits. He is a traditionalist in that his poems are more reader-oriented than is now customary. The demands he makes on the reader are the demands of language itself, not private allusion or confessional minutiae: Davie insists that the reader be alert to histories, resonances, and boundaries of words. Another way in which Davie might be considered a traditionalist is that his poems are in the service of cultural conveyance. In these intellectually lively poems, the self is subordinated to the issue, the observation, the business of living in a complex world in which civilization's networks are always informing one's experience while simultaneously undergoing change.

The self, however, the reflecting, reacting persona, is what enlivens *The Shires*, itself a back-and-forth movement through British civilization. The poet's interaction with place, whether it be casual and incidental or deeply affective, gives these poems an edge over the best guidebook verses. Most of these were probably finished after Davie made the United States his primary residence in 1968, allowing memory a useful distance, a distance from which the whole of Davie's England is beheld.

In the Stopping Train and Other Poems (1977) is as impressive in its range as *The Shires* is in its purposeful limitations. Art and artists are a central concern in this collection; poems such as "Rousseau in His Day," "Mandelstam, on Dante," and "Death of a Painter" remind one how much, for Davie, art is made out of art. In this way, too, he is a traditionalist—always ready to bring the history of art into present relevance or to make one artist's accomplishment the springboard for a new poem. "Orpheus" and "Ars Poetica" are contemplations on the motives for and functions of the creative act and the artwork itself. The reader learns in "Ars Poetica," an elegy for the sculptor Michael Ayrton, that

> Most poems, or the best,
> Describe their own birth, and this
> Is what they are—a space
> Cleared to walk around in.

Other poems respond to Davie's contemporaries; for example, "To Thom Gunn in Los Altos, California" and the "Judith Wright, Australian" section of the book's title poem.

"In the Stopping Train" is the most ambitious and successful of a number of poems in which Davie works at self-understanding and self-correction. Not modishly confessional, "In the Stopping Train" develops an almost outlandish analogy in imaginative and moving ways. The man in the train that both stops and goes becomes a figure for the poet's (and most readers') obsession with destinations and purposes and with the paradoxical way in which stopping, starting, going, and ending are linked experiences. Also, the poem questions the humanity of the word-lover who may be living only at the level of language:

> Jonquil is a sweet word.
> Is it a flowering bush?
> Let him helplessly wonder
> for hours if perhaps he's seen it.
> ....
> He never needed to see,
> not with his art to help him.
> He never needed to use his
> nose, except for language.

Here, and in poems such as "His Themes," "Morning," and "To a Teacher of French," Davie approaches an uneasy peace with his own habits of mind.

Formal disciplines are more noticeable in this collection than in *The Shires*. There are many tightly rhymed stanzaic poems, though Davie is so addicted to enjambment that there is not always a lyrical payoff. In fact, Davie's lyric gift, if judged only by *Collected Works, 1970-1983,* may be questioned. Few poems, even the rhymed and measured ones, give forth a pleasurable music. Davie seems to resist musicality; he either mistrusts it or cannot achieve it. Given the satiric, critical impulse that lies behind many of the poems, the auditory flatness may be a conscious choice. Still, there is too much awkwardness and off-key phrasing. Davie's writing rises to the status of poetry in part because he would otherwise be giving us excellent prose. He is an amazingly agile sentence-maker (as any reader of his criticism will discover), yet this skill alone would not be sufficient for poetry. Added to it is Davie's ability to focus complex issues and experiences through powerful language and imagery; it is through such concentration and condensation that Davie reveals himself a poet.

In many of his poems, Davie is a man of ideas and a social critic. "Depravity: Two Sermons" finds him in this role. His affinities with the Augustan poetic stance, affinities to be expected from a survey of his critical undertakings, affect the kind of singing that Davie achieves. There is a constant search for sense, a constant application of reason that is antithetical to lyric outbursts.

Like the Augustans, and like T. S. Eliot, Davie is a learned and allusive poet. "Horae Canonicae," more euphonious than most poems in this collection, shows many of Davie's strengths and predilections at once.

Before taking leave of *The Stopping Train and Other Poems*, one must notice the five-part revisiting of so many shires, the most overt connection between this volume and its predecessor. Finally, "Townend, 1976," another return to Yorkshire, concludes the book with a characteristic blending of objective and subjective history. It is also one of those poems in which Davie's endless curiosity about words is given play, here on the name "Townend" itself. *The Shires* and *The Stopping Train and Other Poems* reveal a mature poet of diverse gifts, one who shows his alertness to the passing spectacle and to passing poetic fashions but who has found his own way to go.

Three for Water-Music (1981) is an arresting grouping that has marginal connection to contemporary poetic manners, though the poems superficially resemble the modern poetic sequence. These poems are best characterized as irregular odes in the manner of Dryden, the several parts of each composition formally distinctive and unlike the others. Each of the odes is divided into five parts, and in each ode the opening section employs couplet rhyme to announce the theme. After this common opening, the odes develop differently: Some stanzas are carefully rhymed, while others use subdued rhymes or no rhymes at all.

In his title, Davie may be alluding to the *Water Music* of the great neoclassical composer, George Frederick Handel. *Water Music* was written at the request of Handel's patron, King George I of England, and was so titled because it was meant to accompany the movement of the royal barge along the Thames. Handel, who set a number of Dryden's lyrics to music, would be a congenial eighteenth century figure to inspire Donald Davie, though Davie may have had quite another kind of water music in mind. Because two of the poems in this grouping refer to fountains, the movement of the fountain water could be considered a kind of visual music to which the poems are responsive.

Each poem addresses sexual aggression, and the first and last retell, in part, ancient myths of rape. In one case, "The Fountain of Cyanë," tears of grief turn Cyanë into a pool when she learns of her friend's rape. "The Fountain of Arethusa" is a similar "explanation" of how a certain body of water came into being. The middle poem, "Wild Boar Clough," tells a modern British story of brutishness, its celebration, inevitability, and consequences. Moving backward and forward in time in each poem, Davie weaves a complex triptych that involves considerations both transient and universal, political and aesthetic, personal and public. *Three for Water-Music* shows the fire and wit of Davie's other work, but here there is more virtuoso display of craft and even more homage to literary traditions.

Davie's most recent title to be housed in this collected works is *The Battered*

Wife and Other Poems (1982), a considerably larger assemblage than either *The Shires* or *In the Stopping Train*. The poems here are even more splendidly varied, the level of achievement quite high, and the faults and strengths shine through even more intensely. When Davie does manage to sound lyric, he sounds least original—sometimes like Hardy, sometimes like an anonymous balladeer. More often, he exhibits a concern for craft that is effective in diction and compactness, but almost tone-deaf. There is a poem in *The Battered Wife* that may be a clue to Davie's limitations. "Having No Ear," while it concerns appreciating music, may have application to the oral and auditory qualities of poetry:

> Having no ear, I hear
> And do not hear the piano-tuner ping,
> Ping, ping one string beneath me here, where I
> Ping-ping one string of Caroline English to
> Tell if Edward Taylor tells
> The truth, or no.

The poem is one of many concerned with moral integrity and religious fervor; as such, it mirrors Davie's critical studies of religious writers and movements, reminding one once again of how essentially unified his career has been:

> Dear God, such gratitude
> As I owe thee for giving, in default
> Of a true ear or of true holiness,
> This trained and special gift of knowing when
> Religious poets speak themselves to God,
> And when, to men.

Davie, most often, speaks to men. He is entertaining and always careful to be clear, but not at the expense of his genuine complexity of thought. The current of thought is the shaping current of his best work, whether or not it be supported by rhymes or stanzaic scaffolding. In poems such as "Artifex in Extremis," Davie shows his talent for this kind of meditative verse, and he shows that he is a poet still improving, still finding the occasional grand success that justifies the marginal achievements.

The Battered Wife and Other Poems is divided into four parts, the last of which is a group of "Translations and Imitations" that testifies, once again, to Davie's sense of poetry as a continuum of many voices. These exercises suggest how Davie's poetry and criticism feed each other, how the critical and creative faculties can merge rather than be at war. Davie's models in this section are Pierre de Ronsard, Boris Pasternak, and Osip Mandelstam, while he addresses his contemporaries on both sides of the Atlantic, Robert Pinsky and Seamus Heaney.

Two final poems—one on nineteenth century England ("Lady Cochrane") and one on the poet's relationship to his homeland today ("To Londoners")— and Davie's *Collected Poems, 1970-1983* comes to an end. It is a winning performance, an honest, intense series of probings into language and thought, culture, history, and personality. If Davie's lines go flat too often, if his line breaks are often suspect, if his sense of language's music is weak, one can forgive him for his true and able concern with the making of literature: his versatility in prosodic forms; his accurate sense of what makes a proper subject for his poems; his care in the development of complex issues and experiences; his respect for tradition, for language, and for his readers.

Philip K. Jason

Sources for Further Study

Christian Science Monitor. December 2, 1983, p. Bl.
Listener. September 1, 1983, p. 22.
London Review of Books. August 18, 1983, p. 23.
New Statesman. August 5, 1983, p. 23.

THE COLLECTED POEMS OF ROBERT CREELEY
1945-1975

Author: Robert Creeley (1926-   )
Publisher: University of California Press (Berkeley). 671 pp. $28.50
Type of work: Poetry

Thirty years of Creeley's poetry, including early volumes long out of print and several uncollected poems

Born in 1926 and reared in the Great Depression, Robert Creeley published his first poem in 1945 in *Wake*, an upstart Harvard University literary magazine created as an alternative to the established forums. The poem "Return" tells tersely of a son come home to proper people and subdued streets. "Enough for now to be here, and/ To know my door is one of these." Since 1945, Creeley has wandered widely—Mallorca, New Mexico, London, California, New York City—always at home in the world but never quite finding home itself: Ulysses without followers, engaged in the quiet heroism of daily life. Quite consciously, he rejected the allusive poetic model that so dominated the American scene in his youth. Instead, Creeley drew on native American rebels—William Carlos Williams and Charles Olson—in his search for a cultural home. In *The Collected Poems of Robert Creeley*, that search—in technique, subject matter and attitude—reads like a history of postmodernist American poetry. Taken as a single work, this volume stands as an updated version of Walt Whitman's *Leaves of Grass* (1855, first publication).

From the dust jacket of his collected first thirty years, Creeley stares intently with his one good eye—the left eye, lost very young, is shut, sunken, almost asleep: a face divided as his poetry. Coming of age as he did in the midst of the last good war, Creeley began early to reject the tenets of T. S. Eliot and to embrace the newly forming American postmodernist poetry. He attended Harvard, but with few ill effects; he was never graduated. His Massachusetts roots do not betray themselves. Born to a physician-father and nurse-mother, New England to the core, Creeley seldom writes about his early years directly, seldom is concerned with the past or the future. What matters most is *now* and *here*, for he is existential, a son of the contemporary disorder which he takes to be the norm. When he was four, his father died; supported by his working mother, Creeley was reared by a semiretarded motherly housekeeper—almost an orphan and, like Huck Finn, able to create himself in his own image.

In 1944, Creeley took a leave of absence from Harvard to volunteer for the American Field Service in Burma, the only way a one-eyed man could get to the war. When he returned in 1945, he reentered Harvard, married, and moved to the artist community in Provincetown, a long commute to the Harvard campus. He soon dropped out, never to return. Determined to become a poet, he and his wife and the children that quickly followed lived precariously on his wife's small income from her trust fund. By 1950, Creeley had discovered the beginnings of his American root system. He corresponded with Ezra Pound, Charles Olson, and William Carlos Williams; and Olson and Williams in turn led him back to their prototype: Walt Whitman. (In 1973, Creeley edited *Whitman* for Penguin Books.)

Olson, who dedicated *The Maximus Poems* (1983) to Creeley, wrote him in 1950, saying: "creeley says, he's a boll weevil, olson, just a lookin' for a lang[uage], just a lookin' nuts, and i says, creeley, you're off yer trolley: a man god damn well has to come up with his own lang[uage], syntax and song both, but also each poem under hand has its own language, which is variant of same." This is the same advice that Walt Whitman read in Ralph Waldo Emerson's seminal essay, "The Poet," a hundred years earlier: The poet must generate his own voice, his own form; no two poems must or should look the same. Creeley learned the lesson early and practiced it late. By 1952, he was living cheaply on the Mediterranean island of Mallorca, running his own Divers Press and finding his poetic voice and form. From Olson, Williams, Pound, and Whitman, he learned that line length should not be dictated by outworn poetic measures. In 1913, Pound had argued for a natural, musically driven line. Olson, with his Projectivist theories, said that line length should be no longer than the stress that formed it: a subjective length felt by the poet. Williams had long been conducting his own experiments with a native American line length.

All of these forces came together in Creeley to produce a poem such as "Le Fou" written for Olson:

> who plots, then, the lines
> talking, taking, always the beat from
> the breath
>   (moving slowly at first
> the breath
>   which is slow—
>
> I mean, graces come slowly,
> it is that way.

Here are Olson's open parentheses, broken sentences, and unconventional spacing, all of which look and sound a lot like William Carlos Williams; here, also, one sees Creeley's typical avoidance of end-stopped lines. The subject matter is the poet in the process of writing the poem, as in so much of modern poetry. Indeed, throughout these collected poems, Creeley is much preoccupied with the life of the poet in the act of writing poetry.

Words, for Creeley, are more than symbols; in the poet's eye, they become the thing itself, the very world of his creation, for he must "think it all into/

reality, that world, each time, new." The poet is more than the name-giver; he is the creator, the magician, the magus. Reality, as modern physics suggests, is perpetually changing, shifting. The poet's task is not to think too deeply or meditate too long: "There is nothing/ but what thinking makes/ it less tangible." Rather, the poet must make concrete in words his own reality: "The mind,/ fast as it goes, loses// pace, puts in place of it/ like rocks simple markers. . . ." Creeley celebrates words, the title of his third major book published in 1967, "Words/ are/ pleasure./ All/ words." Beginning in the early 1950's with carefully crafted, tight poems, Creeley by 1969 was jotting down the fragments of his world into notebooks as quickly as the words came, revising as little as possible. The results were published as *Pieces* (1969). The poem was no longer an object or a necessarily distinct unit; it had become his life and the poet a sensitive barometer and seismograph tuned to his times. "There is no trick to reality—/ a mind/ makes it, any/ mind."

The deeper one reads into *The Collected Poems of Robert Creeley*, the more Whitmanesque and existential they become, for Creeley recognizes a major truth of the age: "No one lives in/ the life of another—/ no one knows." People exist in isolation, strangers among strangers, knowing only themselves. The words and the pieces become a life record, filled with contradictions. "Do I contradict myself?" asked Whitman. "Very well then, I contradict myself. I am vast. I contain multitudes." The neo-Romantic poet is less sure of containing multitudes, but he is certain that his own reality is multitudinous and significant: The self matters still. The fabled heroes who spoke to olden times may be dead, but the poet-hero remains a possibility: "This is Robert Creeley . . . the mountains/ and the desert are waiting/ for the heroes. . . ." Creeley becomes the poet-hero that Emerson and Whitman demanded for America.

Above all else, Creeley remains the poet of love, the recorder of the male-female conflict. Williams did not need to tell him, "Divorce is the sign of our times." Creeley learned it the hard way. His first marriage ended in divorce, giving him material for a wealth of poems that record all too humanly the little conflicts that make and mar a marriage: "since the day we were married/ we have never had a towel/ where anyone could find it. . . ." To withhold love, Creeley knows, is to be lonely; to love is to be vulnerable: "If you never do anything for anyone else/ you are spared the tragedy of human relation-/ ships." His prototypical husband finally "gave up loving/ and lived with her." One of the final results is Creeley's wonderful "Ballad of the Despairing Husband," which begins

My wife and I lived alone,
contention was our only bone.
I fought with her, she fought with me,
and things went on right merrily.

Creeley's ability to remain detached and yet passionate, his sense of controlled indifference to emotionally charged situations produce the ironic stance so typical of his mature work.

Like D. H. Lawrence, Robert Graves, and William Carlos Williams—all of whom he read and enjoyed—Creeley, too, is driven by worship of the female principle, the fleshy muse, the life force, the White Goddess, Kore, the lady accompanied by goat men: "Her hair held earth./ Her eyes were dark./ A double flute/ made her move." She is the ideal woman, whose real manifestations never quite match the poet's desire. In "The Wife," the poet is torn between two women: One is a woman of flesh and bone, human and flawed, and "The other in my mind/ occurs./ She keeps her strict/ proportion there// . . . how shall he/ who has a wife/ yield two to one/ and watch the other die." Driven by love yet knowing that real and ideal are never one, knowing that the self is ever isolated, Creeley's lover is frequently a lonely man, much aware of his loneliness in rainy streets or furnished rooms.

Less accessible than his love poetry are those poems written to, for, and about the artists and poets whom Creeley knows so well. In 1954, Creeley became the editor of Charles Olson's famous but short-lived *Black Mountain Review*, the voice of Black Mountain College, where Creeley taught briefly from 1955 to 1956 just before that experiment went under. At Black Mountain, Creeley connected with many of the major artists of the postwar generation. In late 1956, he was in San Francisco, where he met Allen Ginsberg, Gary Snyder, Jack Kerouac, and Kenneth Rexroth. Ginsberg's infamous *Howl* had just been published, and the Beat Generation was under way. Louis Zukofsky and his lifework, *"A"* (1978), influenced Creeley, as did Robert Duncan, Kenneth Patchen, and Robert Bly. Throughout Creeley's collected poems, these names appear, frequently leaving the uninformed reader wondering. Painters from the period—Robert Indiana, Chuck Hinman, Jim Dine—also find their place in the poetry. To read Creeley's "Numbers" sequence, it helps to know a similar sequence of paintings by Indiana, whose phrase "Peace, brother," runs through a part of Creeley's work. The poem "Chuck Hinman" is unintelligible unless the reader is aware of Hinman's three-dimensional canvas color-planes. These poems are important, for they suggest that the poet does not write in a vacuum. To understand Creeley, one must first know the literary and artistic history of his time.

The reader of Creeley's collected poems must proceed on faith: Not every poem is accessible, but enough of them are so close to the bone that the effort is rewarded. Like all men, Creeley is sometimes silly, sometimes vain; he fails and falters. Always, however, he is looking for order in a world of entropy, coming finally to believe, as Whitman professed, that there is a grand scheme, a meaning to diverse experience: "One day after another—/ perfect./ They all fit." Like Whitman, Creeley insists, "The plan is the body." Order is natural, it is there to find if only one looks: "Place/ a lake/ on ground, water/ finds a form." Form is order; the poet creates his world inside of forms and thus imposes order on what seems chaotic. Water, a favorite source of imagery for Creeley, imposes form, and "Everything is water if you look long enough." For love, then, and for order and form, for pain and loneliness, for failure and friendship, this collection becomes a life of its times, offering readers a way to know themselves.

Michael S. Reynolds

Sources for Further Study

Choice. XX, July, 1983, p. 1594.
Christian Science Monitor. May 13, 1984, p. B8.
Harper's. CCLVII, September, 1983, p. 67.
Library Journal. CVIII, March 1, 1983, p. 503.
Los Angeles Times Book Review. April 17, 1983, p. 8.
The New York Times Book Review. LXXXVIII, August 7, 1983, p. 13.
Publishers Weekly. CCXXII, October 29, 1983, p. 38.
Virginia Quarterly Review. LIX, Summer, 1983, p. 96.

THE COLLECTED STORIES OF COLETTE

Author: Colette (Sidonie-Gabrielle Colette, 1873-1954)
Translated from the French by Matthew Ward, Antonia White, Anne-Marie
 Callimachi, and others
Edited, with an introduction, by Robert Phelps
Publisher: Farrar, Straus and Giroux (New York). 605 pp. $19.95
Type of work: Short stories

A passionate dissection of the disguises and objectives of love for oneself and others

Colette's career as a writer spans most of the first half of the twentieth century, and she gives the reader not only a glimpse of her own life during that period and earlier but also of the intimate lives of the people she observed as a child in Burgundy, a music-hall performer in various French towns, a traveler in the south of France and in North Africa, and a resident of Paris. She often includes herself—or a version of herself—in her stories, and when she does, she emphasizes the idea of the narrator looking closely at her material until she sees more and more of its meaning. The majority of Colette's stories, in fact, are about perception in one form or another—appearances and the truth behind them, characters seeing what they can or want to until they are forced by their own actions or those of others, or by circumstances, to see truly, or the reader himself drawn to a climax in which he sees the characters' personalities and actions with sudden clarity.

If Colette's stories are a mode of observing closely and in detail, often what is observed and revealed is the nature of character. Colette presents in her stories a rich variety of women who show their nature through dialogue and action. In "My Corset Maker," the main character (who does all the talking, as the characters in the monologue stories do) at first seems to betray cattiness by insisting that her client has put on weight, but in the end she betrays conceit and a touch of avarice by extolling the corset she herself has invented to hide the bodily flaws of the women who come to her. The proprietress in "The Sémiramis Bar" seems a vulgar ogress to outsiders such as the narrator's female friend Valentine, but she is really tenderhearted and maternal to her poor, bohemian regulars. Among the women who perform in the music halls, of whom Colette presents an extensive array, there are those who stand out as vivid paradoxes. Bastienne in "Bastienne's Child" is young, beautiful, and lives to dance, but she turns out to have the plainest of tastes and to have a genius for and a dedication to the domestic life. The lesbian in "Gitanette" has an idyllic affair with her fellow performer, and then she not only reveals to the narrator that she has been deserted but also that her sorrow is what keeps her alive. The actresses in "The Victim" take pity on Josette, a lovely girl whose actor boyfriend is killed in World War I; they give her sewing jobs and finally she gets a bit part in a play. In short, Josette's loss and her poverty endear her to the people who know her, but then her life takes a dramatic turn which casts her into a condition opposite to the generous and excited one that used to be hers. She marries a rich man whom she does not love and is bitterly jealous of him because he is hopelessly in love with her—that is, because he has everything.

The aging woman is a type to which Colette often returns in her stories. The narrator's acquaintances in "Alix's Refusal" make fun of the main character, but this gives the narrator an excuse to lay bare the kind of woman who refuses to hide her age, to come to terms with it by doing so, for as the narrator insists, "the true Alix . . . is the young one." In "In the Flower of Age," Madame Vasco, a widow, does everything she can to appear young and succeeds in marrying a young man; despite all odds, including the revelation that her new husband is a stay-at-home like her first husband and "just another old man," she shows herself triumphant in her desperate masquerade of youth. A grimmer facet of aging, however, is highlighted in "The Rivals," where what keeps Clara's sexual vanity afloat is less the fact that she seduces a famous playwright than that she does so in competition with her old friend Antoinette.

Colette's stories are often as interested in the nature of men and children as in the nature of women. The "Clouk" stories show the stages of numb disbelief, loneliness, fear and desperate hedonism that a husband deserted by his wife can go through, whereas "A Dead End" catalogs a man's unfound fear of desertion, "The Omelette" and "The Murderer" his self-destructive appetite for mastery over women, "The Respite" his craving for a self-pity stronger than his physical pain, "The Tenor" his sexual narcissism, and "Monsieur Maurice" his care to protect his sexual vanity as he ages. The psychology of childhood is amply recorded by Colette in such stories as "Literature," "The Seamstress," "The Hollow Nut," and "The Sick Child," where children escape the realistic world of adults to one of their own making in which ordinary objects and acts become fabulous. As for adolescence, a story such as "The Tender Shoot" reveals the animal cunning and abruptness a teenage girl can bring to sex and love.

Colette extends her fastidious sense of character to animals as well as humans. She personifies animals, skirting the pathetic fallacy by dwelling on those domesticated in the human world. The barely suppressed rivalry of the show dogs in "Clever Dogs," the unreserved gratitude and affection of the dogs in "Lola" and "The Bitch," the frustrated but smooth ferocity of the pet fox in "The Fox," the sexual diplomacy of the cats in "October," and the self-conscious intelligence of Colette's dog Pati in "Bella-Vista"—all of these animal traits are convincingly described by a narrator who pays strict attention to her subjects.

Setting is as important to Colette's stories as the characters who inhabit them. It often provides the imagery of a mood, as in "Sleepless Nights" (where a memory of nature describes the narrator's sexual feelings) and in "Gray Days" (where the narrator is "sick and cranky, like the sea"). Colette is also fond of highlighting small objects in their settings in order to focus a plot or theme. In "The Hand," a young bride focuses on her sleeping husband until she comes to a shocking realization of the brutality of the male sex. Madame Augelier in "The Bracelet," bored by the expensive jewelry to which she became accustomed in her married life, ransacks the shops for the kind of blue glass trinket she loved as a child, only to find that it is no longer fascinating now that she is an adult. The blister of window glass in "The Rainy Moon," which casts a rainbow sphere on the wall of the apartment where Colette used to live, symbolizes not only the future she once looked forward to but also the past that a disappointed woman cannot cling to without causing tragic damage to herself and others. In "The Photographer's Wife," the strings of pearls that Madame Devoidy repairs for a living become the image—paradoxically precious—of the endless string of dull days that Madame Armand, the photographer's wife, lives through, the domestic chores of which cause her to attempt suicide, to find in death the excitement she misses; when she finds out she is wrong, the implied image for the wonder she seeks is the fake pearls featured earlier in the story.

Illumination of one kind or another is invariably the point of Colette's stories, and more often than not it is the result of a sudden or gradual change in appearances. The narrator's friend Valentine in "Morning Glories" is the slave of makeup and fashion, but it is precisely this illusion which her lover desires, not the real woman underneath, just as the harvesters in "Grape Harvest" are happy with the women who dress up for them, not with the women who come to help them in work clothes. The illuminations here, as elsewhere in *The Collected Stories of Colette*, are that appearances are preferable to ordinary reality. In the stories that make up "Backstage at the Music Hall," the reader is made to realize what the show girls are really like behind their costumes, but also how crucial masquerading is to them and their audience. Further, Colette's stories often turn on unmasking itself. The young husband in "Chéri," blinded by his narcissism and bored by his wife, finally sees, through a trick of light, that his mistress is truly old under her cosmetics and (by implication) that his true place is with his young wife. In putting on her lover's hat in "The Kepi" after they have made love, Marco paradoxically strips away the illusion of beauty and shocks her lover with the fact of her aging. The dressmaker in "The 'Master'" reveals himself at the climax as a formerly "impoverished clerk" who expresses his hatred of the women who have made him rich by putting a touch of ugliness in the finery he designs for them. In "The Hidden Woman," a wife's disguise at a masquerade party reveals to her husband a cold restlessness in her character that he has never before noticed. A butler reveals to his mistress in "The Judge" that her new hairstyle is an appalling confession of her age, and in "The Portrait," a group of middle-aged women must face the fact that the famous heartbreaker who once wrote to each of them is not the idol in the portrait they keep of him, but faded and ugly. In "The Find," Irene shows off her wonderful apartment to her friends, and they envy her for it; when they are gone, however, she is revealed as a lonely woman longing for the disorder and imperfection that love would bring to her life, and she ends the day curled up in her bathroom with an exciting book. Finally, the narrator in "Bella-Vista," posing as Colette herself, dramatizes the aspects of her blindness which terminate in understanding: She sees that the house she wants built in the South of France is more a dream than a reality; she sees, relying on her dog Pati's perception, that Monsieur Daste is bad and Madame Ruby good, but not until the end of the story does she see that the former is truly a violent hunter and the latter a man. Her dog is beyond expressing such truths because it is beyond complicating them with moral fantasies, which are the ironic province of the storyteller as obstacle and subject.

Few fiction writers in the twentieth century have so thoroughly manipulated physical texture as a source of insight into character as did Colette, and few have put themselves into their stories so wholeheartedly.

Mark McCloskey

Sources for Further Study

Los Angeles Times Book Review. January 10, 1984, p. 6.
New York. XVI, November 7, 1983, p. 90.
The New York Times Book Review. LXXXVIII, December 25, 1983, p. 3.
The New Yorker. LIX, December 19, 1983, p. 137.
Newsweek. CII, November 21, 1983, p. 100.
Publishers Weekly. CCXXIV, September 23, 1983, p. 62.
Time. CXXIII, January 9, 1984, p. 70.
Virginia Quarterly Review. LX, Spring, 1984, p. 56.

THE COLLECTED STORIES OF SEAN O'FAOLAIN

Author: Sean O'Faolain (1900-   )
Publisher: The Atlantic Monthly Press/Little, Brown and Company (Boston).
   1304 pp. $29.95
Type of work: Short stories

A collected edition of ninety stories which constitute this Irish writer's complete work in the short-story genre

It is an interesting cultural-literary puzzle that the short story has always been a particularly irresistible form for Irish writers, even as it has never been a particularly successful form for their cultural cousins, the British. George Moore, James Joyce, Frank O'Connor, and Sean O'Faolain are only a few whose names have become identified with what has often been called a minor art form. O'Connor and O'Faolain, who grew up together, as it were, within the so-called Irish Literary Revival, have made similar suggestions about the origin of the Irish preference for the short story. In his well-known study of the form, *The Lonely Voice* (1963), O'Connor has said that whereas the novel demands a classical concept of a civilized society, the short story is remote from a sense of community and is therefore romantic, individualistic, and lonely. O'Faolain has similarly suggested that the more firmly organized and established in tradition a country is, the less room there is in its literature for the short story.

Although such a judgment may seem somewhat facile, it may partially explain why an organized country such as England would be cited as the birthplace of the novel, while a largely rural and somewhat parochial country such as Ireland (and the United States in the nineteenth century) would be a fertile breeding ground for the short story. Whereas O'Connor, after several failures with the novel, seemed to have accepted the personal and lonely voice of the short-story form, leaving such memorable examples of the form as "My Oedipus Complex," "First Confession," "Guests of the Nation," and "Judas," to name only a few, O'Faolain seems rather to have battled the Irish predilection for the form. Few of the ninety stories collected here demonstrate the memorability and staying power of the great examples of the form in Western literature.

In his autobiography, *Vive Moi* (1965), O'Faolain indirectly offers an explanation for his relative failure. He laments that a complex society is needed to set a writer in motion, for he recognizes that Ireland remains an unshaped culture with its roots still within the folk. In a 1949 essay on the "Dilemma of Irish Letters," he suggests that whereas in Ireland there are many subjects for little pieces, the novelist becomes lost in "general amorphism" and "unsophistication." He admits with a sense of defeat that the realism necessary to deal with such material reaches a dead end, and thus reluctantly he resigns himself to making the short story his form. Thus, O'Faolain's collected stories reveal a continual battle between his cultural predilection for the short story—with its roots in the folk, its focus on the odd and romantic slant, and its emphasis on the culturally cutoff character—and his own artistic conviction that realism, not Romanticism, is the preferred artistic convention.

The problem is made clear in a relatively late story entitled "How to Write a Short Story." The piece focuses on an aspiring writer who listens to an older doctor friend tell a story about his own youth. As he listens, the young man "writes" the story mentally, watching for the "telling detail" and trying to get the doctor to structure his reminiscence in the terms of the Guy de Maupassant style within which the young man wishes to write. At the end, the young man admits that the story is too convoluted, that there is too much in it, that he can never capture the story in all of its complex reality. He finally laments that Maupassant oversimplified everything, that he was a "besotted Romantic." This is a telling judgment, for O'Faolain has worried that he too is no more than a "besotted Romantic." Applying the term "Romantic" to O'Faolain, however, is more complicated than suggested by the usual judgment that the stories in his first collection, *Midsummer Night Madness and Other Stories* (1932), infuse the natural world with a lyric emotion or that they focus on the romantic young man trying to come to terms with the world.

Instead, the issue concerns basic assumptions about how fiction captures reality—indeed, about what the nature of significant reality truly is. It might be said that the novelist perceives reality as "experience" conceptually abstracted from the temporal plenitude of life, whereas the short-story writer focuses on significant reality as the capturing of "an experience," lifted away from the temporal flow and frozen, as it were, in a spatial moment. Those who hold the second assumption see the short story as the most "natural" and adequate form to capture reality as it is actually experienced. Those who hold the first assumption see the short story as the ultimate artifice, characterized by a radical choice of event and selection of details, inevitably charged with the emotion of the teller, and therefore "Romantic" in the most basic sense of the term.

O'Faolain seems self-confessedly to be the latter type. In his book on writing, *The Short Story* (1951), he says that there are no such things as short stories in life; rather, the short story is one vast convention, an immense confidence trick. Although this may not be as negative as it sounds, it still suggests that for O'Faolain, the most adequate convention for capturing reality is "realism," not the obvious artifice of romance. Consequently, O'Faolain's short stories dwell uneasily within the dualistic realm of the Romanticism to which he was born and the realism for which he yearned. His technique might be characterized as "poetic realism"—a mode which James Joyce, O'Faolain's overshadowing precursor, mastered completely. Poetic realism at its most ambitious and most successful might be described as prose in which, even as objects and events seem to be objectively presented, they are transformed by the selectivity and unity of the story itself into metaphoric meaningfulness. Thus, in Joyce's *Dubliners* (1914), the seemingly trivial becomes charged with meaning in a subtle, unobtrusive way.

To write poetic realism does indeed require artifice, does indeed exhibit the conventional rather than the naïvely natural, and does indeed seem characteristic of the short-story form at its most representative. Nevertheless, the line between complex conventionality as the essential basis of art and conventionality as a highly formalized trick has always been a troublesome one for the short-story form—and indeed it has always been a particularly troublesome one for Sean O'Faolain. Critical judgment suggests that although he is one of the best-known Irish short-story writers of the twentieth century, O'Faolain is too "conventional" to be one of the best.

It is clear, in the thirteen hundred pages of this massive collection of O'Faolain's stories, that the author is a consummate craftsman, one who has an accurate vision of his country and its people and knows the various conventions of the short story and its tradition. At the same time, this collection reveals the limits of a writer who has never raised the form beyond its various conventions or mastered that unique blend of romantic vision and significant reality which exemplifies the form as practiced by Ivan Turgenev, Anton Chekhov, or Joyce.

The stories in this collection can perhaps be sorted, albeit in an oversimplified way, into the two types that O'Faolain himself sees as typical of the short story. In his preface to *Heat of the Sun* (1966), the only authorial comments about his work one will find reprinted here, he suggests that his work falls into the dual categories of short story and tale. He says that the short story is like a child's kite, which, because it is held taut, may not wander far, obeying the restrictions of place, time, character. It is "concentrated stuff," he says, "an essentialist art"; Maupassant and Chekhov invented it. The tale, however, is more relaxed, more free; instead of a kite, it is like a small airplane, can carry more cargo, and can rove farther away; its master is Prosper Mérimée.

Throughout his career, O'Faolain has moved back and forth between these two extremes, beginning at first with the Turgenev-like Romanticism of both nature and violence in the tales of his first collection, then moving to the tight Chekhovian short stories in *A Purse of Coppers* (1937) and *Teresa and Other Stories* (1947). Typical of this second stage, and perhaps the best known of his stories, are "The Man Who Invented Sin," "Innocence," and "The Trout." Whereas the technique of the first collection is one of indulging in the relatively free romanticizing of the tale form, the technique of the next two collections is one of radical limitation of detail and authorial comment and emphasis instead on the economy of metaphor.

In *The Finest Stories of Sean O'Faolain* (1957), which also contains two relatively well-known stories, "Childybawn" and "The Fur Coat," O'Faolain loosens up the previous economy and presents a fuller focus on social and phenomenal reality, while still maintaining the metaphoric nature of seemingly mimetic detail. The stories here incline more toward Joyce than to Turgenev or Chekhov, although they are not informed by the complex and profound theological-aesthetic issues that characterize the stories in *Dubliners*. The collections of stories that make up O'Faolain's work in the 1960's and early 1970's continue to play with the conventions of his three primary precursors, although O'Faolain's work never reaches their level of excellence. In the late 1970's and early 1980's, as O'Faolain nears the inevitable end of his career, a fourth primary influence has been explored, Henry James, as O'Faolain strives to leave the realm of external detail and chart, by means of the syntax of language itself, the complexities of conscious thought processes. This effort is most pronounced in a previously unpublished story, à la James, entitled "The Wings of the Dove—a Modern Sequel," in which the technique of James's nineteenth century novel is imitated and parodied in twentieth century short-story form.

This final self-conscious imitation of a literary precursor makes explicit what has always been characteristic of O'Faolain's work in the short story— that is, he has always been an imitator, unable to transcend his masters. As T. S. Eliot made clear years ago, and as Yale critic Harold Bloom has emphasized more recently, no individual talent can be born except from within the literary tradition that makes it possible. The problem with O'Faolain is that he has never been able to find a distinctive voice of his own, has never been able to deviate from or extend his precursors to manifest, as did Turgenev, Chekhov, Joyce, and James before him, an "individual talent" that stands out from craftsmanship and literary borrowing. Sean O'Faolain has indeed done some good work in the short-story genre, but he has never achieved the excellence that will make him a powerful precursor to short-story writers that follow him.

Charles E. May

Sources for Further Study

America. CXLIX, December 31, 1983, p. 437.
Christian Science Monitor. October 12, 1983, p. 21.
Library Journal. CVIII, October 1, 1983, p. 1890.
Los Angeles Times Book Review. December 28, 1983, p. 6.
The New York Times Book Review. LXXXVIII, October 30, 1983, p. 11.
Publishers Weekly. CCXXIV, August 19, 1983, p. 68.

CONSTANT DEFENDER

Author: James Tate (1943-   )
Publisher: Ecco Press (New York). 63 pp. $13.50; paperback $7.95
Type of work: Poetry

Forty-two poems that demonstrate the continuing decline of the winner of the Yale Younger Poets Award for 1966

In James Tate's new volume, *Constant Defender*, one finds poems that aspire unsuccessfully for the most part—and in a highly (even archly) literary way—to be explosively antiliterary. In most of these poems, one looks in vain for emotional or logical coherence, not to mention a sustained narrative line. Tate is bent on surprising his reader, repeatedly, not with the shock of recognition but with the recognition that meaning has once again been given the slip, absolutely and unequivocally. Unfortunately, this sort of surprise becomes simply monotonous when it crops up in line after line and poem after poem. The waters of Mr. Tate's silliness must be sampled to be believed—for an example:

> Why are we so bad? I hear them
> faintly knocking, neutral ducks,
> and I am reprimanded.
> I am thinking "scalloped potatoes"
> are of absolutely no use.
> I'm thumping my canteen
> and pointing at my nose.
> Yes, I lied about "her,"
> there wasn't one, but for
> that moment a gourd drifted
> down the chimney on the pretext
> of weeding a peninsula
> and nourishing the articulation
> of a single bud. Am I forgiven?

Perhaps Mr. Tate will forgive himself, but one may doubt that many readers will be so generous.

Tate's poetry is surrealistic only in the loosest sense of the term. He distorts space and time and ordinary logic in ways superficially reminiscent of the original Surrealists of the post-World War I generation, but his fantastic and disjointed images, though they bespeak a boundless capacity for invention ("I am disabled/ by the slender blowing of that cucumber/ and am forced to hiccup at the reality of my flashlight"), militate against the Surrealist faith that apparently unnatural juxtapositions and combinations of images can unlock the riches of the unconscious. In that faith, the true Surrealist affirms a realm of feeling and meaning not available to ordinary modes of discourse and of perception. Tate's poems bespeak a threat more than a faith, and that threat is meaninglessness—not the thematic, *meaningful* expression of nothingness of a William Shakespeare's *King Lear* or a Samuel Beckett's *Waiting for Godot*, but a programmatic denial that language is referential to anything outside of its own arbitrary order. Thus, if Tate's poems are about anything except themselves, they are about their author's intelligent, chilly despair of poetry in general, indeed of all discourse, and hence, of all humanity.

Poetry about poetry need not be sterile, of course: Witness, for example, among the great poems of our century, William Butler Yeats's "Adam's Curse," Robert Frost's "Two Tramps in Mud Time," Wallace Stevens' "Notes Toward a Supreme Fiction," W. H. Auden's "On the Death of W. B. Yeats," A. R. Ammons' "Essay on Poetics," and John Ashberry's "Reflections in a Convex Mirror." In some sense, perhaps, great art is always about great art. What the poems just mentioned all express, however—despite their wide and numerous differences from one another—is the poets' belief in the importance of their art. By contrast, when the poems in *Constant Defender* are explicitly about themselves, they announce their own indecipherability and incoherence (in what are, paradoxically, among the few straightforwardly coherent utterances in the volume): "This is the constellation/ of my own bewilderment" ("Interruptions"); "All things seem to be charged/ with a menace or a riddle which must be solved/ at all costs" ("Jelka"); "I know there are/ contradictions in all that I say" ("To Fuzzy"); "Suspicions are almost confirmed./ Denials are swiftly circulating" ("It Wasn't Me"). The idea of a riddle "which must be solved/ at all costs" would seem to promise meaning, however difficult it might be to discover, but the word "seem" subverts that promise: Not only is meaning not disclosed, but even the apparent presence of disguised meaning, the riddle, is only a seeming, an illusion, an apparition, or, one might say, an absence.

One might conjecture two possible sources of the corrosive spirit of denial that characterizes Tate's recent books, including *Constant Defender*. One is biographical: The absences in Tate's poetry might be traced back to the absent father in Tate's life, the pilot lost in World War II whose death was mourned in the powerful title piece of the poet's first book, *The Lost Pilot* (1967). Tate was born in 1943, his father lost in 1944:

> When I see you,
> as I have seen you at least
>
> once every year of my life,
> spin across the wilds of the sky
> like a tiny, African god,
>
> I feel dead. I feel as if I were
> the residue of a stranger's life. . . .

The other conjectural cause of Tate's abnegations is literary: He may be seen as a practitioner of an aesthetic committed to self-deconstruction, as one of the epigones of a dead-end literary movement that vociferously promulgates an inability to confer meaning on experience, the movement of late Beckett, of Alain Robbe-Grillet, and of Donald Barthelme. Personal and literary history may thus be supposed to have attained a baleful convergence in Tate's recent poetry.

Tate's development since *The Lost Pilot* has been predominantly negative. There were many excitingly energetic and delightful poems in the poet's first volume, and many moving ones, such as "The Lost Pilot" itself. "Coming Down Cleveland Avenue" and "Rescue," for example, are representative of that award-winning book (volume 62 of the Yale Series of Younger Poets) in being astonishing *jeux d'esprit*, poems full of surprising imagery, to be sure, but poems also openly celebratory of love. The progress of the poet from *The Lost Pilot* has been a gradual emptying out of the possibilities of meaning and of pleasure. The titles of Tate's collections (with the exception, perhaps, of *Hints to Pilgrims*, 1971) testify to his growing negativity: Consider, for example, *The Oblivion Ha-Ha* (1970), *Absences* (1972), *Hottentot Ossuary* (1974), and *Riven Doggeries* (1979).

One would be hard put to understand why Tate continues to write poetry in the face of his prevalent subversion of the scope and significance of his art were it not for the handful of poems in *Constant Defender* that demonstrate, in spite of all the negation, this poet's abiding, if only occasional, power to evoke feeling and wonder. Tate's poems succeed when they achieve an emotional and thematic coherence that arises from and overrides their discontinuities of image and narrative line. The poems that work in this way are few and far between, and they are perhaps only partial recompense for the agonies of dissonance, mystification, and just plain ugliness to which a complete reading of *Constant Defender* commits the reader. Nevertheless, one can be grateful to a poet who evokes the mysterious but resonant scenario of the first poem in the volume, "Land of Little Sticks, 1945":

> Where the wife is scouring the frying pan
> and the husband is leaning up against the barn.
> Where the boychild is pumping water into a bucket
> and the girl is chasing a spotted dog.
>
> And the sky churns on the horizon.
> A town by the name of Pleasantville has disappeared.
> And now the horses begin to shift and whinny,
> and the chickens roost, keep looking this way and that.
> At this moment something is not quite right.

Several other poems in *Constant Defender* might be cited as similar in their power of emotional suggestion and sensitivity, though none is as admirably lean as "Land of Little Sticks, 1945"; among the better pieces in this atmospheric mode are "Tall Trees by Still Water," "Five Years Old," "Summer Night," and "Tending the Sheep at Big Baas Flip." Elsewhere, Tate charms now and then with zany, self-deprecating humor, notably in "The Dream of Returning to School and Facing the Oral Exam," which opens with this stanza:

> I am wearing huge antlers
> which have sprouted overnight like mushrooms,
> and singing a ritual song.
> My neatness is measured at the door:
> I'm blissfully handsome, poignantly chaste,
> and given a goat to ride the last few hall-miles.

For the most part, however, the poet denies himself and his readers either recognizable feeling or sustained wit, preferring, apparently, to contrive admittedly clever short circuits of feeling and meaning.

Tate is not, to be sure, a merely clever poet. He is ferociously intelligent. He knows what he is doing, and he knows all that his antipoetic poetry is undoing. In a savage effusion titled "Poem to Some of My Recent Poems," he describes both his poems and his muse:

> My beloved little billiard balls,
> my polite mongrels, edible patriotic plums,
> you owe your beauty to your mother, who
> resembled a cyclindrical corned beef
> with all the trimmings, may God rest
> her forsaken soul, for it is all of us
> she forsook. . . .

Addressing his poems in the last line of this curiously lucid and accurate indictment of his own work, Tate says, "You are beautiful, and I, a slave to a heap of cinders." Well, beauty, after all, is in the eye of the beholder. Many readers will find beauty sadly lacking in *Constant Defender*, though they may concur that the muse to which Tate is apparently enslaved is "a heap of cinders." Some may find a sort of morbid fascination in poems that are the spoor of a ruined poetic intelligence. Above all, however, one ought to feel sadness that Tate so freely serves such an incinerated muse; because he allows her to undergo such immolation, it is all of us she forsakes, and James Tate forsakes us all with her.

Daniel Mark Fogel

Sources for Further Study

Best Sellers. LXIII, January, 1984, p. 381.
Booklist. LXXX, September 1, 1983, p. 23.
The Georgia Review. XXXVIII, Spring, 1984, p. 186.
Library Journal. CVIII, August, 1983, p. 1487.
The New York Times Book Review. LXXXVIII, September 4, 1983, p. 8.
Publishers Weekly. CCXXIV, July 15, 1983, p. 45.
World Literature Today. LVIII, Spring, 1984, p. 270.

THE CRAZY YEARS
Paris in the Twenties

Author: William Wiser
Publisher: Atheneum Publishers (New York). Illustrated. 256 pp. $27.50
Type of work: Cultural history
Time: The 1920's
Locale: Paris

A broad, informal survey of the more sensational aspects of international art and culture in Paris in the 1920's

In an attempt to give a sense of order to things, there is a tendency to seek a closed pattern to events within arbitrary time units—years, decades, centuries. One such unit which has received a great amount of retrospective attention is the decade of the 1920's. Because this period was roughly bracketed by the end of World War I and the beginning of the Great Depression, there is perhaps more justification than usual for isolating it as a block of time, and if there was one place in which the spirit of this time was most fully embodied, it was Paris. In his book, *The Crazy Years: Paris in the Twenties*, William Wiser tries to capture the frenetic activity of an international cultural capital during an especially significant and colorful time.

Perhaps no decade and no place has been so exhaustively remembered, relived, and recounted as Paris in the 1920's. (The only rival might be the less-focused reminiscences of World War I.) The approach to the topic ranges from highly subjective, self-serving memoirs by people who were part of the scene to exhaustive, objective scholarly tomes. *The Crazy Years* is somewhere in the middle. Wiser adds little or nothing to what is available elsewhere, contenting himself with retelling familiar stories about familiar people always with an eye to the titillating or conventionally scandalous. He succeeds in giving a sense of the desperate energy of the time but more in the style of the literate gossip columnist than the historian of ideas or culture.

Clearly intended for a wide audience, *The Crazy Years* goes out of its way to focus on those topics which justify its eye-catching title, with no attempt to explore serious cultural or artistic questions. The reader is offered many piquant details, for example, concerning the mistresses of famous artists and writers but almost nothing about the significance of any of their paintings or books. With no documentation, the book does not pretend to serious cultural history and should be taken as a potentially entertaining gloss of the more notorious aspects of Paris in the 1920's.

Economics played an important part in Paris becoming an international mecca at this time, especially for the ever-present Americans. As a result of the devastation of the European economy by World War I, the dollar brought better than twenty-five francs for most of the decade and as much as fifty at one point (it currently commands about eight). The undiscovered writer, artist, or musician could afford both to eat and explore his craft, and the well-to-do from abroad could live like kings.

In some cases, the members of the cultural scene almost were kings. Wiser pays special attention to the Russian contribution to Paris life. After the Russian Revolution of 1917, the coteries of exiled Russian revolutionaries in Paris went home, to be replaced by even greater numbers of disenfranchised, and often impoverished, Russian aristocrats. This greatly varied cast of Slavs included men with titles but no money looking for women in opposite straits, quack doctors and spiritualists, and talented avant-garde painters, composers, and writers.

The most visible Russian presence in Paris was Sergey Diaghilev's Ballets Russes. *The Crazy Years* devotes significant space to Diaghilev and the cast of characters that surrounded him—Vaslav Nijinsky, Igor Stravinsky, Sergey Prokofiev, and the like. Wiser touches on the rivalry between Stravinsky and Prokofiev but, typically, does not explore the historical or musical significance of their work or of the Ballets Russes in general. Instead, he offers intermittent sketches of Diaghilev in his various roles as discoverer and manipulator of talent and as impresario.

The most conspicuous internationals, however, were the Americans. Often flush with cash, sometimes with talent, they came to France by the boatload looking for the latest in art and literature or in nightclubs and dissolute living, sometimes both. Wiser details the changing attitudes of Parisians toward the inescapable American presence. The early goodwill left over from the war yielded to a grudging tolerance of those whose big mouths and boorish manner were compensated for only by their equally big wallets and free spending. Disdain sometimes turned to anger regarding such issues as American insistence that France repay its war loans and the execution in the United States of Nicolo Sacco and Bartolomeo Vanzetti. The exploits of Americans such as Josephine Baker and, especially, Charles Lindbergh provided brief moments of universal good feeling.

One possible advantage *The Crazy Years* has over many better books on the same topic is its breadth. It attempts in a few strokes each, for example, to give a sense of the life of painting and sculpture, literature, ballet, and music, focusing on the social lives of the producers rather than on the nature of their product. As a symbol for avant-garde painting, Wiser offers life at La Ruche (the hive), a decaying Montparnasse housing project that offered a seamy, bohemian residence for the likes of Marc Chagall, Constantin Brancusi, Chaim Soutine, and dozens of others who worked and died in impoverished anonymity.

The coverage of writers is limited largely to the expatriate Americans and British. Wiser touches base with Ezra Pound, Gertrude Stein, and Ernest Hemingway, as well as with Ford Madox Ford, James Joyce, and the young

Samuel Beckett. Wiser mistells the oft-repeated story of T. S. Eliot and Wyndham Lewis delivering a pair of old shoes to Joyce, thereby missing the insight the anecdote offers into Joyce's character, but Wiser does better in giving a sense of the role that well-to-do amateurs played in financing and sometimes editing the little magazines that were such an important part of the modernist movement.

Along with the arts, *The Crazy Years* also surveys popular culture. Wiser devotes a chapter to the various loves of Coco Chanel and to her influence on the fashion industry. He skillfully re-creates the outburst of enthusiasm, somewhat difficult to understand today perhaps, regarding Lindbergh's successful solo flight over the Atlantic. Wiser also catalogs the sudden appetite for black entertainment and culture, symbolized by jazz and the primitive sensuality of Josephine Baker.

One of the important factors in the modernist movement in the arts was the instant cross-fertilization among those within an art form and among those in different art forms, made possible by the concentration of many talented people in a few major cities. Writers, painters, and musicians saw and heard one another's work in progress. Influence crossed traditional boundaries among art forms, and institutions such as the Ballets Russes allowed avant-garde painting, music, and dance to work toward integrated wholeness.

This crucial intermingling of the arts was often nourished in the salons of the rich and influential patrons of art. Wiser paints brief portraits of wealthy women who sought self-expression and offered badly needed financial support to those, usually young men, whose experimentation and daring brought few material rewards. Two of the most important salons were presided over by rich American women: Winnaretta Singer, heiress to the Singer sewing machine fortune, and Natalie Barney. By a not unusual marriage of title and money, Singer became the Princesse de Polignac, and her salon and support was an important part of the avant-garde Paris musical scene.

Natalie Barney's interests were primarily literary and sensual. Openly lesbian, she was almost a caricature of the rich, self-indulgent dilettante, attracting to her soirees the likes of Paul Valéry, Ezra Pound, Virgil Thomson, Colette, and James Joyce, along with many women who would participate with her in brief plays or rhapsodic dances. Here, writers and artists came into contact with publishers or potential patrons who could play important roles in their careers.

The other great meeting places were the Paris cafés. Cheap food and drink and frequent contact with peers made these important parts of the story of the modern arts and general culture. Certain cafés became known for their particular circle, and tales of café life fill every memoir of the time. Hemingway, for one, made known the importance of cafés in the beginning of his own career and his disgust at their takeover by pseudo-artists and tourists.

Wiser succeeds in conveying, whether it was his intention or not, the edge of desperation that characterized this time. There is a hothouse, artificial quality to much of what he describes. Artists, dilettantes, and tourists alike frequently exhausted themselves, their resources, and sometimes their talent in a fervid, sometimes childish pursuit of the newest, the latest, the most unconventional. The dissolution of traditional boundaries, in progress for decades but greatly hastened by the war, brought many new freedoms and for some a sense of liberation, but it also increased a sense of rootlessness and insecurity which fast living could only mask temporarily.

One of those new freedoms was sexual liberation, especially for women, and particularly for homosexual women. Winnaretta Singer, Natalie Barney, Gertrude Stein, and Nancy Cunard were only a few of the prominent women who found French indifference to sexual deviance an important reason for living in Paris. Though sexual attitudes and practices are a significant part of the story of Paris in the 1920's, one eventually tires of Wiser's preoccupation with such matters. Very few pages pass without some account involving mistresses, prostitutes, lesbian or homosexual affairs, naked parties or wrestling matches, and the like. That this conforms to many readers' expectations of "naughty" Paris does not keep it from becoming tedious, making one wish for something more substantial.

Stylistically, *The Crazy Years* begins miserably and only slowly recovers. The opening sentence is as bad as anything that could have been written by the pseudo-writers about whom Hemingway complained: "He was Modi, she was Noix-de-Coco—or he called her Haricot Rouge that winter of the Great War when the lovers ate nothing but red beans." The rest of the first chapter is more of the same, but despite slipping back to such depths from time to time, Wiser generally manages to tell his story fairly directly. The book is organized topically but in a roughly chronological way, so that one gets some sense of the rise and decline of Paris as the center of international activity.

That decline had started even before the disastrous stock-market crash of 1929. More than one expatriate, tired of the rootlessness that Hemingway captured in *The Sun Also Rises* (1926), decided to go home to a different kind of life. The crash simply made obvious what many had already felt— that the party was over and things would never quite be the same. Wiser's depiction of the initial reaction to the collapse is one of the better parts of the book, as is his epilogue, in which he searches through Paris for the present-day remains of those lost but not forgotten years.

There are better books about this period than *The Crazy Years*. One, focusing primarily on the literary scene, is Noel Riley Fitch's *Sylvia Beach and the Lost Generation: A History of Literary Paris in the Twenties and Thirties* (1983; see review in volume 2). Similarly, one would do better to read a few of the memoirs of the time, such as Hemingway's *A Moveable Feast* (1964), than Wiser's distillation of those memoirs. William Wiser's book, however, does give to the reader a broad, if superficial and somewhat sensationalized, sense of this continuingly fascinating and influential period in modern culture.

Daniel Taylor

Sources for Further Study

Christian Science Monitor. December 2, 1983, p. B14.
The Economist. CCLXXXIX, December 3, 1983, p. 104.
New Statesman. CVI, October 21, 1983, p. 25.
The New York Times Book Review. LXXXVIII, October 30, 1983, p. 13.
Publishers Weekly. CCXXIV, September 9, 1983, p. 56.

DASHIELL HAMMETT
A Life

Author: Diane Johnson (1934-   )
Publisher: Random House (New York). Illustrated. 344 pp. $17.95
Type of work: Literary biography
Time: 1894-1961
Locale: Primarily the East and West coasts of the United States; also the Aleutian Islands

Her work well-timed to coincide with a recent resurgence of interest concerning Hammett and his fiction, Diane Johnson approaches her often elusive subject with considerable wit and skill, achieving a biography that is both entertaining and informative

> *Principal personages:*
> (SAMUEL) DASHIELL HAMMETT, the largely self-taught author of acclaimed detective fiction
> RICHARD THOMAS HAMMETT, his father
> ANNIE DASHIELL HAMMETT, his mother
> JOSEPHINE (JOSE) DOLAN HAMMETT, his wife from 1921 to 1937
> JOSEPHINE (JO) HAMMETT MARSHALL, the younger daughter of Jose and Dashiell Hammett
> MARY JANE HAMMETT MILLER, the older daughter of Jose and Dashiell Hammett
> LILLIAN HELLMAN, an accomplished American playwright, and Hammett's longtime friend and sometime lover
> NELL MARTIN, a moderately successful American novelist of the 1930's
> ALBERT SAMUELS, a San Francisco jeweler who hired Hammett to write advertising copy, thus getting him started as a writer
> ALFRED AND BLANCHE KNOPF, Hammett's first hardcover publishers
> JOHN EDGAR HOOVER, Director of the Federal Bureau of Investigation

Alternately lionized and vilified in life, Dashiell Hammett remained virtually ignored by critics and biographers alike until some twenty years after his death in 1961. The publication during the 1970's of three volumes of memoirs by his longtime friend and companion Lillian Hellman occasioned a mild renewal of interest in Hammett and his work, but it was not until the end of the decade and even into the 1980's that Hammett's remembered presence began to assert itself in films, television documentaries, and works of criticism dealing in whole or in part with the mystery genre. Peter Wolfe's *Beams Falling: The Art of Dashiell Hammett* (1979) brought fresh attention to Hammett's contributions both as storyteller and as stylist, and in 1981, the first biography of Hammett appeared: *Shadow Man: The Life of Dashiell Hammett*, by Richard Layman, who two years earlier had compiled a useful Hammett bibliography. *Shadow Man*, although acknowledged by critics as a necessary prolegomenon to future Hammett studies, was generally seen as an assemblage of facts already known rather than a work based on original research. A second Hammett biography—*Hammett: A Life at the Edge*, by William F. Nolan—appeared early in 1983, several months before Johnson's book. Nolan, like Layman, had been denied access to the voluminous correspondence between Hammett and Hellman; his account of Hammett, as one reviewer observed, "magnified the legend, thus losing the man." Diane Johnson's insightful and innovative volume, although not an authorized or official biography of Hammett, was written, unlike Layman's and Nolan's, with Hellman's full contribution and cooperation. Written at times with the freedom and innovation of a novel, *Dashiell Hammett: A Life* manages the unusual feat of keeping the general reader entertained while keeping the specialist well supplied with meticulously documented facts.

Originally projected for publication as early as 1980, Johnson's biography of Hammett was several years in the making and may well antedate, at least in its research, the preparation of Layman's *Shadow Man*. Johnson's effort, profiting from the delay, corrects several errors of fact in Layman's account while avoiding duplication in certain areas where *Shadow Man* provides adequate coverage. Johnson does not, for example, feel the need to explain that the name Dashiell, Hammett's mother's maiden name, is French in origin and therefore bears the accent on the second syllable; regardless of how he signed himself in print, Hammett was generally known to his friends as Sam or—as Hellman called him—Dash. Where Johnson excels is in her organization and presentation of the ironies in Hammett's life. All the details of his life and career are here, but what seems to interest Johnson even more is the texture that emerges from those details.

An accomplished novelist as well as a scholar in her own right, Diane Johnson begins her account of Hammett's life as one might begin a novel, *in medias res*. Hammett is fifty-seven years of age, burned out as a creative writer, and serving time in a federal prison for refusing to name contributors to the bail fund of the Civil Rights Congress, of which he had served as one of four trustees. The reader's first glimpse of Hammett will prove artistically valid as the rest of the picture comes into view, portraying as it does, a man of strong principle set off from society less by his deeds than by his character. Even at close range, however, Hammett remains an enigmatic and maddeningly elusive figure, oddly inaccessible even when present, vaguely admirable at his best and at his worst, most unlovable indeed. To her credit, Johnson ultimately manages what is perhaps as fully rounded a portrait of Hammett as we are likely to get.

Returning, after her initial chapter, to a generally chronological account, Johnson proceeds to sketch in Hammett's origins in rural Maryland, where he was born, in 1894, into a well-settled but less than prosperous Roman Catholic family. Around the age of sixteen, Hammett, like his sister before him and his brother after him, cut short his formal education to help with the family finances. Relations between Hammett and his father remained strained up until the latter's death in 1948, and Johnson is quick to draw inferences from the prevalence in Hammett's work of "a theme unusual in literature," the murder of a son by his father. Drifting from job to job, young Hammett by the age of twenty secured a job as an office worker for the Pinkerton National Detective Agency, which soon thereafter sent him out into the field as an operative. At last, Hammett had found a line of work that suited him, and he would remain with Pinkerton, serving mainly in the Western states, until America's involvement in World War I.

Johnson traces the origins of Hammett's left-wing politics to his experiences with Pinkerton, whose operatives were often hired by management to defend itself against the burgeoning labor movement. One incident, in particular, appears to have loomed large: Hammett, along with other Pinkerton men, was approached to assassinate a labor leader for a fee but declined. Shortly thereafter, the man in question, Frank Little, an organizer for the International Workers of the World, or "Wobblies," was dragged from a neighboring room in Hammett's own hotel by hired thugs and lynched, presumably to set an example of what would happen to union leaders in Montana. Hammett was never to forget the incident and would often refer to it later, both in conversation and in writing. In any case, Hammett soon thereafter perceived his true civic duty and enlisted in the Army.

As Hammett was quick to tell people, once he became famous, he served in the Army during World War I but did not serve in the war; he was never shipped overseas. Not long after his enlistment, he contracted the epidemic flu and was discovered at that time to be suffering also from tuberculosis, presumably contracted years earlier from his consumptive mother. Mustered out in 1919 with the rank of sergeant and a full-disability pension of forty dollars per month, Hammett soon returned to work for Pinkerton's. His health, however, remained poor, and shortly after returning to his familiar Western territory, he was obliged to seek treatment at the Public Health Service hospital in Tacoma, Washington; there he met Jose Dolan, a nurse who, though barely twenty-four years of age in 1920, had served in World War I as a commissioned officer. What began as a simple dalliance—a common occurrence in Hammett's life—turned to something more serious when Jose became pregnant, and Hammett, oddly in character, saw fit to do the honorable thing. Despite his precarious health, Hammett was still employed at Pinkerton's and apparently calculated that his salary, supplemented by his pension check, would suffice to maintain a small household. In a now-famous incident, however, Hammett proved too proficient at detective work for his own good and soon thereafter resigned from Pinkerton's in a fit of pique and disgust: Hired by Pinkerton's to sail for Australia on the liner *Sonoma* to search for a quarter-million dollars in gold presumably hidden aboard, the twenty-seven-year-old operative somehow managed to find the contraband before *Sonoma* even left the harbor, thereby cheating himself out of a trip to which he had been looking forward with delight. As Johnson notes, Hammett's health had by then deteriorated to a point where he was in fact too ill to continue working for Pinkerton's; the *Sonoma* incident may well have provided little more than a convenient excuse. Besides, she observes, Hammett's fleeting glimpses of another, richer world had raised his sights beyond the daily grind of a hired detective. In the meantime, though, the Hammetts needed money. A daughter, Mary Jane, had been born to them in October, 1921, and Hammett's disability pension was proving somewhat less reliable than had been promised or anticipated.

One of Johnson's more effective, if initially unsettling, expository devices is her inclusion of documentary matter, printed verbatim at intervals in the text without prelude or undue elaboration. Thus does she illustrate her account of Hammett's post-Pinkerton life in San Francisco with press clippings ranging from help-wanted ads to obituaries of Hammett's grandmother and mother. Included also are samples of the advertising copy written by Hammett for Al Samuels of Samuels Jewelry, who gave Hammett a job that actually paid him to write. It was not long before Hammett developed an apparent compulsion for writing, applying his Pinkerton experience toward improving the quality of the detective fiction that he liked to read in his spare time. As Johnson points out, however, Hammett's efforts were by no means confined to the mystery genre. During the early 1920's, he tried his hand, with varying degrees of success, at a wide range of styles and genres, including occasional light verse. In time, his work found acceptance in an equally wide range of publications, from H. L. Mencken's *Smart Set* to the trade periodical *Western Advertising*, which for a time kept Hammett on its payroll. Increasingly, however, his real talent and interests lay with detective fiction, particularly of the sort published by Mencken and George Jean Nathan in their secondary publication, *Black Mask*. It was *Black Mask*, indeed, that developed and maintained Hammett's early reputation as a writer, printing his short stories almost as fast as he could write them. Later, when Hammett came to contemplate the longer form of fiction, he would test-market his novels via serial publication in *Black Mask*.

Here, as elsewhere, Johnson documents her narrative with excerpts of Hammett's expository prose and letters. Although undereducated in the formal sense, Hammett in his early thirties stands revealed as a rigorous, scrupulous grammarian and stylist more than ready to match wits with the literary establishment of the day. One of his more interesting occasional pieces, reproduced in its entirety from *Smart Set*, consists of heavily ironic recollections of his career as a detective.

Hammett's growing fame perplexed his wife even as it pleased her, and the marriage began to show strain even after the birth of a second daughter, Jo, in 1926. In fairness, however, Johnson points out that Hammett's frequent physical separation from his family resulted in part from the advice of his doctors who recommended that the children be reared in the country—and away from their father—in order to protect their own health.

Believing, with some reason, that he had but a short time to live, Hammett in his mid-thirties began a period of intense creative activity. Between 1927 and 1930, in addition to short fiction of the sort that he had already perfected, Hammett turned out four well-received, distinguished novels that more than sufficed to establish his name as a household word. Although somewhat uneven in quality, all were well above the market standard for genre fiction: *Red Harvest* (1929), perhaps the archetype of hard-boiled fiction, covers territory familiar to Hammett from his work as a Pinkerton man during the early days of Prohibition; *The Dain Curse* (1929), set in San Francisco, was equally well received but has since lost some of its apparent luster. With *The Maltese Falcon* (1930) and *The Glass Key* (1931) Hammett advanced to the front rank in both critical and popular success, achieving even wider fame through the sale of film and broadcast rights. Not long thereafter, Hammett, along with many of his contemporaries, was lured to Hollywood by the deceptive prospect of writing for the screen. His projected fifth novel, *The Thin Man*, remained unfinished.

By the time Hammett returned to *The Thin Man*, his work had acquired the indelible stamp of his friendship with Lillian Hellman, who had emerged as the most important woman in his life. Initially attracted, during the late 1920's, to an assertive, liberated novelist named Nell Martin, Hammett met Hellman (then married to Arthur Kober) late in 1930 and found in the twenty-five-year-old novice writer many of the same qualities that had drawn him to Martin, with few of the attendant defects. As Hellman is free to admit, it was Hammett who "forced" and encouraged her to develop her talents as a writer, even suggesting the theme and subject matter of her first successful play, *The Children's Hour* (1934). Thereafter Hammett would remain involved, as coach and play-doctor, with Hellman's career as a dramatist, even as his own career waned. *The Thin Man*, finally published in 1934, was lighter in tone than his previous novels and appeared to mark a new direction in the genre; it would, however, be Hammett's last novel. Hammett published nothing from the age of forty until his death at sixty-six, although his name was kept before the public by numerous adaptations of and sequels to *The Maltese Falcon* and *The Thin Man*. Apart from sporadic work on film scripts, work often delayed or deferred by heavy drinking, and on continuity for a short-lived comic strip called "Secret Agent X-9," Hammett was finished as a writer. By the late 1930's, however, Hammett had found a new and consuming passion in the practice of radical politics.

Although leftist politics were very much the fashion among Hollywood screenwriters from the mid-1930's onward, fueled in part by the civil war in Spain, Hammett appeared to have in his temperament and background more basis than many others for a commitment to liberal causes. For one thing, he had been resolutely antimanagement for at least twenty years, following the assassination of Frank Little in Montana. Perhaps unbeknown to him, however, Hammett was already under surveillance by the Federal Bureau of Investigation (F.B.I), having first attracted their attention as a writer of continuity for "Secret Agent X-9."

Curiously, Hammett perceived no contradiction between his politics and patriotism; presumably, in his view, the Land of the Free was, or ought to be, free enough to tolerate all segments of the political spectrum. Nevertheless, Hammett was quick to reenlist in the Army after Pearl Harbor despite the obvious impediments of advancing age and precarious health. Another, more personal reason, suggests Johnson, might well have been a brief falling-out with Hellman, who one evening had fended off his amorous advances because he was inebriated. Hammett, although surprised, would never again approach Hellman in that manner and no doubt perceived military service as an interesting break in the routine. As in the previous war, Hammett entered the Army as a buck private and left it as a sergeant, spending most of his stint in the Aleutian Islands where he served as editor of the base newspaper.

Among Johnson's more effective insertions of documentation without comment are those involving the F.B.I., whose interoffice memoranda record a continuing, humorless, and hilariously ineffective surveillance of Hammett's activities. Reaching the attention of the director himself as well as of Herbert Philbrick (the agent whose career later formed the basis for the television series *I Led Three Lives*), the correspondence shows the Bureau spending most of the war years searching for Hammett throughout the Armed Services in which he was known to have enlisted.

By the time Hammett returned to civilian life, his frail health all but ruined, the Bureau had recovered its efficiency and was watching him closely indeed. Also watching was the Internal Revenue Service, which within a few years would present Hammett with a staggering bill for the payment of back taxes. The circumstances of Hammett's political arrest and imprisonment in 1951 are described by Johnson in considerable detail; in brief, along with a minority of Americans under fire for their convictions, Hammett declined to name names. For the last decade of his life, Hammett, by then permanently sober, attempted to resume writing but had more success with occasional teaching. During the final five years or so, increasingly infirm and without financial resources, he returned to live with Hellman, with whom he had maintained, since 1942, a completely Platonic relationship. Even in his last years, however, Hammett remained sexually active, frequently visiting prostitutes. Johnson suggests that Hammett was in fact incapable of love, at least as most people understand it. At the same time, however, he remained attached to Jose and continued to regard her as his wife even after years of separation and eventual divorce.

Although Hammett wrote nothing of consequence after the age of forty, Johnson appears less puzzled by the long years of silence than by the short years of prodigious activity. There is, indeed, little apparent explanation of Hammett's rapid, compulsive rise from the status of wage-earner to that of celebrated author, all during the decade of his thirties. Johnson observes, placing Hammett within the context of his generation, that such tales of rags to riches were by no means rare in the 1920's; still, ambition alone can hardly account for Hammett's sudden rise to prominence or for his development of a singular narrative style that was to influence the work of such disparate, young talents as Ernest Hemingway and John O'Hara. Although Hammett might have written more, and might have wanted to, he had by 1934 accomplished all that was needed to assure himself an enviable place in the history of American fiction.

Dashiell Hammett: A Life is exactly that, making no claim to examine the author's works as well. Although Johnson is intimately familiar with all of Hammett's writings, she mentions them only in passing, as needed to illustrate the author's life, often assuming on the part of the reader a knowledge as thorough as her own. Seen as a literary biography, Johnson's effort is perhaps best appreciated by specialists or at least by those with more than a passing interest in Hammett's literary contribution. As general biography, *Dashiell Hammett: A Life* is bound to secure and please a far wider audience, composed of those seeking to discover Hammett's place in the cultural history of America between the two world wars. Any biography, however, is necessarily limited by its subject; in the end, Johnson is left with the fact that Hammett's works are simply of greater interest than his life.

David B. Parsell

Sources for Further Study

Christian Science Monitor. November 18, 1983, p. 25.
Harper's. CCLXVII, October, 1983, p. 61.
Library Journal. CVIII, December 1, 1983, p. 2246.
Los Angeles Times Book Review. October 16, 1983, p. 1.
Nation. CCXXXVII, December 17, 1983, p. 639.
The New Republic. CLXXXIX, November 7, 1983, p. 39.
The New York Times Book Review. LXXXVIII, October 16, 1983, p. 1.
Newsweek. CII, October 17, 1983, p. 86.
Publishers Weekly. CCXXIV, August 26, 1983, p. 376.
Saturday Review. IX, September, 1983, p. 376.

THE DAY LASTS MORE THAN A HUNDRED YEARS

Author: Chingiz Aitmatov (1928-   )
Translated from the Russian by John French
Foreword by Katerina Clark
Publisher: Indiana University Press (Bloomington). 352 pp. $17.50
Type of work: Novel
Time: The not-too-distant future
Locale: Kazakhstan, Soviet Central Asia

A two-stranded narrative in which an old man's recollections of native Kazakh traditions are juxtaposed with a science-fiction subplot relating the fearful joint response of the Soviet Union and the United States to contact with an extraterrestrial intelligence

Principal characters:
    YEDIGEY, an old Kazakh railroad worker
    KARANAR, his camel
    KAZANGAP, his friend, whose death evokes memories of steppe life
    ABUTALIP, also Yedigey's friend, a victim of Joseph Stalin's purges

On the whole, Western publishing has not been favorably disposed toward Soviet writings of the post "thaw" period, on the assumption that censorial restrictions render that literature unworthy of translation. Nevertheless, for the past fifteen years, a small but persistent and influential group of authors has managed to get pieces into print which defy or at least considerably modify the concept of Socialist Realism, the official guideline for Soviet literature. Because these works have appeared with censorial approval, they reflect an evolutionary process in current Soviet writing which gives unusually wide scope of theme and style to authors, and which is as remarkable as it is diverse. Chingiz Aitmatov is both a prominent and unlikely member of this literary trend. While other innovative writers keep their political involvements to a required minimum, Aitmatov is an accepted and politically active member of the governing establishment, serving as delegate to national Communist Party congresses and to the Supreme Soviet, the country's legislative chamber. He also functions as occasional correspondent for the Communist Party organ *Pravda.* His literary qualifications likewise find official application. He serves on the editorial board of several journals, participates in the affairs of diverse cultural institutions, and heads the film producer's union of his region. The Soviet Union has honored Aitmatov with many awards and privileges, among them the Lenin Prize for Literature in 1963 for the collection *Povesti gor i stepei* (1962; *Tales of the Mountains and Steppes,* 1973). In addition, the author often appears as the Soviet Union's emissary at international, predominantly Third World, cultural conferences. None of these allegiances and activities has affected the high quality of his literary output.

    As a native of the small Central Asian republic of Kirghizia, Aitmatov represents the literature of the non-Russian national minorities who make up almost half of the Soviet population. While much of Soviet ethnic literature remains regional, Aitmatov's work transcends native boundaries, because he writes in Russian as well as Kirghiz and often aims at national and international audiences. The setting of his works, however, is firmly fixed in Central Asia, and his plots give generous space to the people, customs, and traditions of that region.

I dol'she veka dlitsya den' (1980; *The Day Lasts More than a Hundred Years*, 1983) is in many ways a continuation and recombination of earlier Aitmatov themes. These themes center on unsophisticated laborers and peasants who cope poorly, both physically and psychologically, with intruding technology, modernization, and bureaucracy. They cling firmly and stubbornly to their cultural heritage, rich in legend, folklore, and poetry; they indulge their love for animals and natural surroundings and attempt to neutralize foreign influences by preserving their native mythology. Aitmatov usually places them in confrontation with alien Soviet life-styles. Though he permits them to emerge as moral superiors, they are seldom the victors. Tragedy, defeat, or simply a strong feeling of loss inevitably await Aitmatov's bewildered heroes. The author does not express an overt anti-Soviet bias, yet certain recurrent notions, transmitted subtly and metaphorically through clever use of literary devices, leave the impression of a modern Soviet governing structure slowly eradicating Kirghizia's cultural heritage and rendering the surviving bearers of that culture superfluous if not ridiculous.

The extent to which *The Day Lasts More than a Hundred Years* is linked to Aitmatov's earlier work is easily apparent when one recalls the ethical touchstone of his most important pieces. *Proshchai Gul'sary!* (1966; *Farewell, Gulsary!*, 1973) weaves a delicate parallel between an abused Kirghiz peasant and his mistreated horse, both victims of Stalinist excesses. After receiving the 1968 State Prize for Literature for this work, Aitmatov stressed the destruction of Kirghiz mythology in his next major story, *Bely parakhod* (1970; *The White Steamship*, 1972). This poetic tragedy, which associates the senseless killing of a sacred deer with the death of a sensitive native boy, provoked an outcry among Soviet citizens against cavalier treatment of ethnic sensibilities. Despite the attending ideological controversy, this tale too was honored with the State Prize for Literature in 1977. Aitmatov's drama *Voskhozdenie na Fudziyamu* (1973; *The Ascent of Mount Fuji*, 1975), coauthored with fellow Central Asian Kaltai Mukhamedzhanov and staged at the Moscow Sovremennik Theater, as well as in English at the Washington, D.C. Arena Stage Theater in 1975, likewise buries politically delicate statements in generous doses of native lore. In this powerful play, Aitmatov indirectly but unmistakably suggests that Stalin-era informers are still politically prominent without having changed their ethical orientation. *The Ascent of Mount Fuji* did not receive the wide critical acclaim normally lavished on an Aitmatov work in the Soviet Union, and there were suggestions that he had gone too far.

Not surprisingly, then, the appearance of *The Day Lasts More than a Hundred Years* created a literary sensation. It became clear that the author had not only retained his influential position but also had been singled out for special accolades on behalf of this work, which the head of the Soviet Writer's Union acclaimed in 1981 as the best contemporary Soviet novel. Moreover, the book has been evaluated by Soviet ideologues as a good example of modern Socialist Realism, featuring as it does an honest, hardworking railroad laborer from the harsh Kazakh steppe. In his preface, Aitmatov himself extends the narrow parameters of Socialist Realism by insisting that a real Soviet hero must be a distinct individual, one who perceives the present through the prism of his particular ethnic history and traditions.

Such a moral giant is Aitmatov's main character, Yedigey, whose task in the novel is to arrange a traditional burial for his friend Kazangap. Yedigey uses the day of the funeral to recall the main legends and mores of Kazakh culture and to chronicle the region's history through an entire age—hence the title. These memories are periodically interrupted by reference to the community's hardships during the Stalin era. Some of the political allusions are unusually candid. Among Yedigey's memories during the wake is that of the arrest and subsequent mysterious death of a gentle poet friend, Abutalip. The author gives poignancy to this death by making it coincide with Stalin's own, thereby underscoring the capriciousness of the time. In a powerful scene, Aitmatov depicts the widow's sorrow as being incongruously mistaken by outsiders for grief over the dictator's death. Aitmatov also stresses the irrationality of the indictment: Abutalip was charged with forbidden writing for chronicling native tales and accused of treason for having fought with Yugoslav partisans when the latter were still Soviet allies. To be sure, this gloomy episode is brought to an uplifting conclusion when Yedigey manages to secure the dead poet's rehabilitation during the "thaw" under Nikita Khrushchev, but the effect of the tragedy on family and community is allowed to stand in the novel.

In other scenes, Aitmatov starkly traces the bleak postwar period in images rarely permitted in Soviet literature. Thus, there are glimpses of legless veterans in rags, maneuvering little homemade trolleys, of blind returnees aimlessly crawling about, of angry cripples turning to violence. Slender, doe-eyed Kazakh women perform the backbreaking labor of coal transport, and they are rendered almost indistinguishable from their surroundings by the all-pervading soot. By depicting the types of employment brought to Central Asia by Soviet modernization in such unattractive terms, Aitmatov gives ancient nomadic ways a clear edge.

The steppe community's reverence for and dependence on animals are embodied in Yedigey's Karanar, a camel of legendary renown. Karanar even becomes a major character, as the narrative voice shifts at times to let readers perceive the steppe through the eyes of the animal. Yedigey himself enjoys the reputation of an honest, dependable traditionalist among the older population. For the younger natives, however, who prefer Soviet tractors and trucks to camel transport, Yedigey is a relic. As readers are led into earlier decades and ages through Yedigey's recollections, a close parallel between man and beast emerges. The camel's freedom to roam at will in the open spaces is paralleled by his owner's far-reaching journey into steppe lore. When Yedigey must give up a beloved woman because of local convention, Karanar's destructive chasing of she-camels is similarly circumscribed. In the burial procession, Yedigey and his magnificently decorated camel are perceived as merely ceremonial, largely useless appendages. Nevertheless, throughout the narrative, Aitmatov, comparing the camel's elegant gait with the clanky, grimy freight trains and the awesome rockets alighting from the nearby space station, accentuates the superiority of the steppe-bred creature to more modern means of transport. Man and camel are tied to and dependent on each other in an inseparable bond, while trains and rockets distance and alienate people from one another.

Easily the most striking contrast in the novel is that between Yedigey's settlement and the nearby secret United States-Soviet rocket base. The Soviet Union's actual launch site, Baikonur, is located in Kazakhstan, which may be the reason why Aitmatov has shifted his usual Kirghiz locale to the neighboring sister republic. In this novel, the author has introduced elements of science fiction with a subplot concerning a joint American-Soviet space venture. The superpowers are depicted as sharing world domination absolutely equally, including management of a space station sarcastically called *Parity*. When the American and Russian astronauts onboard *Parity* make contact with a superior, humanlike civilization, actually visiting the home planet of these seemingly friendly beings, both superpowers agree to exile the astronauts to that distant world and to censor all news of this contact. Aitmatov structures the episode in such a way that the arrest and death of Yedigey's friend Abutalip in the Stalin era are connected with these dictatorial superpower decisions. Readers are left with the feeling that the illogicality, paranoia, and cruelty of Joseph Stalin's reign have become the everyday components of international dealings. The brief episodes of the science-fiction subplot break suddenly into Yedigey's recollections, as if signaling interference with native ways. They parallel the interruptions caused by memories of the Stalin era in other sections of the novel.

Aitmatov also finds resonance in an ancient Kazakh tale related in the novel, telling of how ancient invaders tortured Kazakh males by stretching udders from freshly slaughtered camels over the men's shaven heads: In the process of drying, the udders constrict, causing loss of memory. The amnesiac survivors, bereft of knowledge of their past, become hapless allies of their torturers. Aitmatov permits this theme to echo in his account of ambitious Kazakhstani who act as representatives of Soviet authorities, losing all genuine contact with their native culture. On yet another level, the confining animal skin evokes comparison with the satellite barrier planned by the superpowers to block the extraterrestrials from contact with Earth.

The terrifying effect of modern technology on steppe life is foregrounded in the climactic ending of the novel. As the long day of the memory-laden wake draws to a close, Yedigey camps with his camel and dog in the dunes, bent on saving an ancient tribal cemetery which the rocket base plans to use for a subdivision. At that moment, with an earsplitting explosion, the superpowers launch the rockets for the satellite barrier from the nearby base, enveloping the peaceful camping group in clouds of flame and smoke. Aitmatov saves the disoriented Yedigey from mental collapse by placing a mythical white Kazakh bird in his field of vision. The image of the gracefully soaring animal mercifully blots out the eruptions of the rocket launches; the novel's last words hint that Yedigey has survived the nightmare to continue, against all odds, his effort to preserve the ancient burial ground.

Official Soviet approval of this unusual book may well be due to Aitmatov's literary talents. Even noncontroversial episodes, such as Yedigey's falling in love with a married woman, are related through retelling an ancient Kazakh story with a similar theme. Aitmatov employs this method of indirection and implication throughout the novel. Indeed, since the greater part of the book is devoted to Kazakh legend, readers must work at extracting its contemporary relevance. Those favoring a fast-flowing narrative may become impatient with the slow pace of Yedigey's reminiscences. For American readers, the theme of the shared ethical failure of the superpowers provides added interest. Aitmatov's quiet pleading for peaceful exploration of space, coupled with his vision of a balance of power and influence between the two superpowers, reflect one aspect of current Soviet rhetoric and possibly encouraged censorial approval. John French's translation expertly manages to reproduce the linguistic incongruities inherent in a Russian-language novel featuring Kazakh characters who switch between Russian and Kazakh dialects.

While Aitmatov is Soviet Central Asia's most prominent writer, he is not universally admired. His native Kirghiz colleagues have criticized him for writing some pieces first in Russian to appeal to Union-wide readership, while following with Kirghiz versions only after some prodding. They also dislike the way he modifies ethnic themes to fit larger concerns. In addition, Aitmatov has on occasion denounced native mores where he regarded them as harmful; in his first significant work, the novella *Dzhamilia* (1958; English translation, 1973), he attacked the patriarchal custom of forcing young Kirghiz women into arranged marriages. Aitmatov is generally regarded as somewhat of a maverick who defies easy categorization. With *The Day Lasts More than a Hundred Years*, he has once more demonstrated that he can appeal to very diverse constituencies without compromising his artistic integrity.

Margot K. Frank

Sources for Further Study

The New Yorker. LX, April 23, 1984, p. 129.
Observer. August 21, 1983, p. 24.

THE DESERT ROSE

Author: Larry McMurtry (1936-   )
Publisher: Simon and Schuster (New York). 254 pp. $14.95
Type of work: Novel
Time: The 1980's
Locale: Las Vegas, Nevada

Narrated in the third person, McMurtry's novel chronicles the fading career of a Las Vegas show girl primarily from her own point of view, focusing upon a backstage, after-hours Las Vegas that the tourist never sees

Principal characters:
> HARMONY, a twenty-year veteran of the Stardust chorus line
> ROSS, her estranged husband, now living in Reno
> PEPPER, their daughter, age sixteen
> JESSIE, Harmony's friend, also a show girl at the Stardust
> GARY, costumer for the Stardust floor shows
> JACKIE BONVENTRE, choreographer-director at the Stardust
> MYRTLE, Harmony's aging next-door neighbor
> WENDELL, Myrtle's boyfriend, a maintenance man and gas jockey
> MEL, Pepper's much older admirer, a well-heeled former fashion photographer
> BUDDY, the man who is chief among Mel's younger rivals for Pepper's attentions

Departing from the Texas setting and characters familiar to readers of his first half-dozen novels, Larry McMurtry has in recent years expanded the scope of his observation to include such other quintessentially American locations as Hollywood (*Somebody's Darling*, 1978) and Washington, D.C. (*Cadillac Jack*, 1982). In *The Desert Rose*, McMurtry turns his attentions to Las Vegas, with results that at first glance leave a great deal to be desired.

Throughout his career as a novelist, McMurtry has experienced considerable difficulty with the handling of narrative voice, operating most successfully (as in the recent *Cadillac Jack*) through the recorded perceptions of a first-person, limited-viewpoint narrator. Elsewhere, as in his otherwise exemplary *The Last Picture Show* (1966), McMurtry tends to strain the reader's credulity by speaking for too many of his characters at once. In *The Desert Rose*, while cannily avoiding the trap of multiple viewpoints, McMurtry nevertheless disconcerts his reader by limiting his third-person narration to the viewpoint and vocabulary of the novel's principal character, a Las Vegas show girl in her late thirties whose formal education ended in high school.

However laudable in its intentions, in its efforts toward realism, McMurtry's narrative technique tends ultimately toward condescension, affecting characters and reader alike. It is difficult, after reading more than two hundred pages of barely literate narrative, to care about characters whose author has presented them with such readily apparent, if veiled condescension. One suspects that, in real life, a character such as Harmony would be both more literate and more perceptive than she is in McMurtry's novel. If indeed she would not, McMurtry then faces the more serious charge of treating his characters utterly without compassion. A similar charge, incidentally, might be leveled against McMurtry's earlier novel *Terms of Endearment* (1975), which was adapted into a powerful motion picture. Those who have seen and enjoyed the 1983 James Brooks film will probably be disappointed if they turn to McMurtry's novel, where the characters are portrayed with so little compassion as to appear downright disagreeable and undeserving of the reader's empathy.

To be sure, those readers with sufficient interest or patience to look beneath the repellent surface texture of *The Desert Rose* will find amused, amusing social satire of the sort that has made McMurtry justly famous, with entertaining glimpses of American characters of a sort which other writers tend to overlook. A case in point in *The Desert Rose* is Harmony's neighbor Myrtle, an aging borderline alcoholic who keeps a dog-sized pet goat named Maude; her life, apart from Maude, appears to revolve around garage sales. Notable also, in general, are the cast and crew of floor shows at the Stardust Casino, where glitter hides a daily grind of quiet desperation. One of the novel's few memorable incidents occurs when Harmony's friend Jessie is incapacitated by the collapse of the suspended platform upon which she regularly performs; by the time Jessie's broken ankle heals, she will in all likelihood have lost her job. Harmony, too, stands to be fired from the show, on the occasion of her upcoming thirty-ninth birthday.

The major plot device of *The Desert Rose* is that of increasing conflict between parent and child. Harmony's adolescent daughter, Pepper, trained after school throughout most of her short life in the arts of song and dance, is approaching full maturity both in talent and in beauty, if not necessarily in judgment. Harmony's forced retirement, perhaps indeed somewhat overdue, has been engineered by the Stardust's choreographer-director, Jackie Bonventre, who wants to train Pepper as a lead singer-dancer and finds it inappropriate for a mother and daughter to perform nightly on the same stage. The narrative, at times approaching stream of consciousness, hunts back and forth in time, with frequent flashbacks to Harmony's own start in Las Vegas at age seventeen and her discovery by an aging French-born director, grossly overweight, whose fatal heart attack some six months later might well be traced to his enjoyment of Harmony's favors in bed. Thus launched, Harmony's career, notable mainly for its stability, has proceeded more or less without incident for more than twenty years. Harmony, lacking vocal talent, has never aspired to more than a secure spot in the Stardust chorus line, which under normal circumstances provides sufficient income to pay her modest bills.

At the time of the novel, however, circumstances in Harmony's life are somewhat less favorable than normal. Her most recent live-in boyfriend, a foul-tempered, foul-mouthed drifter named Denny, has wrecked her car beyond repair and misused her bank card to the point that credit privileges have been withdrawn. Although he has moved out, Denny returns to Harmony's rural mailbox just in time to retrieve her car-insurance check and thank her for the "loan" before speeding away in a cloud of dust; there will be little or no remedy, as Harmony knows Denny to be an accomplished forger.

By one of the novel's several unexplored but conscious ironies, Harmony's daughter, Pepper, is in a position to help her mother financially but somehow neglects to do so; instead, she "deposits" with a school chum the impressive sums of money paid to her by an older male admirer, Mel, a photographer who asks nothing in return save that she pose for pictures in antique-style underwear.

As the novel's modest action develops, Pepper receives not only a job offer from Jackie Bonventre but also a marriage proposal from Mel, who still has not touched her. She weighs both offers, confiding only in Myrtle and leaving her mother to hear the information secondhand. In time, Pepper will move toward acceptance of both proposals, incidentally precipitating her mother's forced retirement from the Stardust chorus line. Harmony, meanwhile, begins trying to reestablish communication with her husband, Ross, who left her when Pepper was little more than a baby but to whom she remains legally married. Ross, a skilled lighting operator who now plies his trade in Reno, has never seemed to want a divorce and has been known to "come through" for Harmony and Pepper in the past. Although loosely attached to a young woman from the counterculture who is about to bear his child (and rear it in a commune), Ross remains more than a little in love with Harmony and welcomes her, at the end of the novel, to his bed and board in Reno—at least until she finds another job.

Pepper, meanwhile, moves from predictable adolescent rebellion toward a gathering awareness of powers both professional and personal. Very much a child of the 1980's, Pepper has long resented and criticized her mother's comparatively more garish tastes in jewelry, clothing, and hair style. Too self-absorbed and self-centered to suspect that she has in fact been competing with her mother, Pepper indeed symbolizes and personifies a "new wave" that washes away everything in its path, not excluding such traditions as have thus far existed in Las Vegas entertainment.

Mel, the rich, reclusive, erstwhile fashion photographer who ends the novel as Pepper's fiancé, is perhaps the most masterful and ambiguous of McMurtry's creations in *The Desert Rose*. Perceived largely through the eyes of Harmony and Pepper, Mel is a shadowy, secretive, and even sinister figure who continues to astonish characters and reader alike with his spontaneous expressions of sensitivity and disinterested generosity. Even as Pepper and her mother speculate upon Mel's sexuality (he is known to have kinky tastes and has never been married before), the reader is invited to speculate upon the sources of his fabulous wealth; it does not seem to occur to the women that Mel might have grown rich through pornography or through ties with organized crime. At most, Pepper is somewhat nonplussed when Mel tells her that his father is a high-school swimming coach; until that point, she had rather imagined his wealth to be inherited. From what little can be seen of him, however, Mel emerges as one of the more decent male characters in a novel populated largely by thieves, cads, and bounders.

Another generally affirmative male character is the husband and father, Ross, who appears primarily as a voice over the telephone on those rare occasions when Harmony can manage to locate him. When she finally comes face-to-face with him at the Reno bus station in the novel's closing scene, Harmony is somewhat alarmed by Ross's loss of hair and gain of weight, but she consoles herself with the thought that perhaps she too has changed in appearance during the past fourteen years. Ross, although clearly a weakling by the standards of earlier generations, is nevertheless a decent man and in his own way a survivor, a master "light man" who finds his work in demand wherever he chooses to go. Such stability is indeed rather rare in the world around Harmony, who herself has managed to survive most of her contemporaries in the field of casino entertainment. Among her few fellow survivors is Gary, a costumer and out-of-the-closet homosexual who has managed to attract more than his share of (hopeless) female admirers because of his basic decency. Harmony's friend Jessie, for example, harbors a crush on the nondescript Gary even as she keeps regular company with Monroe, the loutish proprietor of an eponymous muffler shop. Myrtle's regular boyfriend Wendell, although fundamentally decent, is a burned-out hulk of a man who, far from his original home, is apparently just waiting to die, unable to come to terms with either his son's suicide or his wife's subsequent desertion. Somewhat more typical of the available male companionship is Dave, a youngish employee of the casino with whom Harmony opts to spend the night after Jessie's incapacitating accident. An ex-Marine, Dave lives in a nearly bare apartment and can offer his guest nothing more than his usual diet of K-rations washed down with beer; since joining the Corps, Dave has lost all interest in regular food, and Harmony wonders if he might not have lost his mind as well.

In keeping with the general tone and viewpoint of the novel, few characters are given the benefit of surnames—with the notable exceptions of director Jackie Bonventre and a visiting entrepreneur named Dub Dooley, who tries to take advantage of Harmony's impending unemployment by offering her a job at his "total nude" club in Houston. Predictably, given the scruples already revealed, Harmony refuses Dooley's offer, preferring to face a dubious future in Reno with the man to whom she is still legally married.

As a slice of life or even a satirical pastiche, *The Desert Rose* is not without its good points, but as a novel it ultimately fails, a slight effort brought down under the weight of its own pretensions. As a stylistic exercise, *The Desert Rose* may arrest the reader's interest but cannot retain it for long. This failure is partly the result of what is left unsaid but mainly the result of the author's patronizing approach toward characters that might otherwise have elicited the reader's concern and ready empathy. It is to be hoped that McMurtry, in future efforts, will once again assert his well-earned authority as an interested, and consequently interesting, observer.

David B. Parsell

Sources for Further Study

Library Journal. CVIII, September 1, 1983, p. 1721.
Los Angeles Times Book Review. September 4, 1983, p. 7.
National Review. XXXV, November 25, 1983, p. 1495.
New Leader. LXVI, November 14, 1983, p. 18.
The New Yorker. LIX, October 24, 1983, p. 162.
Saturday Review. IX, September, 1983, p. 46.

THE DEVIL'S STOCKING

Author: Nelson Algren (1909-1981)
Publisher: Arbor House (New York). 308 pp. $16.95; paperback $8.95
Type of work: Novel
Time: The 1960's and 1970's
Locale: Primarily New Jersey and New York

A posthumously published novel that transcends the author's original intention, becoming a modern morality tale in which the issues of right and wrong and justice in society are held up for close scrutiny

> *Principal characters:*
> RUBY CALHOUN, a middleweight prizefighter
> ED "RED" HALOWAYS, Ruby's friend and sparring partner
> JENNIFER BOGGS CALHOUN, Ruby's wife
> DOVIE-JEAN DAWKINS, Ruby's and Red's mistress
> VINCE LE FORTE, a small-time criminal
> LIEUTENANT VINCENT DE VIVANI, a Jersey City police officer
> BARNEY KERRIGAN, state investigator with the office of the public defender
> ADELINE KELSEY, a black businesswoman interested in Ruby

An angry indictment of social injustice, *The Devil's Stocking* is in the direct tradition of the Naturalistic novel. Nelson Algren's protagonist, Ruby Calhoun, bears more than a slight resemblance to Frank Norris' McTeague and Theodore Dreiser's Carrie Meeber, and, like Dreiser's *An American Tragedy* (1925) and many other Naturalistic novels, *The Devil's Stocking* is based on a true story: the widely publicized murder trial of middleweight boxer Rubin "Hurricane" Carter. Like Dreiser's Clyde Griffiths, Algren's Ruby Calhoun is a victim of the society in which he struggles for survival. Both men, through initiative and grit, begin to beat the odds and make something of themselves, and both are tricked by circumstances and slapped down harder than ever. The lesson—among others, for these are complex novels—is that some people never can be victorious over the situation in which chance has placed them, because the social structure will not *let* them win.

Algren was significantly influenced by Dreiser, Norris, Stephen Crane, and Upton Sinclair, but he was also deeply affected by the generation of writers who achieved prominence during his youth: the leftist, socially conscious writers of the Great Depression. Algren may have been liberated stylistically by Ernest Hemingway, but his content reflected the times in which he lived. Algren learned that the studied objectivity of the journalistic style actually heightened the emotional impact of his angry fiction. At the same time, there is a strong romantic streak running through his work. Although, like many leftist writers of the 1930's, he considered "pretty" writing to be aligned with political conservatism, he could not suppress his rough lyricism.

Nelson Algren was a major—possibly great—writer who did not always write well. Just as Dreiser, Norris, or Sinclair Lewis could startle the most sympathetic reader with an awkwardness of phrase, an infelicity of diction, so Algren was capable of writing very clumsy prose. Stylistic nuance, however, was not essential to Algren's literary purpose. Compassion and narrative drive propel his stories and engage his readers. It is impossible for an open-minded reader not to become deeply involved in the story that Algren is telling; Algren makes readers *care* about his characters and their ultimate fate. Almost against one's better judgment, one suffers along with Algren's seedy, victimized, often raunchy characters, wanting life to work out fairly for them even while disapproving of much of their conduct, and one becomes angry at the forces that oppress these grimy pawns of social injustice.

All of these strengths are evident in the posthumously published novel *The Devil's Stocking*, a fitting conclusion to Algren's long career. The book begins with and often reverts to a retrospective structure, with chracters remembering and commenting on past action, as if in a collection of reportage from various sources. This technique serves to create an objective distance between the subject—some unpleasant truths about American society and the American judicial system—and the reader, without diminishing the force of the narrative.

At times, Algren is eloquent, plunging into vivid descriptive passages or rhetorical flourishes. His description of Big Benjamin, the bouncer in the brothel where Ruby Calhoun's girlfriend works, is written with just such flair:

> This Delancey Street alley fighter, this ghetto lumberjack in the faded plaid shirt, this matzohfied Marciano with a broken nose, this pimpified kingfish who knew nothing of the Talmud and less than that about women, was nothing more, in fact, than a muscular schlemiel who went up and down stairs a dozen times a day fetching Cokes, coffee and hamburgers to the house's whores.

Similarly, Algren uses the vernacular of his characters to intensify his portrait of them both as individuals and as pieces of a larger picture. "You're an uptown up-tempo woman," Ruby tells Adeline Kelsey as he breaks off their brief affair, "I'm a downtown down-beat guy."

Algren undermines the impact of his lively, realistic dialogue, however, with overexplanatory tags: "Calhoun marveled sadly," "asked him, in a courteous tone," "Calhoun reflected, cocking his head," and so on. Algren wants to be certain that readers understand his message, but his failure to trust his material to speak for itself damages an otherwise compelling and admirable book. When Dovie-Jean takes a tour past the Statue of Liberty, the guide recites the verses at the statue's base, welcoming immigrants to the New World. Dovie-Jean's eyes fill with tears, for she feels that she has been included "among the homeless and tempest-tossed yearning to be free." To this, Algren adds, "She hadn't even been invited."

Indeed, as an all-seeing, omniscient author, Algren frequently comments on the events of his narrative. For example, after describing the suppression of a prison rebellion, he remarks: "For the most heinous crime, that of demanding that men be broken to dogs, committed by society against the criminal, no mention was made." He adds, "The confrontation was the state's. Because men are everywhere going to resist at being treated as less than men"; insisting that "the uprising had not been a race riot until the correction officers made it into one," he cannot resist underlining the point: "No reference was made to Governor Nelson's demonstration of physical and moral cowardice." Finally when Algren talks about the Jersey City police lieutenant who helped to entrap Ruby Calhoun, he does not let the man's actions speak for themselves. Instead, he says, "Vincent de Vivani, a corrupted racist, arrogant, contemptuous and cunning, was the living epitome of what had gone wrong with justice in New Jersey."

Nevertheless, Algren's vision and the magnitude of his themes transcend his lapses. Algren holds up the entire American judicial system for scrutiny, but this is not strictly his subject. He attacks racism and hypocrisy, but even these subjects only serve to illustrate still larger themes. In *The Devil's Stocking*, Algren above all is preoccupied with the nature of human dignity. He confronts the struggle that every aware human being must wage to discover and hold onto his own dignity as an individual. There is no crime worse than that of depriving a man of his dignity as a unique person, yet the legitimate assertion of individuality threatens those who are not sure of their own worth. Such people cannot tolerate free, equal, unbowed human beings. After his years of ordeal, Ruby Calhoun knows this very well: "I remain a threat," he says, "because I remain uncrushed."

It is the *perception* of Ruby Calhoun's strength that threatens those who would crush him. The theme of perception as more important than reality runs strongly through the novel. Just as the prison inmates indulge in role-playing before the television cameras, so some black characters pass for white—or choose not to pass. In every case, the actual condition is less important than how that condition is viewed.

In the same way, the perception of justice, the perception of freedom, the *belief* in man's dignity, and the *belief* in innocence are the forces that dominate and control the lives of Ruby Calhoun and the other characters in the novel—and, by implication, all human lives. In *The Devil's Stocking*, a bouncer who cannot even fight passes as a great warrior; the guilty seem to be innocent, and the innocent appear to be guilty. Two respectable lawyers own a brothel that they refer to, between themselves, as their "Forty-eighth Street property." All that matters is the façade. Keep up appearances; hide any flaws behind a layer of hypocrisy; convince the world that you are pure and the others are evil: This is the rule of the modern, urban jungle in which Ruby

Calhoun and Red Haloways and Dovie-Jean Dawkins battle for survival.

At first glance, *The Devil's Stocking* might appear to be a journalistic novel in which Algren has merely returned to his familiar collection of street guerrillas, junkies, drunks, and sleazy women. In fact, however, it is a complex and sophisticated book, a novel of great wisdom rich with insight into the human condition. In this day of authors continually "biting off less than they can chew," it is refreshing to discover a book that takes such major risks—and that, more often than not, succeeds so well. If Algren had lived, he might well have revised or polished this novel before its American publication, but even as it is *The Devil's Stocking* stands as an impressive achievement.

Bruce D. Reeves

Sources for Further Study

The Atlantic. CCLII, October, 1983, p. 122.
Library Journal. CVIII, August, 1983, p. 1500.
The New York Times Book Review. LXXXVIII, October 9, 1983, p. 9.
Publishers Weekly. CCXXIV, July 8, 1983, p. 56.

DJUNA
The Life and Times of Djuna Barnes

Author: Andrew Field
Publisher: G. P. Putnam's Sons (New York). Illustrated. 287 pp. $16.95
Type of work: Literary biography
Time: The late nineteenth century to 1982
Locale: The eastern United States and Europe

A brief narrative of Barnes's life accompanied by a series of sketches about people who figured prominently in her life and literary works

Principal personages:
DJUNA BARNES, a Bohemian writer
THELMA WOOD, the lover and friend of Djuna Barnes
T. S. ELIOT, a critic and playwright
PEGGY GUGGENHEIM, a patron and friend of Barnes
DAG HAMMARSKJOLD, a statesman and translator of *The Antiphon* into Swedish

Djuna Barnes, the elusive, eccentric woman best known as the author of *Nightwood* (1936), is the subject of Andrew Field's biography *Djuna: The Life and Times of Djuna Barnes*. Chapter 1 of the biography provides a sketch of Barnes's life, while the rest of the book approaches its subject only obliquely, focusing on the people who were important to her. It is almost as if Field had sought to protect Barnes's privacy in his literary biography as she did in her life. The reader is not told the final cause of her death, and the details of her relationships with her lovers are left vague. The biography begins with broad strokes, adding very little brush work to fill out her profile. Like the moon, Djuna Barnes is only partially revealed. She lived almost half of her life alone in a tiny apartment on Patchin Place in New York City. Months would go by without conversation; a biographer can only guess at what these silences meant. In the end, Barnes as literary subject remains as incomprehensible as she was in real life. What is not clear is how much Andrew Field has augmented rather than helped unravel the mystery.

Djuna Barnes was, in many ways, a typical descendant of her unusual family. Barnes's grandmother, Zadel Barnes Budington, divorced her husband, Henry—a strict Methodist moralist who wrote religious tracts—after twenty years of marriage. A newspaper journalist with strong feminist leanings, Zadel Barnes was one of fourteen children, many of whom were given strange names of uncertain gender—among them Niar and Unade. These odd names suggest a pretentiousness with spiritualistic leanings—a combination evident in the character of Djuna Barnes.

Zadel Barnes was not traditionally religious, but she enjoyed a mystical or visionary outlook combined with an active pursuit of feminist ideals. While there is no clear evidence of her bisexuality, there is some likelihood that she possessed a sexual disposition toward women. She traveled to Europe with her second husband, changed her name back to Barnes, and conducted a literary salon in England. Her life, like her granddaughter's, is shrouded in mystery and half-truths; it is known, however, that eventually Zadel Barnes lived with her son, Wald, and his wife, Elizabeth Chappell, and was primarily responsible for the education of her granddaughter, Djuna.

Djuna Barnes never attended school. She lived until sixteen in a house which her father had built in Cornwall-on-Hudson, New York. She was an excellent equestrian as well as a gardener, and she lived in circumstances which might have been idyllic. At sixteen, she started a career as a writer which continued until her death at ninety; like her grandmother, she began as a newspaper reporter and journalist. Despite her great gifts, however, Barnes remained psychologically blighted. She was married briefly and lived with another woman, Thelma Wood, for almost ten years, and she had numerous affairs with both men and women. She never formed a permanent attachment, never had or wanted children, and died alone.

It is not clear what happened in Barnes's childhood to permanently cripple her spirit. Field says that she possessed "a negative attitude towards her father" and held "strongly ambivalent feelings towards her mother." Wald Barnes was an incorrigible womanizer who often lived with his mistresses in the house with his children, wife, and mother. Zadel was the matriarch of the family, tolerant of her son's wanderings but also keeping him in an angrily dependent position. Apparently, Djuna Barnes was either molested by her father or sexually assaulted by neighbors with her father's complicity; Barnes's work is filled with vituperative sketches of her father, whom she clearly despised. As is the case with many victims of molestation, Barnes in turn was confused in her own sexual identity. Her writing has the sting of a woman acutely aware of her heritage, snarling and enraged and trapped. She told her family's story repeatedly in her work and freed herself only through silence.

Barnes lived during an exciting period of literary history. She knew most of the important artists of the 1920's and 1930's and enjoyed a reputation as a witty and charming woman. Although never rich, she dressed with style, wearing a black cape which became her hallmark. When she went to Paris in 1919, she was a well-known New York journalist; she carried letters of introduction to James Joyce and Ezra Pound. Joyce was the one contemporary writer she admired without reservation, and her major work, *Nightwood*, owes much to Joyce. As a present, Joyce gave her his annotated manuscript of *Ulysses*, but she sold it a short time later when she was desperately in need of money.

Sometime during the early 1920's, Barnes met Thelma Wood, a six-foot-tall artist who has been described in many memoirs of that era as strikingly beautiful. She was clearly the prototype for Robin Vote, the lover of Nora in *Nightwood*. Barnes and Wood lived together on the Left Bank on Rue Sainte Germaine until 1931. Their relationship was tempestuous and tortured. Wood, an alcoholic and sexually promiscuous, would go out at night and cruise the bars. Barnes, sometimes accompanying her, sometimes retrieving her from alleys or bars, drank also. Their days were filled with recriminations and apologies, their nights with lust and jealousy. Their apartment was filled with mirrors, tapestries, and religious objects: "The salon was scattered with ecclesiastical pillows. The curtains were silk and cotton, yellow with red blossoms. . . . There were three gold-framed epinals: Saint Claude, Saint John, and Gargantua." Although physically removed from her New England and New York heritages, Djuna clearly had re-created that strange mixture of spirituality and pretentiousness which had marked her family. She drank and she went to church; she was austere and abandoned. The contradictions in her past were embedded in the environment of her present.

During the 1920's, Barnes wrote a considerable amount. In 1923, she published *A Book*, containing drawings, poems, stories, and plays; in 1928, *Ryder*, a mock-heroic chronicle of her family, appeared; and in 1929, she completed *Ladies Almanack*, a comic letter to lesbians living in Paris. In addition, she was a regular contributor to *Vanity Fai*, the *New York Tribune*, *McCall's*, *Theater Guild Magazine*, and other periodicals. When she finally was able to leave Wood, she began writing *Nightwood*, most of which was written in England. Wood eventually took up with another woman, called Jenny Petherbridge in *Nightwood* (Field does not supply Jenny's real name).

When Barnes ended her relationship with Wood in 1931, she left Paris, traveled through Europe, and lived for a short while in Algeria with her new lover, Charles Henri Ford. The living conditions were horrible, and when Peggy Guggenheim invited her to come to England in the summer of 1932, Barnes accepted. The large manor house, Hayford Hall, with its servants and eleven bedrooms, spacious lawns, and gracious, hospitable hostess, allowed Barnes both the privacy and the intellectual stimulation she needed to complete *Nightwood*. Still, she was depressed, surly, and melancholy, troubled by debts and by the memories of an impossible series of love relationships. When she returned to Paris and read parts of *Nightwood* (originally titled "Bow Down") to Wood, Wood "threw her teacup at Djuna and attacked her, punching her twice in the mouth." Barnes completed the novel after the summer of 1933 and sailed back to New York to find a publisher.

The manuscript had been rejected by seven major American publishers by the time Barnes returned to Hayford Hall in 1934, but fortunately Emily Coleman, one of the residents at the Hall, became Barnes's "agent." With the help of Edwin Muir, Coleman succeeded in persuading T. S. Eliot to read the manuscript. The rest of the *Nightwood* story reads like a literary fairy tale. Eliot, an editor at Faber and Faber, became convinced of the great literary merit of the novel. He fought the editorial board at Faber and Faber, eventually writing a powerful introduction to the novel. (Indeed, it was Eliot who gave the book its final title.) *Nightwood* was published in London in October of 1936 and in New York in 1937. Even before publication, the novel enjoyed a kind of underground literary fame; copies circulated among the literary avant-garde, and group readings were not uncommon. *Nightwood* has remained almost a cult novel, read by the literary elite since the 1930's. Because of this small but persistent readership, the novel, after nearly fifty years, is still in print.

In some ways, *Nightwood* marked a turning point in the life of Djuna Barnes. Her psychological health, already weakened by several breakdowns, was undermined by physical problems. She drank and smoked a considerable amount, suffered from asthma, did not eat well, and often found herself on the edge of bankruptcy. When she returned again to New York in 1941 after selling her flat in Paris, she was destitute. Peggy Guggenheim literally rescued her and started to provide her with a small monthly allowance which continued through most of her life. She found a small apartment on Patchin Place and lived there for the next forty-one years.

Barnes's last major work was *The Antiphon*, a play about her relationship with her mother. The work was conceived during the last years of her mother's life when, in addition to her own psychological and physical concerns, Barnes was responsible for caring for her mother. Barnes's distressful personal life probably prevented her from responding positively to offers to promote herself as an artist. Although Eliot tried to arrange another book contract immediately after the publication of *Nightwood* and made other professional contacts for her, she refused these opportunities. In New York also, she became increasingly reclusive. When her mother died in 1945, she began writing *The Antiphon*. She patterned the drama on Eliot's *The Family Reunion* (1939) and sent it to him in 1954. Eliot's silence and his belated reticent praise distressed Barnes; still, he helped her to edit the work and came to a special performance of the play at Harvard University in 1956. It was published by Faber and Faber in 1958 and later in New York by Farrar, Straus and Cudahy. Although reviewers tried to be sympathetic, the play was too purposely obscure. Barnes's continued commitment to concealment ultimately condemned her as a literary artist. Even friends who loved and admired her work had difficulty in supporting her. The two great exceptions were Edwin Muir and, later, Dag Hammarskjold. Both men loved *The Antiphon*; Hammarskjold, in fact, cotranslated the play into Swedish. It opened in Stockholm in 1961 and was a great success. Unfortunately, that success was not repeated in the United States.

Barnes lived for more than twenty years after the Swedish performance. Although she gave up drinking and eventually smoking, she suffered from asthma, then emphysema and arthritis. She became more and more unsociable, often not answering her telephone or door bell. Many of her friends were dying; her neighborhood was becoming run-down. Writes Field: "As her contemporaries died Miss Barnes felt like George Sand, ready to pull down the curtain and shut the door on a life that had passed in a time that appalled her."

Barnes continued to write—mostly letters to friends. Peggy Guggenheim sent her three hundred dollars a month, and that, along with occasional gifts, allowed Barnes to survive. Her final work published in her lifetime was a small book of animal alphabet rhymes, *Creatures in an Alphabet* (1982). She dedicated it to Emily Coleman, the woman primarily responsible for the publication of *Nightwood*.

Faith Gabelnick

Sources for Further Study

American Literature. LVI, May, 1984, p. 292.
Harper's. CCLXVII, July, 1983, p. 76.
Library Journal. CVIII, May 1, 1983, p. 907.
Ms. XI, April, 1983, p. 35.
The New York Times Book Review. LXXXVIII, June 26, 1983, p. 9.
The New Yorker. LIX, June 20, 1983, p. 102.
Publishers Weekly. CCXXIII, April 22, 1983, p. 90.

DOCUMENTS RELATING TO THE SENTIMENTAL AGENTS IN THE VOLYEN EMPIRE

Author: Doris Lessing (1919-   )
Publisher: Alfred A. Knopf (New York). 179 pp. $12.95
Type of work: Novel
Time: An unspecified period of time unrelatable to human history
Locale: The planet Volyen, its two moons Volyendesta and Volyenadna, and the
   two nearest planets in its system, Maken and Slovin

The fifth book in the series collectively titled Canopus in Argos: Archives *asserts that
propagandists may manipulate people by the unscrupulous use of language*

> *Principal characters:*
>   KLORATHY, the Canopean agent in charge on Volyen
>   INCENT, an incredibly naïve Canopean agent
>   KROLGUL, chief agent of Shammat in the Volyen Empire
>   GRICE, the Volyen governor of Volyenadna and various other natives
>   of the five planets

All human languages have certain common characteristics, called "universals" in linguistics. All, for example, have a class of words translatable as English nouns and another class translatable as English verbs. All have a means of asking questions and making statements. The universal of interest to readers of the fifth novel in Doris Lessing's series *Canopus in Argos: Archives* is "displacement"—that is, that all languages have the capacity to refer to something not physically present to the speaker and hearer. People can talk about what happened yesterday, about what may happen tomorrow, or even fantasize about what cannot possibly ever happen. Baboons, to select one example as a contrast, use verbal signals to alert the pack to the presence of food or danger; however, the baboon never gives the call for food unless it actually sees or smells food, and it never gives the call for danger simply because it is lonely or nervous. Baboons always tell the truth.

From the possibility of displacement in human speech springs the ability to lie, but from displacement also springs all verbal art, all history, all planning for the future, all science dependent on hypothesis. Indeed, a society built on a language lacking displacement seems inconceivable.

Doris Lessing's *Documents Relating to the Sentimental Agents in the Volyen Empire* is about telling lies, specifically political lies—propaganda. Like fish in water, humans live in an atmosphere of words, seldom thinking about the nature of this surrounding element. We trust that our whole speech community shares a common understanding of the words we use—and in this trust rests the strength of propaganda. Thus, the rulers of every new nation call their state a democracy, not because they believe that the sounds that make up the word have some innate power, but because they want to take advantage of the common associations of the word in the speech community. When people discover (usually as children) that a word may mean different things to different people—that is, when children discover that some people will lie to them—they may react in many ways, and surely the least sensible way to react is to assume that because someone has lied to one, no one tells the truth. Or, to put it into the political context of *The Sentimental Agents* (as the work will probably always be called), the least sensible way to react is to assume that because "freedom" may mean different things to different people, that the word has no meaning at all.

Unfortunately, this reaction seems to be the lesson of *The Sentimental Agents*. The agents of Shammat or Puttiora, the galactic bad guys, are up to their usual nastiness, causing trouble apparently only for the evil it brings about, and their chief instrument in several spectacularly vulnerable societies is lying. Krolgul, one of Shammat's agents, sets up an Academy of Rhetoric in which the locals are trained to respond with the utmost emotion to high-flown but empty phrases—the reaction which George Orwell in *Nineteen Eighty-Four* (1949) called "duckspeak." This particular species of lying—using the emotional appeal of words to cover an emptiness of substance—is in Lessing's novel always referred to as "rhetoric" and described as a disease: People suffer from "undulant rhetoric" and are sent to the "Hospital for Rhetorical Diseases," which has departments such as that of "Rhetorical Logic." The metaphor of disease is the basis for what humor the book has to offer.

Against the flood of diseased language stand the good guys—the agents of Canopus, and chiefly Klorathy. His younger assistant, Incent, has some redeeming features in his eagerness and folly, but Klorathy's eternal wisdom and cool benevolence after a while become suffocating. It is mainly Klorathy who supplies the remedies for rhetoric and who likewise supplies many examples of its most virulent outbreaks. (In this review, Klorathy will be referred to as "he"; it is a measure of the book's character development that it is never specified whether Klorathy is a woman or man.) Some readers may find Klorathy's examples of diseased rhetoric the most repellent parts of the book: Among the works held up for the reader to see through and be disgusted by are Winston Churchill's address to the British people during the Battle of Britain (Lessing, it might be noted, moved to Britain only in 1948) and the song of the Civil Rights movement, "We Shall Overcome," described as "a lament or dirge, of the most dispiriting sort." Elsewhere, Klorathy, speaking specifically about Earth, refers to the Christian religion as "one of the most savage and long-lasting tyrannies ever known even on that unfortunate planet."

It is unfortunate for science fiction that Lessing's present series has been given that label: The second novel in the series, *The Marriages Between Zones Three, Four, and Five* (1980), is better described as a fable and the third, *The Sirian Experiments* (1981), as a fantasy. The others—*Re: Colonized Planet 5,*

Shikasta (1979) and *The Making of the Representative for Planet 8* (1982)—
contain curious scientific errors, a failing also found in *The Sentimental Agents*.
John W. Campbell, Jr., long-time editor of *Astounding Science Fiction*, is
reputed to have maintained that if a so-called science-fiction story could have
taken place on a submarine rather than in a spaceship, then it was not science
fiction at all. The genre had to offer something distinctive, something more
than a transplanetary adventure story or horse opera. For most of Lessing's
novel, nothing happens that could not have taken place on Earth in the
historical past: Indeed, take away the sometimes very thin fictional veil, and
most of what is related did take place in the historical past. The single exception—the episode that might arguably make the book science fiction—is highly
implausible.

On one of the planets in Volyen's system, Maken, each child is reared in
close harmony with a flying reptile—the pipisaurus—who then becomes the
child's mount and companion. These reptiles are truly unusual, having many
features not associated with reptiles, including intelligence, edible "glandular
secretions" (one wonders what evolutionary purpose they serve), and fur.
Their diet consists of birds and insects (on their home planet, the insects are
"often the size of a Maken infant"). Despite the bounty Nature has provided
them, however, their appetites have been awesome enough to threaten the
birds and insects of Maken with extinction. Their owners therefore invade
another planet solely for the purpose of finding more birds and insects for
the reptiles to eat. The picture of someone getting out of an interplanetary
spacecraft and getting on a flying reptile is more than a little hard to swallow.
In any case, the reader is told that the people have joined the reptiles in a
"social osmosis," when presumably "symbiosis" was the word meant.

To be sure, the story of the Makens and their flying reptiles is only a few
pages in an extraordinarily convoluted plot wherein all sorts of political movements, all uniformly ridiculous, are being swayed left and right, feverish with
disease of rhetoric. All sorts of governments are planning invasions and various mischief, people are strutting around in uniforms, orators are saying
senseless things, and no one ever seems to see through the nonsense except
Klorathy. From time to time, his lieutenant, Incent, catches rhetoric and has
to be cured, in one episode by the very curious means of looking at something
like automated shadow pictures on the white ceiling of his hotel room.

The novel lacks life; for all the transparency of the fiction, not many parallels
between the troubles of Earth and the troubles of the Volyens may be drawn.
One reason is that Klorathy always has a rabbit to pull out of his hat. The
moon Volyenadna, for example, has long suffered economic domination
because of its cold, barren tundras. Unable to feed themselves, the Volyenadnans work in the mines to extract minerals that they can exchange for food.
Appreciating their plight and seeing that a bloody revolution may be
approaching, Klorathy solves both problems by giving the Volyenadnans a

plant—Rocknosh—which grows from spores and multiplies explosively (in a period of no more than months, it spreads over enough of the planet to change its color when seen from space). Not only is Rocknosh edible and not only can a variety of useful products be made from it, but also it lessens the severity of the planet's climate. In short, Klorathy gives the Volyenadnans the secret of perpetual motion.

Or, to take another example, when the birdmen of Maken invade Volyendesta, they simply want food for their pets. The Makenites in fact have never before seen Volyendestans, and vice versa. It is difficult to find a lesson in this situation applicable, say, to the long history of warring between France and Germany.

Doris Lessing is a writer with a high reputation; whether that reputation is justified is a question better left for time to answer. What may be asserted now, though, is that she is certainly a writer whose works are out of the ordinary, for better or worse. The scope of her stories is enormous: thousands of years, tens of planets. One danger with stories of such magnitude is the temptation to find swift and easy solutions to resolve plots; another is the temptation to allow characters to remain caricatures. The narrative rushes the principals along from planet to planet, meeting this or that other character whose whole portrait must be rendered in a few sentences. Finally, Lessing is not a very pictorial writer: There is in her later work, beginning in the 1970's, much less description than many another writer provides, and few vivid images. The blurb on the book jacket compares Lessing to Jonathan Swift, but the comparison is more inept in this particular than in any other: Swift's prose is highly colorful and concrete.

Many will argue that the theme of *The Sentimental Agents* is paramount in importance, and that all other considerations are secondary. If so, the book must be compared to others dealing with the same subject. Given the time of the book's publication, it is bound to be measured against Orwell's *Nineteen Eighty-Four*. In that work, it is Winston Smith the character, and Julia, and O'Brien, and even Big Brother, that one remembers. The characters are alive, and the best of them—Smith—cares passionately about truth, believes strongly that language should reflect external reality. O'Brien tortures Winston Smith until he wholeheartedly agrees that words mean whatever Big Brother wants them to mean—"War is Peace," "Freedom is Slavery"—and although he is alive at the end, the party has had to kill all that was uniquely Smith to control him. Orwell's plea is that language matters so much that it must be vigilantly guarded: One fears that Lessing advises that it be disregarded.

Walter E. Meyers

Sources for Further Study

Book World. XIII, April 24, 1983, p. 8.
Booklist. LXXIX, February 1, 1983, p. 698.
Christian Science Monitor. June 22, 1983, p. 11.
Library Journal. CVIII, March 1, 1983, p. 517.
Los Angeles Times Book Review. July 6, 1983, p. 6.
New Age. VIII, April, 1983, p. 63.
New Statesman. CV, May 27, 1983, p. 23.
The New York Times Book Review. LXXXVIII, April 3, 1983, p. 7.
Publishers Weekly. CCXXIII, January 28, 1983, p. 71.
Times Literary Supplement. June 3, 1983, p. 562.
Village Voice. XXVIII, April 26, 1983, p. 45.

DOSTOEVSKY
The Years of Ordeal, 1850-1859

Author: Joseph Frank (1919-   )
Publisher: Princeton University Press (Princeton, New Jersey). 320 pp. $25.00
Type of work: Literary biography
Time: 1850-1859
Locale: Russia, with concentration on Saint Petersburg and Siberia

The second volume of a projected five-volume study of a turbulent, enigmatic literary genius

> *Principal personages:*
> FEODOR MIKHAILOVICH DOSTOEVSKY, the great Russian novelist and literary figure
> MIKHAIL DOSTOEVSKY, Feodor's devoted older brother
> MARYA DOSTOEVSKY, Feodor's unstable first wife
> MIKHAIL PETRASHEVSKY, head of a progressive discussion circle
> NIKOLAY SPESHNEV, leader of a revolutionary secret society
> VISSARION BELINSKY, an influential literary and social critic
> ALEXANDER HERZEN, an influential social critic and editor
> BARON ALEXANDER WRANGEL, a close friend of Dostoevsky during his Siberian exile
> ALEKSAY PLESHCHEEV, an idealistic poet and fellow member of the Petrashevsky Circle
> MAJOR KRIVTSOV, a sadistic commandant of Dostoevsky's prison camp in Omsk, Siberia

Feodor Dostoevsky's tumultuous, complex life and works have been subjected to a towering mountain of description and analysis by scholars from a variety of disciplines: straightforward biography (Leonid Grossman, Konstantin Mochulsky, David Magarshack, to cite only a few); literary criticism (R. P. Blackmur, Philip Rahv, Edward Wasiolek); intellectual history (Edward Carr, Ronald Hingley, Isaiah Berlin); psychology (Sigmund Freud, Karen Horney); and philosophy of religion (Nicholas Berdyaev, Vyacheslav Ivanov, Lev Shestov). Joseph Frank, a sixty-five-year-old professor of comparative literature at Princeton University, seeks to harmonize several of these areas by weaving biography, literary evaluation, and social-cultural context in an ambitious work projected to run to five volumes.

The first volume published in 1976 and subtitled *The Seeds of Revolt, 1821-1849*, highlighted the rapturous reception of Dostoevsky's initial novel, *Bednye lyudi* (1846; *Poor Folk*, 1887), but also described the relative failure of his second book, *Dvoynik* (1846; *The Double*, 1956)—a judgment now generally reversed. Frank's second installment deals with a decade in Dostoevsky's life when he wrote no significant works but experienced monumental changes in his life, spending four of these years as a convict in Siberia and another four as a soldier in one of the Siberian regiments of the Russian

Army. Because Dostoevsky was perforce remote from his country's intellectual and social life during most of this time and lacked the opportunity and
energy for much creative writing, Frank has had to alter the main design of
his magisterial project, concentrating on a fuller biographical study than in
his first and future volumes.

The author is obviously loath to load his book with day-by-day chronicles
of commonplace occurrences, yet he must deal with crucial years during which
his isolated subject was cruelly deprived of books, letters, and even privacy,
and was thousands of miles removed from the hub of his country's literary
activity. Despite occasional longueurs and padding, Frank acquits himself
admirably of his critical task. He takes pains to tell the reader that the second
installment "will be followed shortly by a third devoted to the next five years
of Dostoevsky's life"—years which brought to life such vital texts as *Zapiski
iz myortvogo doma* (1861-1862; *The House of the Dead*, 1915) and *Zapiski
iz podpolya* (1864; *Notes from the Underground*, 1913) and which, as Frank
makes plain in his second volume, could not have borne such splendid harvest
but for their germination in the harrowing experiences of the 1850's.

Dostoevsky's darkest decade began the night of April 22-23, 1849, when
he was taken into police custody in Saint Petersburg as a member of a circle
headed by Mikhail Petrashevsky. Czarist investigators regarded the group of
about sixty as a dangerous "overall movement for change and destruction";
most historians have pooh-poohed such a view, seeing the Petrashevsky Circle
as a talking shop along the lines of a debating-and-discussion society, concerned with improving the lot of the still-unemancipated peasants and
exchanging ideas on literary matters. Frank, making extensive use of Soviet
research published in the past twenty years, reveals that there *was* a small
secret society active within the much larger Petrashevsky structure. Under
the leadership of Nikolay Speshnev, it planned not only to publish propaganda
against serfdom but also to incite an insurrection between both the peasantry
and religious dissenters. Dostoevsky belonged to this active inner circle, but
the Czarist Commission of Inquiry never learned of the Speshnev group's
existence—it simply moved massively to imprison the entire Petrashevsky
group in the notorious Peter and Paul fortress. Then it spent five months
investigating charges of subversion and conspiracy against the society before
reaching the conclusion that twenty-three of the prisoners were guilty of
criminal action.

Czar Nicholas I then took charge of the proceedings and orchestrated them.
He appointed a mixed military-civil court on September 25, 1849; it handed
down a verdict on November 16, condemning fifteen of the accused, including
Dostoevsky, to death by a military firing squad. (He was principally charged
with reading aloud and circulating a letter to Nikolai Gogol from the leading
social-literary critic of the era, Vissarion Belinsky, in which Belinsky stated
strong denunciations of the Russian throne, state, and Church.)

The Czar's next step was to have his highest military court review the sentences; it asked Nicholas to show mercy on such grounds as the defendants' repentance, youth, and cooperation with the authorities and recommended a list of lesser punishments on December 11. Nicholas approved them: "It was well-known that [he] enjoyed playing the role of all-powerful but clement ruler." In Dostoevsky's case, the amended condemnation to eight years of hard labor in Siberia was reduced to four, after which he would have to serve in the Russian Army stationed there for an indeterminate time. Such military service, albeit harsh, would enable him to regain the civil rights—particularly the right to publish—that he would forfeit as a result of his prison term. Hence, Frank notes, this conviction "helps to explain some of Dostoevsky's later favorable utterances about Nicholas, which commentators have usually found either baffling or have attributed to Dostoevsky's unhealthy penchant for masochistic submission to authority."

The Czar, however, had to play mock-executioner before he could manifest his mock-kindness. On the icy morning of December 22, the prisoners were taken to Semenovsky Square, where troops and thousands of spectators surrounded them. They were reunited with their comrades for the first time in eight months, only to be separated into groups of three. The front-row trio, including Petrashevsky, was tied to the execution stakes and the firing squad was ordered to take aim; Dostoevsky, in the next row of three, expected his turn to die in a few minutes. (In *Idiot*, 1868; *The Idiot*, 1887, he would have Prince Myshkin describe in graphic detail the sensations of a man who believed he would be executed in five minutes.) According to the account of a fellow prisoner, Dostoevsky turned to Speshnev and said, "We shall be with Christ," only to have the atheistic Speshnev retort, "A bit of dust."

After a minute of calculated suspense, drums beat retreat. The three men were untied from the stakes; one of them never recovered his senses. An aide-de-camp galloped to the Square with the Czar's pardon and the real sentences. The prisoners were given convict clothes and returned for a brief stay in the fortress before setting out for Siberia. Dostoevsky immediately wrote his beloved brother Mikhail a letter in which he described the most profound experience of his life.

Frank insists that from this moment on, the secular, progressive influences from such writers as Victor Hugo and George Sand, which had determined Dostoevsky's previous philosophy, receded before the onrush of a spiritual vitality, indeed ecstasy, that overwhelmed him as a revelation. "Life is a gift," he wrote Mikhail. "Every minute can be an eternity of happiness. . . . I will be reborn for the better." From that moment, Dostoevsky, always a believing Christian, strove to emphasize an ethic of expiation, forgiveness, and all-embracing love:

Dostoevsky's morality is similar to what some theologians, speaking of the early Christians, have called an "interim ethics," that is, an ethics whose uncompromising extremism springs from the lurking imminence of the Day of Judgment and the Final Reckoning: there is no time for anything but the last kiss of reconciliation because, quite literally, there is no "time." The strength (as well as some of the weakness) of Dostoevsky's work may ultimately be traced to the stabbing acuity with which, above all, he wished to communicate the saving power of this eschatological core of the Christian faith.

On the midnight of Christmas Day, Dostoevsky began his hazardous journey, in shackles, to the military stockade in Omsk, Siberia. He was not to hear from his family for the four years of his imprisonment. He was to be at the mercy of an alcoholic, sadistic, petty camp commandant, a Major Krivtsov, who would invade the convicts' barracks at night, awaken the men exhausted after an arduous day of hard labor, and order them to be flogged for sleeping on their right sides or their backs. From another prisoner's memoir, Frank cites the reason presented by Krivtsov: "Christ always slept on his left side, consequently everybody was required to follow his example."

His encounters with the other inmates at first shocked Dostoevsky. Almost all of them were peasants—the very people he had hoped to free from serfdom—but they struck him at first as thieving, brawling, ill-natured brutes who had no understanding of or tolerance for political dissenters; they categorized Dostoevsky and the few other prisoners of gentry origins as belonging to the enemy class of nobility, "iron beaks that used to peck us [the peasantry] to death." For the first year of his captivity, Dostoevsky was consequently in traumatic shock, forced to recognize that the romantic notions of the common people he had adopted in the 1840's, nourished by the humanitarian concepts of Friedrich Schiller, Hugo, and Sand, simply failed to square with the viciousness and vindictiveness of most of his fellow convicts. These peasant-prisoners contradicted the behavior which Dostoevsky had imputed to his low-life characters in *Poor Folk* and *The Double*: They showed no sign of repentance or remorse for their past crimes; a sense of right and wrong seemed foreign to them; ordinary norms of morality apparently did not apply.

Frank does his best writing in narrating the depths of Dostoevsky's despair at the relentless, abusive class hatred to which he was subjected and the loneliness he felt as a result, with the camp dog his only faithful companion. Some critics, including the religious philosopher Lev Shestov, interpret Dostoevsky's consequent right-wing conservatism and mistrust of human nature as a fundamental psychic-emotive transformation caused by his disillusioning prison camp experiences. Shestov even identifies the underground man's misanthropy and rejection of Schillerian idealism as Dostoevsky's autobiographical repudiation of his earlier faith in tenderhearted humanism. Frank refuses to follow this interpretation all the way.

Frank centers his analysis of Dostoevsky's manifest shift to mystical and reactionary views on what he calls the writer's crucial "conversion" experience, described by Dostoevsky in an article, "The Peasant Marey," embedded in his *Dnevnik pisalelya* (1873-1874, 1876, 1877-1881; *Diary of a Writer*, 1949). Frank reminds the reader that Dostoevsky never adopted, even in his radical preprison years, the Left Hegelian atheism held by many other followers of Belinsky and Petrashevsky. Instead, he regarded progressive social idealism in the 1840's as "the application of the divinely inspired Christian doctrine of love to the modern world," with Jesus a Socialist reformer. In "The Peasant Marey," Dostoevsky recalls a childhood episode when, as a nine-year-old boy, he became frightened of wolves that might be roaming on his father's small country estate; the hysterical boy ran out of the estate's small wood to be comforted and calmed by a nearby peasant known as Marey, who smiled at him gently "like a mother" and blessed him with the sign of the Cross.

Twenty years later, in the Siberian labor camp, Dostoevsky suddenly recalled the "Marey" experience. It elevated him above involvement in a drunken brawl and somehow enabled him to recast totally his former aversion to his fellow inmates: "that despised peasant with shaven head and brand marks on his face, reeling with drink, bawling out his hoarse, drunken song—why, he may be that very Marey; after all, I am not able to look into his heart." He took a "leap of Faith," underwent a striking change of sensibility, and came to regard each downtrodden convict as a potential Marey, capable of the most sublime Christian virtues of compassion, love, and forgiveness.

How did such a perspective differ from Dostoevsky's earlier meliorism? Frank shows that the new humanitarianism was both more intense and more narrowly focused, concentrated on the *Russian* peasant, with Dostoevsky looking on men and women outside the Slavic culture and Orthodox faith as historically and religiously outcast. What had been a general, pan-Western Utopianism condensed to a vibrant commitment to the singular genius and messianic destiny of the divinely favored Russian people. For the rest of his life, Dostoevsky was a fervent Slavophile, insisting that religious and cultural isolation from Western materialism had enabled the Russian people to avoid Europe's alleged demoralization and decadence.

In studying the causes of Dostoevsky's conversion, Frank is delighted to do battle with Sigmund Freud, whose famous essay, "Dostoevsky and Parricide," interprets Dostoevsky's behavior as Oedipally motivated. According to Freud, Dostoevsky felt a sense of enormous guilt when—as he believed—his father had been murdered by mistreated peasants who had enacted the deed about which the son had only fantasized. Freud proceeded to view Dostoevsky's arrest, conviction, and imprisonment as triggering his masochistic need to accept punishment from the Czar-Father as a way of relieving this unconscious parricidal drive.

In his first volume, Frank devoted numerous pages to contesting Freud's Oedipal theory; he was particularly delighted to demonstrate the probability, adduced from evidence recently discovered, that Dostoevsky's father had died of natural rather than criminal causes. In a footnote included in an early chapter of his second volume, Frank withdraws to a safer position: He agrees with Freud "in assuming that Dostoevsky felt a sense of guilt and complicity in his father's murder"—after all, whatever the facts of the father's death, what matters is that Dostoevsky all of his life *believed* in his father's killing. Frank insists, however, in a later section of his text that Dostoevsky did not seek forgiveness for his parricidal wishes from a fatherly, punitive czar but from the Russian people at large—partly because he felt ashamed of his initial aversion to his fellow prisoners, but mostly because

> Dostoevsky felt obscurely that his exorbitant demand for funds had contributed to bringing on those exactions by his father that may have driven the peaceful peasants to desperation. Since it was against the people that Dostoevsky had doubly sinned, it is by them that he wished to be forgiven; and the peasant Marey memory fulfilled this precise function.

One is amused to find Frank stringently correcting what he regards as Freud's erroneous psychoanalytic explanations, only to engage in similar speculations that could well be regarded as Freudian.

As a conscientiously comprehensive biographer, Frank feels duty-bound to chronicle his protagonist's calamitous attachment to Marya Dimitrievna Isaev, unhappily married to an alcoholic, disreputable customs official. He met her in 1855, when a private in the dreary Siberian town of Semipalatinsk, a year after his release from the prison stockade. She was vivacious, cultivated, and passionate; Dostoevsky fell in love with her, to the curious degree of borrowing money that helped the Isaevs move to another backwater, one hundred miles distant, so her husband could attempt a fresh start. Isaev died within a few months, but instead of accepting Dostoevsky's marital offer, Marya then tantalized him by having an affair with a younger schoolmaster. After many stormy scenes, she finally did agree to marry Dostoevsky; the wedding took place February 7, 1857; on their honeymoon he had a severe attack of epilepsy which frightened and alienated her. Soon both came to regret their union, with Dostoevsky becoming increasingly despondent as a result of Marya's violent temper tantrums, mercurial moods, domestic extravagance, and chronic irascibility. She was to die of tuberculosis in 1863. Perhaps her most damning epitaph is that she sat as the chief model for the self-righteous, wrathful Madame Marmeladova in *Prestupleniye i nakazaniye* (1866; *Crime and Punishment*, 1886).

Another biographer would have—and many *have*—relished the rich psychological substance furnished by Dostoevsky's pathological relationship with Marya, but not Frank. His preferred ground is the history of ideas, with special attention to his subject's ideological and artistic evolution. He therefore spends more space on Dostoevsky's sycophantic efforts to obtain civic rehabilitation than on his disastrous marriage, and he takes pains to link

Dostoevsky's Slavophilism with a strongly chauvinistic trend in Russian social-cultural attitudes during the 1850's and 1860's. Symbolic of this change was the transfer of intellectual preeminence from Belinsky to Alexander Herzen, who changed his position from Westernization to Slavophilism after he saw the French working class pitilessly repressed during the June, 1848, uprising. Herzen wrote a forceful meditation, *Vom Andern ufer* (1851; *From the Other Shore*, 1956), which concluded that Western Europe would never attain the new millennium because its progress was hobbled by attachment to private property, the corrupt Roman Catholic Church, and venal civic authority. Provincial Russia, on the other hand, possessed in the village commune and its collectivist culture the embryonic stage of a new and better society which really could lead the world into a new Socialist era.

The radical Herzen thus joined a common ideological substratum of convictions about Russia's role in history with more conservative Slavophiles who believed that their mission was to combat the materialism of modern civilization. Frank stresses that this underlying shared belief in Slavic manifest destiny was more important than superficial ideological clashes between the political Left and Right, and he therefore regards Dostoevsky's reborn sense of "Russianness" as not merely subjective but paradigmatic of Russia's nineteenth century struggle between its Western head and native heart.

In analyzing two mediocre novellas that Dostoevsky wrote in Siberian exile, *Dyadyushkin Son* (1859; *Uncle's Dream*, 1888) and *Stepanchikovo i ego obitateli* (1859; *The Village of Stepanchikovo*, 1887, also as *The Friend of the Family*), Frank is hard-pressed to discover literary merit. Instead, he concentrates on a significant shift in Dostoevsky's psychological understanding of his characters: No longer does he see them as victims of their harsh environment and lowly social status; rather, he now insists on placing moral responsibility directly on the person. In existential terms, the individual is the sum of his action. He is not allowed to answer oppression and resentment with the same coin or to dominate and humiliate others in revenge for his own painful history. The answer to injustice is now love and charity, open-heartedness and transcendence of egoism. Through his brilliant delineation of a buffoon in *The Village of Stepanchikovo*, Foma Fomich, Dostoevsky sketched the outline of his soon-to-emerge underground character, luxuriating in self-destructive self-indulgence.

Dostoevsky's penitential decade is thus shown as not only a period of regenerative suffering but also as an apprenticeship for major literary productions. The psychodrama of his near-death in Semenovsky Square urged him to appreciate life with a renewed vibrancy. His encounters with a diverse range of behavior among his fellow convicts deepened his awareness of the nature and mystery of suffering. Insofar as a great writer is one capable of diving into the most tangled zones of human motivation, Dostoevsky's painful, parabolic stay in Siberia had prepared him to become one. The "years of ordeal" have been mastered by Joseph Frank. He—and his subject—are now eager to enter the era of genius that was to see the composition of matchless novels founded on the death-and-rebirth pattern witnessed in this volume. Should the remaining installments equal the illuminating level of his first and second, Professor Frank's study of Dostoevsky's career will become one of the century's monumental biographies.

Gerhard Brand

Sources for Further Study

The New York Review of Books. XXXI, February 2, 1984, p. 12.
The New York Times Book Review. LXXXIX, January 1, 1984, p. 1.
Newsweek. CIII, January 23, 1984, p. 65.
Publishers Weekly. CCXXIV, October 14, 1983, p. 50.
Time. CXXIII, January 30, 1984, p. 75.

DURING THE REIGN OF THE QUEEN OF PERSIA

Author: Joan Chase
Publisher: Harper & Row, Publishers (New York). 215 pp. $13.95
Type of work: Novel
Time: Primarily the 1950's, with flashbacks to earlier decades
Locale: Northern Ohio

A story of tensions within an extended family during the last years of their family farm

Principal characters:
> LIL BRADLEY "GRAM" KRAUSS, called "the Queen of Persia," farm owner and matriarch
> JACOB "GRANDAD" KRAUSS, her husband, farm manager
> "AUNT" LIBBY KRAUSS SNYDER, their daughter
> "UNCLE" DAN SNYDER, Libby's husband, a butcher
> CELIA SNYDER and
> JENNIFER SNYDER, the daughters of Libby and Dan
> "AUNT" GRACE KRAUSS, also a daughter of Lil and Jacob, a trained teacher
> NEIL, Grace's husband, a failed writer
> ANNE, the elder daughter of Grace and Neil
> KATIE, the younger daughter of Grace and Neil
> "AUNT" ELINOR KRAUSS, another daughter of Lil and Jacob, an advertising executive and Christian Scientist
> "AUNT" RACHEL KRAUSS and
> "AUNT" MAY KRAUSS, Lil and Jacob's other daughters

During the Reign of the Queen of Persia won the 1984 Ernest Hemingway Foundation Award, an award given annually to recognize a distinguished first novel. In her debut, author Joan Chase has constructed a complex and innovative narrative. Her subject matter is traditional—a family saga of sorts—but her angle of vision is not. This is a challenging and rewarding novel that demands from its readers an imaginative act of synthesis, pulling together its disparate parts into a meaningful whole.

Each of the novel's five parts is named for a character or pair of characters; from one point of view, the parts can be seen as separate, self-contained stories. Each has its own sense of time; notable are part 1, "Celia," which is in chronological order, and part 4, "Elinor," in which persons awaiting Elinor's arrival by train reminisce about her last visit to the farm. If they were to be read separately, these two sections might not be considered as pieces of the same novel, but, in the final pages of part 5, "Gram," it becomes clear that *During the Reign of the Queen of Persia* has a story line—if not a plot—and that only a reading of the entire novel can tie the story line together.

Tradition divides most works of fiction into two classes—those told in the first person and those told in the third person. Use of the first person was commonplace in the eighteenth century, when prejudice against fiction made it necessary to disguise novels as memoirs. The first-person narrative also has the advantage of immediacy, conveying the feeling of an eyewitness account. The third person allows the author to assume omniscience and to let the reader know things which would have to be kept hidden in a first-person account. Rarely can a third-person novel be disguised—even for effect—as a memoir.

During the Reign of the Queen of Persia fits into neither of the traditional classes. There is no narrating "I," as in a first-person novel, but most of the novel is told as recollection by characters in it. The recollections are attributed to a collective—"we"—but who are "we"? At most, four persons are "we": the four granddaughters who are the third generation of permanent residents on the Krauss farm during the period of approximately five years between the death of Jacob "Grandad" Krauss and the farm's sale.

The first generation on the farm is represented by Lil Bradley Krauss, usually called "Gram" in the narrative, called "the Queen of Persia" by her son-in-law. The actual owner of the farm, having bought it with an inheritance from an uncle, Gram acts like a queen. The death of her husband, Jacob Krauss—the bane of her youth, later an efficient farm manager—removes an alternative focus of loyalty.

The second generation of permanent residents are Gram's daughter, Libby, known as "Aunt Libby," and her husband, Dan Snyder, called "Uncle Dan." Other daughters and sons-in-law of Lil and Jacob, however, often arrive to disturb the serenity of Gram's reign. The third generation—"we"—are four girls, born less than two years apart: Celia and Jennifer, the daughters of Libby and Dan; and Anne and Katie, the daughters of Libby's sister, Grace, and of Grace's husband, Neil.

It is from the perspective of these four that life on the Krauss farm is seen—not always, however, from the perspective of all four. There are episodes about tricks which "we"—meaning two or three of the girls—play on one of them. Some episodes begin with "we" meaning three or four girls and end with one of them separate from—and antagonistic to—the others, who remain "we." In part 1, "Celia," "we" includes the oldest granddaughter at the beginning, but she gradually becomes distinct from the other three. Celia, the first to become an adolescent, is a high school beauty popular with boys and an object of curiosity and espionage of the other three girls. In other parts, however, "we" frequently includes Celia. In some aspects of her life, Celia remains part of the foursome until she marries and leaves the Krauss farm. In other aspects, she is distinct from the other three girls and their world.

Futhermore, the absence of an "I" is not the only distinction between *During the Reign of the Queen of Persia* and ordinary first-person novels. Some sequences of the narrative are told as if from the perspective of an omniscient author. Sequences of family history—the lives of Gram, Grandad, and their daughters before the granddaughters' births—contain facts which could hardly have been part of the family history and gossip available to the granddaughters; so do some accounts of events within the granddaughters' lifetimes to which the girls were not witnesses. In the taxonomy which divides first-person from third-person fiction, *During the Reign of the Queen of Persia* defies classification. The author has managed to give herself the advantages of both kinds of storytelling.

Logically, the story cannot be. It does not read like a memoir, but it contains too many reminiscences of those actually on the scene to be an omniscient account. Nevertheless, this logically impossible story works. It works because storytelling is not necessarily an exercise involving logic, and it works because the reader wants it to work. The ambiguous, shifting nature of the group from whose perspective the story is told, their knowledge of what they ought not to know, invites the reader to take an active role in making sense out of these characters' lives. Chase is adept at briefly introducing characters, leaving tantalizing hints about their pasts. The hints demand answers, and the reader must work through the whole story in order to find them.

Part 1, "Celia," describes a superficially stable rural existence, beneath the surface of which are conflicts not readily resolved. The focus of this section is the increasing separation of Celia, the oldest girl, from what has been a foursome. This process intensifies rivalries. The nearness of the girls' ages makes Celia's efforts to appear grown-up seem trivial, but the narrative makes it plain that neither these efforts nor other occasions of conflict seem trivial to those involved. Celia is the first of the foursome clearly to graduate into the adolescent world and then into adulthood, even though she is not much older than the other three. The arbitrary nature of the distinctions between childhood and adulthood is indicated, and the bickering of the older generation is made more clearly childish.

Part 1 introduces the family, although it keeps the two older generations in the background, to be described in depth later. Uncle Dan calls Gram "the Queen of Persia" (because of her imperiousness and her collection of Persian rugs). The use of this sobriquet in the title gives the impression that the novel is about a period of time when Gram can be said to reign, but part 1 is, in a sense, about Celia's reign. Celia is described as regal, and the other three granddaughters hold her in a kind of awe. So do the boys who court her, and so, to a degree, do her parents, considering themselves fortunate to have a popular daughter. The quality of her reign, however, is clearly tarnished by her need to let boys take liberties with her. Her reign almost ends in disaster with the revelation that her well-regarded fiancé has made another woman pregnant. Face is saved by marriage to a man who is almost as well regarded as was the first man before the scandal.

Parts 2, 3, and 4 describe events leading up to the time of Celia's reign.

Part 2 tells of Gram's marriage to Grandad. A drunkard and a financial failure, Grandad—like many men in similar circumstances—acts out his frustrations by beating his wife, but his story takes an unusual turn when the wife whom he punishes for his failure makes him a success. She inherits a fortune and buys a farm for him to run; he runs it and ceases to beat her. There is a bizarre irony in this success story, underlining the irony of Gram's misfortune in being punished for what she could not prevent.

Part 3, "Neil and Grace," is about the parents of Anne and Katie, two of the foursome called "we." Although not supposed to be permanent residents of the Krauss farm, Neil and Grace return frequently because of their unhappy marriage—which resembles somewhat the unhappy marriage of Gram and Grandad in its earlier years. Finally, stricken with cancer, Grace returns again to the farm for care from her extended family, bringing along Anne and Katie to join the granddaughters already there, Celia and Jenny.

In Part 4, "Elinor," Grandad dies. Grace's illness causes the members of the extended family to descend on the farm and allows Aunt Elinor, a Christian Scientist, to minister to their spiritual needs. Gram's weakness in the face of Elinor's comforting doctrine resembles that of many monarchs; the religion of the people often dilutes their loyalty to their monarch.

Part 5, "Gram," begins with Grace's death and Elinor's departure. This section covers approximately the same time span as that depicted in part 1. Celia's reign as the glamorous member of the third generation is a kind of challenge to Gram. Moreover, Gram is virtually forced to take custody of Grace's daughters: Gram is a queen who can be imposed on. Indeed, although Elinor is gone, her power remains. The two younger generations continue, despite Gram's disapproval, to practice Christian Science—though apparently not with deep conviction. Gram reigns; it is not certain that she rules.

Although exact dates are not given, various references indicate that the bulk of the narrative is set in the 1950's, a period marked by the decline of the family farm and family values. In the fate of the Krauss farm, the reader can see this decline in microcosm. Grandad has sold the dairy herd in anticipation of his own death. The barn, a reminder of the farm's past glory, burns down, and Gram ends her reign by selling the farm to a developer who intends to use it for a residential subdivision. Meanwhile, Aunt Rachel, a daughter of Gram and Grandad, violates traditional family values by planning a marriage while her former husband is still alive. At the very end, the once regal Celia attempts suicide; the miseries of the two older generations had never pushed them to that extreme.

Nevertheless, the novel is not at all nostalgic about farm or family life. The price paid, particularly by women, in sustaining a family is made clear. Gram is abused by Grandad until she buys him success. Rachel is abused by her first husband, and her fiancé is unlikely to be better. Grace is ill-treated by Neil. Even the outwardly successful marriage of Uncle Dan and Aunt Libby is marred by mutual sniping and by Libby's apparent resentment of her last two—unsuccessful—pregnancies, which she has endured because of Dan's desire for a son.

During the Reign of the Queen of Persia is a powerful first novel, introducing an ambitious new voice in American fiction.

Charles Johnson Taggart

Sources for Further Study

Commonweal. CX, July 15, 1983, p. 405.
Library Journal. CVIII, June 15, 1983, p. 1273.
Los Angeles Times Book Review. October 2, 1983, p. 8.
Nation. CCXXXVII, September 3, 1983, p. 187.
The New York Times Book Review. LXXXVIII, June 12, 1983, p. 9.
Publishers Weekly. CCXXIII, April 22, 1983, p. 86.
Time. CXXII, July 18, 1983, p. 66.

THE EARLY DIARY OF ANAÏS NIN
Volume III: 1923-1927

Author: Anaïs Nin (1903-1977)
Publisher: Harcourt Brace Jovanovich (San Diego, California). Illustrated. 297 pp. $17.95
Type of work: Diary
Time: 1923-1927
Locale: Primarily New York City and Paris; also London, Florence, Brussels, and various locations in Spain

The third volume of Anaïs Nin's Early Diary *treats her adjustment to marriage; her frustrating attempts to complete two novels; her wide range of intellectual and aesthetic interests; and her continuing struggle to define her goals in life*

Principal personages:
ANAÏS NIN, a writer and critic
HUGH (HUGO) PARKER GUILER, her husband
JOHN ERSKINE, a writer, teacher, and critic; friend of Anaïs and Hugh
RICHARD F. MAYNARD, a painter and sculptor; also a friend of Anaïs and Hugh
ROSA CULMELL DE NIN, Anaïs' mother
JUAQUIN J. NIN, Anaïs' father
JUAQUIN NIN-CULMELL, Anaïs' brother

The third volume of Anaïs Nin's *Early Diary* covers the years from 1923 to 1927. Continued from volume 2, which Nin had subtitled in her ledgers "Journal d'une Fiancée," this segment of the projected four-volume work is subtitled "Journal d'une Épouse" ("The Diary of a Wife"). When the complete diary is published, the work will cover the years from 1914 to 1931. "Mon Journal," as Nin affectionately called most of her more recent ledgers, was first composed in inexpensive "date books," but around 1923, she began using commercially printed diary books bound in red leather that had a finer quality paper—with the exception of journal twenty-one. Not until 1931, according to Rupert Pole, did she "use titles on a regular basis and to a more dramatic effect." These "early diaries," anticipating the famous seven volumes of literary diaries, also published by Harcourt Brace Jovanovich and dated from 1931 to 1974, reveal an artist first asserting herself and testing her capabilities.

Volume 3 begins after a brief hiatus from the previously published volume that concludes with an entry from February, 1923 (in the middle of Nin's nineteenth journal). At that point, she was waiting for her fiancé Hugh (Hugo) Parker Guiler to arrive in Cuba, where they planned to wed. The present volume begins with the entry of March 20, 1923; Nin has already settled down to married life in Richmond Hill, New York, near to her close-knit family.

If readers are inclined to regret the diary lapse involving this month of crowded events centering on the writer's union with Hugh, they should understand that Nin never confided in her diary intimate sexual feelings—at least not in the first three volumes of the *Early Diary*. Although her writing on the level of psychological introspection is extraordinarily frank, she simply (at this stage of her life) was too puritanical to express in her personal journals any feelings that touched upon sexuality. Readers familiar with the author's later elegantly erotic books (for example, *Little Birds*, 1979) might be surprised to discover Nin's reticence, but deeply ingrained in her character as a young woman— and, in this volume, as a youthful wife—is her delicacy in treating subjects that arouse vulgar emotions, especially sexual vulgarity.

In the third volume of the *Early Diary*, Nin treats two principal themes: that of the full expression of emotions (excepting sexual ones) in becoming the wife of Hugh Guiler and, as a counterpoint theme, that of her struggle to attain independence as a woman and an artist. Throughout the four-year period covered by the volume, Nin expresses a single dominant emotion of happiness, but other, sometimes contradictory, emotions involving her marriage also play fitfully below the surface at times—envy of Hugh's business success and freedom, resentment at his apparent self-assurance, and (at the lowest point of her negative feelings) fear that the couple's happiness is fated in time to diminish, as though by a curse.

Nevertheless, these negative feelings, often heartfelt and disturbing, are not the true measure of her love for Hugh. From the first entry (March 20, 1923), she speaks of her husband's quality of constant variety: "He evolves continually, so that I can understand him without knowing all of him. I foresee the exclusion of one generally accepted misfortune befalling the married ones—we shall escape monotony." Certainly she retains throughout the volume a sense of her loving acceptance of her husband. Some readers who are familiar with Nin's later journals or her fiction might be surprised—or dismayed—to discover in this writer, who expressed such strong feminist opinions on the need for sexual freedom and independence, a contrary demand for a woman's submissiveness in the marriage relationship. In numerous diary entries (especially those for March 3, 1924; April 1, 1924; January 19, 1925; and May 29, 1926), she emphasizes her complete devotion to her husband in terms that cannot be mistaken. In the May 29th entry, for example, she writes: "Marriage is itself a Destiny which decides the character of the wife's life by that of her husband. Even in an enlightened age, she must follow him wherever he pleases. I have made my choice."

In her entry for January 19, 1925, she describes the aftermath of a lover's quarrel: "My Love and I have passed through the first crisis of our marriage— passed triumphantly. But forever after I shall never be at rest—the fear has come too close to me, and I am a fatalist." In this reflective mood, she asserts her total submission to her husband: "My love for him is tyrannical because it is ideal, because I love his soul, his thoughts, because I could no more bear the sullying of his body than of his mind. I want not only his love but his ideal self preserved, stainless." This key section of the *Early Diary* is significant moreover because Nin contrasts her absolute love for her husband with her still-ambiguous feelings toward her father, the musician and composer Juaquin J. Nin.

Her father, after all, had served as the impetus for writing her journals. Unable to communicate with him fully in her youth (although he had separated from the family, he continued to correspond, at irregular intervals, with Anaïs and several of his other children), she compensated for his absence by composing the diaries. Her frustrated affection for her father, often distorted into resentment and anger, served also to unify her vision as an artist. By the time of her third volume of the *Early Diary*, however, Nin could—at least partly—appreciate her father's estrangement from her mother. In the entry for December, 1924, she describes a meeting with Juaquin in Paris: "I understood my father in a flash. He met me with tears, to which I could not sincerely respond; he talked to me with a show of emotions I could not feel; he told me things which a year ago would have killed me with unreasonable horror and disgust." Now, at the age of twenty-one, she could write: ". . . yesterday I listened calmly, finding no answer to his irreproachable and vicious logic—in fact, I logically approved him, although I forgave, consoled and deceived him for the most illogical causes—pity!—the heartrending pity I feel now for what I once hated."

If Nin's softened yet still ambivalently resentful attitude toward her father was marked by pity for his failures as a family man, she hardened her feelings toward her mother, Rosa Culmell de Nin. From the early entries of volume 3, Nin sensed that her mother, self-pitying and miserable, was manipulating her sense of guilt in marrying Hugh. Nin feared that she was deserting her mother. In time, however, she came to understand that Rosa's demands upon her time and affections were unreasonable. Indeed, when her father attempted to secure a formal divorce so he could be free to marry again, Nin's sympathies were with her father—not, as in the past, with her mother.

It is a sign of Nin's growing maturity, as well as of her more flexible attitude, that she could in time evaluate even her beloved Hugh with an eye judiciously focused upon his faults as well as virtues. For his virtues, Nin (and any fair-minded reader) would set store by his sensitive, compassionate nature; his capacity to forgive (and Nin was surely as temperamental and "difficult" a young wife as she was also beautiful, clever, charming, and high-spirited); his willingness to work at labors not entirely congenial to his desires so that Nin would have sufficient free time to pursue her interests in literature; and finally, his expansive, protective love for her—unconditional and free from jealousy. Notwithstanding these virtues (which Nin appreciated and fullyommunicated in her diary), she was able to judge his limitations; she came to believe that her inner strength was greater than his.

One source for Nin's self-assurance was a belief—as yet untested but res-olute—in her powers as an artist. If she was not entirely happy with her role as an adored, even pampered wife, the cause was that she lacked a vocation. Restlessly, she continued to read and philosophize, to model, to write and revise novels that failed to satisfy her demands for perfection. Always an assiduous reader, she records in her entry for January, 1927: "I read 75 books. I recopied about 300 pages from my Journal. . . . I re-arranged the books in the library about 10 times. . . . I wrote about 200 dutiful letters." Also she accomplished such domestic tasks as making six decorative pillows and forced herself "to rest and relax, thereby gaining a little weight." Over this comic recitation of small tasks accomplished is the heavy burden of uncompleted objectives, although she continued to pursue two avocations—dancing and modeling—that dated from the years before her marriage. As photographs from this volume evidence, Nin in her early twenties (as indeed throughout her life) was exceptionally beautiful, graceful, and vital, favored with a willowy frame that was much admired for its elegance by artists and photographers. For the distinguished sculptor Richard F. Maynard, who was also a family friend, she posed for portraits and a Grecian-like sculpture and a statuette. Reversing roles, she became an art student in Paris and, in a touching entry for March 16, 1927, shows how well she empathized with the feelings of a starving model. To advance her more pressing literary ambitions, she showed—with considerable hesitation—drafts of her fiction to the American critic and professor John Erskine, who also became a close friend to the young couple. Erskine approved of her writings, but she was by no means satisfied with her progress.

During the years covered by this volume, she attempted to complete two novels, "Aline's Choice" and "The Blunderer"—both unpublished. Her approach was always the same: She would begin with enthusiasm, confidence, and fluency; then her confidence would wane. Either she would discover flaws in the construction, or she would read the work of a more accomplished talent and despair. In particular, she envied the artistry of Edith Wharton, whose structural skills she contrasted with her own fledgling efforts. Nevertheless, she recognized that her journals, written for herself both as an artistic dis-cipline and a means of self-expression, had authentic literary merit. In her entry for August 31, 1923, she apologizes to her "dear journal" that she has "mangled and cut into you mercilessly, have left you deprived of half your belongings." She continues: "I have no longer added pages to your book; rather, I have torn them from you. And even in your poverty you have still that elusive and inexplicable way of retaining your power and your character." With insight she judges: "You are still alone and unsurpassed in that you are the most intimate, if not the most complete, of the reflections of my changing self."

As her character develops in strength and wisdom, her *Early Diary* faithfully records the minute psychologically significant changes from youth to maturity. Indeed, the journals provide one of the most interesting, comprehensive, and beguiling accounts of a woman's soul. To be sure, this human record is all the more valuable because Anaïs Nin would in time become a writer and personality of considerable achievement—a novelist, critic, and essayist; a friend of many notable literary and socially prominent figures; and a center in her own right of feminist causes—but these triumphs were to occur later, to be recorded in the *Diaries* by an artist more confident of her powers. Volume 3 of the *Early Diary* reveals as yet only a tentative view of the master. Nevertheless, the work has great charm because the diarist possessed the qualities both of intensity and luminosity.

As yet, few "important" figures appear in her life. Apart from her friendship with John Erskine, she has few links to the publishing world of New York. Most of her experiences are focused upon her husband, her family, and a close group of intimate friends. In her travels throughout parts of Europe, particularly during her long sojourn in Paris, she writes as one without roots. At first, she is uncomfortable in Paris (mostly because of what she perceives as a spirit of sexual license); later—as her entry for May 6, 1925, shows— she succumbs to the city's beauty. Even so, as she had predicted in her entry for August 11, 1924: "I have reached the period when I feel dissatisfied with every country, while loving much in each. Paris will not satisfy me completely, any more than New York has." Only her art—which requires the fullest expression of her individuality—could accomplish that goal.

For the reader, a grasp of Nin's delicate individuality is the chief delight of the *Early Diary*. Quite apart from understanding the writer's ideas or feeling vicariously her emotions, a sensitive reader is bound to touch a quality deeper infused while turning pages of the book. One touches the reality of Anaïs Nin's being. Like few other literary figures who have chosen the diary form to express their intimate souls, Nin is able to compose a complete human document. Because so much of her vitality is transmitted through her journals, a reader may sense a connection with Nin, as though she were indeed alive. To her editors—her executor Rupert Pole, who contributes a brief objective note, and her brother Juaquin Nin-Culmell, who contributes a warm personal (yet not idolatrous) preface to this handsome volume—such a sense of illu- mination must not seem strange. Juaquin writes of his sister as though her presence were still alive for him. Many a reader of volume 3 will feel that same vital presence.

Leslie B. Mittleman

Sources for Further Study

Booklist. LXXX, November 1, 1983, p. 392.
Los Angeles Times Book Review. January 8, 1984, p. 5.
The New York Times Book Review. January 29, 1984, p. 22.

EASE MY SORROWS

Author: Lev Kopelev (1912-   )
Translated from the Russian by Antonina W. Bouis
Publisher: Random House (New York). Illustrated. 256 pp. $17.95
Type of work: Memoir
Time: 1947-1954
Locale: A prison on the outskirts of Moscow

A memoir of the seven years Kopelev spent in a special prison after his conviction for bourgeois humanism

> *Principal personages:*
> LEV KOPELEV, a former Communist Party member and intelligence officer in the Red Army imprisoned for bourgeois humanism
> ALEKSANDR I. (SANYA) SOLZHENITSYN, a mathematician and fellow prisoner
> DMITRI (MITYA) PANIN, an engineer and fellow prisoner

On December 7, 1954, Lev Kopelev left the Marfino *sharashka*, the prison in a former church called Ease My Sorrows, as a free man. In the hell which was the Stalinist prison system, the *sharashkas* were the first circle: special scientific and technical institutes staffed by prisoners. The prisoners, including engineers, mathematicians, and other technicians, spent their time on research, experimentation, and translation.

It was the last which enabled Kopelev to find himself in such relatively comfortable surroundings instead of in the forests and uranium mines of Siberia. In the *sharashka*, Kopelev translated technical articles from German, English, Italian, Polish, and other languages, worked on linguistics, and devised a method of recording and reading voiceprints. It was there that Kopelev met Aleksandr Solzhenitsyn; the two became close friends, and Kopelev later served as the model for Lev Rubin in Solzhenitsyn's *V kruge pervom* (1968; *The First Circle*, 1968); In fact, Kopelev's connections with the Russian intelligentsia were helpful in publishing Solzhenitsyn's first book, *Oden den' Ivana Denisovicha* (*One Day in the Life of Ivan Denisovich*), in the literary journal *Novy Mir* in 1962.

This volume, however, is much more than the recounting of time spent in prison. It is the story of a man's life. *Ease My Sorrows* is the third volume of Kopelev's memoirs, following *I sotvoril sebe kumira* (1978; *The Education of a True Believer*, 1980) and *Khranit vechno* (1975; *To Be Preserved Forever*, 1977); it is the story of a man grappling with his own best beliefs and thoughts. It was exactly those higher feelings that placed Kopelev in prison, as a result of his attempts to prevent looting and rapine as the Red Army moved through Poland and Germany. His crime was one of aiding and abetting the enemy. He was a "58er," which was prison slang for political prisoners sentenced under Article 58 of the penal code of the Soviet Union.

This entire trilogy could easily be entitled "The Reeducation of a True Believer," for Kopelev was indeed a true believer. In the 1930's, he had been exceedingly active in the forced collectivization of the farms and during the war had served in the propaganda section of army intelligence, where he was responsible for the interrogation and de-Nazification of captured German soldiers. Kopelev did all of this while serving in the front lines. He was quick to denounce that with which he disagreed or believed was wrong, but at no time did he deviate from his faith in Joseph Stalin. When hundreds of thousands suffered and starved during the forced collectivization, Kopelev saw the error and stupidity involved yet rationalized the suffering as historical necessity, believing that it would be "rectified" in the end.

Kopelev maintained this belief during his arrest and imprisonment. In his first trial, he was found innocent, but after a review this verdict was set aside and he suffered through a second trial. At this second trial, he was found guilty and sentenced to three years. Once again, however, the verdict was set aside, and at his third trial Kopelev was given the normal sentence under Article 58—"ten and five," ten years in prison and an additional five years suspension of civil liberties. Like many other true believers, he attributed his mistreatment to the need for increased vigilance against counterrevolutionary forces. Such flukes or mistakes, he believed, did not expose any inherent flaws in the Soviet system.

Kopelev maintained his dogmatic Leninism-Stalinism even against the constant badgering of many, including that of Solzhenitsyn and his other close prison friend Dmitri Panin. The cool, rational, and scientific Solzhenitsyn and the religious and passionately anti-Soviet Panin provided good counterparts to the faithful and morally impassioned Kopelev. If Kopelev's beliefs caused his problems, however, they also gave him the strength to endure his imprisonment.

It is these beliefs that have compelled him to write his memoirs, to recount as accurately as possible the lessons learned. In this volume, he recounts the kindnesses, the expressions of human want and need that made life in the *sharashka* bearable. He tells of the relationships that developed between the *zeks* (prisoners) and the free female employees who served as technicians, assistants, and supervisors in the *sharashka*. He describes the stoolies, those who spent their time informing on their fellow prisoners; who returned evil for good, and who preyed on those weaker than they were. The stupidity of an irrational bureaucratic system also feels the lash of Kopelev's pen—a system capable of informing a man that his appeal has been denied four months after he has been freed; a system in which much-needed technical apparatuses are destroyed because they do not appear on an inventory. To question the correctness of such orders was to be guilty of anti-Soviet agitation and, if done in concert with another, to be guilty of conspiracy as well.

Kopelev did speak out and narrowly escaped punishment for it; the arbitrary terror of Stalinist Russia swept his would-be accuser away, for reasons totally unrelated to him.

Despite the privations of imprisonment and the irrational tangle of bureaucracy, the *sharashka* was an island of genuine comradeship. The *zeks* were reasonably well fed, and their lives were not dominated by a search for food and warmth. There was sufficient time and energy for discussions of art, literature, politics, and philosophy as well as for the animated conversations that take place among people engaged in the same project, struggling to accomplish the same goal.

While the *zeks* were physically separated from the rest of the world by prison walls and guards, they were not mentally cut off. Indeed, they were much better informed than their free counterparts. They had newspapers, radios, and even televisions which they had built themselves, salvaging parts from discarded and defective apparatuses. Kopelev's desk had a miniature radio receiver permanently tuned to the BBC. The men worried over the Cold War and the Korean conflict, with the threat of another world war.

The prisoners' work also connected them to the larger world. Kopelev's main duty was the translation of technical articles into Russian; he easily met his quota of twenty-four pages every four days. At the same time, he was engaged in attempts to develop a secret telephone. In the course of these experiments, the Marfino *zeks* created the first machine capable of recording voiceprints; Kopelev called them "word pictures." The prisoners also built the first machine capable of speaking. These accomplishments were, unfortunately, to be lost out of stupidity and bungling; the bureaucracy could see no use in such things, although voiceprints were used to catch a spy.

Another connection with the larger world was the free employees, many of whom were university students writing their dissertations on work being done at the *sharashka*. These students had to be tutored and trained; this was especially imperative after prisoners were forbidden to appear as authors or coauthors of articles. The only way to make their work public was through these assistants, and this they felt compelled to do. They believed that their work was important, that the motherland needed it, and that their actions served their country. Kopelev's work, however, never made it into a dissertation; his assistant failed to pass her examinations.

Kopelev's memoir is full of pain: the pain of separation from family and friends; the pain of seeing one's children grow up as strangers; and one's parents growing old without being there. Kopelev was able to see his wife and parents only two or three times a year; years passed between visits with his daughters. Kopelev evokes the prisoner's constant anxiety, the beautiful and pleasant dreams of the night dashed to pieces in the cold gray of the morning, when one awakens in a prison dormitory and realizes that he still has years left to serve. Then there are the nightmares, dreams of never leaving prison, of dying there. One hides from these fears and immerses oneself in work, music, books, conversation—anything to fill the time and distract one's thoughts as the seconds turn to hours, to weeks, and eventually to years.

Ultimately, however, this is a book about lessons. Kopelev is not a Solzhenitsyn and has not felt compelled to embrace reaction. Certainly, he has repudiated his earlier Leninism-Stalinism as well as the later scientific Karl Marx—but not the early Marx. He has learned those lessons which are imperative if the world is to survive. They are the lessons of tolerance, free expression, and peacemaking. As Kopelev puts it, "I tried to overcome my inability to listen to people who disagreed with me, my inability to look from a point of view other than my own—that deafness and blindness that I used to think was ideological adherence to principle." These are lessons for all humanity.

Edward L. Queen II

Sources for Further Study

Choice. XXI, January, 1984, p. 711.
Library Journal. CVIII, September 1, 1983, p. 1702.
The New York Review of Books. XXX, October 13, 1983, p. 9.
The New York Times Book Review. September 18, 1983, p. 7.
Publishers Weekly. CCXXIV, July 22, 1983, p. 126.

THE END OF THE WORLD NEWS

Author: Anthony Burgess (1917-   )
Publisher: McGraw-Hill Book Company (New York). 389 pp. $15.95
Type of work: Novel
Time: 1890-1939, 1917, and the twenty-first century
Locale: Vienna, New York, Australia, the United States, and space

A novel which recounts, in separate strands, incidents from the lives of Sigmund Freud and Leon Trotsky, and an imagined future in which the world is destroyed

> *Principal characters:*
> SIGMUND FREUD, the founder of psychoanalysis
> CARL JUNG, his disciple and rival
> LEON TROTSKY, a Communist revolutionary
> OLGA, his secretary in New York
> VAL BRODIE, a science-fiction writer
> HUBERT FRAME, the planner of the *America* project
> VANESSA FRAME, his divorced wife, an ouranologist
> COURTLAND WILLETT, an unemployed actor

The End of the World News is a provocative work, by intention and in structure. It consists of three entirely separate strands of story, two of them historical fiction, the third science fiction. The more prominent of the historical strands tells the story of Sigmund Freud, beginning with the notorious moment in 1938 when the Nazis, invading Austria, seized Freud's publishing house in Vienna only to be confronted with and momentarily ejected by the furious psychoanalyst. From 1938, the narrative returns to the 1890's and then follows the whole sequence of Freud's failures, successes, and rivalries to his death in England in 1939. By contrast, the second historical strand—recounted very largely as the libretto for a Broadway musical—focuses on one very short stretch of time, a brief and (apparently) unimportant interlude in the life of Leon Trotsky: the two months, from January to March, 1917, which he spent in New York waiting to be recalled to Russia to take his part in the Revolution. The science-fiction strand, finally, tells a relatively conventional story about the arrival in the solar system of a rogue planet, Lynx, which first sweeps past and then collides with Earth, leaving no survivors except those who escape in spaceships.

The question one must ask, evidently, is whether these strands relate to one another at all; the answer is both yes and no. The strands are given a kind of connection at the very end of the book, when one learns that all of these stories have been or are being told to a class of adolescents on the spaceship *America*, descendants of those who fled generations before. The stories of Freud and Trotsky just happen to have survived. They, together with the account of the building of *America*, are the only memories of Earth that the space-exiles have left. The reader's uncertainty about the way these stories relate to one another, then, is a pale analogue of the complete bewilderment felt by the space-born. The adolescent class in fact simply refuses to believe the stories at all, reclassifying them instead as myth. The building of *America* is a kind of Genesis to them; as for Freud and Trotsky, they become images of god and demon: Fred Fraud kept people strapped to a couch while Trot Sky wanted to liberate everyone and let them run through space as they, the spaceship-people, do. One can see that the connection offered in Burgess' epilogue is a fortuitous and pointless one.

In any case, there is something to be said for the theory that there are no connections at all except for those imposed (probably all in different ways) by different readers. In a feigned introduction to the book, Burgess suggests that one inspiration for it was a picture of President Jimmy Carter and his wife in the White House watching three television sets simultaneously. What connection will there be among three randomly selected television programs? Evidently none. Although there seems to have been a pleasure in watching three things at once, at least for the Carters; therefore, there will perhaps be a pleasure—or so the analogy goes—in following three stories at once. "The family of the middle and late 1980's," declares Burgess in the publisher's blurb (written, against convention, by the author), "will have to be a three-screen family."

Once again, one may suspect that this, too, is provocation, not to be taken seriously: As a prophecy, it certainly seems very unlikely. Nevertheless, the question remains: Can one find, is it legitimate to try to find, any linkages among these three different and separate accounts? Do they not, for example, all deal with the end of the world, or the end of *a* world, as the title suggests? If so, should one not see in them a kind of "counterpoint," a term which Burgess uses both in the blurb and in his feigned introduction? The answer to both questions must surely be yes, yet the whole structure of the book makes any such "counterpoint" difficult to see. The author, one often feels, is simply mocking, or tantalizing, his readership.

For one thing, *The End of the World News* is full of false trails (though in this case, one reader's false trail may be another's key linkage). Freud is quite clearly shown smoking himself to death—he died of cancer of the mouth— with a strong suggestion, in his own terms, that this is a case of infantile oral gratification. When one realizes that Hubert Frame, planner of the *America* project, is doing the same thing, the interpretative faculty leaps into action. After all, both Frame and Freud are also seen as Moses-figures, people who lead their followers to the Promised Land but do not themselves enter it. Freud, furthermore, was famous for his neurotic insistence on getting to railway stations two hours early and then usually almost missing the train. Surely, all of these facts must add up to some statement about human weakness or the urges that make people pioneers. Trotsky, too, surely had a vision of promise in the perfect Socialist state . . . but the connections at this stage peter out. No stress is laid on Trotsky smoking or missing boats, or being a Moses. The whole sequence of thought may be merely a string of coincidences, like the fact that hypnosis, a Freudian technique, is used once in the launching of *America*, or the quotations from William Shakespeare are occasionally interjected by different characters, or the fact that many scenes are set in New York. It seems uneasily significant that even the theory of coincidences comes up on one occasion when Carl Jung outlines his notion of "synchronicity" to Freud, only for Freud to reject it, only for that rejection itself to be (apparently) refuted by an immediate sequence of poltergeist phenomena.

The meaning of *The End of the World News* is not to be reached, in short, by dissection. Even its title, one should note, is an exercise in ambiguity. On a book jacket, the phrase sounds at once comic and ominous: On another level, however, it is utterly familiar, and especially so to British exiles such as Burgess, because it is a phrase used every day by the announcer on the BBC radio World Service. "The end (of the World News)" though, is something entirely different from "the end-of-the-world-news." Burgess' readers are continually challenged to make similar exercises in mental gymnastics, seeing things first one way, then another, coming in the end to relish not the arrival at a fixed conclusion so much as the awareness that there are many possible conclusions, or connections, none of them to be dwelt on too long.

Mental agility is indeed a necessity for reading any one of the strands of this book, leaving alone the question of how they are to be related. The account of Sigmund Freud which Burgess offers, for example, is correct in all biographical details and yet marked by a strong and sardonic irreverence. There is a natural urge to fit Freud into the stereotype of "great scientist, persecuted for his beliefs," and Burgess provides the raw material for this in scenes where Freud is refused publication by his superiors, slighted by those who have reached the rank of professor, accused of writing "dirty books," and promoted only as a result of intrigues and favors that have nothing to do with his real merits. In absolute opposition to this Galileo- or Darwin-image, however, there is a strong suggestion that one could see things as Freud's opponents do. Was Freud not, in fact, himself almost mad? His delusions about the beneficial effects of cocaine are brought forward as well as his strange gullibility—for years he believed that anything which people confessed to him (especially as regards rape or incest) was true, though one imagines any experienced policeman could have corrected him. There is a strong black humor in his relationships with women. Freud's mother becomes very nearly a caricature of the "Yiddische momma," all but saying, in the words of the traditional joke, "Oedipus, Schmoedipus. Who cares so long as he's a good boy and loves his mother?" Freud's wife, Martha, meanwhile acts as a reservoir of common sense, recognizing long before her husband the symptoms of psychological transference and dependence on the analyst as also the prodigious gap between his theory and his practice. There is a richly comic scene as Martha Freud and Emma Jung quietly eat cake and deplore their husbands' stubbornness while their menfolk agonize outside. Of all this, Freud remains utterly unconscious, coming out even at the end of his life with sheer imperceptions such as his belief that women had less libido than men, and so less energy to sublimate, all of which led in his view to the notorious female trait of enviousness.

Was Freud an innocent, a madman, a genius? This is like asking for the meaning of "the end of the world news." One may say, though, that in spite of the black humor of Freud's personal life, and the even blacker farce of his quarrels with Alfred Adler and Jung, Freud is not entirely diminished in Burgess' account. One is conscious of the fallible man, conscious, also, of the seed in him of mythic greatness. The two, together, produce an effect at once droll and rueful.

Much the same could be said about the book's other two strands. Leon Trotsky is a flawed hero of the same type as Freud, like him woefully bad in his relationships with women, the gaps between his theory and his practice continually exposed. Over Trotsky, as over Freud, there hangs a sense of doom, in Freud's case anti-Semitism, in Trotsky's the specter of Mexico, where he fled after his defeat and expulsion by Joseph Stalin, and where he was assassinated, possibly on orders from Moscow. Trotsky's fate seems to be presented by Burgess, though, as pitiful in a way that Freud's was not, for with him there falls—or will fall inside the chronology of this novel—a vision of the perfect Socialist State, in which the excesses both of Stalinism and of capitalism would be resolved. Where did that vision (stigmatized by the *Great Soviet Encyclopaedia* of 1973-1983 as essentially "petit bourgeois") come from? Burgess suggests that perhaps it was the mere experience of New York, where workers were exploited and misguided but at the same time free and even encouraged to better themselves any way they liked.

When it comes to the final story in this trio, of the planet Lynx and its destruction of Earth, one might expect ruefulness to outweigh comedy by some degree, yet this section of the novel is populated even more than the others by a cast of grotesques. The designated captain of *America* likes to pretend that he is Captain Bligh and plays with a cat-o'-nine-tails in private. The final assault on *America* is launched by a revivalist preacher, who thinks he has been called to reenact Noah and is backed by Mafia gunmen who are terrified of Hell. The central character is a fat, cynical science-fiction writer and critic dedicated to seducing students in return for A grades. His main assistant is an alcoholic, Falstaffian, unemployed actor. There is, one may say, almost no notion of normal humanity here at all, and the image given of the United States reads like a caricature by Franz Kafka or Stalin. Is this meant to be set against the Trotskyite vision? Is Burgess saying, in effect, that since the world has rejected and murdered its prophets and visionaries, it deserves in some way to die? Better a Lynx than a universe of multiple television programs, showing mostly commercials?

Once again, the reader is faced with the problem of relating three separate strands to one another, an exercise continually provoked merely by the fact that one is continually switched from track to track and back again but is continually checked by the evident dangers of subjectivity and overinterpreting coincidence. It seems in the end that the major unifying factors of *The End of the World News* are its tone and its author's personality, both of them mordant, cynical, evasive—even potentially irresponsible. In the introduction to the book, Burgess is allowed to say, in a letter, that he is writing about what he considers to be the three greatest events of the century: the discovery of the unconscious, the doctrine of world socialism, and the invention of the space rocket. The book's "editor" (Burgess in another mood), though, dismisses this selection as "eccentric," and when one thinks of the atomic bomb, the concentration camps, the rise of totalitarianism, or the double helix, it looks as if the editor is right. Interpretations of history are free to all. What *The End of the World News* does is to offer a sequence of original sidelights.

T. A. Shippey

Sources for Further Study

America. CXLVIII, May 21, 1983, p. 406.
Christian Science Monitor. May 11, 1983, p. 9.
Commonweal. CX, September 23, 1983, p. 503.
Library Journal. CVIII, February 15, 1983, p. 411.
New Statesman. CIV, November 19, 1982, p. 27.
The New York Times Book Review. LXXXVIII, March 6, 1983, p. 3.
The New Yorker. LIX, April 11, 1983, p. 134.
Publishers Weekly. CCXXIII, January 14, 1983, p. 70.
Time. CXXI, March 21, 1983, p. 76.
World Literature Today. LVII, Autumn, 1983, p. 636.

THE ENTHUSIAST
A Life of Thornton Wilder

Author: Gilbert A. Harrison (1915-   )
Publisher: Ticknor & Fields (New York). Illustrated. 403 pp. $19.95
Type of work: Literary biography
Time: 1897-1975
Locale: Primarily Madison, Berkeley, New Haven, and Chicago

In the first full-scale biography of Thornton Wilder to be published since his death at age 78, Gilbert Harrison deftly explores the many ambiguities inherent in the life and work of an extremely public yet intensely private figure, one of the most reclusive celebrities in recent American letters

Principal personages:
THORNTON NIVEN WILDER, an American novelist and playwright
AMOS PARKER WILDER, his father, a journalist and sometime diplomat
ISABELLA THORNTON NIVEN WILDER, the author's mother
AMOS NIVEN WILDER and
ISABEL WILDER, two of Thornton Wilder's siblings
ROBERT MAYNARD HUTCHINS, an American educator and writer
AMY WEIL WERTHEIMER, a friend and correspondent of Thornton Wilder
RUTH GORDON, a noted American stage actress
JED HARRIS, a successful Broadway producer in the years between World War I and World War II
GERTRUDE STEIN, an expatriate American writer and theorist

Already famous as a novelist by the age of thirty, Thornton Wilder was clearly among the brighter lights in a literary generation noted by Malcolm Cowley and others for its uncommon brilliance. His career, however, remained strangely at odds with the rest of his generation, resisting comparison or assimilation with the careers of such illustrious contemporaries as Ernest Hemingway, F. Scott Fitzgerald, and John Dos Passos. Emerging in his forties as a gifted playwright to boot, Wilder achieved with his dramatic efforts a degree of exposure and near-celebrity afforded few contemporary writers. By the time he reached his sixties, his name had become an international household word yet inevitably followed by a question mark. For all of his demonstrable successes, critics both amateur and professional remained somewhat uneasy in the presence of his work, unable either to dismiss it or to deal with it. Indeed, it was not until the 1960's that critical studies of Wilder's novels and plays began to appear, initially in Germany and only later in his native United States; of the latter studies, those of Malcolm Goldstein and Donald Haberman have proved most perceptive and most durable, although Haberman's study deals exclusively with Wilder's plays. Even at his death, however, Wilder remained a relatively obscure and somewhat misunderstood figure in contemporary American letters, his reputation further clouded by a premature biography prepared without his help and published against his wishes.

Implicitly assuming that Wilder's works have by now been amply discussed, Gilbert Harrison confines most of his exposition and analysis to Wilder's often enigmatic life, quoting extensively from the works but seldom attempting to discuss them. A journalist and sometime editor, Harrison appears wary of the academic establishment, favoring Wilder's own erudite but resolutely extramural approach to the study of literature. To the degree that he lets his sentiments be known, Harrison emerges as a staunch supporter of Wilder's published work, assuming the work as more than sufficient occasion and justification for his inquiries into Wilder's life. The problem is that the facts, thus baldly stated, tend to disparage the work by implication. Harrison, meanwhile, does little or nothing to impede or alter the process, often conveying the disturbing impression that he has somehow lost control of the topic to which he has addressed himself, leaving the reader to supply or reconstruct the biography that might have been written. The conclusions appear to be in evidence, yet Harrison hesitates to draw them.

Beginning his account with a disconcerting assemblage of family letters dating from Wilder's childhood, Harrison sketches a group portrait of the gifted, somewhat eccentric Wilders, a clan dominated and all but determined for life by the stiff, no doubt stuffy *paterfamilias*. Amos Parker Wilder, as Harrison later recounts, was a former New England schoolmaster with a doctorate in political science from Yale University. The degree appears to have overqualified him for most useful work, including a journalistic career which he sought through his purchase of part ownership in the *Wisconsin State Journal*. His much younger wife, Isabella, whom Amos married on the rebound from two prior engagements, appears to have been as lively and versatile as Amos himself was not. Dissuaded by her pastor father from pursuing a career in medicine, the New York-born Isabella Niven lost little time in developing compensatory interest and competence in music, literature, and art. The five surviving children born to their unlikely union were exposed from the start to curious tensions as well as a broad education. Thornton, the younger of two brothers and a surviving twin, showed an early interest in art and letters that increasingly aligned him with his mother. Indeed, the last letter that Harrison quotes by way of introduction shows Wilder as a preparatory school teacher in his middle twenties addressing his mother as "Dear Wun" and observing, "If the school knew I spent so much time writing to my mother, I should be fired." Here as elsewhere, it is left to the reader to draw the evident conclusions.

Responding to shifts in Amos Wilder's career, the family moved frequently during Thornton's childhood, providing a wide range of experiences upon which to draw during his career as a novelist and playwright. Born in Madison,

Wisconsin, he was reared partially in Berkeley, California, educated partially at the elite Thacher School in Ojai, California, as well as in China, where his father had obtained a diplomatic post. During the summers, Harrison recounts, Wilder proved monumentally inept at farm work and other jobs arranged in advance by his father. Entering Oberlin College in 1915, Wilder for the first time in his life took an active interest in academic subjects; it was also at this time that he began writing plays, initially brief one-act plays of the sort which he would never really abandon. Before long, Wilder's writing took precedence over his course work, a condition that persisted even after he transferred to Yale University in accordance with his father's wishes in 1917—having lost a year of class standing because of low grades. Enlisting in the army during the summer of 1918, Wilder served several months of Stateside duty before and after the armistice; returning thereafter to Yale, he was graduated in the class of 1920 with future plans unclear.

After a year of archaeological study in Rome (an experience that later would serve as the basis for his first novel, *The Cabala*, 1926), Wilder returned to the United States, teaching French at the Lawrenceville School in a position found for him by his father. Although only marginally prepared in French pending study toward a master of arts degree, Wilder displayed a distinct flair for teaching; he did not, however, aspire toward an academic career as his father might have hoped. Although Wilder, later in life, became deeply immersed in scholarship, finding odd recreation, for example, in attempting to date the many plays of Lope de Vega, he preferred creative to scholarly writing and always remained an outsider to the academic community. Indeed, the strong implication is that Wilder was temperamentally ill-suited to any form of regular employment and was fortunately able to derive, from the age of thirty onward, a sufficient and at times substantial income from his writings.

Later in life, Wilder would recall that his happiest years were those spent on the faculty of the University of Chicago where he was hired in 1930 at the behest of its president, his friend and Yale classmate Robert Maynard Hutchins. It was Wilder himself, however, who terminated the association after six years, no doubt responding to a restlessness that lay deep within his temperament. Both before and during his tenure at Chicago, he had traveled widely; in 1928, he had made a much-publicized hiking tour of the Swiss Alps with heavyweight champion Gene Tunney and had often revisited Europe. In addition, Wilder had seen much of the United States as a lecturer on the Lee Keedick circuit and came to enjoy living, as it were, in transit. The immediate cause of his departure from Chicago was to join the burgeoning group of novelists hired to write scripts in Hollywood; Wilder's sojourn in Hollywood was, however, uncommonly brief, and he was soon back in Europe working on the play that would become *Our Town*.

Although it is for *Our Town* (1938) that Wilder is perhaps best remembered, his reputation during the 1930's was that of an unconventional but highly entertaining novelist. The critical success of *The Cabala* was followed just a year later by the popular and critical success of *The Bridge of San Luis Rey* (1927), a speculative fantasy set in eighteenth century Peru that may appear dated but was long considered his masterpiece. Appearing to be the work of a much older and more experienced writer, *The Bridge of San Luis Rey* sufficed to establish Wilder both as a novelist and as a private citizen: "the house *The Bridge* built," constructed in Hamden, Connecticut, with proceeds from the book, provided a long-needed home base for the peripatetic Wilder clan, although Thornton himself would not spend much time there until his later years. Wilder's third novel, *The Woman of Andros* (1930), was less well-received and came under fire from leftist critics because its classical setting showed little or no contact with contemporary problems. Perhaps in response to such criticisms, Wilder's fourth novel, *Heaven's My Destination* (1934), was firmly rooted in Depression-era America; even so, the book remained as baffling to many readers as had its predecessor. As Wilder would later observe, he had unwittingly written a political novel without knowing much about politics. Nevertheless, Wilder's *Candide*-like parable of a fundamentalist traveling salesman did much to restore his reputation as an intriguing if unpredictable novelist. Unknown to most of his reading public, he had turned to the writing of plays, his initial literary interest and the one that would yield his greatest successes.

As studies such as Donald Haberman's have noted, Wilder's talents and concerns were perhaps uniquely suited to the theater; it is perhaps just as well, however, that he established himself first as a novelist, awaiting full maturity before launching his full-scale assault on the Broadway stage. In some of his earlier efforts, cited almost reluctantly by Harrison, the dialogue is precariously balanced between the precious and the stultifying. Beginning with the one-act plays of the early 1930's, including *The Long Christmas Dinner* and *The Happy Journey to Trenton and Camden*, Wilder's ear for dialogue was increasingly "on pitch," showing a rare if late-blooming instinct for both aptness and economy. Well-acquainted by then with the innovative work of such European directors as Max Reinhardt and Michel Saint-Denis, Wilder in his late thirties knew that in *Our Town* he had written a mold-breaking play; his sole error lay in the choice of Jed Harris as producer-director. Among the most phenomenal successes of his generation, the Yale-educated Harris may well not have understood the play; in any event, the bickering that ensued nearly stopped the play short of production and survived the eventual first performance by more than thirty years, until the two aging men finally returned to speaking terms. With *Our Town* at last well launched, Wilder turned his attentions to the adaptation first known as *The Merchant of Yonkers* (1939), revised and revived in 1955 as *The Matchmaker*, which in turn served as the basis of the enormously successful musical comedy *Hello, Dolly!* (In his later years, Wilder would marvel at his mounting share of royalties derived from the musical version, in the writing of which he had taken no active part.) Besides *Our Town*, however, Wilder's major contribution to the dramatic repertory was *The Skin of Our Teeth*, completed in 1942 shortly before his entry into the army as an officer attached to military intelligence.

After World War II, from which he emerged with the rank of lieutenant colonel, Wilder drew upon his recent European residence to write *The Ides of March* (1948), an epistolary novel re-creating the last days of Julius Caesar. Strongly infused with the Existentialism of Jean-Paul Sartre and others, *The Ides of March* managed to be both historical and contemporary at the same time, showing that Wilder the playwright had not lost the knack for writing fiction. Thereafter, he continued work on *The Alcestiad: Or, A Life in the Sun*, a mythological play that he had put aside to write *The Skin of Our Teeth*, but *The Alcestiad* was never completed to Wilder's full satisfaction and would not be published until 1977, after his death, with an introduction prepared by his sister Isabel.

The decade of the 1950's, according to Harrison, was a period of sharp ironies and contrasts in Wilder's life, marked on one side by high acclaim and on the other by massive writer's block. A brief teaching stint at Harvard University in the early 1950's proved far less satisfactory than his earlier tenure at Chicago, with Wilder leaving unfinished the printed collection of his lectures stipulated in the original contract. Although many projects (both drama and fiction) were planned and even publicly announced, Wilder seemed unable to write much of anything, even as his prior accomplishments were hailed around the world with colloquiums, honorary degrees, and revivals of his plays. Part of the explanation is that Wilder by then had become a figure of such prominence that he had little time to himself, a problem compounded by his temperamental disinclination to refuse demands upon his time: Only later did he go into near-seclusion, allowing his unmarried sister Isabel to serve as a congenial buffer between himself and his public. Isabel was well trained for the job, having long since taken over the details of her brother's contracts and correspondence.

Early in the 1960's, Wilder departed on an extended sojourn in the American Southwest, eventually beginning work on the long novel that would be published in 1967 as *The Eighth Day*. Other projects, meanwhile, were picked up and discarded as Wilder sought in vain to recover the momentum of his middle years. Wilder's last novel, and the last of his works to be published during his lifetime, was *Theophilus North* (1973), a curious blend of novel and memoir dismissed by most of his critics (including Harrison) as slight and somewhat disconcerting. In Harrison's view, *Theophilus North* is useful mainly for the light it sheds on the perennial and bothersome question of Wilder's sexuality. At the time of his death in December, 1975, Wilder had few pending projects and had given his unexpected approval for a commercial telecast of

Our Town. Of late, however, he had been considerably nettled by the publication in 1975 of Richard Goldstone's *Thornton Wilder: An Intimate Portrait*. Although casually acquainted with Goldstone for more than thirty years, Wilder was persuaded that Goldstone did not understand him, and Wilder reiterated his long-held conviction that no biography should be published during its subject's lifetime.

In his coverage of the Goldstone incident, Harrison often assumes an incongruous, gloating pose, inviting the reader to join in heaping contumely upon the hapless academic who may or may not have understood his subject. To be sure, Harrison's contribution amounts to a better book than Goldstone's and was not written until after Wilder's death. The problem of professional rivalry remains, however, and is not easily dismissed; at times, Harrison appears to be reproaching Goldstone for the selfsame sort of probing that he does himself, and that is, after all, the appropriate task of any would-be biographer either during or after the subject's lifetime. Moreover, it is doubtful at times whether Harrison himself has understood Wilder well.

"Characteristically," wrote Donald Haberman of Wilder in his 1967 study, "no gossip has attached itself to him." Gregarious though he may have been, Wilder was among the most private of persons, easy to know slightly but perhaps impossible to know well. Harrison, in preparing his biography, has indeed managed to dredge up some gossip, but the results remain oddly inconclusive. In the case of Wilder's sexuality, as with everything else about his subject, Harrison presents evidence to support conclusions that the reader must draw for himself. No doubt excessively attached to his sensitive and somewhat neglected mother, Wilder developed frequent crushes on girls and women throughout his adolescence and early adulthood yet was apparently repelled by the physical consequences involved in going further. His few recorded homosexual contacts, in his late thirties, were curiously devoid of tenderness or intimacy. Indeed, concludes Harrison, Wilder was in all likelihood too principled, too prudish, and too self-controlled to abandon his reserve with either sex and was perceived by most of his closest friends as utterly asexual.

Given Harrison's earlier portrayals of the Wilder family, such conclusions are hardly surprising. Even during his long absences, Amos Wilder continued to rule his brood with an iron hand, discouraging his two elder daughters from any semblance of social life. Although the first son, Amos, Thornton's elder by nineteen months, and the youngest daughter, Janet, thirteen years his junior, went on to enjoy the double benefits of marriage and career, the three middle children remained marked for life by the odd aftereffects of their parents' marriage. Isabel, born in 1900, neither went to college nor married; Charlotte, born in 1898, who apparently shared her brother's writing talent, resigned a promising academic career for a bohemian life of lesbianism and political activism. In her early forties, Charlotte suffered a nervous breakdown from which she never fully recovered. She survived her brother Thornton by nearly five years, spending the last half of her life in institutions.

Denied normal expressions, Wilder's inevitable passions no doubt found their outlet in his work, providing some of the most emotionally satisfying scenes to be found in contemporary fiction or drama. At least in his public persona, Wilder remained unflaggingly enthusiastic about life, thus accounting for the title of Harrison's book. Among friends and the children of friends, he was generous with his presence and support, both material and spiritual. Like his alter ego Theophilus North, he was a frequent if beneficent meddler, intervening to straighten the tangled threads of his friends' lives. Harrison does not, however, draw the inevitable conclusion that *Theophilus North* is in fact closer to autobiography than most readers seem to think, a testament and memoir of the mind in which Wilder recapitulates under thin disguise the motives and themes of his life and career. Like Theophilus, like the Stage Manager of *Our Town*, Wilder obviously felt himself oddly on loan from his own life, hence free to straighten out the lives of others—audiences and readers as well as friends. As Harrison notes, such a life was not without its strains: Wilder chain-smoked throughout his life and, although never an alcoholic, consumed more spirits than could possibly have been good for his health, often from noon until midnight. What matters, however, is the result visible in his published work. Significantly, Wilder never drank when he was working; another item in his Puritanical personal code suggested that alcohol was incompatible with good writing.

Wilder wrote well indeed, and perhaps a subsequent biographer will pick up where Gilbert Harrison left off, using *Theophilus North* as the point of departure for a retrospective re-fusion of Wilder's life and work rather than a simple assemblage of the facts.

David B. Parsell

Sources for Further Study

America. CXLIX, November 26, 1983, p. 335.
American Literature. LVI, May, 1984, p. 286.
The New Republic. CLXXXIX, December 12, 1983, p. 32.
The New York Times Book Review. LXXXVIII, November 6, 1983, p. 11.
Publishers Weekly. CCXXIV, September 16, 1983, p. 109.
Smithsonian. XIV, October, 1983, p. 188.
The Wall Street Journal. November 7, 1983, p. 32.

EROSION

Author: Jorie Graham (1951-   )
Publisher: Princeton University Press (Princeton, New Jersey). 83 pp. $12.50;
   paperback $6.95
Type of work: Poetry

*Graham is at her best in poems in which experience is met directly, passion is allowed
to vent itself, and her well-trained art connoisseur's eye plays upon not art, but life*

With this new collection, Jorie Graham becomes only the second author
to have a second book in the Princeton Series of Contemporary Poets (Robert
Pinsky was the first). Her earlier volume, *Hybrids of Plants and of Ghosts*,
published in 1980, won the Great Lakes Colleges Association New Writer
Award as the best first book of poems for that year. The thirty-three poems
in *Erosion* are organized into a single, unbroken sequence in which appre-
ciations of the rough and gentle aspects of time's abrasive action are counter-
pointed by forays into man's more calamitous behavior. The acknowledgments
page shows that Graham has pleased a variety of editors but has overwhelmed
others. A third of these poems first appeared in *The American Poetry Review*;
seven others first appeared in *Antaeus* and *New England Review*. For the
most part, then, Graham has found favor with a somewhat restricted range
of editorial taste, a range compatible with that of recent readers for the
Princeton series. Graham's propensities define this taste as one that rewards
a sophisticated, Europe-facing sensibility, suggestiveness rather than precision, and a skill with various distancing devices that assures a bland result
whatever the subject.

Indeed, it is with almost too much sophistication and world-weariness that
Jorie Graham rehearses the moral decline of the West. The examples are
well chosen, the ideational level is impressively pitched, but the tone rarely
becomes fervent. *Erosion* is a kind of depressant; it makes one aware without
arousing anger. The treatment of calamity seems icy, and, though at times
effective understatement is at work, on the whole the bad news is presented
as tolerable. The wounds of the world are not Graham's sole concern. She
writes, too, of tenderness and of delicate response to environments and
situations of many kinds. Still, the book has a clear direction, a theme that
its title insists on and that emerges quite emphatically—much more emphatically than do the attendant emotions.

Graham's cool, reflective stance is annoying, given her ostensible subjects.
She writes of extremes of the human condition in ways that call for other
than contemplative reactions, but she holds back, content to have the events
she chooses become material for her art—and that is that. In this way, the
poetry becomes an end in itself, failing to reach out beyond the poets who
can admire Graham's assortment of skills. This book is important because it

so intelligently, so assuredly represents the inward-looking stance that does nothing to increase the audience for poetry, but rather confirms the common notion that poetry has turned away from engaging anyone but a barely self-sustaining community of its practitioners.

Graham finds many ways to distract the reader and undermine communication. These include constant and intrusive self-reference; irrelevant formal decisions that mask the real cadences and rhetoric of the poems instead of revealing them; and unnecessarily difficult diction and syntactical formulations.

The reflexive element is more of a style than a philosophy, though maybe in poetry, style is philosophy. Graham presents repeatedly an issue, an image, an event, as if it existed solely for her contemplation and transformation into poetic material. Many poems have the speaker intruding upon material that is interesting enough in itself and insisting on making it interesting only as it affects her or leads her to contemplation: "from any window/ I learn/ about freedom"; "You win when everything is used and nothing's/ changed is how it was explained/ to me"; "How late it is, I think,/ bending,/ in this world. . . ."; "The fragile stem/ from here// to there is tragedy, I know"; "I would not want, I think, a higher intelligence"; "But this too/ is a garden// I'd say"; "Because I think the human/ souls are in a frenzy/ to be born."

These examples could be multiplied. Such constant qualification has the end result of destroying intensity. No truths are insisted upon, and what might pass for reticence or modesty turns into something else: endless equivocation and endless projections of self into poems that might have a more vivid and appealing life if left to their own images and observations. All apprentice writers are reminded that it is deadly to repeat "I think," that the reader knows whose ideas are being presented. Graham's habit could be an attempt to underscore a rampant relativism, a late Berkeleyan hypothesis of reality: To be is to be perceived. She may be insisting, that is, on the subjective perspective that gives knowability to things—and even to nothings. Still, this outlook is so much a part of the modern sensibility that it does not require such an unattractive mannerism.

Another way in which Graham makes her work difficult or distant has to do with her decisions about typographical format. A great many of the poems in this collection are printed in series of six-line stanzas. The first, third, and fifth lines of each stanza begin at the left-hand margin while the alternate lines are indented. Usually, but not always, the even-numbered lines are shorter. The unfortunate thing about this format—it could never be a compositional habit—is that it masks the true rhythms and syntax of Graham's work. It is an imposed visual form, rarely having any communicative value. At worst, Graham's decision to wring her cadences and ideas through this torture makes her work difficult to follow because sentence parts and relationships are obscured. Certainly this typographical version of her work has no resemblance to how she would read the poems aloud.

In this determination to build stanzas for the eye, Graham is following, with little imagination, one of the most questionable practices among contemporary poets. For readers who value the true discipline, the hard-won mastery of strophic composition, work like Graham's can seem outrageous and deceitful. Why pretend to this kind of control—or even a genuine interest in it? Though in some poems, the tension between the formal look and the work's more sinuous structure becomes mildly interesting (as in "The Daffodil"), usually the result is not creative tension but confusion. Perhaps Graham's most effective use of this six-line stanza is in "Kimono," a poem in which the interplay of abstract and concrete seems to be echoed by the interplay of the visual poem and the aural one. The shaping reminds one, appropriately in this case, of the formalism of Japanese manners and art. Moreover, this poem's suggestions of constant and variable elements in perception, especially in the perception of shapes in motion, are heightened by a stylistic interplay of constant and variable language structures: the constant visual pattern against the shifting rhythmic and syntactic patterns.

Given Graham's more characteristic disregard of such matters, however, "Kimono" might be merely a happy accident. The relentless enjambment of lines and stanzas leaves Graham's poems with no sure background prosody against which meaningful variations can be played. The shame is that her writing is so much better, so much more rhythmically evocative than the form in which she so often, mistakenly, has chosen to reveal it.

The poems in *Erosion* are meditative poems. Graham offers from a reading of history, of art, and of her own experience a kind of wisdom poetry that links her with such contemporaries as Dave Smith and such distant predecessors as George Herbert. In *The New York Times Book Review* appraisal cited below, Helen Vendler gave high praise to Graham for a book that "brings the presence of poetry into the largest question of life, the relation of body and spirit, a relation more often considered by theologians and philosophers these days than by poets." Indeed, these are Graham's concerns. Poems with such titles as "In What Manner the Body is United with the Soule," "At the Exhumed Body of Santa Chiara, Assisi," and "At Luca Signorelli's Resurrection of the Body" attest this probing, as they do Graham's Italian upbringing and her immersion in art.

There is a tendency to be respectful toward work that is this ambitious, but complex questions require complex answers, and complex answers require a struggle for utmost clarity. Here Graham falls short. Given repeatedly to aphoristic punch lines, she often leaves the reader feeling as if a philosophical shaggy dog story has just revealed itself. One learns in "I Watched a Snake" that "Passion is work/ that retrieves us,/ lost stitches. It makes a pattern of us,/ it fastens us/ to sturdier stuff/ no doubt." There is enough vagueness and equivocation here for anyone's truth to find a home; as a resolution to a poem that presses toward an epiphany, this passage comes as a letdown. In "For

John Keats," the conclusion warns: "We live a harsh fecundity, it seems/ to me, the symbol tripping much/ too freely/ over everything/ it signifies." Although this passage has a certain power (despite the characteristic "it seems to me"), it is difficult to find it all hanging together as a clear idea clearly expressed. To the extent that the lines themselves worry about undisciplined habits of mind and language, they suggest that Graham is aware of her own limitations as Keats was of his.

Mary Kinzie, writing in the same periodical that first published eleven of these poems, was given room to complain that "the filmy uncertainties of the verb constructions and the reaching for authority from ethical categories without being able to explore or apply them, are evidence of an undisciplined and unripe apprenticeship" (see *The American Poetry Review* citation below). Kinzie worried, convincingly, about "sleights" of "diction and rhetoric" which remain fuzzy while they posture authority. Harsh words, but they have a greater accuracy than many stretches of language found in *Erosion*. By creating—or settling for—unnecessarily difficult or imprecise diction and syntactic formulations, Graham has put one more barrier between herself and the reader.

Another barrier is allusiveness. Given Graham's noble purposes, there is too much hiding behind other artists and works of art. Exactly what she is taking a stand on becomes blurred by her decision to handle many of her treatments of human grotesquerie in a special subgenre: the poem about the painting. The issue now becomes not *what are humans capable of* but *how do artists treat such problems*. Using the works of other artists to keep experience at one remove, Graham's stance remains cool, her tone flat (Helen Vendler calls this "serene depth"), and the moral issues become transformed into aesthetic ones.

Jorie Graham is at her best in poems such as "Salmon," in which experience is met directly, passion is allowed to vent itself, and her well-trained art connoisseur's eye plays upon not art, but life. In "Salmon," no false packaging buries the rhythms of thought and language. Here, Graham's speculations and their self-referential language find vitality rather than muzzle it, and her diction is often sharp, breaking through the mannered haze of lesser achievements. It is recognizably her work, but it is a poem for all readers. More such poems as "Salmon" would be welcome.

Philip K. Jason

Sources for Further Study

The American Poetry Review. XII, November/December, 1983, p. 44.
Commonweal. CXI, March 9, 1984, p. 155.

Library Journal. CVIII, May 1, 1983, p. 909.
The New York Times Book Review. LXXXVIII, July 17, 1983, p. 10.
Times Literary Supplement. May 20, 1983, p. 506.
Virginia Quarterly Review. LIX, Autumn, 1983, p. 133.

EXILED IN PARADISE
German Refugee Artists and Intellectuals
in America, from the 1930's to the Present

Author: Anthony Heilbut (1938-   )
Publisher: The Viking Press (New York). 506 pp. $20.00
Type of work: Cultural history
Time: The early 1930's to the late 1970's
Locale: The United States; primarily New York City and Los Angeles

A study of the talented waves of immigrants who fled Nazi Germany and Austria in the late 1930's and came to the United States, deeply affecting American society in the arts and sciences

Principal personages:
ALBERT EINSTEIN, a theoretical physicist
THOMAS MANN, an author
BERTOLT BRECHT, a playwright and poet
THEODOR ADORNO, a cultural sociologist
HANNAH ARENDT, a philosopher and cultural historian
BRUNO BETTELHEIM, a psychoanalyst
LEO SZILARD, a theoretical physicist
HANS BETHE, a theoretical physicist
DOUGLAS SIRK, a film director
MAX REINHARDT, a stage and film director
HANS HOFMANN, a painter

The waves of refugees who fled Central Europe in the 1930's to escape Hitlerism may well have constituted the most talented tide ever to wash ashore in America. They included many of the world's most renowned scientists, writers, musicians, philosophers, psychoanalysts, and filmmakers, encompassing such diverse and distinguished people as Albert Einstein, Thomas Mann, Arnold Schöenberg, Bertolt Brecht, Fritz Lang, Erik Erikson, Theodor Adorno, and Hannah Arendt. Dissimilar in temperament, they were united in their self-conscious awareness of the bitter pain of exile, their despair at being uprooted from a native soil where they had made illustrious marks. They were also bonded by a satiric sense of humor, as shown in a story popular among the émigrés: Two of them are sailing on the Atlantic, one headed for America, the other headed back to Europe. As their two boats pass each other, the old friends shout simultaneously: "Are you crazy?"

Anthony Heilbut has undertaken to chronicle this diaspora and has written an eloquent, memorable book that registers the resonance of half hope and half despair, of biting wit and sophisticated neurosis common among those brilliant but shipwrecked survivors of the darkest period in modern history. His credentials consist of Berlin-born parents who migrated to New York in the mid-1930's, a Harvard University doctorate in English literature, and an enormous amount of research in refugee lore. His work is likely to remain an outstanding achievement in a complex category of cultural and social history.

Heilbut takes pains to note the unique nature of these refugees from Nazism and Fascism: They were largely but not wholly Jewish; they had been successfully assimilated in Germany or Austria, only to be despoiled of their identity and confidence by ruthless dispossession and expulsion; they came to serve their new land, applying rigorous standards to their professions and exerting the authority of often brilliant gifts. Nevertheless, they carried the vulnerability of the wanderer in their blood: a paranoid disposition to view the unfamiliar with alarm and to scent betrayal and incipient persecution, especially when the McCarthy period of post-World War II America struck what seemed to many of them as ominously recurring chords of intolerance, distortion, and terror.

Heilbut reminds the readers how quickly Adolf Hitler victimized intellectuals, artists, and other radicals as well as all Jews. As soon as he assumed power, in March, 1933, he dismissed Jewish academicians from their positions; on May 10, 1933, the Nazis organized their first massive book burning; on October 10, 1933, the purchase of any book by any proscribed author was declared an act of treason. Eventually, 300,000 Jews left Germany between 1933 and 1939; 132,000 of them came to the United States. (Heilbut fails to furnish the number of exiled non-Jews or of Austrian Jewish and non-Jewish refugees.) The world knows only too well the fate of all but a handful of "non-Aryans" who were unable to flee. Nevertheless, the world of the mid-to-late 1930's was far from eager to welcome victims of this purge: The Swiss, for example, closed their borders to Jewish would-be immigrants—their persecution was declared "unpolitical." In France, some political parties were openly anti-Semitic; one campaigned under the slogan, "Better Hitler than Blum." Almost every European nation, as well as Great Britain, had indigenous Fascist movements. Austria's Nazis often outdid their German comrades in anti-Jewish fanaticism. During Joseph Stalin's purges in the late 1930's, many Central European refugees were executed or imprisoned in Soviet *gulags*.

Even the Statue of Liberty's torch of welcome proved wobbly and dim: American immigration laws imposed strict quotas, and the Immigration Service insisted that each applicant for admission to the United States have an American citizen furnish an affidavit in his or her behalf—documentary proof that the émigré would not require financial assistance. In June, 1940, the State Department ended virtually all immigration from Central Europe, even though many refugee rescues remained possible for another year. One historian has estimated that this policy alone resulted in the needless loss of twenty thousand to twenty-five thousand lives. The only prominent non-Jewish public personality who consistently championed the émigré cause in the United States was Eleanor Roosevelt, while her husband, admired by most refugees to the point of veneration, refused to urge expansion of the quota numbers, did not publicize the existence of the Nazi death camps, and waited until January, 1944, to establish the Wartime Refugee Board—by which time rescues were no longer feasible.

No wonder that some exiles from Hitlerism committed suicide before they could find a haven. Most brilliant among them was the literary and cultural critic Walter Benjamin, friend of Brecht and associate of Adorno, who fled Germany for France, then tried, in September, 1940, to cross from German-occupied France to Spain, only to learn that Spanish border officials refused to honor visas made out in Marseilles. Benjamin killed himself that night. Had he traveled one day earlier, he would have been permitted to cross unchallenged.

Those refugees who did manage to enter the United States found their reception variable, depending on the marketability of their skills. Intellectuals with international reputations were, in the early-to-mid-1930's, hospitably welcomed by such institutions as Manhattan's New School for Social Research, Princeton's Institute for Advanced Study, the California Institute of Technology, and various University of California campuses. Later comers and those with uncompleted advanced degrees had far greater difficulties, and many, whether academics, writers, or artists, never resumed their Continental careers. Composer Paul Dessau worked on a chicken farm; writer Walter Mehring became a warehouse foreman; philosopher Heinrich Bluecher shoveled chemicals in a factory; actress-writer Ruth Berlau tended bar; the greatest German stage actress, Helene Weigel, found herself unemployable in Hollywood.

Except for legal scholars, whose training in Roman law proved useless, many European academics had distinguished careers in America. Karl Deutsch and Heinz Eulau excelled in political science; Lewis Coser, Paul Lazarsfeld, and Theodor Adorno in sociology; Paul Tillich harmonized Friedrich Nietzsche's ideas with those of Protestant theology; Franz Neumann, Hans Kohn, and Peter Gay became leading historians; Erwin Panofsky did notable work in art history; Hans Hofmann became the most influential art instructor of his era, with his students including Larry Rivers, Louise Nevelson, and Helen Frankenthaler; Erwin Piscator inspired disciples in the theatrical program he directed at the New School for Social Research; Herbert Marcuse assimilated Karl Marx's theories into Sigmund Freud's with hotly controversial results; Wilhelm Reich, Fritz Perls, Erik Erikson, and Bruno Bettelheim made towering contributions in distinct areas of psychology and psychoanalysis, sometimes under institutional sponsorship, sometimes not. Most people are aware that Albert Einstein, Leo Szilard, Edward Teller, and Hans Bethe were among the ambivalent progenitors of the nuclear age. Long as this list is, Heilbut's is even longer. He sums up the émigrés' intellectual imprint neatly:

"Fifty years ago, the American upper classes had 'come of age' abroad. Now, European educators came here to complete the education of young Americans."

The reception of many of these newcomers was less than heartening, even among American Jews. Such assimilated luminaries as Bernard Baruch and Walter Lippmann preferred to ignore their presence, partly out of fear that it might cause an outburst of not-so-latent anti-Semitism in the United States. Right-wingers discerned the familiar target of "foreign-born radicals," with such demagogues as Father Charles Coughlin making anti-Semitism and anti-Communism twin causes for paranoid crusades. Many hard leftists, on the other hand, abandoned the refugees after Vyacheslav Mikhaylovich Molotov and Joachim von Ribbentrop signed their infamous nonaggression pact in August, 1939. There were, of course, a few humanists of goodwill who did their best. Native-born scholars such as William Alan Neilson, Lewis Mumford, Van Wyck Brooks, Kenneth Burke, and Malcolm Cowley organized rescue efforts; so did Central European film directors who had established themselves in the early 1930's in American cinematic circles: William Dieterle, Fritz Lang, Fred Zinneman, and Billy Wilder. The agent Paul Kohner eloquently represented refugee writers in their negotiations with Hollywood studios, so that a number of them were employed at relatively modest salaries, including Heinrich Mann, Alfred Döblin, Leonhard Frank, and occasionally Bertolt Brecht. German-born Salka Viertel, writing American films since the 1920's, made her Santa Monica Canyon house a come-every-Sunday salon for many gifted émigrés. It was there that Thomas Mann celebrated the seventieth birthday of his older brother Heinrich by reconciling their relationship via a fifteen-page formal address.

Heilbut devotes several chapters to close-up profiles of the most gifted or influential of these immigrants. Paul Lazarsfeld became director of the Bureau of Applied Social Research, pioneering in industrial psychology and sociology; his most famous work was a series of analyses of the tastes and characteristics of radio listeners. Lazarsfeld's sometime colleague, Theodor Adorno, was in equal measure brilliant and arrogant, pompous and profound. One of the great social philosophers of his generation, he wrote illuminating articles on American jazz, radio, television, dance, and film, deriving psychosocial generalizations from a popular culture that he despised. For him, market mechanisms corrupted American pretensions toward idealism; the accumulation of property sabotaged most relationships; mass distribution devalued high culture, while low culture vulgarized every human response. Unsurprisingly, Adorno returned to Germany in the late 1940's.

So did Bertolt Brecht, Germany's greatest twentieth century dramatist, who lived unhappily in Santa Monica from 1941 to 1947. As a Marxist who toed the Stalinist line, Brecht was disposed to and did find the United States materialistic, racist, economically vicious, and culturally shallow. He was hardly known in America and made little effort to master its language or soften his caustic, coarse, spiky personality. Forced to apply for writing jobs in the film industry, he wrote this bitter ballad:

> Every day to earn my daily bread,
> I go to the market, where lies are bought.
> Hopefully
> I take up my place among the sellers.

The only Hollywood project that materialized for Brecht was the Fritz Lang-directed film, *Hangmen Also Die* (1943); however, he quarreled bitterly with both the director and his American cowriter, ending up with no credit for the screenplay. Still, Brecht did achieve a remarkably fruitful collaboration with Charles Laughton, as they revised his favorite play, *Galileo* (1947), with Laughton incarnating the lead role. The production lasted three weeks in Los Angeles and no longer in New York; nevertheless, *Galileo* has come to be regarded as second in merit only to *Mother Courage and Her Children* (1948) in the Brechtian canon.

Brecht also starred in perhaps the most famous of émigré episodes: his testimony in October, 1947, before the Red-baiting House Committee on Un-American Activities. He coolly denied that he was a Communist, and explained that the apparent party-line dogmatism of his play, *The Measures Taken* (1930), was the result of a distorted translation into English. He then confused matters by attributing the plot of an inoffensive work, *The Yea-Sayer* (first produced in 1930) to the stridently Stalinist *The Measures Taken*. Because none of the Congressional investigators knew German or knew Brecht's career, his strategem succeeded. When he stepped down from the witness stand, the chairman praised him for his exemplary testimony. That very evening, Brecht left for Europe.

While some difficult personalities among the émigrés would have been discontented anywhere outside Berlin or Vienna, others proceeded to put down firm roots. The economist Peter Drucker became an enthusiastic advocate of corporate capitalism, welcoming a pluralistic, nonideological American culture and even finding models of integrity in the lives of such magnates as John D. Rockefeller, Sr., and Andrew Carnegie. The historian Hans Kohn did several magisterial studies which culminated in *American Nationalism: An Interpretive Essay* (1957), an anglophilic work that regarded the United States as having universalized the British tradition of political liberty. The psychoanalyst Bruno Bettelheim studied American children and adolescents from a Holocaust-conscious perspective controlled by his internment, for a year, in Dachau and Buchenwald. Just as he found concentration-camp inmates regressing from adulthood, mired in the moment's needs, so he found autistic children unable to reach emotional maturity, with their parents as hostile to them as prison guards had been to him. He came to affirm traditional American values as far worthier than the deep flaws of European Romanticism and Marxism. Heilbut gives short shrift to German-born Henry Kissinger, son of refugee parents: He does term him "the most famous German Jew of his time," but he proceeds to damn him through the observations of unnamed immigrants for whom "it was an unspeakable irony that the country they had loved so much should achieve what they regarded as its moral ruin largely under the auspices of a fellow emigre."

Heilbut pays closest attention to two refugees he clearly admires: Thomas Mann and Hannah Arendt. Mann was world renowned when he arrived in New York in 1938 and shortly thereafter received an honorary degree from Harvard University and a dinner invitation to the White House. During the World War II years, he served willingly as public spokesman for anti-Fascist causes and became a naturalized American citizen. He never learned English well, however, continuing to write in German, and he struck many Americans, in person or in print, as pompous, priggish, narcissistic and hypochondriacal. "Where I am, is Germany," he declared with as much arrogance as accuracy. Neverthcless, Heilbut takes care to note that Mann was indeed seriously ill during the 1940's, and that he managed to write, while in Pacific Palisades, California, the most ambitious novel of his late period: *Doctor Faustus: The Life of the German Composer Adrian Leverkuhn as Told by a Friend* (1947). This complex book signifies on several levels: It deals with the career of a German composer, Leverkuhn, as narrated by his best friend, Zeitblom. Leverkuhn is clearly identified with modern Germany's character and fate as he encounters a variety of people, including the Devil (whose conversation resembles Adorno's). The Devil gives Leverkuhn musical genius along the lines of Schönberg's twelve-tone technique. In exchange, the composer is damned with syphilis and degenerates—like Hitler's Germany—into madness. Living out the 1930's as a senile invalid, Leverkuhn enters his second infancy and is nursed by his mother.

The novel sold poorly in the United States, and its rejection, as well as the chilly cultural blasts of the Cold War, disillusioned Mann sufficiently with his adopted homeland so that he left it for Switzerland in 1952, a thoroughly embittered man. His insistence on being "non-Communist rather than anti-Communist" sat poorly with McCarthyites. "Only three major intellectuals might be counted on to defend political heretics by 1950," states Heilbut: "Linus Pauling and two emigres, Mann and Einstein." A less strident judgment would be that Thomas Mann, as a traditional European artist and intellectual, had always been culturally and temperamentally isolated in America. With Nazism crushed, he could safely return to his proper zone of comfort.

As for Hannah Arendt, she became—Einstein excepted—perhaps the most celebrated of émigré academics, although she did not receive her first university appointment until she was forty-nine. The daughter of wealthy Prussian Jews, she studied philosophy with Karl Jaspers and Martin Heidegger, became a Zionist while in France after fleeing Germany but established herself as an independent-minded, brutally honest, brilliantly perceptive and snappishly opinionated thinker once arrived in the United States. She challenged many of the basic assumptions of Freudianism, Marxism, and Adorno's sociological Hegelianism while working as an essayist and editor. While promoting English translations of such great European writers as Franz Kafka and Hermann Broch, she also adapted herself to the American cultural scene and became friendly with the *Partisan Review* group, particularly Mary McCarthy, Dwight MacDonald, Randall Jarrell, and Irving Howe.

Arendt's major study was *The Origins of Totalitarianism* (1951), which received great acclaim as an interpretation of what she regarded as a totally new form of social oppression. She saw imperialist colonialism as a forerunner to Fascist terror; dramatized the heavy cost for Jews of their preferring art and psychology to politics; described the change of the masses' mood from anomie to mob frenzy; lashed Marxism for ignoring the power of racism. Like George Orwell, she condemned Bolshevism alongside Nazism and Fascism. Unlike Orwell, Heilbut sadly notes that her equation of the hard Left with the hard Right "provides the most blatant justification for hard-line Cold War politics." He tries to repudiate her perspective by contrasting it with that of Franz Neumann's massive study of Nazi Germany, *Behemoth* (1942), whose angle of vision is Marxist.

This consistent pull toward a left-wing view of the contemporary world is the only flaw in Heilbut's impressively comprehensive text. He has otherwise achieved a significant chronicle, narrating the odyssey of a superbly gifted and ineradicably tainted group of exiles, cursed with caustic self-awareness but blessed with enormous resilience of mind and spirit.

Gerhard Brand

Sources for Further Study

Business Week. July 4, 1983, p. 11.
Commentary. LXXVI, December, 1983, p. 88.
Library Journal. CVIII, April 1, 1983, p. 740.
Los Angeles Times Book Review. May 15, 1983, p. 1.
Nation. CCXXXVI, June 25, 1983, p. 805.
The New York Times Book Review. LXXXVIII, July 10, 1983, p. 12.
Publishers Weekly. CCXXIII, April 22, 1983, p. 90.
Time. CXXI, June 20, 1983, p. 76.

THE EYE OF THE HERON

Author: Ursula K. Le Guin (1929-   )
Publisher: Harper & Row, Publishers (New York). 179 pp. $11.95
Type of work: Novel
Time: Early in the twenty-second century
Locale: Victoria, a prison planet

Conflict between a pacifist, egalitarian society (Shantih) and an aggressive, hierarchical society (the City) is the occasion for intellectual and moral growth in a young woman

> *Principal characters:*
> LUZ MARINA FALCO COOPER, a young woman
> LUIS BURNIER FALCO, chief councillor of the City
> HERMAN MACMILAN, a young aristocrat
> VERA ADELSON, a leader of and spokeswoman for the Shantih people
> LEV SHULTS, a young man and a spokesman for the Shantih people
> ANDRE, a leader of the Shantih people

Two small groups of people live on the prison planet, Victoria. One group, the inhabitants of the City, are descendants of criminals exiled from South America early in the twenty-first century, while the other group, the inhabitants of Shantih (peace), are descendants of protesters exiled about forty years later because of their refusal to cooperate in a long East-West war. In the sixty years since the arrival of the Shantih people, the two groups have not intermixed, but they have become to some degree interdependent.

In time, however, the City people have come to think of themselves as masters of the planet, though they only control a few square miles. They think of the "Shanty-Towners" as peasants, a labor pool over which they rightfully exercise power. The Shantih, on the other hand, are largely self-sufficient. They provide basic raw materials to the City: food, fuel, and fiber. Though their original agreement was for exchange, the Shantih have come to receive almost nothing for their work. The villagers continue to provide materials out of inertia and out of a faith that a unified community will eventually emerge. The City's view of unity differs from the Town's. Luis Falco, chief councillor or boss of the City, plans to complete the formation of an oligarchy in which the Shantih will become a permanent peasant class. For their part, the Shantih expect the City to be converted to their pacifist and egalitarian principles. A crisis grows from these differing points of view.

This crisis becomes the occasion for the maturation of Luz Falco, daughter of Luis. Her efforts to break free from various forms of ideology reveal Ursula Le Guin's thematic concerns in this novel.

Luz is a prisoner in her father's house, as all women are prisoners in the patriarchal society of the City. Through her contacts with the Shantih, especially Vera Adelson and Lev Shults, she has come to see that her position at home mirrors the relation of the Town to the City. She is expected to suspend significant choice and to be the willing tool of the men to whom she belongs.

Luz breaks away from her father and the City when she comes to understand her father's plan to subjugate brutally the Shantih. In a scheme which also implicates an attractive potential husband for Luz, Herman Macmilan, Falco intends to provoke violence, label the violence rebellion, and sentence the rebels to forced labor on the new estates. Repelled by this cruel design, Luz impulsively reveals the plan to the Shantih. Once she has made this break, she finds herself unable to return to Casa Falco, and she joins the Shantih.

The Shantih, however, are also imprisoned in a set of ideas. While they do not organize their society around ideas of dominance and submission, their tradition is tied to the City's system. They are enormously proud of their nonviolent philosophy, derived from Mahatma Gandhi and Martin Luther King. Nonviolent resistance, however, is appropriate and effective only when a powerful group oppresses a weak group *and* when confrontation is unavoidable; the Shantih fail to realize that their situation only meets the first of these conditions.

The emergence of Lev Shults as a spokesman for the Shantih shows that these people have failed as yet to understand their new situation on Victoria. To rebuild their society, they need to reject the old polarities that they have brought from Earth. Lev's leadership is characterized by the female characters as *male* leadership: rational, dualistic, and tending to prefer the testing of principles in confrontation. For this reason, Le Guin's narrative voice grows ironic as Lev becomes "boss" of Shantih, talks of *victory* over the City and of the *conversion* of the City people to the Shantih point of view. Even the *rules* for nonviolent confrontation are ironically undercut.

The women point out the folly of confrontation more directly. They argue that nonviolence provokes violence. Luz argues that they can avoid confrontation by simply leaving, but Lev insists on viewing the two communities as one. Luz and others point out that this amounts to dying unnecessarily for a principle and, furthermore, whether violent or nonviolent weapons are used, to fight a war is to fight the City's war. The feminine viewpoint makes preservation of life central, while the masculine viewpoint makes the affirmation of principle central. These views are complementary, and neither is valid alone. In the present circumstances, the gesture of confrontation is unnecessary, but the male leaders are unable to understand their new situation, to see that they can simply walk away from this conflict. In the ensuing confrontation, Lev is killed and his people react violently, betraying their sacred principles.

Luz sees clearly that the City and the Town are locked in their opposing roles, and she again breaks away, persuading those who share her perception to found a new settlement, secretly, in the unknown wilderness. They hope to build an egalitarian society without the necessity of confrontation. To do so, they must become like the animals of the planet, especially the one they call the heron. The heron is associated with the irrelevance of the human ideas of order which the opposing groups have sought to impose on Victoria. When Lev argues against running away, he asserts that to surrender principle will mean to die like an animal. A woman replies that all people die like animals because people are animals. Lev represses his mortality, exactly as the City represses women and its awareness of its dependence on Shantih. To accept mortality means to be able to understand the universe's indifference to ideology and to become free to leave principles unasserted, free of the need to see one's beliefs mirrored in another.

The Eye of the Heron is a novel of ideas. The central idea is expressed in the one common trait of all Victorian animals: To cage them is to kill them. Each human character who allows himself or herself to be caged in a structure of thought suffers a literal or figurative death. The central issue is how to escape such intellectual cages. Luz becomes aware that such ideologies are a masculine-rational defense against an indifferent universe. Humanity attempts through ideology to assert immortality, to assert absolute truth by forcing others to acknowledge it. When Lev asserts that if the Shantih hold fast, the City's power will melt away like shadows at sunrise, a woman responds that Victoria is "the world of shadows." To impose a form on life is to create an opposition to that form, to hold back but not to defeat chaos. The women are especially aware of the shadow, of the fundamental alienness of human order in an indifferent universe. Because they tend not to see the protective walls of ideology as absolute, they also tend to be able to criticize masculine overassertion of principle. To escape the thought patterns of the past, one must be open to the new. Women on Victoria offer access to the new, perhaps because a male-dominated culture, which represses the nonhuman, forces women, by repressing them as well, into an intimate knowledge of the nonhuman.

Such ideas are consistent with the themes that have dominated Le Guin's fiction. *The Eye of the Heron* originally appeared in a collection entitled *Millennial Women* (1978), edited by Virginia Kidd. In *The Dispossessed* (1974) and *The Beginning Place* (1980), Le Guin explores the problem of escaping oppressive patterns of thought, and in her fictional worlds she often sets up opposing cultures in order to work out a "thought experiment." In her essay, "Is Gender Necessary?" (reprinted in *The Language of the Night: Essays on Fantasy and Science Fiction*, 1979, edited by Susan Wood), Le Guin describes her best-known novel, *The Left Hand of Darkness* (1969), in exactly these terms: as a thought experiment. Many of these experiments have involved the relations between a feminine-anarchic culture and a masculine-hierarchic culture.

Also apparent in *The Eye of the Heron* is the Taoist thought which critics find in most of Le Guin's work. The protagonist of *City of Illusions* (1967) preserves his double identity and his people in part by studying from the opening of the *Tao Te Ching* (late third century B. C.):

> The way that can be gone
> is not the eternal Way.
> The name that can be named
> is not the eternal Name.

The people of Shantih are only gradually coming to understand that the names and ways they brought from Earth are not eternal. They must open themselves to new names and ways or remain imprisoned in the language and the thought patterns of confrontation.

The Eye of the Heron is not as impressive as Le Guin's most admired works: *The Left Hand of Darkness*, the Earthsea trilogy (1968-1972), and *The Dispossessed*. Here, Le Guin seems more interested in working out ideas than in telling a good story, and the characters are accordingly one-dimensional. Nevertheless, this novel stands up well against much current fiction, demonstrating Le Guin's capacity for provocative exploration of social and philosophical issues.

Terry Heller

Sources for Further Study

The Atlantic. CCLI, February, 1983, p. 105.
Los Angeles Times Book Review. January 16, 1983, p. 1.
The New York Times Book Review. May 22, 1983, pp. 15.

THE FEUD

Author: Thomas Berger (1924-   )
Publisher: Delacorte Press/Seymour Lawrence (New York). 265 pp. $13.95
Type of work: Novel
Time: The 1930's
Locale: Middle America

A slapstick tragicomedy about two feuding families

Principal characters:
DOLF BEELER, a plant foreman
BOBBY BEELER, his wife
BERNICE BEELER, their daughter
TONY BEELER and
JACK BEELER, their sons
BUD BULLARD, the owner of a hardware store
FRIEDA BULLARD, his wife
JUNIOR BULLARD, their son
EVA BULLARD, their daughter
REVERTON KIRBY, Bud's cousin
WALT HUFF, Bud's brother-in-law
ERNIE KRUM, a Hornbeck fireman
CLIVE SHELL, police chief of Millville
HARVEY YELTON, police chief of Hornbeck
RENO FOX, a bank robber

The Feud is Thomas Berger's twelfth novel and one of his best. In his previous book, *Reinhart's Women* (1981), Berger seemed to be mellowing, giving his hero, Carlo Reinhart, less chaos to deal with than in the previous three Reinhart novels. This tendency continues in *The Feud*, set in Hornbeck and Millville, somewhere in middle America, during the Depression; the novel recalls the world of *Sneaky People* (1975) but presents it with more humor. There is a desperation in the lives of these seemingly ordinary people, but it is softer around the edges. Most important, *The Feud* offers yet more evidence that Berger is a genuinely original novelist. He has said he agrees with Vladimir Nabokov's contention about *Lolita* (1955) that what is significant in such a work is "aesthetic bliss." *The Feud* provides such bliss.

The troubles in *The Feud* begin when beer-bellied Dolf Beeler, a plant foreman, decides to revarnish a walnut dresser several years after promising his wife, Bobby, that he would do so immediately. Dolf goes to Bud's hardware store in neighboring Millville for paint remover (because the store in Hornbeck is closed following its owner's unexplained suicide), and he gets into an argument with Junior Bullard (Bud's teenage son) and Reverton Kirby (Bud's cousin) when he refuses to dispose of his unlit stogie. Rev, who tells his relatives that he is a railroad detective—though actually he is unemployed—pulls a gun on Dolf and humiliates him. When Bud's store burns down that night, the disagreement between the Bullards and the Beelers becomes a full-scale feud. Numerous other misunderstandings and disasters follow, creating a combination of *Romeo and Juliet* (1595) and the Hatfields and McCoys.

Bud's problem is not merely that he has lost his business, but that it was uninsured—unbeknownst to his many relatives, who have invested in the store and who think insurance will pay for the damages. Unable to face them, Bud tries to kill himself and later has a breakdown.

Tony, Dolf's seventeen-year-old son, has developed a crush on Bud's fourteen-year-old daughter, Eva, because she has "such a big milk fund." When he tries to visit her after the fire, Rev pulls his gun again: "This is our town, and we don't want you in it." Then someone blows up Dolf's car.

Dolf, according to his daughter, Bernice, is the kind of man who "took life too seriously and often thought somebody was cheating him or insulting him when probably they never had the least intent to do so." His natural paranoia, a characteristic he shares with his enemy Rev, intensifies after the bombing. When he goes to work the next day, he picks a fight with kindly Walt Huff, Bud's brother-in-law, who tries to talk Dolf into making peace with the Bullards. After winning the fight by bloodying Walt's nose—only one of several bloody noses in *The Feud*—Dolf has a heart attack. Ironically, the same ambulance that takes Dolf to the hospital carries Bud to the mental ward immediately afterward. As readers of *Who Is Teddy Villanova?* (1977) are aware, Berger delights in devising such coincidences; thus, it turns out that Dolf's son Tony had fought Walt's son the year before.

The Feud quickly develops into what Tony—borrowing from his more literary younger brother, Jack—calls a comedy of errors. Tony knocks out Clive Shell, the Millville police chief, for insulting his mother. Junior Bullard, who believes that he is ultimately to blame for the fire that destroyed his father's store, impulsively robs a lunch counter with Rev's gun and is arrested. Rev surprises Bernice Beeler and fireman Ernie Krum having sex in the backseat of a car and, defenseless without his gun, is beaten up. Sexually aroused by this battle, Bernice and Ernie engage in "marathon back-seat lovemaking," after which they run away to be married. (Bernice fears that she is pregnant and is looking for a father for her child.) Meanwhile, Tony also finds himself carried away by passion and asks Eva to run away with him to Canada to be married: "he had no intention of doing anything illicit to Eva until they were married." Their elopement ends abruptly, however, when he discovers that the girl is more concerned with doughnuts than with him and that nothing about her is interesting except her breasts.

By a strange twist of circumstances, Rev finally becomes a real, if temporary, policeman. Given a chance to prove himself, this lifelong bully and misanthrope dies a hero after killing notorious bank robber Reno Fox in a shoot-out. Around the same time, Dolf dies in the hospital of a second heart attack, and the feud is over, but Berger's coincidences, ironies, and slapstick humor continue for forty more pages.

Despite all the violence and death, *The Feud* is a surprisingly lighthearted, charming novel primarily because Berger so obviously enjoys what he is doing, and because he refuses to condescend or sentimentalize his characters. Like so many Berger creations, especially Jack Crabb in *Little Big Man* (1964), they are both victims and victimizers, searching, usually blindly and ineptly, for freedom and self-respect.

In particular, Bernice and Rev are masterful comic characters. Bernice, with her "famous cocky but not snotty grin," is the most innocent of sluts, the most undevious of manipulators. She is refreshingly unapologetic about her nymphomania: "As the saying went, it was good for the complexion." She feels that men "were all liars and cheats and had a yellow streak up their back, and if they ever had a feeling that wasn't purely selfish, she had never detected it." This view seems to change when she meets the sensitive Ernie, yet when she discovers that her pregnancy has been a false alarm, she runs off to the bright lights of the big city. She writes her mother, "Think I can get an anulment [sic] since we weren't intimate."

Rev is not merely a loudmouthed bully; he spends much of his free time in the public library engaged in scholarly research into such subjects as "the extraction of gold from seawater, Asiatic techniques for training the will, magnetism, and the Pope's secret plan to introduce into the non-Catholic areas of the world an army of secret agents whose mission it was to poison the public reservoirs." He is also a man of principles; these range from *"Don't let anybody get away with anything without calling him on it"* to *"Worship the Lord, but never trust a preacher any farther than you can throw him."* The ironically named Rev is in the tradition of such comic villains as William Faulkner's Flem Snopes.

Berger described *Neighbors* (1980) as "absolutely pure fiction . . . with no taint of journalism, sociology, and the other corruptions." The same is true of *The Feud*. Although it is set in small-town America in the 1930's, Berger is not interested in recapturing or explaining this time and place but simply uses them to fulfill his novelistic purposes.

These purposes, according to Berger, include exploring language as "a morality and a politics and a religion." That exploration in *The Feud* involves writing in a style simpler than that of any of his previous novels—some readers may miss his ornate sentences—and his Mark Twain-like celebration of the American vernacular (with whom he is often compared). The matter-of-fact style intensifies the impact of the narrative's wonderful absurdities. Berger frequently employs dialect—*genmum, champeenship, Sairdy, sumbitch*—but not so often as to be irritatingly cute. More important is the use of clichés: "I think that one was supposed to have my name on it"; "That's just between you, me, and the gatepost"; "The rest is in the hands of the Guy Upstairs"; "Maybe he'll have to go on the lam for a while till this blows over"; "You oughta thank your lucky stars you get good fresh eggs to eat, with all the starving people in China." Such statements are not clichés to those who use them but ways of ordering their chaotic universe. There is also the pleasure Berger takes in occasional linguistic self-indulgence, as when Rev comes upon Bernice and Ernie: "You think you can come up here where innocent women and children are living and corpulate like unto animals of the field, make a spectacle of yourself, hold up to mockery all the principles of God-fearing men, roll in slime and throw it in our face? I'd like to see you both kestrated."

Despite Berger's claim that he is not interested in plot, character, and theme, all of these, in addition to language, are important in *The Feud*. The novel is a comic examination of—one might even say tribute to—contemporary paranoia.

Michael Adams

Sources for Further Study

Library Journal. CVIII, April 1, 1983, p. 756.
Los Angeles Times Book Review. May 15, 1983, p. 1.
Nation. CCXXXVI, June 11, 1983, p. 741.
The New Republic. CLXXXVIII, May 23, 1983, p. 39.
The New York Times Book Review. May 8, 1983, p. 1.
The New Yorker. LIX, May 23, 1983, p. 120.
Newsweek. CI, May 23, 1983, p. 77.
Publishers Weekly. CCXXIII, March 18, 1983, p. 53.
Time. CXXI, May 23, 1983, p. 78.

FIRST LIGHT

Author: David Wagoner (1926-   )
Publisher: Little, Brown and Company (Boston). 114 pp. $14.45; paperback $7.95
Type of work: Poetry

Eighty-seven poems that demonstrate David Wagoner's mastery of his craft and his extraordinary range of feeling and subject matter

David Wagoner is a major American poet: That recognition has been growing steadily among fellow poets and critics over the past three decades, during which Wagoner has published twelve volumes of poetry. *First Light* is the thirteenth and, to date, the finest in a most impressive series. Everywhere throughout this volume Wagoner demonstrates the sharpness of his eye and his mind and the depth and strength of his feeling for the terrors and beauties of the world. *First Light* is a very generous gathering of poems, not only in number (eighty-seven poems, with new pieces beginning on the same pages where the preceding ones end) but also in the range of poetic forms and strategies, tonalities, and topics purveyed by the poet.

The range, indeed, is extraordinary. Wagoner is a virtuoso. His subjects range from family history ("The Bad Uncle") to national myth ("The Author of *American Ornithology* Sketches a Bird, Now Extinct"), from fairy tales in sardonic retellings ("Jack and the Beanstalk") to almost archetypal encounters with wilderness terrain ("Backtracking"), from exacting observation of animals ("Loons Mating"), of people ("A Woman Standing in the Surf"), and of both ("To a Farmer Who Hung Five Hawks on His Barbed Wire") to metaphysical conundrums in a lofty strain ("Walking into the Wind"). His forms are no less various: Though most of Wagoner's poems do not rhyme, a few do, including a modified villanelle ("Canticle for Xmas Eve"), a poem that uses near-rhyme impressively ("Danse Macabre," in which, for example, "elbow" rhymes with "meadow," "hoarfrost" with "harvest," and "borrowed" with "buried"), and a poem ("Stump Speech") that builds incrementally like "The House That Jack Built" through a series of rhymed couplets:

> And this is the stump I stand beside,
> Once tall, now short as the day it died
> And gray as driftwood, its heartwood eaten
> By years of weather, its xylem rotten
> And only able to hold the rain
> One cold inch (roots withered and gone)
> In a shallow basin, a cracked urn
> Whose cambium and phloem now learn
> To carry nothing down to the dark
> Inside the broken shell of the bark
> But a dream of a tree forever dead.
>
> And this is the speech that grew instead.

As for the prevalent unrhymed poems, they come in all shapes and sizes, long poems and short poems, long-lined and short-lined poems, poems that mix long and short lines, and poems in triplets, in quatrains, in five-line stanzas, and in long verse paragraphs.

Wagoner's poetry is quintessentially in the American grain. In many of his earlier poems, his persona was a sort of Emersonian man in quest of a right relation to the natural order around him. These poems might be classed in the broad field of metaphysical poetry about nature and terrain that runs as a central line through the American tradition from William Cullen Bryant, Henry David Thoreau, Ralph Waldo Emerson, Walt Whitman, and Emily Dickinson through Wallace Stevens, Robert Frost, Robinson Jeffers, Theodore Roethke, and A. R. Ammons. The opening stanza of "The Words," the first poem in Wagoner's 1966 collection *Staying Alive*, might be taken as a keynote of this aspect of his poetry:

> Wind, bird, and tree,
> Water, grass, and light:
> In half of what I write
> Roughly or smoothly
> Year by impatient year,
> The same six words recur.

Wagoner's poetry of nature, however, is almost always more richly variegated in its verbal texture than this lovely stanza might suggest. One of the seven sections of *First Light*, titled "The Land Behind the Wind," a sequence of poems about wilderness experience that draws largely, as Wagoner has done in the past, on native American lore, typifies this continuing strain in his work. One observes, for example, that only one of the six words appears in the third poem in the sequence, "Their Shelter," and that that word "wind" by no means strikes the dominant note. Witness the last two stanzas of the poem:

> The tree was their house, its trunk their lodgepole,
> A single wall spreading its pungent needles
> To waver over their half-sleep, their rooftree
> With down-swept rafters whispering
> As high as they could hear and far underground.
>
> It spoke all night to them out of the earth,
> Out of the sky. It said *the rain*, said *wind*,
> Said *snow and ice*, said *deep* and *here*. Their hearts
> Were drumming against the night like the wings of grouse.
> Their only fire was their hearts against the night.

Wagoner's materials here are American, his mythos is American, and so is his poetic. Indeed, the Frostian cadence of Wagoner's verse is sometimes unmistakable, as in the lines from "Stump Speech" and "The Words" quoted above.

Another American element that has always been part of Wagoner's poetic (again belying the monotony he seems to attribute to himself in "The Words") is his use of a kind of hard-boiled, clipped American speech, reminiscent of the dialogue of 1930's B pictures but raised to a pitch of intensity that becomes poetic, much like the practically transcendent use of the same kind of language in William Kennedy's Albany novels, *Legs* (1975), *Billy Phelan's Greatest Game* (1978), and *Ironweed* (1983). A poem in *Staying Alive*, "The Shooting of John Dillinger Outside the Biograph Theater, July 22, 1934," could practically be a blueprint in its diction, tone, and overall mythic thrust for Kennedy's *Legs*, as in these Wagoner lines about Dillinger: "Was Johnny a four-flusher?/ No, not if he knew the game. He got it up or got it back./ But he liked to take snapshots of policemen with his own Kodak,/ And once in a while he liked to take them with an automatic." In *First Light*, this sort of diction runs in and out of the fabric of the poems, least of all in the meditative nature pieces, most insistently in three juxtaposed poems about derelicts and drunks, "In the Booking Room," "Breath Test," and "The Rules," but also in some of the poems about family history—in, for example, "The Shocking Machine" ("Oh boy, the big idea/ Was to find the dumb ones/ Daring enough to hang/ On hard, and then you pushed/ The switch and rang their doorbells!").

Another very American element in Wagoner's work, related perhaps to the slangy, hard-boiled diction of some of his poems, is a recurrent impulse to debunk, a penchant for the sardonic and even for the cynical that balances (though it does not undermine or deconstruct) the often reverential, affirmative themes of the poems about wilderness and about love. This angry and at least partially satiric strain is found in some of the poems about the misuse and despoiling of nature—in, for example, the fine poem "The Author of *American Ornithology* Sketches a Bird, Now Extinct" and in "A Remarkable Exhibition" (about "eight gentleman hunters in tweeds and gaiters" blasting away at a single loon). The fairy tales ("Medusa's Lover," "Pandora's Dream," "Sleeping Beauty," and "Jack and the Beanstalk") are retold with kindred sardonic twists. One is reminded, in the relentless, antisentimental, disillusioned vision of such poems, of the hard-as-nails Robert Frost of "Provide, Provide."

Wagoner may strike some readers as an old-fashioned poet. He writes with a conviction that words may be made to refer reliably to real objects, real experiences, and profound feelings. He writes poems of presence, not of absence, and they are about staying alive in a recognizable world (and collaterally about the enduring power and importance of poetry). A few readers may find Wagoner's organization of *First Light* into seven thematically unified sections to be sadly antique, though most should rejoice in the clarity and coherence thus conferred on the volume. Section 1 presents eight poems about the poet's youth, his parents, and time (and lives) past; section 2, seventeen poems about the terror, beauty, instinctual rightness, and nonhuman otherness of the world of animals; section 3, sixteen poems unified by the recurrence of the sardonic, bitter, satirical voice just discussed; section 4, fourteen poems of precise observation (such as "The Water Lily," "The Flower," and "The Caterpillar") in another, as-yet-unmentioned American tradition, William Carlos Williams' legacy of "no ideas but in things"; section 5, the nine poems of "The Land Behind the Wind" (the only titled section of *First Light*); section 6, thirteen poems of finely concrete description that become allegories or moralized landscapes bearing on Wagoner's central themes of staying alive and of doing so through poetry; and section 7, ten poems about a love between a man and a woman upheld by an organic view of human wholeness with other humans and with nature and consecrated by its commemoration in verse.

Above all, the poet of *First Light* celebrates poetry as the vital foundation of freedom and of love. The very first poem in the volume, "The Truant Officer's Helper," relates how the poet's impulse to imaginative writing originated in his secret sympathy for hooky-playing boys that he watched his truant-officer grandfather round up:

> That night in a shed loft
> I flew with a featherbed
> By lamplight, writing my first
> Short story full of lies
> About a secret country
> And a boy who disobeyed
> And ran away in a dream.
> I tried hard to be good
> And smart and made it up
> Out of my own head
> On that stolen paper,
> My stolen pencil trembling.

The very last poem, the title piece, comes back to a dream of song, a dream shared by the speaker and his lover:

> I see you wake, not moving
> More than your eyelids
> To listen, still half-held
> By your dream, which was also mine
> Between the owl and the wren:
> That we'd learned how to fly
> And sing by dark, by daylight.
>
> You see my eyes have opened
> With yours. Each of us turns

> To the other, arms outstretched,
> Then closed, both newly fledged
> But as wing-sure at wakening
> As owl-flight or wren-flight
> And as song-struck as this dawn.

Throughout the remarkably fine length and breadth of *First Light*, it is clear that David Wagoner is a poet who has eyes constantly open to the world and the poetic skill and power to keep our eyes open with his.

Daniel Mark Fogel

Sources for Further Study

Booklist. LXXX, September 1, 1983, p. 23.
The New York Times Book Review. LXXXIX, January 22, 1984, p. 12.
Publishers Weekly. CCXXIV, August 12, 1983, p. 62.

THE FIRST MAN ON THE SUN

Author: R. H. W. Dillard (1937-   )
Publisher: Louisiana State University Press (Baton Rouge). 287 pp. $19.95;
   paperback $8.95
Type of work: Novel
Time: February, 1977-February, 1978, and an indefinite time in the future
Locale: The Roanoke-Dublin area of west central Virginia

A "post-Einsteinian novel" which combines space fantasy with the author's day-to-day meditations, making the transcendentalist point that man is one with his world

Principal characters:
> THE UNNAMED NARRATOR (R. H. W. DILLARD), one who ponders
>   his world and himself, using a journal to record his observations
> SEAN SIOBHAN, a poet, solarnaut, and the author's alter ego
> FLANN "BLACKIE" O'FLYNN, a man ruled by his sexual appetite
> PEGEEN O'ROURKE, the woman loved by Sean Siobhan and Flann
>   O'Flynn in their various ways
> XHAVID SHEHU, an Albanian exile

Only toward the end of *The First Man on the Sun* does the reader learn the genesis of the joke from which Richard Dillard's odd and interesting second novel has sprouted. It is an ethnic joke told one summer day by the author's English friend David about a Russian, an American, and an Irishman. The first toasts his native Russia, which put the first man in space; the second the United States, which put the first man on the moon and the third Ireland, "who'll put the first man on the sun!" When the others protest that it cannot be done, the heat being too great, the Irishman replies, "Do you think we're stupid? We're sending him at night!" From such seemingly unpromising material, Dillard has woven his own 180-page shaggy-dog story in which a secret and largely Irish group headquartered in Dublin (Virginia, that is; just down the road from the author's own Roanoke) prepare and launch a peat-powered spaceship, the *Wandering Aengus*, manned by three solarnauts who, protected by bonded slices of Irish potato, do manage to survive the incredible heat and land on the sun's surface, which they discover (or perhaps only dream), is covered with talking trees borrowed from one of Robert Louis Stevenson's *Fables* (1896).

If this sounds exactly like the kind of novel one ought to expect from the author of the original screenplay, *Frankenstein Meets the Space Monster* (1965), there is good reason. Dillard's story is very funny and very absurd—as funny and absurd as its character Xhavid Shehu, the thirty-year-old commander of all six of Albania's submarines who had them stolen by a Russian agent; that Shehu falls into a Rumpelstiltskin-like rage whenever he is reminded of his disgrace only confirms the reader's image of him as a cartoon character or perhaps a straight man in a Marx Brothers film. Just as this slapstick Albanian becomes something of a tragic figure, however, his life darkened by the murder of his young bride, so too does the larger story become similarly complex and multifaceted. It is clearly a fantasy, as Ursula K. Le Guin has defined the term—that is, "an alternative technique for apprehending and coping with existence."

In part, Dillard's story concerns the ways in which ones life is shaped by that vast ethnic joke known as international politics. As the major and minor powers bicker and bite, Dublin sends its solarnauts to the very center of the solar system, not to claim it for Ireland but to discover how to influence sunspot activity for the benefit of all mankind. It is not only the nations of the world divided among themselves, however, but also individuals, and this is the reason so much of Dillard's space fantasy takes the form of a love story—the wooing of Pegeen O'Rourke by her two very different lovers, Flann "Blackie" O'Flynn and Sean Siobhan. Blackie is, as his name suggests, something of a blackguard, willing to betray Pegeen as he also betrays his countrymen's greatest (and funniest) dream, of putting a man on the sun. It is not really Pegeen that he loves but sex, which is "his one true joy, his only joy," "the very thing above all things in the world, in the very cosmos, he values most." His love is lyric, to a degree, but it is also limited and very definitely untranscendent. He is earthbound: man as mere matter. Sean is everything Blackie is not: poet, dreamer, lover of Pegeen, world, and spirit. Unlike Blackie, who puts the hapless Shehu, clubbed unconscious, in his place aboard the *Wandering Aengus*, Sean is a willing explorer and a solarnaut in a double sense: not only one who travels *to* the sun but also a creature *of* the sun. He is associated with light, space, and the expansive spirit, whereas Blackie is associated with darkness, rooms, and chairs, with all forms of human limitation.

The brief joke that gives rise to the futuristic yet oddly old-fashioned Dublin (Virginia) fantasy, which includes a variety of substories (love, political intrigue, space travel, and even forty-six pages of selected poems from Sean's book, *Confessions of an Irish Solarnaut*), form only a part of Dillard's inventive "post-Einsteinian novel." As defined by the author, the "post-Einsteinian novel" is "concerned with events rather than characters in the usual sense" and is "composed of small, apparently discrete particles or fragments," and at first glance, *The First Man on the Sun* certainly does appear fragmented. There is a seven-page list of quotations from Dante to Leigh Brackett that recalls the "Extracts" opening of Herman Melville's *Moby Dick: Or, The Whale* (1851); the Dublin story interwoven with entries from the author's journal (or chapters in the form of journal entries); the confusion of verb tenses, the future-tense fantasy ("They will be in an Owl Bar") and the present-tense journal entries; the incongruity of a space fantasy peopled by the likes of such traditional Irish (literary) types as Deidre O'Sohr (John Milton Synge's Deidre of the Sorrows), Flann O'Flynn (Flann O'Brien, author of that wild Irish novel, *At Swim Two Birds*, 1939), Seamus Heanus (the contemporary Irish poet Seamus Heaney), and the mayor's erotic daughter Mollie Mulligan (James Joyce's Mollie Bloom and Buck Mulligan); the variety of styles, such as the Nabokovian chapter "Getting Off," replete with footnotes, that follows the news of Vladimir Nabokov's death in the previous journal-entry chapter; the inclusion of such seemingly extraneous material as the complete box scores from two baseball games between the Salem Pirates and the Winston-Salem Red Sox played on August 27 and 28, 1977; and finally the discrepancy among such matter-of-fact details as baseball scores and the quotations and theories drawn from a multitude of writers and scientists from Amos Bronson Alcott to Harold J. Morowitz and Saints Mark and Paul.

This is clearly literary gamesmanship, but Dillard does not play the game merely for its own sake. Although one might expect the sheer variety of styles, subjects, and narrative lines to have a disruptive effect on the reader, there is nothing arbitrary or even distinctly postmodern about Dillard's method of juxtaposition. Not only do places, events, and people from Dillard's real-life journal appear in the Dublin fantasy, in effect creating bridges between the two narratives, but also the seemingly discrete stories form a seamless whole—or, because this is a "post-Einsteinian novel" and therefore under the rule of relativity, they form various wholes depending on the point of view from which they are observed. For example, the fantasy that adds up to two-thirds of the novel's complete length can also be said to form only one-third of the entire work in terms of the total number of chapters (every two chapters of journal are followed by one chapter of space fantasy). The seemingly distinct strands of Dillard's novel combine and merge and even reverse themselves as the one documents the unreality of the real world, and the other follows "the rational absurdity of a good dream."

The First Man on the Sun, the journal chapters in particular, recall Henry David Thoreau's *Walden: Or, Life in the Woods* (1854), a book in which Thoreau set out to answer the question of how he should live his life. Dillard asks the same question in a slightly different way: How can he *see* the life he is living? Like Thoreau, Dillard is torn between the two sides of his human nature, which are as well the two sides of his world: the sensual (Blackie O'Flynn and Thoreau's woodchuck) and the spiritual (the sun and Thoreau's "higher laws"). "We yearn to look directly on the sun," Dillard writes, "to see its face, its rough or smooth. The squints of our eyes stay on the ground. We see what is around us, and suddenly that is enough," to which he adds this significant postscript: "For now." When "what is around us" is not "enough," the transcendentalist turns to higher things. Others are less fortunate; for them the world is all in all, at once too little and too much, a whirling chaos in which the individual has lost his place in the order (now perceived as disorder) of things and succumbs to "the reductionist trap that defines you as an accidental collection of random, cast somehow into motion but running down, down into the ground."

Meditating on the 344th anniversary of Galileo's recantation, Dillard realizes "How easy it is to recant, under pressure to cast aside what we have seen and what we have heard, to bend to the force of entropy, to run down and allow yourself to be run down"—that is, to run down as a machine does but also to "run down" in two other senses: to be run down by a machine, an automobile, for example, meaning to be run down by a mechanistic theory of the universe; and also to demean oneself, to think of oneself as a lesser person. Entropy is but another name for death, as Henry Adams understood so well; to accept entropy, Dillard implies, is to accept death, to recant one's faith in life. Against this recantation, Dillard posits the life-process itself; this is why he begins his book on the 413th anniversary of Galileo's *birth* and ends it exactly one year later, on the 414th. The structure of the novel effectively moves from birth through recantation and death to birth again. The process continues; the system does not run down.

Dillard, in the role of narrator, follows a similar pattern, his moods keyed not only to the cycle of Galileo's life but also to changes in the weather and the seasons. The discovery of patterns and parallels in nature and man, of orders within orders, like the orbits of planets revolving around the sun, is one of the most compelling aspects of this novel. It affirms, updates, and reinforces the point made by Ralph Waldo Emerson in his essay "Circles": "The eye is the first circle; the horizon which it forms is the second; and throughout nature this primary figure is repeated without end. It is the highest emblem of the cipher of the world." Emerson went on to cite Saint Augustine's description of the nature of God "as a circle whose centre was everywhere and its circumference nowhere." For Emerson and for Dillard, that center is the individual man, whom Dillard imagines as a sun around which friends and lovers, and events and places revolve, held in place by the sun's gravitational field, the still point around which the rest of the universe whirls in orderly fashion. In such a world, there are connections and Emersonian correspondences but no truly random events. In such a world, Werner Karl Heisenberg's uncertainty principle is supplanted by the law of gravity—not the old law of Isaac Newton but the new law of the Grand Unification Theory—which applies to apples, planets, and human relationships equally well.

There is much to admire in *The First Man on the Sun*, though not quite enough to outweigh completely certain stylistic weaknesses. Dillard's prose, like his poetry, is lyrical and meditative, learned as well as playful. By avoiding subordination and using instead conjunctive phrases and clauses, parallel constructions, and Whitmanesque catalogs, Dillard forces the reader to make for himself those connections between seemingly disjunctive elements upon which he bases his vision as well as his aesthetic. The writing is very clear, very precise, very sure but all too often stiff and inert, unequal to the task of making the author's transcendental ideas come alive in the reader's mind. At such moments, the prose degenerates into poetic cliché ("The March lion stirs in his chamber, and everything darts away in terror") or, worse, what one reviewer has all too aptly termed "glutinous pastoral," which reads a good deal like either self-parody or some of the less restrained writing of the author's former wife, the essayist Annie Dillard. More characteristic are those passages in which Dillard appears to have drained the ideas of Emerson, Thoreau, and Walt Whitman of all of their freshness and vigor: "Silent and empty, the day filled with snow . . . ribs and twigs, sticks and hieroglyphs, tracks across the day. That is, of course, the point of days, the point I always seem to forget, that they surprise you. A February day, and it is cold and snowing, Oliver is asleep, and I am puzzled and surprised." The problem is that the reader is neither puzzled nor surprised; the reader is only bored and impatient with an author who seems to have little to say and who says it often and at length. "Many things are not worth doing, but almost anything is worth telling," quotes Dillard in his prefatory "list," to which he might have added that anything worth telling is worth telling *well*. The syrupy rehash of stale ideas is writing, to be sure, but it is far removed from those passages in which Dillard uses his metaphoric imagination to fuse together the cosmic and the quotidian dimensions of life, the poetic and the prosaic. "Like the planets and stars, we do our slow dance, too, circle and bow, touch and part, bid our partners adieu, circle and sway, and touch again" is but one example of Dillard writing well. More of the same would have been appreciated.

Robert A. Morace

Sources for Further Study

Best Sellers. XLIII, September, 1983, p. 198.
Choice. XXI, November, 1983, p. 420.
Kirkus Reviews. LI, March 15, 1983, p. 320.
Library Journal. CVIII, March 15, 1983, p. 600.
Los Angeles Times Book Review. August 21, 1983, p. 11.
Publishers Weekly. CCXXIII, March 25, 1983, p. 46.
Virginia Quarterly Review. LX, Spring, 1984, p. 54.

THE FORTIES
From Notebooks and Diaries of the Period

Author: Edmund Wilson (1895-1972)
Edited, with an introduction, by Leon Edel
Publisher: Farrar, Straus and Giroux (New York). 369 pp. $17.95
Type of work: Journals and diaries
Time: The 1940's
Locale: Various locations in the United States; also Italy, especially Milan and
  Rome; London, England; Greece; and Haiti

In this collection of notebooks and journals from the 1940's, skillfully edited by Leon Edel, Edmund Wilson not only records his experiences during travels throughout several places in the United States and abroad but also confronts mid-life-cycle events that further develop his intellectual and moral growth

Readers familiar with Edmund Wilson's *The Twenties* (1975) and *The Thirties* (1980) are aware that this recent publication is not intended to chronicle the social history of the 1940's. Rather, the volume comprises notebooks, some polished and others rather fragmentary, that Wilson kept for his own use. To be sure, the author recognized the high literary quality of his notebooks and appreciated as well their potential value for eventual publication. Their primary purpose for him, however, was to record impressions, facts, and autobiographical memoranda that might later be incorporated in various projects that he was considering. Some of the journals (or diaries) were quite complete, although all were written rapidly and without revisions; some were incomplete.

Before his death, Wilson prepared and partially edited transcripts of the journals which covered the two earlier decades. From these transcripts, Leon Edel skillfully reedited material and provided useful introductions. In editing *The Forties*, however, Edel had to examine the notebooks of that decade without the benefit of the author's help; the volume, he writes, ". . . is a wholly posthumous book and lacks the retrospective passages Wilson would have written had he been able to put it together." Nevertheless, *The Forties*, like the previous two volumes, is an extremely important work, helpful to social historians and scholars of literature, above all to readers interested in the ideas and impressions of perhaps the most influential of American critics writing between the two world wars.

Wilson's notebooks from this decade cover a wide variety of subjects. From 1940 to 1945, he composed fourteen journals, which Edel has compiled mostly from loose pages and sporadic entries on the back covers of his notebooks. From 1946 to 1949, Wilson composed sixteen journals (the last, "Haiti, 1949," Edel assembled "from almost illegible scrawled notes—put down on the spot in a kind of semi-shorthand, like a reporter's notes"). Usually, however, Wilson "clear-copied" notes like these into his journals. Indeed, a few sections of the volume once existed in typed form. In several notebooks, Wilson treats ideas for books that he was presently writing or planning to write: "Notes for *The Wound and the Bow*" and "Notes for a Novel." Other journals are true diaries, treating such topics as "Thoughts, 1943-1944" or "London, 1945." In several journals he records primarily his impressions of place fixed at the moment: "Italy, 1945," "Trip to Milan," "Rome," "Greece," and so on. Other journals detail his meetings with distinguished personages or friends: "Visit to Santayana," "Katy Dos Passos," and "Visit to Edna Millay." Still others are set pieces, notes designed for later inclusion in articles or books, such as "Trip to Zuñi." Many of the journals did, in fact, serve as material for fuller development. The European notes, for example, were revised in the preparation of *Europe Without Baedeker* (1947), and the account of the Zuñi was amplified for *Red, Black, Blond and Olive* (1956).

For Wilson, the 1940's were a time of reassessment. Edel suggests that when Wilson turned forty-five, at the end of 1940, he "suddenly found himself reckoning with his mortality." Edel's splendid introductory essay, "Edmund Wilson in Middle Age," charts for the reader the high and low points of this "reckoning." The essay is particularly illuminating because a reader might not—without Edel's help—detect in the journals certain signs of the writer's internal conflicts. As readers of *The Twenties* and *The Thirties* are already aware, Wilson was not a diarist to wear his heart on his sleeve. His journals are subjective and impressionistic, to be sure, but rarely introspective. Indeed, although Wilson effectively employed depth psychology in his criticism, he generally avoided any serious investigation of his own motives. Either he felt no need, in recording impressions for his journals, to examine closely these motives, or (curious to say) he was incapable of turning upon himself the same searching light that he had directed toward his literary subjects—then most recently in *The Wound and the Bow* (1941). At any rate, the journals lack a dimension of self-realization that is all the more surprising from a writer of Wilson's acumen.

Four other surprises—or disappointments—await readers of *The Forties*. Wilson reveals almost nothing about his personal life with Mary McCarthy, his third wife, nor does he discuss events leading up to their divorce in 1946. Readers will also be disappointed to learn that Wilson neglects to discuss in detail the writing, reception, or the impact upon his later life of *Memoirs of Hecate County* (1946), his most controversial (and financially rewarding) publication. Similarly, he speaks only briefly about his literary acquaintances. With the exception of the brilliant and touching journal "Visit to Edna Millay" (which is anecdotal rather than critical), he treats major literary personalities only in passing. Literary historians interested in Wilson's private opinions about notables are bound to be disappointed. To be sure, he mentions, usually in a trivial context, such writers as John Peale Bishop (who died in 1944), Louise Bogan, Ernest Hemingway, and Evelyn Waugh, but only two notables, the philosopher George Santayana and Wilson's longtime friend John Dos Passos, are discussed at some length—and even these journal entries treat the writers as personalities rather than artists. Finally, some readers are bound to be disappointed by Wilson's indifference to political-historical events of the 1940's. A great social historian (as *To the Finland Station*, 1940, amply demonstrates), Wilson paid scant attention—at least in his journals—to history shaping itself during World War II. Although he was not, strictly speaking, a pacifist, he was more deeply concerned with the impact of the war upon people than with formulating theories about the socioeconomic basis for that war. In the journals he is, indeed, a disinterested observer (not without compassion for human suffering nor anger at the crass stupidity of war), rather than an activist or propagandist.

To understand reasons for the writer's conspicuous omissions (or selective examples of reticence) in his choice of subjects, the reader should keep in mind the fact that Wilson had never intended his journals to serve as an intimate diary—such as that of Anaïs Nin or of Simone de Beauvoir. Instead, the journals were written to jog his memory for details later to be included in fully developed works, to record amusing or revealing anecdotes, and to serve as literary practice to hone sharply his powers of observation and fluent composition. Moreover, a reader should understand that Wilson was not a writer inclined to share his deepest secrets with certain scholars who would later examine his notebooks. Hence, he keeps his silence on Mary McCarthy and chooses not to gratify a casual reader's curiosity about *Memoirs of Hecate County*. Finally, a reader should keep in mind the fact that Wilson had a keen sense of his permanent value as a literary chronicler. Whatever private feelings he had about his friend F. Scott Fitzgerald (to cite one example) would appear in public form in Fitzgerald's remarkable *The Crack-Up* (1945), planned as early as 1941—not as gossip composed in unguarded moments.

Despite these omissions, such as they are, *The Forties* is an extraordinarily vivid and entertaining book, a pleasure to the heart as well as the mind. Individual passages are composed with great literary pungency. Perhaps the most moving entries are those in the journal "Visit to Edna Millay," from August 6, 1948. Wilson describes the poet, now fading and fragile, her vitality and beauty alike drained by time. Wilson had once been her lover, had always admired her talents as poet and free-spirited revolutionary; now he perceives her—and himself—caught in a moment of time, both past their glory, Edna pitiful and he (the stronger) pitying. Another fine valedictory essay is the journal on Katy Dos Passos; Wilson writes with insight and rare affection about the doomed wife of his friend—as well as of Dos Passos' failing capabilities.

These elegiac passages contrast against those from other journals, many marked by sharp observations, wit, some sagacity and some foolishness, some profound judgments and a few absurdities. Nevertheless, after forty years, the whole mosaic of this book seems remarkably pertinent today. Wilson's notations, except those touching politics, are less dated than one might suppose. One reason for the vividness of the notebooks is their universal concerns. What Wilson lacks from the standpoint of strict historicity, he makes up in his feeling for humanity. His writing is generally precise, colorful, incisive. In such notebooks as "Trip to Zuñi," "Gull Pond, 1942," and "Wellfleet, 1947," he writes as an artist, with a poet's eye for sharp details, a novelist's eye for meaningful gestures. One cannot help but observe in "Trip to Zuñi," for example, Wilson's attempts to empathize with the Indians; instead of describing their dances as spectacles, he tries to feel the mysterious power of their rites, to become drawn into their ceremonies as a participant, not as a viewer. Nevertheless, with his free flow of imagination—a gift of the creative artist—is always the critic's restraining, measuring eye for precision. Wilson tries to get the Indian words precisely right—their spelling and their significance. He tries to sense rhythms, shapes, and colors as an Indian might, while at the same time recording details with a photographer's faithfulness to reality.

Still more impressive is Wilson's achievement in recording the nuances of his own temperament. Although reticent to examine his personality from the vantage of depth analysis, he takes a lively interest in his actions, is always on the lookout for meaningful and varied experiences. His courtship and marriage to Elena Mumm Thornton Wilson, his fourth wife, is recorded in lively (and fairly frank) passages. He is attracted to her elegance, her European graciousness, above all her submissiveness. After a (presumably) stormy marriage with Mary McCarthy, a strong personality whose career objectives as a novelist might have sometimes clashed with his own interests, Wilson settles with Elena into a routine, comfortable domestic life that he comes to cherish. The self-portrait that he offers in his journals is that of an unusually perceptive, clever, curious, and tolerant man; an intellectual attracted as much to life as to letters.

In describing his commerce with a London prostitute, Odette ("London, 1945"), he reveals a robust good humor and unaffected kindliness. He is eager to learn from everyone, to experience, to perceive. In a discussion with his friend Philip Hamburger on the Italian front ("Italy Again"), he learns for the first time about "American jelly bombs, the most formidable weapons yet invented, which could cut a way right through a jungle, so that the army could march through and burn people to a cinder in thirty seconds." The weapon was napalm—or an early formula of that bomb, as yet not called by its now-familiar name. In their uneasy discussion, Wilson writes: "Hamburger grinned at this, and I probably did too." Then he catches himself. His next sentence reveals much about the humanity of Edmund Wilson: "This is the *new sadism*, irresponsibility about human life." In *The Forties*, Wilson continues to record impressions that show, in the face of the tragic realities of that decade, a lively but measured, responsible attitude toward the values of human life.

Leslie B. Mittleman

Sources for Further Study

American Literature. LV, October, 1983, p. 494.
The Atlantic. CCLI, April, 1983, p. 126.
Book World. XVIII, April 17, 1983, p. 3.
Choice. XXI, October, 1983, p. 284.
Christian Science Monitor. June 24, 1983, p. B6.
Contemporary Review. CCXLIII, October, 1983, p. 218.
Kirkus Reviews. LI, March 1, 1983, p. 301.
Library Journal. CVIII, April 1, 1983, p. 737.
The New York Times Book Review. LXXXVIII, May 22, 1983, p. 1.
The New Yorker. LIX, May 23, 1983, p. 121.
Publishers Weekly. CCXXIII, February 25, 1983, p. 77.
Time. CXXI, May 2, 1983, p. 73.

FROM THE FIRST NINE
Poems, 1946-1976

Author: James Merrill (1926-   )
Publisher: Atheneum Publishers (New York). 362 pp. $20.00; paperback $10.95
Type of work: Poetry

A selection of 139 poems by a master who uses his brilliant technique to convey a wide range of crystal-clear perceptions and deeply felt understandings

When he was about eight, James Merrill opened a random book and read that the husband of a character named Alice was "in the library, sampling the port." From the perspective of nearly half a century later, he writes: "If samples were little squares of wallpaper or chintz, and ports were where ships dropped anchor, this hardly clarified the behavior of Alice's husband." Long after his governess had resolved the ambiguity of this particular phrase, Merrill recalls, the episode continued to haunt him: "Words weren't what they seemed. The mother tongue could inspire both fascination and distrust."

Learning thus that "the everyday sounds of English could mislead you by having more than one meaning," Merrill became acquainted with the volatile instability of the world. Things were not simple, set, and sure. The experience of the boy whose sense of language's fixity was swept from under his feet by this tiny epiphany became the dominant thrust of the poetry of the man, as change—of perspective or of actuality—holds sway.

Mutability was a major concern of Renaissance poets—"The Mutability Cantos" of Edmund Spenser's *The Faerie Queene* (1590, 1596) are among his best-known works—as was appropriate for a time when the extremely stable medieval world was rapidly being displaced by the widening horizons and multitude of new facts of the modern world. The changes Merrill writes about, however, are not so earthshaking. Until his recent trilogy, *The Changing Light at Sandover* (collected into one volume at the same time as his selection of poems from his first nine books was brought out by his longtime publishers, Atheneum), Merrill's concerns were on the human rather than the global scale. He dealt with the kinds of change that every human from the dawn of time has had to confront: loss of loved ones through death, loss of youth and vigor, loss of love, loss of dreams and innocence and ideals. Such themes constitute Merrill's persistent concerns, often giving his poetry a sense of melancholy and bittersweet. This is, however, no *fin de siècle* sadness, for a pronounced sense of humor also invigorates much of his work.

A master craftsman, Merrill knows very well how to convey the ceaseless change that is his recurring subject. One cannot do so in the casual free verse so prevalent today. Rather, there must be something to deviate from; hence, Merrill's reliance upon form. Just as his subjects are rooted to those of the Renaissance masters, so in fact are many of his forms, from sestina to sonnet—

forms which he manipulates with endless ingenuity. His sonnets would rarely be recognized as such by a casual reader of this volume. They may often be in lines shorter than the usual iambic pentameter (though Merrill is certainly no slouch with this meter, varying the sounds and rhythms of such lines with the subtlety and skill of John Milton or John Donne); enjambed lines are far more common than end-stopped ones; rhymes and rhyme schemes are seldom obvious.

"The Broken Home," which appeared previously in *Nights and Days* (1966), is actually a sonnet sequence, though not labeled as such. The seven fourteen-line sections are set off from one another by spacing, and each has its own focus and rhyme scheme, making a complete poem by itself, always reaching a strong conclusion with a rhymed couplet or a striking line or two in a closing tercet or sestet. Here, the juxtaposition of what are essentially individual poems to create a single longer poem (a method Merrill uses in many other poems in *From the First Nine*) conveys a clear and touching picture of the poet's relations with his parents.

The second sonnet of this sequence focuses on Merrill's father. The meter and the rhyme scheme are as regular as the most rigid poetaster could wish (if one accepts the use of consonance in two of the words in each quatrain), yet the poem steers clear of the singsong quality that modern users of traditional forms must consciously avoid. Merrill accomplishes this by prosaic, conversational diction ("time was money in those days"); by the use of consonance (and who would ever look at the page and see that *I* and *win* were meant to rhyme?); and, most important, by generally keeping the exactly rhyming words apart except when a particular effect is sought, as in the final couplet which responds to the speculation that the old man would take a new bride: "He could afford it. He was 'in his prime'/ At three score ten. But money was not time."

Thus, the reader discovers that the poem is actually about the death of Merrill's father, yet the true rhyme of this closing couplet inserts a wry comic touch with the clever inversion of the familiar aphoristic equation used earlier in the poem. Suggesting the death indirectly, Merrill avoids sentimentality. Thus, using rhyme, which today is more commonly associated with light verse and song lyrics than with serious poetry, he can have the best of both worlds— he can produce a shapely structure and use rhyme's current capacity for humor and yet simultaneously make a serious point, letting the rhyme contribute to the irony.

The reason for selecting the sonnet form—here, in other parts of "The Broken Home," and in several other poems throughout the volume—becomes clear: It allows considerable flexibility in effects. Merrill's employment of verse forms, whether drawn from the rich Anglo-American poetic tradition or created for his own use, offers him the advantage of myriad effects which can help him to convey and even to create his themes; though the usual free-verse writer might find such forms constraining, Merrill revels in them.

"Form's what affirms," Merrill writes in "The Thousand and Second Night," and although he puts these words in the mouth of a pompous literature professor whom he imagines to be explicating this very poem, the words can be used as a motto for Merrill's work as a whole. In its root meaning, the verb "affirm" means to make firm or strengthen: Form, after all, is structure and shape, and through his form Merrill gives shape to experience, so changeable and unpredictable. This does not mean that he molds everything into a frozen perfection—indeed, life and art wage a perpetual tug-of-war throughout his work—yet through the forms of art, he is able to get a handle on what might otherwise be chaos, to capture a sense of life and reality in art, which is the only form of permanence the human race can know.

Such a tug-of-war is present throughout "The Thousand and Second Night," one of Merrill's longest poems outside his mammoth trilogy. Written, according to Merrill, originally as "rather unrelated poems" until "an afternoon of patchwork saw them all stitched together," the poem opens in Istanbul, the city where East meets West. Once known as Byzantium, this ancient and seductive city served William Butler Yeats as a symbol for a world of perfect art and order. Yeats's "Sailing to Byzantium," in fact, is answered by a later Merrill poem, "Flying from Byzantium," a poem that takes the poet away from a lover and back home and yet also urges the continued embrace of life: "The point's to live, love,/ Not shake your fist at the feast." Yeats's desire to escape from the life of change into the immortality of art is not for Merrill.

Indeed, the effect of Byzantium's modern counterpart on Merrill is literally paralyzing: "The whole right half/ Of my face refuses to move." After assorted peregrinations—to Hagia Sophia, a Turkish bath as cure, recollections of friends and lovers of the past, his own home, and the classroom of the poetry-explicating professor noted above—the poem ends with four lovely, perfectly rhymed envelope-quatrains that convey the reader to the world which the title of the poem has suggested, that of the framing story for *The Thousand and One Nights* (c. 1450). Scheherazade has completed her thousand-and-one nights of engrossing storytelling, as she needed to do to save her life, and the Sultan who had originally threatened her has now become her slave. Each releases the other, and the Sultan at last reemerges into the real world, having relegated both Scheherazade and her tales to the world of the mind and its fantasies and dreams.

Dreams and fantasies and the power of the mind to create them (and of the pen to evoke them) represent the world of permanence, the world of art. From such exquisite early creations as "The Blue Eye" and "The Green Eye" (both of which themselves have undergone change from their 1946 version to this volume, as the reprinting of the original version of "The Blue Eye" at the back of the volume makes clear—changes for the sake of precision of both diction and sense) to the considerably longer, masterful meldings of sensory details, autobiographical experience, poetic form, and theme in the poems at the end of this volume such as "Yánnina," "Chimes for Yahya," "Lost in Translation," and "Clearing the Title," Merrill has shown his concern for the power of the mind to perceive reality and to shape reality. He refuses steadfastly to twist reality into utterly unrecognizable shapes. Though the balance of art and reality remains as tenuous as ever, he has declared a truce, and both are fully accepted in his world.

In the closing poem, "Clearing the Title," Merrill writes about leaving his "lucid icebound book of winter"—literally his Connecticut home, but figuratively a frozen notion of reality—for the tropic splendors of Key West, where his longtime lover David Jackson (the "DJ" of the poem's dedication) is about to purchase a house for them. He sees it as a mistake for them—"past fifty and behaving/ As if hope sprang eternal." In the course of the poem, however, Merrill is increasingly drawn to the vitality and glory of this new place, and at the end he writes, "tonight we trust no real/ Conclusions will be reached"—ostensibly about the purchase of the house, but suggestively about a static view of life. Like the balloons at the end of the poem, "juggled slowly by the changing light," Merrill's work may "float higher yet" in the sunset sky, reaching no real conclusions but affirming the multifarious richness and ever-changing faces of life itself.

Scott Giantvalley

Sources for Further Study

Antioch Review. XLI, Spring, 1983, p. 244.
Hudson Review. XXXVI, Winter, 1983, p. 731.
Los Angeles Times Book Review. February 13, 1983, p. 8.
The New York Review of Books. XXX, June 16, 1983, p. 41.
The New York Times Book Review. LXXXVIII, March 13, 1983, p. 6.
Newsweek. CI, February 28, 1983, p. 70.
Virginia Quarterly Review. LIX, Autumn, 1983, p. 135.
Yale Review. LXXIII, Autumn, 1983, p. R9.

F. SCOTT FITZGERALD

Author: André Le Vot (1921-   )
Translated from the French by William Byron
Publisher: Doubleday & Company (Garden City, New York). 393 pp. $19.95
Type of work: Literary biography
Time: 1896-1940
Locale: The United States, France, and Italy

The troubled life and career of a major American novelist

Principal personages:
F. SCOTT FITZGERALD, an American novelist
ZELDA SAYRE FITZGERALD, his wife
SCOTTIE FITZGERALD, their daughter
SHEILAH GRAHAM, Fitzgerald's mistress
EDWARD FITZGERALD, his father
FATHER SIGOURNEY FAY, Fitzgerald's adviser
CHRISTIAN GAUSS, a Princeton University professor
EDMUND WILSON and
JOHN PEALE BISHOP, Fitzgerald's Princeton classmates, later famous
    writers
MAXWELL PERKINS, his editor
HAROLD OBER, his agent
GERALD MURPHY, an American painter
ERNEST HEMINGWAY, an American novelist
JUDGE A. D. SAYRE, Zelda's father

Charming and obnoxious, success and failure, genius and hack, F. Scott Fitzgerald had one of the most compelling lives of all American writers. Fitzgerald's wife, Zelda, was diagnosed as schizophrenic, but her husband also had a dual nature as man and artist. He could be both a generous, compassionate friend and a self-destructive show-off, both a major talent who created two of the greatest American novels, *The Great Gatsby* (1925) and *Tender Is the Night* (1934), and a writer who turned out dozens of trite stories for slick magazines.

Thus, a problem facing any biographer is to strike the proper balance between Scott the drunk and Fitzgerald the artist, and André Le Vot does that well. Another problem is that this life has been frequently chronicled; Le Vot's is one of five major biographies of Fitzgerald, the others being Arthur Mizener's *The Far Side of Paradise* (1951), Andrew Turnbull's *Scott Fitzgerald* (1962), Matthew J. Bruccoli's *Some Sort of Epic Grandeur* (1981), and Scott Donaldson's *Fool for Love* (1983). There have also been Nancy Milford's highly regarded *Zelda* (1970) and three memoirs by Sheilah Graham, Fitzgerald's mistress during his last years. Le Vot, director of the Center for Research on Contemporary American Literature at the Sorbonne, is the leading Fitzgerald authority in Europe and worked on this biography for twenty years before its publication in France in 1979. Le Vot says that he is correcting "certain errors and gaps" in the accounts by Mizener and Turnbull, but Bruccoli's has become the most extensively researched, most complete Fitzgerald biography. While Le Vot's book, as translated by William Byron, is generally well written, none of the biographies are as stimulating as that by Turnbull, who presents Fitzgerald as a sort of Fitzgeraldian hero.

The virtues of Le Vot's study derive less from his presentation of the facts of Fitzgerald's life than from his interpretation of them. Le Vot provides extensive background concerning Fitzgerald's ancestors, the aristocratic Southern Keys and the mercantile Midwestern McQuillans, to help explain one of the splits in his subject: "These patrician forebears' moral heritage, reviewed and revised by a romantic imagination, can be summed up as an idealistic attitude contrasting with America's postwar materialism—the Southern aristocracy's traditional panache, inherited from the English Cavaliers and sharply different from the down-to-earth mercantilism of the Puritans' descendants." Fitzgerald is both "the thrifty Puritan who stores his harvest and thinks to prove his membership in the Elect with the marks of his success" and "the libertine cavalier who squanders his heritage and, knowing he is damned, perseveres in his folly."

Fitzgerald's role model in failure was his father, an unsuccessful traveling salesman who "saw himself as representing a higher order, raising his good manners and slightly restrained elegance to the status of rules of living." Fitzgerald initially sympathized with his father's view of himself but eventually turned against the man's weak ineffectuality. His dislike of his father may help explain why he devoted much of his adult life to breaking those "rules of living."

Edward Fitzgerald also caused his son to be "drawn toward men with more assertive personalities. . . . He assessed the personal weaknesses revealed in this search for strong men, this nostalgia for a missing paternal image, and remodeled himself accordingly." The first of these strong men was Father Sigourney Fay at the Newman School in Hackensack, New Jersey. Fay was both Fitzgerald's spiritual and intellectual adviser, making him aware of the cultural traditions of Catholicism: "The priest brought him comfort and hope, restored his confidence in his destiny, transposed his naive ambitions to a higher plane and gave him the feeling of belonging to an elite group that expected much of him." Fay was succeeded by Christian Gauss, professor of Romance languages at Princeton University, who impressed Fitzgerald "by his tranquil certainty that great writers were the salt of the earth." Other influences included Fitzgerald's Princeton classmates Edmund Wilson and John Peale Bishop, both later to become prominent writers; Maxwell Perkins, his editor at Charles Scribner's Sons, and Harold Ober, his agent, on both of whom he relied heavily, too heavily, for advances and loans; painter and expatriate Gerald Murphy; and, of course, Ernest Hemingway.

Le Vot sees the Fitzgerald-Hemingway relationship as being rather one-sided, with the younger writer more antagonist than friend. Fitzgerald helped Hemingway to advance his career, but Hemingway soon smugly saw himself as Fitzgerald's superior as man and writer: "once Hemingway was established, Fitzgerald seemed to become his whipping boy." The two were more alike than Hemingway wanted to believe, because each was inhibited by trying to live up to his early success. Le Vot strongly condemns Hemingway for being the only one of Fitzgerald's literary friends not to write something positive about him following his death.

The most important person in Fitzgerald's life, however, was a woman. Zelda Sayre inspired his art; Daisy Buchanan, Nicole Diver, and most of the other Fitzgerald heroines are based on Zelda. According to Le Vot, Fitzgerald became the first American writer since Henry James to show serious interest in "the American girl, to put her across as a model for his contemporaries, to show her no longer as a victim, but victorious, as bold as the Daisy Millers of the past, but successful, independent, invulnerable." Nevertheless, Fitzgerald created this "woman-idol" so well that she quickly developed into an easy formula for his magazine fiction, making him "advance man for the flapper." To pay the debts which the extravagant and impulsive Zelda helped to accumulate, he had to churn out slick stories when he should have been slowly and carefully constructing quality fiction: "He labored like a prisoner digging a tunnel under the wall."

Le Vot explains their attraction to each other: "Who better than Zelda could understand Scott's inordinate ambition to cash in richly on a romantic life-style? Who more indulgently than Scott could ignore Zelda's frivolity and her apparent flaws and see only her basic nature, her intense feeling for life, her perfect freedom of spirit and her disdain for whatever is not felt and experienced acutely?" The problem was that each failed or refused to see what the other really was: "Scott, dreaming, like Gatsby, of a king's daughter, fell in love with a shepherdess, and Zelda, awaiting the marvelous prince who would take her out of her ordinary world, gave herself to an impecunious cavalier who could build castles only in the air."

Zelda's drinking, adultery, suicide attempts, and madness drove Scott into like behavior, except for insanity, and away from his true art. When no one would buy his increasingly second-rate, dated stories, he turned to Hollywood to pay his bills, increased by the cost of psychiatric care for Zelda. Ironically, Fitzgerald seriously wanted to write good screenplays but was not given the opportunity.

F. Scott Fitzgerald is full of fascinating anecdotes from a troubled life. Because Fitzgerald was such a bad student at Princeton, one of his professors, later to become head of the English department, refused to believe that he wrote *The Great Gatsby*. In the army, Fitzgerald forced a conscientious objector at gunpoint to go through the regular training course. Told by a physician that his heavy drinking would kill him, Fitzgerald was given a small, measured glass that represented his daily limit. He left the doctor's office, visited a friend, told him the story, and repeatedly filled the glass with gin and drank it, carefully measuring the amount each time. He and Sheilah Graham went to Los Angeles bookstores to buy for her copies of his books but were unable to find any in stock. He stole Sheilah's silver fox jacket to give it to his daughter, Scottie, for Christmas. The bishop of Baltimore refused to allow him to be buried with his ancestors in Rockville because he considered Fitzgerald's novels immoral. (Scott and Zelda were moved to that Catholic cemetery in 1975.)

Such details, combined with Le Vot's insight into Fitzgerald's character and the clarity of his style, make this biography effective, but there are problems as well. Le Vot spends twenty-nine pages on a brilliant analysis of *The Great Gatsby*, focusing on Fitzgerald's use of color and music, but he offers only a few scattered sentences on the rest of the fiction, with absolutely no analysis of *Tender Is the Night*. Fitzgerald wrote a dozen or so excellent short stories, but Le Vot's reader has no way of knowing this.

Numerous other mistakes, contradictions, and gaps occur throughout the book. Le Vot says that no one would produce Fitzgerald's play *The Vegetable* (1923) and explains how bad it is; then suddenly the play is being staged. After saying that Scott and Zelda fell in love two months after they met and not at first sight as legend has it, Le Vot describes their first meeting: "the love born that evening was to become legendary in American literary lore." Many—but not all—American readers will question the statement that college football "no longer has the sacred status it once enjoyed on American campuses." Finally, what does Le Vot mean when he writes that in New York in June, 1935, Fitzgerald "spent a weekend with Mickey Mouse"?

Le Vot succeeds in capturing the sadness of an artist who died thinking of himself as a failure because his two best novels had not sold well. That, finally, may be Fitzgerald's greatest tragedy.

Michael Adams

Sources for Further Study

America. CXLIX, July 9, 1983, p. 36.
Christian Science Monitor. May 4, 1983, p. 9.
Library Journal. CVIII, April 1, 1983, p. 744.
Los Angeles Times Book Review. May 15, 1983, p. 2.
The New York Times Book Review. LXXXVIII, April 3, 1983, p. 8.
Publishers Weekly. CCXXIII, February 11, 1983, p. 60.
Saturday Review. IX, June, 1983, p. 58.

Virginia Quarterly Review. LX, Spring, 1984, p. 337.
Wilson Quarterly. VII, Winter, 1983, p. 143.
World Literature Today. LVIII, Spring, 1984, p. 273.

A GATHERING OF OLD MEN

Author: Ernest J. Gaines (1933-   )
Publisher: Alfred A. Knopf (New York). 214 pp. $13.95
Type of work: Novel
Time: The late 1970's
Locale: Bayonne County, Louisiana

Faulknerian in plot and thematic focus, this novel is a frequently brilliant, but ulti-mately flawed meditation on violence, Afro-American dignity, and the possibility for repudiating the stereotypes and paternalism of the Southern past

Principal characters:
CHARLES BIGGS, a black farmhand
CANDY MARSHALL, a member of a plantation-owning family
MATHU, the old black man who reared Candy
MAPES, a Southern sheriff
BEAU BOUTAN, a Cajun farmer and murder victim
GIL BOUTAN, his brother, a star fullback at Louisiana State University
WILLIAM "FIX" BOUTAN, the patriarch of the clan
LOUIS ALFRED "LOU DIMES" DIMOULIN, a white journalist and
  Candy's suitor
LUKE WILL, a poor white leader of vigilante action
ROBERT LOUIS STEVENSON "CHIMLEY" BANKS,
GRANT "CHERRY" BELLO,
ALBERT "ROOSTER" JACKSON, and about a dozen other old black
  men

A Gathering of Old Men marks the culmination of Ernest Gaines's long-standing literary debate with William Faulkner. Although he has set each of his five previous books in the Yoknapatawpha-like Bayonne (Louisiana) County, never before has Gaines so directly confronted his problematic white predecessor's vision of the Southern heritage. Insisting on a thorough repu-diation of the paternalistic tradition of the Old South, including the ostensibly benevolent aspects of that tradition, Gaines presents a brilliant critique of the limitations of Faulkner's understanding of Afro-American humanity. When Gaines departs from the emphasis on literary revision of the Southern past and attempts to portray the realistic complexities of the New South, however, A Gathering of Old Men flounders badly. Curiously, the failure derives pri-marily from Gaines's somewhat naïve and distinctly un-Faulknerian belief that the poor white community can be convinced to enter the New South without a direct confrontation with and physical expression of its violent past.
   Thematically and structurally, A Gathering of Old Men draws on several Faulkner novels, including The Sound and the Fury (1929), As I Lay Dying (1930), Absalom! Absalom! (1936), and Go Down, Moses (1942). Its primary point of reference, however, is clearly Intruder in the Dust (1948), Faulkner's controversial response to a proposed federal antilynching law. Both novels

concern the murder of the son of a powerful but distinctly unaristocratic white family; both focus on the presumed guilt of an aging and somewhat aloof black man (Gaines's Mathu and Faulkner's Lucas Beauchamp) who has earned the grudging respect of his community by refusing to surrender his dignity to a repressive social system and who says very little in his own defense; both generate a vision of salvation based on interracial cooperation. Whereas Faulkner emphasizes the role of whites able to maintain some sense of innocence (his saviors are a young white boy, his black companion, and an elderly white woman), Gaines emphasizes the need for an Afro-American self-assertion predicated on direct confrontation with past experience. Gaines does, however, acknowledge the participation of whites in the metaphorical salvation of the Southern soul: Candy, the young heiress to the Marshall plantation where the killing takes place, sets in motion the machinery leading to salvation because of her deep, if paternalistic, love for the accused Mathu; Mapes, a Southern sheriff in the mode of Faulkner's Hope Hampton, respects Mathu's dignity and, despite his personal racism, does everything in his power to discourage violence against the black community; Lou Dimes, a Baton Rouge journalist and frustrated suitor of Candy, is perceptive, but his insights, like those of Faulkner's Quentin Compson and Gavin Stevens, are rendered nearly useless by an inability to take action.

Gaines's focus, however, remains firmly on the group of about fifteen black men, all past seventy, who gather at the scene of the shotgun killing of Beau Boutan, whose father, Cajun patriarch William "Fix" Boutan, has terrorized the black population on and around the Marshall plantation for a half century. Summoned by Candy, who claims to have killed Beau herself, the old men— identified both by given name (Robert Louis Stevenson Banks, Matthew Lincoln Brown, Cyril Robillard) and nickname (Chimley, Rooster, Clatoo, Dirty Red)—arrive at Mathu's cabin with shotguns and discharged five-gauge shells. When Mapes arrives, each claims responsibility for the killing. The old men's explanations of their motivation testifies to a past of submission and a present and future destroyed by mechanization. Having watched the younger generation either move away or being driven into jails and asylums, the old men commit themselves to resisting the expected lynching of Mathu, who embodies the dignity salvaged from past suffering. Johnny Paul both summarizes this past and embodies this determination when he stands up to Mapes, the symbol of white power, for the first time in his life:

I did it 'cause that tractor is getting closer and closer to that graveyard, and I was scared if I didn't do it, one day that tractor was go'n come in there and plow up them graves, getting rid of all proof that we ever was. Like now they trying to get rid of all proof that black people ever farmed this land with plows and mules—like if they had nothing from the starten but motor machines.

Once awakened, this fierce dignity transforms the endurance of the Faulknerian black sufferers into a repudiation of both black passivity and white paternalism.

From the beginning, Candy predicates her determination to shield Mathu from Mapes and the Boutans on the premise that the residents of Marshall are "black and helpless." Even Jack Marshall, the titular owner of the plantation—who, like numerous Faulknerian aristocrats, lives in an alcoholic stupor, fixated on a vanished past—identifies Candy as the new slaveowner: "I have no niggers. . . . They belong to her." Despite her good intentions, Candy lives up to her historical position when she angrily, and unsuccessfully, rejects the desire of the black men to meet without her: "You know where you're at? You know who you're talking to? Get the hell off my place." Her words reveal an ironic commitment to the Old South's social structures even more extensive than that of the Boutans, whose association with the tractor identifies them in part with the mechanized and indifferent New South. Deepening the irony, Mapes accurately expresses the contradictions of Candy's contemporary paternalism when he accuses her of enforcing the silence against which Johnny Paul spoke: "you want to keep them slaves the rest of their lives. . . . At least your people let them talk. . . . Now you're trying to take that away from them."

In fact, Candy has no desire to silence the black community; she simply cannot conceive of any action not predicated on paternalistic attitudes. Whatever her sincerity, whatever the depth of the love she feels for Mathu, she cannot protect anyone, including herself, from the system in which she plays a central role. Rather, the full burden of protection—ultimately the burden of emancipating both blacks and whites from psychological enslavement—falls to the Afro-American community, which must overcome the fear that has circumscribed its past actions. Repeatedly, as the old men claim responsibility for Beau's death, their stories focus on their past evasion of confrontations. After Tucker admits to watching his brother being beaten (as punishment for winning a John Henry style competition with a tractor), Rufe describes the communal response: "none of us looked back at him. We had all done the same thing sometime or another; we had all seen our brother, sister, mama, daddy insulted once and didn't do a thing about it." By standing up to Mapes and Candy, by demonstrating their willingness to resist any Boutan violence, the old men strike a blow for freedom, their own and that of the whites equally tied to the old roles.

Gaines's masterful resolution of the "murder mystery" in *A Gathering of Old Men* extends the themes of confrontation and responsibility to the individual level and cautions against accepting any version of truth at face value. Throughout the first three-quarters of the novel, each character—Candy, Mapes, the Boutans, the old men—assumes that Mathu shot Beau. Because Mathu resisted the Boutans previously, all assume that only he can initiate resistance in the present. Nevertheless, Mathu, like Faulkner's Lucas, is innocent. Whereas Faulkner developed his theme of white guilt by revealing a fratricide, Gaines extends the theme of black responsibility, revealing that the shooting was committed by Charles Biggs, a fifty-year-old plantation hand who despite a huge body has spent his entire life running away from confrontations. Although several characters comment briefly on Charlie's absence when they arrive at Marshall, all assume he has simply run away until, as Mapes prepares to take Mathu into custody, Charlie reappears to claim the dignity he first earned by resisting Beau and then forfeited by asking Mathu to accept the consequences. A direct literary descendant of Richard Wright's protagonists Big Boy (in "Big Boy Leaves Home") and Bigger Thomas (in *Native Son*, 1940), both of whom ran after killing a white person, Charlie infuses the Faulknerian Bayonne with a central motif from the Afro-American literary tradition. Claiming responsibility for his actions, as did Bigger Thomas near the end of *Native Son*, Charlie earns the right to be addressed as "Mister Biggs," completing the transformation of the racial slurs ("boy" and "nigger") into an emblem of respect.

Even as it reinforces Gaines's vision of Afro-American assertion, the unsuspected revelation of Mister Biggs's responsibility reiterates the Faulknerian resonance of *A Gathering of Old Men*. Employing a narrative structure derived from *As I Lay Dying*, Gaines presents his story through a series of brief monologues—more insistently oral in expression than Faulkner's stream-of-consciousness sections—that emphasize the need for multiple perceptions and corroborations of any statement regarding racial relationships. Even then, as the common assumption of Mathu's guilt intimates, the force of history may elevate a stereotyped perception to the status of social truth. *A Gathering of Old Men*, like *Absalom! Absalom!*, asserts the ambiguous substructure of all truth and insists on a continuing exploration of the impact of tradition on contemporary consciousness.

Ultimately, Gaines draws together the numerous Faulknerian elements of *A Gathering of Old Men* in a climax that explicitly echoes "The Bear" in *Go Down, Moses* (1942). Imaging the destruction of the Old South in the death of Old Ben, a bear of mythic dimensions, Faulkner lamented the destruction of the values of the old people, black, white, and red, especially of their profound respect for nature and for one another. The climactic segment of *A Gathering of Old Men*, narrated by Dirty Red, opens with a description of Charlie as a "big bear," a description repeated three times in two pages. Shortly thereafter, Charlie is shot by the leader of a group of drunk rednecks—significantly not Boutans—and the description of his final movements recalls the death of Old Ben: "I saw Charlie still going toward that tractor, but he wasn't shooting now, just falling, slowly, slowly, slowly till he had hit the ground." Charlie's death, like Old Ben's, entails the replacement of one set of values with another—in this case a movement from the "big nigger" stereotype to a new era predicated on the courage and dignity of Mister Biggs's final day. Where Faulkner lamented the passing of the Old South, Gaines insists that even its real values were inextricably involved with the denial of Afro-American humanity. Where Faulkner's vision of the New South, as expressed in *Intruder in the Dust*, rested primarily on black silence and the ability of whites to transform their heritage, Gaines's vision emphasizes black assertion, expressed verbally and through physical actions. In symbolic terms, Gaines responds respectfully, directly, and ultimately successfully to Faulkner's courageous but limited perspective on the traditions of the Old South.

Gaines's realistic portrayal of the New South, especially as it involves the psychological and social relationships of the Boutan clan, however, is much more problematic and ultimately diminishes the impact of his response to Faulkner. Reflected both in a somewhat unconvincing plot development and in a clear diminishment of verbal power, the problems appear approximately halfway through the novel when Gaines shifts attention from the black men gathered at Marshall to the response of Beau's brother Gil, a star fullback for Louisiana State University (L.S.U.) who forms half of the interracial backfield nicknamed "Salt and Pepper" ("Pepper" is black halfback Calvin Harrison). Symbolizing a New South relying on interracial cooperation, Gil repudiates his family's tradition of vigilante violence with little discernible emotional reaction to his brother's death. After learning of the shooting, Gil drives to Marshall, where he sees the old men armed with shotguns and apparently recognizes the full implications of the image. Continuing on to the Boutans' bayou home, Gil confronts his father and argues against violent retribution, partially because any scandal would ruin his chances for all-American recognition. Gil's statement to his father, who will ride only if the majority of his sons support him, seems intended as a moral analogue for the blacks' decision to resist further degradation: "Beau is dead, and I'm sorry, Papa. . . . But I would like people to know we're not what they think we are. They all expect us to ride tonight. They're all waiting for that. I say let them wait. Let them wait and wait and wait." Just as the black men have cast off their stereotyped roles, Gil speaks for a new freedom that will benefit both blacks and whites.

Whatever its validity as a moral ideal, however, the scene holds little of the power of Johnny Paul's testimony or Mister Biggs's apotheosis. Perhaps the clearest indication of the failure is the surprisingly unenergetic language of the sections focusing on the Boutans. Narrated by Thomas "T. V." Sullivan, a teammate of Gil, these sections tap little of the power of the rich regional vernacular, Afro-American or Cajun, at which Gaines typically excels. In fact, Fix Boutan's Cajun voice carries a great deal more conviction and passion than Gil's educated voice, creating the impression that Gil's ultimate triumph rests on an evasion of emotional experience rather than actual moral confrontation. As a result, the plot development that limits the participants in the vigilante action to a group of clearly unsympathetic drunken rednecks seems more a matter of symbolic convenience than of realistic insight. Reducing the psychological power of family values and the sociological impact of a violent past, Gaines avoids the complexity inherent in Gil's situation. Never forced to confront a situation in which he must choose between the assertion of old values and emotional ties and his rhetorical commitment to the New South, Gil simply returns to his pursuit of the all-American dream. Everything in Gaines's treatment of the situation at Marshall implies strongly that such a naïve evasion will be doomed to failure, yet the comic conclusion of the novel indicates no awareness of unresolved psychological tensions or moral dilemmas. This unresolved contradiction keeps *A Gathering of Old Men* from assuming a truly major position in the Southern literary canon.

Clearly, as Faulkner prophesied and as Gaines confirms, the Old South based on segregation and subservience is passing into history. To imply that it is passing from consciousness, however, requires at best a willing suspension of disbelief and at worst a willing immersion in naïveté. Gaines's response to Faulkner is intricate and compelling inasmuch as it addresses the psychological situation of the black and aristocratic elements of the New South, precisely because it requires no such separation of consciousness and history. His understanding of the Cajuns, like Faulkner's understanding of the Snopses, remains fatally externalized and historically shallow. Like Faulkner's aristocratic white descendants and the emerging writers with roots in the poor white culture, Gaines recognizes the confusion generated by the collapse of legal segregation; no one has yet created an essentially new formulation of the racial tensions in the New South. Thirty years after the Brown decision, the dominant fact of interracial contact in the South appears to be an increasing estrangement between Euro- and Afro-American realities. At great and unacceptable cost, the Old South forced blacks and whites at least to recognize each other's presence and to learn to interpret at least the social dimension of each other's behavior. Proximity and familiarity, even as they created and perpetuated the stereotypes Gaines repudiates, at least would have discouraged the naïve optimism reflected in the Boutans' decision not to ride. Gaines's failure to penetrate the depths of poor white psychology, paralleling Faulkner's failure to penetrate beneath the surface of the Afro-American mind, suggests that silence may be replacing violence as the constituting experience of interracial relations in the New South. To the extent that this involves the repression of felt violence, the silence summons up the specter of the very estrangement from history that the old men refuse to accept.

Craig Werner

Sources for Further Study

Christian Science Monitor. December 2, 1983, p. B13.

Library Journal. CVIII, August, 1983, p. 1501.
Nation. CCXXXVIII, January 14, 1984, p. 22.
The New York Times Book Review. LXXXVIII, October 30, 1983, p. 15.
The New Yorker. LIX, October 24, 1983, p. 163.
Publishers Weekly. CCXXIV, July 15, 1983, p. 41.
Saturday Review. IX, December, 1983, p. 61.

THE GIFT
Imagination and the Erotic Life of Property

Author: Lewis Hyde (1945-   )
Publisher: Random House/Vintage Books (New York). Illustrated. 327 pp. $17.95;
   paperback $7.95
Type of work: Literary criticism and anthropology

An examination of the concept of gift exchange (as opposed to market exchange), through many cultures and fields of study but concentrating on poetry

> Behold I do not give lectures or a little charity,
> What I give I give out of myself.

So Walt Whitman wrote in 1855, and so he gave out of himself a remarkable gift to the world, the incomparable "Song of Myself." After having immersed himself in the life around him, in all of its sensory pleasure and plenitude, he was not content to keep it all to himself: *"Walt you contain enough, why don't you let it out then?"* Let it out he most assuredly did, in thousands of glorious lines, perpetually giving of himself:

> Me going in for my chances, spending for vast returns,
> Adorning myself to bestow myself on the first that will take me,
> Not asking the sky to come down to my goodwill,
> Scattering it freely forever.

Whitman's characteristic response to the world—both receptive and bestowing—is the quintessence of what literary critic Lewis Hyde, following numerous anthropologists, calls a "gift economy." Such an economy is not, however, the characteristic mode of exchange in the United States or most of the modern world. In contemporary life, as in the America that Whitman knew a century and more ago, it is the market economy that prevails, with everything and everyone having a carefully calculated value.

It was this more modern spirit that was captured by another great American poet, Ezra Pound, writing in a more cynical age, the 1930's, when the world was suffering economic collapse and the banks, in which people had put their trust (and their life savings), simply failed. Pound's Canto 45, written and published in the mid-1930's, bitterly castigates the mentality that seeks profit and usurious interest above all, where gifts are casually slighted:

> With usura hath no man a house of good stone
> . . . .
> no picture is made to endure nor to live with
> but it is made to sell and sell quickly
> . . . .

There are certain labors, writes Lewis Hyde in his penetrating study *The Gift: Imagination and the Erotic Life of Property*, for which profit-and-loss accounting is utterly inappropriate. Nevertheless, such accounting dominates contemporary attitudes. Witness the 1984 book written by Joanna T. Steichen, *Marrying Up: An American Dream and Reality*, in which women (primarily) are encouraged to boost their status in an entirely profit-oriented quest, a total perversion of the spirit of Eros, which presumably motivates most modern relationships. However, the spirit of Eros is clearly being overwhelmed by the spirit of Logos, the analytic powers of the mind.

Hyde's book is a fascinating work of analysis, examining the contrasting economies of the gift and the market, and, even more notably, a synthesis of tribal customs, folk tales and myth, economics, contemporary behavior, and literary criticism to comment on a significant lack in today's world: the lack of a true feeling for the gift.

The book's springboard was Hyde's concern that the labors of art rarely receive compensation commensurate with their absolute worth (as opposed to calculable value) in a world dominated by market exchange. As a poet and translator (among his credits are translations of the Nobel Prize-winning Spanish poet Vicente Aleixandre), Hyde knows this imbalance at firsthand, yet like other poets, literary critics, visual artists, performance artists, musicians, even actors (in unpaid equity-waiver work such as dominates the Los Angeles theater scene, where professional actors seek fresh challenges between commercials and network series), he continues in his proverbial "labor of love."

Love *is* the motivator, and this is the reason for Hyde's subtitle, "Imagination and the Erotic Life of Property." Eros is a force for union, for sharing. Moreover, it is endlessly renewable. Property in a gift exchange can have an erotic life, because it too is renewable, generating further exchange and producing unity among the people involved in the exchange.

Providing examples of both the ideal gift economy and perversions of it, Hyde draws from a diverse group of sources, notably studies of the gift customs of various tribal groups and the folktales and myths of several cultures. These diverse narratives emphasize the importance of consciousness of the gift and of exchanging it in order to prosper in life's endeavors and (here the other part of the subtitle appears) to release the gift of the imagination. The key story in this respect is "The Shoemaker and the Elves," in which the elves embody the gift, unexpected and unsought, given to any artist—talent, inspiration, or what the classical or Romantic poet would call the Muse.

It is not enough, however, merely to possess a gift; one must, like Whitman, "scatter it freely forever." The important lesson that Hyde draws from the anthropological studies he cites is that the gift is nothing without *increase*— the quality a gift achieves as it is passed on. The Massim peoples in the islands east of New Guinea, for example, pass jewelry from island to island. Foodstuffs may be offered, as with the Uduk in northeast Africa, but the recipient is expected not to keep the goats, say, for milk or breeding, but rather to kill them for a feast, not for the gift-giver but for others. Thus, Hyde emphasizes, true gift exchange involves at least three parties: the giver, the recipient, and the person to whom the recipient gives in turn. Without the third party, the gift is no longer a gift; the exchange becomes incestuous, with no increase of feeling or worth and no sense of surprise or true gratitude possible.

Hence the application to art—specifically literature. The writer receives the talent and inspiration—from the Muse, from genes, from writers of the past—but the writer must then express it and create the work of literature. It is significant, however, that the genre on which Hyde focuses is poetry; the novelist and the playwright labor more frequently for a well-defined audience and the resultant monetary reward. Whitman and Pound, on the other hand, the two poets whom Hyde considers in detail, lived in virtual poverty for most of their lives, yet they never ceased their labor.

Hyde's discussions of Whitman and Pound are fascinating and well-grounded in study of the poets' works and lives; the biographical information is important in examining the connection of the poet as individual (recipient and giver) to his actual poetry (the gift, both as received—from the world around him and from his spiritual sense and insight for Whitman; from the great masters of thought and art of the past for Pound—and as given to its readers). Hyde's analysis of Whitman's "Song of Myself" is one of the most cogent and useful in a long time; it is both fresh and down-to-earth, allowing the reader to see the poem in a new light but one that is familiar as well because it makes such perfect sense. Whitman's giving of himself to the hospitalized soldiers of the Civil War is rendered beautifully, but Hyde's discussion of the poet's later life and some of his homoerotic attachments seems missing a few connections—a paragraph or two of synthesis. (Hyde might also have been a bit more careful in his spelling of names associated with Whitman.)

The Pound discussion offers a poignant view of a brilliant intellectual and poetic genius warped by animosities which were actually grounded in solid, valid criticisms of the profit motive and its distorted notions of the value of art. Benito Mussolini, Pound believed, recognized the importance of supporting artists. (Never mind that he kept one of Italy's greatest writers, Gabriele D'Annunzio, a virtual state prisoner in a lush, well-funded villa for fear of his potential political magnetism.) A broken man in his eighties, Pound was visited by the poet Allen Ginsberg, to whom he admitted his "worst mistake"—"the stupid suburban prejudice of anti-Semitism." As Ginsberg left, after giving Pound *his* blessing, he requested Pound's upon him. Nodding, Pound gave it, "for what it's worth."

What is important is that Pound gave it. The gift moves on—from poet to poet (constantly drawing from the poetic offerings of forebears) on to the reader.

How then does the poet, or any artist, survive in the modern world? Hyde really has no solution, other than the standard compromise, as represented by several alternatives in his conclusion: partaking of both gift and market economies, without allowing the latter to obtrude upon the precious exchange of the former.

There are certain kinds of labor, says Hyde—including nursing, teaching, social work—that cannot be undertaken in the adversarial spirit of the marketplace. Such labor, generally underpaid in America in the 1980's, should receive adequate compensation, but there are values that cannot be measured in dollars and cents. The human spirit operates on a plane different from that of the marketplace, and it and its gifts can never be transformed into commodities.

Scott Giantvalley

Sources for Further Study

Library Journal. CVIII, March 1, 1983, p. 514.
Los Angeles Times Book Review. May 29, 1983, p. 4.
Nation. CCXXXVI, June 4, 1983, p. 709.
National Review. XXXV, April 15, 1983, p. 448.
New England Review. V, Spring, 1983, p. 417.
The New Republic. CLXXXIX, October 24, 1983, p. 40.
The New York Times Book Review. LXXXVIII, May 15, 1983, p. 16.
Publishers Weekly. CCXXIII, February 4, 1983, p. 364.

GREAT TRANQUILLITY
Questions and Answers

Author: Yehuda Amichai (1924-   )
Translated from the Hebrew by Glenda Abramson and Tudor Parfitt
Publisher: Harper & Row, Publishers (New York). 90 pp. $11.95; paperback $7.95
Type of work: Poetry

Reflections by an outstanding Israeli poet on life, love, war, and death

In Yehuda Amichai's latest translated collection of poems, *Great Tranquillity: Questions and Answers*, the author continues to focus upon the motifs that concerned him in his earlier works: the challenge and anguish of continual eruptions of war, the constant awareness of the distant and recent past, and of the historical significance of daily events. He is particularly preoccupied with the themes of time, memory, biblical tradition, and the relationships of lovers and of fathers and sons. In emotional tone, the poems range from despair to buoyancy, from melancholy to a zestful celebration of life.

In poem after poem, Amichai's lovers are caught in the trap of time. They are "poor in years and even days" but rich "in minutes and seconds." For them, time is always rushing by. The passing of a day makes changes as irrevocable as the passing of thousands of years. Sometimes it seems to the poet that all things pass without leaving a trace. People picnic where once a battle was fought and, as the reality of the battle has passed, so too when the picnickers leave, all marks of their having been there will disappear as well: "the view will be smooth as oblivion." Similarly, "An hour turns into a knife/ To be used only once."

More often, however, Amichai stresses the endless continuity of events and the significance of the individual's role in history, which is made up of today as well as of yesterday, of anonymous little people as well as of heroic great ones. The man who sits with his shopping baskets near the gate at David's Tower is equal in importance to the Wailing Wall and Rachel's and Herzl's tombs. History passes, but it remains as well.

For the Israeli, experiences of life and love are measured by and sandwiched in between wars. Amichai speaks of meeting with his father in a café "in one of the intermissions/ Between two wars or between two loves" and describes himself as "an actor resting backstage in half-darkness." Tossed between war and love, he sees these extremes as the only significant realities.

The poet's memories torment him, not only the memories of his own personal experience but also the memories of his nation and his people. The power of recollection is so overwhelming that he feels he must "march against" his memories "like a man against the wind," and that he must put them out like a fire. In these feelings, the poet faces a major dilemma. Memory is one of the significant materials from which a poet constructs his poems, just as it constitutes an important component of the material from which a human being's life is constructed. Without memories, a person is empty and a poet loses dimensions important to his creativity.

A significant portion of memory for an Israeli poet is the remembrance of history, not only of ancient biblical times but also of all the more recent tragic events of Jewish existence in the Diaspora and the Holocaust. Amichai asks the bitter question: "What's Jewish time?" and answers, "God's experimental places/ Where he tests new ideas and new weaponry." He asks, "What's the Jewish people?" and he answers, "The quota that can be killed in training."

In another poem, in the earlier volume entitled *Amen* (1977), there is an angry condemnation of God. The heavens, Amichai complains, are empty. Nevertheless, Amichai is not entirely without hope and a sense of celebration. He finds great beauty in the sight of a family gathered together from all the countries of the world enjoying the scent of jasmine in Jerusalem. The 'family" is the remnant of the Jewish people rescued from exile and returned to the Holy City. The air of Jerusalem is scented, not only with jasmine; for the poet, it is saturated with prayers and dreams and the sense of history-in-the-making. "From time to time," he writes, "a new consignment of history arrives."

Another poem tells of a Jewish father seeking a lost child and an Arab shepherd seeking a lost kid. Calling out for their lost charges, their voices meet in the valley. Though the two men do not meet, they share the experiences of loss and of the seeking and rejoicing in finding what they have lost; the poet describes the essence of their common humanity in their seeking, the kind of seeking which, in history, has led to the beginnings of new religions.

Amichai also refers repeatedly to the Jewish concept of the holiness of all aspects of existence, the physical and sexual as well as the spiritual. In "A Memory in Abu Tor," he observes that God supplied water for both the showering of soldiers' dust-covered bodies as well as for the ritual washing of hands before prayer, and the water was supplied for both with ample abundance. He describes how the Sabbath hymn from the assembly meeting in the lower portion of the building mingles with the shouts of the men in the showers and, presumably, both are equally acceptable to God.

Perhaps more insistently than any other theme, Amichai stresses the contradictory demands made upon a man who must be all things in a very demanding and complicated life, in which he is challenged to be soldier, lover, parent, citizen, and poet. He tries to balance the demands of society that he not show weakness with the inner feelings of a man which are as sensitive and delicate as "the white veils/ Of Jewish women who faint/ At weddings and on the Day of Atonement."

The poet also has a constant double awareness of the desire for private self-indulgence and the need for public responsibility as he describes the appeal of "a pleasant and luxurious bath" and the concern lest when he take the plug out of the tub, the whole city of Jerusalem "and with it the whole world" may "empty out into the great darkness."

In this same poem, Amichai also writes about the role of the poet. He believes the poet must "lay traps for memories" and examine the range of possibilities in experience: the curse in the blessing and the blessing in the curse. The poet, caught between his own anguish and that of those around him, suffers and cries out, but his cry is not understood. "People think it's normal speech."

The "great tranquillity," of which the poet speaks, would seem to be not a state which he has succeeded in achieving but rather one into which he seeks to enter. He appears to yearn to draw apart from the clamor of the excited voices of others and, in the tranquility of his own privacy, to be free to question and to seek for answers.

Roseline Intrater

Sources for Further Study

Booklist. LXXIX, August, 1983, p. 1441.
Jewish Frontier. LI, no. 4, April, 1984, p. 26.
Library Journal. CVIII, September 1, 1983, p. 1708.
The New York Times Book Review. LXXXVIII, November 13, 1983, p. 27.

THE HEMINGWAY WOMEN

Author: Bernice Kert (1932-   )
Publisher: W. W. Norton and Company (New York). Illustrated. 555 pp. $20.00
Type of work: Literary biography
Time: 1872-1961
Locale: The United States, France, Italy, Spain, and Cuba

*An important addition to the body of literature about Hemingway, detailing the parts
played in his life and his writings by his wives and other women he loved*

> *Principal personages:*
> ERNEST HEMINGWAY, a major American writer
> GRACE HALL HEMINGWAY, his mother
> HADLEY RICHARDSON HEMINGWAY, his first wife
> PAULINE PFEIFFER HEMINGWAY, his second wife
> MARTHA GELLHORN HEMINGWAY, his third wife
> MARY WELSH HEMINGWAY, his fourth wife
> AGNES VON KUROWSKY, his World War I sweetheart
> LADY DUFF TWYSDEN,
> JANE MASON, and
> ADRIANA IVANCICH, other women in his life

Women were necessary in Ernest Hemingway's life, but not constantly.
They had their uses for him—in bed, in the kitchen, as listeners, as comforters,
as typists, as hunting and fishing companions, sometimes as money sources.
For their services they were repaid in occasional kindness—particularly when
they were away and he wanted them back. They were expected to be grateful
for his affection or love, to cater to his vanity, to endure his jokes, to forget
or ignore the occasions when he embarrassed or humiliated them either in
private or before relatives and friends, and to forgive his indifference, his
quarrels, his obnoxiousness (especially when he was drinking), and his verbal
and mental cruelty.

The women who played their roles in the drama and the melodrama of
Hemingway's life are the subject of Bernice Kert's excellent account, which
covers nearly a century, from the birth of the writer's mother in 1872 to his
bloody suicide in 1961. The women had their entrances and their exits, many
of them, in the sixty-two years (minus three months) of his adventure-filled,
famous, violent, and finally pathetic life.

The five sections of Kert's book are chronological but with many glances
both forward and backward in time as one woman or another appears, dis-
appears, or returns after an absence, sometimes of years. A sentence from
Hemingway's *To Have and Have Not* (1937) warns the reader of much that
will follow: "The better you treat a man and the more you show him you
love him, the quicker he gets tired of you." The words are from a novel, but
the speaker might well be the author in a confessional mood.

Grace Hall Hemingway, the first woman in her son's life, was the object of his scorn and contempt for most of his years. His favorite epithet for her was "that bitch," and he saw her as a selfish wife who drove her husband to suicide. For many years after Ernest left home, she continued to write to him, offering advice and moral counsel. Though he set up a trust fund for her after the publication of *A Farewell to Arms* (1929), he paid her little attention except to answer her letters with anger, arguments, complaints, and perfunctory thanks for presents. When she died senile at seventy-nine, in 1951, he did not attend her funeral.

Agnes von Kurowsky entered Hemingway's life as a result of his being seriously wounded in World War I, having volunteered for the ambulance service of the Red Cross in Italy. The nineteen-year-old American was brought to a hospital in Milan, where he quickly fell in love with Agnes, his nurse, and he expected to marry her following his recovery and his return to the United States. She led him to think that she would, but a later affair and her expected marriage to a young Italian officer disillusioned and embittered Hemingway when he learned the news by letter. Interference by the officer's aristocratic mother caused the breaking off of the engagement, and Agnes returned to the United States not long after Hemingway did, but there was no renewal of their love affair. Hemingway later fictionalized the experience in "A Very Short Story" (1923) giving it a sordid ending. In *A Farewell to Arms*, he treated it at much greater length, transforming it into a romantic tragedy and making of the idealized Catherine Barkley a woman who physically resembles the Agnes he had loved, but whose life history, mannerisms, and name were drawn from other women he had known.

Hemingway married Hadley Richardson, the first of his four wives, after a courtship of a little less than a year which was carried on mainly through letters. Hadley's inheritance of eight thousand dollars after the death of an uncle enabled the couple to move to Paris, from which Hemingway was to mail articles on sports and politics to the *Toronto Daily Star*, for which he was a reporter. The marriage was happy at first, with trips to Italy and Germany and with the excitement of living in a part of Paris where frequent contact was possible with men and women who provided intellectual and aesthetic stimulation as well as social companionship.

The birth in 1923 of John Hadley Nicanor Hemingway, nicknamed "Bumby," limited the freedom of movement Hadley had known earlier, but she knew such freedom was necessary to her husband in his journalistic work. A disturbing element entered the marriage, however, through the development of Hemingway's interest in two women in his Parisian circle of friends.

Lady Duff Twysden, twice married, with one divorce and another pending, was living with the latest in a stream of lovers. Hemingway was attracted to her, remarks Kert, by "her insouciance, her style, her unerring charm." She was briefly in his life as a confiding friend though not as a lover. He gave her an enduring literary life as the promiscuous Lady Brett Ashley in *The Sun Also Rises* (1926). Married in 1928 to a young American painter, Clinton King, Duff gave up her disordered life and lived quietly with her husband until her death from tuberculosis in 1938 at the age of forty-five.

The other woman who diverted Hemingway's interest from his wife was Pauline Pfeiffer, who presented a much greater danger to the marriage than Duff ever did. Pauline, a journalist writing for the American magazine *Vogue*, was highly intelligent and full of youthful enthusiasm, though she was four years older than Hemingway. Her Parisian friends included John Dos Passos, Scott and Zelda Fitzgerald, Archibald and Ada MacLeish, and Gerald and Sara Murphy. All would later be enshrined, along with the Hemingways, in literary histories of the 1920's.

Pauline decided she wanted the handsome young author, and she set out to get him. In his Parisian memoir, *A Moveable Feast* (published posthumously in 1964), Hemingway pretends that he was duped by the woman who took him from Hadley, but says Kert, "In spite of his later disclaimers, he was not the passive innocent, preyed upon by a scheming Pauline."

Though Hadley was troubled and hurt by what was happening, she was generous. She agreed in writing that if Hemingway and Pauline were still in love after a hundred days, she would consent to a divorce. The lovers concluded that they could not be happy without each other, the divorce was granted, and, in Paris in May, 1927, Pauline became the second Mrs. Ernest Hemingway.

Hadley actually found some relief in being freed from the turmoil of her marriage. She became friendly with Paul Mowrer, a Paris correspondent for the *Chicago Daily News*. They were friends and lovers for five years until they were married in 1933. The happy marriage lasted forty years until Mowrer's death in 1973. Hadley died at eighty-nine in 1979.

Hemingway's marriage to Pauline produced two sons, Patrick and Gregory; was marked by extensive travel and plentiful hunting and fishing; and was ended by separations during the Spanish Civil War and by Hemingway's love affair with Martha Gellhorn. Pauline appears as P.O.M. ("Poor Old Mama") in *Green Hills of Africa* (1935) and, many years later in *A Moveable Feast*, as the woman who took Hemingway from the best wife he ever had, the one he continued to love in memory the rest of his life.

During his marriage to Pauline, Hemingway indulged in one love affair before he met Martha Gellhorn, who would become his third wife. Jane Mason was the unhappy wife of G. Grant Mason, head of Pan American Airways in Cuba. She met the Hemingways on the Île-de-France when they were returning from Spain to New York shortly before the birth of their second son. They met again in Cuba, and Jane joined Hemingway on marlin fishing trips, in which Pauline was uninterested. How far the love affair went is unclear, says Kert, who interviewed Jane fifty years later and was told that she had almost married Hemingway, but both were married at the time. Jane was the model for the sportswoman Margot Macomber in "The Short Happy Life of Francis Macomber" (1936).

When he was young, Hemingway fell in love with women older than himself—Agnes, Hadley, Pauline—but by the 1930's, he had reached a time in life when he called women "daughter" and enjoyed being called "Papa"; Jane Mason was twenty-two when he met her. She soon dropped out of his life, however, to be replaced by Martha Gellhorn, a writer whom he met in Key West when she was twenty-eight and he was thirty-seven.

Martha was a journalist with strong political views who covered both the Spanish Civil War and World War II. In Spain, she was often with Hemingway, who had coaxed her to come there to report on the war which was destroying many of the people in a country he loved. Martha developed from "daughter" into mistress, and Hemingway rationalized that Pauline, with her Catholic views about birth control, had denied him sex that he was now justified in getting from a new and willing young partner.

Hemingway wished to marry Martha if he could get Pauline to agree to a divorce, but Martha resisted for four years of what she called "living in sin." She wanted her independence, but Hemingway insisted; Pauline gave in (with a strict stipulation about support payments), and the third Mrs. Ernest Hemingway began in 1940 her short and stormy marriage to a man she wanted when she was away from him, but who often angered and exasperated her when they were together.

Martha firmly resisted her husband's attempts to dominate her as he had his first two wives. There were many clashes both in private and in public, and the marriage was dissolved in 1945. Hemingway had already been carrying on for some time a love affair with Mary Welsh Monks, who would later become his fourth and last wife.

Mary, like Pauline and Martha before her, was a professional journalist. When she met Hemingway in London in 1944, she was writing feature stories for *Time.* Married young, she had divorced her first husband and in 1938 had married Noel Monks, a London *Daily Mail* correspondent in the South Pacific.

By the time Mary married Hemingway in 1946, she had known him long and intimately enough to be well acquainted with his anger, his rudeness, and his bullying ways, as well as his charm and his prowess in bed, of which he was quite vain. Unlike Martha, though, she submitted to his callous treatment, particularly after he had helped save her life during a hospital emergency following the bursting of one of her fallopian tubes.

During his marriage to Mary, Hemingway had his final fling at extramarital love, a fortunately one-sided affair with Adriana Ivancich, a young woman from a wealthy Venetian family. She was eighteen when Hemingway met her, and though she later said she never fell in love with him, he became infatuated with her. He romanticized the situation in *Across the River and into the Trees*

(1950), in the love affair of Colonel Robert Cantwell and young Renata. Because Adriana was widely recognized as the original of Renata, she suffered considerable embarrassment. Hemingway, meeting her sometime later, apologized and told her, "You are not the girl in the book . . . and I am not the colonel. . . ."

Hemingway had taken Pauline to Africa in 1933. With Mary he went on another African safari in 1953, and this ended with two plane crashes, in the second of which Hemingway suffered a concussion and numerous external and internal injuries. His behavior afterward was at times irrational, apparently as a result of the concussion.

In the final years of Hemingway's marriage to Mary, both his mind and his body revealed that age and his turbulent life-style were finally producing signs of disintegration. He restlessly traveled—from Cuba to Idaho to Spain to Cuba to Spain to New York to Idaho—and Mary tried to keep up, but the pace was wearing, as frequently was her difficult husband's treatment of her. She asked if he needed her any longer and offered to leave him. When he begged her to come from Cuba to Madrid to keep him from "cracking up," she did not realize the seriousness of his condition.

Hemingway developed a persecution mania, thinking that FBI agents were after him; he experienced depression and delusion; and finally attempted suicide. He was twice taken to the Mayo Clinic in Minnesota and twice released. At his home in Ketchum, Idaho, on July 2, 1961, he put a shotgun to his head and fired. Mary reported his death as an accident though she knew it was not. She did not publicly admit the truth until after it had been revealed in A. E. Hotchner's *Papa Hemingway: A Personal Memoir* (1966), the distribution of which she had failed to prevent.

Because it gathers together and expands or updates much information hitherto scattered in many places or only sketchily treated in earlier books, *The Hemingway Women* is an important addition to the body of literature about Hemingway; it will be required reading for all serious students of his work.

Henderson Kincheloe

Sources for Further Study

American Journal of Psychology. CXL, December, 1983, p. 1636.
Choice. XXI, November, 1983, p. 424.
Library Journal. CVIII, May 15, 1983, p. 1004.
Los Angeles Times Book Review. July 3, 1983, p. 2.
National Review. XXXV, August 19, 1983, p. 1027.
The New York Times Book Review. LXXXVIII, July 17, 1983, p. 8.
Publishers Weekly. CCXXIII, May 6, 1983, p. 94.

HIS MASTER'S VOICE

Author: Stanisław Lem (1921-   )
Translated from the Polish by Michael Kandel
Publisher: Harcourt Brace Jovanovich (San Diego, California). 199 pp. $12.95
Type of work: Novel
Time: The future
Locale: The United States

Several scientists are assigned by the government to interpret a tape of a message from outer space

Principal characters:
> PROFESSOR PETER E. HOGARTH, a mathematician and the narrator of the story
> DR. SAUL RAPPAPORT, a colleague of Hogarth and a survivor of the Holocaust
> YVOR BALOYNE, the head of the Project and accountable to Washington
> LEE REINHORN, a physicist who also worked on the Manhattan Project
> DONALD PROTHERO, the discoverer of the nuclear elements in the message
> TIHAMER DILL, a physicist with the Project and the son of a former professor of Hogarth

Although Stanisław Lem's *Głos pana* was published in Poland in 1968, it did not appear in English translation—as *His Master's Voice*—until 1983. Such, however, is the quality of both Lem's perceptiveness and his scientific insight that most readers, especially those not familiar with Lem's other fiction, are unlikely to be aware of the time gap. In total effect, *His Master's Voice* is midway between *Solaris* (1961; English translation, 1970), a philosophical novel about a sentient planet, dealing with the relation of the creator to the created and the ever-shifting nature of reality, and Lem's satiric novels and short stories, which range from broad comedy to mordantly black humor.

At first, *His Master's Voice* appears to be a philosophical essay in the form of a novel, but soon the voice and character of the narrator, Professor Peter E. Hogarth, become distinctive as he recounts events, his impressions of the people involved, and his own shortcomings with analytic, Voltairean detachment and many ironic, aphoristic asides to the reader. Upon initial acquaintance, Lem's fiction, often narrated in the first person, would not seem to have characterization as one of its strong points. Perhaps it would be more accurate to say that in his works, he has created essentially three characters: the detached observer, a scientist who is entangled in events and theories that enter his life by accident rather than design; the inventive genius, ranging from charmingly eccentric, if bungling, to completely mad and malevolent; and the inanimate or nonhuman that acquires a life and character of its own.

There is Solaris itself, a sentient and protean planet, the most remarkable creation in the novel of that title; Ijon Tichy, a robot whose voice resembles that of Professor Hogarth and a number of Lem's other narrators; and in *His Master's Voice*, the two unearthly creations of animate matter, synthesized in the laboratory—Frog Eggs and Lord of the Flies.

Reviewing a novel with a similar theme, Lem pointed out the difficulties in the creation of alien beings. Only by maintaining a complete mystery about the subject or by anthropomorphic analogy, creating contradictions, can one describe a truly other being, such as God. To describe reasonable nonhuman beings, the first science-fiction writers, beginning with H. G. Wells in *War of the Worlds* (1898), chose to create monsters, differing from human beings only in appearance. Aliens, then, became primarily malevolent invaders, and science fiction became, claims Lem in *Science-Fiction Studies*, a "fantasy of imposture and paranoid delusions." In the final analysis, Lem observes, such an outlook is "antithetical to science."

In *His Master's Voice*, Lem explores various human responses to a mysterious communication from space. No matter how objectively the scientists attempt to approach the problem of interpreting the tape of electromagnetic impulses, the presumption of invasion, of a coded weapon, of a genetic super-being, or other concepts of warfare are ultimately at the root of their interpretations. Through a series of twists and turns of logic, Professor Hogarth, with patient, baffled analysis of the nature of language, the nature of reasonable beings, and the layers upon layers of research and concealment arising from the project, accepts and discards one hypothesis after another. As both Professor Hogarth and Lem suggest, a genuine alien must remain forever a mystery, and Hogarth concludes his adventure no wiser as to the true nature of the Sender of the message.

In actual fact, serious research into extraterrestrial intelligence has been going on, intermittently at first and with increasing public awareness and scientific respectability, since the physicists Philip Morrison and Giuseppi Cocconi suggested the possible use of radio telescope to detect signals from outer space. The theory is that because natural emissions of electromagnetic radiation occur at random in nature, a consistent and regular signal must have been sent from outer space for the purpose of establishing communication. NASA's SETI (Search for Extraterrestrial Intelligence) research is funded at only $1.5 million (Americans paid more than three hundred million dollars to see the film *E.T.: The Extra Terrestrial*, 1982); even this modest allocation was challenged in 1978 by Senator William Proxmire with one of his notorious Golden Fleece awards. The efforts of Carl Sagan and others restored the funding, however, and the research continues, with plans to orbit a telescope sometime in the 1980's. In addition, the Planetary Society, an organization of "grass-roots space activists" numbering 100,000, have funded an independent search at Harvard University. Lem's novel, of course, appeared when such research was still new enough to be equated in many minds with science fiction rather than science fact.

His Master's Voice, published during the nadir of the Vietnam War and at a time when, in Poland, science fiction had become more acceptable to the authorities and was dealing with the relationship of humankind's relationship to technology is, among other things, a satire on the Manhattan Project. Not least of the novel's disconcerting aspects, and a telling comment on both the state of the world and of human nature, is its contemporaneity. Pentagon-based scientists and other government-sponsored scientific researchers still regard one another with suspicion; duplication, waste, and bureaucracy persist; and people are as likely in the 1980's as they were in 1968 to regard a message from the stars as inevitably related to conquest, colonization, and warfare. The His Master's Voice Project, with its isolated location, its massive security precautions, and lack of awareness by any of the participants as to the precise nature and intent of the research, parallels the Manhattan Project at Los Alamos. The massive amounts of sophisticated hardware and equipment initially available to the researchers do not.

Professor Hogarth is a mathematician, and Lem depicts his wrestling with the problem of decoding the message on the tape as, among other things, a detailed and sophisticated insight into and analysis of the process of scientific creativity. Lem himself became interested in science at an early age; his father was a physician, and Lem as a boy read many of his books, though forbidden to do so. After surviving the World War II years in Poland—as he says in *The New Yorker*—"only the Nazi legislation . . . brought home to me the realization that I had Jewish blood in my veins," he became a junior research assistant for Konwersatorium Naukoznawcze (the Circle for the Science of Science), which was, among other things, a clearinghouse for scientific information for all the Polish universities. Even as a boy, Lem recalls, his fantasies were complete with documented imaginary worlds, and when he began to write serious science fiction, it was with both a respect for and knowledge of scientific theory, training in medicine, and a perception of science fiction as dealing with human beings as a species. During the war years, he observes that he came to "understand the fragility that all systems [of government and society] have in common, and . . . learned how human beings behave under extreme conditions." Impressed with the role of both chance and order in the universe, he nevertheless, because of his experiences, can "well imagine . . . a preëstablished disharmony, ending in chaos and madness."

Lem's philosophy and experience, particularly his interest in the relationship between chance and survival and his determination to "incorporate cognitive problems in fictions that do not oversimplify the world, as did [his] earliest, naïve science-fiction novels" are especially evident in *His Master's Voice*. The latter observation, indeed, is a major understatement with regard to this novel: The scientific problems and possibilities inherent in a kilometer-long tape (upon which the message from space is recorded) are presented in a dizzying series of contradictory alternatives. Also, a hint of the relationship of chance to any order and reason in the universe is suggested when Dr. Saul Rappaport describes to Hogarth his experiences during the Holocaust, but the full significance of the scene becomes clearer in the light of Lem's own experiences.

At the opening of the novel, contact has been established with space, and scientists must solve the problem of what message, if any, is encoded in the signals preserved on the famous tape. Two groups of scientists, one consisting of mathematicians and biophysicists, the other of biologists, philosophers, and sociologists, are gathered for the His Master's Voice Project. The title of the English translation of Lem's novel obviously refers to the venerable RCA advertisement of a dog listening to a phonograph record, an ironic comment on the relationship of humanity to the Sender of the message. Michael Kandel, who has translated a number of Lem's novels (two of which were nominated for the National Book Award in 1975), is adept at rendering Lem's idiosyncratic language, including his wordplay, into English. Lem's style is both masterful and distinctive; in Kandel's renderings one often forgets that one is reading a translation.

Translating the tape from the stars is a considerably more formidable undertaking, complicated by the preconceptions that human beings bring to the task. Through Hogarth, through whose account the other researchers' thoughts are presented, Lem describes the extreme difficulty of freeing oneself from all basic presuppositions. Only thus will one become receptive to new concepts.

The biologists produce a biological entity, a mass of protoplasm synthesized in the laboratory from the "instructions" interpreted from the tape; they name their creation "Frog Eggs." Working from the same data, the biophysicists create a similar substance but one larger and more menacing; they dub it "Lord of the Flies" and house it in a suitably sinister underground vault. Lem summarizes the technology for the reader in a supposed manual for distinguished government figures who tour the facility. The biologists and the biophysicists quickly become two mutually hostile groups; Lem satirizes the infighting and mutual ignorance among members of the scientific community as well as the incomprehension of the outside world. Inevitably, the demonic aspect of the outcome is the one that the researchers choose to emphasize and explore. When Hogarth and his colleague Prothero learn that the mass of matter is capable not only of producing a nuclear explosion but also of transmitting it to any portion of the globe with the speed of light, they are confronted, both as scientists and as human beings, with several dilemmas. They must verify their hypotheses first, yet maintain secrecy all the while. If they do not follow through with the research, someone else will. Just as they learn that the theory is flawed, they are discovered; they also learn that the entire Project, the "real" one, has been duplicated all along by the Pentagon.

In a further irony, it is only when the weaponlike possibilities are discovered that they begin to think of the consequences of another nation discovering the same information from the same radio waves.

Lem, however, downplays the Cold War aspect of the problem, concentrating instead on the interplay between the ideal of the pure and detached scientific mind and the human fallibility that keeps earthlings earthbound mentally and spiritually as well as physically. The novel ends with a debate among all the scientists who have worked on the Project; their theories contradict one another, and not one offers significant progress toward a solution of the message of the Sender. Hogarth muses, in conclusion, "Wrapped in a network of bugs and taps, we were supposed to establish contact with an intelligence that inhabited the Cosmos," consoling himself with the conviction that the Senders, if of superior intelligence, would never send a lethal message to a civilization "where the finest brains out of a billion beings address themselves to the task of sowing universal death, doing what they would rather not do and what they stand in opposition to, because there is no alternative for them." Or, he muses further, the whole thing could have been chance, a random series of electromagnetic impulses that seemed coherent. Oblivion and death are the inevitable end of human endeavor, and if "even a single atom" of each person's feelings remained behind, "the world would be full of raw, bowel-torn howling." Hogarth (and Lem) end with a quotation from Algernon Charles Swinburne, which thanks "whatever gods may be" that no one lives forever and that beyond is "Only the sleep eternal/ In an eternal night."

Katharine M. Morsberger

Sources for Further Study

Library Journal. CVIII, January 15, 1983, p. 147.
The New York Times Book Review. LXXXVIII, March 20, 1983, p. 7.
Observer. December 18, 1983, p. 28.
Publishers Weekly. CCXXII, December 17, 1982, p. 65.

HOLY PICTURES

Author: Clare Boylan
Publisher: Summit Books (New York). 201 pp. $13.95
Type of work: Novel
Time: 1925
Locale: Dublin

A story of two girls approaching puberty whose moves in and out of the adult world,
though surprising, disconcerting, and even frightening, result in a kind of magical growth

Principal characters:
>NAN CANTWELL, a fourteen-year-old child about to grow up
>MARY CANTWELL, her younger sister
>MR. CANTWELL, their father, trying to provide for his family and
> to avoid and do penance for an old sin
>MRS. CANTWELL, his wife and Nan and Mary's mother; she hides
> behind her cigarettes and books
>NELLIE, the family housekeeper
>DOLL, a part of a new kind of trinity with Ivor, her husband, and
> their baby
>IVOR "SHYSTER" SCHWEITZER, a young Dublin Jew who befriends
> Nan and marries Doll

In the Roman Catholic Church, holy pictures are reminders of the lives of persons or saints. On the front side of such an artifact is the picture itself, beautifully detailed in radiant colors; on the back side, one finds indulgences or prayers, the recitation of which buys remission of temporal (purgatorial) punishment for sins pardoned by the receiving of the sacrament of penance. This custom provides the title and the organizing principle for Clare Boylan's first novel, *Holy Pictures*.

When her father dies, halfway through the novel, Mary Cantwell receives from her friends numerous holy pictures. Sitting by her father's trunk, Mary examines each of the pictures with pious attention, after which she places them on the floor of the empty trunk, closes and locks it, and places the key exactly where a jackdaw comes each night to carry shiny things away to his "heavenly lair." Mary is surprised to find the trunk—her father's secret hiding place—empty. When she first opened it, some weeks previously, she discovered a picture of a girl with a dark brown face, some brightly colored women's clothing, and a bunch of old letters with one new one whose ink was still bright green and whose words promised: "Soon I come." The trunk is kept in the Indian Room, a repository for Mr. Cantwell's military treasures, mementos of the time he spent in India. Mary, while looking for some straw from last year's crèche, had been drawn to the locked trunk and opened it. What she found—the picture, the clothing, the letters—was a surprise to her, as is almost everything revealed to a child from the world of adults, for no message is delivered to children straight.

Mrs. Cantwell does not even tell fourteen-year-old Nan, Mary's older sister, that she is being groomed to be offered to an older man in the sacrament of marriage. Nan believes that her mother is to be the bride and is surprised to find out that the man wants her instead, as he forces his kisses on her and pleads that she touch him. Nan's mother is by turns outraged and impatient. She regards Nan's coming of age as a means to an end, a way to pay not only for Christmas luxuries this year but also for housing and food in years to come. Indeed, Mrs. Cantwell takes it for granted that Nan should be sacrificed, for all Dublin women are sacrificed in one way or another to the male ethos and male-dominated religion of their culture.

It is the "touch of the ole relic," the Cantwells' housekeeper Nellie says. Her husband long gone, her own children unseen, Nellie is the only person to tell Nan and Mary anything, but what Nellie says is all a mystery to the girls, for Nellie's repertoire consists of a series of salacious hints which the girls do not understand and some half-truths about the eccentrics of Dublin— Hammer, who roams the streets at night, Shyster, dressed in rags, who abducts children and sells them into slavery, and a "darkie watching this house." "I'll say no more," Nellie says, having said already both too much and not enough.

Hammer helps Mary to her own secret knowledge. In an attempt to make money so that she and her older sister can go to a showing of *The Four Horsemen of the Apocalypse*, Mary tries collecting loose hair which has fallen or been combed from heads. Although Mary brushes her own hair until her scalp is red and collects what she can from her schoolmates and family, the going is slow, so she takes to the streets, trying to get hair from the neighbors. There Mary meets Hammer, who towers over her, twisting a dish towel in his hands. Hammer takes Mary to his house and there shows her something that she will not reveal to Nan and Nellie because she will not break her promise to Hammer. Mary's secret is not what Nellie guesses, although there is a symbolic relationship. Totally bald, Hammer has been trying to collect hair, too; he has collected all of his, a scant supply, and when Mary finds out his secret, she leaves him her tiny bag.

Mary seems too direct and honest to make the money she schemes to get. Her recital is a failure because she pays an adult who demands remuneration although she performs at her own initiative. Mary saves Bertie the cat when her father tries to teach him to be aggressive, mean, and strong. Mary saves Betty the hen when it is discovered that she is not really laying the egg Mr. Cantwell eats for breakfast. Mary has faith in herself. She knows that she can organize an event and make a profit, but events seem to conspire against her. Nevertheless, she acts responsibly in spite of her own losses.

Nan, too, has her problems. Because she is older than Mary, Nan's problems relate more specifically to the sexual—her body is rapidly changing. The parties that she attends are different. Boys and girls are hanging over one another, though Nan still does not understand why, and she is hurt when her best friend, Dandy, begins to prefer a boy's company to hers. When she was younger, Nan wanted to be a nun, a vocation smiled upon by everyone, but as she grows up she gives up the idea and falls into the company of mischievous girls.

The novel's parade of scenes, largely comic and proceeding by abrupt juxtaposition, with little attention paid to chronology but much attention to pattern, form a series of pictures similar to Mary's holy pictures and similar to the family pictures hung in the room that Nan shares with Mary. Around the walls in the cramped room are pictures of ancestors celebrating births or weddings or holidays. Nan says goodnight to them, her own gallery of pictures, with greater regularity and feeling than she devotes to the indulgences taught to her by the nuns for the release of souls in purgatory. Indeed, every scene in the novel is a picture—either a brief image, action caught in stasis, or a series of images with the dramatic continuity of a motion picture.

Snapshotlike images picture the corsets that Mr. Cantwell manufactures; the women who labor over sewing machines, like Doll's cousin, whose knitting needles and position never seem to alter; and the boys leaning over a bridge at Sullivan's Cross waiting for the sight of a dead man. Mrs. Cantwell is captured hiding behind the smoke of her cigarette; Mrs. Graham perched on her luggage; Nan binding her breasts; the Cantwell family and Nellie making a tableau, frozen into place:

> . . . father crouched with his reeking plateful, the children, stiff with anxiety, the cat, under the chair with its ears down, attempting to make itself invisible, and Nellie studying with interest the extraordinary look of disbelief that shrank the points of father's eyes. . . .

Cinematic images bring alive scenes of longer duration: Mother Mary Ignatius pinning paper skirts on girls showing too much leg; Sister Immaculata, apparently fixated on the Immaculate Conception, wanting the girls to deny their bodies or see the changes in them as "por-ten-tous man-if-es-tations of your impending duties as wives and mothers"; Father Percy flirting with the girls; Nan visiting Shyster, whose real name is Schweitzer, and his family; the appearance of Mr. Cantwell's Indian wife; Doll's interminable pushing of the pram; Mr. Cantwell in the middle of a personal power struggle managed by his two wives and a professional power struggle pitting his business against changing styles.

Another series of pictures are those of the movie stars whose images are on the walls of the Schweitzers' house. Immigrants to Ireland, the Schweitzers have values much different from those of the Cantwells—values that are reflected in the way they live and in their own aspirations (or indulgences). Without money or profession and with no English, Jews living in Dublin found things to sell, which is what Shyster does. He sells secondhand clothes and hens hidden beneath the clothes.

Nan's visit to Shyster's house and family opens to her another way of life. She does not feel a sense of danger about which the nuns have warned her. The dining room prepared for the Sabbath is resplendent with translucent candles, gleaming silver, and shining glasses. Shyster is "poor Ivor" to his three sisters, who are all about Nan's age. Mrs. Schweitzer is as friendly as her daughters, and the Schweitzer women feed Nan pudding and explain to her at length the meaning of their gallery of pictures, with movie stars smiling at the world "with radiant happiness . . . in their furs and jewels and shiny top hats." The Schweitzers are a close-knit family. Ivor is working to put his brother through school so that he can become a doctor; all in the family sacrifice to that end. For the Schweitzers, being poor is merely a temporary condition, a means to a well-defined end, not a state of mind. The girls understand the conditions of their world as well as the adults. For the Schweitzers, there are no secrets and no secret knowledge to be kept hidden:

> "We are merely poor. Mama makes our dresses from the best cast-offs. All our money goes to make Sam a surgeon. Becca and me went barefoot until we were twelve but now that men notice us we must wear nice dresses so that we will have husbands."
>
> She put her hands on her hips and stuck out her plump chest. "See! Already there are grown-up men calling to see me."

Nan's second visit to the Schweitzers corresponds with the coming of her first menstrual flow. For the Schweitzers, it is a cause for celebration, a ritual passage to womanhood, not "the curse" to be kept hidden in the way that Nan binds her breasts. For the Schweitzers, the ideal woman is an Earth Mother embracing the whole of life; for the Cantwells and their Catholic neighbors, the ideal woman is wholly spiritual, like the nuns who have given their lives as brides to Christ.

Not all women, however, are as blessed as Mary, who bore a son immaculately conceived. Mrs. Cantwell learns early that she must accept the behavior of her eccentric husband and, in order to save face, lies to her friends about the presence of his first wife. Mr. Cantwell tries to provide, but human failures get in his way, and rather than face a castrating bankruptcy and a family fallen into chaos, he kills himself. After his death, Mrs. Cantwell finds the enormous power to put the family in order again, but when she learns there is no money, her only recourse is to run a boarding house for men and try to find a husband for Nan. After being fired by Mr. Cantwell, Nellie puts blame where she thinks blame must go: "Men . . . I never knew one worth a curse. They go around pestering and pontificating until they've scourged the life outa every woman in sight. . . . They're all the same. . . ." Though Nellie vows to find herself another job where "there's no men to mess me around," the only way she can find to earn money to care for her children is dependent on the lusts of drunken, staggering, belching men.

An incident involving Ivor and Mrs. Roseberg, a forty-five-year-old widow, provides ironic commentary on the Immaculate Conception. Declaring that the New Testament is wrong, that the Messiah will come not to a virgin female but to a virgin male using the body of an experienced female, Mrs. Roseberg pays Ivor to produce the Messiah. Using Mrs. Roseberg's money to purchase a shop, Ivor is happy with his "work" until he falls in love with Doll and tells the widow he cannot continue. Furious, she tries to sue him for not producing the child, though the neighbors believe that the birthing of the Messiah was never her intention in the first place. Curiously, Ivor does produce a miracle in the person of Doll Cotter, the girl with whom he falls in love and impregnates.

Doll Cotter wanders through the novel and through her life pushing a pram filled with one baby after another, her mother's offspring. While she pushes the babies, she grows up, and when she is pregnant she announces with startling clarity the impending birth of her own child and the name of the father, even though she is not yet married to Ivor, who is frantically trying to get his shop established before he marries. Ivor's pushcart is juxtaposed to and then transformed into Doll's pram when it bears the child of Doll and Ivor. At the same time, Doll is transformed into a young woman who knows who and what she is, who feels "secure from outside and in, completely unafraid." She calls herself Minerva and sets out to produce a miracle for Nan and Mary on a Christmas Eve.

The entire novel is structured around this Christmas Eve scene, a fact the reader is not aware of until the final chapter. The opening chapter of the novel is devoted to the procession of three anonymous girls, through the streets and countryside of Dublin to the forest at the foot of the mountains. Two of the girls accompany a third who is pushing a pram with a male baby inside. As they pass through the city, they are enchanted by the shop windows decorated for Christmas. In contrast, the houses on the outskirts of the city are colorless and fronted by neglected gardens. One of the girls carries a paper bag, another a hen. As darkness begins to fall, a frozen mist descends and spectral sheep and cows moan. A man noticing the trio of girls cannot determine in the half-light whether they are children or young women. From this point in the novel, everything is flashback though not necessarily in a chronological pattern. The reader's awareness, therefore, of the importance of the opening chapter cannot be complete until the closing chapter is reached.

This final chapter picks up the earlier scene, making it clear that all that went between is provided to create the situation that would give the miracle meaning. Nan, carrying her paper bag of finger food, is feeling guilty because she has rejected the suitor that her mother provided for her and so has made impossible any Cantwell family celebration of Christmas. Mary clutches her hen because it was, her mother told her, the only possibility for Christmas dinner. Doll leads them into the forest for a private celebration. In the pram beside her baby, Doll has placed tree decorations: balls, angels, candles on tin pegs, and a Christmas fairy to decorate the top of the tree. By the time they find a tree, the ice has turned to snow, making the tree bright against the darkening sky. Because they cannot reach the treetop, they tie the fairy to the highest branch they can reach, and from there it seems to fly in the air. The tree, covered by decorations and lighted candles, becomes a miracle, so beautiful that Nan's heart fills with selfless love and Mary's mind turns away from the voices of souls in purgatory to memories of Nan in her fairy role. After they have eaten, their only reality is "the tall, twinkling triangle of light," so dark has the evening become.

In the presence of the tree, both Mary and Nan decide to use the two shillings that Doll gave them to attend *The Four Horsemen of the Apocalypse* to buy instead a present for their mother. Moved by her younger sister's willingness to give up her dream of attending the film, Nan realizes that Mary, too, is growing up, and that together they will have an easier time of facing the real world, where mysteries will be unveiled to them, secrets exposed to the light of knowledge. This scene in the forest is juxtaposed to the traditional Nativity scene, so that tree becomes substitute for crèche; in Boylan's reworking of the Christmas story, "salvation" is strictly a human affair, a compound of love and imagination, not an act of divine grace.

A brief analysis of *Holy Pictures* can only begin to reveal its complexity. Indeed, one can fault the author for very little in this fine work. If there is a structural flaw, it is that the pacing toward the end of the work seems out of synchronization with the bulk of the narrative, almost as though Boylan hurried too much as she neared the book's end. In general, however, *Holy Pictures* is an unusually accomplished first novel.

Mary Rohrberger

Sources for Further Study

Library Journal. CVIII, September 1, 1983, p. 1719.
Listener. CIX, March 10, 1983, p. 27.
New Statesman. CV, February 25, 1983, p. 28.
The New York Times Book Review. LXXXVIII, November 20, 1983, p. 9.
Publishers Weekly. CCXXIV, August 5, 1983, p. 81.

HOW TO SUPPRESS WOMEN'S WRITING

Author: Joanna Russ (1937-   )
Publisher: University of Texas Press (Austin, Texas). 159 pp. $14.95; paperback
   $7.95
Type of work: Literary criticism

A witty feminist polemic catalogs the ways that women writers have been made to appear minor

Feminists are always annoyed when someone asks, "Why aren't there more great women writers?" After all, the question implies, women in recent centuries have been allowed the opportunity to educate themselves by reading; little girls have the advantage of early verbal facility; even people without money can probably get hold of the minimal tools a writer needs. Furthermore, the question suggests, many women (unlike most men) have not even had to work for income; they could afford to indulge in literature. So why have they not produced more? The answer, Joanna Russ says, lies in the cultural trick of defining great literature so that women do not write it. In *How to Suppress Women's Writing*, she draws on her own experience in the largely male world of science fiction and on the feminist scholarship of the past fifteen years to classify and name the devices our culture has used to diminish recognition of women's literature.

Scholars of various persuasions have been taking a hard look at the literary canon for some years. What is the process by which it is agreed that some books are universally admired? Who defines a classic? What makes a book great? Who decides which books remain in print in editions cheap enough to use in classrooms? Which authors are anthologized? Which are significant enough to be the subjects of graduate dissertations and scholarly reputations? Who ranks the attributes of literature? What values are espoused by saying that tragedy is the most noble dramatic form? What worldview finds irony and ambiguity valuable and sentiment or moral instruction worthless? Why is war an appropriate subject for great poetry and childbirth an embarrassment? Why do most anthologies of "world classics" include only token representation from Africa and Asia and not even that from the indigenous literature of the Americas?

A good many of the answers are also in general circulation. For one thing, the profession of teaching and criticizing literature was established (by men) during the nineteenth century, at a time when the profession of writing literature was, in the United States, dominated by women. Judith Fetterley has suggested that the territory at the center of fiction—the realistic novel about social relationships among ordinary people, with plots and characters that engaged large numbers of readers—was so firmly in women's hands that men's novels could grow only at the peripheries, among the wilds and whales and ambiguities. Scholars appreciated this unpopular literature because it was difficult enough to need critical intervention before readers could appreciate it, thus making scholarship a necessary profession. A considerable amount of the information that can be used to subvert traditional judgment is also available in books such as Ellen Moers's *Literary Women* (1977), Elaine Showalter's *A Literature of Their Own* (1977), Nina Baym's *Woman's Fiction* (1978), Tillie Olsen's *Silences* (1978), and Janet Sternburg's collection of reflections by contemporary women authors, *The Writer on Her Work* (1980).

Russ assembles a generous handful of the arguments that have been used to trivialize women's literary work and names each with a witty and memorable phrase. She argues that our culture has exercised control without direct censorship; she does not believe any deliberate conspiracy keeps women from creating literature or prevents critics from recognizing the literature women produce—but she does believe that cultural biases at every level (including simple, innocent, blindness) have the same effect as a conspiracy:

> In a nominally egalitarian society the ideal situation (socially speaking) is one in which the members of the "wrong" groups have the freedom to engage in literature (or equally significant activities) and yet do not do so, thus proving that they can't. But, alas, give them the least real freedom and they *will* do it. The trick thus becomes to make the freedom as nominal a freedom as possible and then—since some of the so-and-so's will do it anyway—develop various strategies for ignoring, condemning or belittling the artistic works that result.

The first way to suppress women's writing is by prohibition. Laws are unnecessary—illiteracy, poor education, poverty, lack of leisure, the constant fragmentation of attention that results from duties to family, house, and children are some of the more obvious prohibitive forces. More subtle is the climate of expectation—the tacit permission which the culture gives males to be geniuses (though they may expect to be eccentric or unhappy) as opposed to the suspicion that, for a woman, writing is simply a means of wasting time or trying to evade other duties. Many of these external forces, and the self-censorship that grows from them, are movingly detailed in Olsen's *Silences*; they do, indeed, silence women, and they also silence men who are born in the wrong class or at the wrong time.

Because, as Russ says, "some of the so-and-so's will do it anyway," she next analyzes the techniques that have been used (perhaps unconsciously) to trivialize the work that women do produce. One is to deny that it was written by a woman: It wrote itself, it arrived in a dream, it came out of the subconscious, the woman was a mere secretary. (Women trying to overcome invalidation may adapt this ploy for their own purposes; Harriet Beecher Stowe claimed that she did not invent *Uncle Tom's Cabin*, 1852—God moved her pen.) A more subtle version is for the critic to remark that the book was not written by a woman but by her masculine mind; or better yet, that the author is something more than a woman. (Geniuses may not be ordinary people—but how often do critics call a male author "more than a man"?)

Another mode of trivializing a woman's work is to assert that she should not have written it; the woman who could create such a book must be indecent, abnormal, or neurotic. "Confessional" and "autobiographical" are pejorative when applied to women's work, though young men who want to write are usually advised to seek out experiences (go to war, travel, work at the jobs that look interesting on book jackets, explore sexual variety) in order to have something to write about. An implicit standard of content labels some areas of experience second-rate (killing is more significant than giving birth) and, furthermore, assigns different value to the same content depending on the author's sex. In support of this point, Russ summarizes Carol Ohmann's brilliant article from *College English* in 1971 delineating the shift in critical opinion that *Wuthering Heights*'s once-pseudonymous author "Ellis Bell" was known to be female rather than male.

"False categorizing" is Russ's term for the problem of genres and labels that carry built-in value judgments. Why are Kate Chopin and Willa Cather "regionalists" when William Faulkner is not? Cather, after all, wrote about several Western states; Faulkner's region was a single Mississippi county. Why are autobiographies, letters, and journals insignificant forms (unless written by men in classical or neoclassical eras)? There is also the whole question of drawing the lines that divide popular fiction from great literature—particularly because women are the significant writers in several of the "nonliterary" genres, such as children's fiction, the Gothic novel, domestic realism, social melodrama, mystery, and, recently, science fiction.

Finally, Russ identifies two further means of belittling the works by women that do manage to enter the literary canon. One is the myth of the isolated achievement. Charlotte Brontë's *Jane Eyre* (1847) and Mary Wollstonecraft Shelley's *Frankenstein* (1818) are read and taught; Brontë's *Shirley* (1849), *Villette* (1853), and Shelley's *The Last Man* (1826) are seldom in print and are rarely included even on graduate reading lists. Elizabeth Barrett Browning is categorized as "wife" and a few of the "Sonnets from the Portugese" are put in standard anthologies; her political poems are ignored. (Women write about love, not about affairs of state.) Leonard Woolf, as Jane Marcus points out, deliberately suppressed some of Virginia Woolf's socialist and feminist essays, so that her intense involvement with working women and their causes remains virtually unknown.

The other tactic is the imputation of anomalousness. So few women authors are represented in textbooks, anthologies, and college courses that women of achievement appear to be strange and highly atypical. Here Russ comes full circle back to the climate of expectation that may keep women from even trying to write; a rather large number of contemporary authors confess in

The Writer on Her Work that they graduated from college with the sense that women could not be writers because their voices were tiny and their topics always insignificant. Studies of texts, undergraduate courses, graduate reading lists, and major anthologies show that the proportion of women is usually between five and eight percent. What Russ finds most striking is that the proportion holds steady, yet the names seem constantly to change. Here it does begin to look like conspiracy: as if there were some critical mass beyond which there are too many women. Most anthologies give a fairly wide sample of recent women writers, but when the books are updated, women of the generation just past are dropped, though their male counterparts may remain. *The New Oxford Book of American Verse* (1976), for example, omits Amy Lowell, Elinor Wylie, and Edna St. Vincent Millay, who were present in the earlier edition, but retains Vachel Lindsay, John Crowe Ransom, and Yvor Winters. Thus, Russ argues, our sense of a continuity in female tradition is lost; we grow unaware that Emily Dickinson read Lady Georgina Fullerton and Lydia Maria Child and Dinah Mulock Craik; that George Eliot corresponded with Harriet Beecher Stowe; that Stowe wrote an introduction to the 1844 edition of Charlotte Elizabeth Tonna's *Works*—and even once we learn the facts, these authors are no longer a part of our literary heritage, so we cannot understand what influence they may have exerted.

(The problem does not diminish, although freshman anthologies seem to be improving; all too often, adding a section of "Women in Literature" provides an excuse to drop Dickinson, Edith Wharton, and Gertrude Stein from courses in which they used to be taught, so that undergraduate English majors take classes which ought, properly, to be entitled "Nineteenth Century American Men's Poetry" or "The Modern Men's Novel.")

In an afterword, Russ provides an almost comment-free series of snippet quotations from literature by women of color and other minority traditions. The afterword is either a patronizing, racist embarrassment (as some reviewers have said) or an object lesson demonstrating Russ's basic assumption about the way a tradition polices its barriers. Early in the book, she points out that conspiracy theories, though attractive, are hardly necessary, because all of us accept large chunks of our culture ready-made. The afterword catches the reader up short by demonstrating that even Joanna Russ—so fully aware of hidden bias—became a victim of it by failing to notice women whose works are not tributary to the main stream of white literature. She may have refused to analyze her selections in the afterword to make the reader wonder if commentary would imply that writers of color need a white woman's interpretation to be significant.

The book does have flaws. It reads like an entertaining lecture expanded beyond its natural limits. It is padded and often repetitive. The organization is sometimes sloppy; some of the same quotations are used in more than one chapter. One wishes that Russ had expanded her remarks on the material which she finds typical of women's writing. She mentions the vernacular (women usually write books that people can understand), fantasy, mysticism, diaries—but surely there is much more to be said. Men's experience, as she points out, is limited; women writers can do some things that men cannot. On the other hand, despite the fact that almost all of her information is familiar to feminist scholars, Russ has provided useful labels that stick in the mind. "Is it true that *Frankenstein* came to Mary Shelley in a dream?" asks a student. One could answer the question with a perfunctory "yes"—or one could remember that "she didn't write it" is a way to suppress women's writing and explain to the student what image came in the dream, and how much artistic and intellectual power were required not only to communicate the dream's terror but also to expand the simple image into an analysis of science, a criticism of scientists' motives and methods, and an exhibition of the values created by the assumption that science is value-free. For daily service, Russ's categorization of the ways women's writing has been suppressed will probably become part of the common academic tongue.

Sally H. Mitchell

Sources for Further Study

The Atlantic. CCLII, November, 1983, p. 148.
Christian Science Monitor. February 27, 1984, p. 21.
Kirkus Reviews. LI, September 15, 1983, p. 1049.

HUGGING THE SHORE

Author: John Updike (1932-   )
Publisher: Alfred A. Knopf (New York). 919 pp. $19.95
Type of work: Essays, book reviews, and letters

This collection of lectures, reviews, and letters, consisting largely of previously published materials, offers a survey of contemporary literature and a sampling of the author's ideas about major American literary figures of the past century

Since the appearance of his first book, a collection of poetry entitled *The Carpentered Hen* (1958), almost three decades ago, John Updike has published with systematic regularity, and his readers have come to expect a book each year from him. The 1983 addition to the Updike canon, *Hugging the Shore* follows *Assorted Prose* (1965) and *Picked-Up Pieces* (1975) as another generous sample of the author's nonfiction prose. In this latest collection, largely an assemblage of reviews done for *The New Yorker* during the 1970's and early 1980's, Updike displays a truly remarkable range of scholarship and perception about the works of his contemporaries both in the United States and abroad. The grand sweep over the entire field of literature that he makes in *Hugging the Shore* suggests comparison with critics such as Edmund Wilson and T. S. Eliot.

Not all of the pieces in this collection, however, deal with literature; Updike has also included character sketches, lectures, and reviews of books on religion, science, history, and art. One may wonder what prompted Updike to write many of these rather odd bedfellows; he says in the foreword that he was the instigator of some, while others were suggested to him. Nevertheless, it is clear that he is able to handle any assignment with a deftness that is at times almost annoying: He is clearly happy to show off the breadth of his own reading, willing to range the world for the appropriate comparison to make his point. What makes this offhanded brilliance a bit more annoying is that Updike tells the reader in the very first line of the foreword that "Writing criticism is to writing fiction and poetry as hugging the shore is to sailing in the open sea." It appears as if Updike is apologizing for this latest addition to his oeuvre; such apologies are not only cloying, but unnecessary.

Hugging the Shore is divided (far from equally) into two sections. The first, "Persons and Places," consists of seventy-five pages of short sketches, largely of New Englanders and their habitat. In addition, there are two essays on golfing—one a catalog of differing perspectives on the Masters Tournament in Augusta, Georgia, another a golfing fantasy seen from masculine and feminine viewpoints. Also among this potpourri are short pieces about baseball, postal envelopes, and a 1999 visit to the planet Minerva. In many of these sketches, Updike strikes a familiar pose: the gentle satirist, eliciting from the reader a laugh which, as it rings in his ears, makes him recall that among the faces in the crowd at whom he laughs is his own. Updike's descriptive prose is, as usual, precise: The scenes he views are captured in language that makes the reader see what has spurred the writer's imagination.

By far the larger part of *Hugging the Shore* is its second section. Comprising more than seven hundred pages, "Other People's Books" is a compendium of previously published reviews. Here, Updike ranges the world of literature, past and present. The texts of three lectures introduce the section. In these analyses of Nathaniel Hawthorne, Herman Melville, and Walt Whitman, Updike shows his knowledge of the American literary tradition of which he is now a part. There follow reviews of recent publications by and about Edmund Wilson, John O'Hara, Vladimir Nabokov, Saul Bellow, Anne Tyler, Margaret Drabble, Muriel Spark, Iris Murdoch, John Cheever, and dozens of others. In addition to Anglo-American writers, Updike has something to say about Europeans as well: The works of Gustave Flaubert, Raymond Queneau, Louis-Ferdinand Céline, Robert Pinget, Italo Calvino, Günter Grass, Heinrich Böll, and Roland Barthes are among those that fall under the author's gaze. Even Third World and Far Eastern literature is represented; Updike includes reviews of works by African, Indian, Japanese, and Chinese writers. Poetry and fantasy as well as realistic prose fiction receive attention; commentaries on nonfiction—letters, histories, religious studies, biographies, scientific studies—are interspersed throughout the collection. Perhaps the range of Updike's interests can best be illustrated by noting that within the space of thirty pages, one encounters thoughtful and thought-provoking essays on the life of actress Doris Day and on the friendship of theologians Paul Tillich and Karl Barth; these are separated by pieces on silent-film star Louise Brooks and astronomer-turned-television personality Carl Sagan. One is reminded of John Dryden's comment on *The Canterbury Tales*: "Here is God's plenty."

The last forty pages of this imposing tome are given to an appendix, "On One's Own Oeuvre," which Updike himself describes as "a collection, *mercifully incomplete, of written comments, extracted under various goads, pertaining to the one author upon whom and whose work I am an undoubted expert.*" Here, in snippets of interviews, letters, introductions, forewords, and even testimony before the United States Congress, Updike speaks of his own works. Future biographers and critics will be glad for this selection, for in it the author reveals much about himself and his personal values. Some examples: Corresponding with an editor who wanted Updike to send his "best" story for a collection, Updike remarks, "For a reader, the 'best' would be the one that works best, contains the most truth, for him." To answer a similar request from another editor, he says that he is forwarding the story "Leaves" because, though criticized by a reviewer as an example of "lace-making," the story is "taut and symmetrical lace, with scarce a loose thread." Updike is always conscious that he writes for the popular as well as the highbrow audience, and he makes no apologies for his position between these two groups.

"My personal ambition has been simply to live by the work of my pen," he tells the United States House of Representatives Subcommittee on Select Education. He goes on to urge Congress not to subsidize men and women like himself, preferring instead to have as his patrons "a host of anonymous citizens digging into their own pockets." Government grants he sees as the inevitable first step toward governnment control of publication. The American commercial market in which Updike has been so successful is one which he characterizes as paradoxical. Unlike the writer in the Soviet Union (which Updike has visited and about which he has written on occasion), the American writer "enjoys freedom of expression" and access to a competitive market but at the same time suffers "from a sense of irrelevance"—no one really cares what he says or does.

The writer himself cares, of course, and no writer cares more than Updike, who reveals to readers of this collection how he feels about his role. In an interview with Henry Bech, one of his own fictional creations, Updike says that "as long as there is one unhappy person in the world, life is grim"; writing, however, "makes it less so." As a writer, Updike continues, his task is to examine carefully the world around him and to "[bring] the corners [of the world] forward . . . throwing light into them. . . . I distrust books involving spectacular people, or spectacular events." Literature must "concern itself, as the Gospels do, with the inner lives of hidden men. The collective consciousness that once found itself in the noble must now rest content with the typical." Such a creed is not typically postwar American—the majority of contemporary American writers build their fictions on the absurd, the atypical, the neurotic, the insane—but it is, as Updike suggests with his biblical reference, distinctly Christian.

If there is a weakness in *Hugging the Shore*, it arises from the nature of the book itself. Though the author has tried to give some shape to these assorted pieces, taken in its entirety *Hugging the Shore* can best be described as amorphous. Such unity as the volume possesses is a "unity of voice," the voice of Updike himself speaking to his readers directly, as if he were a guide speaking to travelers on a literary grand tour of the United States, Great Britain, and the world at large.

Unlike the voices who narrate his fiction or verse, the voice in these essays sounds like the genuine Updike, the man behind the many masks of his creative works. That voice sounds both sincere and businesslike, generally free of both strident rhetoric and (what seems unusual for someone publishing in *The New Yorker*) of highbrow cynicism for the world of commercial fiction. One is struck, for example, by the lack of petulant commentary about authors whose commercial success has been gained at the expense of genuine literary merit; when he takes such writers to task, Updike presents his criticisms with the dispassionate objectivity of a nineteenth century German philologist. Similarly, when he objects to the neglect that genuinely gifted writers of the twentieth century have suffered, he does so without ranting against the supposed Philistines who have rejected them.

This is not to suggest that Updike is uninterested in what he is doing, or that these essays lack the characteristic wit one has come to expect in his prose. If anything, he seems willing to state his opinions even if they go against generally accepted beliefs. For example, Updike champions Anne Tyler, who, though receiving "less approval in the literary ether" than some of her contemporaries, creates characters that are "persuasive outgrowths of landscapes and states of mind that are familiar and American." He accuses renowned novelist Kingsley Amis of being partly to blame for the "winsomely trivial" condition of the postwar English novel. He attacks Günter Grass for abandoning artistic concerns in favor of sociopolitical ones. He is especially critical of publishers who produce shoddy, ill-made books but is equally quick to praise those who give their readers handsome volumes. Brilliant one-liners pop up on occasion, such as this barb directed at the editor of a book on American art: "This richness of material, unfortunately, is tossed at the reader not much better organized than the print inside a spitball."

From these reviews, one gets a sense of what matters to Updike as an artist; what matters is, predictably, the mastery of style that allows the writer to capture the world around him or the world that he imagines, presenting it in a way that makes the reader share the experience that spurred the creative act.

Whether one can take so much of Updike being himself (or posing as critic) is another matter. Any critic who applies consistent literary and moral criteria to the works he examines tends to sound the same after awhile, and Updike, for all of his stylistic brilliance, is no exception. *Hugging the Shore* is a hard book to read straight through. Nevertheless, for several reasons it is a book worth having on one's shelf, especially if one is interested in "the complete Updike." First, the author has done his readers the service of collecting his scattered gems and stringing them together into a single necklace. Second, because Updike has not yet published a "Theory of Fiction," these reviews permit the scholar to piece together such a theory and hence to judge better Updike's own works as they succeed or fail in the light of their creator's own standards. Third, and perhaps most important, the collection allows the reader to examine in one place the range of Updike's interests, to see how he values literature and belles lettres, and through his evaluation of them, how he values life itself. Those who consider Updike a major voice in contemporary American letters will thank him for *Hugging the Shore*, for—to return to Updike's own metaphor—though he did not venture into deep waters in 1983, his critical beachcombing has produced an interesting and valuable collection.

Laurence W. Mazzeno

Sources for Further Study

Christian Science Monitor. October 3, 1983, p. 32.
Esquire. C, November, 1983, p. 197.
Harper's. CCLXVII, September, 1983, p. 63.
Library Journal. CVIII, September 15, 1983, p. 1798.
Los Angeles Times Book Review. September 25, 1983, p. 3.
The New York Review of Books. XXX, November 24, 1983, p. 26.
The New York Times Book Review. LXXXVIII, September 18, 1983, p. 1.
Newsweek. CII, September 19, 1983, p. 78.
Publishers Weekly. CCXXIV, July 29, 1983, p. 56.

AN ICE-CREAM WAR

Author: William Boyd (1952-)
Publisher: William Morrow and Company (New York). 408 pp. $17.50
Type of work: Novel
Time: June 6, 1914-January 3, 1919
Locale: East Africa, England, and France

Set mainly in the British and German colonies in East Africa during World War I, this novel portrays a set of conflicts within a British military family and the severe changes wrought by the war

> *Principal characters:*
> GABRIEL COBB, an older brother lost in East Africa
> FELIX COBB, a younger brother who searches for Gabriel
> CHARIS COBB (NÉE LAVERY), Gabriel's wife
> MAJOR HAMISH COBB, the militaristic father of Felix and Gabriel
> MRS. COBB, his wife
> WALTER SMITH, an American planter in British East Africa
> ERICH VON BISHOP, a half English, half German planter in German East Africa
> LIESL VON BISHOP, his wife
> WHEECH-BROWNING, British Assistant District Commissioner

While one might say with some accuracy that all serious fiction is about the nature of vision—in all senses of the word—some novels are more clearly so than others. *An Ice-Cream War* is such a novel, one that attempts to combine the forms of the historical and the satirical novels and, in so doing, achieves a generally well-structured and well-narrated whole. The events of the novel occur mainly in East Africa and Kent during World War I, with excursions to Oxford and Trouville, France, and involve a host of characters, some of whom are distinct individuals and some of whom are caricatured types, familiar to readers of Evelyn Waugh and E. M. Forster. At the center of this carefully crafted book is the theme of how people view themselves and their world and the effects of war, even an "ice-cream war," on that vision.

Boyd opens the novel with a page-and-a-half dream in which Walter Smith, an American planter, "sees" Kermit Roosevelt kill his father, Teddy Roosevelt—a "vision" made more realistic by the booming salute of the guns from the German cruiser, *Konigsberg*, anchored in the harbor at Dar es Salaam, where Smith has come to purchase coffee seedlings. The sound of the salute jars Smith from his sleep, drawing him to the window of his hotel room. From that vantage, he observes the cruiser; also visible is the colony's *Schutztruppe*, being inspected by their commander, Colonel Paul von Lettow-Vorbeck. In sum, the scene is emblematic of German pomp and pride, a vision of efficiency and polish that Smith admires both in its military embodiment and in the first-rate hotel and domestic service available in the German colonies. The quite natural duality of dream and real world in this scene serves well to establish the fundamental and classic conflict between appearance and reality.

The novel ends with Felix Cobb, a young Englishman who had come to Africa to search for his brother Gabriel, on board ship in the harbor at Mombasa, gazing back at an Africa from which Germany has been expelled and in which his brother lies buried. Cobb's sight has been seriously damaged by a misdirected mortar round in the war, and as the harbor guns fire a salute from quayside for a batallion of Indian troops embarking for home, his vision disintegrates: "The view before him trembled, misted and then fragmented, as he had known it would. The quay, the ships, the sea, the leaning palms, glimmered fitfully between the swirling chasms of mica dust." He looks up, thinking of the comfort to be afforded his recovering vision by the quietness of the voyage back to England, and sees "the small unfailing clouds dancing quite contentedly in the repercussing air." Between these two scenes lie four-and-a-half years and a war that has changed not only the political map of Europe and Africa but also the lives of millions. The shattering of the old order is reflected exactly in the final image of Felix's shattered vision and is one of Boyd's themes, but to get to that theme, Boyd—as a good novelist must—narrates a tightly crafted story that involves a number of particular conflicts in the midst of these larger ones.

Walter Smith, the American planter, has journeyed from his farm in British East Africa, near the border with German East Africa, to Dar es Salaam to buy coffee seedlings. While there, he meets a neighbor, Erich Von Bishop, decked out in full military uniform, who has come to meet his wife, Liesl, returning from a year in Germany. The three of them, enjoying a degree of camaraderie, return home together. Smith, a short, heavy American in his early forties, is pictured as the frontier American type, hardworking and always ready to continue his efforts despite adversity. He is proud of his farm, grandiosely named "Smithville," and especially of his "Decorticator," a threshing machine for processing sisal, one of two main crops that Smith grows on his rough-hewn plantation. His efforts to begin growing coffee are typical of his attitude. When questioned by the British District Administrator, Wheech-Browning, an ebullient if misguided young man, Smith suggests that one cannot know whether coffee can be grown until one has tried it. Boyd paints Smith as one of the few generally admirable characters in the novel. Wheech-Browning, on the other hand, Boyd fashions as a near-farcical target for an attack on a species: the colonial functionary, thoughtless and fundamentally inept. As the novel develops, Wheech-Browning becomes a cheerful messenger of doom, with mishaps and death occurring whenever he is on the scene; Boyd mordantly describes Wheech-Browning as one who could sentence a man to death and then go "out for a game of lawn tennis with the police inspector without a qualm."

The scene then shifts to Stackpole Manor in Kent, where Boyd introduces the Cobb family, representatives of the moderately wealthy upper-middle class, crochets firmly in place, about to be plunged into the Great War. At a marvelously drawn family dinner on the eve of the wedding of the eldest son, Gabriel Cobb, twenty-seven, to Charis Lavery, the momentous events of the summer—including the assassination of Archduke Ferdinand in Sarajevo—form a conversational counterpoint to the vapid posturings of the Cobb family and attending friends, mostly military, about various elements of rank and privilege on the one hand and the mad behavior of Major Hamish Cobb on the other. Retired from the Duke of Connaught's own West Kents, the Major reminds one of a Squire Western gone further toward the brutal and mad end of the scale. In this competent set piece, Major Cobb is seen mainly through the eyes of Felix, eighteen, and soon off to Oxford. In open conflict with his son, Major Cobb "looked like a tiny, black and white, angry box . . . a diminutive ambassador about to present his credentials at the court of Saint James." Short, fat, and furious, the Major, choleric in the beginning, insane at the end, dotes on Gabriel, leaving Felix to find delight in aggravating him further with his plans to go up to Oxford while flirting with Socialism and dressing in the foppish fashions of the time.

Boyd is skillful in creating characters of this sort, who not only have a sufficient life of their own but also function as effective symbols of classes and values that Boyd wishes to criticize. Even the newlyweds, Gabriel and Charis, do not escape the satirist's eye. After the wedding, they go off to honeymoon in France, the wedding trip suggesting not only the ignorance and immature sexuality of Gabriel, ranging from incompetence to impotence, but also something of the character of his class. The tone is sharply satirical in the bedroom scenes, but the effect is pity for this fine-looking but thoroughly inept young Captain. The outbreak of war saves Gabriel and Charis from having to confront the sexual problems of their marriage; he is immediately posted to his regiment in India to escort a detachment of Indian soldiers to a disastrous participation in the African campaign. He and his men are disgraced in their first action, and, in the confusion, Gabriel wanders distractedly over the battlefield only to be bayonetted and captured by the German askaris (African troops in service of their German colonial masters).

After the wedding, Felix, an ardent and nearsighted pacifist, goes to Oxford to pursue his scholarly career, but Oxford is much changed by the war, and his guilt over nonparticipation in the war grows. Word of Gabriel's capture and wounding reaches Stackpole, and Felix returns home, where he finds himself comforting Charis, the relationship eventually developing into a liaison. The guilt from their affair drives Charis to suicide and Felix to volunteer for service in Africa in hopes of finding Gabriel before Charis' letter of confession reaches him. It is in Felix's search for his brother that the novel finds its focus in an otherwise episodic sequence of events governed by the progress of the war in East Africa: a series of small encounters between British troops, largely colonials under the command of less than effective British officers, and their German counterparts as they march south into Portuguese West Africa, then doubling back northward for Uganda. In this archetypal search for his brother, Felix becomes the central figure of the novel, searching not only for his brother but also for release from the guilt he feels over his affair with Charis and her death.

The book abounds in ironies, handled with enough deftness to continue the story but lacking in the power to resonate thoughtfully. Gabriel, reduced to a kind of infantile dependency by his wound and incarceration, falls in love with Liesl Von Bishop, who is a nurse with the German forces while her husband commands another unit. Gabriel, however, is no more able to express his feelings to this woman than he was able to perform satisfactorily with Charis and is thus reduced to voyeurism. His three years as a prisoner are oddly happy ones for him, freed from the responsibilities of the military, of living up to an image of self imposed upon him by his class and his father.

Indeed, the entire character and career of Gabriel is ironic. He is not the virile man Felix (and everyone else) thinks him to be; he is not the successful and brave military leader his family and colleagues think him to be; and he is quickly disabused of notions of glory by the realities of his first battle. His end, too, is ironic. With the help of Liesl, he escapes from the German camp just as it is about to be liberated by the British. Pursued by Von Bishop and a squad of ruga-ruga (Africans alleged to be cannibals) because he is thought to be in the possession of important military secrets, he is hacked to death by the colonial troops, and his head is brought back to a horrified Von Bishop. Felix finds the body, assumes that Von Bishop is responsible and vows revenge, but when, after the Armistice, he learns of Von Bishop's whereabouts, he is unable to exercise his retribution: Von Bishop, like half of the German officers, has died of the Spanish influenza just before being repatriated to Germany. In this matter of thwarted revenge, as in so much else in the novel, the vision is essentially comic, the actions and motivations of men being reduced to petty absurdities. Even so, Felix's effort has accomplished something; it has expiated his guilt and provided in the shattered fragments of his old cynicism a firmer, truer understanding of himself.

Boyd writes in a clear, tough style, capable of managing a complex narrative with economy and of characterizing with the keenly observed detail. He is at his best, however, when he infuses with significance the smallest and seemingly most innocuous of events, deftly inserting elements that resonate fully in the total scheme of the novel. For example, on a bright morning in late June of 1916, Felix, home from Oxford for the holidays, joins his family for breakfast. At his place are three letters: "A catalogue from a bookseller, confirmation of an appointment with his optician, and one, unstamped, in a plain white envelope," which proves to be a note from Charis telling him good-bye and leading him to the discovery of her suicide. She threw herself into a carp pond after tying a bust of the Emperor Vitellius to her neck with so many knots that she left herself no room for second thoughts.

Charis' suicide and the disquieting line in her note to Felix that she has "written to Gabriel and told him everything"—all this a necessary manipulation of the plot to get Felix to Africa, but the little touch of the appointment notice from Felix's optician, connecting these awful and grotesque events with the theme of vision and the lack thereof, is deft. Self-knowledge and insight, Boyd assures the reader, is not cheap on any level, whether individual, familial, or societal. The casualties of the Great War are not only the combatants on all fronts but also civilians at home, the Charises and Major Cobbs, and the fundamentally myopic and narrow structures and strictures of the British upper-middle class, ironically symbolized in the plaster bust of the Emperor Vitellius that serves to anchor poor Charis firmly out of this world.

Well researched and skillfully written, *An Ice-Cream War* is William Boyd's second novel. His first, *A Good Man in Africa* (1982), won several prestigious British literary prizes; he has also published a volume of short stories, *On the Yankee Station* (1984). With these books, Boyd, an Englishman born in Ghana, has established himself as a promising young writer.

Theodore C. Humphrey

Sources for Further Study

Harper's. CCLXVI, March, 1983, p. 62.
Library Journal. CVIII, April 15, 1983, p. 837.
Los Angeles Times Book Review. March 27, 1983, p. 12.
The New Republic. CLXXXVIII, April 25, 1983, p. 37.
New Statesman. CIV, September 17, 1982, p. 21.
The New York Review of Books. XXX, June 2, 1983, p. 42.
The New York Times Book Review. LXXXVIII, February 27, 1983, p. 8.
The New Yorker. LIX, April 25, 1983, p. 154.
Publishers Weekly. CCXXIII, January 28, 1983, p. 71.
Virginia Quarterly Review. LIX, Autumn, 1983, p. 28.

IN SEARCH OF OUR MOTHERS' GARDENS
Womanist Prose

Author: Alice Walker (1944-   )
Publisher: Harcourt Brace Jovanovich (San Diego, California). 397 pp. $14.95
Type of work: Essays
Time: 1966-1982

A collection of essays dealing with literature, politics, and community and family life, as experienced by the contemporary black woman

Making a garden requires many gifts: courage, discipline, patience, energy. A garden expresses respect for the land and its history, implies faith in a future the gardener herself may never see. The beauty of a garden depends on its maker's appreciation of detail and variety, on the play between the whole and each of its parts, on a trust in the intuitive creativity of hand and eye. "Your garden at dusk/ Is the soul of love," wrote Anne Spencer, a black poet whose work belongs to the tradition celebrated in Alice Walker's fine collection of essays, *In Search of Our Mothers' Gardens: Womanist Prose.* In this collection, Walker extends the work begun by Virginia Woolf in *A Room of One's Own* (1929): She brings forth and nurtures a tradition in which black women, and especially black women who are writers, can take root and flourish.

Walker's collection includes reviews, articles, essays, and statements, all of them having previously appeared in such periodicals as *The Black Scholar* and *Ms.,* to which Walker has been for several years a contributing editor. Covering the period from 1966 to 1982, the pieces vary in length, voice, and power. Walker's vantage point on the issues she takes up is unique: She is a prizewinning writer (three novels, three volumes of poetry, two collections of stories) and scholar (a biography of Langston Hughes, a Zora Neale Hurston reader); she is an activist in both the civil rights and feminist movements; she is a daughter and a mother. Speaking of herself in the third person, Walker writes, "She rather enjoyed being more difficult things in one lifetime than anybody else." Her experiences authenticate the search that gives her collection its title and governing metaphor and help the reader see Walker's "garden" as a complex and intricate whole, the parts of which must be fiercely and lovingly cultivated.

What is most remarkable and most exciting about these essays is the unity that encompasses their diversity. In her experience and in her writing, Walker must continually confront the fact that, as she recalls telling her mother, "everything around me is split up, deliberately split up. History split up, literature split up, and people are split up too. . . . The truth about any subject only comes when all the sides of the story are put together, and all their different meanings make one new one." To create this new meaning, Walker has divided her collection into four sections. The first, which includes several book reviews as well as essays on Hurston, Jean Toomer, and Flannery O'Connor, deals primarily with literature. The essays in the second part grow out of Walker's involvement in the civil rights movement. The third part examines the relations of black women to one another and to black men. The strong fourth section concludes with one of the most significant pieces in the collection—"*One* Child of One's Own: A Meaningful Digression Within the Work(s)"—and one of the most touching—"Beauty: When the Other Dancer Is the Self." Taken together, these four parts express the rich and complicated relations among literature, politics, and the frustrations and rewards of community and family life, as experienced by the black woman.

Walker's search for a fertile literary tradition takes two different routes. Stressing the importance of models in an artist's life, she scrutinizes a tradition of black literature, and especially black women's literature, which has largely been ignored by the white male critical establishment. Phillis Wheatley, Nella Larsen, Lorraine Hansberry, Margaret Walker, Paule Marshall, Toni Morrison, and many others come in for Walker's sensitive and appreciative consideration. She is at her most enthusiastic when discussing Zora Neale Hurston.

Hurston's work as a novelist and folklorist had long been out of print, her grave unmarked in an overgrown Florida cemetery, when Walker began the search chronicled in "Looking for Zora." Walker states unequivocally that there is no book more important to her than *Their Eyes Were Watching God* (1937), and Hurston is surely a model for the character of Shug Avery in *The Color Purple* (1982). Hurston's importance, aside from the fact that she was "a great gardener," is that she showed blacks "to be descendants of an inventive, joyous, courageous, and outrageous people" who are "complete, complex, *undiminished* human beings." This emphasis on "racial health," on the integrity and positive value of black experience, is significant because, as Walker points out, so many black writers have focused on the antagonism of whites. Certainly, Walker herself must contend with the dominant culture, and specifically with those white writers whose works constitute the literary tradition as education perpetuates it. In "Beyond the Peacock: The Reconstruction of Flannery O'Connor," Walker tackles a painful subject: the portrayal of blacks in the writing of Southern whites. This essay, like so many of Walker's pieces, is structured as a narrative; it is the story of a visit to Andalusia, O'Connor's home near Milledgeville, Georgia. Struggling with the contrast between well-maintained Andalusia and the ruin, nearby, of the Walker family's tenant house still surrounded by the daffodils her mother planted in the yard decades before, Walker manages to appreciate O'Connor's handling of her black characters. "By deliberately limiting her treatment of them to cover their observable demeanor and actions," Walker writes, "she leaves them free, in the reader's imagination, to inhabit another landscape, another life, than the one she creates for them."

These discussions of Hurston, O'Connor, and other writers help to delineate the black woman's literary tradition. Walker considers another means to the same end in the essay which gives her collection its title. "In Search of Our Mothers' Gardens" develops an explicit and persuasive parallel between Woolf's comments in *A Room of One's Own* about the fate of William Shakespeare's sister and the spirituality and creativity of the American black woman. "What did it mean," Walker asks, "for a black woman to be an artist in our grandmothers' time? In our great-grandmothers' day? It is a question with an answer cruel enough to stop the blood." Walker notes that the artistic black woman sometimes lost her mind. In less tragic cases, she expressed her spirituality and creativity in religion and in the domestic arts of quilting and gardening, the value of which is only now being affirmed. Always, the creative black woman told stories, and it is these stories that her daughters must now retell. Walker's sense of urgency lest these stories be forever lost—her feeling of responsibility to her mother and to all the black women her mother represents—is one of the most insistent messages of this book. "We must work," Walker writes, "as if we are the last generation capable of work—for it is true that the view we have of the significance of the past will undoubtedly die with us, and future generations will have to stumble in the dark, over ground we should have covered."

Walker's concern for, and faith in, a future that will recognize the past accomplishments of black women arise in part from her own experience as a mother. In a 1973 interview, she explains that her first book of poems was written, during her senior year in college, out of a suicidal depression associated with an aborted pregnancy. Indeed, much of her work has been motivated by despair, has been her "way of celebrating with the world that I have not committed suicide the evening before." The process of rearing her daughter, Rebecca, has affected Walker's motives for writing. As she explains it, Rebecca's birth brought "the incomparable gift of seeing the world at quite a different angle than before, and judging it by standards that would apply far beyond my natural life." Unlike Virginia Woolf, who made much of the fact that none of the great British women writers had children, Walker maintains that the experience of child-rearing, though certainly not easy, can and must be integrated into a woman's creative life. In a 1976 review of Buchi Emecheta's *Second Class Citizen* (1975), Walker observes that the novel's protagonist, an Ibo woman who emigrates to London, manages to live out "the cultural concept of mother/worker that she retains from Ibo society" and thus challenges the way Western culture "separates the duties of raising children from those of creative work." The important essay "*One* Child of One's Own: A Meaningful Digression Within the Work(s)" discusses this issue at length. Again using *A Room of One's Own* as a point of departure, Walker does not deny that motherhood can threaten a writer's work, but she also contends that the experience of mothering does not necessarily stultify and may actually enrich a woman's creativity. In Walker's view, motherhood does not threaten the woman artist nearly as much as do the repressive social forces of racism and sexism. Set against these forces, she and her daughter are more than mother and child; they are *"sisters* really, against whatever denies us all that we are." More metaphorically, Walker comments in a 1972 convocation address at Sarah Lawrence College that "each woman is capable of truly bringing another into the world. This we must all do for each other."

The use of motherhood as experience and metaphor typifies Walker's feminist consciousness, a consciousness which is alert to connections between the personal and the political and which insists that women be accountable to one another. Stating that black women cannot separate themselves from the women's movement without "abandon[ing] their responsibilities to women throughout the world," Walker also criticizes the racism of those white feminists who appear to believe that "women" and "blacks" are mutually exclusive categories. The black woman's children, says Walker, must always make the white woman "feel guilty. She fears knowing that black women want the best for their children just as she does. But she also knows black children are to have less in this world so that her children, white children, will have more. . . . Better then to deny that the black woman . . . is a woman." Despite racism within the feminist movement, Walker does not rule out the possibility for some sort of sisterhood, however uneasy, between black and white women. Certainly, they have many similar concerns: "the danger of perpetuating stereotypic models of beauty"; the necessity of "naming [their] own experience after [their] own fashion"; the possibility that women might provide "a new kind of leadership" in the effort to save the Earth from domination and destruction by white men, who, Walker says, have "never met any new creature without exploiting, abusing, or destroying it."

Walker's willingness to admit the possibility of an alliance between black and white women, like some facts about her personal life (in particular, her marriage to a white civil rights lawyer from whom she is now divorced) has provoked criticism from those who question her commitment to her race. In several essays in part 3, Walker responds to such attacks, exploring the persistence of colorism among blacks and taking heart from the courage and solidarity of black women. Indeed, questions about Walker's commitment to freedom and equality for black people seem unwarranted, not to say malicious. The longest section of *In Search of Our Mothers' Gardens* recounts her involvement in the civil rights movement. Repeatedly, she extols the work of Martin Luther King, Jr. She recalls that she first saw King on the television set her mother had bought for watching soap operas; from that moment, Walker says, her life was permanently changed. Her own involvement in the movement, like King's, included "beatings, . . . arrests, the hell of battle. . . . I have fought and kicked and fasted and prayed and cursed and cried myself to the point of existing." In a 1972 speech at a newly integrated restaurant in Jackson, Mississippi, she observes that King's gifts to dispossessed Southern blacks included the very land which they had worked but never owned, the much-loved places most blacks believed they had to leave in order to escape the cruelty of racism. Racism, says Walker, dropping another of those references to working the land that recur in her writing, is like "that local creeping kudzu vine that swallows whole forests and abandoned houses; if you don't keep pulling up the roots it will grow back faster than you can destroy it."

Walker's intense awareness of the natural world grows in part out of her upbringing in rural Georgia. "In the cities," she writes, "it cannot be so clear to one that he is a creature of the earth, feeling the soil between the toes, smelling the dust thrown up by the rain, loving the earth so much that one longs to taste it and sometimes does." She also holds a belief, characteristic of both African-American and native American cultures, in the spirituality of the material world. This spirituality, which Shug Avery identifies as God in *The Color Purple*, causes Walker to "weep with love" at the beauty of the Earth as seen from the moon: "bluish, a little battered-looking, but full of light, with whitish clouds swirling around it." It is this lovely world which Rebecca sees in her mother's scarred and useless eye, blinded in a childhood accident movingly recounted in "Beauty: When the Other Dancer Is the Self." It is this same world which must be protected from senseless destruction by those who are not, as Walker's mother has been, "careful to stay on good terms with the earth she occupies."

Loving the earth; acknowledging the spirituality in all things and all people; taking seriously "all partisan movements" because they "add to the fullness of our understanding of society as a whole"; clinging to optimism about the future because one's child must live there; discovering and preserving the past because its value has been overlooked—these are, as Walker sees them, the duties of the artist who is also a black woman. These duties make a heavy burden. Walker lightens it with a prose style that ranges from lyricism to sassiness—what she calls "womanishness"—and that continually establishes connections between what is tangible and immediate and what is not. The review entitled *"Nuclear Madness: What You Can Do"* is addressed directly to "you with the toothbrush, you in the sack, and you there not letting any of this . . . get between you and that turkey sandwich." Walker pauses in the middle of her account of visiting Cuba to "think of myself eating rabbit in a fancy Havana restaurant, talking to Huey Newton about whether I approved of his sharecropper father or not." She can also pontificate, as when she states flatly, "Every affront to human dignity necessarily affects me as a human being on the planet, because I know every single thing on earth is connected." Virginia Woolf, whom Walker greatly admires, usually resisted the temptation to pontificate, even at her most argumentative; Walker may still need to learn that lesson. On the other hand, given the number of difficult things Alice

Walker must be in her one lifetime, given her sense of responsibility to them all, given her intricate and joyful view of diversity within wholeness, perhaps she may be forgiven an occasional lapse. Hers is not, after all, an easy garden to cultivate.

Carolyn Wilkerson Bell

Sources for Further Study

America. CL, February 25, 1984, p. 137.
Commonweal. CXI, June, 1984, p. 345.
Los Angeles Times Book Review. December 4, 1983, p. 1.
Nation. CCXXXVII, December 17, 1983, p. 635.
Progressive. XLVIII, February, 1984, p. 42.
Publishers Weekly. CCXXIV, September 2, 1983, p. 62.
Smithsonian. XIV, January, 1984, p. 133.

IN THE HOUSE OF THE JUDGE

Author: Dave Smith (1948-   )
Publisher: Harper & Row, Publishers (New York). 92 pp. $13.95; paperback $7.50
Type of work: Poetry

This seventh collection by one of America's most powerful and energetic younger poets is his best so far; vigorous, straightforward, and coherent, it awakens the reader's sense of mystery and love

In the past dozen years, Dave Smith has established himself among the best poets born since 1940. Even in those poems that fail to make themselves understood—and there have been several over the years—one could sense the essential compelling power of his vision, his narrative drive, his ability to evoke powerful and complex emotions. All of that power is in this collection, which is nearly free of the clotted images and troubled syntax that in earlier volumes occasionally made Smith's poems elusive. Still, it is noticeable that throughout this book, forms of the verb hunch, suggesting crouched power waiting, occur five or six times; Smith is chiefly a poet whose eloquence springs from great energy just under control. Reading him, one sometimes thinks of hot-rodders who remove the mufflers from their cars to achieve greater efficiency, or the old-time steamboat racers on the Mississippi who tied down the safety valves risking explosion to get speed: When these tactics work, there is no substitute for them, and in this splendid book, they work most of the time.

Smith's sense of place and his attraction to a specific landscape—Tidewater, Virginia—have long characterized his poetry; even when writing about the American West, as he does so splendidly in *Goshawk, Antelope* (1979), there is at least the undercurrent of comparison with what has come to stand in his work for home.

This issue is now fruitfully complicated. A primary theme in the collection is that the search for home can be a considerable preoccupation, and that home can genuinely turn out to be where one finds it, as one looks down on a sleeping child's face or back at the lighted window of a house at dusk.

The book is arranged in four sections, the first, a single poem called "Building Houses." This haunting poem evokes childhood memories of houses going up and of a house burning, possibly as the result of the speaker's mischief; he recalls the events fragmentarily, letting the memorable images—the accusing face and voice of an old woman, fire leaping into the night sky—have their sway so that piecing the events together is difficult. The end of the poem, however, stands as an epigraph to the poems that follow:

> Crone, mother of shades, where did you send them? Tell me
> what house built of blue worksong and truth

casts its undying light of forgiveness.
I want to go there, son and father.
. . . .
The city of men cracks around me.
I know what hope bears, the unbuilt,
that dream of grace raging—
but where are the builders
who nail the dark and the light,
who rose freed, singing together?
Where is our home, our sorrow and love?

The second section, containing fifteen poems, arcs over the country from Tidewater, through Salt Lake City, back to a New York hotel, and finally to an unspecified place, about which the speaker, addressing a lost friend, says,

Jesus God, I'm as far from home as you,
uselessly trotting out sleek words
to make a place real for children.

The third and fourth sections, though they contain separate poems that stand independent from one another, come close to being sequences as they are arranged here. The third section is a group of poems that evoke a distant love given the name Celia. The name's conventional poetic connotations and the often dreamlike recollections of the sequence lift these poems from the realm of autobiography; one ceases to be interested in whether this is something that happened to Smith, because one is so interested in what is now happening to the speaker.

The fourth section contains the title poem; these fifteen poems are based on the author's experience with a house in Montrose, Pennsylvania, where he and his family spent a year making a home in a temporary place of abode.

After the invocation in part 1, then, the collection moves to nine poems which explore the speaker's childhood and youth. The first poem, "Photographic Plate, Partly Spidered, Hampton Roads, Virginia, with Model T Ford Mid-Channel," is as carefully detailed as the title; this photograph, of a time when the Chesapeake froze deeply enough to support a car, turns out to include a figure identifiable as the speaker's grandfather. The poem is a moving instance of the hope that many people harbor—that a thing gone, looked at long enough, will come back—or, failing that, will make itself clear:

Under the ice where they walk the dark is enormous.
All day I watch the backs turned away for the one face
that is mine, that is going to wheel at me the secrets of many.

Other poems—"Snake: A Family Tale," "Running Back," and "Smithfield Ham"—lead the reader who already knows something about Smith's Virginia background to look hard, trying to discern the line between recollection and fiction. The question is finally irrelevant; the speaker of "Running Back" is more nearly a professional player than Smith ever was, but Smith has drawn on what he has lived of the game to do something much more complex and realistic than, say, James Dickey's "In the Pocket." That is not high praise, actually, for it should be added that when Smith settles down to this imaginative act, the first thing he foregoes is any attempt at watered-down metaphorical speech. When this running back speaks, he knows what Smith knows and talks about John Keats, uses words such as "inevitably," and then turns around and says things such as, "I'm paid to crack a rock that growls." The effect, if one thinks in stereotypes rather than in specifics, is momentarily surprising but finally satisfying.

The six poems that end part 2 move out from Virginia, taking various attitudes and tones; for example, "Outside Martins Ferry, Ohio" is a moving tribute to James Wright, and "An Ode to Salt Lake City" is a poem that greets with mixed kinds of anger the news that the prophet Spencer Kimball had received a revelation admitting black males to the Mormon priesthood. The section closes with the first poem quoted here. "No Return Address" is a strong poem about loss and faint hope based on a letter from an old friend from Tidewater days; there is no way to respond to it, because the writer has withheld his address. The letter, like a streetlight the speaker ends watching as he stands in his sleeping son's room, is a "message [he does not] understand. On and off."

Part 3 strikes at least one reader as evasive at times, though several of the seven poems in this section are among the best in the collection. The opening lines of the first poem, "Love Blows in the Spring," demonstrate part of the difficulty:

> How speak of this? How make those words
>   as smoke from the mouth, soft,
>   rises and not entirely is a silence
> but enough so our sighs, like wings, may
>
> spread and be something the face can keep.

There are moments when this syntax almost becomes explicable, but then it slips away again leaving unanswered questions about unsupplied question marks. The passage's persuasive rhythm, however, cannot be denied, and this is one source of the sequence's hold on the imagination: Once again, the reader conditioned by confessional poets will wonder how much of this is fiction, forgetting that it is in fact presented as fiction. That is, the reader is not given the kinds of clues provided by a Robert Lowell, that the poet was the man who suffered and was there; the speaker of these poems observes and remembers but does not add to this any self-indulgent complaints about how hard it is to write poems. So one is left with a convincing character, Celia, a waterman's daughter once loved by the speaker as well as others, who has become lost in a not-quite-specified way and whose image will not let the speaker alone.

The question of Celia's precise fate comes up in "To Celia, Beyond the Yachts," a beautiful account of the speaker's return to the scene of an earlier tryst with her; he remembers her leaping "to lie in that sea." At the poem's end, that image is recalled, and it is not easy to know whether it suggests drowning or a moment of craziness; watching a hawk, the speaker wants

> to know what his eye knows,
> why love made you leap down a turning tide, a looping
> rise and fall of scream I hear you make with him.
>
> I look at the far faces of men who could love you enough
> if you sang up out of the sea . . . each is one I am,
> skidding line in the wake, paying out a huge hunger.

The last poem in the sequence, "Sister Celia," indicates beyond doubt that the character is not dead; the speaker returns to find her, recalls earlier meetings, pronounces energetically and sometimes bitterly on the nature of love and time, and ends with a wrenching expression of the desperate hope that loss and time can somehow be confronted:

> Listen, what
> do we wait for except life's little bell zinging,
> collect, the message a trip home, all the way?
> Fool, before it's too late answer. Say yes. You'll pay.

The constraints against quotation in the present format are hard on this poem; its seventy-five longish lines run to more than seven hundred words—a solid narrative—with room for the narrator's brief reflections on what he sees and remembers. At the same time, the poem is economical, every gesture adding to the tone's slow crescendo. It is not Smith's most elegant poem, but it is among his strongest and most absorbing.

Part 4 of the collection is again a sequence, though each poem's integrity makes it clear that it was not conceived as such. This group of poems gives the book its title and is less obviously fiction than the preceding section. For one thing, *In the House of the Judge* is dedicated "to Sue Smith, who made it possible for me to live in her father's house in Montrose, Pennsylvania." So when one comes to these last poems about the Judge's house, one has some external tag for the feeling that now the poet is speaking for himself. This places on him only a small increment of responsibility to the facts, but fiction and fictionalized autobiography are not quite the same, nor do they seem to be. Smith understands this, and when he tilts toward extravagance in this last section, his management of tone is sufficient to the task of keeping one from wondering whether some image or other is based on what really happened.

Several pressures emerge to exert force on the speaker of these poems; one is the sense of being alien, a Southern accent among strangers who notice such things; another is the weight of the past as it manifests itself in this turn-of-the-century house; a third is the hope that somewhere there is a place where both the speaker and his children can say "home" and mean the same thing.

"Toy Trains in the Landlord's House" and "In the House of the Judge" are the central poems in this section. They reveal, in sharp yet mysterious detail, an old house's ability to make felt the presences of its former occupants. In the first poem, during an excursion to the cellar to contend with the quirks of old wiring, the speaker finds a set of model trains; in the second, he walks quietly through the house at night, the suspicion unshakable that he is in the presence of the Judge's ghost. Both poems give rise to fine meditations on the Judge's character and on the speaker's own need to remember that he is a man alive, wishing he could do more than he can, hoping for the strength and skill to do what is within his capabilities.

The quieter poems in this section suggest that there are moments—jogging, hiking with children, mourning a friend—when living near the limit of capability seems more inevitable than difficult. Making such a theme memorable in quiet poems is not the least of this books's many strengths.

Dave Smith is one of the best younger poets in America, and this book is his best so far.

Henry Taylor

Sources for Further Study

Hudson Review. XXXVI, Autumn, 1983, p. 589.
Library Journal. CVII, December 15, 1982, p. 2342.
New England Review. VI, Winter, 1983, p. 348.
The New York Times Book Review. LXXXVIII, February 13, 1983, p. 15.
Publishers Weekly. CCXXII, December 17, 1982, p. 73.
The Sewanee Review. XCI, July, 1983, p. 483.
Virginia Quarterly Review. LIX, Autumn, 1983, p. 135.
Western Humanities Review. XXXVII, Autumn, 1983, p. 251.

IRONWEED

Author: William Kennedy (1928-   )
Publisher: The Viking Press (New York). 227 pp. $14.95; paperback $5.95
Type of work: Novel
Time: Halloween and All Saints' Day, 1938
Locale: Albany, New York

Francis Phelan returns home to Albany, New York, after twenty-two years of wandering in search of forgiveness and redemption

> *Principal characters:*
> FRANCIS PHELAN, the protagonist, a former professional ballplayer
>   who has become a tramp
> RUDY, a fellow wanderer
> HELEN ARCHER, the woman Francis has been with for nine years
> ANNIE PHELAN, Francis' deserted wife
> BILLY PHELAN, Francis' son
> MARGARET PHELAN, Francis' daughter
> ROSSKAM, a rag and junk man

William Kennedy is a former newspaperman who now teaches writing at the State University of New York in Albany. Each of his four novels has been set in Albany, a town he has made his fictional base. A lifelong resident, Kennedy knows the streets, the people, the history, and the legends of the place; his novels project the palpable reality of the city and its largely Irish population. At the same time, however, as James Joyce did with Dublin in *Ulysses* (1922)—the author and the book most clearly echoed in *Ironweed*—Kennedy goes beyond the straight reality and enriches it through imaginative reconstruction, sees it through his own figures and patterns and myths. In Kennedy's hands, Albany becomes a world in which the past and the present, the living and the dead, the actual and the unreal, all intermix in a portrait of lyric beauty and harsh realism.

Ironweed is loosely connected to Kennedy's earlier books by more than setting. *Legs* (1975), which describes the last days of the gangster "Legs" Diamond, is told by Marcus Gorman, a lawyer mentioned in *Ironweed*. The events of *Billy Phelan's Greatest Game* (1978) are narrated by Martin Daugherty, a newspaperman who also figures in *Ironweed*. Indeed, the events of *Billy Phelan's Greatest Game* have only recently occurred when the present action of *Ironweed* takes place. More directly, the main character in *Ironweed* is Francis Phelan, Billy's roaming father, who returns to Albany and his home after twenty-two years on the bum, and some of the events and characters detailed in *Billy Phelan's Greatest Game* are recounted or reappear in *Ironweed*. Still, *Ironweed* is a separate novel and need not be read in connection with its predecessors, although such knowledge does enhance the book.

Ironweed takes place in Albany over two days and two nights, Halloween and All Saints' Day of 1938. Francis Phelan and his friend Rudy, a dull-witted tramp who is dying of stomach cancer, are earning a few dollars by digging graves. Francis owes fifty dollars to the lawyer Marcus Gorman, who has defended him in court against charges that he registered to vote twenty-one times for the Democratic Party. Francis has gone to work for a short time to pay off Gorman. Buried in this graveyard are Francis' parents and his thirteen-day-old son, Gerald, who died of a broken neck when Francis dropped him while changing his diapers twenty-two years ago, the act that set him on the run and separated him from his wife, Annie, and his two other children, Billy and Margaret. During the intervening years, he has lived with the guilt of Gerald's death and also of others, for Francis Phelan has lived a life marked by violence. As a boy, he witnesses his father's horrible death when Michael Phelan is hit by a train as he walks toward him; Francis is the first to reach his twisted body. As a young man, Francis kills a scab trolleyman named Harold Allen during the strike of 1901, braining him with an expertly thrown rock. That death, only partly accidental, results in others, as the soldiers protecting the trolley fire against the mob of which Francis is a part, killing two bystanders. Later that same day, on the run from possible pursuers, he watches helplessly while an escaped convict named Aldo Campione is shot down as he frantically tries to reach the train on which Francis is leaving town, grasping futilely for his outstretched hand.

Francis is able to return to Albany after the strike, entering underground legend as one of the heroes of the incident. He marries and begins to play professional baseball with the Washington Senators, leaving his growing family each spring for months on the road and adding to his local fame. After Gerald's death, however, he runs away. In his travels, he kills Rowdy Dick Doolan, a crazed tramp who tries to cut off Francis' feet with a meat cleaver in order to steal his shoes. Francis fights viciously with many others over the years to protect himself and his own. In all, he witnesses more than two dozen deaths, "Bodies in alleys, bodies in gutters, bodies anywhere, were part of his eternal landscape: a physical litany of the dead."

Francis' penchant for violence is symbolized by his scarred and mutilated hand, which once caught and threw baseballs with grace and skill but which has also killed and maimed. "If you think I won't fight for what's mine, take a look," he tells Rosskam, the junk man with whom he works on All Saints' Day. "That hand's seen it all. I mean the worst. Dead men took their last ride on that hand." At the same time, he feels almost betrayed by his hands. "I got the idea that my hands do things on their own," he says as he thinks of how many have suffered by his actions. By the end of the book, he has killed and hurt again, breaking the back of one man and crushing the knee of another with a baseball bat when they attack him in a hobo jungle.

Francis knows himself to be a survivor. He is linked with the "ironweed" of the title, which is described in one of the book's two epigraphs as "a member of the Sunflower Family. . . . The name refers to the toughness of the stem." Francis sleeps in the weeds, even on cold nights, for they protect him. He is hard and resilient. In contrast to Francis, Helen Archer, the woman he has traveled with and lived with for nine years, is not meant for survival. She thinks of herself as "the Helen blossom," which she describes as "a seed that germinates and grows into a shapeless, windblown weed blossom of no value to anything, even its own species, for it produces no seed of its own; a mutation that grows only into the lovely day like all other wild things, and then withers, and perishes, and falls, and vanishes." Although he no longer loves her, Francis maintains an allegiance to Helen which ends only with her death.

Francis, in fact, for all of his violent ways, is a protector of others and has a strong sense of integrity. Even though he knows himself to be a bum, he believes that "you gotta be fair in this life." One of the reasons he is drawn to Rudy is that "there was something in him that buoyed Francis' spirit. They were both questing for the behavior that was proper for their station and their unutterable dreams. They both knew intimately the etiquette, the taboos, the protocol of bums . . . they shared a belief in the brotherhood of the desolate. . . ." Although he has deserted his own family, Francis is drawn to people who are weaker than he, and he takes his responsibilities to them seriously.

Above all, Francis is a man with a "compulsion to flight," from the consequences of his violence and from the guilt of his transgressions: "the running of bases after the crack of the bat, the running from accusation, the running from the calumny of men and women, the running from family, from bondage, from destitution of spirit through ritualistic straightenings, the running, finally, in a quest for pure flight as a fulfilling mannerism of the spirit." It is appropriate that Francis' running should end in the graveyard on the day of Halloween, "the unruly night when grace is always in short supply, and the old and the new dead walk abroad in the land." "I remember everything," he tells his buried son, Gerald, when he visits the grave for the first time. In grief, he falls prostrate while the spirits of his own father and the other dead look on. His son offers Francis forgiveness, not for the dropping, the fumbling of the hand but for the "craven flight" from the family afterward. Francis realizes that his running has been a self-imposed punishment, an intentional self-humiliation as much as a fleeing from responsibility. Now it becomes a searching after grace and expiation. As he leaves the cemetery and moves through the streets of Albany, Francis faces the various dead of his past. He encounters and acknowledges the ghosts of Harold Allen and Aldo Campione and Rowdy Dick Doolan and others whose lives have intersected with his own.

Thus, *Ironweed*, for all of its realistic depiction of life on the bum during the Depression, is essentially a story of spiritual regeneration. The second of the book's two epigraphs comes from the *Purgatorio*. Francis is, at the beginning, filthy, clothed in rags and flopping shoes, looking for a shoelace. He is aware of his "own uncanceled stink." On Halloween night, after a day of digging graves, he washes his face and hands at the mission where he has gone for coffee and soup. There, he is given a new pair of socks. Later that night, he shaves, washes his genital region, and is given new underwear. He spends the first part of All Saints' Day working on a junk wagon and uses his earnings to buy a turkey, which he takes to his old home. There, he "knew he had to wash as soon as possible. The junk wagon's stink and the bummy odor of his old suitcoat was unbearable now that he was among these people." Going through his trunk long kept in the attic, he finds an almost forgotten suit of clothes. He bathes. "He felt blessed. He stared at the bathroom sink, which now had an aura of sanctity about it, its faucets sacred, its drainpipe holy, and he wondered whether everything was blessed at some point in its existence, and he concluded yes." Washed and dressed, he is transformed, his "resurrectible good looks" brilliantly apparent. His physical cleaning, his new apparel, parallel his sense of forgiveness and spiritual rebirth.

Francis finds redemption in the course of his wanderings. On All Saints' Day, he is forgiven by Gerald, Rowdy Dick, and all the other ghosts from his past. As he sits in the kitchen of his former home, he sees them assembled in the backyard, a "garden of acolytes" holding candles and singing the Dies Irae, the requiem hymn for the dead. He is also forgiven by the living. His son Billy tells him that Annie, his wife, never revealed the manner in which Gerald died. "I can't figure that out," Francis says. "Woman keeps a secret like that for twenty-two years, protectin' a bum like me." His family gather around him and offer him the chance to return.

Some critics have objected to this conclusion, arguing that Kennedy gives in to sentimentality after holding a tough edge throughout the rest of the book. There is some justification for this complaint from a point of absolute realism, but the entire thematic substructure of the work demands that Francis find redemption. Kennedy does not lapse into either the maudlin or the improbable. Francis is ready for expiation; life has carried him to this necessary resolution. Moreover, his return is not without its irony. He has, after all, killed again, and is, in a sense, still running, although this time toward home rather than away. He seeks sanctuary, but there is no absolute assurance that he will stay, that the dance of flight will not overtake him again. He does seem to have found grace after a lifetime of suffering, and that blessing is emotionally satisfying.

Ironweed was the winner in the category of fiction of the 1983-1984 National Book Critics Circle Award and the 1984 Pulitzer Prize. It is a worthy choice, a strong and original retelling of one of man's oldest and most compelling tales.

Edwin T. Arnold

Sources for Further Study

Antioch Review. XLI, Spring, 1983, p. 248.
Commonweal. CX, September 9, 1983, p. 472.
Hudson Review. XXXVI, Summer, 1983, p. 375.
Library Journal. CVII, December 1, 1982, p. 2269.
Los Angeles Times Book Review. December 26, 1982, p. 1.
The New York Review of Books. XXX, March 31, 1983, p. 11.
The New York Times Book Review. LXXXVIII, January 23, 1983, p. 1.
The New Yorker. LVIII, February 7, 1983, p. 121.
Newsweek. CI, January 31, 1983, p. 72.
Time. CCXXI, January 24, 1983, p. 86.

JAMES GOULD COZZENS
A Life Apart

Author: Matthew J. Bruccoli (1931-   )
Publisher: Harcourt Brace Jovanovich (San Diego, California). Illustrated. 343 pp.
$15.95
Type of work: Literary biography
Time: 1903-1978
Locale: Chicago, Illinois; New England; Virginia; and Florida

A first and comprehensive biography of possibly the least read and discussed of America's major modern novelists, who was victimized by the very literary world whose ways and wars he attempted to avoid

Principal personages:
 JAMES GOULD COZZENS, an American novelist
 BERNICE BAUMGARTEN, his wife and literary agent
 THE REVEREND FREDERICK HERBERT SILL, headmaster of the Kent
  School
 DUDLEY FITTS, Cozzens' friend at Harvard University
 LUCIUS BEEBE, a Harvard eccentric and dandy
 WILLIAM JOVANOVICH, a publisher

The complex ironies surrounding the life and literary career of James Gould Cozzens continue long after his death in 1978 as they seem more and more with each passing year to apply to the lives and literary careers of all serious American writers. Cozzens attempted to live a life apart from the doings and undoings of the literary world, an artist's life, but the popular and critical success of his novel *By Love Possessed* (1957) plunged him unwillingly into the stew of literary politics and cast a shadow over his literary reputation. He was one of the first victims of the shift in American publishing and critical assessment away from the literary merit of works themselves and toward the transitory values of celebrity. The dark days of Cozzens' last years become our own when chain bookstore shelves are stuffed with nonfiction nonbooks, romances, and fantasies, when novels have a shelf life of six weeks, and when it has become practically impossible to find the works of serious writers at all. It is, then, somehow appropriate that the year in which this very fine biography was published ended with Stephen King's *Pet Sematary* (1983) squatting toadishly at the top of an undistinguished best-seller list.

The story that Matthew Bruccoli tells in this fully researched and clearly written biography is really three stories: one, the relatively uneventful private life of an artist who lived apart, who did not socialize or participate in the literary scene, who did not seek adventure or travel the world, and who was involved very closely only with his wife and his work; the second, the development of Cozzens' craft and art from florid romanticism through a period of solidly realistic "professional" novels to the remarkably complex and stylistically brilliant novels of his later years; and third, the shape of Cozzens' literary career from brilliant boy novelist to reasonably successful craftsman to Pulitzer Prize-winner to best-seller and finally to silent victim of a literary reassessment.

James Gould Cozzens' private life, although a quiet one, is not uninteresting. Born in Chicago in 1903 of a New England family, he began to write as a child and began to write seriously and to see himself as a writer while attending the Kent School in Connecticut. His years at Kent, as he recorded in a thorough and revealing diary, were marked by the usual turmoil of adolescence and the struggle of a bright and rebellious young man to both learn from and gain his independence from a brilliant and opinionated headmaster, the Reverend Frederick Herbert Sill. Kent and Cozzens' rebellion from Kent very much made him the writer he became; for the rest of his life, he referred back to his Kent years and the values inculcated by Father Sill much more than he ever did to his time at Harvard. He began his first novel, *Confusion* (1924), while at Kent and set forth on his long literary career.

Confusion was published during Cozzens' sophomore year at Harvard University and made him a central figure in a rather dandified literary crowd of undergraduates that included Dudley Fitts and the somewhat older Lucius Beebe. These friends, the rarefied Harvard atmosphere of the day, and Cozzens' romantically overwritten first four novels are much of a piece. Even his leaving Harvard after his second year (never to return), months spent as a tutor in Cuba, and a year in Europe did not free him from either his personal or aesthetic romanticism. It took meeting, falling in love with, and marrying Bernice Baumgarten in 1927 for him to grow up in both his life and his art.

Bernice was at the center of the rest of Cozzens' life. She was a literary agent, reputedly "the best agent in New York," and she helped Cozzens shape both his style and his career. She supported him financially and emotionally, sacrificing herself in many ways to his talent but willingly and enthusiastically; their relationship, a very private one which remains private to them even after this thorough biography, is the clearly apparent key to Cozzens' becoming a major American author.

During World War II, Cozzens was in the Army Air Corps, working mainly in the Office of Information Services (OIS) in the Pentagon in a job which "gave him access to virtually anything he wanted to see—bombing statistics, policy decisions, misconduct in high and low places, reports from the theaters of war, and matters such as the menstrual difficulties of women pilots." Bruccoli concludes, and apparently quite correctly, that "Cozzens may well have been the best-informed officer in the Air Corps—certainly the best-informed officer below the high command." The remarkable insight into and knowledgeability of command problems and decisions of Cozzens' novel *Guard of Honor* (1948) are a direct result of his responsible position at OIS.

After the war, Cozzens returned to his writer's life. The Pulitzer Prize which *Guard of Honor* received in 1949 changed his routine very little, but the extraordinary success of *By Love Possessed* in 1957 and the critical brouhaha that followed it did bring about a number of changes. The Cozzenses moved first to Virginia and then to Williamstown, Massachusetts, and Cozzens found it harder to write to his satisfaction. His isolation from the literary community continued, but it took on an embattled quality that it had never had before. He drank more heavily, and, in 1971, he stopped abruptly on the advice of his doctor. This sudden shock to his system led to a blackout while he was driving his car, resulting in a very bad crash. He was never really the same after that, confessing to William Jovanovich in 1972: "I really died in that car . . . this is someone posing as me."

The Cozzenses moved to Florida in the fall of 1971. For the next seven years, Cozzens lived in a state of chronic depression and anhedonia (the inability to take pleasure in anything), battling cancer and writing only in his notebooks. "Dismayingly," he wrote in February of 1974, "I just can't seem to give a damn about doing anything except somehow getting thru to bedtime." Bernice died after three years of serious illness in January of 1978, and Cozzens, finally losing his struggle with cancer, followed her six months later. He believed that he had resisted the temptation to commit suicide only because, as he put it in May of 1978, "subliminally I suspect the ghost of FHS [Father Sill] in the boy still in me will give me crap about *Kent Boys Don't Quit.*"

The story of Cozzens' progress in his art is, in contrast to the peaks and valleys of his life, one of steady development and improvement, a lifetime of work resulting in a major body of fiction. In the years between 1924 and 1968, he published thirteen novels and one collection of short stories. He disowned the first four novels as he outgrew them, but the nine remaining novels and the stories constitute more than a worthy achievement for any serious literary artist.

Cozzens' first four novels—*Confusion* (1924), *Michael Scarlett* (1925), *Cock Pit* (1928), and *The Son of Perdition* (1929)—were the work of a prodigiously bright boy and young man, romantic, undisciplined, florid in style and attitude. They were critically well received at the time of their publication, and they are far from being bad books; it is in the light of the work that followed them that they came to look unworthy both to Cozzens and to his readers.

S. S. San Pedro (1931), a sharply written short novel concerning the sinking of a ship, marked both Cozzens' maturity as an artist and his moving into what Bruccoli rightly describes as "his unembellished middle style." It and the other short novel of this time, *Castaway* (1934), establish clearly the special gifts that would inform the larger novels to follow: an ability to describe complex events with clarity and accuracy, an awareness of the great subtlety and intricacy of the interrelationship of lives and events in either the narrowest or broadest of circumstances, and a concern with the interdependence of fact and perception, language and meaning—a concern reflected in scrupulous attention to style and form as well as to content and structure. Cozzens was never, from this time on, merely realistic, as *S. S. San Pedro* might suggest to an inattentive eye, or merely symbolic (or allegoric), as the eerily Kafka-esque *Castaway* might suggest to that same eye; he forged in his developing art a complex symbolic realism, one which was true to fact and just as true to the aesthetic shaping of fact into meaning. He admired both Somerset Maugham and John O'Hara but was always doing a great deal more in his fiction than either of those masters of reductionist realism ever did. They described the world as they saw it honestly and directly and accurately, but Cozzens explored the world with his fictive imagination, knowing always that art is so much more than description, that the very act of artistic description transforms that which is being described.

This philosophical and aesthetic understanding required that Cozzens move into longer and more complex narrative forms in order to express that understanding properly. The so-called professional novels of his middle period, by using the worlds of the professions, gave Cozzens the ground upon which to explore his central concern, what Bruccoli calls "the attempt to depict the effect of interlocking simultaneity of events." By using the worlds of doctors, ministers, novelists, lawyers, and soldiers in these novels, Cozzens pressed the style of his middle period as far as it would take him in his exploration of that simultaneity of events and of fact and perception. These novels—*The Last Adam* (1933), *Men and Brethren* (1936), *Ask Me Tomorrow* (1940), which he considered to be "the novel in which he came closest to fulfilling his intentions, *The Just and the Unjust* (1942), and *Guard of Honor* (1948)— form as clear-eyed and intelligent a view of what it is to be alive in our time as the work of any modern writer, culminating with *Guard of Honor*, Cozzens' great exploration of war as the vast testing ground of all values (and quite possibly the best book to come out of World War II in any language).

Perhaps knowing that in *Guard of Honor* he had pressed the techniques and approaches of his professional novels to their extreme, Cozzens turned in his last two novels to a more direct exploration of the interior world, of the mind itself in its labyrinthine complexity. The style of *By Love Possessed* and *Morning Noon and Night* (1968) is as complicated and snarled and difficult and brilliantly exciting as the subject with which it is dealing. Reflective, allusive, syntactically intricate, obscure, and immensely intelligent, the language of both novels is as much the subject of the books as the events of the stories, for the language is the mind, and Cozzens' language creates the mind of his characters on the page, exasperatingly, annoyingly, dizzyingly, and richly. No wonder they met with critical misunderstanding from critics who failed to see that these books were concerned not with sociology or politics or even ethics but with the moral center of all experience, the working of the human mind in the world it inhabits and informs. They are extraordinary books; they, along with *Guard of Honor*, deserve to be ranked with the best of American novels of this century.

The third story that Bruccoli tells in this fine book, however, lets his readers know, without special pleading, why Cozzens' superb novels are not found on college reading lists or the usual compilations of best books or even in print. After the enormous popular success of *By Love Possessed* and a very unfortunate *Time* magazine cover story that made Cozzens out to be a kind of waspish New England Scrooge, the literary establishment, led by Dwight Macdonald, turned on Cozzens with a fury that was shocking (and apparently convincing) at the time, but has since become all too familiar both in American literary politics and American politics: the ritual making and breaking of major celebrities (writers and presidents being subcategories). From the making and breaking of Cozzens and J. D. Salinger to the rise of *People* magazine is not such a long way, and the story that Bruccoli tells of Cozzens' career must stand as a kind of paradigm for so much that has happened since.

Still, all is not lost. This excellent biography, along with Bruccoli's anthologies, *Just Representations: A James Gould Cozzens Reader* (1978) and *James Gould Cozzens: New Acquist of True Experience* (1979), may cause critical attention to turn anew to Cozzens' work. Cozzens' books do remain available to be found and read and reread and studied long after all of the critical and publishing aberrations are gone. "To simplify," James Gould Cozzens wrote in his notebook in 1962, "will be to falsify." He remained true to that belief. Matthew Bruccoli honors that belief in his biography. May they both find readers worthy of them.

R. H. W. Dillard

Sources for Further Study

Antioch Review. XLI, Fall, 1983, p. 508.
Commentary. LXXVI, September, 1983, p. 68.
Library Journal. CVIII, May 15, 1983, p. 1003.
Los Angeles Times Book Review. June 5, 1983, p. 1.
National Review. XXXV, May 27, 1983, p. 632.
The New York Times Book Review. LXXXVIII, July 5, 1983, p. 4.
Publishers Weekly. CCXXIII, April 22, 1983, p. 89.
The Wall Street Journal. June 16, 1983, p. 30.
West Coast Review of Books. IX, July, 1983, p. 31.

JOHN CHEEVER
The Hobgoblin Company of Love

Author: George W. Hunt (1937-   )
Publisher: William B. Eerdman's Publishing Company (Grand Rapids, Michigan).
   326 pp. $17.95
Type of work: Literary criticism

A many-sided critical study that explores the mythological, biblical, and literary resonances of Cheever's fiction, this is the most thoughtful and appreciative treatment of the subject that has thus far appeared

Nearly completed at the time of John Cheever's death in 1982 at the age of seventy, George Hunt's masterly appraisal of Cheever's fiction was prepared with the author's full cooperation, yet without his direct intervention. Unrestricted by the series format common to the two earlier book-length studies of Cheever, Hunt's treatment ranges both wider and deeper than the usual single-author study, providing a most useful "companion" to the work of a somewhat neglected major writer.

Already known as the author of *John Updike and the Three Great Secret Things: Sex, Religion and Art* (1980), Hunt, teacher, editor, and Jesuit priest, has proved to be an uncommonly gifted observer of contemporary life as reflected and refracted in fiction. In Cheever's case, the image of refraction is the more appropriate; although Cheever's often astonishing fictions sometimes reflect experience as in a hall of mirrors, they more frequently serve as a prism that transmits light even through distortion. Hunt, sensitive to even the smallest details of Cheever's thought and style, offers readings of both long and short fictions that invite the active participation of his audience. An experienced reviewer, Hunt observes at one point that whereas "the task of a book review is to tell potential readers what they will find," that of the critic is, in addition, "to tell actual readers what they probably missed. To do this," he goes on, "one must provide sufficient room for re-entry into the book to point up its spaciousness." Hunt's readings, although highly informed, are seldom if ever prescriptive, serving instead as precept and example for confronting Cheever on one's own.

Owing in part to his long association with *The New Yorker*, Cheever has been "discovered" only recently as a major American writer; as Hunt observes, the reputation justly earned by Cheever has been obfuscated at least in part by the host of imitators that crowded in behind his earliest unsung successes. With time, however, the nature of Cheever's talent and the extent of his accomplishment become more readily apparent. The distinction and originality of Cheever's work derive uniquely from its resonance, a quality that continued to elude his many imitators. At times mistaken for an observer, chronicler, or novelist of manners, Cheever proves upon close rereading to have been much more than that, an observer blessed with the rare gift of portraying the topical against the background of eternity. Even the most "current" of Cheever's observations were deeply informed by classical and biblical mythology, further refined by close acquaintance with the work of such gifted storytellers as Charles Dickens and Nathaniel Hawthorne. Given the fact that Cheever's formal education ended at age seventeen with his expulsion from a private secondary school, the depth and breadth of his erudition are little short of astonishing; unlike Jean-Jacques Rousseau, perhaps the most famous self-taught writer of all time, Cheever appears to have had a wise teacher.

The sources of genius, or even of exceptional talent, remain impossible to trace, and Hunt wisely declines to speculate upon how Cheever's work came to be what it is. He does, however, trace the evolution of Cheever's work, particularly noticeable in *The Stories of John Cheever* (1978), collected and published only a few years before the author's death. Unlike many contemporary writers, notes Hunt (citing James T. Farrell as a case in point), Cheever definitely improved with age, transcending in his maturity even the most remarkable of his earlier accomplishments. Hunt acknowledges that a full-scale biography of Cheever is doubtless waiting to be written yet shows little inclination to assume the task himself; although extremely well versed in the facts of Cheever's life, Hunt is clearly less interested in the ingredients than in the finished product. Pending a biography, however, Hunt includes an exhaustive chronology of Cheever's life and work.

In an age of increasing specialization, the traditional life-and-works study may well be approaching obsolescence, and with good reason: In certain recent examples of the genre, such as Deirdre Bair's *Samuel Beckett* (1978), the wealth of biographical material serves ultimately to undermine or trivialize the simultaneous examination of the author's accomplishments. In contrast, a number of current "literary" biographies, even when prepared by established academic critics, eschew discussion of the work to concentrate upon the life; the reader is expected either to know the work or to seek knowledge of it elsewhere. A case in point, and an impressive one, is Diane Johnson's *Dashiell Hammett* (1983), in which only glancing attention is paid to Hammett's fictions. Hunt, indeed, finds sufficient riches within Cheever's work as to render his biography irrelevant.

Taking his subtitle, *The Hobgoblin Company of Love*, from a fictional "letter" in Cheever's first novel, *The Wapshot Chronicle* (1957), Hunt finds all of Cheever's work informed by Christian faith, subspecies Anglican. A lifelong Episcopalian, Cheever may, at first glance, seem an unlikely subject for the occupaton of a Jesuit priest, but the liturgical structure common to both communions soon unites the criticism with its subject. Hunt soon finds and amply illustrates a point of the intersection in the poetry of W. H. Auden, Cheever's close contemporary and quite possibly, as Hunt persuasively argues, the writer whose characteristic themes, concerns, and sense of irony most closely approach Cheever's own. Both authors, in Hunt's view, proceed from the timely through the timeless and back again, illuminating experience in an unequivocal, if often ironic, spirit of affirmation.

Preceded by a lengthy introduction outlining the methods to be used, Hunt's initial chapter deals extensively with Cheever's particular uses of irony, perhaps the single most distinguishing characteristic of his fiction both short and long. Drawing from the work of Northrop Frye and even more from that of Sören Kierkegaard, Hunt isolates a narrative tone that became both sharper and deeper through the years, as Cheever perfected his use of first-person narration. Even in his earliest short stories, however, Cheever the ironist is clearly sharpening his tools, preparing for the mellowness that would come with his maturity. Hunt admits that his personal choices among Cheever's fictions are quite arbitrary; some of Hunt's (and Cheever's) readers may in fact find them too arbitrary, for Hunt dismisses as slight or negligible a number of stories, such as "Torch Song" and "The Hartleys," that are deserving of consideration among Cheever's more impressive efforts. Nevertheless, Hunt's appraisal more than fulfills its stated goal of providing a point of reentry to Cheever's work; the reader thus equipped will be able to revisit even the neglected stories with considerable profit. For example, the Orville Betman segment of "Metamorphoses," almost totally ignored by Hunt, emerges from application of his method as a highly readable restatement of the Orpheus myth.

Although Hunt devotes considerable, and proportionate, attention to Cheever's five published novels, it is clear that Cheever, like John O'Hara before him, possessed talents better suited to the shorter form. The novels are not without their merits—indeed, they contain some of Cheever's best writing—but even Hunt has a difficult task set before him in attempting to defend Cheever against criticisms that he never fully mastered the "architectonics" of the novel. Cheever's compact, often epigrammatic style is in fact somewhat ill-suited to the novel, just as the discursive style of John P. Marquand, for example, was rather ill-suited to the shorter form, as he, too, once depended upon it.

Episodic though Cheever's novels may be, especially the two Wapshot books, Hunt finds unity of purpose and theme where others have found little more than confusion. *Bullet Park* (1969) and *Falconer* (1977), although more unified than their predecessors, are at first glance rather more perplexing; Hunt, to his own and Cheever's credit, explicates both novels in the light of Cheever's sustained preoccupation with the Cain and Abel theme, overlapping at times the Gemini myth of Castor and Pollux. In these stories as well as in the novels, Cheever, as Hunt amply demonstrates, employed both structures "to dramatize the existential divisions within humanity." Considered in the light of Hunt's thoughtful exposition, all four of Cheever's major novels acquire a far deeper resonance than was originally ascribed to them by reviewers, many of whom persisted in perceiving Cheever as a social satirist. Although Cheever's use of satire is highly effective, Hunt is correct in perceiving it as the means to an end rather than an end in itself: As a forger of contemporary myth and parable, Cheever made frequent use of satire, but to consider him as a satirist in the same vein as O'Hara or Marquand is to see little more than the exposed tip of the iceberg.

Just as Cheever did his best work in the shorter genre, Hunt is at his best as an explicator of *The Stories of John Cheever*, finally collected in rough (yet, as Hunt warns the reader, not exact) chronological order in 1978. Bearing out Hunt's assumption of gradual development, the stories in fact group themselves chronologically into four thematic categories, duly noted and labeled by Hunt as "The Urban or New York Stories," "The Exurban or Vacation Stories," "The Suburban Stories" (by far the most significant group), and the generally lesser but still engrossing "Expatriate Stories," most of which are set in Italy. In the strongest of the stories, as Hunt indicates, the four basic loci are intermingled to illustrate the contrast of city and suburb as perceived by a real or imagined outsider or expatriate.

Perhaps predictably, Cheever's earliest stories were set in the New York of his own residence, where, as Hunt notes, he lived in a high-perched apartment overlooking the Queensborough Bridge. As if stressing the detachment of his observation, Cheever wrote the most characteristic of his "New York Stories" in an objective third-person voice, purporting to speak for all of his characters at once: "The Enormous Radio," perhaps the most famous (and certainly the most frequently reprinted) of Cheever's urban tales, emerges oddly diminished from Hunt's close examination, considerably overshadowed by the stronger, if less pretentious work that lay ahead. Of the "Vacation Stories," portraying archetypal (and futile) attempts to escape what one has left behind at home, Hunt singles out "The Day the Pig Fell into the Well," although other readers might opt for "The Summer Farmer" or "The Hartleys." It was in the suburbs, however, that Cheever would discover his strongest and most distinctive narrative voice, speaking most often from a limited first-person viewpoint. Still, some of his most effective suburban stories, such as "The Country Husband," "The Swimmer," and "The Wrysons," are narrated in the third person, as are the impressive retellings of Ovid in "Metamorphoses."

As Hunt argues, the developing institution of suburbia found its true and most natural poet in Cheever. Among the few biographical details that Hunt stresses is that of the Cheever family's removal, in 1951, to a small rented house on the Vanderlip estate in Westchester County, northeast of New York City. Cheever's best short fiction began to develop soon after this move, and most of it explored in cosmic terms the unfolding suburban experience. Although such satirists as Marquand (especially in *Point of No Return*, 1949, and *Melville Goodwin, U.S.A.*, 1951) had already ventured outward into suburban territory, it remained for Cheever to relate that specifically American adventure to its universal antecedents. With considerable help from Surrealist poetry, Ulysses' voyage emerges from Cheever's informed consciousness as "The Swimmer" (an attempt was once made to adapt it to a major motion picture starring Burt Lancaster), a mind-boggling oneiric parable of success and failure, memory and repression that anticipates the later plays of Eugène Ionesco.

Other tales, their mythological origins more diffuse and therefore less readily traceable, carry nevertheless the full authority of archetype, transcending the topical satire that floats above their surface: The emotional and intellectual impact of "The Brigadier and the Golf Widow," for example, has survived the passing vogue of bomb shelters. The same is true of "The Wrysons," in which an admittedly strange couple finds an even stranger fusion of their suburban anxieties concerning the ashes of a Lady Baltimore cake. As Hunt notes, the blend of myth with observed reality is perhaps even stronger, albeit stranger, in "The Scarlet Moving Van," in which the vagaries of suburban mobility are portrayed against the barely perceptible background of New Testament theology. Irony prevails throughout, as best exemplified in "O Youth and Beauty," where the will to live and stay young takes a perhaps unwitting turn toward suicide.

Oh What a Paradise It Seems (1982), Cheever's last published novel—more properly a novella, or perhaps an extended short story—receives more attention from Hunt than it probably deserves; thematically and stylistically, however, the mid-length fiction compares favorably with the best of Cheever's later short stories and may even be seen as a kind of last testament. In an epilogue, Hunt includes the eulogy delivered at the family's request during Cheever's graveside service by John Updike, his erstwhile competitor and perhaps his worthiest successor in the art of fusing observation with archetype. "His religious faith," said Updike, "mysterious as all faiths are, must help account for his artistic integrity and his air of artistic freedom." Updike's use of the word "air," together with the word "Seems" that concludes the title of Cheever's last published fiction, may well strike an unwelcome note of false appearance; George W. Hunt, however, bears with Cheever's implied faith, expressing what Cheever himself called "a love of light and a desire to trace some moral chain of being." Multiple ironies notwithstanding, Hunt credibly concludes this study with the thought that John Cheever more than succeeded in his chosen task, which was to produce a body of work that invites reading and rereading by reason of its resonance.

David B. Parsell

Sources for Further Study

America. CXLIX, September 17, 1983, p. 134.
Best Sellers. XLIII, January, 1984, p. 380.
Booklist. CXXIX, September 15, 1983, p. 129.

JOSEPH CONRAD
A Chronicle

Author: Zdzisław Najder (1930-   )
Translated from the Polish by Halina Carroll-Najder
Publisher: Rutgers University Press (New Brunswick, New Jersey). Illustrated.
647 pp. $30.00; paperback $14.95
Type of work: Literary biography
Time: 1857-1924
Locale: Primarily the Polish Ukraine and England

Departing from the usual thesis-ridden interpretation of Joseph Conrad's life uncritically derived from the novelist's fiction as well as his autobiographical pieces, Najder winnows fact from legend and meticulously portrays Conrad's development

Principal personages:
JOSEPH CONRAD, the Polish-born English novelist
WILLIAM BLACKWOOD, English magazine publisher of Conrad's serialized novels and tales
TADEUSZ BOBROWSKI, Conrad's uncle and guardian
JESSIE EMMELINE CONRAD (NÉE GEORGE), Conrad's wife
STEPHEN CRANE, an American novelist, poet, and journalist, and a friend of Conrad
FORD MADOX FORD, an English novelist, critic, and editor, and Conrad's close friend and collaborator
JOHN GALSWORTHY, an English writer, and Conrad's friend and source of many loans
EDWARD GARNETT, an English editor and critic, Conrad's "discoverer," friend, and champion
ROBERT CUNNINGHAME GRAHAM, Scots nobleman and member of Parliament, a radical Liberal, and close friend of Conrad
EWA KORZENIOWSKA (NÉE Bobrowska), Conrad's mother
APOLLO KORZENIOWSKI, Conrad's father, a Polish revolutionary poet and patriot
JAMES B. PINKER, Conrad's literary agent
MARGUERITE PORADOWSKA (NÉE GACHET), a Polish expatriate writer, a friend and confidante of Conrad
JOHN QUINN, a wealthy American lawyer and the collector to whom Conrad sold many of his manuscripts

Students of Joseph Conrad have long been indebted to Polish critic Zdzisław Najder, whose *Conrad's Polish Background: Letters to and from Polish Friends* (1964) has for two decades proved an indispensable source of information and insight into the novelist's origins. Now Najder's *Joseph Conrad: A Chronicle* (published in Poland in 1983 as *Zycie Conrada-Korzeniowskiego*), in addition to his other translated volume, *Conrad Under Familiar Eyes* (1984), makes available to English-speaking readers for the first time not only the primary documents but also the full range of facts and plausible inferences necessary for a truly balanced, comprehensive understanding of Joseph Conrad's career as man and writer.

Himself a Polish man of letters, a cosmopolitan well versed in several national literatures, a political activist (he is a director of Radio Free Europe), and an exile from his Russian-controlled homeland, the biographer has much in common with his subject—so much, indeed, that one approaches the book half prepared to find a subjective bias or a political slant shaping the account. Before many pages have been turned, however, such fears are dispelled. Najder's reconstruction of Conrad's life, a richly detailed chronological narrative anchored by prodigious documentation, is nothing if not objective. In fact, so scrupulous is Najder's adherence to verifiable facts and so calmly skeptical is his attitude toward Conrad's autobiographical utterances (full of what Najder calls "auto-mythologizing") as well as the memoirs left by his family and associates, that Najder takes the risk of seeming at times almost as sober and colorless as an income-tax auditor in carrying out his task. Nevertheless, this patient, no-nonsense approach in the long run pays off handsomely in the general plausibility of his portrayal of a dauntingly elusive subject.

With rare exceptions such as Frederick R. Karl's *Joseph Conrad: The Three Lives* (1979), previous biographies have tended to domesticate this elusiveness, offering up reductive images of Conrad as romantic sea-dreamer, guilt-ridden neurotic, misunderstood aesthete, and so on. In contrast, Najder's Conrad is a far more complex and contradictory figure, difficult to categorize. Conrad himself, in such works as *A Personal Record* (1912), contributed to the tendency to reduce his wide-ranging experiences to a kind of logic of teleological necessity, derived from his desire in late middle age to see his life as more the determinate product of conscious choice than it actually was. By emphasizing the episodic, ad hoc circumstantial quality of Conrad's career on land and sea, Najder's biographical method calls attention to the conflicting impulses that drove Conrad to try at every stage but especially in retrospect to impose a shape—a fictive role or identity—upon the recalcitrant opaqueness of life.

If there is a keynote to Najder's Conrad, it is the dynamic tension and the subsequent depression and inertia resulting from the perpetual attempt to recast himself into new personae wherein the illusion of a coherent self continuous with a coherent world might be attained, if only for a brief time. The pattern had its origins in the peculiar conditions of his childhood. Józef Teodor Konrad Korzeniowski was born on December 3, 1857, in the Ukraine. His grandfather Teodor had been a hero in the unsuccessful insurrection of 1830, a distinction that resulted in the confiscation of his estate by the Russians. Teodor's son, Apollo Korzeniowski, a gentleman or *szlachcic*, was many other things besides: playwright, poet, academic, translator of Victor Hugo, and an important underground leader of the revolutionary activists whose political activities resulted in his imprisonment on the eve of the brutally suppressed insurrection of 1861. Condemned to exile in a region of northern Russia noted for its severe climate, Apollo suffered from rheumatism, scurvy, and chronic depression, while the health of his wife, Ewa, underwent an even more precipitous decline; she died from consumption in 1865.

If this loss and the apparent hopelessness of his political cause left Apollo a broken, melancholy man, one can imagine the effect on his only son, who was not yet ten years of age. "Poor child," Apollo confided to a friend back in Warsaw, "he does not know what a contemporary playmate is; he looks at the decrepitude of my sadness, and who knows if that sight does not make his young heart wrinkled or his awakening soul grizzled." Young Conrad's only consolation was found in his reading—William Shakespeare, James Fenimore Cooper, and Frederick Marryat were among his favorites—and it is to this early recourse to imaginative escape that one may trace his lifelong fascination with the sea and with English literature as its fittest vehicle of expression. Actual escape, however, was less easily achieved, and when Apollo Korzeniowski died on May 23, 1869, the eleven-year-old orphan walked alone at the head of a massive procession honoring the fallen poet and patriot. This legacy of doomed heroism was a shadow from which he would never completely emerge.

Nevertheless, by the age of fourteen Conrad had decided to become a sailor, an intention staunchly opposed by his pragmatic maternal uncle and guardian, Tadeusz Bobrowski. Within two years, however, Bobrowski relented, and Conrad, supported by a generous two-thousand-franc allowance from his uncle, left Poland for Marseilles to find work aboard ship. Although he had considerable difficulty securing a job as a seaman and drew ever more heavily on Uncle Tadeusz' support, Conrad was to pursue this livelihood—first as simple crewman, then as third, second, and first mate, and finally as captain—for almost twenty years, most of them spent in the service of the British merchant marine. "If a seaman, then an English seaman," he would write many years later. Najder demonstrates, however, that this was less a deliberate decision than a result of circumstance, for as a Russian subject Conrad was liable to military conscription and could not serve on French vessels without asking for official permission, a request which would itself undoubtedly have resulted in his conscription. Great Britain, in possession of the amplest merchant fleet in the world at the time, did not require official permission and had made a practice of hiring foreigners among its ships' crews.

Thus, in his twenties, Conrad found himself living in reality the escapist fantasies he had imbibed as a lonely child, save that the hard and tedious work, the rebuffs he inevitably suffered as a foreigner trying to learn a new language, the often lengthy periods of unemployment between voyages, the initially unsuccessful attempts to pass the examinations for his first officer's certificate and later his master's certificate, the periodic illnesses and fits of depression amounted to a far less romantic and heroic existence than his readings in Cooper and Marryat had suggested. Conrad's trip up the Congo River in 1890, this time in the employ of a Belgian trading company acting upon the mercenary motive sanctioned by King Leopold II's lofty but hollow, altruistic rhetoric, was the nadir of his experience. Doubtless it marked a decisive shift of mental energies toward the vocation he would enter permanently from 1894 on. *Almayer's Folly*, his first novel, was published in 1895, although he had begun working on it as early as 1889.

The change from helmsman to penman, from peripatetic wanderer to shore-bound wonderer, is inevitably the pivotal juncture in any account of Conrad's life. This is so not only because it marks the transition to the literary achievements which provide the motive for interest in the life, but also because it brings into sharp focus the puzzles and contradictions evident in one form or another at every stage of Conrad's career. The distinction of Najder's biography lies partly in his ability to show the operations of a behavioral pattern extending out in both directions from this decisive event (or series of events) without sacrificing the sense of open-ended, trial-and-error struggle against the vicissitudes of fortune that is the essential quality of daily life seen from within. For the lonely son of a defeated Polish patriot to become certified captain in the greatest merchant fleet in the world was, simultaneously, the fulfillment and the denial of the child's dreams of escape. He had freed himself from one set of constraints only to find another requiring yet another form of escape, albeit a form similarly associated with his youthful reading. Paradoxically, his search for escape was, in both cases, also a search for a home: that still center of spiritual security and certitude in a world of inalterable flux which Conrad had never known and never would know on this earth where, as he later wrote, "we are camped like bewildered travellers in a garish, unrestful hotel."

Isolation, then, was both the cause and the eventual result of every major action or decision in Conrad's life. Fitfully employed, scorned by his fellow sea captains for his aloof manner of speech and dress and his saturnine, "foreign" disposition, he turned to a profession with even fewer prospects for financial security and a sense of belonging—a profession, moreover, requiring an odd mixture of solitude and dependence upon others. Again, his foreignness only exacerbated these difficulties, and throughout his career as writer Conrad was bedeviled by the "Slavic" tag upon which contemporary English reviewers relied to account for many of the unconventional qualities of his books. This was one reason, as Najder sensibly notes, for his frequent use of the Maylayan Archipelago for his fictional settings. He was able to write authoritatively about a locale unfamiliar to his English readers, thereby satisfying their appetite for the exotic while also avoiding the risk of directly treating either the domestic scene—which they knew far better than he—or the Polish scene—which held little interest for them (and from which, in any event, he was removed by more than half a lifetime). The choice of Charles

Marlow as observer-narrator in "Youth," *Heart of Darkness* (1902), *Lord Jim* (1900), and *Chance* (1913) was similarly a strategy for mediating between the homeless wanderer and the exaggeratedly English identity which Conrad imaginatively projected for himself but could never attain in actuality.

It is tempting to view even Conrad's choice of spouse as another means of assuaging his sense of estrangement from his adopted country. In Jessie George, he had evidently selected the very type of the English housewife, yet as Najder's highly unsympathetic portrait of Jessie suggests, her resentful, self-absorbed peevishness and incomprehension of her husband's devotion to his art only served to seal him up still further in his isolation, even in his own home. Conrad's collaborative associations with Ford Madox Ford, Edward Garnett, John Galsworthy, and James B. Pinker, among others, all followed this pattern of dependence-avoidance, of affection exchanged at arm's length. Najder argues that Conrad's crucial decision to write in English can itself be seen in a similar light: "writing in a foreign language . . . leaves uncommitted the most spontaneous, deeper reaches of the psyche, and allows a greater distance in treating matters we would hardly dare approach in the language of our childhood." Thus, Conrad's self-imposed artistic constraints amounted to an extension of the perpetual search for identity that was at the same time a perpetual escape from it, an expression of the central paradox of his life no less than those of Lord Jim, Kurtz, and Nostromo.

If, to paraphrase T. S. Eliot, the end of all exploration is at last to arrive where one began and to see the place for the first time, then there is a special pathos to the last decade of Conrad's life. His final years were as fraught with restlessness, solitude, and self-doubt as his years of wandering, and as anguished and conflict-torn as the decades of his greatest literary achievements. What distinguishes the years from 1914 to 1924, however, is that Conrad's glance was no longer even ostensibly directed toward the elusive horizon before him but was fixed obsessively on the path behind, which led so far back as a patriot's grave in Cracow. To be sure, he continued to produce stories and novels of the sea with a far more overt romanticism that gained him the popular audience he had failed to reach in his earlier works, but this development he received bitterly, for he knew that he was cashing in on second-rate literature and that he was no longer able to write as he once had. Increasingly, he became preoccupied by the idea of fidelity, of human solidarity and devotion to a code of honor, traditional values he had always celebrated in his fiction but which now took on a more overtly political meaning in the face of a world shaken by war and revolution.

There is acute irony in the disparity between these ideals and the reality of Conrad's lifelong spiritual and cultural isolation. That they can be traced to the legacy of his father is confirmed by his final, fitful, and largely futile attempts to reestablish contact with his homeland. Conrad happened to be visiting Poland when World War I broke out. One of the most moving images in Najder's biography is that of Conrad, who was not a religious man, kneeling prayerfully at his father's grave. As an extension of this gesture of attempted reconciliation, Conrad allowed himself to sympathize with the political struggle of Józef Piłsudski and his followers, who were fighting for Polish independence at this time. The outbreak of war cut short his visit, but he agreed to do what he could never bring himself to do before: to champion the Polish cause when he returned to England. The subsequent alignment of Russia with Great Britain, however, made this position conspicuously unwelcome back in England, and although Conrad followed through to the extent of composing a four-page memorandum which argued that an autonomous Poland would be consistent with long-range British interests, he soon muted his advocacy and withdrew behind his customary stance of complete hopelessness toward the perennial illusions of the doomed Poles.

Homeless to the end, Conrad aptly characterized himself in mid-life as "homo duplex," one whose viewpoint and sense of values were irreparably divided. As Najder demonstrates, Conrad's life can be seen as a prolonged attempt to resolve this breach by imagining a series of new identities that seemed to transcend or deny it. Each of these fictive selves, however, sooner or later proved to be illusory, a recapitulation of the original breach which only grew wider—except when arrested by the power of art. It is Najder's distinction to have rendered the tensions that made (and nearly unmade) Conrad and to have done so with such authority that we seem to see him before us whole.

Ronald G. Walker

Sources for Further Study

America. CL, April 21, 1984, p. 303.
The New York Review of Books. XXXI, March 1, 1984, p. 3.
The New York Times Book Review. LXXXVIII, December 11, 1983, p. 7.
Publishers Weekly. CCXXIV, September 30, 1983, p. 103.

THE JOURNEY TO THE WEST
Volume IV

Author: Wu Ch'êng-ên (c. 1500–c. 1582)
Translated from the Chinese and edited by Anthony C. Yu
Publisher: University of Chicago Press (Chicago). 469 pp. $35.00
Type of work: Novel
Time: The seventh century
Locale: China, India, and the Buddhist Heavens

A Buddhist monk makes a hazardous and fabulous journey from China to India to obtain scriptures, assisted by the magical powers of a monkey, a hog, a river monster, and a dragon horse

> *Principal characters:*
> TRIPITAKA T'ANG, the Buddhist monk who is chosen to bring scriptures to China
> SUN WU-K'UNG, a monkey king who becomes the chief disciple of the monk; also known as Pilgrim or Great Sage
> CHU WU-NÊNG, the second disciple who is the Marshal of Heavenly Reeds incarnated as a hog
> SHA WU-CHING, the Curtain-Raising General of heaven who has descended to Earth as a river monster and is the third disciple

With this volume, Anthony Yu finishes his acclaimed translation of a major Chinese epic, the *Hsi-yu chi* (*The Journey to the West*). There have been several English versions prior to this, but none before has been a translation of the entire text. Yu has succeeded wonderfully in translating accurately the poetry and prose of this difficult text into flowing, readable English. He also brought his wide knowledge of Chinese literary and religious traditions to the text, both in the interpretive act of translation and in numerous scholarly footnotes. From the appearance of the first volume in 1977, Anthony Yu's work on this project has received the highest praise, and this fourth volume has already won the 1983 Gordon J. Laing Prize for adding the greatest distinction to the publication list of the University of Chicago Press. It is a well-deserved honor.

The Journey to the West is a classic of Chinese literature which details the adventures of a Buddhist monk, Tripitaka T'ang, who travels to India to bring sacred scriptures of Buddhism back to China. He travels for fourteen years and 108,000 miles, undergoing eighty-one ordeals on the way. He is accompanied on his journey by four supernatural helpers: a monkey king, a hog, a river monster, and a dragon horse. On their way, the T'ang monk and his companions are hindered by countless monsters, ogres, and demons. The monk's animal companions are indispensable in this regard, for they possess magical powers and weapons; Monkey is especially valuable, because he can change himself into numerous creatures and can even transform the hairs on his body into additional creatures to create a one-monkey horde of warriors.

This favorite Chinese tale has been told for centuries in various versions. The story is based upon an actual journey by Hsüan-tsang in the seventh century. This particular version, published in 1572, was probably written by Wu Ch'êng-ên, a poet and humorist. The work is the culmination of more than nine hundred years of telling and retelling the story of Tripitaka (an honorific title) as a legend and folktale. In his synthesis of this vast tradition, the author created a complex work of religious allegory, supernatural adventures, and alchemical lore, all pervaded by a sense of humor.

The text is a mixture of prose and poetry, gracefully interwoven. The use of poetry to emphasize and enhance prose is a technique common to Chinese literature, and especially to Buddhist writings. The author of *The Journey to the West* goes beyond this conventional strategy, skillfully employing poetry to further the narrative and give an interpretation of events. Even when merely describing scenery or creatures, the rich and vivid poetic passages are valuable adjuncts to the prose. One can almost feel the surroundings in passages such as this account of the arrival of winter:

> The peak's jadelike plums half-blooming,
> The pond's water slowly icing.
> The red leaves have all dropped away
> And pines turn verdant and gay.
> The pale clouds are about to snow;
> Dried grass on the mountain lies low.
> What frigid scene now fills the eyes
> As bone-piercing wind multiplies!

Anthony Yu has indeed done a superb job with the difficult task of rendering not only prose but also poetry into fluent and contemporary English.

At the very beginning of the text, the story of the origin of the Monkey King, Sun Wu-k'ung, is told. This tale discloses the primary role he is to play in the story, unlike earlier versions of the Tripitaka legend. After his birth from a great stone egg, he frolics for a time as king of the monkeys at the Water-Curtain Cave in the Flower Fruit Mountain. Amid a carefree life of abundance, he begins to worry about the impermanence of life. Longing for the knowledge of immortality, he undertakes a journey which brings him under the instruction of the Taoist Patriarch Subhodhi. Through this tutelage, Monkey attains immortality as well as magical abilities. With these powers, he becomes intolerably disruptive and proud and remains so even after he is called to the heavens in an attempt by the heavenly immortals to control him. The immortals put him in charge of the heavenly stables, but he demands the title of Great Sage Equal to Heaven. Eventually, he ruins the Festival of Immortal Peaches by eating the peaches, getting drunk on stolen wine, and stealing elixir reserved for the use of the Jade Emperor of Heaven. Monkey successfully fends off heavenly troops sent to subdue him until the Buddha himself must punish him by imprisoning him under a mountain.

The story goes on to detail the Buddha's decision to give holy scriptures to China for the people's enlightenment. The Bodhisattva Kuan-yin is dispatched to the East to find a suitable scripture pilgrim; she is also to enlist the aid of any monsters with any great supernatural powers that she encounters. On her journey, she meets the monkey, hog, monster, and dragon and prepares them for discipleship. After reaching China, she chooses Hsüan-tsang as the scripture seeker and he receives a commission from the T'ang emperor. He is given the title Tripitaka T'ang, which refers to his role as imperial searcher for the Buddhist canon of scriptures.

As the T'ang monk travels, he meets his animal disciples one by one. He frees Sun Wu-k'ung from under the mountain and begins to win the loyalty of this Prometheus-like ape. A dragon swallows their horse, but, proving to be the very dragon that Kuan-yin recruited, he transforms himself into their horse. They next meet Pa-chieh, the hog monster of Cloudy Paths Cave. Monkey battles him, but once Pa-chieh learns that the scripture pilgrim is Monkey's master, he joins them as a disciple. Finally, they meet Wu-ching, or Sha Monk, a river monster of the Flowing Sand River. The scripture pilgrim now has his full traveling party of immortals with miraculous powers. Only with such aid could Tripitaka T'ang hope to complete such a lengthy and hazardous journey.

The travelers meet with incredible troubles at every turn. Monsters threaten to eat them or kill them in various horrible ways. Demons attempt to seduce and entrap them. They also are often asked to assist innocent people who are plagued by the local ogres and monsters. Furious and bloody battles occur, and Monkey frequently resorts to bodily transformation to win these struggles. He becomes hundreds of sleep-inducing insects, armies of monkeys, a cricket, or even a piece of clothing. He can enlarge or reduce his size, somersault thousands of miles in a wink, and perform other amazing magic. Such tricks get the travelers through many tight spots.

As they move across China, the animal guardians of Tripitaka also pursue their own spiritual journeys. The T'ang monk tries to control them, but ultimately they must learn to control their own beastly inclinations to progress, however slowly, toward spiritual perfection. The inner journey is indeed a rocky one for these disciples, who had already earned immortal status once but fell from favor through their evil actions. Their aid to the monk and to others they encounter also forwards their own redemption.

Chapters 75 to 100 are contained in the fourth and final volume of *Journey to the West*, continuing the tale from where it left off in the previous volume. As this volume begins, Monkey is trapped in the stomach of a green-haired lion fiend. If he tries to climb out through the monster's mouth, he will be chewed to pieces. Instead, he makes a rope of his hair, ties it firmly around the beast's heart, and then shrinks himself and crawls out the lion's nose. Once he has escaped, he enlarges to a height of thirty feet and is able to control the fiend by tugging on the rope attached to its heart. He can then return to his companions, who are mourning his supposed demise, and assist them as they meet attacks by the lion fiend's brothers: a yellow-tusked white elephant and a golden eagle-roc or "Garuda Monster."

In these final chapters, the travelers are accosted by lions, rhinoceros fiends, a king who kills monks, and various monk-eating monsters. A female rodent spirit captures Tripitaka in order to seduce him as her mate. This would destroy the monk's mission by causing him to transgress his monastic vow of celibacy. The group saves the lives of 1,111 young boys whose hearts are about to be eaten for the sake of adding a thousand years to the life of a dissolute king. They encourage a town to return to the way of Buddhism and by so doing end a drought sent as punishment. The three disciples also take on their own three followers, training them in martial arts.

Through many other adventures, the travelers finally arrive at the Thunderclap Monastery of the Spirit Vulture Peak in India. To reach this residence of Buddha, they must cross a raging river in a bottomless boat. Here it seems that Tripitaka has at last lost, as he falls through the boat and his body floats downstream. Nevertheless, congratulations are given him, because he has now become a Buddha who watches his own corpse float away. They receive the scriptures, deliver them to the Chinese emperor, and return to heaven to be given their appointments as Buddhas and other dignitaries.

Time and again in this volume, as in the preceding ones, the Monkey King serves as the savior of the others. His ability to change into numerous forms, to somersault into the heavens to plead for assistance from the immortals, and to wage fierce battle with his mighty rod gets them through the horrible ordeals which they must face. Old Monkey also has the discernment to detect the presence of demons and monster spirits even when they are disguised in other forms. He is occasionally a bit high-spirited, proud, and unruly even though his demeanor does gradually improve along the journey. He is also ingenious, daring, insightful, and fiercely loyal to his master.

The pig, Pa-chieh, is not nearly so versatile as his "Elder Brother" the monkey, yet Pa-chieh can be a powerful warrior, striking down monsters with his nine-pronged muckrake. Often, however, his central concern is consuming vast quantities of food, bickering with Monkey, and generally being a slave to his own desires. The pig is quite frequently unmannerly, impulsive, cowardly, greedy, lazy, and lustful. It is especially in such failings that he provides the perfect foil for the clever gibes of Sun Wu-k'ung, whose favorite name for Pa-chieh is "Idiot."

Sha Monk is a more obscure figure in this volume. His most common activities are leading the horse and guarding the luggage with Pa-chieh's assistance. He can be a strong fighter, wielding his priestly staff with a vengeance.

In general, however, he is more passive, observant, and reflective than the others, often acting as the voice of restraint or remonstrance to his more impulsive fellow disciples.

Tripitaka T'ang is often overshadowed by his colorful companions, especially by the fantastic monkey king, who steals the central role in this magical retelling of the Tripitaka legend. The T'ang monk remains in the background but does so as the master for whom hardships are undertaken. He maintains a controlling influence over his assistants' unruliness, symbolized by the headband (or "fillet") which he deceives Sun Wu-K'ung into wearing, and which he can tighten painfully by reciting a "tight fillet spell." Monkey is the most in need of control by Tripitaka and, as the senior and most powerful disciple, in turn commands the others. In this work, however, the master plays an ambiguous role. He is often seen cowering as his disciples do battle for him or complaining of the hardships and lacking the will to proceed on the journey. He is, after all, a mortal human facing fourteen years of immense trials, monstrous adversaries, and incredible adventures. He tends to become overwhelmed. Without the assistance of his immortal and magical disciples, he would have been unable to persist on the journey. It is he, however, and not his animal helpers, who must travel more than 100,000 miles to India for the scriptures. Sun Wu-k'ung explains this to Pa-chieh when asked why he does not simply put the master on his back to soar above the clouds and avoid the river monster (actually Sha Monk before his discipleship).

> "Take this monster here: he can use spells and call upon the wind, pushing and pulling a little, but he can't carry a human into the air. And if it's this kind of magic, old Monkey knows every trick well, including becoming invisible and making distances shorter. But it is required of Master to go through all these strange territories before he finds deliverance from the sea of sorrows; hence even one step turns out to be difficult. You and I are only his protective companions, guarding his body and life, but we cannot exempt him from these woes, nor can we obtain the scriptures all by ourselves. Even if we had the ability to go and see Buddha first, he would not bestow the scriptures on you and me. Remember the adage: 'What's easily gotten, is soon forgotten.'"

The Journey to the West is a complex allegory informed by the religious syncretism of the late Ming dynasty, uniting Taoist alchemy, Mahāyāna Buddhism, and Confucianism. Clearly, it is a tale of spiritual quest and pilgrimage. The travelers have both inner and outer quests for salvation. Externally, the pilgrims deliver the scriptural canon of Buddha's law for the instruction of the Chinese people. Their internal quests lead them to discover their own Buddha natures and escape the Wheel of Transmigration. At times, they almost succumb to doubt and despair, but their way is protected by the benevolence of the Buddha and the Bodhisattva Kuan-yin. They cannot frustrate the will of Buddha even through their personal failings and bunglings. This is symbolized at the very start of the story when Monkey haughtily tries to usurp the title of the Jade Emperor of Heaven. Tathāgata Buddha challenges him to prove his superiority by leaping out of the palm of Buddha's hand. Monkey uses his 100,000-mile somersault to reach five great pink pillars which he marks with his name as proof of his success. Disrespectfully, he urinates on one pillar before leaving. When he returns to claim his title, he looks down at Buddha's hand, only to find his graffito and the aroma of monkey urine on Buddha's fingers. The remonstrance received from Buddha serves as a backdrop for the rest of the tale: "'You stinking, urinous ape!' scolded Tathāgata. 'Since when did you ever leave the palm of my hand?'" Despite Monkey's protests, Buddha flips over his hand, imprisoning the ape under his fingers, which in turn become the Five-Phases Mountain.

The Five Phases of Taoist alchemy play a large part in this allegory. Water, fire, wood, metal, and earth are related to the five forces of the body: essence, spirit, soul, vigor, and will. The last three of these are allegorically represented by Pa-chieh, Wu-k'ung, and Sha Monk respectively. Monkey is the unruly "monkey of the mind" which must be controlled for the Master to gain Buddha nature. Hog represents bodily desires and Monster is the will. Indeed, the symbolism is incredibly rich and complex throughout this text; Anthony Yu's scholarly footnotes help sort out many of the allusions and offer references for further study of this fascinating aspect of *The Journey to the West*. In general, his competent handling of the translation enables untutored readers to begin an understanding of the religious and symbolic depths of the work.

A reader entering the world of these volumes is embarking on a wondrous personal journey, a journey into a magical time of long ago and far away, as well as a journey into self. For the Western reader, this will be at times a difficult pilgrimage, fraught with unfamiliar names and faces, unknown places and allusions. Yu assists the reader admirably with his lucid introduction to the first volume and with the numerous explanatory footnotes. Throughout, his notes and translation facilitate the reader's interpretation of the religious and alchemical allegory. At first, however, the profusion of details can be frustrating. Names can be particularly difficult. Monkey alone, for example, can be referred to by more than a dozen names. This confusion is overcome within a few chapters of this volume, however, and is made considerably easier if one has read the preceding volumes.

Their length and complexity should not discourage anyone from becoming thoroughly engrossed in these volumes. Just as the intricate world of J. R. R. Tolkien's lengthy *Lord of the Rings* trilogy has been mapped and explored by countless readers, so this saga should become familiar to a wide range of Westerners. Better parallels may be drawn, perhaps, with Dante's *The Divine Comedy* or the various versions of the Arthurian legends. Despite all of its differences from Western literature, *The Journey to the West* has underlying themes of universal appeal. Pilgrimage, good and evil, self-discovery, and heroism are seen amidst a fabulous tangle of magic, religion, alchemy, adventure, poetry, and humor.

The reader can approach this text at whatever level of difficulty desired. Children of Eastern heritage have been reared on tales derived from *The Journey to the West* as children in the West have been reared on Grimm's fairy tales. Now, Western children can be told these stories of a different culture. Older readers can enjoy the work simply as a fabulous, often humorous, adventure series, while those willing to spend more time and thought with the text will be exposed to a wealth of Chinese wisdom, history, and imagery. Scholars will find a rich resource for interpretation and further research. This work will be read with great pleasure by students of alchemical lore as well as fans of fantasy novels, by researchers of Eastern religions as well as those looking for good fiction for leisure reading. This is to say, finally, that *The Journey to the West* has all the characteristics of any true literary classic. It can be read, reread, and subjected to differing interpretations. One can learn from it in proportion to the energy one is able to expend on it. Above all, at whatever depth the reader becomes immersed in the story, he or she will be rewarded with hours of enjoyment. Anthony Yu has indeed performed a great service in so skillfully making this Chinese classic accessible in full to English-speaking readers.

Mary J. Sturm

Sources for Further Study

Christian Century. CI, March 7, 1984, p. 258.
The New York Times Book Review. LXXXVIII, March 6, 1983, p. 7.
Parabola. VIII, August, 1983, p. 122.

KHODASEVICH
His Life and Art

Author: David M. Bethea (1948-   )
Publisher: Princeton University Press (Princeton, New Jersey). Illustrated. 375 pp.
$27.50
Type of work: Literary biography
Time: 1886-1939
Locale: Moscow, Petrograd, Berlin, Sorrento, Paris, and other cities in Western Europe

An analysis of the relationship between the life and work of a Russian poet and critic

Principal personages:
VLADISLAV FELITSIANOVICH KHODASEVICH, a poet and critic
VALERY BRYUSOV, a Russian Symbolist poet, novelist, and critic
ANDREI BELY (BORIS BUGAEV), a Russian Symbolist poet, novelist, and critic
ALEKSANDR BLOK, a Russian Symbolist poet
ANNA CHULKOVA, Khodasevich's second wife
NINA BERBEROVA, Khodasevich's third wife, a Russian émigré writer
VLADIMIR NABOKOV, a Russian émigré writer
MAXIM GORKY (ALEXSEY PESHKOV), a Russian writer

The brilliant and intriguing poet and essayist Vladislav Felitsianovich Khodasevich (1886-1939) shared the general fate of many Russian émigré writers, who tended to slip through the cracks between their homeland, with readers living under an oppressive regime, and the West, which offered freedom but no audience. (It was this dilemma that, in part, prompted Vladimir Nabokov to become an English-language novelist.) Khodasevich's long eclipse, however, appears to be ending—a fact attested by a forthcoming collection, edited by Robert Hughes and John Malmstad, that will include such books of verse as *Molodost'* (1908; *Youth*), *Schastlivyi domik* (1914; *The Happy Little House*), *Putem zerna* (1920; *Grain's Way*), *Tiazhelaia lira* (1922; *The Heavy Lyre*), and *Evropeiskaia noch'* (1927; *European Night*). There is a general consensus that Khodasevich's work has long been undervalued, and efforts have been made to assign to him his rightful place among modern Russian poets.

David Bethea's study of Khodasevich is a pioneering attempt to ascertain the relationship of the poet to his contemporaries during a period of rapid artistic development in Russia, noting those events that had an impact on his verse and thought, and finally arriving at an appreciation of his work in the context of overwhelming political and social changes. Bethea has worked intensively on Khodasevich, having published portions of the present book as separate essays, and he has edited Khodasevich's letters to his third wife, the writer Nina Berberova. The latter had in fact read the manuscript of *Khodasevich*, and her intimate acquaintance with Khodasevich and with the émigré community during the 1920's has been a valuable asset to this study. In *Khodasevich*, Bethea writes on Khodasevich's life and art, but his study is not divided into the conventional two-part work with a biography in the first part and a literary analysis in the second. He instead uses a chronological framework to link the historical context, and particular episodes in Khodasevich's life, with the poetry of each specific period of development. The resultant work not only furnishes the background associated with biography but also links biographical data with literary analysis in a well-integrated study.

Bethea suggests that certain occurrences in Khodasevich's early life had an enormous impact on his later writing. The poet was the sickly child of a Polish father who worked as a photographer and a Polish-Jewish mother who had converted to Catholicism. The child, however, identified with Russian culture, not Polish, and the determining factor here was his nurse, Elena Alexandrovna Stepanova. It was Elena Alexandrovna who was his wet nurse when no one else would care for the child, and in so doing she sacrificed the life of her own infant, whom she had given to a foundling home. Just as the nineteenth century poet Alexander Pushkin, to an extent Khodasevich's model and a writer he deeply revered, found his nurse's folktales to be a source for some of his own work, so, too, did Khodasevich assert that he had imbibed Russian culture with the milk of his nurse.

Khodasevich began his literary career early in the twentieth century during the ascendancy of Symbolism. Valery Bryusov, one of the founders of the school and a mentor for younger poets, was his role model. Khodasevich became disillusioned with Bryusov, however, particularly with the older poet's exploitation of art to enable him to play the "role" of poet, and the younger writer drifted away from Symbolism. Khodasevich's position in relation to Symbolism is complicated further by the fact that he was only twenty in 1906, a period when the school was beginning to decline and to be wracked by internal dissension, but, in addition, Khodasevich was too much the ironist to be either a poseur, like Bryusov, or to subscribe to mysticism, as did such younger Symbolists as Andrei Bely and Aleksandr Blok. Bethea presents a careful synopsis of the Symbolist movement, and he discusses Khodasevich's later aloofness from the school with sensitive insight.

Khodasevich, however, was to be closer to the Symbolists than to any other group in modern Russian poetry; he disavowed himself from the Acmeists and Futurists, both groups having risen to dominate Russian letters with the demise of Symbolism around 1910. His verse combines the searching lyricism of the Symbolists with the irony that would be his trademark particularly during the emigration. Because Bethea's biographical comments are interspersed with poetic analysis, the reader can follow the development of Khodasevich from the young poet blindly following the "decadent" stylistic excesses of Symbolism to the mature writer whose melodious verse gradually gave way to stark visual images that would dominate his poetry at the end of his career. His first book of verse, *Youth*, heavily influenced by Symbolism, contains references to crypts and an emphasis on sound characteristic of Symbolist poetry; it is, of course, the work of a very young writer. Soon, Khodasevich began to evolve away from decadent images and an emphasis on sound toward the concrete images found in the later verse, images very different from those of the Symbolists.

Khodasevich's next stage of development, beyond his involvement with Symbolism, was linked to a growing interest in Pushkin that culminated in an essay on Pushkin's *Gavriiliada* (1822) in 1922. It was in Pushkin, Bethea maintains, that Khodasevich found a cultural homeland, comparable to Greece for Osip Mandelstam or Byzantium for William Butler Yeats. It is important to note here that Khodasevich's respect for Pushkin is in striking contrast to the Symbolists' preference for the nineteenth century writers Nikolai Gogol and Fyodor Tyutchev, indicating Khodasevich's aesthetic independence from Symbolism.

In contrast to the Symbolists and linked with his attraction to Pushkin, Khodasevich sought to incorporate into his poetry concrete details from his everyday existence that would never have graced his earlier verse. Bethea provides analyses of specific poems from Khodasevich's second collection, *The Happy Little House*, to illustrate this point. Like the first chapter, this one is enriched by the addition of biographical material, including a recounting of Khodasevich's passionate but ultimately unhappy affair with Zhenya Muratova, wife of the art critic Pavel Muratov; the affair left its mark in a poem Bethea considers to be one of Khodasevich's worst, "Materi" ("To Mother"). In spite of this one rather embarrassing lyric, Bethea correctly believes that this was an important evolutionary period for Khodasevich, for he was conscious of having outgrown the confines of Symbolism and of finding his own voice.

Khodasevich's next collection, *Grain's Way*, was written between 1914 and 1920. It spans, therefore, the years of war and revolution that were traumatic both nationally, for Russia as a whole, and individually for Khodasevich. Bethea considered *Grain's Way* the first of Khodasevich's mature collections, noting that the poet had by then developed sufficiently to draw on his two most important sources, Pushkin and Symbolism, synthesizing them into his own work. The extravagance of Symbolism was exchanged, with a degree of finality, for the irony of the mature poet and the emphasis on the banal world of everyday objects that hearkens back, ultimately, to Pushkin and his poeticizing of ordinary life. As in earlier chapters, Bethea notes events in Khodasevich's life that influenced the verse of this period, and he provides painstaking, sensitive analyses of the poems, illustrating the poet's mood and aesthetics of that particular time. Bethea notes, for example, that Khodasevich was "working on" Pushkin during the composition of *Grain's Way*.

The collection *Grain's Way* is distinguished, first of all, by a multitude of visual images antithetical to the Symbolists' emphasis on sound; Bethea has in fact informed the reader earlier of Khodasevich's interest in the plastic arts, especially in painting. The "grain" of the title is not simply a gratuitous image; it stands for the cultural seeds sown by poets, seeds that take root and nourish the art of the following generation. In germinating (dying), Bethea observes, the poet gives life to future artists. Bethea correctly describes Khodasevich as a transitional figure between Symbolism's searching after truth and the Acmeists' use of everyday objects. He links Khodasevich's prosaic environment specifically to Pushkin rather than to Acmeism, and his otherwise excellent analysis of this facet of Khodasevich's verse would have been further enriched by a comment on the Acmeists' style and by a discussion of their place as continuators, like Khodasevich, of the traditions of Pushkin. In spite of this omission, however, Bethea provides a thorough, valuable summary of Khodasevich's life and art during the extremely trying period of war and, particularly, revolution. He notes especially the poet's gradual disenchantment with the Bolshevik regime that would eventually lead him to emigrate to Western Europe.

Conditions in Moscow during the revolutionary period became so trying for Khodasevich and his wife, Anna Chulkova, that they moved with her son to Petrograd, formerly Saint Petersburg. The importance of Saint Petersburg as the dominant city in Russian literature, central to the aesthetic visions of Pushkin, Gogol, Fyodor Dostoevski, Bely, and Blok, was evident to Khodasevich, and it was there that he produced his most significant work. The Saint Petersburg that symbolized the apex of Russian culture, a sign both of autocratic power and of Westernization, was now dead, and Bethea correctly believes that Khodasevich identified the corpse of this city with that of Pushkin. The image of the sower in *Grain's Way*, the wise disseminator nourished by a culture of the past who transferred that growth to future generations, was gone, replaced by the poet who works in a vacuum.

The sense of doom saturating Saint Petersburg immediately after the Revolution was lightened somewhat by the feverish intellectual activity at the Dom iskusstv (House of Arts), immortalized by Olga Forsh in *Sumasshedshii korabl* (1931). It had been Catherine's winter palace and was now the residence of such writers as Osip Mandelstam and Mikhail Slonimsky. In spite of the exciting atmosphere and relative comfort after the harshness of life in Moscow, Khodasevich was well aware that this period was only an interlude during which the culture with which he had identified was coming to be dominated by a new Soviet culture antithetical to him both as poet and intellectual.

It was during this period that Khodasevich met Nina Berberova, the writer who became his third wife and accompanied him out of Russia into exile in Western Europe. Discussing the poems written at this time, which appeared in the collection *The Heavy Lyre*, Bethea notes Khodasevich's awareness that his poetic gift was rewarding but had resulted in a painful separation from others; Bethea's discussion of "Muzyka" ("The Music") is a sensitive treatment of Khodasevich's predicament. The poet's departure from the Soviet Union in the summer of 1922 was the concrete result of his realization that he could not fit in the new society, and this awareness was to be translated into poetic death, for Khodasevich eventually fell silent.

The chapter "Seeds of Wrath and Impotence" is aptly titled, for in poems written during emigration, Khodasevich expresses his rage at being unable to pass on his cultural seed to younger poets, as well as his anger over being cut off from his audience and forced to live in alien cities. Bethea's comments on the poems "Net, ne naidu" ("No, I Won't Find"), "Skvoz' nenastnyi zimnii denek" ("Through the Foul Winter Day"), and "Pod zemlei" ("Underground"), all part of Khodasevich's last collection, *Evropeiskaia noch'* (*European Night*), stress Khodasevich's bitterness toward the jarring atmosphere of Western European cities and the loneliness of emigration. He augments his commentary with background information on Khodasevich's relations with Bely and Maxim Gorky during this period.

Bethea's treatment of Khodasevich during emigration is an able summation of the poet's final years. As with the earlier chapters, the discussion of events and related poems provides insight into both the poet's life and work; this book is a most valuable analysis of the verse and times of a brilliant poet who has been neglected for too long.

Janet Tucker

Sources for Further Study

Library Journal. CVIII, September 15, 1983, p. 1797.
The New Republic. CXC, February 13, 1984, p. 38.
The New York Times Book Review. LXXXVIII, November 27, 1983, p. 9.
Publishers Weekly. CCXXIV, July 8, 1983, p. 53.

THE KINGFISHER

Author: Amy Clampitt
Publisher: Alfred A. Knopf (New York). 149 pp. $11.95; paperback $6.95
Type of work: Poetry

Everywhere, Clampitt's book is chock full of lavish soundplay, inventive word combinations, startling imagery, learned and playful wit

Up through the Renaissance, earth, air, fire, and water were considered to be the basic elements of the created universe. In various states of balance and imbalance, they were also believed to be the causal factors of human personality. Long after scientists and the educated public had abandoned such notions, poets continued to exploit the metaphorical power of these states of matter. Whenever one lets one's senses work upon the natural world, one can understand why these explanations have had such a long hold on the imagination. Earth, air, fire, and water are generative images in Amy Clampitt's highly acclaimed volume *The Kingfisher*. In taking advantage of their power and allusiveness, Clampitt finds a convenient and telling link between her own baroque sensibility and the Baroque art of the seventeenth century.

The book's first two sections, "Fire and Water" and "Airborne, Earthbound," announce this sensibility while simultaneously announcing the all-encompassing range of a nervy artist. As one might expect, section 1 includes poems on coastal settings, while section 2 provides inland scenes and descriptions of birds. The third, fourth, and fifth sections are called "Heartland," "Triptych," and "Watersheds." These deal, in turn, with the American Midwest, religious holidays and motifs, and foreign travels. The sixth and last section, "Hydrocarbon," echoes the opening movements of the collection. By thus presenting the new science's name for the key molecular combination necessary for mankind's major energy sources, Clampitt suggests that her book is an encompassing journey that tests the old and new sciences against each other, asking the reader what has changed and what has remained constant over long stretches of human history. Provocatively, this last section has a strong political focus.

The plain style has found an aggressive challenger in Amy Clampitt. She dares the reader to contend with poems seasoned with such word choices as: dado, trig, gemütlich, ombré, repoussé, panicled, campanula, chrysoprase, velouté, ruching, clepsydra. Even crossword puzzle fans will find themselves reaching for the dictionary to get through a number of Clampitt's poems. This baroque diction is an antidote to plainness, to dullness, and to the barely literate stuttering that is so often taken seriously today. Indeed, her work is extravagantly ornamented: sometimes wonderfully rich, sometimes too rich. Her antidote carries its own poisons—hothouse poisons in which style does a dance further and further removed from communication. One can admire phrases such as "damascene-/ sealed bizarrerie of fernwork" and "a totem-/ garden of lascivious pheromones" and yet wonder if this is luxury or overgrowth. Everywhere, Clampitt's book is chock full of lavish soundplay, inventive word combinations, startling imagery, learned and playful wit, but there is almost no room to breathe, and sometimes straightforward sense is forsaken. In these poems, the reader is summoned by a strange, idiosyncratic voice. Time will tell if the author of *The Kingfisher* sounds fresh notes of genius or only precious notes of wastrel extravagance.

One poem, at least, indicates that Clampitt herself is well aware of her poetic manner and the possible objections to it. "Marginal Employment" records the extravagances of the Duc de Berry, evoking his "choicest curios" and telling how his tastes

> . . . added value
> to the hours of no one knows
> how many lapidaries, couturiers,
> embroiderers of passementerie
> with gilt and pearls, and wielders
> in gold leaf of the minutest
> marginal punctilio.

The duc's *Très Riches Heures* "is burdened with a fossil gilding," and the reader is asked to consider the effort, the human toll that went into "the scandal/ of such squandered ornament." This last phrase could represent an extreme stance toward Clampitt's poetic style. Her argument is this: "The earth's hours/ are weightier, for all this lightness,/ than the sum of human enterprise's/tumbledown fiascos." High claims for the value of high artifice.

Amy Clampitt is a pleasing technician; indeed, something of a virtuoso. Her instinct and care for expressive shapes are evident in both open and closed forms. Most often, she sees to it that her stanzaic poems work honestly—a rare attribute today. "A Hairline Fracture," for example, uses its loosely defined seven-line stanza to frame shifting centers of focus, this even though the five-stanza poem contains only two sentences. (It could have been otherwise punctuated to reveal many more dependent clauses, but dependencies appropriate to theme and speaker's perspective are created by running clauses together.) The short last line of each stanza prepares for resolution while it holds a space anticipating the next movement. Distant echoes of sound ("weather"/ "Square"; "character"/ "barrier") enclose the first two stanzas, a full stop terminates the third, and separation of subordinate from main clause justifies and announces the break between stanzas 4 and 5. More important, there is true distinctiveness to the material, the part of the argument, in each stanza. In these ways, Clampitt holds onto a modernist formal integrity that gives her work a chance of survival.

Formal play and displays are everywhere in *The Kingfisher*. "Balms" employs three short-lined sonnets as stanzas. Two other sonnet experiments are "The Cormorant in Its Element" and "The Local Genius." In the title poem, all the end words in the third stanza conclude with *rd* or *ld* consonant patterns, while other true and slant rhymes define the other stanzas. "Exmoor" employs a consonant-echo envelope rhyme that plays against the poem's constant enjambment:

> Lost aboard the roll of Kodac-
> olor that was to have super-
> seded all need to remember
> Somerset were: a large flock

One notes here Clampitt's fun with splitting words, something that continues through the poem's closing triplets. The stanzas here do not have the integrity of those in "A Hairline Fracture." They work in quite another way, moving the reader around corners and over spaces to suggest the rhythms of the described journey. The unrhymed, unclosed tercets of "A Procession at Candlemas" work on a visual level and by their distant allusion to the terza rima of Dante. The processional quality is enhanced by Clampitt's decision, though this feature is lost when the poem is heard rather than read.

The Kingfisher provides such a great range of subjects and attitudes that it is difficult to label Clampitt's central concerns. She is skillful in creating physical and psychological environments in which moral action takes place— or fails to take place. Many of her poems, especially toward the end of the book, embrace philosophy, politics, science, history, art, and the evocativeness of places in complex, highly charged, and demanding ways. There is a vision of America's national conscience and consciousness in "The Dahlia Gardens" that rivals any in the last ten or twenty years. The aforementioned "A Procession at Candlemas" is almost as powerful, with its striking images of "street gangs// amok among magnolias' pregnant wands."

There are poems about music, about dancing, about the lore of art-rich Europe. There are poems about ecological history, such as "The Quarry," and even one about "Botanical Nomenclature" that explains Clampitt's fondness for the kind of language with which some of her poems are overstuffed. The relationships between creature and environment are explored in "Camouflage," a poem that pulls another thread, a moving human story, through its tapestry. "Salvage" blends the natural world, the man-made world, and the world of ideas. One of the shorter poems in the collection, "Salvage" has great reach and suggestibility through its dazzling image making. In the poem, the speaker watches flatbed trucks haul squashed-down junked cars to their destination and enjoys the

> ceremonial removals

from the category of
received ideas
to regions where pigeons'
svelte smoke-velvet
limousines, taxiing

in whirligigs, reclaim
a parking lot

The fifty poems of *The Kingfisher* take up 130 pages, considerably more than is customary in poetry collections today. The length of the book is a problem. Many of the individual poems are long and difficult, leaving a reader to wonder if making it through the whole book is going to be an ordeal that brings rewards. In fact, there *are* rewards, but it would have been wiser for Clampitt to have presented a slimmer collection. While her achievement is impressive, the sheer bulk is off-putting. Perhaps she is aiming too quickly at the place in history that Frederick Turner, in his jacket blurb, has already assigned her. At any rate, the effect of the collection is jeopardized by its length, in part because the shape of the book loses certainty as the reader loses touch with the earlier poems. Books of poems depend on the reader's memory for some of their important effects, and few readers will hold on to what they need from the early parts of this collection by the time they reach the later stages. Another problem is simply reader exhaustion.

Following the poems are thirteen pages of notes. These include comments on sources, glossings of obscure allusions, and explanations of specialized knowledge. In one case—the notes for "Rain at Bellagio"—Clampitt gives the reader hints on how to read the poem. While this placement of notes is preferable to distracting footnotes, the problem they admit to is a problem of some consequence. Who is Clampitt's audience? Would not these poems live more completely in themselves? What does one do with the notes? The implied answer is that one must read the poems over again because surely something was missed.

Clampitt's readers will miss many things the first time through, and the second. Patience brings rewards; certainly the difficulties in these poems can be overcome by a diligent, committed reader. The only question is whether such risks need be run in the first place. There is simply too much here—too much exotic diction, too much allusiveness, too much density, too much material—for most readers. Even though Amy Clampitt is a highly original poet, she does little to extend or even maintain the shrinking audience for poetry. *The Kingfisher* is an elitist performance, and it is difficult to know whether to applaud Clampitt's integrity or to accuse her of self-indulgence.

Her "guilt," it is only fair to add, is not greater than that of William Butler Yeats or T. S. Eliot, or any number of the great, learned, and highly individualistic moderns. Supreme makers, they are bad influences for most writers who come under their spell. Clampitt, too, may be a major voice and a bad influence, but that part of her art demonstrating a great and spirited love for language can do much good.

Philip K. Jason

Sources for Further Study

Commonweal. CXI, March 9, 1983, p. 155.
The Georgia Review. XXXVII, Summer, 1983, p. 428.
Hudson Review. XXXVI, Autumn, 1983, p. 582.
Library Journal. CVIII, January 15, 1983, p. 134.
Los Angeles Times Book Review. March 6, 1983, p. 6.
New England Review. VI, Winter, 1983, p. 336.
The New York Review of Books. XXX, March 3, 1983, p. 19.
The New York Times Book Review. LXXXVIII, August 7, 1983, p. 12.
Virginia Quarterly Review. LIX, Autumn, 1983, p. 132.
Yale Review. LXXV, Autumn, 1983, p. R14.

KLEIST

Author: Joachim Maass (1901-   )
Translated from the German by Ralph Manheim
Publisher: Farrar, Straus and Giroux (New York). Illustrated. 313 pp. $22.50
Type of work: Literary biography
Time: The late eighteenth and early nineteenth centuries
Locale: Germany

A narrative of the major events in the life of Kleist, emphasizing his personal traumas and disasters with comparatively little analysis of his works

> Principal personages:
> HEINRICH VON KLEIST, a German Romantic writer
> ULRIKE, his half sister
> HENRIETTE VOGEL, the woman with whom Kleist committed suicide
> ADAM MÜLLER, a German Romantic writer, an associate of Kleist
> ERNST VON PFUEL, a close friend of Kleist

Unlike their English contemporaries (William Wordsworth, Percy Bysshe Shelley, John Keats, Samuel Taylor Coleridge, and Lord Byron) and German rivals (Johann Wolfgang von Goethe and Friedrich Schiller), the German Romantics have not, on the whole, received much attention outside the borders of their own country. Their impact on humane letters in the English-speaking world has been negligible. Many of their principal works remain either untranslated or available only in archaic and generally out-of-print versions; only occasionally do they merit inclusion (and then only in brief snippets) in standard anthologies of Romantic literature. Nowhere is the general neglect of the German Romantics more strikingly illustrated than in the case of Kleist's well-nigh canonical essay, "Über das Marionettentheater." Enthusiastically received by E. T. A. Hoffmann at the time of its original publication in the *Berlin Abendblätter*, the essay has provoked widespread admiration and occasioned some famous borrowings (notably by Rainer Maria Rilke in the fourth of the *Duineser Elegien*, 1923; *Duino Elegies, 1930*) among the great figures of German letters. Despite the text's considerable reputation in the literary and cultural history of central Europe, the only adequate English translation extant at the moment of writing was published some years ago in the *Times Literary Supplement*—an odd place for the enshrinement of a classic text, to be sure.

It is with some pleasure, therefore, that one contemplates the translation into English of a full-scale biography of Kleist. Originally published in 1957, revised and reissued in 1977, Joachim Maass's *Kleist* covers the ground of Kleist's brief and troubled life in copious detail. Would that the energy and excitement of its subject's life were matched by the narrative of this biography. It may be that the plodding, tedious quality of Maass's book is unnecessarily accentuated in the translation—although Ralph Manheim is highly regarded as a translator—but for whatever reason, this book has taken an important, neglected, and potentially lively subject and turned it into an extremely tiresome read. Readers with only limited German but diligently devoted to the study of German culture and interested in the Romantics will find the book a useful source of new information, but for those whose command of German is good, reading Kleist's own letters would be preferable to plowing through this biography.

Nevertheless, the record, such as it can with confidence be established—as Erich Heller has remarked, "Kleist's life, more than that of any other celebrated figure in the literary history of his epoch, abounds in unsolved puzzles, both factual and emotional, and biographies of him, therefore, often engage in purely speculative constructions"—is all there in Maass's account. He draws liberally upon Kleist's correspondence and on legal and political documents, and his knowledge of the day-to-day details of Kleist's dealings with friends and associates is considerable. Most valuable, perhaps, is the knowledge one gains of the history of composition and publication of Kleist's major works. Maass has obviously done his bibliographic homework with some care.

Setting aside the somewhat lugubrious incidents of Kleist's personal life, including his suicide à deux with Henriette Vogel (which Maass draws out with all the excessive sentiment and morbid fascination for details that Kleist himself, a distinguished writer of drama and clearly in his final hours preternaturally concerned with the theatricality of his own death, could have wished for its presentation to posterity), the real interest of the present study lies in the glimpse it affords of literary life in late eighteenth and early nineteenth century Germany. Above all—in both the spatial and idiomatic senses of the phrase—there is Goethe.

Relations between Goethe and Kleist were stormy and, Maass speculates, perhaps ultimately responsible for the personal tragedy of Kleist himself. Kleist's boast that he would "tear the wreath off [Goethe's] head" has not been vindicated in the ensuing one and three quarters centuries. Goethe, it would seem, treated Kleist rather badly, and posterity, whatever its praise for individual works, has scarcely been more kind. Kleist was undoubtedly a difficult man to deal with, and surely some of Goethe's distaste for his work stemmed from his sense of the destructiveness of Kleist's personality. *"Die verfluchte unnatur!"* Goethe is supposed to have exclaimed upon reading Kleist's play *Penthesilea* (1808; English translation, 1959), consigning it to the fire as he did so. It may be that Goethe's instincts in the matter were correct, but one might speculate that what most moved the elder poet to rage was a clear recognition that in Kleist he beheld something like a former incarnation of himself. Goethe had, after all, done a considerable amount to popularize the Romantic cult of early death in his own youthful novel, *Die Leiden des jungen Werthers* (1774; *The Sorrows of Young Werther*), the autobiographical dimensions of whose character are well-known.

In addition, one learns much about the literary mode of production in Germany at this period. What Jürgen Habermas, referring most often to the eighteenth century (and frequently more to France than to Germany), has dubbed the "public sphere" operated in this period with somewhat less force, though not without consequence to literary production. The salons (or, in England, coffeehouses) where educated men and women mixed and discoursed about politics and culture had, by the time Kleist began to publish, been overtaken by forms of cultural dissemination more directly controlled by the state. Kleist's efforts to have his works printed (or, in the case of the plays, performed) encountered repeatedly the coercive power of the Prussian state apparatus. True, it was ultimately public opinion that doomed Kleist's literary (and personal) life to oblivion, but the force of this opinion was frequently felt in the refusal of licenses to print or in the unwillingness of state-supported institutions to make his works public. The forms of overt censorship that would characterize the Prussian (and other German) states for much of the nineteenth century had already emerged in Kleist's lifetime. It is instructive to learn that the notorious forms of political repression under which Karl Marx would later suffer in Germany applied at this period equally to cultural matters, particularly when, as was the case with many of Kleist's works, conventional manners and morals were affronted (see, for example, Maass's account of the reaction to *Die Marquise von O . . .*, 1808; *The Marquise of O*, 1960).

Where this biography fails most noticeably is in its treatment of the literary character of the works themselves. Maas falls back repeatedly on empty phraseology about Kleist's "genius" and the "artifice" of his language, as well as on nebulous references to "Kleistean themes" (whatever they might be). Nowhere is there a single sustained reading of a text, nor is there any effort to describe Kleist's writings at a more profound level than the thematic. Where plots are given, Maass is content to recount the incidents, leaving even a rudimentary formal analysis of structure to be inferred by the reader. One might dismiss this objection as mere carping, because Maass does not lay claim to literary critical analysis but seems to have intended merely to give a full and relatively unspeculative account of Kleist's life, both in and out of the world of letters. Nevertheless, it is fair to fault a biographer who consistently makes claims for the literary genius of his subject for neglecting to give more than passing attention to the texts on which the claims for genius rest. Because Christoph Martin Wieland's judgment (after hearing Kleist recite fragments of his *Robert Guiskard, Herzog der Normänner* in 1804) that "Kleist was born to fill the wide gap in our dramatic literature which, at least in my opinion, even Goethe and Schiller have failed to fill" has proved exaggerated, if not simply wrong, it would seem incumbent upon Maass to justify his high opinion of Kleist's achievement with critical interpretation of some of the major works.

This demand is warranted not only by the judgments expressed in Maass's text but also by similar judgments in the larger body of literature dealing with Kleist, which has failed notably to do more than honor him. Indeed, genuinely critical reading of Kleist has hardly begun (although the impending publication of the late Paul de Man's essay on "Über das Marionettentheater" may begin to redress this imbalance). Only after more careful exegeses of his texts have shown the actual rhetorical and aesthetic complexity that has often been attributed to them will the large claims for Kleist's literary genius be supportable. Maass's biography does nothing to advance this cause and is therefore something of a disappointment.

Michael Sprinker

Sources for Further Study

Library Journal. CVIII, July, 1983, p. 1364.
New Leader. LXVI, October 3, 1983, p. 13.
The New York Times Book Review. LXXXVIII, July 24, 1983, p. 3.
The New Yorker. LIX, September 12, 1983, p. 157.
Observer. January 8, 1984, p. 50.
Publishers Weekly. CCXXIII, May 13, 1983, p. 44.
Time. CXXI, May 30, 1983, p. 79.

LANGSTON HUGHES
Before and Beyond Harlem

Author: Faith Berry (1939-   )
Publisher: Lawrence Hill & Company (Westport, Connecticut). 376 pp. $19.95
Type of work: Literary biography
Time: 1902-1967
Locale: The United States, Africa, Mexico, Russia, Europe, the Far East, and the Caribbean

A detailed account of the restless, prolific life of the famous and often controversial black writer

> *Principal personages:*
> LANGSTON HUGHES, a leading black writer of his time
> ARNA BONTEMPS, Hughes's frequent collaborator, and an important author in various modes
> COUNTEE CULLEN, a poet and leader of the Harlem Renaissance
> RICHARD WRIGHT, the author of *Native Son* and other impassioned fiction
> ARTHUR KOESTLER, a thinker and writer of politically grounded works
> JACQUES ROUMAIN, a leftist Caribbean writer and activist
> ZORA NEALE HURSTON, an author of works distinguished by their elements of humor and folklore
> ALAIN LOCKE, a critic and intellectual leader of the black literature movement

By the time of his death in 1967, Langston Hughes should have had every reason to feel secure about his place in the history of American culture. No one could have been a more prolific or versatile writer. For more than forty years, he had written successfully in every conceivable mode. Most of this writing took the form of poetry, drama, autobiography, or fiction, but Hughes was also accomplished in such unusual areas as song lyrics, librettos, and comic journalism. When he was not writing creatively, he was expressing his feelings and concerns as an editor, translator, and world-traveling activist. Nevertheless, he apparently died a disappointed man. As a sensitive black man trying to make his way in a hostile society, he continually dreamed of justice, and most of his work was inspired by an obsessive need to confront the inevitable consequences of entrenched racism. Because he finally doubted that his efforts had accomplished much, however, he seems to have concluded that the sum of his work was perhaps only a "wasted song."

Today, this melancholy self-assessment may hardly sound credible because Hughes's reputation has been on the ascendancy for a number of years, thanks in large part to a critical change in attitudes toward Afro-American literature as a whole. The definitive history of the rise of Afro-American literature has yet to be written. When it is, it very possibly will show that Hughes was the single most important figure in the movement, since he embodied more fully than anyone else its energy, variety, and idealistic goals. Faith Berry invites this conclusion in *Langston Hughes: Before and Beyond Harlem*, the first full-scale attempt to trace Hughes's life.

Although Berry's biography has its flaws and weaknesses, it is still an important book—the first to add up Hughes's enormous achievements and put his impact in perspective. In doing so, Berry worked against great odds. When she first planned the project, she had luck on her side. After meeting Hughes not long before his death, she was promised by his literary executor, Arna Bontemps, that she would be provided with all the help she needed in her research. This promise, however, never materialized, and after Bontemps' death in 1973, Berry was refused access to important collections of Hughes's papers. A less determined person might have given up at this point. Instead, she decided to search out all the other sources. For more than a dozen years (inspired, she says, by the tenacious example of Hughes himself), she persisted. She appears to have researched every available written item by or about Hughes; she also appears to have interviewed practically all of Hughes's surviving friends and associates. The result is a book that has the heft and density of first-rate historical scholarship.

As one follows Hughes's story, one begins to get a full picture of the times from a black person's point of view. There were years of constant struggle, interspersed with brief periods of exhilaration and real hope. Like most of his counterparts, Hughes was hounded by money problems for much of his life. In the United States, the lot of the black writer was to have a limited reading public and few outlets for publication—especially if, like Hughes, one was not only black but also politically militant. For many years, Hughes had to place much of his work with such appreciative but financially unrewarding journals and newspapers as *New Masses* and *The Daily Worker*. Even after Hughes became internationally famous, he still thought it was a great accomplishment when he managed to get enough money together to buy a brown suit.

If money worries nagged him constantly, the problems of racial and political harassment were even more oppressive. Because of his militant activism against racial prejudice, he often faced the hostility of white supremacists. This situation frightened him, but never enough to make him stop writing and speaking on the subject of injustice. It was when he sensed the direct pressure of official disapproval that Hughes felt most vulnerable and fought most desperately to keep his moral courage. Because of his leftist politics, Hughes felt such pressures especially keenly during the years when Communism was perceived as a living, pernicious threat in various parts of the world. Thus, in the United States, he was frequently targeted by J. Edgar Hoover's FBI as an agitator with Communist Party connections (Hughes *was* a sympathizer, but he never joined the Party). Even in Japan and the Caribbean, he was at times harassed for his liberal politics. Hughes, however, was a survivor; he held on during the bad periods, and when more opportune times came, he took full advantage of them.

One of the best times for Hughes as well as for many other black writers and thinkers was the era that produced the Harlem Renaissance, an explosion of black creativity and consciousness in the 1920's. Before this intellectual and artistic movement died with the onset of the Great Depression, black America went a long way toward a full discovery and definition of itself. Hughes was not a leader in this movement—he was then an impressionable, shy young man still trying to establish himself as a writer—but after meeting many of its most important figures and learning a great deal by way of involved curiosity and quiet analysis, he eventually came out of the experience with perhaps the clearest and most persistent vision of what constitutes the distinct power of black art. Consequently, an understandable misconception surrounds Hughes: He is often thought of as having been the most personally active and prominent leader of the Harlem Renaissance—a good example of how the strength of a fulfilled vision can distort mundane facts and yet still, in a sense, serve the truth.

In terms of danger and ultimate disappointment, the Spanish Civil War was one of Hughes's worst experiences, but it was also one of the most rewarding times for him in certain ways. As a journalist, he was actually paid to side passionately with a proletarian cause he believed in. He more than satisfied his appetite for extreme adventure while reporting from active war zones, and he mixed with many people whom he could admire for their political involvement. One of these was Ernest Hemingway, a man so fundamentally different in personality that Hughes evidently surprised himself when they became friendly.

Hughes made friendships easily all during his life. He had the kind of natural charm and sensitivity that attracted people to him. Thus, at one time or another, he seems to have been acquainted with practically everyone who was prominent in the world of art and culture in the United States during his lifetime, and many more besides around the world. The list barely begins with such important names as W. E. B. DuBois, Countee Cullen, Richard Wright, Ralph Ellison, Carl Van Vechten, Arthur Koestler, Jacques Roumain, and Arna Bontemps.

Bontemps and Roumain were two of Hughes's most loyal friends. Two other writers, who at first befriended him and later turned violently against him, were Zora Neale Hurston and Alain Locke. Hurston, it seems, turned against Hughes out of creative envy, Locke out of sexual jealousy. Behind Hurston and Locke stood a rather unlikely white woman known as Godmother, who pulled their strings with the combined power of bribery and sinister emotionalism. For a while, an indigent Hughes was under Godmother's sway, too, but when he rebelled and broke ties with her, Hurston and Locke, encouraged by this powerful woman, seemed to make it their business to vilify Hughes at every opportunity. A strange chapter—in fact, the strangest in a long, dramatic life of almost constant movement and change.

Hughes was constantly on the go until he finally settled down in Harlem during his last years. This fact is certainly reflected in the nervous energy and the experimental approaches characteristic of his work. This restless desire for travel and new experiences also helps to explain the appeal of Berry's biography. In tracing Hughes's life so carefully and thoroughly, it was inevitable that she would tell a dramatically interesting story, because Hughes led one of the most exciting lives imaginable. Berry's biography, however, is not without its flaws; in fact, there are serious ones. However admirable Berry's exhaustive research may be, in the end the reader remains somewhat unsatisfied. One comes away from Berry's account knowing a great deal about Hughes's life and his accomplishments and yet not really knowing the man himself. Berry certainly provides all the facts, but a thoroughly successful biography requires penetrating analysis of the essential uniqueness or genius of its subject as well.

Every great person has a "mystery" that finally explains him. Berry is perfectly aware that Hughes had an essential hidden side, but the most she manages to do is to provide the reader with occasional clues, sometimes with truncated stories that excite one's interest without fulfilling it. One is led to believe that Hughes's complex character could be explained by such factors as his unusual relationship with his parents, his ambivalent sexuality, and his divided nature as a man who was at once intensely private and socially committed. These are tantalizing revelations, but it is natural for the reader of a biography to want some convincing conclusions. It is the task of the biographer not only to point the reader but also to lead him, toward the discovery of the subject's "mystery," even at the risk of perhaps being later proved wrong or imprecise. As long as the biographer, in the absence of dependable proof, applies factual knowledge and unbiased speculation and also shows a determination to uncover the secret of greatness, the reader should not complain.

Given the limitations under which Berry had to do her research, the best approach for such speculation would have been to go by the suggestive evidence of Hughes's writings. She does use many quotations as useful indicators of Hughes's developing concerns. She should also have applied the kind of serious literary analysis that provides at first the key to stylistic imperatives and later to the inspired mind. Even if she had already unlocked the writer's mind, however, some serious literary analysis would have been called for; a book about a writer must finally try to explain the greatness of his creative work. Thus, Berry's work must be regarded as a valuable but limited pioneering effort, preparing the way for the kind of critical biography that Hughes deserves.

Georg Gaston

Sources for Further Study

Booklist. LIX, August, 1983, p. 1440.

Choice. XXI, October, 1983, p. 272.

Christian Science Monitor. October 19, 1983, p. 23.

Library Journal. CVIII, May 1, 1983, p. 906.

Los Angeles Times Book Review. July 3, 1983, p. 3.

The New York Times Book Review. LXXXVIII, September 11, 1983, p. 14.

The New Yorker. LIX, July 18, 1983, p. 99.

Publishers Weekly. CCXXIII, April 15, 1983, p. 38.

Virginia Quarterly Review. LX, Spring, 1984, p. 359.

LECTURES ON DON QUIXOTE

Author: Vladimir Nabokov (1899-1977)
Edited by Fredson Bowers, with an introduction by Guy Davenport
Publisher: Harcourt Brace Jovanovich (San Diego, California). Illustrated. 219 pp.
$17.95
Type of work: Literary criticism

Nabokov rebuts the sentimentalized interpretation of the Spanish classic and offers a fresh perspective based on his own close reading

Years afterward, Vladimir Nabokov recalled how in the spring of 1952, as a Harvard University guest lecturer, he had taken "delight" in "tearing apart *Don Quixote*, a cruel and crude old book, before six hundred students. . . ." He might have omitted this vastly influential work from his syllabus—he had omitted it during the twelve preceding years at Wellesley College and Cornell University—had not Harvard insisted that he make it the starting point in his discussions. Nabokov approached his new task with characteristic alacrity and thoroughness but also with an obvious distrust of the book's reputation. In *Lectures on Don Quixote*, admirably edited and prefaced by Fredson Bowers, one may trace the growth of Nabokov's esteem for his subject. The lectures also stimulate intriguing speculation as to *Don Quixote de la Mancha*'s possible influence on the lecturer's own literary productions.

What prompted Nabokov's initial suspicion was the highly sentimentalized view of *Don Quixote de la Mancha* prevalent in the early 1950's, when scholarship of Miguel de Cervantes was at a low ebb. Was the man Quixote indeed the sweet, charmingly befuddled but admirable idealist that critics made him out to be? Was Sancho Panza truly a levelheaded peasant with a flair for pithy, comical observations about life? Above all, how should one characterize the world of seventeenth century Spain in which they had their adventures? When Nabokov delivered these lectures, the accepted notion of the Don Quixote milieu was epitomized by Aubrey F. G. Bell, a critic for whom Nabokov reserved particular scorn. In *Cervantes* (1947), Bell remarks that "the general character that emerges" in *Don Quixote de la Mancha* "is that of a sensitive, keen-witted nation, humorous and humane." On the contrary, retorts Nabokov. The characters of the novel display a barbarous, sadistic nature in subjecting Quixote and Sancho to "a veritable encyclopedia of cruelty." Anyone who thinks otherwise simply has not read the book attentively or perhaps not read it at all. Indeed, the novel has inspired so many films, ballets, and musicals that many who have never laid eyes on it could supply a reasonably accurate plot summary, along with the popular sentimental interpretation.

To clear the interpretive ground, Nabokov presented his six hundred Harvard students with his own chapter-by-chapter synopsis based upon an extremely close reading. (Bowers has appended this lengthy classroom handout to the text of the lectures, making the book a highly useful crib sheet as well as a fresh interpretation of *Don Quixote de la Mancha*.) The synopsis serves as an empirical foundation for Nabokov's attempts to demolish the body of myths surrounding *Don Quixote de la Mancha* and its author.

The notion, for example, that *Don Quixote de la Mancha* is "the greatest novel ever written"—or even *one* of the greatest novels—Nabokov dismisses as utter nonsense. Nor, unlike many other critics, will he grant Cervantes any Shakespearean powers of mind or imagination. Aside from his influence on posterity, says Nabokov, Cervantes is in no respect the peer of the Bard. Nabokov does not even find *Don Quixote de la Mancha* particularly well planned or well constructed, except for the very first and last sections, which he contends were originally intended to stand alone. Otherwise, the novel is merely a picaresque tale, stringing together stories, episodes, and jests as the protagonist moves from place to place. Nabokov's commentary on the book is studded with phrases such as "an artless composition" and "a very patchy haphazard tale."

Another myth he rebuts is that of Sancho Panza as a down-to-earth character whose witty proverbs serve as a foil to Quixote's high-minded delusions. There is no true symmetry between the two characters, says Nabokov, partly because Sancho is more a foreshortened version of the Don than his opposite. For example, despite Sancho's "peaceful disposition, he enjoys a fight when he is really aroused; and when drunk he looks upon dangerous and fantastic adventures as excellent sport." The Don, of course, embodies chivalric courage, whether because he is insane or for some other reason. Again,

> At first Cervantes stresses the lucid quality of the fat squire's common sense, but we soon discover in chapter 26 that Sancho is curiously absentminded, a dreamer in his own right: witness his forgetting a certain letter that would have given him three ass-colts. He persistently tries to correct Don Quixote's delusions, but suddenly in the beginning of part two plays the part of an enchanter himself and in a most cruel and grotesque manner helps to deepen his master's main delusion—the one referring to Dulcinea. But then he becomes confused about his responsibility for that delusion.

Finally, attacking a different aspect of the Sancho myth, Nabokov finds that the squire's "cracks and proverbs are not very mirth provoking either in themselves or in their repetitious accumulation. The corniest modern gag is funnier."

Nabokov's insistence upon detailed examination of the text gives him a clear advantage over his contemporaries who stick with the traditional critical wisdom about *Don Quixote de la Mancha*. His barbed comments, however, may lead the reader to wonder what constructive purpose his iconoclasm will eventually serve. Indeed, he was justly criticized for relentlessly underrating authors such as Jane Austen and Fyodor Dostoevski in two earlier volumes to which the present one is a companion: *Lectures on Literature* (1980) and *Lectures on Russian Literature* (1981). Such a criticism, however, does not apply to his treatment of *Don Quixote de la Mancha*. Instead, in cutting through the growth of generalizations about the book, he finds concrete (though modest) examples of excellence overlooked or exaggerated by his scholarly predecessors, and in the process, he apparently comes to like the book and its hero much more than he might have expected.

In what are practically asides throughout his lectures on the novel's themes and "structural devices," Nabokov alludes sympathetically to the Don, at one point describing a moment of near-lucidity when a "real melody" makes him wonder if his beloved Dulcinea really exists—"a very vague, very secret doubt is forming cloudlike in the otherwise limpid heavens of his madness." At another point, Nabokov calls attention to a particularly affecting speech of Quixote's when he sends his squire with a message to Dulcinea: "Observe if she repeats two or three times the answer she gives you and if her mood varies from mildness to austerity, from the harsh to the amorous. She may raise a hand to her hair to smooth it back, though it be not disordered." After reading this passage aloud, Nabokov remarks, "A charming detail, this."

Nabokov is at his most perceptive when he raises points such as this, for, in the absence of overall cohesion in *Don Quixote de la Mancha*, he focuses admiringly on its "structural devices"—"the ways and means that Cervantes will think up to keep the story going." These "ingredients," as listed by the lecturer, range from the author's superb dramatic dialogue (Cervantes was "a frustrated playwright") to "the chivalry theme" and "the mystification theme, the cruel burlesque jest." Cervantes' handling of chivalry and mystification, however, constitutes Nabokov's other main objection to the book, and, although he avoids the embarrassing denigration that marked his discussion of Dostoevski, Nabokov still betrays a stubborn prejudice against Cervantes' abilities as a thinker.

The problem is Nabokov's refusal to credit Cervantes with any satirical motive in his treatment of the society in which he lived. To Nabokov—who meticulously catalogs the "wallops, punches, sundry blows and bangs" suffered by the embattled hero in one day and night—all the instances of cruelty in *Don Quixote de la Mancha* seem to be recounted with approval, with no sense of irony. Nabokov notes that the heroes of *Le Morte d'Arthur* (1485) by Thomas Malory and *Amadís de Gaula* (1508)—two more of his classroom handouts—are, like Don Quixote, subjected to enchantment, humiliation, and physical cruelty; therefore, *Don Quixote de la Mancha* resembles these works in every respect. The only difference Nabokov will acknowledge is: Whereas medieval knights who believed in magic potions were considered sane, in an age of gunpowder one who held such a belief, as did Quixote, must be insane. That, of course, enhances the cruel laughter that Nabokov insists *Don Quixote de la Mancha* was designed to elicit.

It is not surprising that Nabokov, a Russian émigré with bitter knowledge of Communist and Nazi atrocities, would deplore what he believed to be their equivalent in a past age, but his contention, however original, that *Don Quixote de la Mancha* represents no "distortion" (that is, ironic criticism) of chivalric romance remains unconvincing, not only because of his failure to consider any alternative but also because of the cavalier arguments he uses to support his reading. An example: "Being by nature a storyteller and a magician, but not a preacher, Cervantes is anything but a fiery adversary of social evil. He does not really give a hoot whether or not books of chivalry are popular in Spain; and, if popular, whether or not their influence is pernicious."

His loathing of the book's supposed cruelty even leads Nabokov to misinterpret one scene: the "strappado" episode of book 1, chapter 43, in which a servant girl whips Don Quixote's horse out from under him, and he is left hanging by his hands from a balcony. As Nabokov sees it, Quixote remains in this position for "two hours, despairing, bewildered, and bellowing like a bull, while the maid servant and the innkeeper's daughter, and presumably millions of readers, are doubled up with laughter." Though Nabokov is surely right in deploring the cruelty of the prank, a careful reading suggests that the Don is actually suspended for no more than a few minutes. In any case, there is no justification for supposing, as Nabokov does, that Cervantes condones the trick.

It is strange that the author of *Kamera Obskura* (1932; *Laughter in the Dark*, 1938)—in which a blind man is tormented by his wife and her lover—should deplore gratuitous cruelty in any book. Even more strange is that Nabokov should deny Cervantes any "second sight" on the cruel society he portrays. After all, the reader of *Pale Fire* (1962) is afforded second sight on the action through such devices as the "chroniclers theme," also found in *Don Quixote de la Mancha*.

While refusing to grant Cervantes any true literary sophistication—other than "the intuition of genius," again an unsatisfying explanation—Nabokov nevertheless judges *Don Quixote de la Mancha* to be great because of its influence, because of the "long shadow" it casts upon the works of authors as diverse as Charles Dickens, Gustave Flaubert, Nikolai Gogol, and Leo Tolstoy. Might not Nabokov add his own name to the list of those influenced? In particular, *Lolita* (1955; a diminutive of the Spanish "Dolores") is, like *Don Quixote de la Mancha*, a novel about the power of delusion and the quest for an elusive, and illusive, paragon of female innocence. Undeniably, *Lolita* develops some uniquely Nabokovian themes, but, as it was published only three years after the Harvard lectures, perhaps its possibilities were enriched by Nabokov's meticulous investigation of *Don Quixote de la Mancha*.

In any case, there is no mistaking the impact on Western literature that Nabokov attributes to the Don—the character, not the book:

We are confronted by an interesting phenomenon: a literary hero losing gradually contact with the book that bore him; leaving his fatherland, leaving his creator's desk and roaming space after roaming Spain. In result, Don Quixote is greater today than he was in Cervantes's womb. He has ridden for three hundred and fifty years through the jungles and tundras of human thought—and he has gained in vitality and stature. We do not laugh at him any longer. His blazon is pity, his banner is beauty. He stands for everything that is gentle, forlorn, pure, unselfish, and gallant. The parody has become a paragon.

Nabokov has been criticized for intimidating students with his *ex cathedra* manner, for making them incapable of independent thought. That is not a just criticism of one who made thoroughgoing skepticism the foundation of his own investigations—or, for that matter, of one who was sometimes prone to such obvious human error. An equally valid contention is that Nabokov goaded students into questioning all pronouncements, even his own. *Lectures on Don Quixote* certainly questions received ideas, and, whatever the flaws of Nabokov's reasoning, it certainly challenges reader and student alike. Nabokov has achieved his own intended effect, for one can never look at *Don Quixote de la Mancha* the same way again.

Thomas Rankin

Sources for Further Study

Christian Century. C, August 3, 1983, p. 724.
Christian Science Monitor. June 15, 1983, p. 11.
Library Journal. CVIII, February 15, 1983, p. 398.
Los Angeles Times Book Review. April 17, 1983, p. 11.
Nation. CCXXXVI, March 5, 1983, p. 276.
New Statesman. CV, June 17, 1983, p. 22.
The New York Review of Books. XXX, March 3, 1983, p. 3.
The New Yorker. LIX, May 2, 1983, p. 131.
Publishers Weekly. CCXXII, December 17, 1982, p. 69.
Time. CXXI, April 25, 1983, p. 115.

LETTERS

Author: Sylvia Townsend Warner (1893-1978)
Edited, with an introduction, by William Maxwell
Publisher: The Viking Press (New York). 311 pp. $26.00
Type of work: Letters
Time: 1921-1978
Locale: England

Letters by one of England's foremost fiction writers and essayists

Sylvia Townsend Warner came to a literary career after first pursuing music and musicology, encouraged in this later ambition by David Garnett and T. F. Powys. A slender volume of poems in 1925, *Espalier*, was followed by a novel, *Lolly Willowes* (1926), her first but by no means last foray into the supernatural. The distance between these early productions and the last volume published in her lifetime, *Kingdoms of Elfin* (1977), is at once enormous and yet small. Like so many writers of the 1920's, she showed a preference for the delicate and fanciful, which she abandoned in midcareer for a more worldly and naturalistic style, only to return to the original manner late in life. During these more than fifty years, she published seven novels, nine volumes of stories, four volumes of poetry (and a fifth in collaboration with Valentine Ackland), innumerable essays, and a brilliant biography of T. H. White. She could hardly be called a prolific writer, however, often laboring through several revisions before releasing a novel or story. Her style is marked by the utmost clarity and smoothness, music to the eye and ear, and her gift for metaphor is startling and original.

In spite of these qualities, there is nothing precious, arty, or *fin de siècle* in Warner's matter or manner, although she was sensitive to people of all kinds, to nuances of gesture and emotion, and to nature. It is sensitivity, in fact, that makes her such a charming correspondent—charming in the sense that she desired to please and hence wrote to and for her recipients. Moreover, these are intensely personal letters; those looking for tidbits about the famous and infamous figures of her time will be disappointed. Recipients are often well-known figures such as David Garnett, Llewelyn Powys, and Marchette Chute, but a great many more are unfamiliar—American composer Paul Nordoff, Mrs. Chute's daughter Joy, and *Vogue* artist George Plank. To read these letters, therefore, is to be taken into the private world of their author, not the public arena of literary politics; and because the author is Sylvia Townsend Warner, the letters stand in their own right as examples of the dying epistolary craft and as mementos of an extraordinary life.

The early letters are those of a struggling young author, grateful to David Garnett and Charles Prentice for encouragement, excited by new books and writers, enthusiastic about a new acquaintance or residence in the country.

In the background at this time is Warner's developing relationship with the poet Valentine Ackland, with whom she lived for nearly fifty years. Already one ascertains the jumble of contradictions that make up a person of character: confidence and humility, gratitude and disappointment, delicious parody and sympathetic criticism. Through the 1920's and early 1930's, Warner's tone is often gaily humorous or bemused; the reader finishes a letter with a quiet smile at a clever observation, a turn of phrase, a metaphysical image. In a moment of anger, Warner swears eloquently. By the time of the Spanish Civil War, her tone is more serious, though nevertheless engaging. She finds pleasure in learning to heckle at political rallies and to speak publicly; there are serious letters about writers' congresses and an appeal to fellow artists for money to aid Republican Spain. She becomes furious at being denied a passport by the British government and visits the front anyway. Between these public concerns are semiprecious gems of character study, recollection, nature description. After a brief flight to New York at the outbreak of war, she is impelled by a sense of duty to return to England.

The war, Warner found, was a "middle-aged pursuit," but it failed to dampen her sense of humor. There is a comic description of the house she shared with Ackland being requisitioned by the armed forces, a wry and amusing rumination on the future occupation of those who censor the mail, and a hilarious passage that describes Red Cross officials instructing ladies in how properly to undress a wounded man. Scarcity, rationing, bureaucratic idiocy, volunteer work for the Workers Educational Association and the Women's Volunteer Service convey the day-to-day sense of wartime Great Britain. By that time, Warner was publishing in *The New Yorker*, in which more than one hundred of her contributions were to appear. Tending to her precious garden, her cats, and her friends, she maintained, despite the war, a zest for the small good things of life—a spirit that must have been encouraging to those who received her letters.

Although Warner writes that she felt "no particular elation" at the end of World War II, one can detect in her letters of the next two decades another shift in tone or, to use the musical imagery she herself often employed, a modulation to another key, not minor, but richer and deeper in feeling, occasionally tinged with melancholy. There is a period of struggle with her best novel, *The Corner That Held Them* (1948), and a wittily peevish letter to *The New Yorker* complaining of delays, followed by that ancient litany of writers, "I have no money." Postwar prices bedevil her budget, relations with Valentine Ackland deteriorate temporarily, her mother dies, she suffers a spell of writer's block. Through these difficulties, Warner remained basically sympathetic and even optimistic, not in some vapid Rotarian way, but with a simple love of life. A letter to Alyse Gregory must be one of the most charming thank-you notes ever written; one paragraph in a long letter to Paul Nordoff evokes the feeling of being deliciously exhausted, while writing to

Marchette Chute, Warner follows a paragraph on the encumbrances of property with a vivid description of a holiday in southern France. Everything delights her: At the age of sixty, she savors the taste of icicles; she has fond recollections and praise for a former neighbor lady who drank too much; Ackland's foray into antique dealing provides occasions for innocent delight; cats are an endless source of fascination and imagery; even a bicycle race excites admiration, "it was ravishing to see them flash past and stream away down the avenue like a flock of macaws." There is poetic delight in these pages, for Warner succeeds in making her readers see the world anew, with eyes never clouded by custom or ennui.

In 1953, in a letter to Alyse Gregory, Warner comments on continuity, observing that a cracked, old teapot may provide more sense of one's past than any written record. Perhaps she is right, but another pleasure of these letters is precisely that sense of life's flow. By the 1970's, the river of her own life had reached that broad, level, and smooth quiet near its estuary, yet she retained even then an astonishing capacity for wonder and an unquenchable desire to learn. Valentine Ackland's death in 1969 was an irreparable loss. Of their relationship, Warner says simply, "I might so nearly have lived unblessed. Even now my desolation is enriched by her." As if her life were destined to come full circle, Warner resumed correspondence with David Garnett, kindred spirits still after fifty years, and she turned once again to stories of fantasy and fairy. In the letters of her last years, she worries about diminishing stocks of wildlife, reveals a still lively wit, and continues to surprise the reader with fresh and vivid scenes from nature.

Credit for the success of this volume must go in part to the intelligent editing of William Maxwell. Whether the letters printed here are representative, the reader may never know, for Warner wrote thousands in her lifetime. The effect of the letters included may also be enhanced by Maxwell's selecting and pruning, but such concerns are irrelevant. His unfussy editing, free of annoying pedantry, permits the writer to speak for herself. Maxwell's introduction is excellent, his notes unobtrusive and informative, and the index is full and accurate.

The letters of Sylvia Townsend Warner are a delight awaiting anyone interested in good writing, humane living, and, yes, continuity.

Dean Baldwin

Sources for Further Study

Antioch Review. XLI, Spring, 1983, p. 251.
Boston Review. VIII, June, 1983, p. 28.
Library Journal. CVII, December 15, 1982, p. 2340.

Nation. CCXXXVI, March 19, 1983, p. 343.
New Statesman. CIV, December 3, 1982, p. 26.
The New York Times Book Review. LXXXVIII, April 17, 1983, p. 11.
The New Yorker. LIX, May 30, 1983, p. 98.
Publishers Weekly. CCXXII, November 19, 1982, p. 69.
Saturday Review. IX, March, 1983, p. 58.
Virginia Quarterly Review. LIX, Autumn, 1983, p. 123.

LETTERS OF ARCHIBALD MACLEISH
1907 to 1982

Author: Archibald MacLeish (1892-1982)
Edited, with an introduction, by R. H. Winnick
Publisher: Houghton Mifflin Company (Boston). 471 pp. $20.00
Type of work: Letters

A selection from the correspondence of an important American poet, spanning seventy-five years

Was there really only one Archibald MacLeish? In the 1920's, he practiced law and later moved to France and consorted with Lost Generation writers. In the following decade, he was a staff writer for *Fortune* magazine. During the 1940's, he held several high-level federal positions in Washington. Later, he joined the faculty of Harvard University. His career was unique for an American poet, but it was as an American poet that he wished to be recognized.

R. H. Winnick has garnered nearly four hundred letters spanning three quarters of the twentieth century, a few by the poet's parents at the beginning, the rest by the poet himself. Winnick indicates neither the number of letters which he read nor the basis of his selection. Of materials in the poet's possession, the editor reports that he was denied access only to correspondence between the poet and his wife. Although one might expect difficulties with correspondents still living or with the families of those recently deceased, Winnick reports no instance of unwillingness to cooperate in the endeavor, while his list of acknowledgments suggests an assiduous search. The reader is left to guess how representative the published letters are, but they obviously constitute a substantial wedge of MacLeish's epistolary life. The footnotes are generally informative and unobtrusive, and the index appears complete and accurate. Unfortunately, the letters are unnumbered.

More letters to Ernest Hemingway are printed than to any other single correspondent, a round three dozen from 1926 to 1958. The other correspondents most often represented are the poet's mother, his college friend Francis Hyde Bangs, Ezra Pound, Dean Acheson, and Robert N. Linscott. Those to the last-named, MacLeish's editor at Houghton Mifflin Company, suggest that the editor resisted the temptation to include merely perfunctory business letters. The ones to Acheson, a Yale University classmate and lifelong friend, cover more than fifty years, MacLeish's self-searching letters of the 1920's being the most interesting. Both MacLeish and the future Secretary of State were cultivated young men who studied, practiced, and showed unusual aptitude for the law, but unlike Acheson, MacLeish could not devote himself to it for love of another vocation.

Whereas the poet and his Ada, whom he married in 1916 while still a law student, were willing to accept a financially precarious life of poetry and music (she was an accomplished soprano) and the necessity of accepting support from his parents, MacLeish could not endure the possibility of being second-rate at his craft, but suspicions that he could not be first-rate persist in the letters of the 1920's. Many of the best were written from France in the middle of that decade. Although he and his wife spent five years in France, MacLeish never considered himself an "expatriate," despite a number of friendships with Americans who have been so labeled.

From late 1923 until her death in 1925, MacLeish wrote to Amy Lowell, who had earlier encouraged him, about his efforts to write "poetry with salt in it," efforts which naturally enough at the time led to study of Pound, T. S. Eliot, Marianne Moore, and poets of the Imagist movement. His struggle to find his own poetic voice also became the subject of several letters to the American poet John Peale Bishop, with whom he had established a firm friendship by the time of Bishop's return to the United States in 1924. Despite his doubts of success, these years, when the poet was in his mid-thirties, resulted in four books of poetry and relations with two towering literary men, Hemingway and Pound. Both relationships were tempestuous, though in different ways. The letters to Hemingway, who quickly became "Pappy" (the novelist was seven years younger), reveal a deep affection punctuated by frequent quarrels. With Pound, the situation differed. It appears that MacLeish met him only once in Europe, but he admired Pound's poetry and critical acumen and regularly risked his cantankerousness for the sake of his criticism, although it is clear that Pound never considered MacLeish a successful poet. MacLeish's high aspirations and self-doubts rendered negative criticism painful, especially when delivered by the young but already influential Edmund Wilson, against whom MacLeish nourished the only deep and abiding grudge visible in this volume, usually expressed in asides to Pound and other literary friends.

Only occasionally do the letters adumbrate the themes of MacLeish's poems, some of the most celebrated of which (the anthology favorites "Ars Poetica" and "You, Andrew Marvell," for example) date from his European period. Winnick is certainly correct in devoting more than a third of the book to letters of the 1920's.

The letters of the 1930's and 1940's disclose another side of MacLeish. As he approached middle age, he can be seen becoming more like his father, a canny Scottish immigrant turned successful Chicago merchant. He can be seen driving hard bargains with his publisher and dickering with Maxwell Perkins, Hemingway's editor at Charles Scribner's Sons, over rights to his epic *Conquistador* (1932): "I am determined that it shall not puddle into oblivion like the rest of my books." Scribner's did not get it, but neither did it puddle, earning MacLeish his first Pulitzer Prize. He had already struck a deal with Henry Luce, by which MacLeish might serve as staff member of *Fortune* with several consecutive months off each year for uninterrupted writing at his new home in Conway, Massachusetts. Subsequently, he bargained for yet better terms, and he did not scruple to lecture the publisher occasionally on articles in Luce's other journalistic bastion, *Time*, to which he took exception.

Although MacLeish became a controversial figure at the outbreak of World War II, when his book *The Irresponsibles: A Declaration* (1940) assailed the American literary establishment for failing to oppose Fascism vigorously enough, the focus of the correspondence in this period shifts to his own public service. There are letters to associate justice of the Supreme Court Felix Frankfurter and President Franklin D. Roosevelt concerning MacLeish's appointment as Librarian of Congress; revelations of his concurrent duties as director of the wartime Office of Facts and Figures (the tribulations of which occasioned two of his most impassioned and eloquent letters, one to Frankfurter in 1942 and the other the next year to an assistant director of the organization that superseded the OFF); and attempts to solicit Adlai Stevenson as his assistant upon his appointment to the position of Assistant Secretary of State for Public and Cultural Relations. Winnick also prints one of MacLeish's replies to Stevenson's frequent appeals for assistance in preparing speeches for his presidential campaigns of the 1950's.

The most extensive postwar correspondence concerns MacLeish's sustained efforts to free Pound, the Fascist sympathizer, from Saint Elizabeth's Hospital in Washington, D.C., Despite Pound's past scorn for MacLeish's work and MacLeish's own contempt for the cause to which Pound had dedicated his services, MacLeish considered Pound's incarceration a blot on America and an unnecessary insult to a man who, though a traitor to his country in time of war, was now widely considered a harmless old man. Readers familiar with the efforts of such luminaries as Hemingway, Eliot, and Robert Frost in Pound's behalf will find convincing evidence that MacLeish's role in the delicate negotiations with Washington officialdom was most important. It was also the most thankless. Fourteen letters to Pound between August, 1955, and March, 1958, show how thoroughly Pound himself tested MacLeish's diplomatic skills.

There are also rather fatherly letters to younger poets and to students at Harvard University, where the poet served as Boylston Professor of Rhetoric from 1949 until his retirement in 1962. Only a relative handful of letters represent the last twenty years of MacLeish's life, during most of which he remained active as writer and lecturer.

A chronology of letters can reveal the stages and changes in a life, and these will undoubtedly buttress Winnick's projected biography of his subject. Even more vividly than biography, however, letters communicate a writer's substance—that part which endures through the zigzags of maturation, a full career, and the subsequent decline of creative energy. Opinions and interests change, but the voice remains. It is what successive generations of readers find in the great letter-writers to whom their modern brethren are so often unfavorably compared—Horace Walpole, Lord Byron, Henry Adams. While they adjust their style to different readers, they retain an unmistakable epistolary presence. They are always recognizably themselves.

It is probably unfair to compare any twentieth century letter-writer to those who learned the habit before the days of routine air travel and global telecommunications. The differences go far deeper than the development of a preference for picking up the telephone or zooming away to visit one's friend. It may be doubted whether the development of an epistolary personality is possible in a culture which charges more for a letter than for an electronic message and takes longer to deliver it than the postal service of a century ago, and which reserves the right to interrupt electronically at any moment the concentration of anyone who might be practicing the older and slower form of communication.

With his roots in an earlier age, MacLeish may have escaped or resisted many of the century's assaults on the habitual writer, but he did not develop the epistolary presence of a great letter-writer. What several reviewers of this volume have described as a "public " quality in his letters, as though he sensed the possibility of a larger audience peering over the recipient's shoulder, may in fact be a function of that failure, which he feared as a young poet in Paris, to develop his own voice. His letters often take on the coloration of their intended readers, especially those with highly idiosyncratic styles, such as Hemingway and Pound. They read as though he were trying to gratify his correspondents even while disagreeing with them. Close readers of MacLeish's poetry may find, in his best work, an authentic voice, but whether because of a temptation to pose for an anticipated audience or because he could not overcome the mimicry of a derivative writer or for some other reason, these letters fall short of the highest standard.

They reveal a developed human being with some negative and many admirable traits—a proud, shrewd, versatile man intensely conscious of his duty as a citizen, keenly aware of the claims of his muse; a man whose achievements stand as a monument to industry and human engagement. They also reveal a poet whose reach exceeded his grasp, a man of many letters and friends who, in being different things to different correspondents, never becomes, for the reader of Winnick's selection, an authentic epistolary personality.

Robert P. Ellis

Sources for Further Study

American Literature. LV, October, 1983, p. 475.
The Atlantic. CCLI, March, 1983, p. 116.

Choice. XX, April, 1983, p. 1139.
Library Journal. CVIII, February 1, 1983, p. 202.
Los Angeles Times Book Review. January 30, 1983, p. 1.
The New Republic. CLXXXVIII, January 24, 1983, p. 28.
The New York Times Book Review. LXXXVIII, January 2, 1983, p. 3.
Publishers Weekly. CCXXII, November 12, 1982, p. 62.
Western Humanities Review. XXXVII, Autumn, 1983, p. 268.

THE LETTERS OF HENRY ADAMS

Author: Henry Adams (1838-1918)
Edited by J. C. Levenson, Ernest Samuels, Charles Vandersee, and Viola Hopkins
  Winner, with an introduction by J. C. Levenson and a bibliographical note by
  Charles Vandersee
Publisher: Harvard University Press (Cambridge, Massachusetts). Illustrated.
  3 volumes. 2016 pp. $100.00
Type of work: Letters
Time: Volume I: 1858-1868, Volume II: 1868-1885, and Volume III: 1886-1892
Locale: Berlin, Rome, London, Washington, Boston, Samoa, and Tahiti

The first three volumes of a projected six-volume edition which will provide a generous
although not complete collection of the letters of Henry Adams

As any student of American history knows, the epistolary talents of the
Adams family are a great and still only partially mined national natural resource.
For more than a hundred and fifty years, the pens of this small group of
curious, articulate New Englanders scratched out descriptions of the events
and discussions of the ideas that shaped the intellectual and political consciousness of their country. Narrow, bitter, and contentious as they sometimes
are, the Adams letters have provided a unique record of the American past
and a fascinating study in the interplay of personality and politics.

Publication of *The Letters of Henry Adams* makes available to the general
reader for the first time an important vein of this mine hitherto only glimpsed.
In the past, scholars or casual readers who did not have access to the Adams
family papers could read the letters of this celebrated grandson and great-
grandson of presidents only in highly abridged or selected editions, notably
the two-volume collection published in the 1930's by Worthington C. Ford,
which deleted comments that might have been an embarrassment to the still-
surviving members of the Adams family and their immediate circle of friends.
According to the current editors, more than fifteen hundred letters survive
from the period covered by these three volumes; of these, 1,277 appear here,
710 of them published in a complete text for the first time. The letters, which
begin with Adams' first European trip in 1858 and end with his decision to
return to Washington in 1892, cover his sojourn in the London embassy during
the Civil War, his years in Washington and at Harvard University, his marriage, his hopeless infatuation with Elizabeth Cameron, and his retreat to the
South Seas with John La Farge. They present, as well as a touching personal
history, a vivid report on the rise and fall of the Gilded Age in the United
States and the birth of what Adams identified as *fin de siècle* despondency
throughout the world.

It would be worth reading these letters if their contributions to the historical
record were their only value. Little of the information about Charles Francis
Adams' diplomatic maneuvering in the 1860's or the attempt of the reform

Republicans to take power in the presidential elections of the 1870's can be new to the scholar, but Henry Adams' unique perspective on the period lends a sharp immediacy to his observations. He was an involved participant in the political life around him, especially in his early years, sometimes fascinated and sometimes bored, but always acute and often eager. The four sons of Charles Francis fully expected him to be nominated for the presidency in 1872, and Henry's letters to Carl Schurz and others during this and subsequent years show him to be as full of intrigue and excitement as any other partisan insider. It is not until the late 1880's that he can confess that he has, for the first time, no personal friend in the Cabinet and thus knows little of what the inner circles are up to. He had ambivalent feelings about these circles, but his views on their unpredictable revolutions are always interesting and sufficiently snappish to retain their historical bite. Similarly, his letters from Tahiti and Samoa, which he visited in the 1890's, several decades before Margaret Mead, present a highly individual view of island customs observed carefully at a time when they were rapidly changing.

Adams' historical and anthropological observations, valuable as they may be, provide only a small part of the interest of these volumes. The letters are a pleasure to read. They are witty, eloquent, and precise. Adams was clearly lucky in his choice of friends, for he was able to write to them on a wide range of subjects, assured of their common interests and affections. Childless himself, he keeps up with the activities of their children. He jokes about himself and about shared memories and mutual friends. No answers to Adams' letters are provided here, except where they are quoted briefly in notes, but it is clear from, for example, Adams' letters in block capitals to little Martha Cameron and to his nieces that he was warmly accepted in his immediate world and was more relaxed and open to experience than his famous autobiography would lead the reader to expect.

There are many significant differences between letters and autobiography as literary genres, and it is difficult to imagine these contrasts more clearly illustrated than they are in the juxtaposition of *The Education of Henry Adams* (1907) with Adams' correspondence. The former is a fixed rhetorical structure, carefully planned, polished, and unified by a distinctive narrative voice. Written by a disappointed elderly man for a select audience, it distorts, or at least shapes experience into illustration. The letters by contrast offer change, uncertainty, fluctuation. They are alive. The reader becomes absorbed in process rather than fascinated by product. The sharp perceptions and intelligence that characterize the autobiography are never absent, but they seem part of a developing personality, a lively response to an unstable world instead of exemplary aspects of an American character. What was Adams like as a young man? Was he flirtatious? Or passionate? What did he do after his wife's suicide? How did he feel? One goes to Adams' letters for answers to such questions raised by *Mont-Saint-Michel and Chartres* (1913; privately printed,

1904) and *The Education of Henry Adams*, brilliant but slightly inhuman works.

Henry Adams was born in 1838, the fourth child and third son of a family that was inextricably involved with American political life. Born, as he says in his autobiography, "under the shadow of Boston State House," he perhaps carried a lighter burden of expectation than his older brothers, but he was never without the sense of being an Adams and thus caught, willy-nilly, in history. The middle-child consciousness that he was somehow out of place and perpetually in need of self-definition, and which would later be expanded into a full-scale philosophical position, pursued Henry from an early age. He was temperamentally drawn to his rebellious older sister Louisa but was closest in age and interest, at least while he was young, to his brother Charles, who had been his Harvard roommate and to whom the majority of the letters in the first volume are written.

Henry rather indirectly escaped the legal career that seemed to loom ahead of him in 1858 by persuading his parents to let him study civil law and languages in Europe. He left suddenly, apparently without consulting Charles, who was reading law in Boston and bored to death with it. Thus, the early letters home from Berlin, a place Henry soon found tedious and dismal, are both defensive and filled with that kind of anxiety about his own and his brother's career choices that only the very young and the very self-absorbed can feel. Henry insists at first that he wants to stay with law, envisioning himself and Charles working together in Boston in spite of Charles's contention that the two of them "are not adapted to make great lawyers." At the same time, although he claims that he does not want to be a writer, he follows his brother's suggestion to try journalism and write letters for American newspapers about his European experiences. It is impossible not to read the future into his comments from Rome in 1860, when he has just read Edward Gibbon's autobiography—an event that is described with great care in *The Education of Henry Adams*, because it provides one of the controlling thematic ideas of that book:

> Do you know, after long argument and reflexion I feel much as if perhaps some day I too might come to anchor like that. Our house needs a historian in this generation and I feel strongly tempted by the quiet and sunny prospect, while my ambition for political life dwindles as I get older.

Adams was only twenty-two at this point, and it would take a long time for his ambition for political life to become entirely negligible, if it ever did, but he did begin early to relish his role as an observer and to take it seriously. Like Henry James, Adams was to discover that his success in life would depend on the quality of his perceptions, and that the critical eye he could turn upon experience would be his most valuable and reliable personal resource. Even the earliest letters, homesick and filled with pleas for news from Boston, display his fondness for description and a slightly pompous analysis of the society around him. As he moves south in his second year abroad, he warms to the excitement of revolutionary politics in Italy, admires Giuseppe Garibaldi in person, and is thrilled to take official dispatches to Palermo. He writes excited letters to Charles about his adventures, then reorganizes the material into formal reports to the Boston *Courier*, impersonating very successfully the seasoned political commentator.

When Abraham Lincoln was elected in 1860, he rewarded Charles Francis Adams for his support by making him Minister to Great Britain, a post which at that moment required considerable diplomatic tact. Henry, who had already been persuaded rather easily to postpone the study of law a little longer to become his father's private secretary, went along to London with some reluctance. While Charles and older brother John struggled with hateful superior officers and inadequate supplies on the battlefield, watching their contemporaries die around them, Henry took his younger sister to balls, suffered the snubs of the English aristocracy, and watched his father in action. The skill of Charles in surmounting repeated crises and keeping Great Britain out of the war is described at length in *The Education of Henry Adams*. Here, what one is most conscious of is Henry's frustration and annoyance. He feels guilty about being away from the fighting and repeatedly threatens to enlist, but he also bewails the futility of the bloodshed. He is lonely, and his moods are uneven, swinging from triumphant to depressed in accordance with the war news or the progress of official business. He dutifully reports the family news, but predictions of imminent disaster abound.

The letters of this period are very much those of a son and brother. Henry is still defining himself to Charles and looking for direction. He is sure he has wasted his life and confesses to Charles, "I have steadily lost faith in myself ever since I left college." Gradually, however, a sense of purpose and direction begin to emerge. He begins a history of Pocahontas and Captain John Smith, searching the British Museum for documents and quizzing other scholars. Flashes of prescience illuminate his comments. After noting the obsolescence of the British naval force, he predicts, "Some day science may have the existence of mankind in its power, and the human race commit suicide, by blowing up the world"—an idea he would develop in his later works.

Volume 1 ends with Adams' return to Boston with his family in 1868; volume 2 begins with his decision to move to Washington alone and try his hand as a writer on contemporary affairs. In this volume, which traces the emotional growth and professional commitment of the mature man, the circle of correspondents widens. Charles, who was often living near Henry and from whom, in any case, he was often estranged, is replaced by Charles Milnes Gaskell, a close friend from the London period, and by Adams' contemporary and neighbor, John Hay. Adams seems immediately more self-assured and confident, a formed person rather than a dependent middle son.

After two years in Washington, watching with amusement and dismay the peculiar shenanigans of the Ulysses S. Grant Administration, Adams moves back to Boston to take on the editorship of the *North American Review* and to assume the duties of a professor of medieval history at the newly re-organized Harvard University. He meets and marries a Boston woman, Marian Hooper, buys a house on Back Bay, and absorbs himself in the problems of editing, teaching, and research. Soon, however, he begins to find the demands of academic life annoying (several of his letters are written during faculty meetings), and by the end of the 1870's, he is happy to return to Washington as editor of the Albert Gallatin papers, the first in a series of projects that would culminate in his massive history of the administrations of James Madison and Thomas Jefferson. In Washington, until his wife drinks photographic fluid one December Sunday morning, Adams is happy, sur-rounded by friends and challenged by his work. He arranges for the anony-mous publication of his two novels, *Democracy: An American Novel* (1880) and *Esther* (1884), and reports with glee the reactions of Washington society to the books. He buys land with John Hay, commissions Henry Hobson Richardson to design a house, and spends time poring over the plans and choosing rugs and furniture to fill it.

The mystery of Marian Hooper Adams' sudden death is not solved here. Adams' comments about his fiancée, when he announces his wedding, are characteristically defensive—he notes that she is "certainly not handsome" but is nevertheless "so far away superior to any woman I had ever met"— yet there is no indication here that the marriage was anything but happy. One biographer suggests that Adams was covertly patronizing toward women (and there is some evidence of this in the letters, particularly the early ones), yet this was hardly unusual in Adams' period, and it is really necessary to stretch one's imagination beyond the confines of these pages to guess the underlying causes of Marian's depression and suicide. Perhaps the cozy inti-macy of the Adamses, the Hays, and Clarence King, who called themselves the "Five of Hearts," concealed unpleasant pressures; perhaps being childless and thus relatively unoccupied while Henry worked in his study was simply too much for this clever woman. In any case, the letters written to Marian— she was usually called "Clover"—when she was nursing her father in his final illness only a few months before his death, and subsequently hers, are the most touching documents in the three volumes. Henry talks about the dogs, her friends, the progress of the house. His brief notes after her death are, by contrast, abrupt and painfully controlled.

Critics tend to view the omission from *The Education of Henry Adams* of any reference to the author's marriage and its aftermath as a kind of structural coyness: It breaks the book neatly into the kind of antithetical pattern that fits Adams' general theory of history. From the letters in the third volume it becomes clear, however, that his reticence reflected reality: Adams could not or would not speak of his wife and the years of their marriage, even to his closest friends at the time. Some diary entries that are included by the editor suggest that Adams suffered miserably, but as far as the public was concerned, his mourning took the form of boredom, restlessness, and a general sense of his own lack of worth. With the emergence of Elizabeth Cameron as the principal recipient, a reborn Henry Adams appeared, but it is never quite clear that this is the same man who wrote the earlier letters. The descriptions of life in Samoa and Fiji are sometimes almost impersonal, but they suggest a more responsive writer and display a far broader emotional range. The tension between the descriptive surface of the travel letters and the complicated interior turmoil of the man writing them make this the most compelling volume of the collection.

A few months after his wife's suicide, Adams was persuaded to go to Japan with his friend, the painter John La Farge. Adams' letters home are not pleasant to read. Although he is too well-bred to impose his sufferings directly on his friends, his observations of the world around him are sour, his attitudes unyielding and uncharacteristically provincial. He was a sophisticated traveler by this time, one with highly developed tastes in Oriental art, but he could not open himself to the Japanese character. Japan was a disappointment; its population seemed to him doll-like, its women repulsive, its culture second-hand. Longing to get as far away as possible from Washington, he craved exoticism but could not bear it when it confronted him. Perhaps he had not gone far enough. Perhaps China was the answer. He was committed to return to the house in which Clover had died and to finish the history he had planned and begun in the early years of their marriage, but he would study Chinese and try again to escape.

Life, however, does go on. In spite of his misery, or possibly because of it, Henry Adams fell in love. It is not clear from the letters precisely when he acknowledged his infatuation with his beautiful young neighbor, Elizabeth Cameron. (Otto Friedrich's suggestion in his biography, *Clover: A Love Story*, 1979, that jealousy prompted Marian Hooper Adams' suicide seems far-fetched, although not impossible.) It is clear, however, by the end of the 1880's, that Mrs. Cameron and her baby daughter are playing an important part in his life. He writes to her with increasing frequency and with such obvious emotion that the departure for Samoa, a trip he had planned for months and which she had possibly suggested as a solution to the problem, comes as a relief.

This time, the letters of observation are rich and appealing. Unlike the Japanese, the Samoans and Tahitians please Adams. They are graceful and beautifully proportioned, sensual without being provocative, and their attentions soothe his jangled nerves. Passion seems to have opened his senses and relaxed his hypercritical responses. He describes to John Hay and Gaskell, and especially to Elizabeth Cameron, the languorous beauty of the sunrises, the native dances, the lush vegetation, and the food, which he religiously samples and learns to like. His curiosity about the growth and decline of the culture in the islands is intense. He questions the inhabitants about everything and even inspires in them a desire to record what they can remember of their history. He begins to paint, taking lessons from La Farge, and he sends his watercolor sketches—nicely reproduced in this work—home to give his friends some idea of the view from the veranda of his native hut. Until his teeth start to rot, the trip is a real restorative: Adams seems a new man.

As the voyage comes to an end, however, Adams' thoughts return to Washington. He arranges to meet Mrs. Cameron in Paris, but she is with her daughter and stepdaughter, and the meeting is not a success. In London, she apparently rebuffs him again but gently enough to inspire a passionate letter to her on shipboard. One wonders how the two will be able to resume an ordinary social relationship at home where Adams, surrounded as he will be for the rest of his life by a bevy of real and honorary nieces, must see her and her husband nearly every day. The sources of that mystical power attributed to the Virgin in *Mont-Saint Michel and Chartres* begin to seem evident. The as yet unpublished volumes of letters will presumably provide the denouement.

The accomplishment of J. C. Levenson and the other editors of these letters is admirable. The notes are brief and sometimes leave the reader unsatisfied, but considering the scale of the enterprise, it is hard to see how they could have been more informative or detailed. They follow at the end of each letter, an arrangement that is generally convenient; although when the letters are long, the reader must sometimes scramble around to find the relevant pages. Levenson's introduction, supplemented by the paragraphs which introduce the various chronological divisions of the books, tells the reader almost everything about the text and the characters that he needs to know. The index, placed at the end of volume 3, is particularly well-organized and easy to use.

One final comment might be made: The first three volumes of *Letters of Henry James* (1843-1895), edited by Leon Edel and also published by the Harvard University Press, cover roughly the same period of time and describe some of the same people and events as this collection. Comparison between the personal writings of these two men, so alike in some ways and so profoundly different in others, might help to illuminate the peculiar qualities of each. Both men were intricately bound to their families, particularly to their retiring mothers and overbearing brothers; both were observers and analysts, comfortable with women, whatever their hidden feelings about them may have been, and uncomfortable with the open brutality of American popular culture. It is interesting to note, however, one significant difference that becomes apparent through these letters: Adams was rich, at least comparatively so, while James had to write to live. There is nothing in the Adams letters remotely like the polite negotiations over contracts, payments, debts, and serial rights that take up so much space in the James volumes. In fact, at one point, Adams even offers to subsidize his publication, a gesture which reveals much about his relationship to his own work and to the society around him.

Jean W. Ashton

Sources for Further Study

Chronicle of Higher Education. XXV, September 15, 1982, p. 27.
Los Angeles Times Book Review. August 21, 1983, p. 6.
New England Quarterly. LVI, September, 1983, p. 472.
The New York Times Book Review. LXXXVIII, March 6, 1983, p. 9.
Newsweek. CXXI, April 11, 1983, p. 95.
Time. CXXI, April 11, 1983, p. 95.

THE LETTERS OF MARGARET FULLER

Author: Margaret Fuller (1810-1850)
Edited, with an introduction and notes, by Robert N. Hudspeth
Publisher: Cornell University Press (Ithaca, New York). Volume I: 374 pp. $25.00.
   Volume II: 276 pp. $25.00
Type of work: Letters
Time: 1817-1838 and 1839-1841

The initial volumes of the first complete edition of the correspondence of one of America's foremost women of letters

Although Margaret Fuller is widely recognized as one of the outstanding literary figures of nineteenth century America, there is still no modern collection of her personal papers. Robert N. Hudspeth's work, which will eventually include the more than one thousand of her letters that have survived, will make available an important new resource for students of this period. Hudspeth, professor at Pennsylvania State University and biographer of Fuller's brother-in-law, Ellery Channing, faced a formidable task in undertaking this project, for many of the autograph letters were lost, damaged, or altered by the well-meaning but careless friends and relatives who compiled the *Memoirs of Margaret Fuller Ossoli* (1852) shortly after her death. The extensive textual notes testify to the care with which Hudspeth has searched out the most reliable version of each letter.

Hudspeth's service to his readers goes far beyond meticulous attention to the text. His thirty-page introduction to volume 1 is a superb essay on Fuller's life and work, as well as an incisive assessment of the letters and what they add to our knowledge of her complex personality. He notes the restlessness that kept her moving from place to place throughout her adult life and deprived her of the roots that sustained her Transcendentalist friends Ralph Waldo Emerson and Henry David Thoreau. For Fuller, Hudspeth suggests, "having a home meant having a life that lacked renewal," and her Romantic spirit kept her constantly questing after new goals. She was committed throughout her adult life to improving education and the arts in her native land. As she matured, she turned her attention to larger social questions as well; she spent the last years of her life working for Giuseppe Mazzini's republican revolution in Italy.

The 344 letters printed and annotated in these two volumes show the gradual, often painful, development of this remarkable, revolutionary woman. Volume 1 covers the years from 1817 to 1838, showing Fuller first as a child of seven writing dutifully to her father, Timothy Fuller, and concluding with her as a mature woman, the mainstay of her widowed mother and six younger siblings, preparing to embark upon her first major literary project. This volume is both tantalizing and frustrating. Even as a child, Fuller expressed herself well and provided important insights into her thoughts and feelings, but no more than eight or ten letters have survived from any year up to 1834, and consequently one receives only glimpses of the author's interests and experiences during her early years. Hudspeth's introduction and copious notes help to put the letters in context, but to be fully appreciated, they should probably be read in conjunction with a full-length biography.

The earliest letters reveal a child of formidable mental ability. At nine, Fuller was reading the fifth book of the *Aeneid* and translating Oliver Goldsmith's poem "The Deserted Village" into Latin. Four years later, she wrote her father that she was pursuing her study of Greek but thought it might be easier with a teacher. Her literary style was equally precocious. In 1819, not yet ten, she wrote Timothy Fuller, "I enclose you my composition and specimen of writing. I assure you I wrote the former off much better and made *almost* as many corrections as your critical self would were you at home."

Fuller's sometimes pathetic desire to please her father is visible through much of her early correspondence with him. She frequently apologizes for the quality of her penmanship and for remarks he has criticized. Her affection, however, is often expressed, and she keeps him abreast of news of friends and her younger brothers and sister, who were something of a trial to her then and later. As Hudspeth notes, these letters suggest that Fuller's childhood was happier and better-balanced than she later remembered. She sounds like a typical older sister of any generation in reporting to her mother of her brother Eugene: "He was a good boy till he went to meeting. There he behaved very ill. To punish him I did not let him go to meeting in the afternoon and ever since he has behaved as bad as he possibly can. He says he will spoil this letter if I write how he has behaved."

While there are enough surviving letters to give a rounded, if fragmentary, picture of Fuller's childhood and early adolescence, only a half-dozen remain from the period from 1826 to 1830, when she matured from girl of sixteen into woman of twenty. Her formal education ended when she left Susan Prescott's school in Groton in 1825, but she continued her studies with great intensity. Among the few extant letters are ones to Miss Prescott describing Fuller's reading in classical philosophy, English, Italian, French, and Spanish poetry, and the works of Madame de Staël. Rhapsodic descriptions of nature in letters from the early 1830's suggest that she also fell under the influence of the Romantic poets at this time: "The holy moon and merry-toned wind of this night woo to a vigil at the open window; a half-satisfied interest urges me to live, love and perish!" By 1830, she was also familiar with the work of Johann Wolfgang von Goethe, the writer who was to dominate her studies for years. She frequently expressed her enthusiasm for his work, writing a clergyman friend, James Clarke, "It seems to me as if the mind of Goethe had embraced the universe. . . . I am enchanted while I read."

The early 1830's brought emotional distress as well as intellectual development. Fuller sought intense friendships with both men and women, and she was often rebuffed. With Clarke, whom she may have hoped to marry, she was able to maintain a long-distance intellectual companionship when their emotional ties weakened. Her break with another potential husband, George Davis, was more nearly complete, but two letters included show the depth of her feeling for him. She often veiled her distress with men, but she felt free to communicate more openly with women. Their marriages were often hard for her to accept. To one friend she wrote, "Somehow your engagement seems to have changed our relation to one another and we have not been sufficiently together yet for me to feel easy under this change."

It is often hard to remember in reading the letters from these years that the author was only in her early twenties. Occasionally, however, Fuller's youth shines through the philosophical discussions and the prickly emotions. She seems youngest and happiest in her correspondence of the summer of 1835 when she first begs her parents to allow her to go with friends on a trip to the Catskills, then, their permission granted, writes them of her "three weeks of such unalloyed pleasures as are seldom allotted to mortals."

Fuller was to see very few weeks of "unalloyed pleasures" for years to come. In October of 1835, her father died. Although she wrote of her regret that her sex prevented her from being guardian of the younger children and administrator of the estate, she in fact assumed both of these responsibilities psychologically if not legally. She began writing her brothers letters filled with the same admonitions about penmanship, behavior, and studies that their father had earlier directed at her, and she regularly corresponded with her mother about buying and selling property and about plans for the education of the younger children. The stresses of these new responsibilities evidently exacerbated already existing physical problems; from this time on, she writes frequently of headaches and other ailments.

Even though Fuller viewed her father's death as the end of "all youthful hopes of every kind," it initiated a new and fruitful period in her life. The letters include her request to Bronson Alcott for a teaching position in his experimental school in Boston, as well as accounts of her later responsibilities at the Greene-Street School in Providence, where she taught languages to sixty boys and girls. Her correspondence also shows the development of her friendship with Emerson at this time. Their relationship was not without occasional strain; she desired emotional intensity that he could not or would not provide. He and his family, however, welcomed her as a frequent house-guest, and he encouraged her literary pursuits.

By the end of 1838, Fuller felt the need for a change. She wrote her friend Almira Barlow, "I have gabbled and simpered, and given my mind to the public views these two years back, till there seems to be no good left in me." She resolved to rejoin her family, now living in Groton, for a few months in the winter of 1839 and complete her first major work, a translation of Johann

Peter Eckermann's three-volume work, *Gespräche mit Goethe in den letzten Jahren seines Lebens, 1823-32* (1836-1848; *Conversations with Goethe in the Last Years of His Life*), which she published in May of that year. She promised to give her brother Richard and her sister Ellen lessons twice a week, but she was adamant in her resolve to take on no more pupils for the time being. She had not altogether abandoned the idea of teaching, however, for she wrote a friend who was minister of a church in Cincinnati to consider whether it would be feasible for her to open a school for girls there in a year or two. "I am not," she wrote, "without my dreams and hopes as to the education of women."

Fuller's plans for educating women were not, however, to take the form she expected. The letters printed in volume 2, covering the years 1839 to 1841, show the beginnings of the conversations she established for Boston matrons who were interested in finding "a place where they could state their doubts and difficulties with hope of gaining aid from the experience or aspiration of others." Her plan, outlined to one of the early participants, was to pick a broad topic, such as Greek mythology, give a brief statement of her own views, then encourage discussion. The conversations, which provided a welcome source of income as well as intellectual stimulation for Fuller, continued with considerable success to 1844.

Fuller's second occupation during these years was editing the *Dial*, a journal established by Emerson and other distinguished Transcendentalists. She and Emerson corresponded regularly about both contents and business affairs, a continual anxiety. She solicited writings from many of her acquaintances and occasionally offered astute editorial advice; one letter contains extensive criticism of a poem of Thoreau. Though the *Dial* created a steady series of problems, she was pleased that it "brings meat and drink to sundry famishing men and women at a distance from these tables." Her letters give some sense of the range of her own contributions to the magazine—from reviews of books, concerts, and art exhibits to prose meditations on the magnolia and the yucca.

With many more letters available from each year covered in volume 2, it is possible to see Fuller in much more detail than volume 1 provided. Her emotional life continued to be turbulent. On a visit to Newport in 1838, she met Charles Newcomb, a young man who was later to join the well-known experiment in communal living at Brook Farm. Obviously infatuated to some degree, for several months she wrote him glowing descriptions of scenes of natural beauty. Then he suggested that they not correspond regularly. Characteristically, she replied in a hurt but dignified tone and offered him lifelong, disinterested friendship. On the heels of this break came a rift with her closest woman friend, Caroline Sturgis. With her Fuller was more direct. The terms in which she expressed her feelings were hardly ones designed to smooth over conflict: "Only for a moment did I cease to love you. I wept at the loss you were to sustain in me. I would have given all but self-respect to save you."

She added later, "When I am dissatisfied or feel repelled by any trait of yours I feel also that I can wait." These tensions were eventually overcome, for both Newcomb and Sturgis continued to receive and save her letters.

Far more damaging to Fuller's emotional stability was the end of her close relationship with Samuel Ward, an aspiring artist who had been a friend since his student days at Harvard University. Few of her letters to him have survived, but, as Hudspeth comments, those that have show that she was in love with him and suffered deeply when he abandoned her and his art in 1839. His decision to become a banker seemed a repudiation of her highest values, and his engagement to Anna Barker, another intimate friend of hers, seemed a double rebuff. Her reaction was to suppress the anger she must have felt and instead to romanticize and idealize the marriage of her friends, to whom she referred as "Raphael and his Madonna." The intense spiritual experience she underwent a few weeks before their wedding can also be seen as a psychological defense against despair. She wrote to Caroline Sturgis, "Of the mighty changes in my spiritual life I do not wish to speak, yet surely you cannot be ignorant of them. All has been revealed, all foreshown yet I know it not. Experiment has given place to certainty, pride to obedience, thought to love, and truth is lost in beauty." This exalted mood helped to bridge the separation from Sturgis and sustained her at a point when she felt that there was no one capable of fully responding to her needs.

The advantage of so complete a collection of correspondence as this one is that it allows readers to see the writer in different moods and different relationships. Fuller was hurt deeply by Ward, but she was not totally absorbed by emotional crises. She continued with the conversations and her editorial duties and focused her attention increasingly on the needs of her family. Her letters of 1841 are as apt to be practical instructions to a brother about paying bills and collecting laundry as they are to express her conviction that "I must die if I do not burst forth in genius or heroism." It may in fact have been her need to provide strength for her family that saved her from emotional collapse. Of special concern during this period was her sister Ellen's engagement to Ellery Channing, the talented but unreliable poet who was the son of a distinguished New England clergyman. Fuller confided to Emerson her serious doubts about the wisdom of this marriage, but once it was an accomplished fact, she wrote graciously to her new brother-in-law: "Should you prove the wise and faithful guardian of my sister's happiness; should you be the means of unfolding what is beautiful in her character, and leading her tenderly to her true aim, you will have conferred on me a benefit, beyond requital, and only to be answered in prayer."

Volume 2 ends with a series of letters dealing with family business affairs and arrangements for the education of Fuller's brothers. Plans of Ellen and Ellery continued to concern her; she had by this time established a comfortable enough relationship with Ward to consult him about the possibility of buying a farm for the young couple. Her life seems at this point to have been burdensome, constricted, and rather sad, but the letters also show the intelligence, dedication, and enthusiasm that were to open new opportunities to her during the last decade of her life. The remaining volumes of Hudspeth's edition should be even richer sources of information about Fuller and her circle.

Elizabeth Johnston Lipscomb

Sources for Further Study

Choice. XXI, November, 1983, p. 422.
Library Journal. CVIII, May 1, 1983, p. 901.
New Leader. LXVI, September 19, 1983, p. 16.
The New York Times Book Review. LXXXVIII, June 19, 1983, p. 1.
The New Yorker. LIX, July 18, 1983, p. 98.
The Wall Street Journal. August 15, 1983, p. 16.

LIFE & TIMES OF MICHAEL K

Author: J. M. Coetzee (1940-   )
Publisher: The Viking Press (New York). 184 pp. $13.95
Type of work: Novel
Time: An unspecified future
Locale: South Africa

A novel that explores the responses of a poor simpleton to his victimization by a civil war he does not understand

> Principal characters:
> MICHAEL K, a poor, homeless simpleton
> ANNA K, his ailing mother
> A MEDICAL OFFICER, Michael's sympathetic doctor

Since publishing *Dusklands* in 1974, J. M. Coetzee has come closer and closer to writing a novel in which he plainly comments upon the injustices of white dominance and apartheid in his native South Africa. In *Dusklands*, his first novel, Coetzee juxtaposes two aggressors, an American bureaucrat designing a method for propagandizing the Vietnamese and a white South African hunter seeking elephant tusks, both of whom misunderstand the peoples they seek to control. *In the Heart of the Country*, Coetzee's second novel and winner of the 1977 Central News Agency (CNA) Literary Award in South Africa, is a mad spinster's narrative of violations of the sexual taboo between white sheep farmers and their black hired hands. *Waiting for the Barbarians*, Coetzee's most celebrated novel to date, which also won a CNA award in 1980, concerns the unprovoked brutality with which a remote white government treats the docile natives whom it rules. His first three novels are violent depictions of white domination, connected only allegorically to present-day South Africa.

In *Life & Times of Michael K*, winner of Great Britain's top award for fiction, the Booker Prize, Coetzee is moving away from allegory toward more or less contemporary realism. No longer is he treating racial exploitation in the past or within one household or in a mythical time and place. This novel takes place in an unspecified but not too distant future: South Africa has been ravaged by the civil war between whites and blacks—a civil war in which, according to *The New York Times*, underground liberation movements have destroyed some 432 million dollars of property in five years.

The novel focuses on thirty-one-year-old Michael K, born a simpleton with a harelip and a gaping left nostril. Coetzee never identifies Michael by race but, as various clues suggest—his mother worked as a maid, and a medical officer describes him as "one of a multitude in the second class"—he is probably black. The action of the novel is set in motion when Michael is laid off from his job as a gardener for the city of Cape Town.

When he loses his job, Michael decides to take his bedridden mother, Anna, to the Visagie farm in Prince Albert where she spent her childhood. Michael and Anna apply for an exit permit that never arrives, and so they decide to leave illegally. Michael wheels his mother away from the city in a ricksha that he has built. Because they lack an exit permit, guards of the Free Corps, who, according to an officer, ". . . are fighting . . . so that minorities will have a say in their destinies," turn the couple back. Two days later, they try again—this time they get by the checkpoint—but Anna's illness worsens, and Michael takes her to a hospital, where she dies. A nurse hands Michael a suitcase packed with his mother's belongings and two bags; one contains clean clothes and toiletries, the other, Anna's ashes.

Deciding to take his mother's ashes to the Visagie farm, Michael continues the journey and encounters obstacles along the way. A soldier takes his mother's purse at gunpoint, telling him that he must contribute to the war effort. (The soldier tosses a ten-rand note, about ten dollars, to Michael as a "tip.") At the next checkpoint, Michael, with all others who lack an exit pass, is herded onto a train and carried to a place where he is forced to repair railroad tracks. A day later, Michael slips away and continues his trek to Prince Albert.

Michael arrives at the Visagie farm only to find that the family has abandoned it. He buries Anna's ashes in a field and lives for a time on birds and a wild ewe. His solitude ends when Visagie's grandson returns to the farm, a deserter from the army. Thinking Michael is a servant, the grandson demands that Michael keep him supplied with food. Dissatisfied with the birds that Michael brings to him, he sends Michael into town for groceries; instead, Michael flees to the mountains nearby, where he lives on lizards, grubs, and flowers. Before long, however, sick and malnourished, Michael descends the mountain and goes into Prince Albert.

There he is arrested and sent to a local resettlement camp that is filled with others of the second class. Almost every day, men from the camp are loaded into trucks and hauled away to work on roads, railways, or farms. With their wages of one rand (roughly one dollar) per day, they are expected to pay for their own meals. Michael, resenting his imprisonment, and steadily weakening from the hard labor and meager nourishment, escapes and returns to the Visagie farm once more.

Once again, Michael finds the farm vacant, but, taking no chances, he builds a shelter in a mountain crevice from mud, grass, and stone. He finds a handful of pumpkin and melon seeds, plants them, and lives off of insects and roots, while he waits for his plants to grow and yield fruit. He hides from rebels but is caught by the Free Corps, who interrogate him, mine the farm, and send him to a rehabilitation camp near Cape Town, where he is hospitalized for malnutrition, dysentery, and degeneration of the intestinal wall.

Michael's doctor, curiously, takes special interest in him. The doctor describes him to the camp commander as ". . . a person of feeble mind who drifted by chance into a war zone and didn't have the sense to get out." When the commander receives a call from the police at Prince Albert, who request that Michael be returned for questioning regarding a water pump that has been destroyed, the medical officer convinces the commander to falsify a list of first names of the perpetrators. When Michael escapes, near death after having refused food and intravenous feeding, the medical officer writes a death certificate rather than report the escape to the authorities. Michael had told him, "I am not in the war," and the medical officer respected him.

Michael's final escape takes him to a beach where a group of vagrants give him liquor, food, and sex, but he is no more of their world than he was of the camps. He wants freedom from charity as well as freedom from confinement. He wants to be free to live off the earth.

It is obvious that *Life & Times of Michael K* offers a perspective on apartheid, but the novel suggests no facile solutions. It does not simply pit the owners against the workers, oppressors against the oppressed, rulers against the ruled, nor does it laud the powerful. Indeed, in this very political novel, the hero is decidedly apolitical.

The novel, however, does take a political position, even though its main character does not. Most clearly, it takes a dim view of those who are in power. The Free Corps enforces martial law—specifically curfew and travel restrictions—ostensibly to maintain order in the country, but the real effect of martial law is the maintenance of power at the expense of the disenfranchised. Michael suffers interrogation, imprisonment, and forced labor even though his only crime is being poor and homeless and having compassion for his mother. Perhaps the key to understanding what the powerful represent comes from the only Free Corps representative who treats Michael K as a human being: the medical officer. He has forgotten the original reason for the war, and when he asks, he is told that the Free Corps is fighting for civil rights. Not only has the army, as a matter of course, disregarded civil rights—hence the irony of its name—but it also has actively engaged in fighting the lower-class insurgents whom it claims to be fighting *for*. Class power, this narrative suggests, is thoroughly self-interested and hypocritical; it lacks any justification for the denial of liberty and respect on which it thrives.

Given this perspective on class domination, one might expect the narrative to herald the poor, if only by virtue of their poverty. It does not. The poor offer little hindrance to Michael, it is true, but they offer little help as well. Early in the story, Michael has to defend himself with a steel rod against three poor robbers. When Michael witnesses the stabbing of a policeman in a resettlement camp, only he calls for help; the others care as little for the man as he had cared for them. They, like their oppressors, lack humaneness. There are acts of charity here and there, but not much more than Michael received from the medical officer. The oppressed, that is to say, are morally indistinguishable from the oppressors.

This observation surely has a bearing on contemporary debates in South Africa about whether the black majority should take over the white capitalist system. Coetzee's novel suggests a negative answer: One class's oppression is no better than another's. Michael comes to a similar conclusion when he returns to the farm and decides not to move into the farmhouse:

> Because whatever I have returned for, it is not to live as the Visagies lived, sleep where they slept, sit on their stoep looking out over their land. If this house were to be abandoned as a home for the ghosts of all the generations of the Visagies, it would not matter to me. It is not for the house that I have come.

Michael realizes that the hope of the oppressed does not lie in the patterns of the powerful. There must be a different organization of power—one that ensures liberty and equality—not simply a change in who sits in the seat of power.

If there is a positive moral or political vision in this novel, it is minimal. The hero values freedom as much as he values survival. Both he and the medical officer genuinely respect the well-being of others. Furthermore, throughout the novel is a reverence for the earth. These values are hardly evident in the struggle for social control, but the narrative ends with Michael's daydream about earthly sustenance. Is there justice only in dreams?

John P. Ferré

Sources for Further Study

The Atlantic. CCLIII, February, 1984, p. 105.
Los Angeles Times Book Review. January 15, 1984, p. 2.
Maclean's. XCVII, January 30, 1984, p. 49.
New Statesman. CVI, September 30, 1983, p. 29.
The New York Review of Books. XXXI, February 2, 1984, p. 3.
Newsweek. CIII, January 2, 1984, p. 63.
Time. CXXIII, January 2, 1984, p. 84.
Vogue. CLXXIV, January, 1984, p. 60.

LIGHT

Author: Eva Figes (1932-   )
Publisher: Pantheon Books (New York). 91 pp. $10.95
Type of work: Novella
Time: 1900
Locale: Giverny, France

An account of the imaginary events in one full day in the life of the painter Claude Monet

> *Principal characters:*
> CLAUDE MONET, a French Impressionist painter
> ALICE, his common-law wife
> GERMAINE and
> MARTHE, her daughters
> LILY, Alice's granddaughter
> OCTAVE MIRBEAU, a Monet family friend and prominent journalist

Eva Figes first came to American attention through a feminist tome entitled *Patriarchal Attitudes* (1970), but she has also produced, in addition to other nonfiction such as *Tragedy and Social Evolution* (1976), an impressive array of fiction, most recently the novel *Waking* (1982). In *Light*, she takes on a novelistic assignment that is supposed to be fatal: the treatment of artistic endeavor other than writing. One of the cherished truisms of modern narrative is that works of fiction come to grief when a musician, painter, or sculptor is the subject. The exceptions to this rule, however, should give pause to those who proclaim it. Thomas Mann's *Doktor Faustus* (1947; *Doctor Faustus: The Life of the German Composer Adrian Leverkuhn as Told by a Friend*, 1948) is a classic refutation of the principle; *Light* bids fair, in its more modest way, to be another.

The obstacles would appear quite steep at the outset. To enter the consciousness of Claude Monet, one of the least analytical, least self-conscious, and least verbal of major modern artists, would clearly require extraordinary powers of invention, not to say distortion. Surely the intense examination of the psyche that informs *Waking* would be inappropriate here, and it is not used. Instead, in a spirit very much in keeping with that of Monet's work, the novella seeks the outer world with all the pagan gusto of its principal character. The title, in one sense, does announce the subject of the book, and its dappled prose renders that shifting light which it traces in all of its divagations and quirks. Many of the passages devoted to landscapes and shifting shadows recall the chapter from Virginia Woolf's *To the Lighthouse* (1927) entitled "Time Passes"; the house and grounds of Giverny almost become characters in this text.

"Almost" is the operative word here. Figes realizes that the setting alone cannot be the protagonist, and she begins to sketch out very rapidly the interactions within the Monet ménage. She emphasizes the activities of ancillary figures in the household (such as Monet's common-law wife, Alice, and her daughters, Marthe and Germaine), partly for tactical, partly for strategic reasons. The tactical reason stems from Monet's role as the commonsensical, placid sensualist who believes that things "are, and ought to be, simple," and the consequent need to look elsewhere for human complexity. The strategic reason involves a subversion of the reader's expectations. Instead of providing a guided tour of the Great Man, Figes focuses upon those in the shadows who thanklessly make his sunlit existence as pleasant as possible. There is, at least potentially, a political feature to this shifting of focus. (Particularly curious for this theorist of patriarchy, by the way, is the gerrymandered nature of this patriarch's clan. Monet is not married to the woman of the house, nor has he fathered either of the daughters remaining at home. Nevertheless, as the narrative establishes, his word is still law.) Also, the way the narrative gradually opens out into the household in general, at first emerging as if part of the natural landscape, is one of the chief pleasures of the text.

The culmination of this social treatment occurs in chapter 7, where Octave Mirbeau, a journalist and friend of Monet, visits for lunch. Here one sees the Monet clan truly *en famille*; every modulation in collective mood and every mutual adjustment of demeanor and interaction is noted with precision. Mirbeau himself is admirably rendered as well: a forward-looking, anticlerical fop with a journalist's eye for rhetorical theatrics. Some readers will be reminded of Monsieur Homais in Gustave Flaubert's *Madame Bovary*. Characteristically, Mirbeau twits the Monets for retaining servants yet is unhesitating in being served by them himself. Like so many public men, Mirbeau seems passionate about almost every topic but finally only as a matter of rhetoric; his proclaimed concern has about it a certain weightlessness, an air of self-promotion.

One of those present at the lunch—served, significantly, on the veranda, that intermediate point between inside and outdoors—is Alice's granddaughter, Lily, the member of the household who, at nursery-school age, has most in common with Monet. The story provides many clues to their affinity. Both are in love with the outdoors, and with light itself. Among the most vivid passages in the narrative is the sequence in chapter 5 concerning Lily's attempts, ultimately successful, to blow a large, complete bubble from her clay pipe. When finally the bubble evolves, "round, iridescent, and perfect," it holds only for a moment—"enough for Lily," however: "Memory holds the shining bubble, bright with the newborn glory of the world."

What becomes apparent, to elaborate the crucial link between Lily and Monet, is that the project of Monet's Impressionism, as Figes presents it, is precisely to render a moment, as is always said—but in so doing to defeat the onward rush of time; somehow to hold the bubble, bright with the world's newborn glory. The early chapters involving Monet and his helper Auguste in the lily pond—which to the painter is like "sitting in the middle of an aquamarine bubble"—make this clear. It is not one moment in time, after all, that is Monet's quarry: It is the repetition of that moment over many occurrences. The layerings of the paintings, then, accrete as a similar quality of light strikes the same setting over a period of time. The resulting "impression" is in fact more like a palimpsest of numerous inscriptions, the rough equivalent in painting to what in narrative is called an "iterative event." (One very famous iterative event in fiction opens Marcel Proust's *Remembrance of Things Past*: "For a long time I used to go to bed early," reads the first sentence, followed by a description of moments within these varying experiences of going to bed—but as if they had all been part of one continuous process. The use of "would"—"I would often," "It would happen that," and so on—signifies the iterative event.) Why is this detail of layering so significant for Monet's philosophy as well as his technique? The reason is that this layering process points to the implicit belief in cyclical time which informs Monet's work and which is in sharp contrast to the outlook of his wife, and perhaps of the text itself.

It is true that Monet no longer believes, as in his youth, in the solidity of the world and the consequent irrelevance of the light that envelops it. In her review of *Light*, Joyce Carol Oates has made much of this conversion of Monet to the realization, as Figes puts it, that "light and those things it illuminates are both transubstantial, both tenuous." Oates also highlights Figes' literary ancestry regarding this particular version of the substance-accident problem, citing in her review Virginia Woolf's famous 1919 definition of life as "a semi-transparent envelope surrounding us from the beginning of consciousness to the end." The conversion to Impressionism, however, leaves Monet still a pagan of sorts, a man who still believes that stasis can be effected and time frozen in its tracks. The only difference is that instead of thinking that objects in themselves can endure, he substitutes for that faith the conviction that moments, impressions, or sensations—apart from the objects that may be responsible for them—can indeed repeat themselves. It may be that "each day is a new beginning" where "the miracle of creation was recreated," but what the sun's light re-creates is reassuringly like what it destroyed in disappearing the night before. In embodying successive layered moments on one canvas, experienced by the spectator in one stroke, Monet gives shape to his belief in cyclical time.

Contrasted to her husband throughout the text, Monet's wife, Alice, partakes as much of penumbra and secrecy as Monet does of sunlight and expansiveness. From the first chapter, where Monet bounds out-of-doors while his wife broods crankily in her separate bedroom, the two seem to inhabit different "planes of being," as Oates would have it. In mourning for her dead daughter Suzanne, Alice continually wears black—a color of which Monet distinctly disapproves, both for his own paintings and elsewhere. To Alice, by way of distinction, the sunlight is what is "cruel, an affront"—presumably to her personal suffering. She frets about God's punishments, while Monet obviously has little interest in the subject of God in the first place, let alone His punishment. Figes loads Alice down with night, death, and silence to the point where she becomes a more unpleasant character than may have been intended. The reader cringes a little when Alice hovers into view, knowing that bitterness and *morbidezza* are in the offing. For all of that, Alice does provide the narrative with a suitable counterweight to Monet; her value goes beyond that of merely being the shadow that gives Monet's sunny disposition its chiaroscuro.

Whereas in Monet's world, lost moments can be retrieved and experienced once more, time's onrush somehow stayed; in Alice's world, one can only cling dumbly to memory, to the lost past, knowing that to hold the past in mind is to hold its loss in mind as well. Monet resurrects his past, and Alice lovingly entombs hers. For example, in chapter 2 she visits Suzanne's grave and stays there so long that she loses "all sense of time." In chapter 6, Monet experiences a similar sensation—indeed, it is again called "losing all sense of time"—but for him it is a present incident (Lily coming up the garden path) that evokes a buried memory of another child of his and so breathes new life into that memory for a moment. He says to himself that "if continuity is anything, it is in this . . . an echo of something." In line with his faith that the past can recur and does recur, he calls forth ghosts from the past, both in the above-mentioned passage in chapter 6 and at one point in the veranda-lunch scene. Monet's paintings thus become the visual record of his immersion in the outside world, but also of a curious faith in the ability of that world, combined with human memory, to re-create past moments—to produce, in a way, iterative events. Alice does not see in the ever-changing world of flux the chance to relive any past experiences: She sees change as that brutal force which bears away all that she cherishes, and she hates it.

One interesting result of this difference between husband and wife is that while Monet paints, Alice writes. She addresses her journal entry to Suzanne, and indeed she can "almost hear the swish of her gown" as she does so. This writing is her way of getting the dead to return to life ("Nothing is lost," she thinks briefly and delusively.) The paradox, however, that paralyzes her is that the dead can only be revivified as absences, and she feels "absurd, speaking to the dead." This circumstance—and Alice is the only figure shown writing in this novel—emblematizes the larger question of the novel itself, which as a narrative holds a relation to the past very similar to Alice's. Unlike a painting, which is an experience of sensation in itself and has artistic value as that—therefore laying claim to a more direct access to what it presents—a narrative presents past events *as* past events. They are recounted, but in the past tense, and discursively rather than through sensual rendering. In its resurrection of the past *as* past, as something to be mourned, the narrative may be closer to Alice's world, where loss is genuinely and finally loss, than to Monet's, where echoes of past moments somehow impart a continuity not in the things themselves.

Despite the fact that Claude Monet is the subject of this novella, it contains a gentle, even oblique subversion of the implicit assumptions of the Impressionist aesthetic. For Monet, flux was really only the means that would yield the repetition of moments, the cyclical reality that ensures finally that the past will indeed be prologue. The mourning Alice, and the visiting abbé who visits the Monets and silently reflects on a similar motif of time's irreversibility, both suspect a gloomier truth: What is lost survives, if at all, not in the world but in one's tenacious mind alone, and, in recalling what time has borne away, one inevitably also recalls the fact of its loss as well.

The structure of the narrative may at first mislead in this respect. By concerning itself with the events of one day, it might seem to be alluding to the globe's ceaseless rotation on its axis, producing an identical reality tomorrow and tomorrow and tomorrow, whether for good or ill. As the story progresses, however, the reminders of time's inevitable course thicken: the many references to the technological changes that compromise Giverny's Edenic serenity, the final word from Monet permanently dashing Germaine's hopes for marriage, and so on. Above all, there is the lyric and bleakly lovely chapter 12, after the sun has set at last on the Monet estate in Giverny. This final chapter, which evokes both the later progressive blindness of Monet himself and the Great War which brutally altered the face of France and of Europe, suddenly reminds the reader that he has been passing among people whose lives and whose way of life, however much these have been altered imaginatively by Figes, were nevertheless once very much present and now are not. It reminds the reader, finally, of the destructive power of irreversible time, in spite of the closing image of Monet keeping faith with his lily pond: Figes suggests that sometimes when the sun sets on something, it sets for good.

Mark Conroy

Sources for Further Study

Nation. CCXXXVII, December 31, 1983, p. 706.
New Statesman. CVI, September 2, 1983, p. 24.
The New York Times Book Review. LXXXVIII, October 16, 1983, p. 11.
Publishers Weekly. CCXXIV, August 26, 1983, p. 367.
Times Literary Supplement. August 26, 1983, p. 898.

LITERARY THEORY
An Introduction

Author: Terry Eagleton (1943-   )
Publisher: University of Minnesota Press (Minneapolis). 244 pp. $29.50; paperback $9.95
Type of work: Literary criticism

A brilliant introduction to contemporary literary theory, laced with Marxism and wit

This is an unusual book. It is the best introduction to date for college students to current critical theory. Without standing on the shoulders of earlier works of this kind by Robert Scholes, Jonathan Culler, and Edith Kurzweill—to name only a few—Terry Eagleton manages to do a better job than his predecessors in clarifyiing the theoretical distinctions between New Critical formalism and post-Structuralist ideas. The strength of his approach comes largely from the way he traces the historical movement from the rise of English studies at the beginning of the century to the current critical environment, where traditional academic and cultural values have been superseded by influences from extra literary fields such as linguistics, psychoanalysis, anthropology, and politics.

What makes this book truly unusual, however, is that its pedagogical clarity is in constant struggle with Eagleton's own Marxist theory. At times the Marxism is strident and sounds more like a bias than an intellectual point of view. When Eagleton suggests that literary symbolism, with its aesthetic of organic unity, projected the literary work of art as "an absolute spiritual truth" used to bully the lower classes "to forget their grievances," one becomes skeptical of his objectivity, and when he blames the success of Senator Joseph McCarthy's witch-hunting in the 1950's on the political inertia resulting from New Critical "disinterestedness," it seems that Eagleton has descended to some witch-hunting of his own. When he attacks American ego-psychology for "underwriting middle-class society," it becomes clear that he has descended to something worse. Nevertheless, despite such lapses into sneering humor and below-the-belt polemics, Eagleton's analytical imagination, Marxist or otherwise, seems to thrive on the intellectual complexities he has contracted to elucidate. The linguistic determinism at the heart of so much current literary theory is congenial to the social determinism of his Marxism; a sympathetic dialectic seems to energize his thinking so that when he discusses literary theory he is also thinking social change. His own language reveals the critic. The quotation marks and italics in the following are Eagleton's own: "The hallmark of the 'linguistic revolution' of the twentieth century, from Saussure and Wittgenstein to contemporary literary theory, is the recognition that meaning is not simply something 'expressed' or 'reflected' in language: it is actually *produced* by it." He can be even more explicit: "One of the themes of this book has been that there is no such thing as a purely 'literary' response: all such responses, not least those to literary *form*, to the aspects of a work which are sometimes jealously reserved to the 'aesthetic,' are deeply imbricated with the kind of social and historical individuals we are."

What appeals most to Eagleton in current literary theory is its dethroning of the creative artist. He attacks E. D. Hirsch's intentionalist theories as a step back to feudalism. Authorial intention, Eagleton argues, is no more reliable as validation of meaning than the landed titles of legal inheritance; in both cases, a privileged position is won by force. By discrediting the cult of creativity, the notion of authorial originality and genius, and other intentional theories of the expressive imagination, today's literary theory is bringing down an elitist establishment: By shifting to "reception theory," the most recent development of hermeneutics, criticism has given literature back to the "underprivileged" reader. Eagleton sees this shift from text to reader as a healthy rejection of New Critical text-worship, which, although it deflated intentionalism, elevated the literary work to iconicity, the opiate of the common reader. Hermeneutics liberates the reader to interpret the text on his own terms, but Eagleton is quick to remind one that dethroning the creator does not permit the reader, in any naïve sense, to take his place. The reader, as one knows from Structuralism and semiotics (and Marxism), is a fated creature, as limited as is the artist by the language and society in which he lives.

Eagleton is at his best as a teacher when he explains the basic principles of Structuralist theory. He begins by suggesting that Northrop Frye's "totalization" of all literary genres in *Anatomy of Criticism* (1957) prepared the Anglo-American mind for the shock of Continental Structuralism. Frye's four narrative categories (comic, romantic, tragic, ironic), identified with the four mythoi or seasons, suggested an anthropological equivalence that anticipates the much leaner schema of relations characteristic of Structuralist analytics. Frye's structures come from literature itself; Structuralism's schema derive from the simplest grammatical paradigms or the binary relationships of signs. Eagleton coins a little story, an allegorical tale, and then he changes the characters to clarify the gist of Structuralist theory: "You could replace father and son, pit and sun, with entirely different elements—mother and daughter, bird and mole—and still have the *same story*. As long as the structure of *relations* between the units is preserved, it does not matter what items you select."

Although Eagleton admires the scientific objectivity of Structuralism and its sister discipline semiotics, which he defines as literary criticism transfigured by structural linguistics, his fondness cools when he contemplates the indifference of the Structuralist approach to the human subject. While Structuralism makes the study of literature less subjective and impressionistic, its constant focus on the "literary system" at hand—a whole system of codes, conventions, and genres—tends to blur or oversimplify not only the individual text but also the use of language itself. One can never, insists Eagleton, understand the "intentions of a piece of language" without a grasp of its immediate purpose. No universal formula can be so inclusive as to account for the full thrust of a language act, and that thrust is impossible without a human subject. Eagleton's Marxism pulls him both ways. He is attracted to the debunking of a "creator-capitalist" aesthetics in Structuralism, but at the same time he rebels at the notion that the revolutionary act is a linguistic and therefore, most probably, a metaphysical impossibility. When he distinguishes Structuralism from Deconstruction, it is clear that he is not only tracking the historical path from one to the other but also working out the difference between them as a possible solution to the tensions between determinism and revolution in his own Marxism:

> Structuralism was generally satisfied if it could carve up a text into binary oppositions (high/low, light/dark, Nature/Culture and so on) and expose the logic of their working. Deconstruction tries to show how such oppositions, in order to hold themselves in place, are sometimes betrayed into inverting or collapsing themselves, or need to banish to the text's margins certain niggling details which can be made to return and plague them . . . to dismantle the oppositions which govern the text as a whole.

Transformation in language and/or art parallels radical politics for Eagleton, and so, finally, he praises feminist criticism as the most impressive achievement of current literary theory, because it brings together the liberating possibilities of Structuralism, Deconstruction, psychoanalysis, and various hermeneutical approaches for a revolutionary purpose. He also praises Harold Bloom, who braves Deconstructionist readings in the absolute faith that he can recover a Romantic humanism which will reinstate "author, intention, and the power of the imagination." Eagleton does not really believe that Bloom's enterprise can succeed. The archenemy of Romanticism, rationalism, has been discredited, but the "intolerable skepticism" of post-Structuralist thought renders Bloom's humanism purely an assertion of his own will. The "practical" solution, Eagleton pounds home in his last chapter, lies in what he calls a political criticism. Humanism, despite Bloom's sincere individualism, is only a disguise for a return to bourgeois tyranny. What is needed is a "strategy" of literary inquiry that insists on asking not *what* the object is or *how* one should approach it, but *why* one should want to engage it in the first place. The why must be asked by all men and women of all social classes. Only then will literature transform itself into an object that one can finally understand. Terry Eagleton's closing tone is that of *vates*: teacher *and* preacher.

Peter A. Brier

Sources for Further Study

Library Journal. CVIII, August, 1983, p. 1483.
Nation. CCXXXVIII, January 21, 1984, p. 59.
New Statesman. CV, June 3, 1983, p. 24.
The New York Review of Books. XXX, December 8, 1983, p. 43.
The New York Times Book Review. LXXXVIII, September 4, 1983, p. 9.
Times Literary Supplement. June 10, 1983, p. 587.
Wilson Quarterly. VII, Winter, 1983, p. 151.

THE LITTLE DRUMMER GIRL

Author: John le Carré (David Cornwell, 1931-   )
Publisher: Alfred A. Knopf (New York). 430 pp. $15.95
Type of work: Novel
Time: The 1980's
Locale: West Germany, Great Britain, Greece, Yugoslavia, Austria, Lebanon, and
Israel

Israeli intelligence agents enlist the aid of an English actress to stop Palestinian terrorists

Principal characters:
CHARMIAN (CHARLIE), an English actress
GADI BECKER (JOSEPH) and
MARTY KURTZ, Israeli agents
KHALIL,
MICHEL, and
CAPTAIN TAYEH, Palestinian guerrillas
FATMEH, Khalil and Michel's sister
MINKEL, an Israeli professor

Since the publication of *The Spy Who Came in from the Cold* (1963), his third novel, John le Carré has been regarded as the best living practitioner of espionage fiction, and his seven books since then, all but one of them spy novels, have made him the most acclaimed ever. Le Carré's previous fiction has concentrated on East-West tensions, but with *The Little Drummer Girl*, he has shifted his focus from the Cold War to the very bloody conflicts of the Middle East. For the past decade, in novels such as *Tinker, Tailor, Soldier, Spy* (1974) and *Smiley's People* (1980), his examination of the chesslike maneuvers of British and Soviet spies, featuring George Smiley and Karla, his Russian nemesis, has fascinated both readers of popular fiction and critics who admire le Carré's style and his insight into global politics. Following several visits to the Middle East since 1977, le Carré wanted to deal with the complex political struggles there. Such a subject—with all sides seemingly right and wrong at the same time—appears perfect for this master of moral ambiguity. Abandoning his familiar mise-en-scène and his recurring cast of characters, le Carré has produced one of his most interesting books, combining politics, adventure, and romance and offering a fresh look at his usual themes of betrayal and guilt.

Le Carré's typically labyrinthine plot begins with a series of anti-Jewish bombings in Europe. Israeli intelligence officer Marty Kurtz is assigned to get the terrorist behind all of these killings, an evasive Palestinian named Khalil. Kurtz is preoccupied not only with stopping Khalil but also with keeping his own operation from being shut down and perhaps most important, holding back "the mounting outcry for a military solution." Kurtz chooses an unlikely weapon: twenty-six-year-old English actress Charmian, known as

Charlie, veteran of third-rate touring companies and numerous left-wing causes. Kurtz selects Charlie for her acting ability and radical background. Charlie's involvement comes about as the result of an elaborate charade carried out by Gadi Becker, known to Charlie as Joseph, a truly battle-scarred veteran of several wars. Becker slowly entices Charlie into a meeting with Kurtz— in part because he is the only man she has ever wanted who will not sleep with her.

Kurtz's plot, during the unveiling of which the reader is only one slight step ahead of the naïve Charlie, is to convince Khalil that the actress is the true love of his younger brother, who calls himself Michel, another terrorist. Kurtz's team forges love letters between Charlie and Michel and indoctrinates her in everything known about the brothers and their cause. Meanwhile, Michel is kidnaped, tortured, and killed; his death is made to look like an accident.

The heart of *The Little Drummer Girl* is in the scenes in which Charlie and Becker act out Michel's courtship of her. She is able to "fall in love" with a man she has never seen because his part is being played by a man whom she truly loves—a man who shares all of her intimacies but not her bed. In this strange mixture of role-playing and genuine feeling, Charlie begins to lose her grasp on her own identity. Indeed, le Carré treats the tension between modern man's quest for a firm identity and his need to assume varied roles as well as anyone in postwar fiction, with the possible exceptions of Vladimir Nabokov and Thomas Pynchon. Charlie is never certain why she is going along with Kurtz and hates herself for doing so. Kurtz knows that she participates because "to the uninitiated, the secret world is of itself attractive. Simply by turning on its axis, it can draw the weakly anchored to its centre." There is also the fascination of trying to distinguish what is real: "the only logic was the fiction, and the fiction was a web that enmeshed everyone who tried to sweep it away."

Becker and Kurtz tell Charlie that she can quit any time, but after Michel's death, she is taken in by the terrorists and is determined to play the role to its completion. She goes to Beirut, is interrogated by the feared Captain Tayeh, meets Michel's sister Fatmeh, and, after much questioning, convinces all that she is on their side and is trained in terrorism. Charlie strongly sympathizes with the Palestinian cause and wishes that she could continue playing Michel's bereaved beloved. She is sent to West Germany to kill a moderate Israeli professor and finally meets Khalil, who sees through her only when it is too late. Both Charlie and Becker are overwhelmed by the moral implications of their actions.

As usual, le Carré researched his book extensively, including meetings with Palestine Liberation Organization leader Yasser Arafat, and he has said in interviews that he, like Charlie, became increasingly upset at the injustices done the Palestinians. *The Little Drummer Girl* has been criticized for being pro-Palestinian, and it does show that the Israelis can be as violent as any terrorists, especially in the series of attacks which follow Khalil's death. Nevertheless, throughout the novel, le Carré emphasizes the desperation and absurdity of terrorism. In Lebanon, "some kind of terrorist V.I.P." arrives for target practice in a chauffeur-driven Volvo, and a woman trained in Yemen, Libya, and Kiev is described as "playing the circuit like a tennis pro until somebody decided what to do with her." In le Carré's world, no countries or causes are right or wrong; there are only individuals who must be victims or victimizers.

One strength of *The Little Drummer Girl* comes from its creator's juggling of moral complexities, as when Khalil discusses their target with Charlie:

> They say Minkel's a nice person. Maybe he is. When I read about him, I too said to myself—this old fellow Minkel, maybe he's got some courage to say those things. Maybe I would respect him. I can respect my enemy. I can honour him. I have no problem concerning this.

Another strength is the complexity of the characters, especially Kurtz, Becker, and Charlie. Kurtz's name, the reader is told, invites "laborious comparisons" with the representative of the failure of civilization in Joseph Conrad's tale *Heart of Darkness* (1899). Kurtz is aware of the thin line between civilization and savagery but accepts brutality and deception as part of the game. He is a consummate manipulator who "wheel[s] and deal[s] and lie[s] even in his prayers." Like George Smiley, he exults in the intellectual challenge of espionage.

The charismatic Gadi Becker, who sees himself as the epitome of the cool, detached professional, earns the respect denied Kurtz. It is Becker, however, not Kurtz, who is Conrad's hollow man, "surrounding [himself] with versions of [his] identity because the original somehow went missing along the road." His inability to remove all of his masks, to be what Charlie wants and needs him to be, causes him finally to lose his detachment and appraise "the basic assumptions of his life."

Charlie, partially based upon le Carré's half sister, actress Charlotte Cornwell, is the novel's most complex and interesting character. She is able to order the world only through her art; the world makes sense only when she is on stage. Becker and Kurtz give her a role to play in what she calls the "theatre of the real," only to confuse her even more about her values and her identity. She becomes engulfed in "the complex fiction of her several lives" and desperately wants Joseph to save her from "their shared schizophrenia." She wants moral absolutes in a chaotic universe because "doubt was what she ha[s] learned to fear the most."

Le Carré's only novel not to succeed with readers and critics was *The Naive and Sentimental Lover* (1971), a love story, and in *The Little Drummer Girl*, he tries to combine romance and adventure equally. The novel might have been more powerful with less romance and more espionage; Charlie's mourning for her lost and unattainable loves becomes repetitious. Charlie is also perhaps too much like the heroines of Ken Follett's spy fiction, those average women in love with good-bad men who can save civilization as we know it if called upon to do so.

Le Carré has always been praised for the realism of his novels, especially when compared to the comic-book heroics of Ian Fleming's James Bond, but *The Little Drummer Girl* strains credibility with the near perfection of Kurtz's complicated machinations. The twists and turns of the Smiley books are missed, even if their absence makes this plot easier to follow than is usual with le Carré. A final flaw is that the writing grows tired at times: Charlie's mind is "like a sponge" and "sharp as a flint"; Khalil has "the pallor of the dungeon in his complexion"; Charlie's car "handle[s] like a dream"; and she wants Joseph "more than she ha[s] ever wanted anyone."

Such gaffes detract only slightly, however, from le Carré's exploration of some of the murkier waters of international politics. As Khalil tells Charlie, "Terror is theatre. We inspire, we frighten, we awaken indignation, anger, love. We enlighten. The theatre also. The guerrilla is the great actor of the world."

Michael Adams

Sources for Further Study

Christian Science Monitor. March 30, 1983, p. B9.
Library Journal. CVIII, February 1, 1983, p. 221.
Los Angeles Times Book Review. March 13, 1983, p. 1.
The New York Review of Books. XXX, April 14, 1983, p. 19.
The New York Times Book Review. LXXXVIII, March 13, 1983, p. 1.
Newsweek. CI, March 7, 1983, p. 70.
Saturday Review. IX, June, 1983, p. 52.
Time. CXXI, March 14, 1983, p. 87.
Virginia Quarterly Review. LIX, Summer, 1983, p. 91.
West Coast Review of Books. IX, March, 1983, p. 37.

THE LONDON EMBASSY

Author: Paul Theroux (1941-   )
Publisher: Houghton Mifflin Company (Boston). 248 pp. $13.95
Type of work: Short stories
Time: The early 1980's
Locale: London

In this collection of separate but connected short stories, the American narrator observes a wide range of British and European eccentrics as they weave in and out of his life at the American Embassy in London

Principal characters:

> SPENCER MONROE SAVAGE, the narrator, unnamed until the last page of the book, a Foreign Service officer at the London Embassy
> EVERETT HORTON, the senior American diplomat in London and the number-two man after Ambassador Noyes
> ERROLL JEEPS, a black American diplomat in London
> SOPHIE GRAVENEY, a British friend of the narrator, an actress and real estate agent
> VIC SCADUTO, American Cultural Affairs officer
> CHARLIE HOGLE, a telex operator at the American Embassy
> WALTER VAN BELLAMY, an American poet in Great Britain
> ABDUL WAHAB BIN BAZ, an Arab student living in London
> MARGARET DUBOYS, Foreign Service officer at the American Embassy

The stunning opening paragraphs of the first story in *The London Embassy* collection set the tone for the rest of the book: elegant, worldly, cool, and clever. One wonders, however, how reliable this clever, obviously sophisticated first-person narrator can be. Can the reader trust the observations and judgments so articulately offered in this graceful, understated prose? Anyone who has read many of Paul Theroux's stories soon learns to reserve such judgments. As his masters—Anton Chekhov, Guy de Maupassant, and Somerset Maugham—before him, Theroux relishes the ironic tone, the deceptively limpid narrative, the tale of the wise hypocrite. The more seductive the style, the more confident the tone of Theroux's narrator, the more reserved should be the reader's initial judgment: Theroux may well be playing games with his audience again—delightful, entertainingly wicked games, but games nevertheless.

The world of international diplomacy, of career diplomats, and sophisticated world travelers, lends itself well to the type of fiction that Theroux seems to enjoy producing—particularly when he takes on the shorter forms. The characters who populate the stories in *The London Embassy* know that their initial perceptions very likely are not to be trusted. This is a world of artifice, of role-playing, of intrigue, and of games—games played often for the sake of simply playing them. In some of the stories, the author himself is clearly playing games with the reader. Occasionally, the games are rather obvious, to the detriment of the story, but just as often they are subtle and excruciatingly effective.

The narrator of the stories in *The London Embassy* (unnamed until the last page of the book) speaks in the cool, candid tone of a professional observer. Even when he is involved in the stories he is telling, his narrative is marked by its detachment, as if he is stepping back and watching himself along with the others in the story. His attitude is rather like that of many of F. Scott Fitzgerald's first-person narrators—especially Nick Carraway in *The Great Gatsby* (1925)—or of Joseph Conrad's ubiquitous Charlie Marlow. Theroux's narrator relates his disappointments in love, his education in the labyrinth of diplomacy, and his adventures in the vastness of metropolitan London all with a calm, rather interested manner, as if he is surprised to find himself where he is, having the experiences he is having; but he is determined to make the best of it and, above all, not make waves.

Eccentrics populate all of Theroux's books, from *Saint Jack* (1975) to *The Great Railway Bazaar: By Train Through Asia* (1975) to *The Mosquito Coast* (1982), but he writes about them here with that special fondness that many British authors reserve for oddballs. Perhaps Theroux's long residence in Great Britain has given him this peculiarly British viewpoint toward the eccentrics of the world. Many of his characters, in *The London Embassy* and his other books, could have stepped out of the pages of Charles Dickens or Evelyn Waugh. Here, the eccentrics range from a daffy American poet living in England to a young Embassy telex operator who takes to wearing a single gold earring, thereby scandalizing his superiors; from a grave robber to a beautiful young actress who makes real-estate deals on the side. Still, Theroux, despite his years in Great Britain, is an American, and perhaps because of this he is a bit nonplussed by the very oddities that he seems to find so fascinating in his characters. He does not take their eccentricities as matter-of-factly as would his British counterparts.

Occasionally, Theroux reaches a little too far, straining for effect. Such is the case in "Tomb with a View," the story about a grave robber, and it is most obvious in the weakest story in the collection, "Neighbors." In the latter story, Theroux makes much ado about a mystery of sorts that is very early quite transparent to the reader, so that when the conclusion finally comes, the reader is disappointed that there was not some further twist beyond the revelation of the eccentricity of the neighbor. Eccentricity for its own sake is not enough.

In some of the stories, however, Theroux achieves perceptive insights into his characters and their world. "The n on the Clapham Omnibus" touchingly portrays the pathetic situation of an aristocrat trained for nothing in life but the existence of an aristocrat, to be waited upon and to be amusing at house parties and social occasions. When he has to survive without the financial support required to maintain his accustomed style, he is at a loss, like a child turned loose in the world. The story offers a view of the artificiality of the British class system, showing how even the upper classes can be victimized by it. More important, it illustrates the nature of role-playing in contemporary society. Without their masks, many people believe that they are nothing and— like the poor aristocrat in the story—they will stop at nothing to preserve the last shred of a façade behind which to hide their real condition.

The question of masks and pretense runs through many of the stories in this collection. It appears, for example, in the story of Margaret Duboys, "Sex and Its Substitutes"; in "Neighbors," about the narrator's two unseen neighbors, one violent and noisy, the other invisible and silent; and in "The Exile," about the famous American poet Walter Van Bellamy, who has created an entire persona behind which he hides. It is the theme as well of "Charlie Hogle's Earring," in which Theroux explores what can happen when a simple gesture breaks down society's protective façade. Everything in society rests on perception, on what *seems* to be true. The facts are less important than what one *believes* the facts to be. People are in danger more from what others *think* about them than from what they actually may be guilty of doing.

In "Sex and Its Substitutes," the staff at the Embassy speculates about Margaret Duboys, debating about whether she has a male friend, about the kind of relationship she might have with this unknown friend, and about what other kind of secret life could lurk behind her respectable façade. In "A Little Flame," a character says, "People's secrets are the most interesting thing about them. How could you love anyone who didn't have a secret?"

A lie can be a weapon, an act of cruelty or thoughtlessness, or an act of charity. In the story "A Little Flame"—of all the stories in the collection the one most closely patterned after the models of Maupassant and Maugham— the narrator chooses to lie to preserve the illusions of an acquaintance who would be destroyed if he knew that his dead wife had cheated on him. Once again, the illusion, the appearance of truth, is more important than the actual truth. In this story, there is much talk of the nature of truth and the importance of artifice, but the widowed husband fails to realize just how important the appearance of truth—the well-told lie—is to him. Only the narrator, who knows the truth and chooses to withhold it, has that knowledge. The irony here may be a little heavy-handed, but it is nevertheless effective.

The theme of perception versus reality dominates the bitter little story "Children" as well. In this savage story, the children of Vic Scaduto, the American Cultural Affairs officer, and their young British friends are revealed to be totally concerned with appearances, with the symbols that represent class and position. They are intolerant of foreigners, of people who belong to the "wrong" class, and of anyone in any way different from what they consider to be correct. Like their parents, these brainwashed young snobs lack the sensitivity or the interest to penetrate beneath the surface to discover the authentic value of another human being.

The eighteen stories in *The London Embassy* are all written with the clear, graceful, lightly ironic prose that characterizes much of Paul Theroux's fiction. The stories tend to be uneven in other respects—the plots are sometimes contrived and the conclusions artificial—but they are all highly readable. Perhaps, therefore, this book should be considered minor Theroux, what Graham Greene has referred to as an "entertainment." The merits of the book are real, but Theroux has written and will write better, more important, books.

Bruce D. Reeves

Sources for Further Study

America. CXLVIII, April 16, 1983, p. 304.
Christian Science Monitor. June 24, 1983, p. B6.
Esquire. XCIX, April, 1983, p. 106.
Hudson Review. XXXVI, Summer, 1983, p. 368.
Library Journal. CVIII, March 15, 1983, p. 603.
Los Angeles Times Book Review. March 13, 1983, p. 1.
The New York Review of Books. XXX, June 2, 1983, p. 42.
The New York Times Book Review. LXXXVIII, March 29, 1983, p. 1.
Newsweek. CI, April 25, 1983, p. 85.
West Coast Review of Books. IX, March, 1983, p. 34.

LOOK AT ME

Author: Anita Brookner (1928-   )
Publisher: Pantheon Books (New York). 192 pp. $11.95
Type of work: Novel
Time: The early 1980's
Locale: London

A female file clerk at a research institute takes up with a group of captivating people but is disappointed in her desire to find through them the fulfillment she has missed elsewhere in her life

Principal characters:
FRANCES HINTON, a file clerk at a research institute
NICK FRASER, a paid researcher at the institute
ALIX, his déclassé aristocratic wife
JAMES ANSTEY, the other paid researcher at the institute and Frances' eventual companion
MISS MORPETH, Frances' predecessor at the institute

If George Orwell's avowed motive for writing was to get back at the grown-ups, it could be said with equal justice that Anita Brookner's novel is part of a campaign to get back at the spoiled children. Among these spoiled children, who at first appear charming to the novel's heroine, Frances Hinton, the most prominent are Nick Fraser, who is doing research at the institute where Frances works, and his upper-class wife, Alix. The title of the book under review, then, is interesting for several reasons but above all for a paradoxical one: The moral of the story has much to do with how shallow "looking" really is, and how images can lie.

Such a concern comes naturally to a writer such as Anita Brookner, whose chief scholarly interest is in the field of art history. In fact, her principal reputation—despite such previous novels as *A Start in Life* (1981; published in the United States as *The Debut*, 1981) and *Providence* (1982; whose theme is in some respects quite similar to that of *Look at Me*)—has been as a chronicler of artists, in, for example, *Jacques-Louis David* (1980), or of art critics, as in *The Genius of the Future* (1971). It is not surprising, then, that Frances files "photographs of works of art" with "doctors and patients" in them, with special emphasis on "dreams and madness" and a general concern with "the incalculable or the undiagnosed." (The institute deals with problems of "human behavior.") The opening sequence of the novel depicts the variety of morbid iconography she must file interwoven with descriptions—well-nigh clinical—of the other workers and patrons of the library, whose images begin to meld into those of the art prints, not so much in the narrator's rendering as in the reader's mind.

This melding is quite strategic on Brookner's part. Her heroine inhabits a world of dull routine with an undercurrent of horror and death—a combination that also obtains in her apartment, which has seen the deaths of both of Frances' parents, and which Nancy, the family retainer, lovingly preserves in a style of 1950's kitsch that provokes trendy Nick and Alix Fraser to shameless mocking delight when they visit. Frances' apartment, like the library, is both a prison and a mausoleum, where unchanging rules of etiquette keep the votive lamp burning for the dead, even though this faithfulness to ancestral memory depresses the living descendant. Frances grows restive with the constant reminders that "everyone was, more or less, dying" and begins to feel she has "lived with all this for far too long."

The chosen vehicle of escape becomes the Frasers, who bestow their gracious attentions upon Frances for a while. Frances' coworker, Olivia, observing how she is swept up by the Frasers, sees the bourgeoisie vanquished once again by "the brutal fascination of the upper classes," and her assessment becomes increasingly persuasive as the book progresses. The Frasers' chic Kensington flat stands in sharp contrast to Frances' entirely respectable, entirely stuffy building north of Hyde Park, a building "full of small elderly people." Nick's and Alix's giddy social exuberance, of which noisy, rapacious dining at top-flight restaurants is the repeated emblem, puts into cruel relief Frances' monthly Sunday visits to old Miss Morpeth, her predecessor at the library and thus also her dread alter ego, at which times they share tea, cake, bread and butter, and studiedly pointless conversation. Despite their mutual tolerance, which slips fatally on one last visit, it is clear that Miss Morpeth dislikes Frances and finds the sessions as unendurable as her visitor does. As the polite visitor sits in Miss Morpeth's genteel flat, "eating the bread of affliction," she understands with dawning clarity why, despite Miss Morpeth's persistent invitations, the Frasers have been reluctant to enter the "kingdom of the shades" that the lady's home has begun to resemble. According to Frances, the sympathies of this dashing couple lie always "with the successful, not the unsuccessful, with the moneyed rather than with the poor, with the fortunate rather than with the unlucky."

Even though Frances acknowledges feeling at times like "a beggar at their feast," it is easy to see that the Frasers' very superficiality, their heedless cruelty and assumption of prerogative is precisely what attracts her (and everyone else in the sad library) to these two. She purposes to "see how the others, the free ones, conducted their lives," so that she can begin her own. That same quality of slightly careless brutality which fascinates Frances also leads the reader to suspect a level of Jamesian social intrigue on the Frasers' part, especially given the manipulative skill of Alix. (Both on the first and the last occasions on which she appears in this novel, Alix initially is glimpsed trying out varied arrangements of her hair and asking the assembled men which way is the prettiest: a powerful demonstration of narcissism's power.) Common sense suggests that having swept Frances up in such a whirlwind fashion, the Frasers could well drop her with equal suddenness. The only question becomes when they will do it. When they do, however, the subtle changes in their manner toward her, the tiny snubs that can never be pinned down, the calculated averting of eyes are all brought out with a mordant connoisseur's touch.

The agent that hastens this process of disenchantment is James Anstey, the other researcher being funded by the institute along with Nick. It emerges that Nick and Alix seem interested in Frances as a partner for James: They find a use for her. As Frances and James begin to see each other, Alix calls constantly, wanting all the details. (The voyeurism of the alliance between Frances and the Frasers apparently goes two ways.) Eventually, James's "reticence," which initially Frances finds "very exciting," turns to—was it always?—a kind of finicky disinterest. In a completion of the Jamesian situation, Frances discovers, well after the fact, that another of the Frasers' circle is actually James's lover. The only remaining ambiguity, never resolved, concerns how long the "other woman" has been a factor. Since the novel, in the manner of Henry James's *The Golden Bowl* (1904), centers on Frances' consciousness—indeed has Frances for its narrator—one is left to wonder with her at what point, if ever, James Anstey changed his mind. In any case, Frances has certainly been not only an observer or even a beggar at the Frasers' banquet but also one of the courses. This voracious crowd obviously goes through its people very quickly.

It is for the heroine a doubly bitter return to loneliness: loneliness, incidentally, rendered here about as well as it has ever been. The "Public Holiday Syndrome," especially acute on Christmas, and the horror of Sunday afternoons, along with the paradoxical pleasure of anticipating Monday morning, "that time that other people dread," pass in grimly detailed review. The climax of the novel, Frances' return home after learning the full truth about James—or as much as she cares to learn—is a summation of these motifs. Leaving the Frasers' party after their Kensington restaurant dinner, she walks through London; the narrative intersperses an account of the scenes she encounters with her reflections on her relationship with the Frasers. Frances has caused no embarrassment at the dinner (her characteristic description of herself is "blameless"); crucially, she betrays outwardly none of the murderous hatred she feels. Her "own reflection" in the glass front of the Harvey Nichols store is "small, slight, undeniably chic . . . poised," offering no clue to passersby, as she has scarcely given a clue to the Frasers, of her sense of betrayal and defilement. (The face of Dr. Weiss, a female academic in *The Debut*, with a similarly opaque quality, also elicits "no speculation whatsoever" from the passing observer.) Except for one incident in the Marble Arch underpass, where a drunk tries to grab her sleeve, momentarily banishing her numbness, little if anything happens on this long march to Edgware Road and "the home stretch." One could say as well that little happens in the famous meditation chapter in Henry James's *The Portrait of a Lady* (1881), in which heroine

Isabel Archer begins to add two and two, yet that scene is the pivot of James's novel. In the same way, this long walk is the pivot of *Look at Me*, and the heroine knows it, "my mind kept saying: something has happened."

What, though, has happened after all? Simply that Frances, who has up until now made a hobby of writing short stories, decides this night to "get serious" about it and complete a novel. She commences to live her own life, but ironically—and, one is given to understand, instructively—she has not won self-fulfillment by changing her role to more perfectly emulate "the free ones." Quite the opposite: It is in being rejected by that circle that she is freed to return to herself, to her situation, with the sad wisdom required to be clear about it. In the past, writing has been for Frances merely a way to alleviate loneliness; the Frasers, in throwing her back on herself, inadvertently have given her both a topic and the time to explore it.

Brookner understands well the narcissistic motive behind the writing of fiction (the heroine in fact often repeats the words of the title to herself), but as mentioned at the outset, much of the book's impact stems from a critique of the vanity in that motive. The beguiling perfect couple, Nick and Alix, seem ready for the caption in "those old copies of the *Tatler*" that say "pictured here enjoying a joke." This ceases to beguile once it is clearer that the joke is always at someone's expense. Thus, the description of the Frasers, always vivid, grows more grotesque as the story progresses, until these *enfants terribles* are rendered as "lords of misrule" ensconced amid "the collapsing ruins of puddings" with their "idle hands searching lazily for nuts, sweetmeats, marzipan." Significantly, this scene is actually Frances' fond fantasy on Christmas Day, and it compares favorably to the drear, shabby convocation occurring at her own flat on that day. One of the realizations Frances has is that the appeal of the Frasers, with their grasping hands and open mouths, owes to a childish appetite that the heroine herself possesses but never displays as they do. Their appeal is infantile, though undeniably strong, and their unself-conscious narcissism is part of what compels Frances to write—with the important difference that now she is aware of that fact.

There is also, without much question, an element of revenge in Frances' writing: "These scenes, these actions, to be retrieved, at a later date, intact." The observer becomes a participant, the victim a prosecutor. A clear, accurate portrayal of the beautiful people, fully noting their power to charm and the plain heroine's complicity in that power, makes them nevertheless very ugly. Their images have not exactly been defaced, but they have been revealed for the deceptions they truly are. "Sometimes an image stands for something that will only be understood in due course"; this cryptic remark of the heroine's early in the novel becomes bleakly apposite when applied to Nick and Alix. Michel de Montaigne says in his essay on physiognomy that beautiful people who do wrong should be executed for betraying the promise written on their brows. Whether Frances agrees with that sentiment, there is no doubt that the characters of the Frasers are well executed indeed.

The center of all this turbulence, however, is the relationship between the heroine and James Anstey, and this is the book's major flaw. In a narrative notable for its lively, observant eye for detail, James is a curiously dim and dour figure, lamely drawn, and Frances' attitude toward him, both in her capacity as narrator and as companion, is so understated as to be insignificant. The short shrift given this allegedly central figure, and the mists of vagueness in which he is complacently cloaked, make his loss less an issue than Frances' feeling of humiliation or bad judgment. That he is a figure of scant interest means that his abandonment of the heroine is a shaky scaffolding on which to build a conversion scene.

Despite this problem, Brookner's novel largely rings true. Her depictions of the library, of the heroine's chintz-laden flat, of a sterile and empty London cityscape, make her a veritable virtuoso of dinginess. The greedy glitter of the Frasers is ridiculed in scenes that resonate with the sardonic. Oddly enough, this book, which tells the reader how images lie, knows it must let those images shine forth and seduce first. Given the dingy backdrop, it is unsurprising that the Frasers, and perhaps even James, seem brighter with promise than they could ever really be. As the disenchantment with Camelot proceeds apace, however, all of the virtues that the dingy alternative would have boasted (if it could have) become clearer. The principal bearer of these unheralded virtues is probably the heroine's socialist coworker, the crippled Olivia; Frances' announcement to the disdainful and disbelieving Alix, on their final meeting, that she is spending Christmas with Olivia constitutes a declaration of solidarity, a taking of sides.

The novel in fact closes on the hated day of Christmas, Frances seated at her desk of desolation, writing. As it opened with images of madness, melancholy, and death, so it closes with images which, Frances reflects, "used to throng [her] mind" and which, in her new, unwanted knowledge, she seems "to welcome back." These closing images are of a less fantastical but still depressing sort. She sees the various elderly figures in the library as they pass in mental review, and finally she sees herself. It is easy to read this penultimate passage before her concluding gesture ("I pick up my pen. I write.") as the final triumph of experience over hope, as the narrator's dawning awareness that it is her destiny to grow old and to follow Miss Morpeth to the solitary grave, but it is also the moment of recognition that allows these figures, including herself, to emerge in their own right from the obscure depths of dinginess. To "see," then, is not only to visualize, to grasp the physical; it is to understand, to divine essence and motive. To see in that second sense requires powers not only of observation but also of logic and intuition, not only the instant snapshot but also the extended case history. Although the heroine desires to make her experiences into a "satirical novel," "playing for laughs" and converting everything "somehow, into entertainment," the author of *Look at Me* has done a bit better than that. She has produced a novel which, while very funny (even painfully so), has probed the surface of people's outward aspects, both bright and dull, and has shown by the most appropriate of methods—the written word—how misleading appearances, visual images, can be.

Mark Conroy

Sources for Further Study

Christian Science Monitor. October 19, 1983, p. 24.
Harper's. CCLXVII, July, 1983, p. 75.
Library Journal. CVIII, April 1, 1983, p. 756.
Listener. CIX, April 14, 1983, p. 32.
Los Angeles Times Book Review. May 3, 1983, p. 12.
The New York Times Book Review. LXXXVIII, May 22, 1983, p. 14.
Publishers Weekly. CCXXIII, March 4, 1983, p. 91.

LOST IN THE COSMOS
The Last Self-Help Book

Author: Walker Percy (1916-   )
Publisher: Farrar, Straus and Giroux (New York). 262 pp. $14.95
Type of work: Informal philosophy

A mixture of many genres, this wry meditation on the spiritual malaise of twentieth century man conducts a serious metaphysical inquiry in the playful spirit of a gifted comic novelist

Walker Percy is that rarest of all American writers, a philosophical novelist. Among philosophical novelists of the twentieth century (Albert Camus and Jean-Paul Sartre, for example), he is rarer still, for his existentialism is Christian rather than atheistic, and his method is decidedly comic in two senses of the word: It is satirically humorous, and it tends toward the realm of spiritual harmony typified by Dante's *The Divine Comedy* (1320).

Percy's novels detail the existential predicament in which post-Christian man finds himself: lost in the cosmos. The protagonists of Percy's five novels are all lost: in the microcosms of New Orleans (*The Moviegoer*, 1961); New York City, the South and Southwest (*The Last Gentleman*, 1966); the ruins of Paradise Estates (*Love in the Ruins*, 1971); a Louisiana plantation transmogrified into a movie set and a room or cell in a center for aberrant behavior (*Lancelot*, 1977); and finally Lost Cove Cave (*The Second Coming*, 1980), where Percy's befuddled hero demands that God make an appearance. What distinguishes Percy's protagonists, what wakes them up to their predicament, is their inability to make do in the customary ways. Inauthenticity makes them uneasy even as authenticity continues to elude them. Although Percy's satire can be scathingly funny—Father Kev Kevin reading *Commonweal* while sitting at a vaginal console in a Masters and Johnson clinic in *Love in the Ruins*, for example—most of his writing is tempered by compassion for his lost characters and their fumbling attempts to discover their authentic selves. At the same time, as the Swiftian satire suggests, they try the patience and good humor of the author, who, nearly forty years ago, made his own Kierkegaardian leap from psychoanalysis to Catholicism and from the practice of medicine to the writing of novels.

However different in method, Percy's novels and the essays collected in 1975 under the title *The Message in the Bottle* serve the same purpose: to record and to analyze phenomenologically the modern malaise, the pathology of the spirit. *Lost in the Cosmos*, a work that is neither wholly fiction nor essay does this. As its subtitle, "The Last Self-Help Book," suggests, *Lost in the Cosmos* is a parody, but it is also a wry meditation on a culture given to embracing the queerest kinds of obsessions—television talk shows, newspaper horoscopes, how-to guides such as *The Joy of Sex*, "Dear Abby" columns, and Carl Sagan's *Cosmos*—rather than facing up to its own spiritual poverty. The very structure of Percy's elliptical book is designed not so much to alleviate the reader's anxieties as to increase and so bring to consciousness his sense of dislocation. The two pages of subtitles, a kind of publicity department's idea of a table of contents, are followed by "A Short Preliminary Quiz": The reader must first decide whether he is lost in the cosmos, and then whether he should buy the book, a "Twenty-Question Multiple-Choice Self-Help Quiz," which includes a takeoff on Phil Donahue's daytime television talk show, a forty-five page "intermezzo," "A Semiotic Primer of the Self," that, Percy notes, "can be skipped without fatal consequences," and last, two "Space Odysseys" about the future of man following an all-out nuclear war. Throughout, there are questions, puzzles, diagrams, and alternatives but never any firm answers or resolutions; these, the book suggests, the reader must find for himself. Percy's task is to point to and illuminate the problem, not to solve it for the reader. "The only difference between my book and Aquinas," Percy told his publisher's sales representatives, "is that he gave all the right answers; mine is multiple choice."

The general problem to which Percy addresses himself is summed up in the book's epigraph, drawn from Friedrich Nietzsche: "We are unknown, we knowers, to ourselves." In Percy's usage, "we" refers to those who have come to accept the scientific view, which holds that far from being unique, man is nothing more than an entirely understandable, responding organism situated, as are all other organisms, in a deterministic environment. That man is not merely an organism having only physiological needs should be obvious, Percy claims, to anyone who studies man's odd behavior—for example, his preoccupation with fashionable clothing, "authentic" antiques, "meaningful" sexual relationships, and other aspects of modern consumer culture. What does the salesperson mean, Percy asks, when she fits a customer with a dress or hat and says, "It's you"? Why are so many people in the richest nations of the world so bored and disappointed? Why do people desire so intensely to have their lives certified for them, even in so absurd a way as by hearing their hometown mentioned on the *Johnny Carson Show*?

The behavioristic method cannot adequately treat these matters. What is needed is a "radical science"—semiotics—that will enable man to understand behavior such as shyness and depression not as problems to be solved or conditions to be corrected but instead as appropriate human responses given man's existential predicament, his being lost in the cosmos, which is to say, lost to himself, to his sense of self. Modern man, Percy believes, has surrendered his sovereignty to various experts, whom he expects to cure him of all diseases and all dis-ease. Such faith is misplaced, Percy contends; if one is shy, it is because the "self is indeed unformulable" to oneself, and if one is depressed, it is because, living in a deranged world, one has reason to be depressed—despite what the normative psychologists and the I'm-okay-you're-okay experts say to the contrary.

Percy's study of the nature of language, reflected in the essays of two decades collected in *The Message in the Bottle*, led him to the theories of Charles Sanders Peirce, the founder of modern semiotics. Percy's semiotic analysis in *Lost in the Cosmos*, as well as his advocacy of semiotics as the new and necessary instrument for a complete understanding of man's nature, continues the development in his thought begun in the later essays in *The Message in the Bottle*. In *Lost in the Cosmos*, Percy continues to focus on the absurdity of the scientist's efforts to explain himself and his world exclusively in terms of "dyadic" (stimulus-response) behavior. In forcing the history of the universe and of man into a simple deterministic continuum of causes and effects, the scientist refuses to entertain the possibility that any creature may be unique, as Percy's "sovereign wayfarer" surely is. The scientist's position is at once inconsistent (as a scientist, he should be open to all facts) and inaccurate; as an observing consciousness (what Percy, following Peirce, calls a "triadic" creature), the scientist does indeed stand outside of his own theoretical continuum.

The scientist is unique not only in his having a consciousness but also in his desire to share his knowledge with others by means of the symbolic language which, Percy contends, is wholly unique to man. The songs of whales, the signs of chimpanzees, and the peckings of parrots represent dyadic forms of *communication* rather than examples of triadic *language*. (Triadic behavior, it should be noted, cannot be reduced to a system of dyadic relationships, such as occurs in communication between apes.) Whereas dyadic creatures from amoebas to apes exist in a discontinuous environment, triadic creatures—human beings—are able to use language to create for themselves a continuous world in which "even the gaps are named—by the word *gaps*." In emphasizing man's ability to use language to conjure a world other than his physical environment, Percy comes dangerously close to the postmodernist assumption that language is reality, and reality language. What distinguishes Percy's view from the bleak solipsism of the more extreme postmodernists is his belief that language is social in origin, and that words signify something other than themselves or the user's solipsistic imagination.

Although he escapes, even if barely, the fate of Samuel Beckett's disembodied voices, Percy's sign-user runs his own risks. One is that he can use language to name and therefore know everything in his environment and his world except himself. (Recall that for Percy, the self is unformulable to itself.) A second risk is that signs do not only evolve, they also devolve. Through overuse, a sign can lose its meaning and become a mere abstraction. According to Percy, the language of Christianity has suffered such a devolution, so that "God and religion have a bad name"; in the "post-religious technological society" of the late twentieth century, man is forced to choose between immanence (self as consumer, as a "naught" filling its emptiness with goods and experiences which it in turn drains of all meaning) and transcendence (self as scientist or artist orbiting the world without actually participating in it except occasionally in the unfulfilling sphere of immanence). Neither option can satisfy man other than for the moment, because man cannot be classified as *either* a biological organism *or* a transcending consciousness: He is both.

In Percy's view (he is a practicing Roman Catholic), man can ultimately be saved from this disastrous bifurcation only by the very Christianity that science has devalued. The Christian tradition can become viable in contemporary society if the old theological language is translated into a new and defamiliarized form. (Gabriel Marcel, the French existentialist philosopher—also a Roman Catholic—whose writings have had such a profound effect on Percy, made a similar attempt in *The Mystery of Being*, 1950.) Percy's intent in *Lost in the Cosmos*, however, is not to argue his own theological position, but rather to call for a "new model of man" provided by semiotics, not by religious presuppositions. Such a model would be based on "the study of man as the sign-using creature and, specifically, the study of the self and consciousness as derivatives of the sign-function."

Thus, instead of speaking of the "soul," Percy speaks of the existential "self," defined "in minimal terms as the semiotic entity which is unique in its ability to understand the world but not itself," and the Fall of Man, freed of Christian myth and iconography, becomes man's "turning from the concelebration of the world to a solitary absorption with self." Unfortunately, Percy is not always as successful as he is in these two instances. At times, as one reviewer complained, he sounds "priggish"; in his "Space Odyssey," the fictional abbot's espousal of certain orthodox Catholic views (most notably on the Incarnation) appears, disconcertingly, to be Percy's own. Far more compelling is the abbot's (and Percy's) claim that for man to survive with his self intact, science and religion must be wedded to prevent either from going astray, the one into cosmic transcendence (Percy's image of astronomer Carl Sagan so lonely he must scan the heavens hoping to find an extraterrestrial intelligence to talk to) and the other into superstition (Creationism, for example). Both abbot and author agree (along with Sören Kierkegaard) that "Judaeo-Christianity is indeed a preposterous religion" when seen from the perspective of modern science. However—and here is where Percy's semiotic analysis comes into play—from a different vantage point, it is science itself that appears preposterous, in that it accounts for all of the cosmos except man, the observing consciousness.

In *Lost in the Cosmos*, as in his other books, Walker Percy does not so much espouse "preposterous" Christianity as make clear the need for it. He assumes the seemingly impossible but wholly admirable task of putting the modern Humpty Dumpty back together again—or, more accurately, of leading postreligious man to an understanding of his fallen state. Best of all, although the threat of nuclear destruction is rife in this book, Percy does not lapse into the apocalyptic mood that characterizes the self-righteous—and murderous—protagonist of his fourth novel, *Lancelot*. More a satirist than a Jeremiah, Percy seeks to free his readers so that they may "contemplate the comic mystery" of their existence and concelebrate a world that lies before them—not a nuclear wasteland and nightmare, but as John Cheever once wrote, "a bewildering and stupendous dream."

Robert A. Morace

Sources for Further Study

Los Angeles Times. August 10, 1983, V, p. 1.
Los Angeles Times Book Review. June 5, 1983, p. 1.
The New Republic. July 11, 1983, p. 38.
The New York Times. CXXXII, June 11, 1983, p. 12.
The New York Times Book Review. LXXXVIII, June 5, 1983, p. 9.
Newsweek. CI, June 13, 1983, p. 72.
Washington Post Book World. June 19, 1983, p. 5.